Kathleen June 2002

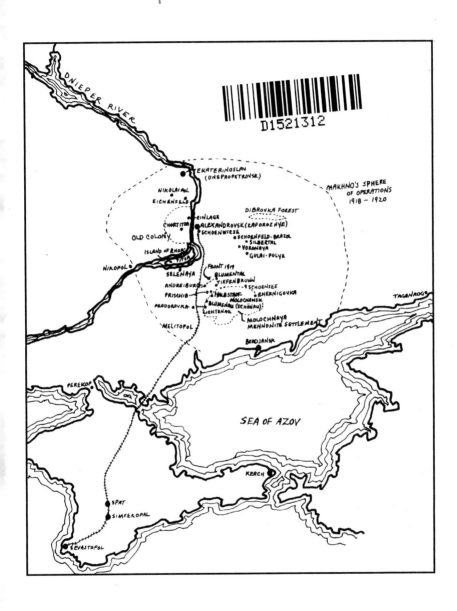

D1521312

DNIEPER RIVER

MAKHNO'S SPHERE
OF OPERATIONS
1918 - 1920

EKATERINOSLAV
(DNEPROPETROVSK)

NIKOLAIABL
EICHENFELD

DIBROVKA FOREST

EINLAGE
CHORTITZA
ALEXANDROVSK (ZAPOROZHYE)
SCHOENWIESE
OLD COLONY
SCHOENFELD-BRAZOL
SILBERTAL
VORONAYA
ISLAND OF RHOR
GULAI-POLYE
TIEFEN
NIKOPOL
SELENAYA
FRONT 1919
BLUMENTAL
TIEFENBRUNN
ANDREIBURG
SCHOENSEE
PRISCHIB
HALBSTADT
CHERNIGOVKA
PRODOROVKA
MOLOCHANSK
BLUMENAU (SCHÖNAU)
TAGENROG
LICHTENAU
MELITOPOL
MOLOCHNAYA
MENNONITE SETTLEMENT

BERDJANSK

PEREKOP

SEA OF AZOV

KERCH

SPAT
SIMFEROPAL

SEVASTOPOL

"Stories must be told and re-told, and the retelling of stories about a place, a person, an act is so much more important than recounting the original facts because the so-called lies — the accretions and deletions of each new telling — are more humanly significant than literal facts can ever be (insofar as they are discoverable or rememberable in any case). The 'lies' of good stories are always, perversely, truer than 'facts.'"

RUDY WIEBE

"In a sense, we haven't got an identity until somebody tells our story. The fiction makes us real."

ROBERT KROETSCH

"The fact is always in the past, but a fiction is what you make of it. And you have to have a certain amount of facts to make a fiction out of them. Something that will last."

RUDY WIEBE

"Fact, in order to survive, must become fiction . . . fiction is not the opposite of fact, but its complement. It gives a more lasting shape to the vanishing deeds of men."

ROBERT SCHOLES

MY HARP IS TURNED TO MOURNING

a novel by

Al Reimer

Windflower
Communications
Winnipeg, Manitoba

MY HARP IS TURNED TO MOURNING
Copyright ©1990, Windflower Communications

All rights reserved. No part of this book may be reproduced, stored in a retrieval system or transmitted in any form or by any means without the prior permission of the publisher, except by a reviewer, who may quote brief passages in a review.

Published by Windflower Communications,
#7-1110 Henderson Highway, Winnipeg, Manitoba R2G 1L1.

Canadian Cataloguing in Publication Data
Reimer, Al, 1927 -
  My harp is turned to mourning
  ISBN: 1-895308-06-2
  1. Mennonites - Soviet Union - History - Fiction.
  I. Title.
PS8585.E554M92 1991   C813/ .54   C91-097193-5
PR9199.3.R45E55M9   1991

Originally published by Hyperion Press Limited. This book is part of a series of publications sponsored by the Mennonite Literary Society Inc., and the Chair in Mennonite Studies, University of Winnipeg.

Design by A. O. Osen
Typography by Raeber Graphics, Inc.
Printed in Canada by D.W. Friesen & Sons, Ltd.

Painting on cover: "Refugee" by Alexander Harder-Khasan, reprinted with the kind permission of Johannes Harder.

International Standard Book Number: 1-895308-06-2

*For the survivors and all their children
and children's children in Canada and elsewhere.*

When I looked for good, then evil came unto me: and when I waited for light, there came darkness.

My bowels boiled, and rested not: the days of affliction prevented me.

I went mourning without the sun: I stood up, and I cried in the congregation.

I am a brother to dragons, and a companion to owls.

My skin is black upon me, and my bones are burned with heat.

My harp also is turned to mourning, and my organ into the voice of them that weep.

Job 30: 26-31

Acknowledgments

For their encouragement and helpful criticism during the years I was working on this novel I wish to thank the following friends and readers: Victor Doerksen, Harry Loewen, Gerhard Lohrenz, Victor Peters, Andreas Schroeder, Jack Thiessen, and John B. Toews. They provided historical and fictional expertise that saved me from many errors and false steps as well as technical and stylistic gaucheries.

Above all I am indebted to my good friend and colleague Roy Vogt, who was instrumental in getting me to start writing fiction and who cajoled and inspired me to write this novel against all the usual odds and more.

Most of the characters and events in this novel are invented but true. Even those characters and scenes based on real people and events are fictionalized and should not be confused with those in the historical record (which is, after all, itself fiction in another guise).

AL REIMER

Contents

Part I
Islands in the Steppe: 1905-1913

CHAPTER ONE

1

Village Blumenau, Molochnaya, May, 1905

Sitting with the other lads on the wooden fence of the horse pen behind Mayor Thiessen's stable, Willie Fast gazed in awe at the new stallion from Germany. A purebred Oldenburger he was, and every boy there knew the village had paid a whopping 850 rubles for him. The shaven heads bobbed with excitement, but Willie was oblivious to the chatter. He had eyes only for the big horse.

He had never seen anything to compare with this magnificent creature, so big yet so calm and controlled.

The young stallion exuded strength and mastery as he stood immobile but alert, quivering nostrils raised slightly, already probing the air for the hot mare's scent of the *tabun* grazing in the common pasture not far away. The glossy sides and flanks rippled and the full-cut tail swished rhythmically as the flies buzzed and settled in the warm May sun.

Majestic — that was the only word for him: this was the way a young prince or king should look, as if power was his by right. Willie's adolescent mind groped for a comparison. Yes, like the war horse in Job, neck clothed with thunder. But no, this horse was different. He did not chew the ground in anger, impatient to run into battle. This stallion had a higher purpose. He was a horse of life, not of death and destruction. He would bring into life many fine horses to help work the black steppe soil and pull the ladder wagons and the Sunday droshkies. He was a creator, not a destroyer.

His brother Kolya was shouting in his ear, but Willie paid no attention. His whole being was concentrated on the stallion. He had been around horses all his life, but for the first time he was really seeing and feeling what a horse was: how the muscle-flanged neck arched up so loftily from the immense bulk of barrel chest and flowed into the surprisingly small, delicate head. All that silken power knotting itself at the noble face, in which the lustrous eyes shone like dark, rich jewels. And the vigor and sweep of the mighty haunches tapering down to the fragile sculpture of legs and hoofs. The unfathomable energy in the mighty body all seemed to flow in the direction of those dainty-looking extremities of the head and legs.

Willie's fingers itched for a pencil to capture this splendid creature on paper. But he was jerked out of his reverie by a loud squabble. One of the boys had dared to suggest that there was an even finer stallion in a nearby village. He was answered with jeers and given a shove by his neighbor that almost toppled him from his perch.

There was more speculation: exactly which mares were worthy of being bred to this champion, when the first foals from him could be expected next year, and whether the stallion would in the long run prove to be worth the money paid for him. Hans Martens, no doubt echoing the pious views of his elders at home, asserted gravely that the 850 rubles could have been more wisely spent on "good works" than on such a worldly luxury as an imported stud horse. A stallion from one of the government stud farms or from a Mennonite estate owner would have served the same purpose and cost much less.

Hans was hooted down in a chorus of derision. The boys forgot about the horse in their eagerness to heap scorn on the whole "Prayer" Martens family, whose aggressive piety was considered unseemly by most villagers.

But the young stallion, as if aware he had lost the boys' attention, drew it back to himself in dramatic fashion. In the warmth of the late afternoon sun his mighty organ began to unsheathe itself with slow luxuriance. The boys watched fascinated. The wits in the crowd began to vie with each other in describing this most interesting part of the stallion's anatomy, and in seeing who could invent the most outrageous comparisons for it. The contest, punctuated by frequent bursts of raucous laughter, became wilder and wilder.

Willie tried not to listen. Not that he was embarrassed by the crudities. Like all Mennonite village boys he was used to the coarsely explicit "horse corral" talk that was rigidly banned from the homes. About farm matters Mennonite males of whatever age were completely matter-of-fact. Willie's irritation stemmed from the very presence of the others. Seeing the beautiful stallion for the first time had turned out to be an experience he wanted to savor without interruption from others. He detested the rough, insensitive behavior and comments of the other boys. They were ignorant clods. *Schwien,* pigs.

The boys were building to a riotous climax of earthy Low German expressions about the stallion's sex and function. Young "Prayer" Martens left in disgust, most likely to "go home and pray for young sinners," as one boy yelled after him sarcastically.

The dead-pan voice of Isaac Klassen — known as "Hinkie" because of the hitch in his walk — cut through the snorts and guffaws in a final burst of inspiration.

"Yeh, his sack looks like Mrs. 'Syrup' Wiebe's big black jelly bag hanging outside her summer kitchen."

"That's her husband's that she hangs out to dry," came the topper like a flash from an older boy who had just stepped up to the fence.

The boys exploded in a gasping hysteria of mirth.

The joke-fest ended as casually as it had begun. Belly muscles weak from laughing, the boys sobered up and began drifting away. Their places were taken by sedately inquisitive men from the village. Having completed the mandatory Saturday afternoon barn and yard cleanup in good time, they too were coming for a quick look at the new stallion before supper.

Willie glanced back just in time to see the big horse veer in a swift side movement as one of the men at the fence whistled sharply to attract his attention.

He would come back when there was nobody else around. Then he would have plenty of time to study the noble animal more closely.

Mayor Thiessen's farmstead lay at the northern or "upper" end of Blumenau while the Fasts lived at the "lower" end, so the brothers had a good half mile to walk home.

Still exhilarated by the beauty of the new stallion, Willie let his eyes wander along the broad village street. He was barely conscious of Kolya trudging beside him as his charged imagination lent newness to his surroundings. Its glow held him like magic. For the moment he saw even the familiar face of the village as new and different. The street was deserted in the late afternoon quiet, the stately acacias on both sides stitched together by neat mulberry hedges and immaculately whitewashed wooden and brick fences. Behind their discreet curtains of greenery lay the farmsteads, the narrow end of each house facing the street with the bulkier connecting barn bringing up the rear. The driveway, with its ornamental gate posts, exposed the whole *wirtschaft* to view, like something freshly cut open with its insides suddenly revealed.

Outwardly, Blumenau differed little from scores of other Molochnaya villages. It had been founded in 1804, the third village in the original north-south string of ten villages established along the Molochnaya River. It contained thirty-two full farmsteads consisting of 175 acres each, plus twenty half and quarter farms. There were also a number of *anwohner*, families of landless workers and tradesmen who lived on small lots consisting of house and small garden. About eighty families lived in the village, giving a population of about 450. A village of average size.

That was the public Blumenau everybody knew. For Willie, the village had also a personal and private reality that fascinated him even though it never fully revealed its mystery. He dreamed about this secret Blumenau and tried to explore it from the moment his grandfather Fast (the Young Daniel) had first told him the story of how the Mennonites had come to the Molochnaya a hundred years ago to what they had been told was empty steppe land waiting for the plow. But it wasn't empty, they found. Not quite.

In the midst of steppe grass so high that even a man on horseback was barely visible, they had found other human beings — strange, fierce-looking heathen called Nogaies. The Nogaies, his grandfather told him, were small, brown-skinned Tatars, seminomads who pitched their beehive tents of black felt wherever they found good grazing grass. Apparently their favorite place to camp in the southern steppe was the marshland around the "River of Milk," the "Molochnaya," whose low eastern bank overflowed in spring and provided lush pastureland.

Grandfather Fast didn't know much more about the Nogaies except that one of their *auls,* or tent villages, had stood on the very spot selected as the site for Blumenau. When the Nogaies found that their fierce shouts and menacing gestures were ignored, they gave way sullenly to the big, stubborn *njemtsi,* the silent foreigners. Angrily, they struck their tents, loaded them onto huge oxcarts, and removed themselves from the accursed intruders.

The clearing where the tents had stood, bare and trampled hard, became part of the rigidly laid out "Meadow of Flowers," Blumenau.

Willie often wondered what the Nogaies had been like. He had never seen a Nogai, of course, except in his imagination. The little Tatars had disappeared from South Russia generations ago. He had never even seen a picture of them. But their memory haunted him. They were an intimate part of his inner, secret Blumenau. When his grandfather had told him about them he was so excited he immediately began to search for traces of their existence. He convinced himself that his father's homestead stood on the very spot where the little beehive tents had stood. He walked around after that with his eyes to the ground, sure that if he searched hard enough he would turn up something — a clue, a sign that the Nogaies had left behind for him alone to find.

After scouring every foot of the farmyard, the orchard behind the house, even the front garden by the street, he still had found nothing. But the feeling that someday he would find evidence of the Nogaies' existence never left him. Even now, at thirteen, he sometimes caught himself with his eyes to the ground, searching for something, some actual thing that would prove the little brown people had really lived on the very spot where he was living.

At such moments he felt inexpressibly sad and bereft. He didn't know why.

The magic was gone. He was back on the deserted street, walking beside Nikolai. He glanced at his brother's freshly shaved head. His own hair was still of winter length. It had been spared the spring shearing because he was going to secondary school in Halbstadt in September. The longer hair was important. It meant he was no longer regarded as a mere boy. Kolya had demanded the same treatment on the grounds that he was only a year younger; but Papa had curtly dismissed Kolya's shrill protests and ruthlessly sheared his head bare with the old handclipper that caught on your hair and hurt like crazy. Afterwards, Kolya refused to speak to Willie, even though they shared the big sleep bench in the summer room.

Kolya's behavior, in fact, was getting stranger every day. There was something frightening about his younger brother, Willie had to admit. Barely twelve, Kolya was so fiercely independent and flew into such violent rages when anyone crossed him that he was becoming the despair of the family. Even the harsh thrashings Papa frequently gave him in the stable seemed to have no effect on him except to make him even more sullen and stubborn. The boy was "growing up wild," which meant, Papa said, he was behaving in a way that brought shame to his family and embarrassed the villagers.

Why was Kolya so angry all the time? He seemed to resent everybody around him. In spite of all the time they had spent together, Willie felt he and Kolya were growing rapidly apart. Kolya was secretive and never confided in him anymore. He rarely even talked about what interested him and kept to himself as much as possible. Like this afternoon: they had finished raking the yard early, but Willie had to plead with Kolya to come to Thiessens with him "to see the stallion from Germany." And he knew Kolya had nothing else to do. That's what was so maddening. Kolya never pleased anybody, not even himself.

Sometimes Willie felt that Kolya was not his real brother, that he had come into the family by mistake. Like the man Papa knew in Lindenau who had been found in a horse manger as a baby, abandoned there by unknown and probably unclean hands. Kolya had a temper like a drunken Russian, Papa said. He could go crazy over nothing. There must be a demon inside him. Mama said God sometimes sent a cross where you least expected it. And then you had to learn to bear and pray.

When the boys entered their yard they spotted an unfamiliar droshky standing there.

"It must be Onkel Lepp, the traveling preacher," Willie guessed. "He's speaking in church tomorrow. He's Papa's old friend. Kolya," he grinned, "that means we'll have something better than Saturday beans for supper. Maybe even chicken and apple *platz.*"

Nikolai merely grunted, although his eyes lit up at the mention of a special supper. Food was one of the few things that could soften the boy's surliness.

"Let's take a look at his horses before we go in, Kolya."

They walked past the front entrance of the house to the huge, steep-roofed brick barn attached to it. Inside the barn they were met by old Anton, the Russian stableman, excited as usual, his sloe eyes dancing above his long gray beard.

"Aha, aha, here you are to see the visiting horses. Over here, *khlopsy,* in the spare stall where they should be. Beauties, ain't they, my cock pigeons?"

The old man's ragged sleeve pointed to a fine pair of slender, matched light bays standing a little tensely in the unfamiliar stall. While the boys appraised the horses, old Anton chattered away in his unique blend of Ukrainian, Russian, and Low German. He regarded his curious lingo as Low German and took great pride in it. In fact, he had mastered mainly Low German nouns to which he attached light, musical Ukrainian verbs and adjectives. Willie took great delight in the old peasant's mixed speech. The mismatched words bumped along unevenly, like buggy horses trying to pull a loaded ladder wagon.

Old Anton had been with the Fast family for decades. He had shown up one day in the early eighties when the Young Daniel Fast was in the midst of rebuilding the old wooden house and barn into larger, more modern brick structures. Without saying a word the little peasant had started laying bricks, swiftly and straight as a string. When the buildings were completed, without directly asking permission, he cobbled together a large box from leftover lumber and suspended it from the ceiling over the horse stalls. There he had slept ever since.

Having been born into serfdom, old Anton still retained the serf's deferential manner and quaintly formal mode of address to his superiors. He was a jolly, talkative old man whose liveliness, Father Fast said, was fortified by secret nips of *samogon,* although no one could ever catch him at it.

Old Anton's duties, never clearly defined, became more nebulous with time, but he ruled over the barn-stable area with a benign but firm hand. The barn was his domain, the animals his subjects. He treated them like people, and a sick horse or cow often made a miraculous recovery under his skilled and loving hands. He rarely left the barn to go outside and refused absolutely to set foot in the house. His meals were brought to him in the barn, and winter and summer alike he slept in his suspended box, removing only his boots for the night. And inside the house, Mother Fast insisted she could tell from the smell exactly when Old Anton went to bed.

For all his prattling, the old man was mysteriously tight-lipped about his past. When queried, he would only say with a sly wink that it had pleased God to release him from serfdom when he was young enough to enjoy his freedom and for that he was eternally grateful to the *Batushka* Tsar. Every two or three months he would disappear for a weekend that would sometimes stretch into a week or longer. He never asked for permission to go nor did he ever say where he had been; but he usually looked a little tired and subdued when he came back, as if he had traveled a considerable distance and slept where he could.

Winter and summer, Old Anton's costume was the same: a long, thick peasant caftan with sleeves so ample that only the tips of his fingers seemed to emerge from them, and on his head a round, black sheepskin cap of indeterminate age and condition but always set at a jaunty angle. His incredibly narrow shoulders sagged almost straight down to a round little belly held in by a narrow leather belt.

Old Anton received no regular wages and had never asked for any. But his devotion to the Fast family was total, and Willie was his particular favorite.

The moment Willie pushed open the connecting door between house and barn, he knew he was right about tonight's supper. The fat, spicy aroma of chicken noodle soup easily overwhelmed the stale barn smells that clung to the short corridor between barn and house.

Willie got his first look at the distinguished guest when they sat down to eat. Father and Onkel Lepp emerged from the living room, where they had been conversing. The visitor, standing beside his short, broad host, looked very tall and angular in his long, black frock coat. But it was the preacher's luxurious side whiskers that made the boys stare. They swept out from his hollow cheeks in majestic black-and-white cones that seemed a foot long on each side. Along with his piercing eyes and high forehead they gave him an air of dignity such as Willie had never seen before. Onkel Lepp looked as though he was used to being stared at and expected nothing less.

With the eight Fast heads bowed around him, the guest of honor said grace in elegant sounding High German. Covertly, Willie studied the visitor some more. So this was what a famous reiseprediger looked like. Here was another special being from the outside world, that exciting world whose mysteries he could only guess at. Imagine! to travel from place to place just preaching and meeting people and seeing new things. Filled with envy and awe, he heard the rich, high voice pray for "our peace-loving Tsar Nicholas and for the victory of our great Motherland against the heathen foe in the East."

The beautiful voice paused at last and they all said a muted "Amen" together.

Willie looked up shyly when he felt the eyes of the visitor on him as Father introduced the children. The dark, deep-set eyes caught and held his for a moment. Willie thought he recognized something in those eyes. They had the same direct yet far-away expression he had noted so often in the faded photo of his great-great grandfather Daniel Fast. He had often puzzled over that look. And here it was again in Onkel Lepp's eyes. What did it mean? And the visitor's smile. That was strange too. It seemed to disappear into the immense side whiskers almost before it was fully there.

The chicken soup steamed in the big white porcelain tureen; Willie waited hungrily for his turn. The Fast children — from Willie's grown-up brother and sister, Heinrich and Maria, to his younger sisters Greta and Lenchen — ate in silence and listened with respectful Sunday faces as the two men continued the conversation they had started in the parlor. When there was company at the table it was not thought proper for children to speak either among themselves or to guests unless they were asked questions. Onkel Lepp had not asked any of them a question.

The two men were old school friends who had not seen each other in some time. They were reminiscing about their years together in the Halbstadt Central School in the 1870s. Willie couldn't help noticing, though, that his father was a little formal with his distinguished schoolmate, as if not quite certain that he could still treat him as an equal. Father considered himself a simple farmer, and talking to teachers and ministers, he said, always made his tongue feel thick. Willie was amused to note that Papa, with his broad face, fleshy nose, and short stiff hair and mustache looked like an English bulldog sitting beside a Russian borzoi. His voice rumbled like a bulldog's too, deep in his chest, while Onkel Lepp's was light and clipped.

"Yes, Gerhard," Lepp was saying, "in our time P. M. Friesen was the most exciting teacher in the Halbstadt school. That man loved the Russian language and taught it with such skill and enthusiasm one couldn't help learning. When I first heard P.M.'s flawless Russian I promised myself that some day I too would speak it without a German accent."

Lepp fixed his sombre gaze on Willie. "Nowadays, of course, it's easy for our youngsters to learn Russian thoroughly, but in those days most of our people were far from being at home with the language of our country."

Papa looked sly, the corners of his mouth drawing down the way they did when he was about to say something amusing.

"Erdmann, I wasn't a scholar like you. To me Peter Martinovich was fascinating just as a character. I had never seen or heard anyone like him. You remember the time the whole school was buzzing with the rumor that P.M. had decided to get married — and to the ugliest girl in Halbstadt too — and that his friends were trying to talk him out of it?"

Lepp smiled his lean smile and nodded. Willie's sister Maria, who was sixteen and very pretty everyone said, blushed but suddenly looked interested. Mother murmured something about the children, but Father went on.

"That was P. M. Friesen all over. There he was, a good-looking, well-educated young man, a very eligible bachelor who could have taken any girl in town. Mothers with marriageable daughters drooled when they saw —"

"Gerhard, please, we're at the table," Mother smiled. She must have heard the story before. Maria suppressed a giggle.

Father glanced at Maria. He was enjoying himself now. "P.M. apparently kept telling his friends that the girl couldn't help the way she looked and that she deserved to be loved as much as any well-favored girl. Without marriage she couldn't achieve happiness. He wanted to marry her so he could make her happy."

"But did he love her, Papa, or just feel sorry for her?" Maria blurted out.

Lepp looked sternly at the girl. "True compassion is one of the finest kinds of love we human beings are capable of." He turned to Father.

"Allow me to point out, Gerhard, that it wasn't really the girl's looks that Friesen's friends objected to so much as her background and character.

How could a man who had studied in Switzerland and Moscow, a man of culture who was used to moving in good social circles, possibly spend his life with a wife who was without breeding or education? They were completely mismatched, and that was the real point of the whole affair."

Willie's father looked thoughtful. "Yes, I suppose you're right," he allowed. "Anyway, in the end P.M.'s friends won. The engagement was broken off and in a short while he married a fine girl who was in every way suitable for him." He turned his attention back to his plate. "That was P. M. Friesen for you. Who else would have wanted to do such a strange thing?"

Lepp sighed as he accepted another fluffy *tweeback*. "Yes," he reflected gravely, "school days are a pleasant oasis in one's life, an oasis always enjoyable to recall, especially with old friends who once shared it. *Schoen ist die Jugendzeit, sie kommt nicht mehr,*" he softly quoted from the old German folk song.

Father and Mother Fast nodded in agreement and looked around the table at their own *jugend.* Willie wondered whether the Halbstadt Central School would be an oasis for him too.

"Yes, those were simple but good times," Onkel Lepp sighed as he balanced his coffee cup and took a delicate sip. He set down his cup. "Now we live in more difficult times. Even P.M. has changed greatly. You may have heard that he has formed his own church in Sevastopol. He calls it the 'Evangelical Brotherhood' and accepts Mennonites of all denominations as members. Even non-Mennonites."

Lepp's austere face betrayed a glimmer of envy. It was well-known that he was deeply interested in the Russian mission himself, but he was closely watched by the authorities and had been warned more than once not to proselytize among the Orthodox population. Such activities were forbidden by law.

Willie hoped the conversation would turn to the war between Russia and Japan. That was a subject which interested him much more than P. M. Friesen or the Russian missions.

As if reading his mind, Onkel Lepp said: "Recently I was in Moscow and you would not believe how gloomy people are about the war. It seems we are actually on the brink of being defeated by the yellow hordes of Japan. Can you imagine the double eagle of imperial Russia humiliated by those little heathens from the East? Who would have predicted it last year when hostilities began? Losing Port Arthur was bad enough, but General Kuropatkin losing 100,000 men killed, wounded and captured — that is almost unbelievable! The latest report is that Admiral Roshdestvensky's naval force has been almost totally destroyed at Tsushima."

Willie's heart thudded with indignation. Russia defeated on land and sea — with so many casualties? How could that be? Wasn't Russia one of the most powerful nations on earth?

"But surely, Erdmann, it can't be a total defeat?" Father rumbled. "Russia is too powerful. After all, even when an eagle loses his feathers he's still far from being a chicken."

Onkel Lepp had more to say. "It's not just the war, my friend. It's the conditions inside our country that worry me even more. Strikes and riots are breaking out all over. It's as though this ill-advised war with Japan has also released the forces of Satan within. You've no doubt heard of the Hoaliganers, the robber gangs making raids all over the country, robbing and killing. These unholy fiends — they've plundered several Mennonite estates, Schmidt of Jarlitza and Klassen of Meerfeld are the most recent ones. Thank God, so far nobody has been killed."

"Yes, we've heard about the terrible raids." Father Fast's blunt face reflected his concern.

Lepp continued, his cherry *platz* untouched on his plate. "So far our Mennonite colonies have been spared violence; here my friends you live in a peaceful village far removed from the outside world. You and others like you live under God's special protection as a chosen people. But there is a trend towards disobedience and lawlessness, towards anarchy and chaos in our cities and elsewhere that is gathering force quickly. As Christians, of course, we need not fear or despair over this evil force. What is now coming is clearly forecast in the Prophetic Books." Lepp's manner and voice had become intense, the preacher in him rising.

Willie and Kolya sat transfixed by the blazing eyes and compelling voice.

"... whom God has placed over us," the voice was saying. "Tsar Nicholas will have to assert himself, take stern measures to control the wild rabble trying to upset the order and stability of our nation. There is much unholy talk in the cities now about socialism, trade unions, the new proletariat —all Satan's work to try and undermine a God-ordained monarchy and government."

The voice paused for effect. "And who are these so-called proletarians loudly demanding what they call their 'rights'? They're ordinary Russian peasants lured into the cities and given factory jobs. What do those poor souls know about politics? They simply swallow the evil poison pumped into them by the agitators — many of them Jews, no doubt. Stuffed full of violent ideas, these peasants-turned-proletarians go back to their home villages and spread unrest and false doctrines. Unless the government takes stern measures, the whole country will be poisoned."

Lepp's voice throbbed with passion, though his manner remained outwardly calm and dignified. The whole family was mesmerized by that remarkable voice. They waited hushed while their eloquent guest took another sip of coffee. Willie again tensed a little as the searching eyes swung towards him then moved up over his head as if discovering there something more important.

"Yes, we are living in prophetic times, times that are all part of God's wonderful plan for mankind. I believe — " again the voice paused dramatically — " we are entering the final phase of this world. We are in the sixth vial of wrath as foretold in Revelations. The seventh and last vial is already at hand. That means, my friends — " the voice soared in triumph — "we are in the last century before the glorious Second Coming of our Lord."

Willie felt faint. He licked his lips wanly, his half-eaten *platz* forgotten. Less than a hundred years till the end of the world? Perhaps in his own lifetime?

"There is still time to repent, but that time is getting short. The unclean spirits have emerged from the mouth of the dragon and the beast and the false prophet, and are at work among us spreading false doctrines and political chaos. That is why we Christians must work harder than ever to spread the Gospel.

"And that is why I have come here to the Molochnaya to solicit your help for the work to come. There is reason to believe the government may at last be ready to lift the restriction against mission work among members of the Orthodox Church. Yes, that may be the one good thing coming out of these turbulent times. Just imagine, dear friends in Christ, what a glorious prospect, not only to work freely among the heathen of the Eastern regions, the Urals and Turkestan, but soon perhaps even in central Russia among the poor lost sheep of Orthodoxy.

"It will be the final harvest, friends, the great witness unto all nations just before the Savior — "

" — I don't believe you! I don't believe you! It's all lies!"

The shrieked words flamed in the air. For a desperate second Willie thought they had been torn from his own burning throat.

There was a commotion beside him as Kolya stumbled to his feet, his face contorted and white as he faced Lepp.

"You're just saying that to frighten us, so we'll give you more money, so you can — "

"Nikolai," Father's voice thundered. "To your room! I'll deal with you later." He shook his grizzled head as though reeling under a blow. "Blasphemy yet!"

Kolya walked out, his back defiant.

With a stricken look, Father turned to his friend and guest in fumbling apology.

Lepp had not moved, nor did he look shocked or angry. He was not visibly embarrassed by Kolya's outburst, but when he spoke, his voice sounded changed.

"The boy seems very emotional for his age," he observed quietly. "Has he said such things — "

" — He's only twelve, Erdmann, but I don't know what to do with him anymore. He's so stubborn and rebellious we fear for his soul. It's as though he's in the grip of the Evil One."

"You have a grief, Gerhard, but you mustn't despair. Rebelliousness of spirit knows no age. Leave him for now. Perhaps I can have a talk with him later. With God's help I daresay we can get to the bottom of what's ailing the lad. He does seem very young, though, to show such bitterness and rage against his elders."

"We've tried everything, Onkel Lepp," Mother faltered through her tears, "but he just seems to get worse."

Willie rose from the table with the rest. Onkel Lepp and Papa went back to the living room. Mother and Maria began to clear the table.

He felt badly shaken. First Onkel Lepp's frightening prophecy about the end of the world being so close, and then Kolya's mad outburst. He felt as though his head would burst. Something felt torn loose inside him. Was he going mad too? He had heard his parents talk in whispers about *seelenangst,* the dread affliction of the soul that sometimes struck sinners, people not right with God, when they least expected it. They would sit in a room and weep uncontrollably or else howl with guilt until they were exhausted. And no one, not even a minister, could soothe or comfort them. Sometimes they stayed that way until they died. He had heard of such cases.

Possessed by evil spirits. He shuddered. Poor Kolya. What would happen to him?

Still trembling, he put on his cap and went into the barn to help Old Anton with the late chores.

2

On the platform the song leader opened his hymn book, cleared his throat with resonant authority and loudly announced the first number. He repeated it even more loudly, paused a few seconds to allow rustling pages to settle, then rolled sonorously into the opening line of "Jesus, Still Lead On." With late-comers still trickling in, the congregation picked up the vocal pulse and filled the church with pleasant sound, female voices on one side, male on the other. The voices blended and soared on the line

"And although the way be cheerless,"

and sank to a quiet close on

"Guide us by Thy Hand
To our fatherland."

Erdmann Lepp looked out over the singing congregation and his heart surged within him, as it always did at the beginning of a service. God would lead him once again to fill hungering hearts with life-giving words. The power of the Word. How privileged he felt during these moments of inner dedication that God had chosen him to do His mighty work of sustaining and strengthening the souls and spirits of His Mennonite people. And winning souls. Among those who had not yet surrendered themselves to Christ, be they Mennonites or others. Particularly others — the benighted ones mired in ignorance and superstition. Work for the night is coming . . .

His eyes fell on his friend Gerhard Fast, sitting stolidly on the men's side with his oldest son. A fine, devout man, Gerhard, but burdened with a son who seemed possessed of a demon. He had gone to the lad's room yesterday to speak to him, but had been rudely rebuffed. The unnatural boy refused even to look at him, let alone answer questions. Try as he might, he had not been able to break the lad down. Never had he seen anything quite like this twelve-year-old boy for evil stubbornness.

He had failed. Yes, and the father's grim threats and the mother's piteous lamentations when he emerged frustrated from the lad's room had only added to his sense of failure. Perhaps with his sermon this morning he could open that young face clenched tight in the boys' pew at the back.

But the other Fast boy — the artistic one, his father had called him —would surely make up for the bad one. He looked promising with his intelligent eyes and sensitive face. One might wish to have such a boy for a son . . . .

Sitting at the back with the other young boys, Willie felt Onkel Lepp's eyes on him and faltered in his singing. Why was he looking at him like that? Or was it Kolya? Kolya had refused to tell him what went on between him and Onkel Lepp. Not one word. Papa had taken Kolya to the barn. They were gone a long time, but he had heard nothing. Kolya never screamed or even cried anymore no matter how hard Papa beat him . . . Now Onkel Lepp was standing in the pulpit. If only he wouldn't preach about the Second Coming and the end of the world . . .

"Dearly beloved, greetings in the name of Jesus, our Lord and Savior. I take as my text this morning the well-known story of the Good Samaritan . . ."

Willie brightened with relief. It wouldn't be about —

" — deals with mankind's fall from grace through sin and its terrible consequences; but it also deals with redemption and the loving care our Lord bestows on the redeemed."

(I feel God's strength moving within me giving me sharp words to pierce the hearts of these humble folks before me)

" 'A certain man went down from Jerusalem to Jericho.' My friends, before man fell through sin he lived in Jerusalem, the city of peace and innocence, but when he started lusting after the forbidden he wilfully departed from God's chosen path for him . . ."

(Expectant faces bared like petals to the sun let my words shine on them so they can feel Your warmth and love)

". . . 'and fell among thieves,' that is, Satan and his fallen hordes, who have robbed and wounded mankind and left it half-dead with black wounds of sin . . ."

(Sin is everywhere even among these good people Satan and his hordes are rampant . . . the sin-twisted face of that Fast boy daring to defy me screaming liar at me a mere child devil-possessed like one of the hellish monsters I used to . . .)

"Yes, man's whole being is full of the cuts and welts of sin and pride.

He is helpless . . ."

(As one they reach out for my words God's Word that rebellious child let my words drain the defiance from his eyes and knead him into penitence)

Willie could feel his brother beside him, stiff and unyielding; Kolya wouldn't listen or submit, Willie knew that.

". . . priest and the Levite, representing the pomp and power of state churches and the wealthy classes 'passed by on the other side.' But the compasssionate Samaritan, Jesus the Savior, did not pass indifferently by but 'went to him, and bound up his wounds . . . and set him on his own beast, and brought him to an inn . . . .' "

(Lord I am Your beast of burden to carry wounded sinners to the inn of salvation bear meekly for Your sake the sinful souls of Russian peasants heathen in the East unsaved Mennonite youth and backsliders let me bear their burden for Christ)

Christ's compassion and love express themselves in action. Gently he approaches the wounded sinner, bends over him lovingly and examines his wounds like a physician . . ."

Watching Onkel Lepp's transfigured face, the morning light bright on the hairy spirals leaping from his cheeks, Willie again thought of his great-great-grandfather, the Old Daniel Fast. He too had been a mighty preacher. And the founder of his own church, the Young Daniel, Willie's grandfather, had told him once. And had the Old Daniel stood like this, like a holy prophet, preaching the word of God?

"And the inn, my friends, is the living church of God, the Congregation, the place of refuge on this earth for the rescued sinner to grow strong . . ."

(Faces shining they sit secure in the warm inn of the congregation these comfortable Mennonites protected from the wicked world the violent road to Jericho teeming with robbers and cutthroats and false preachers)

"And now Christ, the loving rescuer, turns the patient over to the keeper of the inn, the spiritual counselor responsible for the welfare of the congregation, the guests in the inn. And the two pence, the earnest money given to the innkeeper? They stand for Holy Writ and the Lord's Supper, the vital sustenance of all believers.

"Home at last. Jerusalem the golden. Can we even begin to comprehend, beloved friends, what indescribable bliss that will be?"

(All hushed now in glowing rapture as they picture the heavenly glory to come once more Heavenly Father you have led me and these believers to this blessed summit from which to contemplate the Promised Land)

"But what if there are those among us who are not yet safely lodged in the inn? I ask each of you to look into your own heart and ask yourself if you are still a victim on the road. Naked and half dead are all who still live in sin —whether here or elsewhere . . ."

(Oh rebellious young sinner why will you not look up repent and let

your heart be moved by grace so sullen he sits there that hard
lad unmoved unbending)

"We are living in evil, violent times — the end times — and we must all
learn to be compassionate Samaritans like Christ. We must help to reclaim
not only the lost ones among us, but those lost in other places on other
roads. As Christians we can at the very least help fallen victims with our
prayers and practical gifts."

Willie tensed as he heard the plea to give. What if Kolya should suddenly
scream — no, not that. Kolya moved his head slightly, shifted his weight,
shuffled his feet, then sat still.

". . . and remember that the foreign and inner missions are as intimately
connected as twin sisters. By giving these sisters your faithful support, you
will help God's Kingdom grow and thrive in these perilous times just before
His return in glory. Amen."

Erdmann Lepp's visit had left Willie with confused feelings. He was both
relieved and sorry that the great man of God was gone. Never had he
experienced such a disturbing force in his life. As if Onkel Lepp wanted
something from him, but Willie didn't know what it was.

In his unsettled state he sought solitude. He wanted to think about
things. He wasn't even sure what things he wanted to ponder. Instinctively,
he was drawn to the living room, to the photo of the remote ancestor
whose time-stopped visage he had studied so often. There was a puzzle, a
mystery to be explored. He had an obscure, troubling sense of connection
between Old Daniel Fast and Onkel Lepp, but he had no idea what it was.

He held the small, framed picture carefully and gazed at it by the light of
the window. It was a faded, sepia daguerrotype covered with a fine tracery
of cracks that made the image of his great-great grandfather look as if
covered with a spider web. At the bottom, inscribed in lavish Cyrillic was
the name of a Russian photographer and the place and date, "Tokmak,
1852."

Old Daniel Fast was sitting self-consciously in a chair with carved arm-
rests, his shoulders rounded by time, one elbow resting on a fancy looking
little table top. His pale hands looked at home gripping a gnarled stick
between his legs. He was dressed in a heavy, dark frock coat which exposed
an equally dark vest with a double row of buttons right up to the chin. A tiny
flutter of collar stuck out on top.

As always, it was the face that drew Willie's attention, especially the eyes,
slanted like his own. The sunken cheeks were deeply lined (some of the
lines probably cracks in the paper); the hard, straight mouth was wrenched
downward at one corner, as if in pain, or just stubbornness, or perhaps in an
effort to hold in something — but what? The aureole of white hair was cut
abruptly half-way down the ears in the old Prussian style.

The face looked incredibly old to Willie. But the eyes, those strange eyes, looked both old and young, if that was possible. They were large, light in color, and looked as if they had seen everything worth seeing, and perhaps more. Willie was convinced those eyes could have spotted a lost lamb at the other end of the vast steppe. But they also looked as if they could see right through you. In the photo they were not fixed on the camera, but gazing into the distance slightly to the subject's left. When Willie had been smaller he thought he could make those eyes look directly at him by moving the picture in a certain way. But it never worked.

The eyes were fixed on something else than Willie, on something he would never see himself.

If only Old Daniel Fast had written something down about his life. At least then Willie would have had something to go by in trying to find out the mystery of those eyes. Lately, he had tried to draw that ancestral figure, but each time had failed miserably. Oh, he could get a general likeness, get the proportions and the shading right without too much trouble. But he couldn't capture the quality of the face, the expression in those eyes. Once he had worked on a sketch for hours, got excited, thought he had it. Then he looked again at what he had done — the face, the eyes — and realized that they were not alive. The eyes saw nothing. And in the photo they seemed to see everything.

CHAPTER TWO

Daniel Fast Remembers: (1) Flight from Babylon
Blumenau, Molochnaya, August, 1852

"What, Father, weeping again?"

Neetje stooping over me, wiping my cheeks with the corner of her ever-present apron, as though I'm a crying child hurt at play.

"You mustn't be sad on a beautiful summer day like this, my heart. The dear Lord has made this day for you to enjoy too." She smiles, her long, bony head bobbing over me.

What does she know, this daughter-in-law? She has never been my age —not yet — body one long ache, joints that screech like rusty hinges when I move, seeing everything blurred through water, hearing everything muffled through walls. What does she — ?

"Look, I've brought you something to cheer you up." She puts something hard and shiny in my hands. "It's your picture, the one you had made by the photographer in Tokmak. Peter just brought it. See how nice you look in your good coat, eyes and hair shining."

I try to focus my rheumy old eyes on the image before me. This dim, old man's face staring from the shiny paper, is that really mine? I have never seen a living picture of myself before. Can such a thing be possible? My image fixed on paper? I cannot believe it. "Thou shalt not make graven images," I was taught from a boy. Here I am, an old man near death, staring at my own graven image.

"No," I hear myself say, "take it away. I don't want it." I feel my anger rising. This is the Devil's image of me, not God's. In a moment of weakness — senility, more likely — I have let them do this to me. No more. It is sin. I want it destroyed, undone, removed forever, this smooth little graven image.

"No, Neetje, a sin of vanity, a graven image — an affront to God. Burn it, so no one else will see my shame. I — "

"But, Father, I can't do that. You agreed to sit for your picture. And you know why: so your descendants can see what you looked like. It's their right, and God has made it possible with this wonderful new machine."

"No, daughter. The wise man in Scripture says, 'The men of old are not remembered, and those who follow will not be remembered by those who follow them.' That's the way God has ordained things for us mortals. No, this machine is not of God, it's of Satan. Destroy the image. It's my wish and will."

Neetje takes the accursed thing and returns to the house, grumbling. She means well, this long, stringy daughter-in-law, but she understands so little. I am trembling with outrage to see myself exposed on that bit of paper. I am old, yes, but I am still a creature of the Lord God, and will bear myself erect before Him.

What does Neetje understand about my tears? She thinks I'm sad, afraid of dying. She thinks I don't trust enough in the Lord she finds so easy to love and trust because He lets her be young and healthy just now. Foolish woman.

My tears are of anger and frustration. Yes, anger at this life. Just once before I die I'd like to hold my long life clear in my head — my whole past so I can look at it and understand. But it won't hold still; it keeps running through my memory like water through fingers. My head is too old, too feeble, to hold it all in at once.

"Emptiness, emptiness . . . all is empty. What does a man gain from all his labor and his toil here under the sun? Generations come and go . . ."

But still they keep pushing at me, the memories, like a sour stomach pushing up . . . Ach, what's an old used-up man good for except to sit and remember?

Na, ya, a little I can still do this summer, putter around the garden and orchard slowly. I yearn to touch everything one more time, all the familiar things I made and planted here on my old *wirtschaft*. Be near the earth and its growing things . . . "I go the way of all the earth," said the old King David to his son Solomon. And what's left for me to say to my son Peter? It's his *wirtschaft* now, a good full-farm that with God's help I created here on the Russian steppe.

But Peter's not the farmer I was. He wants to, but he can't. He's a dreamer; from a boy he's been light-headed. Always he saw new things in his head and then tried to make them with his hands. Who put such ideas in his head? Like that new-fangled wagon he made once that got me into so much trouble with my old *gemeinde*. That wagon was something new! With all sorts of gears and pulleys so it could be driven from the seat almost. Ach, but that made a scandal. And I was at fault too, the brethren said, for allowing it. Such a contraption, they said, could only come from the Devil, who is always finding new ways to puff us up with pride . . . We had to destroy it. I did a lot of praying over that. Poor Peter. He understands so much how things work, but he never understood how people work in the world. . . .

But the young Daniel, my grandson, he's not like that. He's more like me. Not like his father. A fine lad. He has his feet on the earth, as they say. He will be a proper farmer . . . .

Ah, the sun, the little round sun. So warm here in the backgarden beside the summer kitchen. A light breeze tickling the acacia leaves about me. Such a giant now, this acacia. I remember when I planted it. That was when the mighty Cornies ordered our people to plant acacias and mulberry hedges, and the cuckoo knows what else. He wanted progress and order that Cornies. That's all he cared about. Get rid of every weed, sow, plant, build — all according to his plans. I hate weeds too, but I was concerned more with the weeds that sprang up in the church. Every time I think of

Johann Cornies something sharp goes through me. Not that he ever did anything against me. Still . . . every time I think of Cornies I think of how he controlled our lives from big to little. The Mennonite Tsar, people called him in later years. And now he's gone too . . . .

I like it best sitting here just after *faspa,* like now. Usually Neetje comes out to sit beside me mending or something while Peter and the boys are doing the chores. So quiet and peaceful now. It's *schnorrijch.* So deaf I am when people are talking, but the barn sounds I can hear plain from here . . . Ya, Neetje is a good woman, sober, God-fearing, and hard-working. Her *tweeback* are almost as good as my Anna's were. But she's twitchy, like most skinny people. Can't sit still for long. Won't allow a body to relax. She thinks she has to talk to me. I haven't got the heart to tell her I'd rather be left alone to think and remember. So I pretend I'm dozing. Keep my eyes closed till she goes back to the house with her long steps. So tall for a woman she is and lean. Not like most women who get round and heavy after marriage. She's also a little crooked, one hip higher than the other, her long head hanging to one side like an ailing chicken's.

Na ya, if my schooling had been better when I was a boy in Prussia I'd be able to write down my life properly now. But with my High German it wouldn't give much, even if my hand didn't shake so badly. And Low German is for speaking, not for writing. Anyway, how could I even begin to put down in words all the things God has led me through in my long life. No, now it's too late for that. I'll just have to sit here remembering and trying to understand the Lord's ways with me before He takes me to His bosom — which God grant be soon!

What could I tell them anyway, my children and aftercomers, about the struggles and suffering and hopes and disappointments I've lived through? And what would they care? Everybody has to live his own life, and die his own life too. Only God can fit together all the puzzling pieces in a man's life. . . .

Maybe, if I just sit here and tell it all to myself — or pretend I'm telling it to a great-grandson I'll never see — I'll be able to understand a bit better, to see what exactly God meant for me when He put me on this troubled earth. Ya, tell it all to someone who would be interested and understand. . . .

Schnorrijch, I've lived here in Russia for fifty years — since a young man — and still my ancestral home in Prussia is as close to me as my life here in Blumenau. How can that be? Maybe that is Satan's work too, to make me remember that wicked Babylon so clearly.

Well, then, let's see where it all began — but watch for Neetje, I don't want her to overhear. . . . The little village of Neunhuben in Danzig I can see clear as this garden. My mother I don't remember. She died when my next-brother David was still at the breast. My father was a half-cripple from an accident and too poor to send us to school. I can't remember being just a child playing, with nothing else to do. Our father always made us work at something in the house to sell. For a while we made brooms, then wicker baskets.

Even as a boy I felt a strong pull towards the free life of the world. I taught myself to read in my spare time. Mostly I read in the Bible and the *Martyrs Mirror*. The stories I liked best were the ones about strong faith and miracles. I always had the feeling that those stories contained secrets that were hidden from me. God's mysteries — oh, how I wanted to know them; but always I was ashamed of my own ignorance. And of how my love for the world took my attention away from God.

At fifteen or sixteen I started working with the men of the carpenters' guild. There I fell into evil ways. Smoking and cardplaying and drinking and other unclean habits (even that Polish girl — with the others, in the old shed in Huebner's field) blunted my soul so I didn't even bother reading God's word anymore. My father had died that winter and as the oldest boy I was now the head of the family. I was my own boss and came and went as I pleased. Like a black ram in the field.

Then one day my uncle Jacob Riesner, my mother's brother, who was church teacher in Pordenau, came to our house and talked in earnest with me. I had always liked Oom Jacob and respected him as a man of God. In his slow, drawling voice, the tears standing full in his eyes, he told me my sinful life was leading me straight towards Hell. Now it was time to stop and make things right with Him.

I listened with my eyes on the floor, and I knew inside that I had reached an end and a beginning. Yes, now it was over with my freedom. Oom Jacob's words bit into my conscience like sharp teeth. I felt like a helpless lamb in the jaws of a wolf. And the wolf wouldn't let go no matter how I struggled and tried to tell myself that my life with the carpenters was not really so bad, that they were good men at heart and amusing companions. Oom Jacob had opened my eyes and forced me to see what that world really was. It was Satan's world, impure and wicked and full of vanities. I knew I'd have to submit to the sharp teeth of my conscience.

When I was twenty I took catechism. Then I was baptized and taken into the *gemeinde*. Oh, how happy that made me. But the wolf had let me go too soon. I soon had to admit I still wasn't free of sin or sinful thoughts, that my mind still turned to worldly pleasures with each new sun. In my misery I started to read God's Word and the *Martyrs Mirror* again. My *seelenangst* drove me to read far into the night and then I wept and prayed on my knees till morning. After a while I began to feel easier about my life and ways. God led me to the *Wandering Soul,* a precious old book of spiritual meditations and Christian dialogues printed in the old Dutch times. With its help my soul won through and I experienced fully for the first time the wonderful grace of the Lord.

Now I had peace in my soul, but in my mind I was still restless. I no longer enjoyed working with the godless carpenters. When uncle Jacob Riesner invited me to work for him on his farm in Pordenau I accepted gladly. I worked hard, and soon Oom Jacob hinted that when I was ready to settle down he might sell me half his *wirtschaft*.

And that time was not long in coming. There in Pordenau God led me to my Sarah. She was the daughter of Elder Franz Klassen. Sarah came sometimes to Oom Jacob's house to help out when my Taunte Suess was sickly. When I met Sarah I knew right away it was God's will. Sarah knew it too. But Oom Franz said no, not yet. It was fall, I remember. He took me into his *grootestow* and closed the door. Oom Franz never wasted words. "Boy," he said, "now you listen. If you can get half of Oom Jacob's *wirtschaft* you can have her. But only if. Then you will wait till the work is finished next fall. Sarah will be nineteen then and ready."

The following September Oom Franz read the banns for us in his church at Pordenau. Sarah and I made all our visits in Pordenau and Neunhuben and other places in the Werder. It took us two full weeks. On September 25, 1798, we were married in Klassens' large parlor by Oom Franz himself. It was a large wedding and even the Klassens' yard and barn couldn't hold all the wagons and horses, so some had to be taken to the neighbor's yard. The older people sat in the big room. The young married men sat in the fore room, the front door having been sealed off with benches. Outside, on the front door, a little sign said: "Through the barn, please." The young married women sat in the corner room and tried to keep their babies quiet. Sarah and I sat in the parlor in front of Oom Franz.

Ach, that was a long, choking afternoon! It was stuffy with so many people and the room smelled of camphor balls from all the Sunday clothes. I tried to listen to Oom Franz's sermon, but I kept thinking about Sarah and how it would be with us in marriage. Sarah looked calm and pretty in her black dress and black lace *haube* on her head. I kept my face straight to the front, but she knew when my eyes looked sideways at her and the corner of her mouth twitched a little. There was also a little sweat on her upper lip. My heart glowed with her warmth beside me.

Never could I have imagined how living with my Sarah would be. I had my half-farm from Uncle Jacob and had already built a house and barn on it with my cousin Abram's help. Oom Jacob helped a little too. So we moved in right after the wedding. The furniture was part of Sarah's dowry from her parents.

From the first night I had such passion for Sarah I began to feel guilty. Was it seemly to feel so strongly for another human being? Even though we had been married in the eyes of God and made one flesh, I worried that my strong desire for Sarah was becoming a sin of the flesh. I thanked God daily for having given me such a fine wife. But sometimes I feared I loved Sarah even more than God. Sarah was very happy too and we looked forward eagerly to our first child.

But it was not to be. God blessed us in our work and our love for each other, but he did not send us a child. At night in our marriage bed we prayed earnestly together — both before and after — but our prayers went unanswered.

Sarah and I worked hard on our half-farm and came ahead. The Lord's bountiful blessing had been extended to us in our *wirtschaft,* but after three years of marriage we still had no children. I kept telling Sarah if it was not the Lord's will that we should have little ones, we would still have each other just the same. But she knew I had to say that, and I knew my words could not really console her. Gradually, we talked less and less about this sad matter.

But we still prayed and did not give up hope.

Another problem was also bothering me more and more. When I looked around at our Mennonite villages, I was shocked by the loose living and growing worldliness I saw among God's people. The spirit of Babylon seemed to be let loose among us; we were rapidly becoming "a dwelling for demons, a haunt for every unclean spirit." I observed that even some of our church teachers, who should have led their flocks in purity, were not walking in God's ways. They usually looked the other way when it came to *schnapps*-drinking and other bad habits; they seemed to tolerate even "the fierce wine of fornication," as the prophet says. Just as long as such things didn't become open scandals. From my reading of Menno Simons' writings I knew the only proper punishment for such transgressions was the ban, complete communal shunning and exclusion of the offender. But the church teachers seemed to be less and less disposed to carry out this God-ordained punishment.

Na ya, I recall David Friesen and his stepdaughter. Friesen had married an older woman, a widow with property who had an unmarried daughter not very much younger than he was. When this girl was brought to bed with child, everyone of course suspected Friesen himself. Oom Jacob, my uncle, who was declining rapidly by this time, went with the other teachers to see the girl. They sternly admonished her to tell them who the father was.

"I don't know, I don't know," she wailed. "I couldn't help it. It must have been Satan." And that was all they could get out of her.

Oom Franz and the other two teachers were willing to let the matter rest there, but Oom Jacob, feeble though he was, wanted to get at the truth. He talked gently to the girl, but she only groaned and said she was tired and wanted to sleep.

At last, Oom Franz in his blunt manner said: "Oom Jacob, that's enough. If she won't tell us that's the end of it. It's on her conscience. We won't persecute her anymore."

When Oom Jacob protested that this was giving in to sin, Oom Franz said dryly; "Jacob, maybe you should save your strength to prepare yourself for the next world, and leave this world to younger men."

Oom Jacob felt deeply offended, he told me later, but there was nothing more he could do.

"Daniel," he said to me not long after, "my day is nearly ended. But you and Sarah are young. You must not stay in this accursed Prussia. Here it's almost out with us Mennonites. The German king doesn't want us here anymore. In any case, we are too close to the world here. You must go to Russia, where they are begging for new settlers. There you'll be able to live apart from the world and make a fresh start. I've heard there's good land there in the south, in New Russia, not far from the colony of Khortitza.

"Best of all, you'll be able to begin a new spiritual life there. Here we've lost our forefathers' ways. You've read Menno, you know what he says about finding and keeping the pure way. Once we had that way here, but now we've lost it. Perhaps there you and others like you can establish the pure church once more. A complete way of life — God's way. That is the hope you must take with you."

My uncle's words struck deep into my heart. My feelings for the old man were strong. He'd been like a loving father to me. Not only had he led me to the Lord, he'd helped me get a good foothold in life. Now he was giving me a new dream for the future, a hope for a better life with other true believers in a new land.

Sarah and I discussed leaving and prayed earnestly about it. I could tell that my wife was not as eager to go as I was. And how could I blame her? She knew her family would never leave Prussia and would not want her to go. It was a hard decision for her. I did not press her. She needed time to pull herself through. For days she kept her lips pressed together and said very little. Then one night she looked at me with her deep eyes, tossed the thick rope of her night braid over her shoulder and said: "Where you go, Daniel, I go." I knew by the way she came into my arms that she meant it in earnest.

When we told Oom Franz he was furious, as we'd expected.

"So this is how Oom Jacob gets back at me?" he thundered. "I know this is his doing. That old sheepshead. What does he know? He's been talking about Russia for years, and how all Mennonites should get out of Prussia and move out there to that barren wasteland. Now he's twisted your heads too. Well, Fast, I tell you you're not taking my girl to that treeless wilderness to starve. So get it out of your heads."

It was no use trying to tell him the land was very good in Russia, that the Mennonites who had been there since '89 were sending back favorable reports. To Oom Franz Russia was one big desert without trees, water, or good earth, and nothing I or anybody else could say would change the picture he had. My father-in-law had a large *wirtschaft* and was considered the wealthiest man in the area. At his age you couldn't blame him for not wanting to start over again in a strange country. But that he would try so hard to prevent us from going was very painful, even if Sarah wasn't as eager as I.

Na ya, my father-in-law was a hard, stubborn man used to getting his own

way. He blustered and threatened and once or twice he and I almost came
to blows. But I knew that under his tough bull's hide was a true Christian
and loving father.

And so it came. When he finally realized he couldn't change my mind he
turned right around and said no more, but helped us all he could.

"If you insist on going to those ungodly wilds, you may as well take
something with you," he gruffed, "so you won't have to run around like field
mice looking for something to eat."

And that was that. Now he heaped on us everything from furniture to
horses — all the things he'd threatened to withhold before.

Oom Franz gave us a large, sturdy wagon that I fitted with a rain-tight
canvas roof. We had to repack the wagon many times before we got in all
the furniture, household articles, clothes, and other things we wanted to
take. We also decided to take six horses and two cows. I'd sold my half-farm
to my cousin Abram, who already had the other half of Uncle Jacob's farm.

About 200 families were getting ready to trek to Russia that summer, but
some couldn't get ready in time and had to stay behind. They planned to
leave the following summer. In our group we were thirty families, mainly
from Pordenau and the neighboring villages of Prangenau and Neukirch.

We left after the noonday meal on August 17, 1803. Our group was to
meet at the home of our parents, the Klassens. We were already there the
day before and spent our last night there. In the morning the wagons began
arriving from all directions. Soon Oom Franz's yard was filled with wagons
of all shapes and sizes. The women, made useless with waiting, sat passively
inside and around the house. The men and boys, too excited to sit down,
stood about the yard chatting or fussing around their wagons. Some looked
pale and nervous.

At noon Oom Franz invited us all to the back garden where a long trestle
table stood in the shade loaded with plates of cold ham, *tweeback,* and
bowls of *plumemoos.* When everyone had gathered around the table, Oom
Franz bowed his head and said grace. Sarah, standing beside me, was
weeping quietly, as she had at the farewell service in the church the day
before. She knew this was the last time she'd ever hear her father's familiar
voice asking God's blessing.

After we'd eaten, Oom Franz read a passage from Scripture, and then we
all sang together — those who weren't sobbing:

> Abide, O dearest Jesus,
> Among us with Thy grace
> That Satan may not harm us,
> Nor we to sin give place.

Ach, that was a sorrowful parting! We men hitched up our wagons and
that at least gave us something to do for the last few minutes. The women
just stood there looking at each other, embracing again and again and
breaking into fresh sobs.

Some of the village men and boys accompanied us on horseback that first afternoon. Towards evening they took their leave and went back. Some of our younger men were also on horseback as outriders and came to the wagons only for the night.

The first few days we were still in the Marienburg Werder and could stay with Mennonite people for the night. Then the land began to look less familiar as we continued south along the Vistula until we reached Graudenz. There we left our beloved Vistula behind and swung due east towards the Polish-Russian border.

Our guide was a Heinrich Wall from Ladekopp. This man had moved to Khortitza with the first emigrants, but returned to Prussia a few years later when he found the new country not to his liking. Now he wanted to go back again. He was a restless man this Wall, but a good talker who knew his way around. Some said he wasn't a decent man, but he always treated us well on that long trip. Even though the Russian government had told us exactly what route to follow, we were lucky to have a man like Wall to lead us. At the Russian border, we had been told, there would also be a Russian soldier or two to accompany us the rest of the way.

After the first few days we fell into a routine so regular the days followed each other like echoes. We got up early in the morning when the haze and the dew were still on the ground. After we'd gone a few miles we stopped to feed and water the horses and ate some breakfast ourselves. In the early afternoon we halted for another rest, then traveled until sundown. We then drove all the wagons into a neat circle, with the last wagon placed directly before the first one. After supper around the fire we went directly to bed, except for a few of the women who had to get food ready for the morning or perhaps do a little mending by candlelight.

Sarah, never a loud or talkative woman, became quieter with each day. I began to worry about her, whether I was doing the right thing taking her away from all her loved ones to a strange land where it would be hard at first.

Then one morning she got up feeling sick to her stomach. She told me she wanted to ride in the Fehdraus' wagon that morning. Mumtje Fehdrau had been looking after sick people in Pordenau for many years. She was also our midwife.

When Sarah returned to our wagon that afternoon she looked much better. Her face was so bright and happy I was surprised.

"Daniel, what do you think? A miracle has happened. Mumtje Fehdrau thinks I'm with child. Can the good Lord have blessed us at last — now, after five years?"

I was so astonished I didn't know what to say. "Now you are carrying, Sarah, now? Are you sure? Now, while we have this long hard journey before us?"

I didn't know whether to be happy or sad at this news.

Who could know God's mysterious ways.

From that day Sarah was a changed woman. It was as if the old Sarah had died and a new one born. She was so happy and talked so it was a blessing to hear.

"Now you're like your namesake in the Bible," I joked with her, "but at least you didn't have to wait till you were ninety, did you?"

She only smiled and squeezed my arm.

It took about two weeks of steady traveling to get to the Russian border. At the border town of Grodno we received our immigration money from the Russian government: ten rubles per head and fifty per wagon. A husky young soldier with friendly black eyes joined us there. He knew a few words of German and Wall a few more of Russian. Together they would lead us to our new home.

Now we were in the vast, mighty empire of Russia! Everything felt and looked strange. So much space, so much emptiness, with only here and there a village. So different from the crowded Werder with a village every few miles. And the people so different too. The men with their tangled, uncut hair and beards and long shirts hanging down loose or cinched in with a belt; their women and girls in wide skirts looking drowned in their huge, bright kerchiefs. But they smiled and waved at us and were friendly enough, even though we were *njemtsi,* foreigners. When we stopped at a village for water, before we could even ask the men and boys started hauling up buckets of water from the creaking wooden draw wells with their long poles sticking up. The peasant women invited our women and girls into the whitewashed huts and offered them bread and hot tea.

We let them know as best we could that this was to be our new home too, though we still had far to go.

After two more weeks of steady travel in a southeasterly direction, we reached Ostrog, in the province of Volhynia. Mennonites from the Thorn region in Prussia had settled there a few years before. We decided to stop for a few days with these people. They were quite poor but shared what they had with us and we were grateful to be with some of our own again. Our horses were thin and tired and many of our wagons in urgent need of repairs. We were glad for a chance to rest up.

Our guide Wall told us we had now come a little over half way on our trek. We'd been on the road for over a month and had another month ahead of us. The young soldier, sitting very straight, always rode in front and sometimes galloped on ahead so far we could barely see him. We always felt relieved to see him come back again.

At the large town of Berdichev we caught up with another group from the Werder, a much larger group than ours. They were having a lot of sickness among their children and had lost several. They'd been in Berdichev for three weeks. We decided we would travel together in one long train the rest of the way. We'd been warned there were many wild bandits and outlaws in the southern steppes and we knew the larger our train the less danger there would be of attack. Our one soldier wouldn't be able to fight off a whole gang, we knew.

Praise be to God, it never came to violence. We were never attacked, though several times in the distance we saw large bands of horsemen kicking up clouds of dust as they rode across the plain. At such times, Ivano, our soldier, would tell us to order the women and children to lie down in the wagons while we men kept the wagon train moving and tried to look as unconcerned as possible.

I often wondered what we would have done if we had been attacked. Would we have helped our soldier and defended ourselves as best we could, like other people? Or would we have surrendered meekly to those fierce robbers and let them do what they wanted with us? Na ya, we had a few guns with us — for hunting rabbits and so forth — the younger men and boys mostly. But we were, after all, peace-loving Mennonites, the defenseless ones who believe in following Christ's example of turning the other cheek. Fortunately for us, perhaps, the good Lord chose not to put us to the test. At night Ivano supervised the watch, posting guards who watched the deep, singing murk around us with anxious, straining eyes and ears. But God kept His restraining hand over us.

We reached Khortitza on the Dnieper in late October after a journey of a little over two months. Tongue cannot utter our joy and relief at finally reaching our destination safe and without loss. It had been a long, hard road, especially for my Sarah, who was beginning to swell out a little. I was worried for her. She'd grown pale and listless again in the past few weeks, though she never complained and tried to remain cheerful. I hoped that here in our temporary home she would come back to herself again.

Our relief and happiness did not last long. We were given cramped lodgings and not very good food, for which our Khortitza brethren cheerfully charged us high prices. Even then they made us feel they were doing us a favor by keeping us at all, and that they would be happy to see the last of us. Among ourselves we often quoted the old Mennonite saying,

Two days a welcome guest
After that unwelcome pest.

The Khortitzers had the saying too, we knew. But perhaps we shouldn't have resented their treatment of us as much as we did. They had come here with almost nothing and had a hard start. They saw we had a great deal more with us by way of household possessions, machinery, and animals. They also knew we'd brought money. For money they would shelter and feed us. There had been no one here to do that for them.

Even now I don't like to think about that humbling winter. It was one tedious blur of waiting and watching with nothing to do. Endless hours to think and worry about the future. As Sarah got closer to her time, her health got worse. It was the journey that had done this to her. Or so I believed.

The baby came on a gray, cold March morning, a boy, our Peter. It was a hard birth. Mumtje Fehdrau worked grimly, almost desperately. When it was all over she turned to me, white-tired, and said, "Daniel, for a while there I didn't know if I was fighting for a life or against a death. Maybe both. If I hadn't felt God's hand on mine I would have given up."

The baby was fine. Sarah barely pulled through. That was a bitter time for us.

As soon as Sarah was strong enough we set out for the new Molochnaya settlement, about a hundred miles southeast of Khortitza. The rest of our group was already there. We found that Klaas Wiens, who was to be our *oberschulze,* our administrative chief for the colony, had already laid out the first string of villages in a north-south line on the east bank of the little Molochnaya River.

We took a farmstead in Blumenau because our relatives, the Herman Riesners and the Gerhard Wiebes, had chosen it. They told us when they got there the site of the village was occupied by Nogaies, a heathen tribe that lived in felt tents and lived off the land with their herds of cattle. We got to know these wild creatures all too well. What they wanted more than anything was to get their hands on our horses, bigger and stronger than theirs, and on our women and girls. They were the cleverest thieves we'd ever seen. At night our guards had whips, but even then the tricky little Nogaies sometimes got away with our horses. They never got any of our women or girls, though, Once one of our girls wandered into the man-high steppe grass and there they were, waiting for her. Luckily, her screams were heard by her older brothers, who quickly came to her rescue.

From the beginning Blumenau was one of the best of the ten villages on the north-south line from Halbstadt down to Altonau. Our soil was light and sandy and we had good grazing pasture and hay when the Molochnaya overflowed its shallow eastern bank in spring. The run-off water came our way because the western bank rose to a high ridge. We came to call that ridge the Colonists Hill because the Lutheran German settlers built their villages on that side.

We chose our farmsteads by lot, and my 175-acre full-farm was situated on the lower end of the village. That first year we lived, like the others, in an earthen *semlin,* a hut half in, half out of the ground. We worked hard and soon had the beginnings of a good *wirtschaft.*

When spring came my Sarah was pregnant again. We were grateful that God had blessed us a second time, but also a little fearful of what might happen. Mumtje Fehdrau had told Sarah with her first that perhaps she wouldn't be able to have anymore, at least not for a while. But God not man regulates such matters. We could only hope that the dear Lord would see us safely through this time too.

Ach, the misery and calamity of this life. In November Sarah's child, again a boy, came stillborn. Poor, dear Sarah was so weakened and torn by the ordeal, Mumtje Fehdrau told me, now it was over with her unless God made a miracle.

Heart and soul in anguish, I went to my dear wife's bed. She looked like an angel already, so white and pure on the pillow. My man's heart melted and the hot tears burned my cheeks. I had no words left, but like a dumb beast could only pick up and hold Sarah's thin hand.

She opened her deep eyes for the last time. "Daniel," she whispered, "my pilgrimage is done. I go to the Lord. Take good care of little Peter. And Daniel . . . you are still young. You must marry a good woman and have the children the Lord meant you to have."

Then she closed her eyes and had peace. I gazed at her beloved face and tasted the first bitter fruit of sorrow.

And the words of the prophet shuddered through my riven heart: ". . . if two lie side by side, they keep each other warm; but how can one keep warm by himself?"

CHAPTER THREE

The Loewen Estate "Voronaya," August, 1905

Pain exploded from the welts of his buttocks and back as he tried to shift his body ever so slightly on the straw. He groaned softly, then cursed slowly through clenched teeth. Damn *njemets* cockroach. *Burzhuj* swine. Fat Mennonite bully with his *nagaika,* his double-damned whip. In his rage he tried not to move, just lie motionless on his stomach.

It was getting dusk in the barn loft. The rumble in his gut told him it was supper time. To hell with it! He would stay right here; he didn't need their slop, the rotten *burzhuy* bloodsuckers.

He writhed inwardly as he remembered how the big, thick Papasha Loewen with his red face and terrible black mustache had stood over him with his whip and told him to put his arms around the rubbing post behind the cow barn.

"I didn't know it was wrong to take the chisel, I didn't know," he had sobbed desperately. "I only took it along to try it out. I needed it."

He knew it was useless, but the pain, the horrible pain he knew was coming made him plead. Already he could feel the terrible bite of the whip.

"Then we'll have to teach you that taking along what doesn't belong to you is stealing, boy." The Papasha's iron voice cut through his sobs.

Then it began. Just before the whip whistled he wanted to cry, "Papasha, Little Father, don't hit, I won't take along anything anymore. I'm sorry, don't hit."

But he couldn't get the words out before the first bite of the whip spread unbearable fire through him. His agony was so great he wanted to faint, to slide into stifling darkness, but instead he was screaming and gasping and trying to jerk himself away from the scalding blows.

Time hung black between blows. The fire in his flesh leaped higher and higher until finally, mercifully, he lost the rhythm of strokes and felt the burning subside to throbbing numbness.

He failed to notice the second it stopped. He was in the dust, his body heaving with dry sobs. The Papasha was bending over him, breathing heavily.

The iron voice again. "All right, here's some salve. Get one of the boys to rub it on in the loft. You can stay there or come down to supper. But remember, if you ever steal anything again — anything — I'll send you home and you'll never work here again. Understood?"

He got up slowly, dazed, but he understood. Unexpectedly the black hatred within him gave way to a sudden rush of tenderness that almost choked him. He didn't know why he felt like this. He didn't dare look up at the Papasha, but again he wanted to say something and found he couldn't. He wanted to say, "Papasha, you were right to beat me, I deserved it. You are my Papasha, my Little Father, and I must feel your power when I do wrong." But he just couldn't find the words.

He limped to the loft, trying to fight down the pain, knowing that for the first time in his life he had felt what it was like to have a father, a father who cared enough to hurt you. Not the drunken sots of fathers he saw in the village, beating up everybody in the *khata* in their fuddled rage, from wife to smallest baby. They were *duraki,* idiots. But a real father like this Papasha Loewen, who beat you when he was sober because you had done a bad thing. His tears welled up again at his bad luck in never knowing such a father. He had never had any father, not even a drink-crazed one, that he could remember. Only his mama and his three older brothers.

By the time he had gingerly eased himself down on the straw in the loft, the tender feeling was gone. He was a *durak* to have felt that way at all. To hell with a papasha. The big Loewen was nothing but an accursed landowner who had gotten rich by bleeding the peasants. He often heard his brothers cursing the German landowners, fat pigs swimming in their own suet, demanding more and more while Russian workers slaved for them and made them richer. Savva said now that Russia had lost the war in the East the revolution would start. The peasants would get their land and the workers would go on strike till they got decent wages too.

He was still holding the little box of salve. To hell with it. He tossed it into the straw. He wouldn't use that pig grease. He slid his hand slowly down to his side pocket, feeling for his battered little harmonica, his prize possession. It was all right. Mother-of-God, if he'd had it in his back pocket where he usually carried it, that old swine would have smashed it with his *nagaika.* He ran his thumb along the dented metal, held the instrument to his mouth, and made a few practise sweeps with his full lips.

It soothed him to play, even if the small movements of his head caused twinges in his sore backside.

After a while he slipped the mouth organ back in his pocket. Propped delicately on his side he took out his package of *Troika* tobacco, but found he had no paper. Nothing. Smoking was strictly forbidden in the loft anyway. The big Loewen was as strict about that as he was about taking things along. Hadn't Fedya Maslenko been sent home for smoking in the horse stable?

Yes, and who had caught him? The Loewen son, that stuck-up kid Martin Jakovlevich, who was always snooping around in his fancy blouse and thick belt with the big, shiny buckle. That cocky shit of a student. He even had a long silver pocket chain with a bunch of keys on the end of it that he liked to swing around his fingers as he strutted around trying to be somebody. And he was going to hit me with his belt that time, until the Papasha came along and sent him packing. If he'd only tried. Snotnose. He'd be just like the big Loewen some day.

But the daughter, the little Katya, she was different. He had worshipped her from a distance all summer. She was a little younger than her brother

—about twelve or thirteen — and not the least stuck-up. She was friendly and talked to everybody, even the Russian fieldhands. She was like the Mamasha Loewen, always kind and friendly. Once Katya had passed him in the yard and greeted him, her dark eyes dancing, her voice so gay and lilting he almost melted on the spot. He'd never seen a girl so light and pretty and alive. The girls in his village were cows by comparison. How he'd love to touch that long dark hair and white skin just once. Yes, he would gladly die if he could just once hold the smooth *golubka,* the little pigeon, in his hands.

He moved his hand over his chin, cheek, and forehead and felt with self-loathing the ugly pimple-bumps sprouting there like warts on a toad. Such a beautiful Mennonite girl would never look twice at a pale runt of a *khokhol* who didn't have two kopeks to rub together. He was almost sixteen. Why wasn't he growing anymore, so people wouldn't call him *Maly,* Shorty, all the time and tell him he looked like a dwarf?

Relaxed now, he retreated into his favorite daydream. Some day he would be a real *nalyotchik,* a bandit, with his own gang. They'd live off the fat-assed landowners and do whatever they liked. They'd drink real vodka, smoke good tobacco, ride the best horses, and take all the women they wanted. They would be a *volnitsa,* a band of freemen, like the Zaporozhian Cossacks of long ago. His oldest brother Savva had told him about the Zaporozhian Cossacks. They had lived in an all-male stronghold on the island of Khortitza, all by themselves, as comrades. No women were allowed on the Island but the Cossacks could meet them in other places, like the smaller islands in the Dnieper rapids.

Savva said in the *volnitsa* nobody could give you orders or make you do things you didn't feel like doing. Everybody was equal and everybody followed the voice inside himself that told him what to do. Someday he would be a *nalyotchik* and enjoy this freedom, even if he had to kill all the rotten *burzhuy* around the countryside to get it.

Carefully he shifted his body again and found he could lie on his back without too much discomfort. The shame of his beating flooded back through him. I'm finished with these Loewens, he thought. In a few days when the harvest was over he'd leave for good. Only forty kopeks for driving the wagon loads to the threshing machine all day! At least he'd have enough to get the new sheepskin he needed for winter. Next summer he wouldn't come back to these cursed Germans. Never. He'd get a job at the foundry in Gulai Polye with Savva and Grishka. He would join the factory workers' union and become a secret revolutionary Anarchist like his brothers.

"Nestor, Nestor Ivanovich, where the hell are you?"

It was Petya calling from down below. The hell with him too. He heard more crunching of boots outside, then Petya's irritated voice again.

"Kolya, have you seen that Makhno runt around? If he don't come now, he won't get no supper."

The boy paid no attention. He stared at the darkening rafters and smiled bitterly to himself. No, he'd never work for these filthy *njemtsi* again. And he wouldn't miss any of them, except the little Katya . . . If only he had such a sister. And such a papa. For a few precious seconds he had felt nothing but love and tenderness for the Papasha Loewen, even if he had hurt him with his hard leather whip. The Papasha cared; he hurt you because he cared.

The hell with him, the hell with them all!

CHAPTER FOUR

1

Halbstadt, Molochnaya, April, 1908

"Fast, may I have a word with you, please?"

Surprised, Willie, who was just leaving, turned and paused between the cream-colored Doric columns of the handsome portico which formed the front entrance of the Halbstadt Central School. It was Mr. Burzev, his art teacher, hurrying towards him. What could he want?

"If you are walking home, Fast — Wilhelm, if I may — perhaps you will permit me to accompany you part of the way?" the teacher, a little breathless, asked in his elegant, rather formal Moscow Russian.

Willie murmured a polite acceptance and the two descended the steps and turned into the street.

Alexander Michaelovich Burzev was Willie's favorite teacher. A small portly man with a pale moon face and a finely shaped mustache, Bursev was friendly and encouraging in class. When he liked a student's work he was ebullient, almost bouncy with approval. When he disapproved he grew reserved, stroked his mustache with his pudgy forefinger, and hissed tonelessly through his large front teeth.

Willie felt a little self-conscious walking down Romanov Street with Mr. Burzev. He had expected to walk home with his pals "Snapper" Loewen and "Sparrow" Priess, not with his art teacher. He glanced up at the window-dominated facade of the red-brick school building and wondered where his friends were. Probably behind him somewhere, wondering what he was doing with Burzev.

"Well, my lad," the teacher began as they walked past the school's handsome picket fence, its length neatly sectioned off with thick, square brick posts. "In a few days you'll be graduating. And I suppose then it's home to — Blumenau, is it — for the summer?"

"Yes, sir, I work on the family farm in summer."

"Good, good, exactly what a young man needs after a long winter of studying, some healthy outdoor work to clear away the cobwebs and toughen the muscles, eh?"

Burzev smiled, his prominent teeth flashing above his snow-white collar and dark cravat. He gave Willie a comradely pat on the shoulder, then raised his hand lightly to his gold-framed pince-nez in a familiar gesture.

They passed the squat, weathered granite monument erected by a grateful government for relief services rendered by the Mennonites during the Crimean War. Willie didn't like the monument, considered it ugly and out of place here, a disturbing foreign element. A government official must have designed it. Today he barely noticed it.

"And next year? Any plans for further education?"

"Yes, sir, I'm entering the teacher's training program here."

"Well, well, so you want to become a teacher?"

Mr. Burzev looked surprised. His pale, round face turned blandly serious, as it did in class when he had something important to say.

"Wilhelm, I take the liberty of telling you something. You have been a good all-around student, but as an art student you have been — I speak frankly now — ah, more than that. As an art student you are — exceptional." He considered the word carefully. "Yes, 'exceptional' is the right word, I would say. I don't mind telling you that you are the first art student of real promise I have had in my fifteen years of teaching here in Halbstadt and across the river in Prischib. You show unusual skill with the pencil. You have the kind of feeling for line and form and texture that can only come from within yourself. No one can teach you that."

Willie blushed with pleasure. He was not used to such naked words of praise. He glanced shyly at the white profile under the black bowler. Such words from Mr. Burzev! He didn't know what to say. He stammered his thanks, but Burzev raised his cane suavely and assured him there was no need. But he looked pleased all the same.

The boy felt encouraged enough to mention a problem that had been bothering him for months. "I enjoy your classes very much, Mr. Burzev, but I'm not satisfied with my work this year. I'm trying harder than ever, but my sketches and water colors somehow aren't getting any better. You've taught me valuable tricks of perspective and shading and, and other techniques, but — "

"Wilhelm, please allow me to interrupt," the teacher cut in smoothly. "I think I know what you are trying to say. If I'm not mistaken I struggled with much the same problem at your age. You see, my lad, what you need now are not just new techniques, though you'll always want more of those too. What you need most right now are new ways of seeing."

Burzev's dark eyes were shining and his big teeth bared in a grimace of concentration as he gripped the boy's arm again.

"New ways of seeing, sir?" Willie pondered the words. "Oh, you mean new ways of seeing as an artist?" He was suddenly swept up in his teacher's excitement.

"Yes, yes, that's it. A good technique is indispensable, but in the long run an artist can only develop by growing as a person. That means growing a new set of eyes every once in awhile, learning to see and feel new sensations, impressions, experiences. He can do that best by moving about in the world. Discovering the incredible variety of shapes and images and colors and textures all around him." Burzev opened wide his arms. "The world of the artist is an ocean, Wilhelm, not a shallow pond."

He pulled at the boy's arm as they reached the end of the block and the teachers' residence where Mr. Burzev lived. But the teacher showed no disposition to stop. He tightened his grip and indicated he would like to walk on.

"But, sir, how can I develop new ways of seeing here in Halbstadt, or at home in Blumenau where everything is so familiar, so ordinary?"

As they talked, the boy was overcome by a sense of futility, an awareness that he was powerless to change his lot, to get the freedom he needed. He was bound to a world where most things were ordered and controlled, and very little left to chance. From birth he had been heated and hammered, bent and shaped by family, church, and school to fit his Mennonite world as precisely and serviceably as a properly made horseshoe fitted a hoof.

All very well for Mr. Burzev to talk about growing new eyes, experience new things in the outside world; but what chance did he, Willie Fast, have of ever getting away to explore the ocean of the artist?

I'll always be a small carp stuck in a village pond, he reflected glumly.

Noting Willie's dejection, Burzev was sympathetic. The large teeth retracted slowly under the sculptured mustache. He gazed past the boy and said quietly, "I know there isn't much you can do right now, Willie. But you must prepare for the time when you can. Even here on the remote steppe you can begin to grow those new eyes." He brightened again. "You know, I'd be quite willing to go on teaching you next winter — private lessons in the evenings. I promise to teach you everything I know before you leave here, if you're willing to work. After that" — the voice fell again — "it's up to you . . . and your parents. Sooner or later you must try to get into a good school of art — in Odessa or Kharkov, perhaps even Moscow or Petersburg."

Burzev suddenly swept his arm in a gesture so wide it seemed to include not only the town of Halbstadt but the whole Molochnaya settlement. "You can't grow into a mature artist here, no matter how good a start you make. You must get out as soon as you can — hopefully with your family's blessing, but if not then. . . ."

"If only I could, sir, I'd like more than anything in the world to go to art school. But my parents want me to become a village teacher. My father would never let me go to art school."

Burzev looked reflective. "Willie, you know that aquarelle you did the other day, the one of the open steppe with the road from the village cutting across the foreground and the Colonists Hill in the background with large, soft masses of cloud piled about it?"

Willie nodded. He remembered the trouble he'd had getting the proportions right, the perspective of distant space and height. The sky had kept wanting to get bigger and higher while the foreground kept receding, with the village in the far corner shimmering almost out of sight.

"Do you know what's wrong with that composition?" Burzev pursued. "You lost control of your subject. You wanted to depict a Mennonite village set in an immensity of steppe and sky. What you really did was to show a shadowy, insubstantial ghost village lost and isolated in a world too large for it. Even the road that is supposed to run towards the village — to be its lifeline — is pinched off and lost to the eye before it reaches the remote little village."

Burzev stopped and his eyes held Willie's. "Don't you see, Wilhelm, that sketch expresses more than you meant it to. It reveals your inner yearning for a larger world than the one you know. Your romantic spirit is eager for release from your narrow, confining Mennonite *bauernkultur"* — he gave the German word an odd Russian twist. "Your artistic nature is as baffled as an untamed rook tied to a fence post. Forgive me, my boy, for being so frank," he added when he saw the look on Willie's face.

Willie stared at his teacher in fascination. Never had anyone talked to him like this. It was as though Mr. Burzev had boldly, without knocking, entered the most secret room of his being.

As if Burzev had read the boy's mind, he said in a low, passionate voice, "It's all there in your work, my lad, as plain as if you'd said it in words —plainer even. Your drawings are mostly about the village life you know best — farm buildings, animals, horses, and men plowing — and you have observed accurately enough in a technical sense. Some show real mastery of form and design. But I must speak frankly again, Wilhelm. Forgive me. Most of them are done in a false style. You portray Mennonite village life as romantic with your noble, prancing plow horses and stately barns and trees resplendent under radiant skies. It's a German brand of sentimentality, I suspect. Your people must have brought it with them. Like that water color you did a few months ago of a farm nestled protectively under magnificently arching trees, with the peaceful river curving gently around it in the foreground. In one sense, that picture breathes serenity, love, security. But, Willie, that scene can also be seen as a prison, the farm a lonely island cut off from the rest of the world.

"Don't you see the contradiction? You interpret your world as larger than life, as an unsullied paradise on earth because that's the way you have been taught to see it. But is that the only reality of your world? You are old enough to know something about the ruthless conformity of your village life. What about the stern self-denial and monotonous toil of your people? Their compliant faith and ironclad forms of worship? Their ignorance of art and beauty? Their lofty contempt for the joy and spontaneity of the Russian peasant culture that surrounds them? That's the other side of your world, and it requires interpretation too, and in a more realistic, courageous style than the one you are using now.

"If you really love and believe in your Mennonite world — and I know you do — then you must learn to see it more completely. All sides of it. And the best way to do that is to leave for awhile, to stretch and strengthen your artistic faculties in the inexhaustible world outside."

Willie felt as if a stone had been dropped on him from a great height. His elation had broken like an egg as Burzev talked.

The teacher, sensing that he had stunned where he meant to enlighten, tried to make amends. "Perhaps I've said more than I should, Wilhelm. All I really want to tell you is that you have a rare talent and that you must develop it properly. I am eager to help you in any way I can. Someday, perhaps, I can help you get into my old school, the Stroganovsky School of Art in Moscow. I spent the three best years of my life there." He looked suddenly wistful.

Willie said nothing as they resumed their walk. He had noticed several passersby looking at them with mild curiosity as Burzev held forth. In Halbstadt students and teachers, especially Russian teachers, did not usually talk so intently and for so long on street corners.

Before they parted, Burzev added a final plea. "I ask you to think about what I've said, my young friend. And one more thing. There is a hidden world right here in the midst of your colonies waiting to be discovered. That world existed long before your industrious people created their little oases here. It's the free, boundless, mysterious steppe with its wild floods of grass, its tough wormwood and stunted *krushka* trees, which grew here eons before you Mennonites planted your tame acacias and mulberry hedges. The spirit of this place is that of the wild, nomadic Nogai, not that of the domesticated German. Remember that, Wilhelm."

Burzev raised his cane lightly to the rim of his bowler and turned to walk back to his residence.

As Willie crossed the street, he heard the rhythmic tapping of his teacher's cane on the wooden sidewalk.

"Hey, Rembrandt, you look like an Old Testament prophet with a vision." Martin Loewen, known as "Snapper," stepped grinning from behind an ornate gate post. With him was Jacob "Sparrow" Priess. Willie's pals had been waiting impatiently and were full of curiosity about his long talk with Burzev.

"What did old Pinch-Nose want with you anyway?" Snapper demanded bluntly. He hated Burzev's compulsory art classes with a passion. Snapper was an exuberant extrovert who had neither the skill nor the patience to satisfy the exacting standards Burzev demanded of his students in art and penmanship classes. Snapper detested the little Russian's habit of fussing with his pince-nez as he lectured, and the way he silently stroked his mustache as he bent over Snapper's desk nearsightedly examining his crude drawings or ill-formed lettering.

Willie frowned at the intrusion. He had been left with conflicting emotions and wanted to be alone. For once, he did not feel like confiding in his friends. He knew he must keep Burzev's remarks to himself, especially the advice about getting away from a Mennonite environment if he wanted to grow as an artist. He knew that Russian teachers were tolerated rather than loved in Mennonite schools. No matter how long they stayed they were regarded as outsiders and never fully accepted. Mr. Burzev's frank criticism would be very much resented if it got around.

"Come on, come on, out with it, Rembrandt." Snapper emphasized his impatience by giving Willie a painful snap on the earlobe, the irritating habit that had earned him his nickname.

Willie clapped his hand to his stinging ear, his temper rising. "You won't get anything out of me that way, Snapper. It's a private matter and none of your business."

The two eyed each other belligerently. Both were tall and muscular, though Snapper was heavier in build. They wrestled and fought constantly and had been known to hurt each other. As usual, the smaller Sparrow Priess tried to keep the peace between the reserved but stubborn farmer's son and the boisterous, sometimes haughty estate owner's son.

"If he doesn't want to tell us, Snapper, it's because he's been asked not to. Let it be."

But Snapper was in one of his aggressive moods. There were times when Willie's cool self-possession and Jacob's gentle common-sense had a perverse effect on him.

"He's just being bullheaded again, Sparrow. Look at his eyes, they're as slanted as a Tatar's. They get that way when he's trying to put one over on you."

The slightly oriental cast of Willie's eyes was a family trait about which he was often teased. The teasing no longer bothered him, though as boys in the village school he and Kolya had ferociously gone after anyone who called them "slant-eyes."

Snapper's handsome, open face now wore its usual expression of good-natured bantering. "Old Pinch-Nose was probably telling him what a great artist he is. That's why he's looking so sly."

Willie relented. "All right, Loewen, since you've made such a shrewd guess I may as well tell you a little more. Burzev thinks I've got real talent. He even thinks I should go to art school some day."

But Willie said nothing about Burzev's hints that he must not allow himself to be stifled as an artist in the narrow confines of his Mennonite world. Sparrow would probably understand, but Snapper might blab everything to his father and make Burzev sound like an ungrateful, hostile Russian in Mennonite employ. Mr. Loewen was, after all, a member of the Halbstadt school board.

The boys had reached the small confectioner's shop on Station Street, not far from the Pauls' student residence where Willie and Snapper boarded. Snapper headed for the door. He loved sweets and always seemed to have enough kopeks to buy them.

Sparrow continued on home. He lived in a small backstreet house with his elderly aunt. He was sensitive about his poverty and blushingly refused even the modest charity of Snapper's candy. Sparrow came from an impoverished *anwohner* family in the village of Sparrau (hence his nickname), but he never talked about his family nor had he ever invited his friends to his aunt's house.

Young Priess was a scholarship student who received a hundred rubles per year. The scholarship was really a delayed loan offered by the colony to promising but indigent students. In return, recipients were obliged to serve as teachers in the colony for a period of six years while repaying the loan at the same time. Sparrow was bright and extremely industrious. One of the top students in the school, he looked forward to becoming a teacher. But even teaching was to be only a stepping-stone to the ministry. Priess was a serious-minded youth whose ultimate dream was to become a missionary in a foreign country, preferably Sumatra where the highly respected minister Heinrich Dirks had been the first Mennonite to open a mission a generation ago.

Snapper's invitation came as a complete surprise. "Rembrandt, how would you like to spend a week at Voronaya this summer? I've already asked my parents for permission to invite you, so it's all settled."

"Sounds exciting, Snapper. I'd love to see your place, but I don't know if my father would let me go during the busy season. I'd have — "

"You could come after the harvest, in August. In mid-August we're having a large bible conference at Voronaya. There'll be guest speakers from all over — Germany, Switzerland, even England. We've had conferences before. They're kind of exciting. The speakers I like best are the ones who explain the prophetic books — you know, the Book of Daniel and Revelation — all that stuff." Snapper gave his most winning smile. "And the food's just great, old buddy."

Willie was eager to accept. It would not be easy to get permission from Father but he would try. A trip to Voronaya would be an exciting break in the long summer in Blumenau.

"Oh, and Rembrandt, remember I told you about the motor car — the new Opel we ordered from Germany? Father's promised to let me learn to drive it this summer. By the time you come in August I'll be able to whisk you around at thirty miles per hour. How does that sound?"

It sounded just fine to Willie. This summer would be different. He thought about the things Mr. Burzev had told him. He would follow the teacher's advice and start growing a new pair of eyes. He would spend every spare minute sketching from life. He would go out on the steppe and look for native subjects — anything he could find that would get him away from his "German sentimentality," as Burzev had called it.

Just before he drifted into sleep that night, he recalled that Snapper had made the invitation in the privacy of their room. That meant, of course, that Sparrow Priess would not have received a similar invitation.

2
Blumenau, July, 1908

Under the merciless July sun Willie smeared a grimy paw across his sweaty brow as his body jolted and swayed to the uneven rhythm of the clattering binder. Up front, Kolya, wearing a floppy straw hat, guided the double team of horses, hitched tandem style, from the broad back of Mashka, the left rear horse. Kolya was in a foul mood, as usual. Willie could tell by the rough way he handled the horses and the vicious swipes he took at the horse flies. Kolya hated driving the team. He considered it a kid's job and had mounted Mashka only under the direct threat of a beating from Papa. Well, just as long as Kolya kept the horses on a straight line Willie didn't care what mood he was in. He had his own problems.

Willie was still getting used to the new McCormick self-binder he was using for the first time. Papa had shown him how to operate it and stayed with him all morning to see that he did things right. Now, in the afternoon, he was on his own at least till *faspa* time, Papa had said.

Willie had let out a whoop of excitement when he got home from school in early May to find the new green and red binder gleaming in the shed. It replaced the old Russian-made *lobogreika,* the "brow warmer," on which he had spent muscle-cramping hours last summer pushing off the heavy mounds of wheat stalks with a fork as they flowed in ever-coming streams from the cutters. He had only been spelling off Papa for brief periods, but even then he was constantly assailed by panic as he realized how unequal his young strength was to the relentless task. But he had hung on grimly, knowing that Papa had to rely on him because his older brother Heinrich simply wasn't healthy enough for that kind of work.

Yes, he was grateful for the new binder. It was vastly superior to the primitive *lobogreika.* But it didn't really do much more than change a horrendous task into a merely unpleasant one. The heat and the noise, the dust and the tedium, held him in thrall as before. By mid-morning the novelty of the new machine had worn off and the day once again crawled along like an endless, clanking chain belt.

He shouted at Kolya to take the corner more carefully. They had missed a strip that would have to be picked up on the next round. Papa wouldn't like that if he saw it. He settled back to the long, straight advance upfield.

If only he could believe in farming the way Papa did. Like other Mennonite farmers, Papa believed in his land in the same direct way he believed in God. Working it, he said, was a sacred trust, a divine command from the Almighty. Papa believed there was no higher calling than farming, not even the ministry or teaching, which were necessary only to serve the needs of tillers of the soil and their families. God's chosen ones. Papa always talked about the land as a living thing, as a bountiful mother who never grew old or died. You gave her your life-long devotion and care. In return she supported you and gave meaning to your existence here on earth. "The land may groan, but it never dies," he was found of saying. The land was always there, solid, durable, dependable. When Papa sat on the *schaffott,* the side-porch, in the evening, he liked to talk about the land and conclude by saying, "Always remember, boys, nobody can carry the land away on his back overnight." He always said this as if saying it for the first time. Sometimes Willie felt like asking him if maybe somebody *had* carried away the *anwohners'* land on his back, but he knew that would hurt Papa's feelings.

"Kolya, keep the horses straight," Willie yelled over the din, and then was almost pitched from his seat as his surly brother jerked the horses back into line.

Sometimes he felt guilty about not feeling the same way about farming as Papa did. Not that he disliked everything about farming. Far from it. Something within him responded eagerly to the way the working of the land was intimately tied to the cycle of the seasons. The natural rhythms of farming were deeply satisfying. He also like the purposefulness of farming, the planning required to fit together the different tasks to form a self-contained little world with its own life and personality, related to but distinct from the larger world around it.

What he didn't like was the hard, constant, tedious labor required to keep the little farm world running smoothly. Papa gloried in heavy manual work; Willie did not. He hated it. But he knew that if he were ever to express his true feelings about farming to his parents, their bewildered anguish would be much the same as if he were to run away from home or tell them he didn't believe in God. No, he would hide his feelings as best he could.

It was more than enough for his parents to have one son like Kolya.

Willie looked up at the bobbing young back of his brother. Kolya had completed only the first year at the central school in Halbstadt. His grade and the teachers' reports had been so bad that Papa had not sent him back for a second year. Principal Stefanov had told Papa it was the right decision. Kolya was now working at home, but Willie suspected he was only biding his time and would leave home for good as soon as he could get away. Barely fifteen, he already spent most of his spare time with the Russian workers and youths in the village, and had several times gone to Tokmak with them without permission. A flogging from Papa meant little to Kolya now. Even the threat of a flogging from the mayor of the *volost* in Halbstadt didn't seem to scare him.

Papa said Kolya was hard-necked beyond all belief. Where did he get such a wicked will?

Willie was surprised when Papa and the girls arrived in the wagon with the *faspa.* The time had passed more quickly than he thought. They ate seated on the ground in the shadow of the wagon. Greta, eleven, and Lenchen, only seven, gleefully played hostesses, and kept plying them with *tweeback* and coffee. Papa soon rose to inspect the field and to see whether their rows were straight. After assuring himself that the new binder was working properly, he left with the girls, having given Willie an encouraging slap on the shoulders.

Back on his hard steel seat, Willie thought about how his summer had gone so far. The first big job had been the hoeing and weeding in the *bashtan,* their huge melon and cucumber patch. That was in early June. He and Kolya were condemned to long days of spine-paralyzing toil amidst the myriad green tendrils festooning the black soil in ever more convoluted patterns. Day after day under the blazing steppe sun. Why were there so few clouds in summer? He and Kolya scanned the horizon ceaselessly, looking for the billowing navy clouds that would bring temporary relief from the slavery they had to endure. But rain seldom came to the Molochnaya in mid-summer.

In the second half of June they had been busy with the haying, again a task filled with long days of mind-clenching labor.

And now the harvest, the biggest farm task of all.

He watched the sheaves, neatly tied, drop one by one to the carrier, from where he released them with a lever at proper intervals. This was what intrigued him most about the new machine, how it could tie its own sheaves and deposit them so cleanly. He marvelled at the smooth mechanics of the operation.

More than ever this summer he lived for his sketching. He tried not to be too open about it though. Papa hadn't said much, but it hadn't escaped Willie that his parent gave him a sour look of disapproval whenever he saw his son tuck his precious "portfolio" under his arm to wander off somewhere to sketch. Papa liked his sketches of the *wirtschaft,* but only those.

Last summer Willie had given his father a large oil sketch for his birthday. It showed the family farm bathed in the serene light of a summer sunset, a halo of soft light illuminating the red-tile roofs like a benediction. Papa's eyes grew moist when he saw it. He said it affected him like a prayer. The painting now hung in the parlor, on the same wall as the portraits of the Tsar and Tsarina.

This summer Papa was making it plainer than ever, though, that he regarded his son's sketching excursions as an unmanly waste of time. In an unguarded moment Willie had shown him his nature sketches. Papa looked at them impatiently. "Na, boy," he said curtly, "aren't you a little old to be drawing flowers and birds? Leave that for the *maedchenschule* girls in Halbstadt. Maybe it's time you stopped mooning around with your pencils and crayons and got on with something useful.

Willie almost blurted out that this was his real work and always would be, but his courage failed him when he saw the closed look on Papa's bulldog face. If he tried to tell him, Papa would understand nothing but the shame of having an artist for a son. Nothing else.

His mother was more sympathetic, but she too became guarded and more evasive when he hesitantly confided to her one day his burning desire to pursue art as more than a boyhood hobby, perhaps even as a vocation after he had been trained at an art school.

"Your father would never give consent to anything like that, my dear boy," she said softly, not looking him in the eyes. "You know he has a very different future planned for you. It would grieve him deeply if you ever mentioned such a thing to him. He is reluctant even to let you train as a teacher, but that's as far as he'll go."

Willie guessed that it was his mother who had persuaded Papa to let him train as a teacher. She gazed at him with such affection and concern he felt ashamed. "My darling son, if you only knew how much he yearns to have you follow in his footsteps, take over the farm some day, become a pillar in the community as he is . . . ah, that's what he longs for. You are his only hope. We know Heinrich's lung condition is only a matter of time. And what can we expect from our rebellious Nikolai? If you leave what will become of our beautiful *wirtschaft?* It is one of only two in the village still in the hands of the original family. Did you know that?"

Her voice trailed into silence, and she turned away from him struggling for control. He wanted to comfort her, but he didn't want to lie. So he had said nothing.

The rig had come to a stop. Surprised, Willie realized they had reached the "home" corner again. Kolya, torso twisted on Mashka's back, shouted, "Time to quit, Willie. You want to work all night?"

Willie bristled. It was up to him to decide when to quit. He glanced at the setting sun. Kolya was right. They still had chores to do when they got home. But he was tempted to make one more round. Just to show Kolya. Well, it was late enough. The Russian stookers were trudging across the field from the other side. They also knew it was time to quit.

The boys rode home in silence, weary and hungry. They looked forward to a good supper. Mama and Marie knew how to fill empty harvest stomachs with huge helpings of special dishes they did not often make at other times.

Willie again worried about his invitation to Voronaya. August would soon be here and still he hadn't received permission to go. So far Papa had put him off by saying there was lots of time to think about the matter. He must get Papa's consent somehow, before it was too late. Why was his father so grudging about such things?

Willie helped himself to three thick slices of fried ham, his wearinesss already forgotten. Beside him Kolya was chewing vigorously, face impassive as ever. Father was in a good mood. The new binder had performed up to his expectations the first day.

"Na, ya, boys, if we have a good crop again next year we'll get one of those naptha motors Bock and Riesen make in Schoenwiese for threshing. Think how happy Mashka and Prince and the other horses would be if they didn't have to plod in a circle all day anymore." He beamed around the table. "Doesn't old Anton always say it's unnatural for horses to walk in a circle?"

"But Father," Heinrich said in his delicate, musical voice, "Miller Peters' Jash says in two, three years at most farmers around here will thresh with steam engines, or even with petrol tractors. Wouldn't it be better to wait?"

"Ho, boy, it won't be that soon. We'll have time to wear out a naptha motor before those machines come."

On impulse, Willie decided the moment was right to angle for his visit to Voronaya. He began casually.

"Papa, Martin Loewen told me they've had a steam engine at Voronaya for several years."

"Well, yes, Voronaya, Willie, there you're talking about a harvest operation a little larger than ours. What would they thresh a year — 500 hundred acres of wheat, a thousand.?"

"I don't know exactly, Papa, but it's a lot . . ." He paused. Now was the time. "Papa, have you had time to think about my invitation to the Loewen's *khutor?* Martin says the bible conference is very inspiring."

Father looked interested. "Yes, I've heard very favorable things about those conferences. Apparently the Loewens invite dozens of guests to hear special speakers. And pay for it all themselves. Of course, they're well-to-do. The rich can be expected to carry a larger burden of the Lord's work. That's only biblical."

"Martin wants to pick me up here by droshky and bring me home again too. It's less than forty miles, he says. It wouldn't cost me anything."

The last point was shrewdly calculated. Papa seldom made a practical decision without considering the costs carefully.

"Yes, yes, I'm sure it would be a good experience for you, Willie. We'll see what Mama thinks."

Mama, naturally, said yes and so it was settled. He was going.

Tired as he was, Willie lay in bed that night with his brain churning. Even Kolya's bitter grumbling in the barn that Willie was as usual getting favored treatment, had not deflated Willie's buoyant mood. Kolya was still muttering threats and warnings when they went to bed. Mercifully, he had fallen asleep quickly.

As usual, his thoughts centered on his art. Getting permission to visit Voronaya was an exciting minor victory. Much more difficult was his long-range campaign to persuade his parents to let him go to art school. There he had made little if any progress. But he had not given up hope. Just by working at his art regularly he was keeping his hopes alive.

He had not forgotten Mr. Burzev's advice to start growing a new pair of eyes. Everywhere he looked now he saw dazzling profusions of forms, colors, and textures where he had never seen them before. Earlier in the summer, when he had more time, he had gone on long sketching excursions where he concentrated on the larger forms. He tried to capture the subtle undulation of the steppe, its moods of light and shadow, the ever-changing configurations of cloud overhead. Then his attention was caught by the "forest" that curved in a shallow crescent around the upper end of the village. He wandered for hours in the groves of poplars, oaks and elms that had been planted in Johann Cornies' time and had been the pride of the community ever since. Finally, he moved on to the river bank and the marshy lowlands around it.

Then, with growing excitement, he began to look at smaller, more intimate things, the kind he had never given a second glance before. With rough, almost feverish strokes of his pencil he would try to bring alive a clump of steppe grass in all its tough vitality thrusting up in a dense spiral from the hard, dry crust of the soil. Here and there he came upon delicate wild flowers — an early white crocus, a yellow cornflower, or a rare poppy oozing scarlet from the earth like a drop of blood from a cut finger. He spent hours drawing and shading flowers and vegetation he couldn't even name. Even his mother could provide only homely Low German nicknames for the flowers, and none at all for the small plants and weeds whose subtle shapes and colors fascinated him.

The flora, at least, were stationary subjects. The fauna were more troublesome. When he did see a marmot, or a ground squirrel, or a hare it didn't hold still for him. Nor did the birds.

His favorite sketching spot, the one he went back to again and again, was on the river bank behind Blumenau. There straggly lines of willows drooped in heat-exhausted quiescence and the coarse marsh grasses curved their heads sleepily over the sluggish brown waters. He would seat himself comfortably against the deeply corrugated trunk of an old hermit oak (strangely out of place here where no other trees except willows grew). Facing the summer-shrunken river and beyond it the smoky, blue-green stretches of the long, high ridge of the Colonists' Hill, he would untie his home-made portfolio and take out his sketching materials. Using the portfolio as a sketching board, he drew whatever attracted his fancy.

The spirit of the place. That's what Mr. Burzev had called it. The mysterious Nogaies. Sometimes he fancied he was actually seeing them in their old habitat: lithe, flat-nosed, brown people with wet black cherries for eyes and blue-black hair, and clothes made of shaggy skins and swatches of bright cloth. He tried over and over to draw them that way, but he could never get them right. They always turned out looking vaguely monstrous, and that is not how he saw them in his imagination. He did better with their animals: their horses small and fast, but according to what his grandfather had told him not fit for anything except riding. Their cattle, miserably thin in spring, had always swelled to sleekness on the lush grass around the "River of Milk." He drew them both ways.

But why did these people belong here more than he did? Only because they had been here first? And why had they been chased away? Just to make room for Mennonite villages? It didn't seem fair.

Sometimes, as he sat under the old oak gazing at the Hill in the distance, he dreamt of becoming a famous artist. His friends at school had nicknamed him "Rembrandt" after a teacher had told them that the great Dutch artist had become a Mennonite while living in Amsterdam long ago. Willie didn't know whether there had been other Mennonite painters in Holland, but he did know there had been none in Russia. Perhaps he would be the first one.

But before he could hope to become a famous artist, he would have to find a way of getting to art school.

3
Voronaya, August, 1908

It was a long but exhilarating drive. The slim, high-spirited blacks had maintained a superb trotting pace since the boys had left Blumenau at seven in the morning. They made one stop at a Russian village to feed and water the horses while they sat in the shade in the Loewens' smart black droshky and devoured the substantial lunch Willie's mother had made them. By mid-afternoon they had covered most of the distance and were rapidly approaching Voronaya.

Snapper's handsome face as always radiated confident well-being. He loved to talk, but was an impatient listener. Willie, for his part, was quite content to relax and listen to Snapper's lively chatter. Snapper's sheer animal vitality was so strong that it often had a curiously relaxing effect on Willie. He was content just to bask in the glow of his friend's personality. He liked Snapper and enjoyed his company, but he knew they didn't have similar interests. Sometimes he wondered whether they were merely school chums who would inevitably drift apart when their school days were over.

Snapper, with uncharacteristic seriousness, was now talking about his parents. They had not always been the ardent Christians they now were, he said. Early in their marriage they had grown quite worldly. But shortly after Snapper was born they had both experienced a dramatic conversion while attending revival meetings conducted in the Molochnaya by the young traveling evangelist Erdmann Lepp.

"They went to hear him out of curiosity, Rembrandt, and came back with the love of Christ in their hearts. That's the way Mutti describes it. And the same thing happened to many other respectable church members then."

Willie could well believe it. He remembered the hypnotic effect Onkel Lepp's preaching had on him the time he came to Blumenau.

Since then the Loewens of Voronaya had changed their lives completely. They had thrown themselves body and soul into Christian service, starting with the symbolic act of donating all their jewelry to the foreign mission. The idea for the summer bible conferences had come from the David Dicks at the Apanlee *khutor,* who had been the first to sponsor such events in the

Molochnaya.

"My parents regard them as very important missionary projects and say they receive many blessings from them."

"And what blessings do you get from them besides the good food?"

"You won't mock once you see what it's like," Snapper shot back. "You'll be impressed, I promise you. This time, besides Onkel Lepp, we've invited several foreign speakers. The famous Professor Stroeter from Germany will be there, and also Fritz Oetzbach, who's a tiny hunchback but a wonderful man of God. Oh, and the Reverend Broadbent from England is coming. Imagine, Willie, all the way from England."

Willie was about to ask if the English Broadbent could speak either German or Russian, when they reached the top of a low rise and Snapper exclaimed:

"Look, Rembrandt, there it is on the right — where the trees are."

Willie looked across the rolling fields at what resembled a small park set on a flat-topped knoll which sloped gently down to the broad fields around it. Through the trees he caught glimpses of large and smaller buildings grouped in what appeared to be a loose square. A double row of angular poplars flanked the approach road that wound up to the estate in gentle undulations. It was a magnificent sight.

"Snapper, for once you didn't exaggerate. It's a splendid-looking place. I've seen Cornies' famous Juschanlee and from a distance, at least, it's not as pretty as this."

Snapper beamed with pride. "My grandfather bought Voronaya in the 1870s from a Count Tenietsev, a young nobleman who had frittered away his wealth at European gaming tables. The main part of our house and some of the smaller farm buildings still date from that time. The rest we've either built new or had to rebuild."

The blacks, sensing home, moved swiftly along the approach road. Willie spotted several of the multiple-share plows known as "buggers" at work in a nearby field. On the other side of the road, in a field surrounded on two sides by trees, grazed the largest herd of German red cows he had ever seen.

Willie wondered what it would be like to live on such a place, to be in a position to inherit it some day. No wonder Snapper had so much self-assurance. One day this magnificent *khutor* would belong to him. Willie felt a touch of envy. How superior all this was to a village *wirtschaft,* even a full farm like theirs. This was what Mennonite estate-owners liked to call an *oekenome,* a self-contained "economy," a complete agricultural centre. It was really a farm village which was controlled in every phase of its operation by the will of one man — its owner.

They reached the massive front gate, which was topped by a gothic arch with the name "VORONAYA" painted on it. Then they were inside the spacious courtyard, its centre dominated by a rondell of flowers spreading lavish colors in a luxurious pyramid.

On the far side of the courtyard stood the manor house, its long brick facade painted lemon yellow with white trim. The central part of the house consisted of two stories, with a single-story wing added at each end. The wings were topped by square towers almost as high as the two-story main part. In front there was a long porch covered by a gaily decorated wooden roof supported on slender pillars connected by three archways, the middle one forming the entrance over the steps. Along both sides of the manor running right around the courtyard were numerous other brick buildings — stable, granary, workshop, school, servant quarters and others — so that the whole complex formed a loose square, as Willie had noted from a distance, enclosed by a white brick fence.

Drawn up in neat rows along the sides of the courtyard were wagons of all shapes and sizes, from stately, covered black fourgons to light, sleek kaleshes, droshkies, and even a tiny one-horse "drogger."

"Well, our guests are here, so things must be in full swing," Snapper said as they dismounted. A stable boy came to take care of the horses.

Snapper made for the house. "They're probably all at the back, in the garden, having *faspa*. After we've eaten, I'll take you on a tour of the place."

Inside, they were warmly greeted by Snapper's mother, who was just organizing the kitchen service. Mrs. Loewen was a plump, lively little woman whose black dress and frilly black lace *haube* were set off by a snowy-white apron. Her eyes danced behind wire-rimmed glasses and she had a child's beaming smile, which Willie sensed at once was as natural to her as breathing.

"Well, well, well, so this is the Wilhelm Fast we've heard so much about." Her voice was as warm and intimate as her smile. "Martin says some day you'll be a famous man with your talents. I've heard of the Fasts from Blumenau. They've always had a good reputation, I know." She beamed up at Willie as if the Fast reputation was proof enough of his talents. Hardly pausing for breath, she shrilled an order in Russian to the servant girl just emerging from the kitchen. Still beaming her delight, she invited the boys to come outside to meet all the wonderful guests and "take in a bite" with them.

On the tiled terrace outside several dozen guests, most of them men, were seated at two long trestle tables set with sparkling *faspa* china. From the broad terrace ran a freshly sanded walk bordered by low hedges interspersed with colorful beds of flowers. The hedges were backed by double rows of immaculately trimmed trees — acacias, maples and chestnuts, mostly. Beyond them were informal groupings of various fruit trees, including pears, cherries and apples. Willie was used to fine gardens, but he had never seen one as grand as this.

The two boys quietly took their places at the larger of the two tables. There were no formal introductions and they were hardly noticed in the lively discussion that was under way. Willie immediately recognized

Erdmann Lepp at the other end of the table. He looked as striking as ever, though his flaring side whiskers seemed a little grayer.

Another distinguished-looking gentleman, probably the professor from Germany, Wilhelm guessed, was talking. He was a mild-looking man with deep-set eyes under heavy eyebrows and wore a neatly trimmed Vandyke. He spoke with a soft, slurred German accent that sounded strange to Willie's ears.

"Yes, my friends, I believe the work here in Russia among you Mennonites is bearing a rich harvest. There is a spiritual vitality and hunger for the Lord's Word truly gratifying to a visitor like myself. I'm sure Brother Oetzbach shares my sentiments. If only all of Russia could share the wonderful blessing of the living Word, instead of remaining mired in spiritual sloth and the dead formalism of Orthodoxy."

The others murmured their assent. Lepp set down his coffee cup. "The good professor has touched on an issue of vital concern to our Mennonite brotherhood. The 1905 October Manifesto promised religious freedom for all Russian citizens. Now, three years later, we are still not allowed to win souls for Christ among adherents of the state church."

He looked around the table, his gaunt face intense. "Somehow we must win that right. Russia is ripe for a great spiritual awakening in these last days before His coming."

A husky young man with a blond elegantly tapered mustache had a question for Lepp. He was Andreas Harms, Snapper whispered, a teacher from nearby Schoenfeld. The young man's deferential manner showed his awareness of the company he was in. "But is there not reason to hope, Onkel Lepp, that the Duma now in session will soon make complete religious freedom the law of the land? I've heard that our own Mennonite deputies Bergmann and Schroeder are doing all they can to bring this law into being."

Lepp regarded the young teacher with interest. "Yes, there is that possibility, my friend, but right now it is only that, a possibility. I talked with Hermann Bergmann only last week, and he didn't sound too hopeful. But in the meantime" — Lepp leaned forward and tapped the table for emphasis — "there are things we can do without flouting the Russian law as it now exists. We can start by exerting a spiritual influence on those closest to us, our Russian servants, workers, and neighbors. Without doing any open evangelizing, we can speak to them informally, include them in family worship services, make them receptive to God's Word, and point them to the true, living faith. But of course we must be careful in doing this. Direct, formal evangelizing could have serious consequences for us. And we all know how much civil and political unrest there is in our land already."

There was silence around the table. Lepp's burning conviction always made a deep impression. His zeal for carryng on missionary work against all odds, under the most difficult conditions, was known and respected throughout the Mennonite colonies.

The silence was broken by a fat, hulking man who had kept eating *tweeback* and cheese throughout the conversation. "Speaking of the unrest and violence in our nation," he began, still chewing vigorously, "yesterday I heard of another act of violence against innocent people. Peter Willms and his wife from Halbstadt were attacked by bandits in their train compartment on the way to Alexandrovsk. Willms himself was shot and seriously wounded, but his wife wasn't hit. The poor man's life is hanging in the balance." The fat man wiped his brow with a rather wrinkled-looking handkerchief. He shook his head. "What a terrible experience! How can we permit such terrorism to continue?" He cast a look of outrage around the table.

The blond teacher, Harms, also had news. "Have you heard the latest from Gulai Polye? It seems the police raid on Semeniuta's terrorist gang several weeks ago is still producing results, even though Semeniuta himself got away. The day before yesterday Karachentsev, the police chief, captured four of the escaped bandits in Ekaterinoslav. Under interrogation the prisoners gave more names to the police. Yesterday five more were arrested in Gulai Polye." He turned to his host, Jacob Loewen. "One of them was a Makhno boy — Nestor, I think. Don't you know him, Mr. Loewen?"

"Nestor Makhno? Yes, yes, he was the small, pimply one. He worked for me." Loewen was searching his memory. "A bit of a loner he was, that one. He was here several summers. I always felt a little sorry for him; he looked so miserable and friendless. But young Martin caught him stealing one time and I had to punish the kid. I don't know . . . after that he wasn't much good. He didn't come back the next summer. So he became a terrorist too? Well, well, I'm sorry to hear that."

"What will they do with these bandits and terrorists?" the diminutive Fritz Oetzbach wanted to know.

Young Harms chuckled grimly. "Oh, they'll make an example of them, I'm sure. These fellows have gone far beyond the usual stealing and political agitation. They're murderers and cut-throats. Earlier this summer they attacked the mail carriage delivering money to the Gulai Polye station and killed the guard. A few weeks later they shot a private detective who had been brought in from Alexandrovsk to help with the investigation. When the police raided the house where the gang was holding a meeting, two policemen were wounded in the shoot-out. Chief Karachentsev swore to root out this nest of vipers and it looks as if he's finally succeeding."

Snapper and Willie had followed the conversation with great interest. Snapper was excited by the news of Nestor Makhno's arrest. "Willie," he whispered, "that's the punk I've told you about. Remember? He's the one I caught staring at Katya in a way that made me see red. I was going to beat him up but Father interfered. I also caught him stealing — some tool it was. That time Father did take the whip to him." He dropped his voice even more. "Father's too soft with our workers. He spoils them. Some day, when

I'm running this place, things will be different. I would have sent that *russejung* Makhno packing on the spot, I can tell you. I don't believe in killing workers with kindness."

Willie looked at him coldly. He detested Snapper when he showed the arrogance of an estate-owner's son. "You'd rather kill them with work, I suppose."

Snapper flushed. "Save your sarcasm, Willie. As a future landowner I have to think about these matters. Prepare myself for heavy responsibilities."

"Ah, here you are Martin — and Herr Wilhelm Fast! Welcome to Voron-aya."

Willie looked up into the pretty, smiling face of Katya Loewen. He had met her occasionally with Snapper this past year when she was attending the *maedchenschule* in Halbstadt. At fifteen she was a striking girl with her deep brown eyes and long black hair.

Snapper regarded his sister with the fond, cool superiority of an older brother. "Tell me, Rembrandt, you still think that face is worth drawing?"

Willie pretended to look properly critical. "Yes, I think so."

Katya was unruffled. "Just as long as you don't try to draw me, Martin. I'm sure you'd make me look like a scarecrow." Snapper laughed and gave his sister's black mane an affectionate tug. "All right, Fast, now that the Ugly Duckling is here we'll take the grand tour of Voronaya." He put up a quick arm to ward off Katya's giggling assault.

Willie was very conscious of the dark young beauty walking beside him as they looked at the various buildings around the courtyard. He was sorry when she had to leave a few minutes later to help her mother.

Snapper stopped before the open doorway of the carriage house. "Look, Rembrandt, here she is, the most beautiful female on Voronaya — just don't tell Katya that — our new Opel, black as a raven and twice as fast." Martin patted the sleek, shiny hood fondly.

Willie had seen motor cars before, but had only once had a ride in one, a tired old runabout that barely crawled along. But this shining black Opel with its long slim lines and highly polished metal parts was a thing of beauty. How dashing it looked with its light canvas top folded back revealing its immaculate maroon upholstery. The brass side-lights sparkled in the rays of the descending sun and the round white headlights looked like gigantic eyes. Snapper pointed to the black tool box attached to the running board and the can next to it filled with extra petrol.

"I'll take you for a drive, Rembrandt. Wait here while I get my stuff and see whether anybody else wants to go."

Willie was so intent on examining the interior of the Opel, he didn't hear the approach of another guest behind him.

"Here you are, my young friend Fast. I've just been told who you are. I wouldn't have recognized you. You've grown into a proper man since I saw you in Blumenau."

Willie ducked his head out of the Opel at the sound of Erdmann Lepp's voice. He murmured a greeting and shook hands. He groped for something to say. "I'm just waiting for Martin. He's taking me for a drive." He felt self-conscious under Lepp's appraising stare.

"And your parents — keeping well, I trust?" Lepp remembered something else. "Ah, yes, and your — ah — high-spirited brother? I suppose now that he's older he has matured and become more obedient?"

Willie hesitated. He felt ashamed to tell the minister the truth about Kolya. "I'm afraid he's worse than ever, Onkel Lepp. Father is keeping him at home now, hoping that steady work on the farm will be a discipline for him."

So, so, that's how it is," Lepp murmured. "A pity, a pity. What a cross for your dear parents."

Snapper came back wearing an aviator's helmet with goggles. "Onkel Lepp, you're just in time. Get in. We're going for a drive before it gets dark. Mr. Harms is coming too."

"Lepp drew back, startled. "No, no, my boy. I must decline. You see, I don't approve of these horseless carriages. No. Such pleasure machines do not fit in with our simple Mennonite traditions. They're also very dangerous, I understand. I'm surprised your father would allow you to operate such a machine. In America, I've heard, many people have already been killed by these monsters." Lepp edged away from the Opel, as if it might strike *him* at any moment.

But Snapper had a way with older people. His hearty assurances and brisk manner inspired confidence. Uttering soothing reassurances, he took hold of Lepp and practically pushed the apprehensive preacher into the front passenger seat. Willie and Harms, the chubby teacher, were already seated in the back. Snapper adjusted the controls, dashed around to the front, cranked furiously, and in moments the Opel roared to life.

Lepp's reluctance leaped to dismay as he felt the machine's power vibrating through him. But it was too late. The snorting monster was already moving through the doorway. He clamped a bony hand over his white summer hat in anticipation of a mighty rush of wind. His other hand had a death-grip on the door-top beside him. He looked rigidly ahead, not noticing Snapper's grin. Before he knew it, they were through the front gate and careening into the open road.

Already Lepp felt dizzy from the speed. As the air rushed by like a storm, he kept a tight hold on his hat. He decided that was too risky and placed it on his lap, partly jammed between his knees. His alarm was mounting. This wasn't at all like a train, this frightening machine. In a train carriage one felt safe and enclosed, not open and exposed to dangerous speed like this. Why had he allowed this young rogue to talk him into this?

And still their speed increased. He was dimly aware of fields streaming by, though he didn't dare take his eyes off the narrow ribbon of road stretching ahead so perilously. What if the machine were to go out of control and hurtle off the road? They would all be killed. He stole a quick glance at Martin beside him. He looked calm and competent behind his goggles. Too young and foolish to realize the danger.

Aware of his glance, Snapper asked, "Well, Onkel Lepp, how do you like it?" His voice sounded loud and reckless.

Lepp stared ahead, tight-lipped, his fear laced with anger. Was this wild boy mocking him, God's servant, trapped unwillingly in this dangerous vehicle?

The speed was now so great that he was aware only of impending disaster as the machine, swaying from side to side, seemed about to leap to destruction. His panic and outrage were tipping him towards hysteria. As a boy he had once been caught on a runaway harvest wagon with the demented horses charging crazily along the road until they veered into a fence and snagged to a violent stop. That mad, out-of-control flight had felt just like this.

He was overcome by a sickening sense of despair. God was about to let him perish in this roaring, hurtling beast, to pluck him in the blinking of an eye into eternity. Or was God teaching him another lesson about these wicked times? That this devil's work was another sign of the latter days, the time of the sixth seal, along with earthquakes, floods, falling stars and other disasters? Oh, Lord, he prayed fervently, if it be Thy will to spare me from disaster, I will search Thy prophetic writings once again to learn why such things as this should be. He closed his eyes then in stoical resignation.

The car chuffed up a gentle rise, then began to cough ominously and slow down. Snapper worked furiously pushing and pulling things, and soon they picked up speed again. Lepp wanted to yell to Martin not to speed up again, but the words were jammed back into his throat by the roaring wind. Suddenly the machine lurched dizzily to one side and he was sure they were going off the road. He heard Martin shouting a greeting to the other side and realized they were passing a horse-drawn wagon. He could hear the horses snorting and whinnying wildly as they passed, and then they were shooting through space again as though trying to overtake the horizon itself.

Snapper bawled lustily over the noise: "Willie, you see the needle? It's showing thirty-five exactly. Isn't that something?" Snapper's face as he turned to the back was flushed with excitement.

Thirty-five miles per hour? In an open car! Lepp closed his eyes and prayed fervently. Surely God would not allow His servant's work to end this way. Never. This, too, had to be His divine leading, His purpose, to be revealed in the fullness of time.

Then in a blinding flash it came to him. Yes, yes, of course. Why was he such an unseeing fool and coward? *Ezekiel's magical chariot of God!* "I heard the sound of the living creatures' wings brushing against one another, the sound of the wheels beside them, and a fierce rushing sound. A wind lifted me and carried me along, and I went full of exaltation, the hand of the Lord strong upon me."

God had put him into this motor car for a purpose!

He tried to subdue his terror as he willed himself to accept the wild motion, the noise and velocity. When the car slowed down for a gentle curve, his body stopped rebelling, to his vast relief. Gradually he began to respond to the machine's surge of power, its straining to go faster, faster. He forgot his fear, aware only of this soul's longing to soar, to be caught up in wild, unstoppable movement forever, released into the vastness, boring through space like an eagle, faster than any horse, faster even than the diabolical Nogai horsemen of his old dreams. He felt ecstasy, a more than human power. God was rushing past him in the wind. Take me with you God! Let me race beside you, envelop me in your "fierce rushing sound." He leaned forward eagerly, defying speed, road — everything. He sensed Martin looking at him. He didn't care. God was all around them, the moment holy.

God had spoken in the wind. He wants me to use this machine! It is not Satan's vehicle. It is God's. God wants me to work through this machine. It is to be my Ezekiel's chariot. God said: "Man, I am sending you to the Israelites, a nation of rebels who have rebelled against me . . . But the Israelites will refuse to listen to you . . . so brazen are they all and stubborn. But I will make you a match for them. I will make you as brazen as they are and as stubborn as they are . . . Never fear them, never be terrified by them, rebels though they be."

Yes, yes, with this holy chariot he could go everywhere — from colony to colony, from mission field to mission field. It could take him to places where there was no railway, to remote places from Poland in the West to Turkestan in the East. With it he could travel easily to the Volga region, to Samara and Orenburg, right up to the Urals. No more long, interminable mission trips with horses that had to be changed every twenty-five miles.

Now he would be God's swift messenger, bringing the Word to thousands on the magic wheels of this horseless chariot. Yes, this machine was the answer to his prayers. God had led him to it miraculously. Now he could harness time itself. He would cover great Russia and do the Lord's work as long as strength lasted. And he would never again allow craven terror to overcome him.

Once more God had spoken to him in a vision.

The working sessions of the conference began after breakfast next morning. The last guests were arriving this morning. All except Rev. Broadbent, the Englishman, who had been unavoidably delayed, and would not be able to come in time. Fortunately, he had not been invited as a keynote speaker.

Erdmann Lepp was to give the lead-off sermon in the afternoon. Willie and Snapper had not seen him since the drive in the Opel. They had been surprised to find Lepp in such a hearty mood when they got back. He had seemed so tense and nervous when they left. He asked Snapper eager questions about the cost of such an auto, and about its performance under various conditions. Lepp had not said why he wanted this information and the boys were left to wonder about his sudden change of attitude towards the "pleasure machine."

They did not know that Lepp had spent the rest of the evening meditating on his vision of a ministry built on the motor car. God would vouchsafe to him in His good time how such a vehicle was to be acquired and exactly how it was to be used. One thing was certain. He could never operate such a machine himself. He would have to get an assistant, someone like the young Loewen — or better still, Wilhelm Fast. He liked the Fast boy. He was obviously intelligent and sensitive. Lepp did not know how things stood with the boy spiritually. But he would soon find out. Perhaps God had led young Fast here to Voronaya at just this time for a reason. He resolved to have a searching talk with the lad before the conference was over.

The purpose of the conference was to examine the doctrine of millenialism, the belief in a thousand-year Kingdom of Christ to be established before the end of the world and the final judgement. Lepp was to interpret the apocalyptic events leading up to the Messianic kingdom, while Prof. Stroeter would deal with the millenium and its aftermath. Millenialism was finding growing support among Mennonites frightened by the turbulent times brought on by the new century.

As always Lepp had prepared himself carefully. Over the years he had made a close study of apocalyptic literature. He was also — especially for a Russian Mennonite — an unusually perceptive student of both Russian internal politics and international affairs. He was confident that he had discovered the symbolic and political keys to Revelation, and that God's glorious plan for the salvation of mankind had been revealed to him by the Divine Will. He regarded it as a sacred obligation to help others understand and prepare for the stupendous climax of the human story. He had always hoped that he might be among the privileged elect still alive when Christ came to claim His kingdom. But as he got older his hope of experiencing this unique blessing was waning. Lepp never wavered in his belief in millenialism, but it was characteristic of him to be less interested in that golden, thousand-year experience itself than in the cataclysmic events that were to precede it.

He was well aware that millenialism was regarded as a heresy in conservative Mennonite circles. Such criticism — and some of it had become bitter and personal of late — bothered him not at all. He was utterly confident that the Lord had led him to the truth and that it was his mission to spread that truth wherever he could.

Erdmann Lepp rose with measured dignity to address the delegates and guests assembled on the Loewens' spacious garden terrace. His spare frame immaculate in a well-cut black frockcoat, his side-whiskers flaring elegantly, he was an impressive figure. He was renowned as a conference speaker and the audience of mostly ministers and teachers quickly hushed to respectful attention.

Lepp's deep-set, slightly hooded eyes calmly scrutinized his waiting audience. His mentor Bernard Harder had once told him never to start a sermon until he had compelled every person in the congregation to submit to his gaze. Lepp's sense of timing as a speaker had been honed to perfection during the many years of his ministry. He had faced every conceivable type of audience, friendly or hostile, in German or Russian, both of which he spoke like a native.

In the soft, August air, Lepp's tenor voice sounded controlled but vibrant. "My dear friends and colleagues in Christ: My subject this afternoon is the final period of earthly history as illuminated by divine prophecy. I take as text the sixteenth chapter of Revelation, in particular the sixth phase of human history as described in verses 12-14." He paused a few seconds to allow his hearers to find the passage in their Bibles. He himself left untouched the closed Bible before him. . . .

"I believe, as you do, I trust, that we are living in the last century before our Lord returns to set up His glorious thousand-year Sabbath. There are unmistakable signs that the sixth angel of Revelation has already poured out his vial of wrath. In this next-to-last phase of human history three momentous developments are to unfold: the drying up of the great river of Euphrates; the emergence of the kings of the East; and the appearance of the three unclean spirits shaped like frogs. I am convinced we are already in the midst of this sixth phase, that the time we Christians have to prepare ourselves and others for the Second Coming is getting short . . . May God grant that at least some of us will be privileged to experience this most marvellous of earthly events."

Willie, sitting in the back with Snapper, felt his old fear come upon him again as he listened. He had not forgotten what Onkel Lepp had said about the end of the world on his visit to Blumenau, but he did not think it would be marvellous to experience this event. No matter how well prepared you were it was a frightening prospect. Why couldn't the world go on for a bit longer, as it always had? Was it his terrible luck to have been born too late? He was as scared of the Second Coming now as he had been then. He fervently hoped Onkel Lepp was wrong, that he was misreading the signs. But as he watched the minister and listened to his confident voice he knew with absolute certainty that this inspired man of God could not be wrong. He just couldn't be. Not about something as important as this.

"Yes," Lepp repeated resonantly, "the Euphrates stands for the entire Islamic world, a world that is 'drying up,' losing power and influence in modern times. The Moslem nations, especially Turkey, are much weaker than they once were. Tsar Nicholas I called Turkey 'the sick man.' The rise of Christianity through mission work in Islamic nations is also having its effect.

"But, but, my friends . . ." Lepp held up a long, white forefinger, "we must not think that this is the end of Panislam. No, the forces of Islam will not surrender meekly. The yellow flag will be unfurled in Mecca and a bloody religious war will follow, a war in which a third of mankind will be slaughtered, as foretold in Revelation 9."

Willie and Snapper exchanged nervous glances. Willie wondered what his friend was thinking. He couldn't imagine Snapper being very worried by anything as remote as the Second Coming. But he did look a little apprehensive and for once was listening intently.

". . . and the kings coming out of the East? Dear friends, they symbolize the greatest dangers facing our world today: Japan and China, the masses of Gog and Magog led by Satan. They represent the 'yellow peril' about which the German Kaiser has recently warned the Western world. Yes, my friends, the terrible hordes of the yellow races will all too soon move like a deadly plague through Central Asia in an attempt to conquer the kingdom of Israel, which is to be re-established in Palestine in this final period. And joining these Mongolian armies will be countless mercenaries from other Eastern countries — from Persia, Ethiopia and Libya, as well as the men of Gomer and Togarmah as described by the prophet Ezekiel."

Lepp's figure seemed to loom even taller and his features darkened with wrath as he thundered: "But who will oppose these hideous masses from the East? Apparently not the Christian nations of Europe, who lack the will to unite. Russia learned that the hard way only a few years ago when it was forced to submit to the Japanese wolves because none of the nations of Europe or America would come to its aid. Had Russia received help in its valiant fight against Japan, that heathen nation would not have risen to prominence so quickly and become the growing menace it is today. Yes, my dear listeners, the terrible thunder clouds that blacken the political skies in the time of the sixth trumpet are those of Panislam and Gog and Magog."

The speaker paused and delicately patted his glistening brow with a snowy handkerchief. Eyes probing his audience relentlessly, voice now low but no less intense, he resumed. Willie felt naked and defenseless before that searing gaze and the voice penetrating him like a sharp knife. He shivered in the hot sun, then wondered if Snapper had noticed.

"Frightening as those developments will be, my precious friends, there is another no less threatening and even more immediate. The three frog-shaped evil spirits described in Revelation 16: 13-14 represent the false teachings, conflicting ideologies, the political and moral confusions that will afflict the nations of Europe in this sixth and next-to-last phase. This period of disorder and confusion is already upon us. In strife and upheaval we are staggering blindly towards the final crisis that will herald Armageddon and the coming of King Jesus to claim his earthly kingdom. Not all the nations and states of the world will reach the final phase together. The less enlightened and more lawless ones will get there sooner than the better-ordered Christian nations. But all will arrive at that final stage sooner or later.

"However" — the long, bony hand was poised imperiously — "even during this period of anarchy and confusion God's dynamic spirit will not be absent. Even the powerful forces of worldly materialism and atheism will not prevent that spirit from bringing about much-needed political reforms and moral and spiritual regeneration."

Again the magnetic voice hung suspended over the intent faces. The ascetic face softened momentarily and the ghost of a smile hovered and was gone. "Can we not see that spirit at work here in our beloved Russia? It was present in the October Manifesto proclaimed by our gracious sovereign a few years ago. The reforms proclaimed in it clearly show God's hand at work. Now we have our national Duma, and already we have two able, God-fearing Mennonite deputies looking after our interests there. We Mennonites, blessed as we are on all sides, have particular reason to give our earnest support to the Tsar and his Duma. Our first duty is to be quiet, obedient citizens in our earthly Motherland. Our even greater duty is to be true citizens of the Kingdom of God, alert citizens who keep their garments ready so they will not stand naked when the Great Day of the Lord is at hand."

The rich tenor voice again gathered momentum. "And the Lord's day is coming, my dearly beloved. God will not be mocked much longer. When the sixth vial of wrath has emptied its contents over the earth and the Children of Israel have reclaimed Palestine according to God's plan, then" — the voice soared to a mighty crescendo — "then will come the seventh and last vial and the final, cataclysmic events that will engulf this earth. Then will the brutal forces of Islam be themselves shattered on the mountains of Israel, as foretold by God's mighty prophet Ezekiel. Yes, God will destroy that great horde from the East so utterly it will take the people of Israel seven months just to bury the corpses. And for seven long years Israel shall burn as fuel the weapons — from spear shafts to rifle stocks —that will lie scattered through the land.

"No, my friends, God will not be mocked!" For the first time Lepp's voice threatened to go out of control. It was a near shriek now. The long, gaunt frame trembled with passion and the eyes blazed with a fire that scorched Willie's very soul. The voice was that of Ezekiel himself. It compelled you to listen; it surrounded you like a thunderstorm: there was no escape, only that voice coming, coming, hurling itself at him like a thunderbolt from heaven. Oh, God, he almost whimpered aloud, spare me, let me be one of the saved ones, I don't want to die!

". . . earthquakes, volcanic eruptions, terrible tidal waves, floods, blizzards, typhoons, famines and epidemics — these natural upheavals will be as nothing compared with the noise and destruction and terror of Armageddon. Woe to him who is not that day wearing the righteous armor of God, and woe to him who walks naked that day and exposes his shame for all the world to see!"

The voice sank to a dramatic whisper. "It will be a glorious victory for God and His faithful soldiers. Whoever is on the side of His victorious army that day will feel gratitude and joy so great as to be indescribable. . . . And then shall begin" — the voice seemed now to come from a great height —"the inexpressibly beautiful millenium of the Messianic Kingdom. Christ shall reign with his saints over all the nations. Death will be abolished forever, and 'the times of refreshing' will flow over the earth. . . ."

When the voice came again at last, it was so small and soft, a filament of sound so finely spun, that the least noise would have splintered it to silence. "Who would throw away such a beautiful future? Who among us would not give his very soul to become a citizen of this glorious New Jerusalem? . . . Amen."

It was over. Willie felt weak, drained of all strength, as if he'd been running endlessly in a nightmare to escape some terrible, unknown pursuer. It was as if he had been away to another world so strange that this world, the old world, no longer looked familiar or had meaning. Still in a daze, he felt Snapper's hand on his arm, and for once his touch was gentle, almost tender.

"Well, Rembrandt, what did I tell you? It's a great experience listening to a man like that, isn't it?"

Willie stared at Snapper, then turned back to the pulpit in spite of himself. Lepp, towering over the others, was benignly, graciously accepting expressions of gratitude for his inspiring address. Then he looked up, saw Willie, and beckoned him over.

Willie rose to obey the summons. He seemed to have no will or feelings of his own. He felt nothing, not even fear anymore. It did not even occur to him to wonder what Onkel Lepp wanted of him. He walked towards the pulpit, his mind a blank.

Later he could not remember clearly all the things Onkel Lepp had said to him. He did remember that the minister had been friendly and kind. They had gone for a walk in the garden and sat down in the arbor to talk. Lepp had asked him questions about the state of his soul, whether he had experienced conversion and felt ready to be baptized and taken into the church. Willie tried to answer these questions honestly, but he was still so shaken by Lepp's sermon that he stumbled, unable to find the right words. Yes, he wanted to be a Christian but didn't feel ready for baptism. And he wasn't sure what conversion meant. Onkel Lepp had then explained earnestly and at length all about conversion, but Willie had found it difficult to concentrate on everything he said.

And the more pressing and personal Lepp became, the more desperately beleaguered the boy felt. If only he could get away from that soothing voice and the deep gaze that gripped him like a vise. He didn't know if it was just embarrassment he felt or fear. Later he decided it had been mostly fear.

He remembered Lepp asking him if he'd ever thought of someday dedicating his life to the Lord as a worker in His vineyard. Willie had answered — truthfully — that he never had, but the minister ignored that and said something about needing an assistant some day for the evangelizing he expected to do among the Russians. That he would need somebody to operate his "auto machine" when he went on preaching missions. There had been more of a similar nature, but Willie could not remember the rest clearly. Towards the end Onkel Lepp's words had lost all meaning for him, and he simply waited for the moment when he could withdraw from this strange overpowering man.

Finally, Lepp had asked him to kneel down beside him and said a long, emotional prayer. He urged Willie to consider all these things "prayerfully" and to prepare himself for a life of service. Then he had been dismissed with an affectionate pat on the shoulder.

In bed that night Willie thought about the day's events. He decided that he was afraid of Onkel Lepp because of the power he had over him. The noted *reiseprediger* had come into his life twice now and both times the experience had left him with feelings of guilt and anxiety. He wanted to be an artist, not an assistant to a traveling evangelist.

But he did want to be ready for the Second Coming all the same.

CHAPTER FIVE

Alexandrovsk, August, 1908

"Hey, Shorty, move your stumps, you slimy little serpent, or I'll kick your ass off the bunk." The words were accompanied by a rough push that forced him against the cold surface of the cell wall.

It was that fat bully Matvienko kicking him around again. They all did it, cursing him and calling him sarcastic names like "Shorty," "Monkey," "Runt." He drew his legs up on the bunk and turned his face to the wall. He was close to tears. It wasn't enough that he was in jail waiting for the trial that would decide his fate. He also had to put up with kicks and insults from his fellow prisoners. They treated him like scum.

He couldn't believe it would end this way. He was sure to be found guilty and hung with the rest. And all he had done as a revolutionary Anarchist was attend some meetings, join demonstrations, and help distribute the pamphlets smuggled into Gulai Polye by Volodya Antoni the Czech agitator and Sasha Semeniuta the deserter. And once, only once, he had been a lookout while the gang broke into Priess Brothers factory to steal badly needed money. Even then there had been no violence.

He thought bitterly: I wasn't even a regular activist like the others who were rounded up in the police raid on Vanya Levadney's house. The bastards wouldn't let me into the inner circle in Gulai Polye. Said I was a punk kid. Even Savva and Grishka, my own brothers, told me I couldn't be an activist because I got too excited and talked too much when I was full of *samogon*. My own brothers shut me out!

But he was here anyway, in this cold, stinking cell with these *khlopsey*, these tough guys, who treated him like shit and spit on him every time he opened his yap.

Mother-of-God, he didn't want to die. He wasn't even nineteen yet. And he'd never had a chance to do anything — not like Levadney and his brothers, and Sasha and Prokop and the others who knocked off that police sergeant Lepchenko in the raid. And the time they robbed the mail carriage at the railway station and killed the guard: he hadn't been in on that either. Or when they shot the detective from Alexandrovsk.

And now this. To be hung — for nothing!

He shivered against the dank wall and tried to shift his cramped legs a little. Matvienko, his fat rear clamped against the boy's shins, looked down at him with an evil grin.

"Hey, Shorty, your pimple-face looks paler than a baby's ass. Can you feel the noose tightening around your pigeon-neck? God, they don't even need a rope for you. They could hang you with a girl's hair ribbon, you mangy little son of a bitch."

He stared up at the ugly, grinning face in horror. How did this big brute know he'd been thinking of the rope?"

"Leave him alone, Tima, can't you see he's scared shitless already, the poor little bastard?"

It was Levadney's voice from the next bunk. Vanya was the only one who ever stuck up for him and told the others to lay off. "Don't forget the kid's only eighteen," Vanya added. "If he's lucky he'll get off with *katorga*, life at hard labor. Even the tsarist pigs don't bump off kids."

"*Nichevo!* the rope or *katorga*, what's the difference in the end?" the harsh voice of Lichko ground out cynically. Lichko was another native of Gulai Polye. The boy hated the slimy Lichko even more than Matvienko.

"I'd take my chances at *katorga*," Matvienko growled decisively. "When the revolution comes — and it's coming whether we're around or not — they'll open all the prisons anyway. You wait and see."

"Yeah, we'll see nothing, Tima." Lichko spat on the filthy floor and rubbed viciously with his foot to emphasize his disgust. "You know damn well what they're going to do with us."

Katorga! the boy shriveled in despair at the idea of spending the rest of his life in prison. For once he agreed with Lichko. In the end it was as bad as being hung. He tried to imagine what it would be like to spend year after year in a cell like this. He wouldn't be able to take it, he was dead sure of that. He'd only been here for three days and already he was close to cracking up. He knew it . . . He recalled his old dream of the *volnitsa*, of becoming a powerful *nalyotchik* free to do what he liked . . . .

Now it was over before it had begun. His dream. His hopes. Dead at eighteen — or else swallowed up forever in a rotten jail full of terrifying bullies and cutthroats. He'd never see Gulai Polye again, the old *khata*, and his mother — the only soul in the world who liked him and treated him like a man.

Lying there cramped and miserable, he wanted to scream and scream and curse the whole stinking world for the pigsty it was, full of animals who did nothing but shit on each other and tear each other to pieces!

Katya Loewen! The name tolled in his memory like a church bell. Katya Loewen, the only lovely, pure, happy human creature he had known. How excited and good he'd felt every time he saw her. If only he could have felt like that all the time. She was so beautiful and alive. But even Katya had that big Loewen, that exploiter, for a father. And that shit-ass with his shiny chain for a brother.

After he had left the Loewen *khutor* that summer he had been lucky enough to get a job in the foundry at Gulai Polye. It made him feel like a man. He was one of the workers, a real wage earner living among his own people. The first few weeks at the foundry were exciting. The workers were rising up at last. There were meetings in the town square with lots of fiery speeches, colorful banners with stirring slogans, and angry crowds ready for anything.

Then a general strike was called all over Russia and he went on strike with his brothers and the other workers at the foundry. But at the other end of town the workers at the farm implement factory, they heard, were not going out. The factory was owned by Mennonite bourgeois who warned their workers if they went on strike they'd never get their jobs back. Savva said they wouldn't let the *njemtsi* bastards get away with that. So the foundry workers organized a demonstration and marched through town to the Priess Brothers implement factory.

When they got near the factory they were met by a troop of Don Cossacks on horseback. Mean-looking bastards, their horses squeezed together in tight lines across the road, sabres and *nagaikas* held up straight and menacing. Right there he felt his courage and excitement sink to his belly. But Savva and Grishka and the others up front had enough *samogon* in them not to give a damn about the Cossacks. The Cossacks let them come close and then made a sudden charge, scattering the demonstrators left and right while raining heavy blows on the fleeing and fallen with their long, hissing *nagaikas* and the flat of their sabres.

He was able to get away without getting hurt, but many didn't. Both his brothers, leaders up front, took ugly slashes across the head and back. They came home torn and bleeding. At first Mamasha screamed and cursed them for being stupid, but when she saw how badly hurt they were she shut up and began to wash and dress their wounds.

That was the end of their rebellion. The Cossacks stayed in Gulai Polye for a week. Some people whispered they weren't real Cossacks anyway, but a unit of police militia disguised as Cossacks because the Cossacks aroused more fear in the peasants than the police. Any villager who dared show himself on the street after curfew was cruelly whipped home. The Cossacks even arrested some people at home and beat them up with rifle butts.

That's when Savva and his pals swore they would become real revolutionaries — not just factory rebels and pamphlet Anarchists — and started organizing in earnest. The trouble was that Savva and the others didn't really know where to begin. They had no experience as activists except for a few strikes and demonstrations. If it hadn't been for Volodya Antoni, the Czech, they wouldn't have gotten very far.

Volodya had arrived in Gulai Polye at just the right time. The young Czech had lived in the village as a boy. He remembered Volodya from school as a thin, dark, nervous boy who wore glasses and spoke Russian with a heavy accent. They were almost the same age, though they never had much to do with each other. Volodya was a foreigner who didn't say much and kept to himself. He lived with his uncle who owned a saloon near the market place. After a while Volodya had moved away, and now he was back suddenly. He had changed a lot. He was no longer scrawny and nervous and he no longer acted like a foreigner. He lived in Ekaterinoslav now and boasted he was a secret member of the outlawed Anarchists.

When Volodya Antoni offered to use his connections to help them form a cell of the Anarchist party, Savva and the others agreed, though they weren't too happy having a mere kid as leader. Savva was even more upset when Volodya chose Sasha Semeniuta, a deserter from the army, as his right-hand man. But even Savva had to admit the "Antoni punk" knew what he was doing. One of the first things the young Czech did was organize a "terrorist squad" to carry out "expropriations." They could do nothing without money, Volodya pointed out, and no one would hand them the rubles they needed on a platter. The only way to get them was grab them off a rich man's platter.

He felt proud and important when Volodya selected him as a lookout for their first operation. It was a night break-in at the office of the Priess Brothers factory. It was a slick job, partly inside, partly outside. One of the office clerks, an Anarchist sympathizer, managed to get the combination to the office safe. The only risky part was overpowering the two night guards. But Savva and Sasha took care of the guards without trouble. After removing the cash from the safe they smashed the dial to make it look as if they'd broken the safe open.

His lookout station was in the shadow of a building standing kitty-corner across the street from the factory. From there he had a clear view of the entire length of the street and the side street that cut across it. He had felt nervous, he remembered, though he never came close to panicking. He had one bad moment when a drunken villager suddenly staggered out from the shadows behind him and asked him thickly what he was doing standing there. It was just moments after Savva and Sasha had slipped over the factory wall. The old drunk fumbled out his bottle and offered him a drink, but he put the guy off by telling him he was waiting for a girl who didn't like the smell of *samogon* on his breath. With an evil wink, the old man stumbled off across the street, and he heaved a sigh of relief.

That first "expropriation" provided them with a war-chest of 500 rubles. Now they could buy paper and a hectograph to make copies of proclamations and leaflets. They were privately amused when the townspeople and even the stupid cops assumed that the anarchist literature was the work of professional agitators from Ekaterinoslav or Alexandrovsk.

He was so elated with his part in the operation he went out to celebrate. As usual, he got so drunk he couldn't remember much the next day. But he went to the cell meeting that night sure he would be given an even more important job. Instead he found himself confronting hostile faces. Volodya and Sasha told him he was a drunken blabbermouth who had boasted about his part in the break-in to people who weren't even members of the cell, and that if he ever let his tongue wag like that again he might suddenly disappear from the scene altogether. At home Savva and Grishka gave him another savage dressing down.

He didn't go to the meetings after that, though he still helped distribute pamphlets at night. For the next few weeks he didn't touch a drop and kept to himself. He still hoped that after awhile he would get back into the inner circle again. He knew he could do important — even dangerous — things, if they'd only give him the chance.

But his chance never came. Soon all hell broke loose. They shouldn't have killed that detective from Alexandrovsk. That's when the cops put two and two together and figured out the terrorists were villagers after all. The night the activists held their meeting at Levadney's *khata* on the edge of town, the cops were ready. In the shoot-out one cop was killed and Prokop Semeniuta, Sasha's brother, was wounded in the leg. Before the cops got to him, though, Prokop put a bullet through his brain. The rest of them got away through the nearby wheatfields.

But that police-chief bastard Karachentsev was like a bloodhound. He had managed to flush out four of the guys in Ekaterinoslav. The four were interrogated separately, giving such conflicting evidence they knew the game was up for them. They began singing like steppe larks, naming names. He was sure it was Lichko, the slit-eyed son-of-a-bitch, who had given the police his name.

He would never forget his terror when the police pounded on the door of the *khata* and dragged him off with his mother's screams ringing in his ears.

And now he was here in this stinking prison in Alexandrovsk waiting for trial with the others. And they had no idea how long they'd have to wait. Matvienko said they'd be kept rotting here for weeks, maybe even months, before the tsarist pigs brought them to trial.

Nichevo. What did it matter, he thought in his desolation. It was all finished anyway. The rope or *katorga. Svoboda.* Anarchy. The *volnitsa.* Just words. Lousy empty words with no meaning — like everything else.

CHAPTER SIX

1

Daniel Fast Remembers: (2) Finding the Way
Blumenau, August, 1852

Ach, that is always the way in this life. I lost my dear Sarah just when our new life was beginning to prosper. It was a hard blow from which I did not recover for a long time. But even in my sharpest grief I knew I couldn't remain alone. I would have to take another wife — and soon. The most pressing reason was my little Peter, still under two. But I also needed a woman's hands to help with my prospering farm. And I had not forgotten my Sarah's dying wish for me to have a family.

As always, the Heavenly Father heard my prayers. Right after seeding time the following spring, about six months after the death of my first wife, I took to wife Anna Froese, the oldest daughter of my neighbor Johann M. Froese. Anna was a serious, hardworking girl whose family I had known for many years. She was no beauty, like my Sarah with her dark eyes and hair, her long neck and graceful ways. But I knew that in plain Anna I would get a kind, loyal wife who would sensibly and fearlessly share good and bad with me. I was already past thirty and Anna only twenty-one, but from the beginning we suited each other like hand and glove.

My life was settled and peaceful again and my life with Sarah now seemed almost like a dream. When Anna presented me with a healthy daughter —our Liese — in the summer of 1807 my happiness was complete.

With my *wirtschaft* and domestic life running smoothly again, I began to take an active interest in the spiritual life of our new settlement. We had brought four church teachers with us but no elder. After organizing our *gemeinde* we elected Bernhard Dyck, our senior church teacher, as our elder. Elder Johann Wiebe of the Khortitza *gemeinde* came out to consecrate Dyck as elder. Then, not long after I took Anna Froese, teacher Peter Harder died suddenly and the election fell on me to replace him.

Na ya. It had been my secret hope someday to become one of the Lord's servants. Now that the call had come I could think only of my unworthiness and lack of preparation. But there was no help for it. It was plainly God's will that I should serve. How could I say no? If God had led me to this then I was ready to do what He would give me strength to do. But a heavy burden it would be for someone as inexperienced and unschooled as I was. I consoled myself with the words of Paul: "to shame the wise, God has chosen what the world counts folly, and to shame what is strong, God has chosen what the world counts weakness."

Now that I was in the ministry I could see the church from the inside. What I saw was not all good. Our group had carried with them to Russia the hope of building a new and purer *gemeinde*. Ach, it wasn't to be. Some of the evil seeds of our old Babylon were being resown in the wild steppes. I had not known our new elder that well in Prussia. I now discovered he was a shrewd, energetic man, but with grave faults of character. He had a domineering, interfering nature and a temper that turned him into a raging beast whenever he felt he'd been crossed or defied in some way.

Elder Dyck soon got into a bitter feud with Klaas Wiens, our *oberschulze,* the chief administrator of the colony. It started over a minor matter. Wiens, who lived in Altonau, had flogged a young Mennonite who had been caught in a haystack with a Russian girl. Although not married, the young man was already a member of the *gemeinde,* and that's what angered Dyck. Only he, as church elder, had the right to punish a church member for such a sin. A moral sin, the Elder thundered, was not a secular matter. It was a church matter and only church authorities should deal with it.

So it began. The *Oberschulze* was a headstrong man too. He expected to be obeyed promptly in his attempts to regulate the affairs of the colony. Wiens was quick to punish offenders, though he was not a harsh or an unjust man. He usually handed out a fine or a community work assignment to transgressors, but he didn't hesitate to use the rod when he thought it necessary. And Wiens was a powerful man who could lay it on. He also knew he had the backing of the government officials in Ekaterinoslav.

I soon realized that Elder Dyck would not rest until he had broken the *Oberschulze.* The Elder saw Wiens as a threat to church authority — meaning to himself. Before long he insisted we place Wiens under the dreaded ban. Shunning was a stern punishment and meant total exclusion from Mennonite church and community.

I tried hard to change the Elder's mind. I liked and respected Wiens, a highly competent man even if he had overstepped his bounds a bit in this case. I pleaded with the Elder for a milder punishment such as a public apology before the whole *gemeinde.* But I got nowhere. Dyck had the support of the two other teachers, so he felt he could ignore me.

The Elder called a brotherhood meeting to vote on the ban. Wiens was dumbfounded. He had not expected Dyck to push things so far. The *Oberschulze* insisted on coming to the meeting, but the Elder wouldn't let him enter the meeting house. Through the window I could see Wiens walking up and down the yard nervously. While the brethren were casting their votes I went out to talk to him.

Wiens had a stricken look and his big shoulders sagged in defeat. "What will happen to me, Daniel, if the vote goes against me? Why is Dyck persecuting me like this?"

"He thought you had too much power as *oberschulze,* Klaas. The church and the church teachers must have final authority. He's right about that. You must know that too, my friend. But as your friend and minister of God I sympathize with you and wish you no ill. For what it's worth, I think Elder Dyck is committing a grave sin himself by not giving you a chance to submit gracefully and do public penance for your stubborn and highanded actions.

Perhaps if you had given in sooner this wouldn't have happened. But then he might have found some other excuse to get rid of you. You're a threat to his power as elder, so he has to get rid of you."

Wiens looked at me with such suffering eyes I had to look away. What a misery and calamity to see a strong man broken.

This time Elder Dyck had won, but his feathers would not always stay smooth either. As for Wiens, he was not a broken man for long. He smoothed his own feathers by moving out into the unbroken steppe on the southern edge of the Molochnaya. There he built himself a vast estate that is flourishing to this day. But he remained under the ban as long as Elder Dyck was alive.

Strange are God's ways with us earth-pilgrims.

Two other troubling matters came up during those early years that grizzled me even more and convinced me I'd fled from the old Babylon to a new one almost as bad. My doubts grew about Elder Dyck and the direction in which he was leading the *gemeinde.*

The first trouble came from the Elder's readiness — even eagerness — to apply the rod to erring members of the church. Ya, he was now in favor of the very form of punishment he had persecuted *Oberschulze* Wiens for giving. The difference was that the Elder had not then been fully in control of colony affairs. Now he was. Dyck had the new *oberschulze,* Jacob Buller, in his vest pocket and everybody knew it. The Elder now prescribed the rod even for such minor offences as a farmer beating his horses or a hired man not doing his work properly. The *Oberschulze* and his police assistants were kept busy doing the flogging.

I could no longer remain silent. I reminded the Elder that we Mennonites were forbidden to use or support any kind of physical violence. "You know as well as I do, Ohm Bernhard," I said, "that warnings followed by shunning are the only forms of punishment our forefathers permitted the church to apply. It is deeply wrong for the church or its leaders to punish with physical force even if —"

"Fast, that's enough," the Elder roared, red in the face, "you are still a very green spiritual servant. You will not tell me what Mennonite doctrine is." He glared at me spitefully. "You would be better off not to meddle in matters that are up to me as leader to decide."

That Sunday he preached a snippy, hard-edged sermon on the text "Render unto Caesar," all the while casting meaningful glances in my direction. His shameless performance troubled me greatly, but I made up my mind I would not allow him to wear me down on this issue. And he didn't.

More trouble came when Russia was at war with the French. The Emperor Alexander issued a manifesto strongly urging all citizens to contribute to the war effort by donating swords, guns, foodstuffs, and money. The Elder and the *Oberschulze,* along with the village mayors, were summoned to

Tokmak and asked what we Mennonites intended to give. The mayors were ready to cooperate with the government but Elder Dyck hesitated and finally said it would be wrong for Mennonites to help the war in any way. That to give money to buy swords and guns would be a sin for us. The official was not pleased and reminded the Elder that loyal citizens had a duty to help their country in time of need.

Not long after, the Inspector at Tokmak sent the colony a pledge book in which all givers were to record their gifts. I urged the book be sent back to the government right away. The mayors didn't agree. They were afraid of offending the Inspector. After much talk back and forth, Elder Dyck said he and *Oberschulze* Buller would take care of the pledge book by taking it back to Tokmak themselves.

I left thinking the matter settled. But it wasn't. A few weeks later I heard that the pledge book was actually going around in the lower villages. I was stunned. How could that be? The Elder had promised to take the book back to the Inspector. I went to Dyck and asked him to explain. He got on his high horse right away.

"Are you accusing me, Fast? I gave the book to Buller to take back to Tokmak. If the Inspector sent it back again, that's not my doing. The government officials have the final power here, not we, my friend."

I looked at him in disbelief. He was hiding something. I could tell. I asked him to call a brotherhood meeting so we could resolve the matter once and for all. Reluctantly, he agreed, but not before accusing me once more of being a meddling "old nosc" who had better learn to keep his place.

The brotherhood meeting was a stormy one, with the brethren arguing on both sides of the issue. I sensed that *Oberschulze* Buller would not stand up to much pounding. I went after him in earnest. After much nervous hemming and hawing and angry interruptions from Elder Dyck, Buller finally confessed that the Elder had secretly give him permission to send around the pledge book, but only after the issue had died down a bit. The Elder, of course, tried to smear the whole thing over, but he looked sheepish all the same. I don't think he convinced many of the brethren that he had dealt honorably in the case. I also knew he would never forgive me for bringing his double-dealing to light.

That issue finished Elder Bernhard Dyck for me. Now I was certain he was interested only in keeping personal power, even if it meant surrendering our traditions of church authority into the hands of the secular authorities. As long as we had this treacherous, worldly minded man as our spiritual leader, the pure church we had hoped for would never have a chance to flourish in our settlement.

I began to read Scripture and the works of Menno Simons more carefully than ever to get a better picture of just what the pure church should be. I was determined not to give up the dream we had brought from Prussia.

The more I read the surer I became that a pure Christian church must be founded on the principles of love and brotherhood — not only individual love of God but mutual love for each other. The strength of Christianity lay in the congregation itself, the brotherhood, not in the individual Christian. A *gemeinde* properly founded was not just a church as such, but a family of suffering believers. Not just faith, but following — true discipleship as practised in the Early Church, that was the only way. No man could enter the Kingdom by himself, but only together with his brother.

And the only way to establish such a pure *gemeinde* was in isolation from the world: to follow Paul's warning "not to conform oneself to this world." The hard part was that such a closed community of pure believers would have to be protected at all times from outside pollution. But how to do that? The only way, I became convinced, was to follow a firm, clear set of rules backed up by a strict use of the ban — and only the ban! The task of the church teachers in the pure church was to stand on the walls of the spiritual Zion and blow the trumpet whenever danger came near. And to take care of all matters in a spirit of mutual love — not greed for power, personal ambition, or worldly compromise.

That was my view of the pure church. But, ach, how to bring it about in a world beset by Satan. It was far from clear to me at that time how true believers could live removed from the rest of the world, perhaps even from the rest of the Mennonite community. By strict rules, ya, but exactly what rules? I decided such rules could only be worked out in practise as the lives of true believers called for them.

Full in heart and soul, I began to talk in private to a few trusted friends, including my father-in-law Johann M. Froese, about my yearning for the pure way. I found eager ears in Blumenau as well as in several other villages. But I had no clear idea of how to take the first step. I still felt myself to be too weak and unworthy to lead others. On my knees I daily begged the Lord to open the eyes of the Elder and his secular supporters, to soften their hearts so they would see the error of their ways. In my soul I knew such a miracle could come only from above, that perhaps the Almighty had plans for us all that I knew nothing about. All I could do was wait and pray.

One day Father Froese came to me with several other supporters and said now it was time for us to hold our own meetings. They did not wish to attend Elder Dyck's church any more. By this time the *gemeinde* had two churches, one in Petershagen at the northern end of the colony, the other in Ohrloff at the southern end.

I grieved in my heart over this request, but I now understood it was God's will that those of us who wanted to follow the pure way would have to do it on our own.

So we began to hold meetings in the homes of our tiny group.

When Elder Dyck heard about our meetings he flew into a rage and wanted to ban us all on the spot. Cooler heads persuaded him to meet with us and talk through the whole matter. In the meantime, some of the villagers in our own Blumenau threatened us with beatings if we didn't give up our rebellious "foolishness" right away. What a misery and calamity! Never had I tasted such a scalding soup. How could this be? Our sincere attempt to read God's will and find his pure way was leading us into bitter strife and violence. That was a bitter drink for me to swallow. For years, as a shepherd to the flock, I had tried to lead the *gemeinde* to greener pastures, and now I was myself accused of being a wolf in the fold.

But as I came to fuller understanding of God's plan for us, I stopped worrying about what the *gemeinde* thought about us. I saw that the ruthless opposition from the Elder and his supporters was part of God's plan for us too. It was only through persecution that we could discipline ourselves into a true group of suffering disciples. I reminded our group in a sermon of the Anabaptist aim of achieving *gelassenheit,* serene self-surrender and resignation to God's will. I used as text the words in Corinthians about making "every human thought surrender in obedience to Christ." I also stressed the strength of brotherhood: that bread is made of kernels ground and mixed, and wine of grapes crushed and blended. And what has not been ground or crushed is a husk only fit for swine.

Small as our group was, with only about two dozen adult members, I was not the only church teacher in it. My father-in-law Johann M. Froese had been elected teacher two years after me. Father Froese had become my strong support. He was highly respected in the community and always remained calm and collected when feelings ran high. He was the opposite to Elder Dyck in this as in other ways. Without my father-in-law standing beside me in those difficult days, I would not have been able to cope with the wily Elder and the *Oberschulze,* not to mention the hostility of most of the colony.

The Elder and the *Oberschulze* now decided on more drastic action. Father Froese and I were summoned to a full meeting of the District Council, made up of the village mayors headed by the *Oberschulze.* We were bluntly asked why we continued to hold our own services against the express will of the Elder and the *gemeinde.* Froese and I stated without anger or reproach our conviction that the Elder and the *gemeinde* were following a path contrary to the will of God and the traditions of our forefathers. As a result, our consciences would no longer permit us to follow a spiritual counsel we believed to be wrong, that we didn't want to remain part of a congregation that seemed to be trying to move into the sinful world as quickly as possible. I reminded them of the saying we had heard so often in Prussia: once the Mennonites had lived in the world, now the world was in their midst.

The mayors hotly accused us of sowing strife and disunity and heresy. One of them sarcastically asked if we were trying to be as pure as the old Mennonite elder in Friesland who had banned everyone except his wife and was finally left without a congregation? Hans Heide from Halbstadt, known as a drinker and boaster, even threatened us with a flogging if we didn't give in.

The meeting ended with more noisy threats than calm understanding. Father Froese and I went home saddened but more determined than ever not to give up our principles and convictions for the sake of public peace and unity. That would be hypocrisy and cowardice. We decided never again to discuss religious matters at a council meeting, where they did not belong.

We waited for the next attack. It was not long in coming. Elder Dyck ordered Froese and me to a meeting of the church teachers in Ohrloff. We were surprised to find that the popular and highly respected Elder Johann Wiebe, who had ordained Bernhard Dyck as elder, had come all the way from the Old Colony for the meeting. It looked as if Elder Dyck was going to make a last effort to break us and bring us to heel.

Elder Dyck opened the meeting in a calm and dignified manner, but the crafty gleam in his eye did not escape me.

"We have waited half a year now for you, servants of God that you are, to come to your senses and lead your little flock back to its true fold. In love we have reminded you of your duties to God and our *gemeinde*. But you have shown nothing but stubborn hostility and open defiance." He paused and stared his hatred at me. "I am well aware, Brother Fast, of what you said at the District Council meeting, and of the other bad things you have said about me personally in various places. God will not be mocked, my erring friends. The step you have taken not only disrupts the work of the true church, but will lead, unless you repent sincerely, to your own personal damnation.

'What do you now say in the presence of this assembled body of spiritual servants?"

Father Froese and I looked at each other. I was considered the leader of our group, but I was ready to give place to Oom Johann as my senior in years and family position. But when he remained silent, I felt God's spirit moving me to speak.

"Oom Bernhard," I began, "we have come here in all humility to resolve our differences with you and the *gemeinde*. We yearn to be reconciled to you in the spirit of Christ's love and peace as expressed in the words 'First be reconciled to thy brother.' I humbly confess my own weakness, ignorance, and inexperience. But I cannot be a hypocrite and say to you now that I did wrong and beg you to forgive me and take me back. No, my brothers, that I cannot do. I will not be like the Pharisees who believed but were afraid to confess Christ 'lest they should be put out of the synagogue.' "

"What's that you say?" the Elder roared, already losing all his calm. "Are you saying that we are the false church, the synagogue, that you and your miserable followers are the true believers who follow Christ, and we are the Pharisees?"

Livid with rage, he jumped up and down, snatched his cap from the table and hurled it to the floor. The tiny Elder Wiebe, looking startled, plucked Dyck's sleeve and said, "Brother, brother, calm yourself."

Abruptly, the Elder stopped his antics. His anger seemed to vanish. Again the cunning look came into his eyes. He was trying hard to look humble and sorry.

"Brothers, forgive me, I am sorry I forgot myself." He looked at me for a long moment and held up his hand.

"Brother Fast, I can see that quarreling will get us nowhere. My only desire is to carry forward the work of the *gemeinde* as best I can. I have been consecrated by the Lord as leader of this congregation and I must carry out *all* my duties, unpleasant as they may be at times."

Over the swarthy face stole the look of pious humility again. What was coming now?

The Elder's voice dropped to a hoarse whisper. "Brothers . . ." he stopped, on the verge of tears it seemed. "Brothers, if God permits nothing else to work" — he dabbed at his eyes with a large blue handkerchief — "if love, warnings, even threats cannot move you and bring you back into the fold — then" — again he paused, face contorted in an apparent effort to master his feelings — "then, I am prepared to lay down my burden as leader in favor of one of you."

With a woebegone expression he scanned our faces to see what effect his astonishing offer was having. We waited.

He tried again, his face longer than ever. "Yes, rather than allow this tragic split in the *gemeinde* to go on, I am prepared to step down, if that will bring you back."

I didn't have to look at Froese to know how he was taking this offer. Elder Wiebe looked red and uncomfortable. His face told the whole story. Nobody in the room could believe that Dyck was seriously offering to step down. It was just another trick to win sympathy for himself and make us look like stubborn, ungrateful wretches. He was not the man to resign gracefully for the sake of peace and harmony. And he knew very well we would not take up his offer.

I could hardly hide my scorn in pointing out that his resignation would solve nothing, but leave the issue more muddled than ever.

Clearly, the Elder had expected me to say just that. There was the crafty look again. "So, even when I offer to lie down at your feet, to humble myself in love to you, you will not let your hard hearts be softened." He looked around the room, appealing to the assembled teachers to judge for themselves what the situation was. The piety and self-sacrifice in his face would have moved a Tatar. The moments hung heavy as a funeral. Froese and I sat waiting.

Without warning the Elder flew into another fit. The face that had been full of holy mercy a moment before now flamed with hate.

"All right, you hard-necked sinners, if nothing works with you" — his voice rose to a scream that made Elder Wiebe wince and look even more embarrassed — "there's only one thing left to do and that's to turn the whole matter over to the authorities at Ekaterinoslav. General Contenius and the Guardians Bureau will know how to deal with you scoundrels. You'll be led off to Siberia in chains before the snow flies again." He devoured us with the look of a man possessed. "And we'll elect new teachers to replace you as though you had never been."

I sat there numb and heart-sore. What a misery and calamity to be threatened with banishment to Siberia by our own spiritual leader and fellow Mennonite! I could not believe my ears.

For the first time my father-in-law spoke, his deep voice trembling with sorrow and outrage. "Oom Bernhard, consider what you are saying in God's presence. Banish us, your spiritual brothers, in chains into exile? Is that the act of a Christian, to give us over to the authorities like common criminals, to throw us like Daniel among the lions?"

The Elder said nothing more, but continued to look as though ready to make good his threat.

And so the meeting ended with this terrible threat hanging over us, but with nothing finally decided. Elder Wiebe came over and spoke to us in a kindly way. He allowed that the stand we were taking was not without scriptural basis, but urged us to reach a working compromise with Elder Dyck in the interests of brotherhood and unity. He added that it was quite within Dyck's power to have us banished.

So even this decent, respected man from Khortitza was admitting we were right but in the same breath urging us to compromise our principles and convictions in the interests of a unity that would be like scum covering a stagnant pool.

I went home that day as close to despair as I'd ever been in my life.

In spite of all this brutal opposition our little group carried on. We even gained new members here and there. But our fight for independence was far from over. Not only was Elder Dyck still trying to find ways of breaking us up, but we had other pressing problems to overcome.

As a *gemeinde* we were officially without an elder, therefore officially leaderless. That meant we could not celebrate holy communion or baptize new members. When we tried to get a Mennonite elder to supervise and sanction the election and installation of an elder from our group, he would decline — afraid, I suppose to face the wrath of Elder Dyck. We even considered petitioning for an elder to come out from Prussia, but we knew our mail was now being censored by the District Counsel. So that avenue was closed off too.

We finally persuaded Oom Heinrich Enns, the elder at Schoenwiese in the Old Colony to come out and supervise the election for elder. The lot fell to me, unworthy as I was for such a high office. Elder Enns, however, excused himself from the laying on of hands that would have installed me officially as the elder of our little *gemeinde.*

That left us almost where we had been before. Our brotherhood then decided that Oom Johann, my father-in-law and spiritual brother, would consecrate me as elder. After all, that was how Grebel and Blaurock and the other early fathers had installed one another when they started.

So, almost two years after our break with the *gemeinde,* we were at last complete as a working congregation. But it gnawed at us and caused us much heart pain that we were not yet accepted as an official *gemeinde* by either the big *gemeinde* or the government. Other Mennonites mockingly called us the "little gemeinde" or, even worse, the "crazy church."

But we tried to bear taunts and persecution with meekness of spirit. We still hoped that when feelings had died down with time and we'd proven ourselves to be a true, living, *gemeinde,* we would be accepted even by Elder Dyck and our other bitter enemies.

CHAPTER SEVEN

1

St. Petersburg, November, 1912

August Bock Junior leaned comfortably back in his chair and stretched out a pair of very long legs. He gave a languid wave of his cigarette holder and emitted thin jets of smoke from a patrician nose set high above a generous, full-lipped mouth. His long, heavy face betrayed just a hint of haughty animation, which meant he was enjoying himself. As he always did in an argument that he had started.

"I won't fall into that trap, friend Fast. I'm not condemning Mennonitism as such. I'm simply saying that it's about time we Mennonites woke up to the fact that we're Russian citizens and that we have no right to seal ourselves up in our villages as islands of German culture while pretending that the Russian culture around us is inferior, and that in any case it has nothing to do with us. It's high time we realized that we ought to become Russian citizens in a cultural sense and not just a legal sense."

Wilhelm knew he was being toyed with. He had been through this argument before with the sophisticated young Mennonite across the room.

"August, I know you want me to argue that Mennonitism depends on German language and culture. Well, I won't do that. I agree with you that we need to Russianize a lot more if we are to develop as a people in this country, but —"

"— But nothing, Rembrandt. Don't hand me that stuff about German cultural heritage and the Anabaptist tradition. I was raised a Mennonite, yes, but my mother isn't one. She's of pure German stock. I've got nothing against the Mennonite church, but I could just as easily be a Lutheran or Baptist, or even a Catholic, for that matter."

"Why do we have to equate Mennonitism with the Mennonite church anyway? We Mennonites have become an ethnic group here in Russia. We have our way of life and culture now. We don't need the Mennonite church any more to give us that identity."

The speaker was Abram Schellenberg, a mill-owner's son from Melitopol near the Molochnaya. He was small and dark, almost Semitic-looking. He was a brilliant student in his second year of history and philology at the University. Abram had begun his studies with every intention of returning to the Mennonite colonies to teach after completing his degree, but he was beginning to waver. He had a Russian girl friend, also a student in his faculty. And he was in the process of losing his Mennonite faith.

"We don't, of course," young Bock began, but Wilhelm interrupted him.

"Oh, yes, we do. Remove the church from the colonies and what's left? The church stands at the very center of Mennonitism. Without it you have nothing but German-speaking farmers living in isolated villages in the midst of an alien land and culture. It's the Mennonite church that gives purpose and meaning to the German culture and the simple, rural way of life of the Mennonite colonies. Without the church —"

"All right," August conceded, "as things now stand you may be right. But I see no reason why the colonies couldn't gradually adopt a more Russian culture and way of life and not be so dependent on a German-language church, with its strict demands for obedience and conformity. Unless it's the church itself, of course, that keeps us Mennonites foreigners in our own country." He smiled around the room, enjoying his own daring.

From the corner, Jacob Priess spoke for the first time. "I think you miss the whole point, August," he said with gentle conviction. "You seem to think that a church, a body of believers, is just a kind of social institution, a part of culture that can be changed at will — like switching to another language, or moving to another country and adopting its customs." He paused and leaned forward, oblivious to the scornful look the rich man's son was giving the lowly *anwohner's* son. "Our Mennonite church is not just another church interchangeable with other churches that function mainly as social institutions. No, August. Ours is a living, believers' church. The risen Christ stands at the center of our church. Our people have suffered bloody persecution, and for almost four centuries have stood apart for their Anabaptist faith. Don't —"

"— Don't preach to me, old boy," Bock said loftily. "I've heard all that before. That stuff is for simple farmers and Brethren fanatics. I've got more civilized views and I'd suggest —"

"— And I'd suggest, August, that you try to be a little less condescending." Wilhelm was nettled, partly because of Bock's overbearing manner and partly because he did not like the deep sincerity of his close friend and roommate Jacob treated with such obvious disdain. It wasn't the first time he had come to Jacob's defense against the snobbish Bock. He knew August looked down on young Priess not only as an intellectual inferior, but as a social inferior.

August Bock Junior was the only son and heir of August Bock, the immensely wealthy and influential Mennonite industrialist at Schoenwiese, Old Colony, in the city of Alexandrovsk. The older Bock was the senior partner in the large farm implement manufacturing firm of Bock and Riesen. Young August, though somewhat spoiled and a bit of a snob, was also amiable, generous to a fault, and possessed not only of a keen mind but a well-developed taste for refined living. He was a desultory student at the Institute of Electrical Engineering. Some day he expected to fill his father's massive boots in the firm. In the meantime, he was elegantly marking time by cultivating the social graces and indulging his passion for the arts. He liked to associate with young Russian noblemen and artists of the bohemian type. But he also kept up less fashionable contacts with Mennonite students and was, if anything, proud of his provincial origins. Wilhelm valued August's friendship and realized he had much to learn from the sophisticated young man from Schoenwiese.

Young Bock was an odd physical specimen — although not as odd as his giant father Bock Senior. His large frame was so loosely put together, his gait so shambling, he resembled a bear walking on stilts. Not that he didn't care about his appearance. He was always impeccably dressed. Characteristically, he was wearing his smartly tailored Institute uniform with only the top two buttons undone, even though the room — a typically cluttered, shabby student room — was warm and suffocating with smoke.

"Sorry, Rembrandt. Didn't mean to be rude," Bock apologized casually. "Just getting carried away with the earth-shaking subject of Mennonitism." The flat, cool eyes crinkled and the heavy curve of jaw tilted up disarmingly. He hitched up his slouching torso and took a sip of the Georgian wine he had brought.

Bock's amused gaze swung to the young man who was sitting at a small table near the window. Karl Plett, also in the uniform of a technical institute, had not taken part in the discussion. He had been idly turning over the pages of one of Jacob's textbooks as the others talked.

"Well," Bock said brightly, "and what does our socialist friend from Orenburg say about the Mennonite people? Can they be persuaded to side with the workers and peasants, or will they have to be dealt with as part of the wicked bourgeosie when the next revolution comes?"

Plett looked up at Bock with cool distaste. He disliked August Bock and would not have come to Wilhelm's room tonight had he known Bock would be there.

"You know very well I'm not a socialist, Bock. I'm interested in constitutional democracy of the kind practised in the West. I think our monarchy is corrupt and obsolete, and I would like to see it brought down and replaced by a better system." He gave Bock a long, level stare. "That's the extent of my interest in politics. As for Mennonitism, it's not something I care to discuss. I'll leave such subjects to intellectuals like you. I'm interested only in becoming a good engineer."

Bock took the rebuff good-naturedly. "Well said, Plett, well said. But you better not let a tsarist agent hear you make such remarks about the Romanov monarchy, or you'll be doing your engineering in the Peter and Paul Fortress for a stretch."

The conversation shifted to other things. Shards of cigarette smoke hung overhead or drifted in long comet-tails to the corners of the room. Like most student rooms, it was part barracks, part lounge. The furniture was sparse and worn, but of solid quality. Wilhelm and Jacob had considered themselves fortunate to get a good room at a reasonable rate in a house on the Stredny Prospect. The house was within easy walking distance of both the Teachers Institute and the Academy of Fine Arts on the University Embankment.

The two friends had arrived in the capital in good time for the fall term.

Both had completed the three-year teachers training course in Halbstadt the previous spring. Wilhelm's long-range campaign to persuade his father to allow him to attend an art school had finally succeeded, but only at a heavy cost to his immediate future. The condition was that he would come back to teach school in the colony for a period of no less than five years. On that point Father had been adamant. Father's hand was made even stronger by the fact that Wilhelm would be subject to call-up for alternative forestry service in the summer of 1913. He had long ago decided that he did not want to vegetate in an isolated, boring forestry camp for the required three years. The only sure way out of that was to commit himself to five years of teaching in a Mennonite school. Father and the government both had him over a barrel. His one clear triumph was that he had been accepted by the Academy of Fine Arts in St. Petersburg. It was reputed to be the best in the land.

Jacob Priess was attending the Teachers Institute on a scholarship from the colony. The three-year course would qualify him as a secondary teacher in the colony. But Jacob, like Wilhelm, would be subject to a call-up next summer, and could expect to have his studies interrupted as well. There was a slim chance that either one or both of them could escape the draft altogether either by being physically rejected or by being exempted through the lottery system. Jacob, however, was also reconciled to the possibility of teaching the obligatory five years in a village school. He would then try to get into a seminary in Germany or Switzerland. He had never wavered in his ultimate ambition to become a minister — either a traveling minister and evangelist like his idol Erdmann Lepp, or, better still, a missionary in a foreign country.

Wilhelm admired his friend's methodical, patient planning for the future. Jacob had never even considered life in any other terms than as a life of service to his people. He took it for granted that he must develop his native endowments to their fullest, regardless of how long it took. Jacob was that rare type, a visionary with common sense who would permit nothing he could control to deflect him from his course. He would, of course, get married when the right time came. In the meantime, unlike his roommate, he seemed to have none of the usual young man's romantic inclinations — or if he did he kept them well hidden even from Wilhelm. He did not seek out girls, and had, so far as Wilhelm knew, never been alone with one even for something as innocent as a walk. Jacob seldom if ever even talked about girls in a romantic way, and Wilhelm was half convinced that he didn't even permit himself to think about them in that way.

How different Snapper Loewen, his other old school chum, was in that respect. Snapper was still in Halbstadt, a student in the recently established Business School. He and Snapper wrote to each other frequently, and Snapper was just as voluble on paper as he was in person. His witty, detailed accounts of his social life and his extravagant but innocent flirtations with eligible local belles were highly amusing, although Wilhelm read only the milder portions of these letters to Jacob. Snapper also wrote at length about his future plans for Voronaya. But first he would be obliged to serve his "sentence" in the "accursed" forestry service, to which he expected to be "condemned" in spring.

So far, art school had been everything Wilhelm had expected it to be —and more. From the first day of term he had been overwhelmed by the abundance of artistic talent surrounding him. The students around him seemed so superior to him in natural talent, knowledge and technique, that his confidence quickly sagged. He was stunned by what appeared to be the limitless virtuosity even of the new students like himself. He became so depressed that in the third week he stayed in his room for three straight days rather than face his classes. Jacob had a long talk with him then and persuaded him to give it a good try at least.

Bleak and miserable, devoid of all hope, he went back. That had been his low point. On the edge of despair, swallowing down shame and humiliation, he forced himself to work again. It was all dead at first — stiff and awkward and mechanical. He was on the verge of giving up again. Then slowly, very slowly, it began to come. His work — even the sketching from a nude female model, which embarrassed him at first — began to improve noticeably, grow surer of itself. Now it seemed to him that the very geniuses who had been so utterly beyond him were beginning to look at his work with shrewd appraisal and a certain silent respect. The long hours of extra work he had done with Burzev were beginning to stand him in good stead. He still had a long way to go to catch up with the best of his classmates. He was under no illusions about that. But at least he could face them now — more importantly, he could face himself again. But while he had set at rest some of the doubts he had about his talent, he began to develop other doubts — about himself as a person — doubts he had never faced before. But he kept them to himself.

August Bock was now on one of his favorite subjects — grand opera. "Boys," he drawled between sips of his Georgian red, "you don't know what you're missing by not attending the opera. The other night I heard the great Battistini, the "glory of Italy," singing the Don in *Don Giovanni*. What a voice, as smooth as quick silver, with high notes as free and vibrant as a tenor's. He goes up and down like a flute, without ever seeming to take a breath. The man's a marvel. He's in his mid-fifties and his voice sounds like twenty-five. I've never —"

"Enough of that, Bock." Karl Plett's mouth had been writhing in mounting disgust. "Who cares about that kind of caterwauling? I'd as soon listen to cats mating as to that so-called singing."

August was unruffled by Plett's outburst, but his tone was sarcastic. "I suppose where you come from, Plett, mating cats are about the only kind of music you get to hear — except for a few doleful hymns in church Sunday mornings." He paused to see if Plett would retaliate, but the latter was intent on rolling a cigarette and ignored him.

"Friends, you should have seen that round little Italian dressed up as a youthful lover. That was something. The voice was heavenly, but when he sang his serenade to Elvira's maid with one foot on a bench, plucking his little mandolin, he looked so out of character, his fat little belly pushed up by one thin leg, big nose jutting out and his neck bulging behind, I almost burst out laughing. Then, can you imagine —?" Bock stopped and saw he had captured even Plett's interest. "Right in the middle of his serenade, with the girl looking down from the balcony, the great singer's foot slipped off the bench and he almost lost his balance. The audience tittered, but the great Battistini never missed a note. But when he glanced at the conductor a few moments later, his face looked as black as a rain cloud."

Wilhelm chuckled with the others at August's amusing description. He himself was becoming interested in opera and ballet. A few weeks ago he had gone with August to a performance of *Boris Godunov* at the beautiful Maryinsky Theatre. He had found the singing and acting and stylized sets strange at first, but exciting. The colors and textures of the sets and costumes dazzled his artist's eye. The Russian basso Chaliapin, incredibly tall and regal-looking, made a profound impression on him as the tragic tsar, Boris. According to August, Chaliapin was the greatest singing actor in Russia, and quite possibly in the whole world. Wilhelm could well believe it. During the famous death scene of Boris, he had heard gasps of anguish all around him and people in the audience openly sobbing as the stricken king crashed to the stage in his death agony.

"By the way, Rembrandt, speaking of singers," Bock sailed on, "did I tell you that my sister Clara is coming to Petersburg after Christmas? The girl has a promising voice and will be taking private lessons from Mde. Oda Slobodskaya, who was a soprano in the Imperial Theatres. She's retired now and takes only a few carefully selected students. Clara's very lucky to get on with her."

Wilhelm had heard enough about Clara from her brother to know that he would very much like to meet her. August said she was pretty, lively, and intelligent.

"Will I get to meet her?" Wilhelm smiled.

"But of course, old boy, of course."

There was a firm knock on the door. Wilhelm was a little startled. They weren't expecting anybody else to drop in. He opened the door and found himself staring into the dour countenance of Erdmann Lepp.

"Good evening, Wilhelm. I hope I haven't come at an inopportune time." Lepp smiled his wispy smile. His side whiskers were more luxuriant than ever, but with more gray and less black in them now.

Wilhelm stammered a greeting and an apology. He was dumbfounded by the sudden appearance of Lepp, whom he had not seen for several years.

The young men rose deferentially when the minister entered the room and cast rather nervous glances at each other — all except young Bock, who greeted Lepp with expansive familiarity.

"My dear Onkel Erdmann, how nice to see you again. I have been meaning to visit you at your school. How are things going with your work?"

"Very well, August. I have just returned from an extended trip to the south. I saw your parents in Schoenwiese. They asked me to say hello. In fact, I was going to look you up tomorrow — and now I find you here. Good, good." He patted the younger man affectionately. He turned to Wilhelm. "I also have greetings for you, Wilhelm, from your dear father and mother, with whom I stayed overnight in Blumenau. They are both well and send their love. Your mother also sent you this food package." He handed Wilhelm the neatly wrapped parcel he had been holding under his arm.

The boys sat down, a little self-consciously, in a sort of semi-circle around Lepp. The relaxed student atmosphere was gone. The unexpected visitor had immediately created formality, as though they were now in church. But the smoke was still thick in the room. Lepp's flaring nostrils pinched in and he fanned his long hands before his face to dispel the noxious fumes.

"Well, boys, you seem to be enjoying a typical student evening. I suppose the smoking stimulates thought and the expression of noble ideas, does it?" He looked pointedly at the wine bottle and the half-filled glass at Bock's elbow. Bock smiled back blandly, unaffected by the stare.

The youths snickered politely at Lepp's little sally, and looked even more uncomfortable. After what they considered a seemly interval, Karl Plett and Abram Schellenberg made their student excuses and rose to leave.

August Bock, chatting easily with the older man, stayed awhile longer. Wilhelm was surprised to learn that Onkel Lepp was a close friend of the Bock family. Apparently he was treated like a member of the family in the Bock home. Was it possible, Wilhelm wondered, that August's wealthy father provided Lepp with financial assistance for some of his missionary work? Lepp was telling them about the Baptist seminary for the training of missionaries and evangelists where he was teaching. He also told them about the late evening meetings which he and his colleague Adolf Reimer, a young Mennonite evangelist from the Molochnaya, conducted periodically. The services were intended for an underworld audience, the kind of people who came out into the streets at night to ply their unsavory trades — thieves, purse snatchers, gamblers, and prostitutes.

Wilhelm saw that Jacob was captivated by Lepp and his missionary activities. From the moment the minister had walked into the room Jacob had not taken his eyes off him. August, however, looked increasingly bored as Lepp talked, though he perked up briefly at the mention of the colorful street characters. Soon August also took his leave, after arranging to meet Lepp the next day.

Lepp now turned his full attention to the two roommates. Wilhelm sensed that Lepp's visit was not as casual as it appeared to be. What was his real purpose in coming? Wilhelm recalled the strange, unsettling interview he had had with Lepp at Voronaya several years before. What did the missionary want from him? Did he still want him to be his assistnat, as he had hinted then? Wilhelm winced at the thought. Never. He would not allow this man to control his life, no matter how important and divinely inspired his work was. He braced himself for the confrontation he felt must come.

At the moment, however, Lepp seemed to be more interested in Jacob. "So, you are the Jacob Priess about whom I have heard such good things from the teachers in Halbstadt? It's also my old school, you know. Intelligence and hard work are a mighty combination in a young man. They can lead to great rewards — especially if placed in the service of our Lord." He regarded Jacob benignly, then looked at Wilhelm with what appeared to be a slight frown.

Jacob spoke eagerly. "I have long wanted to meet you, Onkel Lepp. I plan to dedicate my life to the Lord's service, and I would like very much to benefit from your advice and experience."

Lepp looked pleased. Soon he and Jacob were deeply engrossed in congregational and theological subjects. It was obvious that the veteran *reiseprediger* had taken an immediate liking to the spiritually intense and dedicated young student. Wilhelm listened to the two with growing relief, not minding in the least that they were paying less and less attention to him. He was sitting by the table in the chair that had been occupied by August Bock. He pushed the wine bottle aside, drew closer a sheet of paper and began to doodle as the other two continued to converse.

After a few minutes, Wilhelm rose and lit the battered old samovar in the corner. Yes, he was glad that Onkel Lepp and Jacob were hitting it off so well. Already he felt much less threatened by Lepp's presence.

"Then you are interested in the ministry yourself, my young friend?" Lepp was asking Jacob.

"Oh yes, sir, teaching is just a preparation, a preliminary step towards my goal. Didn't you yourself go from teaching to missionary work? More than anything in the world I would like to follow in your footsteps, Onkel Lepp, to do the kind of precious work you are doing." Jacob stopped, afraid he might be showing too much zeal and enthusiasm in Lepp's eyes. His face shining, he searched the older man's face. Wilhelm had never seen Jacob respond so intensely to another's presence.

Lepp, too, felt that he had unexpectedly found something of great value. He regarded the young man before him with studied calm, but inwardly he felt a rapture slowly spreading through him. Could it be that this ardent, zealous young man was the disciple he had sought so long? And here he had thought for years that it might be Wilhelm Fast, who had great gifts, clearly, but who seemed to lack this fine youth's zeal. And thus God led. He had led him to Jacob Priess through the Fast boy. Yes, he was sure now. He knew what he must do. He would train and test young Priess by initiating him into the tract mission. He had just returned from Halbstadt with a large supply of tracts printed by the Kroekers at their Ruduga press. Yes, the tract mission would make a good start for this dedicated young brother.

Wilhelm resumed his doodling as he kept one ear on Lepp's detailed account of the tract mission. His sketch had started as an aimless geometric pattern. Gradually, the abstract doodles flowered into realistic shapes and figures. He worked steadily, only half-conscious of what he was doing. He completed his drawing just as Lepp looked at his pocket watch and announced it was time for him to go.

Before going to bed, Wilhelm looked at his drawing again. It showed an auto driving along a road. Inside the car, on the passenger's side, sat a gaunt, erect figure with side whiskers blowing in the wind. Beside him, driving, was a young man with a happy smile on his face. Behind the car, standing on the road with a bundle over his shoulder, stood another young man who apparently had just gotten off the auto. He seemed to be relieved to have his feet on the ground again.

2
St. Petersburg, January, 1913

"Clara, this is my friend Fast, the great painter." For once, August Bock's long cold face was warm with fraternal pride and affection.

Wilhelm was looking at a very pretty, smartly dressed young woman. Never would he have taken this stunning girl for a Mennonite. How could such a gorgeous creature be August Bock's sister? With his big face and awkward body? It didn't seem possible.

"I'm honored to meet you, Miss Bock." He felt stiff and awkward in the presence of this radiant, graceful young lady. He simply could not believe that this was a Mennonite girl from the colonies.

"Well, Mr. Fast, I feel as if I know you already. I've heard so much about you — and all good, I hasten to add." Her Russian was flawless and her smile revealed small, perfect teeth.

"Listen, Rembrandt," August said, taking charge as usual, "my father is taking the three of us out to dinner. After dinner he has to make a business call. I've got three tickets for *Swan Lake* at the Maryinsky. So — that's settled." He did not wait for an answer. "This afternoon — right now, in fact — we'll show Clara some of the famous sights of Petersburg. She had her audition in Moscow and has never been up here before. What do you say, old boy?"

Wilhelm quickly said yes to the whole plan, though it would mean cutting a class in art history to go sightseeing. The prospect of spending the afternoon and evening with this beautiful girl suddenly made everything else seem unimportant.

The January afternoon was crisp and clear, but not uncomfortably cold. The pearly northern winter light gave an attractive sharpness of focus and outline to the streets, buildings, and people. It was a perfect day for sightseeing, in fact, even though the wintry conditions added a certain starkness to the scene. A dirty layer of hard-packed snow covered the wooden paving blocks of the streets, and the boulevard and park trees stood naked and stiff, devoid of the wavy green masses which in summer softened and complemented the architectural splendors of the elegant capital. August, however, declared confidently that winter made it easier to appreciate the architectural lines and contours of the fine buildings in the famous half-circle that formed the city's core between the Neva and Fontanka Rivers.

They leisurely walked the half mile from August's room on Tverskaya Street along Nicholas Avenue to Nevsky Prospect. Here the grand tour was to begin. Clara, her gray Cossack-style fur hat tilted at a rakish angle, was brimming with delight. The Nevsky Prospect was the very summit of big city sophistication and chic. She stared in fascination at the stately stone palaces, four and five stories high, standing shoulder to shoulder on both sides of the street. The smart shops, cafés, and restaurants squeezed in between delighted her even more.

"Now, Clara," August commanded, "look straight down to the end of the Prospect — that gold building with the colonnaded tower and the spire is the Admiralty. It's the handsomest building in town, for my money. Now here, on your left, is the magnificent Anichkov Palace — see it? And before Clara had finished with the Anichkov, her brother was turning her shoulders the other way. "And there on the right — down the street — is the Comedy Theatre."

Before Clara could turn to ask a question, August shouted "Taxi" and in a few moments a carriage on runners, one of the famous Petersburg horse-drawn cabs, was pulling over to the curb. The thoroughbred horses pranced and tossed their heads impatiently as August bargained briefly with the stout, liveried coachman. Then the three young people got into the sleigh.

"Now we'll see the Nevsky and its wonders in style," August sighed contentedly. Wilhelm smiled and caught Clara's eye. She smiled back and made a wry face at her brother's long profile. Both knew that August hated physical exertion of any kind. He never walked far when he had a chance to ride.

Clara leaned forward and exclaimed excitedly as they made their way down the wide, thronging street, its vertical planes so sheer and majestic it seemed to her to have been cut right through a solid stone mountain. It was impossible to take in everything at once. Wilhelm noted, though, that while she was in a rare state of excitement, she kept her wits about her. A Mennonite village girl would have been stupefied by the dazzling big city sights and sounds. Not Clara. He felt the faint but charged pressure of her body beside him on the seat. What an extraordinary girl, he thought, so charming, so alive, so confident and bright.

Clara suddenly pointed up ahead to the right. "Look, that funny tower with the big ball on top, what on earth is that, Gusha?"

August brayed appreciatively. "That's what it is, *liebchen* — the earth. I thought you'd notice our new landmark, little sister. That's the renowned Singer Sewing Machine Company that makes the little machines that sew your fancy dresses and cloaks."

"It's a vulgar monstrosity," Wilhelm said decisively. "It spoils the whole skyline of the Nevsky. Just look at that ridiculous tower and ball squatting beside the graceful spire of the Admiralty from this angle. It shouldn't be allowed, such a desecration of beauty. One is great art and the other is — is an ugly display of American commercial greed. If the Americans had been allowed to they would have built that building high enough to blot out the Admiralty spire altogether." Wilhelm stopped, suddenly conscious of his outburst. He felt Clara giving him an appraising stare.

· "You seem to have very decided opinions about things, Mr. Fast. Are you always so sure of your judgments?"

Her tone was frosty. She seemed to be annoyed. He didn't quite know why.

August came suavely to the rescue. "He's an artist, Clara, so naturally he has strong opinions about such things. And I couldn't agree more. That tower is an utter disaster." He turned to Wilhelm, his tone carefully neutral. "I may as well tell you, Rembrandt, my sister is an independent little cat; she likes to make up her own mind about things."

Now Wilhelm understood. He had spoken too soon. He should have given Clara a chance to express her own response before he sounded off.

"I don't think it's so bad," she said lightly, the tension gone. "But why the ball?"

"Aha, that's the American ingenuity of the thing," August laughed. "After dark a light goes on inside the globe and the name "SINGER" sparkles round the metal ring."

Just then, on their left, they passed an incredibly long, butter-colored building with white colonnades and many ornate porticoes and arched doorways and a row of expensive carriages and sleighs lined up along its front.

"Look Clara, that's *Gostiny Dvor*, the Merchant's Inn, the largest food and clothing store in Petersburg. You can get foodstuffs there from the ends of the earth. Actually, it's a bazaar, a whole collection of *ryady*, or rows, of private shops all under the same roof. It caters mostly to the nobility and the rich merchants," August added smugly.

Clara gazed intently at the crowds of well-dressed shoppers going in and out of the vast store, arms laden with packages.

"And just beyond the *Dvor,* the building with the handsome tower, that's City Hall. Oh, and over there, on the other side, is the famous Cafe Nord, which is said to serve the finest pastry in Russia. Does that tempt you, my dear?"

"Yes, it does, Gusha," Clara laughed, teeth sparkling in the frosty air. "But for once —" she broke off as she saw the breathtaking, semi-circular facade of Kazan Cathedral opening up just beyond the projecting bulk of City Hall. "Oh, but it's beautiful, overwhelming," she whispered as her gaze swept the majestically curved length of the golden colonnade topped with its splendid gilded dome.

"Yes," Wilhelm put in dryly, "and across the street the beautiful, overwhelming Singer building."

"Please, Mr. Fast, no more of your superior judgments." But she was smiling. "Don't spoil the innocent enjoyment of a naive girl from the provinces."

They arrived at the foot of the Prospect, in front of the Admiralty, where they continued their tour on foot. Clara was eager to see the Winter Palace with its famous square. But first she had to run to Senate Square at the far end of the Admiralty to take a close look at the Bronze Horseman celebrated by Pushkin: the magnificent equestrian statue of Peter the Great by Falconet. Clara moved slowly around the great monument, studying it from all sides. There sat giant Peter, arm regally oustretched to the West, on a horse rearing dramatically, a crushed serpent writhing under its hooves, daubs of grimy snow on its neck, haunches and tail — horse and rider poised forever on a massive wave of gray and pink granite. And behind the Bronze Horseman loomed the gigantic bronze and plum-colored pile of St. Isaac's Cathedral, that prodigious symbol of the splendor and power of the Russian autocracy, Wilhelm thought, as he and August waited for Clara to finish her inspection of royal Peter.

Palace Square and the turquoise, white, and silver winter Palace offered a baroque splendor that was too much even for Clara. As they approached the Palace from the open side of the Square, she almost stopped breathing. She stood stock-still on the winter-swept cobble stones and reverently declared that this was a moment she would treasure forever. She wanted to see nothing else that day, she said, so the effect would remain vivid. Wilhelm, trying to see the sight through Clara's eyes, was alternately amused and enchanted by the direct, fresh way in which this marvelous girl experienced everything around her. Never had he met anyone like her. He ardently hoped they would become friends.

Like most people who met August Bock Senior for the first time, Wilhelm could only stare helplessly at this genial but indelibly ugly giant. He could not believe that a human head could be so large and shaggy, a face so shockingly coarse. Bock's massive jawbone curved down from his elephantine ears in a long, heavy shovel — like a grain scoop, Wilhelm decided. That prow of a chin looked strong enough to push a house off its foundation. Compared with those mammoth jaws, young August's "hayspade" was a puny thing indeed. When Mr. Bock spoke, his voice rumbled from his great chest with a resonance that made the ears vibrate. His voice was so harsh and deep it seemed to come straight up from his stomach in a rumbling column that moved through his lips without having touched his vocal chords. But Wilhelm discovered during dinner that Bock Senior was a gentle, considerate, extremely nice man. He had none of his son's haughtiness, and it was clear that while Clara, thank God, had none of his gross looks, she had inherited her father's frank, open, uncomplicated nature.

Wilhelm tried to hide his self-consciousness as they sat in the elegant dining room of the Astoria Hotel overlooking Cathedral Square. He had never eaten in such posh surroundings, and he had to watch the others carefully to know what to pick up next, what to eat and what to leave. The hovering, deferential waiters discombobulated him even more. He ducked from side to side awkwardly as the various dishes were being served, not sure from which side the uniformed creatures would come at him next. The dinner itself was excellent, and at Mr. Bock's urging Wilhelm had a second glass of wine, although he had not yet acquired a taste for dinner wine.

Clara was as gay and animated as ever. She talked with voluble delight about the afternoon of sightseeing. Bock Senior clearly doted on his charming daughter. At first Wilhelm was a little shocked to see such easy intimacy between two people so ludicrously mismatched physically. They looked like Beauty and the Beast together. But it did not take him long to gauge the depth of feeling between father and daughter, and he soon found himself regarding the elder Bock in a new light. He was ugly only if you ignored everything about him except his physical features.

Wilhelm kept stealing admiring glances at Clara; he noted how regal her bearing was — in fact, her proud bearing made her seem taller than she was. In profile she looked amazingly like a younger Empress Alexandra, he decided, with her high, clear brow, small but determined chin, her long, delicate nose with just a hint of aristocratic hook, and her gracefully curving neck. Her hair was simply but artfully arranged in shining blonde coils about her small head. She not only looked like a princess, but would be as unobtainable for someone like him, he reminded himself.

Dinner over, August Bock Senior excused himself politely, wished the young people an enjoyable evening at the theatre, and left for his appointment. They had plenty of time before the curtain at the Maryinsky, so they dawdled over coffee, and finally, at Clara's insistence, walked across the Square for a closer look at St. Isaac's. They then took a leisurely route to the theatre several blocks away.

The gilt and blue velvet grandeur of the Maryinsky, with its great painted ceiling and sparkling crystal chandeliers created another dazzling effect for Clara. As they settled into their chairs in a side gallery, her face was filled with such rapturous anticipation that Wilhelm couldn't resist whispering, "You could be taken for a native Petersburger, Miss Clara, you look so much at home in these surroundings."

She glanced at him sharply, but saw that he was merely being playful.

"No, Mr. Fast, I do not feel at home here — not yet — but I am enjoying every minute of it. And I can promise you that someday I *will* feel completely at home here — on both sides of the footlights."

He was surprised by the look of grim determination that suddenly hardened her face. She really means it, he thought, she really thinks she will be singing here some day; and again he was conscious of the immense gulf between them.

Then she smiled and added gaily, "And when I'm a famous opera singer you shall paint my portrait full length, like the one of Giulia Grisi in the foyer. And I shall pay you a fat fee and get you other clients and you too will become rich and famous."

Her gay rush of words produced for the first time a spark of warmth, almost of intimacy between them. He leaned back with a warm feeling as the conductor made his appearance and the house came alive with applause. He did not think he wanted to become a rich portrait painter, but he would gladly paint this marvelous girl's portrait. And he would do it for nothing — just to have her near him.

CHAPTER EIGHT

1

Daniel Fast Remembers: (3) "God Hath Chosen the Foolish"
Blumenau, August, 1852

Who can know the ways of the Lord with us earth-pilgrims? Or of Satan who works from the inside with even more cunning than from the outside. When he saw he couldn't ruin us through the unholy wrath of Elder Dyck, he decided to come at us another way. Not through persecution by our enemies, but through our own meekness and humility. From the beginning some of our members were narrow and overzealous in their views. They were very conservative and strong-minded people, these brothers and sisters, and wanted to set up not only strict church rules, but very strict rules of behavior in everyday life too. Na ya, I was in favor of strictness. After all, we were trying to go back to the uncompromising faith and practice of our Anabaptist forefathers.

We set up rules of conduct forbidding all drinking, dancing and, above all, the evil habit of smoking that was so common among our Mennonites in Russia. We also banned all forms of personal vanity such as frockcoats, cravats, polished boots, and watch chains for male members and bright-colored dresses, rings, brooches, and fancy hairdressings for female members. We believed that the color blue was the *duse,* the God-pleasing color, and ordained that blue be the only color used on farm buildings, homes, wagons, and furniture. Our members were urged not to attend weddings or other gatherings where merriment reigned and foolish games were played. We considered joke-telling and loud laughing as idle pursuits invented by Satan to take our minds away from serious matters. We had nothing to do with secular offices such as *schulze* and *oberschulze.*

Some of our more extreme members wanted to set up even more rigid rules. They insisted that bread should only be broken in the biblical way and not cut with a knife. They favored setting aside certain days for fasting, but were for doing away with all religious holidays including Christmas and Easter. They even wanted to break off all contact with our Mennonite brethren in the Old Church. A few went so far as to suggest that we sell all our worldly goods and live as paupers! That was going too far for the sake of spiritual purity, I told them. We still had to live in this world even though we didn't want to be of the world.

Our bickering over rules was, alas, only the skin rash that covered a much more serious sickness underneath. In their hot zeal to create a pure *gemeinde,* some of our members became raving fanatics who believed they could express their own purity only by accusing and attacking others less zealous. Everywhere they looked they saw impure beliefs and sinful conduct. The parents of some young people in Muensterberg were threatened with the ban for having allowed their children to attend a party in Altonau where there was drinking and dancing. Our deacon, Heinrich Friesen, was accused of vanity for having bought his wife a small handmirror at the bazaar in Tokmak. Friesen had to make public apology at the next brotherhood meeting.

The charges and counter-charges flew thick as hailstones. And most of them landed on my head. I was forever being pressed to ban this or that member. The sacred instrument of shunning, the church's rod of chastisement from God, was now to be wielded like a birch rod in the hands of a drunken schoolmaster.

What was happening to my dream of the pure church?

Ach, but sly Satan knows how to make bad things worse. Led by Big Franz Warkentin and "Turnip" Isaac Rempel, several of our families in Muntau now denounced the rest of us as shallow believers and hypocrites and threatened to form their own splinter group. Their practices and conduct became so extreme and foolish that I became truly alarmed for them. They were terrible weepers and groaners who put themselves through one spiritual agony after another. At table they said long emotional graces, trying to move each other to spontaneous weeping. If that didn't work they would leave the table without eating. After hours on their knees in penitence for their "cold spirits" and "frozen feelings," they would finally eat the food they had left on the table, even if already mouldy or tainted. Several of them got quite sick and the Warkentins' youngest girl died from eating tainted food.

Soon they were fasting whole days at a time, all the while accusing themselves of the most horrible sins. Rempel and his family began to go out in the evenings — it was October and quite cold — and throw themselves on the chilly ground of a roadside ditch near their home. There the whole family would lie all night, praying, singing, and beseeching God to be merciful to them, miserable sinners that they were. The Rempels' second son David, only fifteen and a half-cripple with one leg shorter than the other, caught lung infection one night and three days later he was gone.

I went to see these people, hoping the boy's death would bring them to their senses. But it didn't. They read his death as a sign from God that they were lax and filled with pride. They seemed interested only in suffering the pain of remorse without the joy of redemption. They were so joyless and gloomy, these poor creatures, it made my blood run cold. Nothing I said to them made the slightest impression. With tears and sighs and wringing of hands they accused me of being "lukewarm" and "proud" and of not being sincerely interested in finding the pure way.

The foolish conduct of these brothers and sisters caused me much heartache and soul-searching. I blamed myself for not having seen this terrible soul-sickness in time. It was the crafty work of Satan himself. I never doubted that. And he had ensnared me too by encouraging me to tolerate these practices when they first began. I should have taken stern action then.

Instead I had been weak. Now it was too late.

But it seemed Satan had only toyed with me so far. Now he grew earnest. He began by attacking the very pillars of my strength — my father-in-law Johann Froese and my dear wife Anna. In the midst of all this upheaval and strife in our church my mother-in-law, who had been morbid and ailing for years, passed away with scarcely a sigh. Oom Johann, who was past sixty but not an old man, decided to get married again.

It didn't take him long to find a new wife. In Tiegenhagen lived a widow Quiring who was well-to-do and on the lookout for the right man. She was a woman widely known for her gift of second sight. She had already shown some interest in our *gemeinde,* especially during my mother-in-law's final illness, when she had been a frequent visitor at the Froeses.

Oom Johann and the Widow Quiring were married in the spring in the midst of a late, thick snowstorm. Everybody said it was a good match. I was not so sure. In my contacts with the Widow, I thought I detected a certain lack of balance in her, certain extremes of character and behavior. The Widow was an imposing woman physically. So enormous, in fact, and round and broad on top, it was said she could place a full cup of coffee on her bosom without spilling a drop. But I never saw her do that. She was a very loud talker, a pushy woman who liked to control everything around her. The first time we ever met she had a lot of advice for me as elder. She seemed to have an answer for everything, including her own questions. She would be good to take along the next time Elder Dyck or the *Oberschulze* sent for me, I couldn't help thinking.

As a "clear-seer" the Widow Quiring claimed to hear voices from heaven in prophetic dreams. I knew there were such women — they had existed even in biblical times — so I had to wait and see before I tried to judge her. Who was I to question God's methods for revealing Himself to us mortals even if He resorted to noisy old women in dreams and visions. I only hoped she was a good prophetess like Deborah in the time of Judges, and not like Miriam, Moses' treacherous sister or, God forbid, like the Witch of Endor, who could summon dead spirits out of the depths.

Misery and calamity. My worst fears were soon realized. My new mother-in-law's influence over Oom Johann was frightening. Almost overnight he changed from a quiet, devout, loyal friend and helper to a raging fanatic. His wife's visions — which she seemed to have almost every night — became calls for action for the poor old man. The Widow (somehow I could never think of her as anything else) seemed to know the whole Bible from memory. She was particularly strong on Daniel and Revelation.

One night she dreamt the end of the world down to the last detail. Now the fat was in the fire. She considered this dream as a revelation from God, who had vouchsafed to her the time and place of the Second Coming. Oom Johann was now like a man possessed. He drove frantically from *hof* to *hof,* from village to village, his hefty wife seated beside him like an avenging angel, and announced to all and sundry that the world would come to an end that summer, on August 1st, 1820, just after the end of the harvest.

Inspired by his wife's dream, Oom Johann painted such terrible pictures of the last day — how the flames would shoot and crackle through house and barn, how the earth would quake and break open in loud explosions, how people would scream and run around like beheaded chickens in their terror — that he frightened people half to death. He and his wife held meetings in homes and on the streets, not just with members of our *gemeinde* but with anybody who would listen to them. They urged people to prepare for the great day: all the righteous were to meet in the village pasture at the lower end of Blumenau on the evening of July 31st. There the blessed assembly would celebrate a joyous holy communion for the last time. They would wait through the night in their Sunday clothes, their feet freshly washed (we had recently restored the ancient ritual of footwashing in our *gemeinde*), until the heavens would open and the Lord would come down in all His glory for the Last Judgment. The Widow assured everybody that the morning of the last day was to be bright and sunny without a cloud in the sky — except, of course, for the cloud the Son of Man would come down on — so that all the saved would have a clear view of what was happening.

The whole community was so stirred up by the Froeses and their supporters the Rempels and Warkentins from Muntau that we were all in a daze. I didn't know where to turn. People who believed the Widow's prophecy were making public confessions of their sins to purify themselves before the event. All sorts of hideous sins came to light, including a number of hitherto unsuspected cases of adultery and other sins of the flesh. Some members urged me to ban these self-confessed sinners; others said it was now too late for shunning, that God in His glory, soon to be here, would exercise the Final Ban. It seemed that a terrible curse or spell had been cast over us, as in the dark days of Aaron and Joshua. I was sure that my parents-in-law were crazy not inspired, but I couldn't seem to make others see that.

Not even my dear, faithful Anna. Ach, what a misery and calamity it is for me to recall her part in this sad story, even after all these years. My Anna, who had always been so gentle and steady, so level-headed and devoted, now also came under the influence of her fanatical parents. As the Froeses lived next to us, Anna came into daily contact with her stepmother. At first Anna paid little attention to her regular reports of dreams and visions. But even placid Anna was awed by the Widow's vision of the Second Coming. She began spending much of her time at her stepmother's, neglecting the children and her housework. Nothing I said seemed to make any impression on her. I tried to overlook her neglect as much as possible. She was, after all, big with our sixth child and I didn't want to be too hard on her. A woman is never quite herself at such times.

That was another mistake I made.

Anna now began to have her own strange dreams, all of which she eagerly told her stepmother. One afternoon she came home highly excited with the news that her mother was convinced that she, Anna, had the gift of second sight too. Sometimes, apparently, people who had the gift did not know they had it until someone else who had it told them so.

"Daniel," Anna exulted, "isn't it wonderful? Now you will have me to help you with the Lord's work just as Father has my dear mother. There is so much to do to get ready for His coming."

Her words stunned me. So the Widow's disease had now passed into my wife's bloodstream. I tried to reason with Anna by telling her that not all dreams and visions came from God. Satan had that power too. Satan, I told her, liked nothing better than to sow doubt and confusion and false hopes among the weak and trusting. I told her it was unbiblical to try to predict the exact time of the Second Coming. Christ himself said no one knows the day and hour except for God. If God had wanted us to know he would have given the date in Scripture.

I was talking to a stone. Anna looked at me with hurt, sullen eyes and said perhaps what people were saying about me, that I was not a true believer, that I was lukewarm and more interested in keeping power as elder than in advancing God's work, was true after all. She said many other things even more terrible. Abruptly, she swung her heavy belly to the door and went back to her parents' house, where she stayed the whole evening. I finally went to bed with a heavy spirit, but after pouring out my heart to the Savior who sees all, I felt better and prepared myself for sleep.

Ach, *du lieber Gott!* I was torn out of sleep by a moaning voice. Something terrible was happening. I stared up at Anna standing in the darkness beside our bed in her night shift, a crazed look on her face, clutching a butcher knife suspended over her swollen belly. Her voice, even more than the raised knife, froze my body so I couldn't move.

" 'All manner of sin and blasphemy shall be forgiven . . . but the blasphemy against the Holy Ghost shall not be forgiven . . .' "

She kept her burning eyes fixed on me as she said these words.

"Anna, Anna what — ?"

"You have blasphemed against the Holy Ghost." Her voice rose to a shriek.

She looked down at her belly. Then I knew. She was about to plunge the knife into her own womb, into our unborn child. I screamed and lunged at her, grabbing her wrists just as her arms tightened to strike. She began wailing and gibbering as I took the knife from her and forced her to sit down on the edge of the bed.

"Blasphemer, blasphemer, blasphemer," she screeched at me, her face twisted horribly, eyes rolling wild, "I know you, devil, you have defiled the temple of the Lord, you have blasphemed against the Holy Ghost; your black sin is here in my belly. Let me cleanse myself of your foulness, you viper and blasphemer. Let me go. I know you, I know you . . ."

Ach, that was a night so unearthly and hideous I felt the end of the world was already here. Anna kept struggling and screaming to get loose and I wrestled with her on our bed with terror in my soul. She was unbelievably strong and I did not want hurt to come to our poor, unborn child. At long last her swollen body wore out and she agreed to lie down. I sat over her, watching anxiously. She soon fell into a heavy, labored sleep, but still I did not dare leave her alone.

The children had been roused by the screaming, of course, but I knew they would never dare come into their parents' corner room at night unbidden. When daylight came my oldest son Peter, a lad of sixteen, came to the door and asked if there was anything he should do.

"Yes," I whispered, "go fetch Mumtje Fehdrau right away."

She was quite elderly now, but she was still the best person around to look after poor Anna. I did not want Anna's mother there as long as I could prevent it. The old witch would take over the sick room soon enough. And of course she would blame me for everything.

Anna gradually recovered her strength if not her reason. She was never the same again. Something had gone out of her that dreadful night; perhaps the devil that had possessed her had taken part of her with him when he left her: I don't know. She was very quiet and listless after that. She no longer had prophetic dreams and seemed to have lost interest in church and spiritual matters. Though I didn't like to talk about it to others — or even think about it — I could see that poor Anna was now weak-minded, and would probably stay that way. *Schnorrijch,* but she now had a good memory, where before she had been one to forget things easily. Sometimes in the evenings she would sit down and recite aloud all the verses of a hymn from the *gesangbuch.* She would never tell me why she did this, or why she had no interest in the church.

Anna's baby came on August 1st, the very day forecast by her mother as the day of the Second Coming. It was my wife's last child — our dear gentle David, who is now a teacher in Lindenau nearby.

The Second Coming did not happen that day, though the Froeses and their followers sat waiting in the pasture in their bare feet all day, right up until it got dark. Oom Johann and his wife were the last to leave. They walked home alone in the dark, silent for once and looking straight ahead.

But the Widow was not one to hide her light for long. She and her husband did lose some of their influence in the community when the world still stood as before on August 2nd. But she still had her second sight. Ya, she even had a third sight now — hindsight. Her vision had come from God, she declared as loudly as ever, and so had to be true. But being human, she herself had made a mistake. She was out on the date of the Lord's return by exactly two years. How did she know? Here she heaved her broad bosom and with a modest blush explained. At the most sacred moment of her vision, just when the date of the Second Coming was being revealed to her, Oom Johann, sleeping blissfully beside her, had accidentally bumped her in the side with his elbow. That momentary disturbance had caused her to miss the "two" in "twenty-two," and made her think the date was 1820 when it was really 1822, as her latest dream had confirmed. Satan, she said, lowering her voice, could spit even into a sacred vision. Otherwise, all the information had been exactly right.

And so the Widow plucked many lost believers back to her side again to help her prepare for the new Second Coming that was coming without any doubt this time. Satan would not deceive her a second time, she added grimly.

It was time for me to take stock of myself and my role as elder. My problems with the *gemeinde,* I knew, were far from over. I spent much time on my knees beseeching God's guidance and wisdom. Ach, what a shame to know I had been weak and afraid to act at the very time I should have been strong and forthright. I should have punished the rebels in our group long before this, including my wife's parents. Instead, I had tried to be understanding and forgiving. My compassion and tolerance had been seen only as the weakness of a lukewarm believer.

Now I would show them all where I stood. I preached a strong sermon based on Revelation 22, where the Lord Jesus warns every man neither to add nor to take anything away from God's prophetic words. I included supporting passages from Menno and other early fathers. My sermon, I hoped, would bring my flock to its senses.

Ach, how wrong I was. My sermon broke over my own head. As soon as I started on my theme I saw my wife's parents and the Warkentins and Rempels exchanging mocking glances. They were not pleased with what I was saying. Suddenly, in the middle of my sermon, Oom Johann rose to his feet behind me, came to the pulpit, and fixing me with an angry stare hissed, "That's all false teaching. I don't want to hear any more of that. It's enough to make my stomach rise, such crooked thinking." Then, Bible in hand, he stepped off the platform and faced the congregation.

The Widow had also risen from her place near the front. Her large, round face looked black as a cold forge. She scraped and pushed her way past feet and legs to join her husband in the aisle. Together they slowly shuffled to the door. The Rempels and Warkentins and several other people walked out too. I looked at the retreating backs and felt my world crumbling around me. With a heavy heart I finished my sermon, feeling the disapproval in the room. Oom Johann's open, perhaps planned rebellion, meant the end for me as elder of the *gemeinde.*

A few days later I received a written note from Oom Johann asking me to attend a brotherhood meeting in Muntau. I went with deep feelings of foreboding. The night before the meeting I spent hours on my knees calling on God to show me what to do and to give me the strength to accept what would come. The shame I was about to suffer was as nothing compared with the sense of failure I felt. Why was God allowing my dream of a family of suffering believers to turn into a nightmare of squabbling, backbiting, and hatred? Instead of a loving brotherhood we were a pack of wild dogs tearing at each other.

The assembled brothers avoided my eyes when I walked into the room for the meeting. A bad sign. But I already knew what my fate would be, so I was quite calm. God would allow me to get through this misery and calamity too.

There were some bad consciences in that room. I could almost smell them.

Oom Johann looked very stern. As if the Widow was looking through his eyes. His deep voice throbbing, he asked me if I still held to my view that I was right and the *gemeinde* wrong? Or was I now ready to confess openly my wilful pride and error in resisting the will of the brotherhood? All I needed to do was ask forgiveness of the brotherhood and the matter would end here and now. Then his face hardened even more and looking over my head he said quietly:

"If you remain stubborn, the matter will now be settled in open vote." A shuffling of feet and a clearing of throats seemed to back up Oom Johann's harsh words.

"Oom Johann," I answered, "I can only say to you and the brothers what you heard me say to Elder Dyck a few years ago. I have tried to stick to Scripture and the teachings of our forefathers. It's my deep conviction, strengthened by many hours on my knees before God, that what you and certain other members of the brotherhood have been teaching is wrong and directly contrary to the Bible and the traditions of our Mennonite faith. If you can show me, on the basis of Scripture and church teaching, that I am in error, please do so. If not, then I am willing to put the assembled brothers to the test in open vote."

Oom Johann said a few more things but made no effort to refute my position from Scripture. He then solemnly bade me ask each of the brothers in turn whether he supported me or not.

This I did, but with a heart so laden I could scarcely breathe. The result was as I knew it would be. A few of the brothers said "yes" to me through their tears, but the majority muttered "no," most looking uncomfortable as they did so. A few, like Rempel and Warkentin, gave their "no" vote with open satisfaction.

In a loud voice Oom Johann announced that I had been defeated in an open vote of the brotherhood taken in the awesome presence of Almighty God, and that I now stood relieved of my post as elder of the *gemeinde*. In a half-hearted attempt at reconciliation, he added that I was free to remain with the *gemeinde* as a teacher, provided I would not try to teach false doctrine and spread heresy.

Who can know the despair I felt? I had been so certain that I was following God's will for our people. That we were reestablishing the principles of faith and conduct as laid down in the Bible, and in the writings of Menno, Phillips, Peters, and others. Now doubt washed over me in waves as I nursed my sick soul in the privacy of my home. The support I could once have expected from my Anna had shriveled with her poor brain. She cared no more about my defeat and future than she cared about the upkeep of the house that had once been her pride and joy. She had become a pale, withered vegetable. She spent most of her time in the small room singing and reciting hymns and bible verses. She did not bother with anything else, including the children. Our oldest girl Liese, fortunately, was now thirteen and very capable. She looked after the house, the cooking, and the smaller children very well and without ever complaining.

My doubts and misery stayed with me as the weeks and months went by.

What if instead of following God's plan I had really been following my own? Instead of going back to Anabaptist traditions, had I perhaps simply used those traditions to satisfy my own personal ambition? I had professed to love God and my fellow man, but had I loved myself more? Had I been led by Satan to forget that a man can gain the whole world and lose his own soul? Had God deliberately chosen the foolish in our *gemeinde* — including the Widow — to confound me, who had set himself up as wise? Ach, what a humbling lesson I was forced to learn. At last God was opening my eyes to my own vanity. Perhaps I had wanted a church for myself instead of for Him. Through rules and narrow practises I had tried to control the rest, to impose my will on the members.

I had dared to play God!

CHAPTER NINE

1

Butyrki Prison, Moscow, February, 1913

"Well, well — look boys, here comes our little *Skromny,* our Modest One, with another great Anarchist poem he's just written."

It was that sarcastic bastard Abram Gotz, the little Jew who was always boasting about how he had been a leader in the Socialist-Revolutionary Party on the outside.

"Yeah, the great Monk Nestor. He'll soon have us all converted to Anarchism." That cold fish Minor, Gotz's slimy side-kick, had to put his two kopeks in too.

Rude snickers and more sarcastic taunts as he stepped to the center of the large cell, holding up a scribbled sheet. The gibes no longer bothered him. He was used to their crude insults and sarcastic guffaws. They found him entertaining, a relief from the excruciating boredom of prison life. So what? Let them laugh. He was using them too, the bastards. He desperately needed an audience for the ideas boiling over in his brain, the burning words fed by the fire in his gut. His poems came spurting out of him in mighty spasms, like seed out of a man's bag. His revolutionary zeal was a force he barely controlled by letting the fiery words march across the page. Sooner or later these sneering assholes would start listening to him in earnest.

Coolly, he matched their contempt with his own. "All right, you ignorant clods," he began, his full, red lips curling in a mock sneer, "now listen and try not to scratch your lice while I'm reading."

"It better be good, *Skromny,* or you'll be the louse we'll scratch," rumbled the big redhead Korzenko in the corner bunk.

"It's called 'Song of the People's Heroes'," he announced, coughing. It was his damn chest again. His thin shoulders heaved and heaved. At last it stopped and he began.

> Through the forests and over the hills,
> On the steppes between the rivers,
> In endless, eager lines
> Move the freedom-loving peasants.
>
> On high they hold a banner —
> The wind-whipped flag of Anarchism;
> In that bold word the mighty cause
> Of truth and freedom for the masses.
>
> The ancient cry for freedom
> Has become a cry for action;
> The spirits of courageous leaders
> Return to give us strength.

We march in solidarity
A movement of the people,
An army that cannot be stopped.
And who is riding at its head?"
He made the mistake of pausing for effect.
"The brave Makhno, of course," came the mocking answer.
He did not change expression, hid his annoyance. He waited for the laughs and jeers to stop.
"And who is riding at its head?" This time he was not interrupted.

"The first in line is Stenka Razin,
The next is Kondrat Bulavin,
Then comes the Batko Pugachev,
Brave peasant leaders of the past.

With solemn pride these heroes ride,
Their clarion calls inspire
The lines of eager followers
Who bide their time to strike.

We stand for brotherhood and truth,
For freedom and equality;
We are the homeless and the hungry
We fight for holy liberty.

Our cause is just and pure,
Our strength is born of suffering
The bourgeoisie we vow to conquer,
So forward all who dare."

Thin but erect, his boyish head thrown back, he brought his reading to a ringing close. He could tell that his cell-mates were impressed — even Gotz and Minor — because they hadn't interrupted the last part of his reading at all.

His friend and teacher Pyotr Andreevich Arshinov called out from his bunk. "Bravo, well done, Nestor Ivanovich. You are becoming a real poet, I must say."

There were other murmurs of approval, and he basked in a new respect as he walked over to Arshinov, face aglow, his heart full of fire and satisfaction.

He had been in prison for over four years now. He and the other Anarchists from Gulai-Polye had been kept in the Alexandrovsk prison that whole first winter without being brought to trial. All except Vanya Levadney. He had escaped one night in the middle of winter, a blizzard raging outside. But he never made it. They found him frozen stiff beside the road — the road to Gulai-Polye. A new prisoner had told them that later.

In the spring of 1909 they were finally taken north to Ekaterinoslav to stand trial. Four — including Lichko and Matvienko, the bastards — got the rope. The remaining five, including himself, pulled *katorga,* life at hard labor. He remembered feeling only numbness as the sentences were read out. Even when his own name and sentence hung in the fetid air of the courtroom he had felt nothing — no relief at cheating death, no despair over a living death in prison. Nothing. Not even during the long rumbling blur of the train trip to Moscow. But when the big iron gate of the Butyrki had clanged shut behind him, then it came — black despair, bleak hopelessness; he could think only of finishing himself off the first chance he got.

He never got the chance. In the Butyrki they knew how to keep you alive. Nobody cheated the Butyrki. Not unless you could will yourself to stop breathing. The rules kept you alive and suffering. The Butyrki, he discovered, was a punishment prison with regulations so numerous and brutally strict that even the most careful and best behaved prisoners ran afoul of one or more of them daily. It was impossible to be a model prisoner in the Butyrki. As impossible as being a rebellious one. His first punishment had come within hours. He had wandered aimlessly over to the cell window, having already forgotten that you were supposed to stay at least three steps away from the window. Then he rashly tried to tell the guard that he had been accidentally pushed by one of his cell-mates.

That gave him his first taste of the Hole, the dreaded solitary cell in the Pugachev Tower. A taste that lasted for a week.

He didn't like to think of those first weeks and months when he experienced in shock after numbing shock the cold ruthlessness of the Butyrki system. His quick temper kept delivering him into the waiting hands of the bloody guards. He simply couldn't control himself when he thought others — whether fellow prisoners or guards — were picking on him or taking advantage of him. The threat of immediate punishment meant nothing to him. His fits of insane rage struck suddenly, blindly, left him incapable of thinking. The fits terrified him because they made him helpless, defenseless. Always it was the same: the sudden tumult in his blood, his mind racing out of control, the ugly lash of his tongue striking out in stinging frenzy. And then the guards would come to life, moving in with hungry, wolfish grins and swinging clubs.

That first time they dragged him to the Hole he fought like a madman. He realized later that if he had been a big, heavy man he would have had broken bones. Ironically, it was the very puniness of his body that often saved him physical humiliation or injury. For some reason the sadistic guards seemed to prefer working over the bigger prisoners, the stronger ones, even though they were usually the most passive ones. It didn't help his pride, though, to know that he escaped the roughest manhandling because he had the delicate body of a twelve-year-old girl. For other reasons, that girl's body also attracted the attention of some of the other prisoners.

When the door bolt scraped tight that first time, he lay in the darkness feeling the cold, dank breath of the floor seep through him. Not for the first time since his trial he wished bitterly they had hung him instead. A sudden jerk into nothing — better than this dragged-out torture, this shitty vomit of life that wouldn't stop. The soft dreams that floated through his fitful dozing on the chilly stones only sharpened his despair when he awoke.

Black days lost in time and silence; when they marched him back to his cell he had to learn painful light again. He hated his fragile body for still mocking him with unwanted motion, forcing him to feel what he was powerless to shut out. He collapsed on the floor of his cell, not bothering to find his empty bunk. Like a whipped dog he wanted to hurt alone. The voices and movements around him broke against his indifference and did not reach him.

It took him a long time to come back to himself that first time. But he did come back finally. Only to lose himself again in a black rage that got him right back in the Hole. Again and again. He couldn't remember how many times. For a long time he thought he would never get used to the horrors of prison life. Once during that first year he went completely berserk and they put chains on him and threw him into the Hole that way. For he didn't know how many weeks. When they finally hauled him out he had lost his sense of balance and staggered around like a drunk. He suffered dizzy spells and then his chest began to ache and the coughing fits started.

Bit by bit, though, he began to take an interest in what was going on around him. The black spells came less often. He began to listen to Gotz and Minor — whom the other prisoners called the "major and minor Jews" — talking politics. Actually, it was Gotz, who looked like a fussy little office clerk with his bald head, pointed little beard, and small white hands, who did most of the talking. The more sinister-looking Minor was big, had fat, round shoulders and a long, pale face from which pale, hooded eyes glanced suspiciously at everyone except Gotz. Minor didn't say much himself, but he hung on Gotz's every word, then looked around with an air of approval as though he himself had just uttered the wise words. Everyone knew if you disagreed with Abram Rafailovich you were also disagreeing with Minor.

Gotz and Minor belonged to the moderate wing of the Socialist-Revolutionary Party which had been formed in 1900 by the *Narodniki,* the Populists. The party stood in opposition not only to the monarchy but to the radical Marxist party of the Social Democrats. Gotz liked to boast that he was one of the founding members of his party, and represented what he called the socialist right wing. He was convinced that after the rotten Romanovs had been deposed, Russia would undergo a gradual, peaceful evolution to socialism. If he had his way, he said, his party would be called the Social-Evolution Party. It was the party of the peasantry, not of the unstable, urban proletariat. The Russian peasant, he added, had a natural instinct for socialism.

Yes, Gotz was a moderate, but a passionate one. "The road to freedom for Holy Mother Russia," he had begun grandly one day, his tiny hand fluttering mothlike in the air, "is land reform for the peasant. The peasant of Russia has been carrying the monarchy and the idle nobility on his back too long." He paused, his pale little face suffused with a gentle ecstasy, like that of a priest celebrating the mass. Sniffing reflectively, he resumed his formal tone.

"Yes, the 1861 manifesto abolishing serfdom came as too little too late. The peasant was no longer legally bound but he was still bound to the land by economic necessity. And the land he received still didn't belong to him personally. It was only held by him in trust, so to speak. The real owner of the land confiscated from the estates of the nobility was the village *mir*, the commune. The *mir* redistributed the land collectively available to it every few years, but there was never enough to enable individual families to make a decent living. And even when he did get a piece of land, the peasant had to indenture himself financially to the government by taking out a long-term loan. So, the peasant actually got poorer after 1861." Gotz paused again, sniffing more rapidly now, like a bloodhound picking up a steady scent.

"But get to the point, Abram Rafailovich," big Korzenko called out impatiently. "We all know we peasants are forced to live on our own turds. What's to be done about it, that's what we want to know, comrade. We won't be kicked around forever."

Gotz allowed an expression of good-natured tolerance to flit across his face.

"Complex problems demand complex solutions, my friend. The point is that while the *mir* system has failed, we should still be working with the *mir concept*" — he emphasized the last word and paused, as though giving student listeners a chance to catch up with their note-taking. "You see," he continued reflectively, eyes closed, pale face shining, "Marxist socialism is not the answer here in Russia. Marxism may be all right for the West, where they have different traditions. But Russia must develop its own specifically Russian brand of socialism."

"Gotz, you serpent," bawled another voice, "just tell us what you have in mind and don't preach against Marxism, which you don't understand in any case." The speaker was an ardent Social Democrat, a Marxist who saw things only in revolutionary black and white.

Gotz looked pained, but ignored the interruption. "We all know Stolypin's land reform in '06 was not the answer. Stolypin was a politician, a tool of the Tsar, capable of thinking only in terms of political solutions. With a stroke of the pen he dissolved the *mirs* and gave the peasants the right to their own land.

"It sounded fine in theory, but it was the wrong solution. Now, half a dozen years later, the bad results are showing more and more. The peasant got too much freedom too suddenly. Within a year or two the poorer peasants were beginning to sell off their land to the wealthier peasants. I predict, my friends, that within ten years there will be a new class of landowners and an even greater number of landless peasants than before."

"But Abram Rafailovich, you still haven't tole us what you advocate."

"I'm coming to that." Gotz was unperturbed. "What Stolypin should have done was not to abolish the *mir* system but to adapt it, to perfect it." He looked around, savoring his revelation. "Some of our German colonies in the South have that perfect system now."

He had been following Gotz's long-winded argument with casual impatience. The reference to the German colonists made him alert.

"In the German colonies, I understand, the farmer owns his land outright, but is subject to the collective will of the village government. In other words, there are two important conditions set on the farmer's ownership of his land. One is that he can't divide the land, a wise rule. The other is that he can sell the land only with the approval of the other farmers."

He could not remain silent any longer. "What you say is true of the Mennonite villages, Abram Rafailovich. But many of the Mennonite Germans live on vast estates, just like the Russian nobility. I know, I worked for one. Those are the bastards that should be forced to give up their land first."

They looked at him in mild astonishment. He had never joined the political discussions before.

Gotz was amused. "Ah, so our little Ukrainian hot-head wants to make his view known too. And what are you, my young friend? A good Marxist, yes? Menshevist or Bolshevik?" His tone was sarcastic. "Don't tell me you're an Anarchist, God fobid?"

"Yes, comrade, I'm an Anarchist, a pure revolutionary, and I've been listening to you spouting off long enough. You talk big words about changing the land system. But I have a question. How are you going to make those changes without having a revolution first? And what kind of revolution do you favor?"

Gotz looked annoyed. All these radical socialists cared about was revolution, the bloodier the better.

"Revolution? No, evolution first, my friend. As our late leader Pyotr Lavrov used to say, 'Before you can have a proper revolution you've got to educate the masses, show them through slogans and speeches what their objectives should be and how to achieve them.'"

"That's all bullshit," he spat in derision. "The peasants don't need to be told what a revolution is or how to carry it out. Where I come from we know from the cradle what the wrongs are and what to do about them. All we need is the will and the weapons."

Well, well, our little cockpigeon from the south has the true revolutionary fervor," Gotz answered sarcastically." Tell me, my little friend, will you be leading your *khokhols,* your Ukrainians, to victory by divine inspiration from your cell here, or will you wait for a little help from those who have not yet been caught by the tsarist swine?"

"You can laugh, Gotz, but you're as helpless as I am. Besides, what do you know about the peasant? Don't tell me you're one yourself, you soft toad."

Gotz reddened with anger and Minor gave him a murderous look from his hooded eyes.

At that point a new prisoner, Pyotr Arshinov, had stepped forward and smoothly separated the combatants with a few witty, relaxing remarks. Arshinov seemed interested in him, hailed him as a fellow-*khokhol,* and had a long talk with him.

Yes, that had been the day Pyotr Andreevich took him under his wing. Now, a year and a half later, he already owed more to Arshinov than he could ever repay. Arshinov had become his trusted friend and teacher, a fellow-anarchist who was older, more experienced, and knew much more about the cause. Arshinov started by teaching him some proper Russian grammar and then introduced him to Russian literature. Pyotr Andreevich said he too was largely self-taught, and that a man was in a mental prison for life unless he freed himself through education and knowledge about the things that mattered. Now, under Arshinov's guidance, he was even studying a little mathematics and social history. But what he found most exciting of all were the anarchist writings of Prince Kropotkin and Bakunin. He poured over them hour after hour. When he was not writing poetry, that is. Arshinov encouraged him to write some poetry every day. That was the best way to learn how to sort out one's thoughts and feelings and to express them forcefully on paper, he said.

According to Pytotr Andreevich, a political leader must communicate his ideas and feelings to his followers clearly and forcefully, or he would fail.

Someday he'd be a political leader. He was certain. He would get out of this stinking pisshole somehow and go straight back to Gulai-Polye. He'd show all those bastards he was a new man, a man to respect. This time he would do the organizing, he would be the boss. Nobody was going to kick around the pimply faced kid anymore. And he'd get the slimy serpents who put him in here too!

CHAPTER TEN

1

St. Petersburg, April, 1913

It was a mild, softly lit afternoon in mid-April. Clara Bock and Wilhelm Fast were walking hand-in-hand along the University Embankment in front of the long, yellow and white Academy of Fine Arts. Spring had come early to the northern capital, and the Neva was struggling to free its slate-colored waters from the blocks of winter ice lingering along the stone embankments. Across the river rose the massive gilt dome of St. Isaac's. To its left, behind a row of high-shouldered quay buildings, the golden stiletto of the Admiralty spire seemed to impale a low-hanging cloud. Farther left still, foreshortened by distance, the stone and glass length of the Winter Palace and the Hermitage, gleaming turquoise, white and silver, looked like a majestic ship afloat on the river.

Wilhelm, strong broad face animated, was discoursing on his favorite subject of art. For some time now the pretty girl beside him had been his constant companion, a willing listener and sounding board for his ideas and aspirations, a sympathetic critic who could also ask tough questions. The initial reserve between them had quickly melted into a warm comradeship that took them both by surprise. Though they were quite aware of their feelings for each other, they hadn't expressed them openly. For the moment at least, they enjoyed the spontaneity of their relationship, the heady camaraderie of two sensitive young people exploring each other's minds and natures. But Wilhelm was also aware of a certain emotional reticence in Clara. There were moments when he felt a need to declare his feelings for her directly, was on the verge of doing so, but was stopped by something suddenly guarded in Clara's manner, a wariness in her blue-gray eyes, as though she feared that something indiscreet or indelicate was about to be said. He was puzzled and a little disturbed by this evasiveness in her.

For her part, Clara found Wilhelm most exciting to be with when he talked about his art and his dreams as an artist, when he explored realms of thought and feeling that were new to her. She admired the introspective play of his mind, the quick, steep flights of his imagination, the remorseless way he attacked pretension and hypocrisy, his own included. She knew he was in love with her, that he would soon want her to be more than a soul mate. Her own feelings were complex and confusing. She could not quite sort them out. She was very fond of this intense young man, adored him, in fact, but was not quite ready to have him declare his love — not yet. Their relationship seemed so exactly right as it was. As a friend he was exciting to be with, but as a lover he would become possessive, demanding, hem her in. She wasn't at all sure she was ready for that.

They had reached the second of the two handsome ancient Theban sphinxes which had found an improbable resting place here on the embankment of a northern Russian river.

"I'll tell you something else, Clara," Wilhelm said quietly as they sat down on the low wall beneath the sphinx. "Why I'm crippled as an artist and probably always will be."

The girl uttered a low, passionate denial. "You're not crippled, Vasya. How can you say that? Your work is brilliant — everybody says so — and it's getting better all the time."

He smiled and reached out to touch her gloved hand. "I know you mean that, Clara, and I'm grateful. What you say about my work may not be entirely wrong. But I'm talking about something you and the others don't see. You judge me by my work, by what you see in my sketches and paintings. But that's only the end product of the creative process. I have to look at the process itself. Right now I'm more concerned with myself as the machine that produces the art than I am with the product. It's the raw materials I start with that I'm worried about. An artist can only work through his five senses. All the material for the imagination to work on has to be brought in through those five doors."

He drummed his fingers on the brown marble pedestal beside him and frowned in concentration. Clara, her fine eyes intent, waited for him to continue.

"And that's exactly where the trouble starts. Where background and environment come in. For an artist the visual world is all-important, of course, but the other senses are important too." He stopped again, struggling to find the right words.

"But, but what if an artist has the bad luck to grow up in a tiny Mennonite village in the middle of nowhere, a drab, empty place where there is little for the senses to feed on — no beauty, no art, no real variety of life?"

"Vasya, what are you saying?" Clara objected swiftly. "The world is full of sights and sounds and smells — no matter where you are. Your senses are feeding all the time. It's what you do with the sensations you collect that's important, surely."

"Yes, yes, that's true, of course," Wilhelm conceded, "but not all sense impressions are of equal value or of equal use to an artist. How one's senses develop has a lot to do with how they are stimulated and where. Look, Clara, I grew up on a farm. For a long time that was my whole world. I knew exactly how everything looked and felt in that little world: the pure curve of a freshly turned furrow in autumn, the spicy smell and warm feel of a cow barn in winter, the whole gurgling, seeping, chirping, springing-to-life world of the farm in spring.

"But when I got interested in drawing pictures on paper I never even thought of using these homely impressions and sensations. I knew that certain things were considered beautiful in themselves — the pure-bred village stallion I tried to draw over and over, for example, a steppe sunset, a stork carved in silence on a barn roof. But mostly, I thought, art meant making something pretty out of your head — like the lace doilies my mother made, or the fairy-tale creatures my brother Heinrich whittled out of wood. My senses told me what was real, but I never connected those real things with art. As a boy I never saw works of art about the real things in my world . . ." His voice trailed into silence and he was lost in thought for a moment.

"When I was fourteen or fifteen, I did an oil sketch of our farm. For my father's birthday. It was a shamelessly sentimental picture. My father almost wept when I gave it to him and proudly hung it in the parlor. Whenever I looked at it there I felt uneasy, ashamed somehow. I know why now. I was pandering to my father's German sentimentalism. That's how he wanted to see his farm, like a living prayer to God; he even said so. It was a dishonest picture, neither real nor true. I despise myself for it now."

"But, Vasya," Clara said softly, "if the picture gave your father pleasure then surely it was real and true?"

"No, my dear, I don't think so . . . I just thought of my old art teacher in Halbstadt — Burzev. He was the only person who gave me good advice about my art before I came here to the Academy. He took me aside one day and told me I had better grow a new pair of eyes as an artist. In essence he was urging me to escape my world as soon as possible, for my own good. And he was right, though it was dangerous for a Russian teacher to give that kind of advice to a Mennonite boy in the Molochnaya.

"But now I'm not so sure I did get out in time. Here I am with my undeveloped senses, my narrow range of sensory experience, my vocabulary as an artist far too limited. It's like trying to write poetry with the words of a peasant, or painting pictures with your toes."

Clara smiled but her voice was serious. "Vasya, Vasya, you mustn't torture yourself like this. You may be right about your past, but what does it matter now? You're free. You can develop now the way you want to, make up for the time you lost. Perhaps even —"

"No, dear friend, that's only part of it." He looked at her sadly. "It's not just a technical handicap I'm suffering from. In time I might have overcome that. But there's also the whole spiritual thing I've been telling you about. That affects me as an artist too."

Clara saw he was back to what was rapidly becoming an obsession with him. He was beginning to express doubts about the church, about his own faith, even about the traditional Mennonite claim of being a people set apart by God. He was finding it more and more difficult to reconcile the isolated world he had left behind with the much larger, richer, more significant world to which he had come. And his sense of cultural inferiority was complicated by a growing sense of spiritual alienation. With all her heart she wished there was something she could do to help him through this first serious crisis in his life.

"I'm sorry to say it, Clara, but it wasn't just my five senses that were deprived of nourishment: so was my soul. Believe it or be damned. Black and white — the two non-colors. But among us Mennonites they are the primary colors, with only shades of gray in between. That should sound familiar even to a liberated Mennonite girl from Schoenwiese."

Wilhelm rose from his seat and looked out across the Neva. Clara remained seated but twisted her blonde head in the same direction. Neither moved nor spoke for several seconds. He glanced down at her profile.

"Clara, do you remember those words of Christ: 'He that is not with me is against me, and he that gathers not with me scatters abroad'? That is our Mennonite attitude exactly. When it comes to religious belief such an uncompromising attitude may be absolutely essential. I don't deny that." His voice shook with passion. "But that's not true for the artist. Such an attitude is death for the artist. He must remain detached, uncommitted. He must be spiritually neutral, or at least ready to jump from side to side when necessary. Do you follow me, Clara?"

He bent forward and placed his hands on her shoulders. She gazed up at him in mute sympathy. Did she really follow what he was saying? She spoke finally, but her voice was tentative, uncertain.

"I think I follow you, Vasya, but I'm not sure. If you mean that the artist cannot be a believer, a Christian, then I can't agree. I'm trying to be an artist too, but I've never had any serious doubts about my Christian faith. The two don't seem to be directly related, in any case."

"But they are, Clara, they are. The artist must have faith too; he must be a believer . . . But don't you see? An artist can't be a *dogmatic* believer. He mustn't be forced to take sides, not even in religion. His faith must be in his own vision as an artist. That is his religion. That is his first commitment, and his first commandment too. But in such a world as you and I come from not taking sides is unthinkable. Even God takes sides — our side against the world's side, and so on. God speaks High German, not Low German — and certainly not Russian." he was trying to laugh off his bitterness now.

Clara rose and adjusted her coat. He frightened her a little when he talked this way. "You mustn't allow yourself to get bitter, Vasya. I understand your frustration over your background." The shadowy sun was low on the horizon and she shivered as she took his arm for the long walk home. "But even artists have immortal souls, my friend. You won't find salvation in your art. You know that." She glanced up to meet his eyes and squeezed his arm possessively. His lips parted in a smile, but his eyes — those fascinating Oriental eyes — were inscrutable now.

What a strange young man he was. So bold, almost reckless in some ways; so vulnerable and unsure of himself in others. His outburst just now about faith and the artist. Did he really believe that? He must, or he wouldn't have been so passionate about it. She knew he was above trying merely to impress her with the virile drum beat of his ideas. And yet, she couldn't help thinking that he had a bit of a flare for dramatic self-exploration. It was the artist in him. He had a young man's love for — what? Not showing off exactly, but a certain male daring in trying out new ideas and attitudes, rather shocking ones for a Mennonite. On occasions like this she felt small and inadequate beside him. And yet she loved him for being what he was.

But there were also times when she felt differently. When she couldn't help seeing him as someone who mattered very much to her now, but would he be part of her future? It hurt her to think that he might not be.

2
Moscow, Easter, 1913

They were lucky enough to get a compartment to themselves on the crowded train. With his usual panache, August bribed the train attendant with a lofty smile, a pat on the shoulder, and a folded ruble note. Clara and Wilhelm sat by the window, facing each other. August, sitting beside Clara, actually managed to stretch his long legs across the aisle and with a voluptuous sigh prop them up beside Wilhelm.

Clara was radiant with anticipation. she loved traveling, especially by train. She was smartly turned out in a light gray topcoat cut in a semi-military style that managed to look both spruce and trim and softly feminine. It had a high, tight military collar edged with white and pale blue piping. The exaggerated epaulets and broad, turned-back cuffs had the same edging. But the feminine fullness at the sleeves and bosom and, above all, the saucy swirls of her little black hat and matching muff, accentuated the animated grace of her figure.

Once they were settled and underway, Clara sensed that there was something bothering Wilhelm. He was trying to be cheerful, to carry on the usual banter with August, but his eyes kept wandering to the window and he looked sombre as the train rattled into the open countryside. At first he had refused their invitation to spend the Easter break with them in Moscow. Embarrassed, he pleaded shortage of funds. Certainly he could not afford to go home to the Molochnaya for Easter. With her practical streak, Clara had worked out the costs exactly. He would need only the train fare. In Moscow he would be a guest of the family, she and August had assured him. Their parents were coming from Schoenwiese and had rented a large apartment. They had their parents' permission to include him in the family reunion.

"You're not sorry you decided to come, Vasya, are you?" Her smile was a little anxious. Was it selfish of her to make him go to this extra expense?

"Why should he be?" August yawned. "He's traveling to Moscow with the two most charming and interesting people he knows. He'd be an idiot to pass up the chance."

Wilhelm considered a riposte, but let it go. "I suppose I may as well tell you now as later." He hated himself for spoiling Clara's gay mood, but he had to get this off his chest. "I, I've got a difficult decision to make. I received a letter from home yesterday. There's a teaching position open in Schoensee for next year, if I want it."

"And not come back to the Academy?" Clara's disappointment was sharp.

"I probably wouldn't be coming back anyway. Don't forget I'll be turning twenty-one in July and become eligible for service to our glorious motherland. Of course, there's always the chance I might be found unfit, or get off through the lottery, but I don't want to take the risk."

"I don't blame you, old boy," August drawled. "The very idea of serving on some primitive, remote forestry station is enough to chill my blood. I've got about eight months to go and I lie awake nights already worrying about it.

"But Vasya, if you're going to be drafted why are you talking about taking a teaching post?"

"That's my one way out. If I promise to teach for five years, I can avoid alternative service altogether."

Clara gave him an odd look, but made no further response.

Abruptly, she changed the subject to herself. "I'm not sure I'll be going back to Petersburg next fall myself. Not if I can find just as good a teacher in Moscow, or even closer to home in Kharkov or Odessa."

It was the boys' turn to be surprised. "What's brought this on, Clara?" August queried. "Aren't you satisfied with your teacher? Or is it home-sickness?"

"No, no, Gusha, it's neither. I'm just thinking out loud." She leaned forward and gave Wilhelm an intimate little smile and a light pat on the knee. "Besides, without Vasya there Petersburg would be a lot less fun, I suspect."

August looked at her shrewdly. "There's something else, Clara, isn't there?"

"Yes, I suppose there is," Clara conceded with a girlish pout of her lower lip. "I know already that I'll never be a professional singer. I'm just not good enough — no don't either of you interrupt," she cried as she saw that August and Wilhelm were about to reassure her. "Mde. Slobodskaja was a darling to accept me as a student, but it's becoming more apparent with every lesson that she's written me off as a student of real promise. Oh, she's kind and solicitous, but I can tell she's just going through the motions with me now." She stopped, her voice trembling. "It's all Mama's doing, you know. She wants so much for me to have a career." Clara was struggling for control. "She arranged for everything — and now . . ."

The two young men looked at each other. Both had suspected that this was coming, and had wondered together at what point Clara herself would acknowledge it. Hearing her bravely confess her honorable failure, Wilhelm felt a deep surge of love and compassion for the lovely, spirited girl who had started out with such glowing hopes a few months ago. She was not without talent, of course. She had a fine, clear soprano and a natural way with German lieder and Russian folksongs. But even Wilhelm had guessed that her voice was too small for grand opera, and that she was not an accomplished enough musician to become a leading singer with a professional company.

"Don't look so sad, my girl," Wilhelm said gently and reached for her hand. "Your singing career hasn't even started yet. You have no right to talk about failure."

"He's right, darling sister," August said firmly. "You're barely nineteen. Wait till you've studied a few years before making such a stern judgment on yourself. Even if you don't become another Patti or Lipovskaja, you can still become a fine singer if you want to. And you'll give pleasure to many, many people — perhaps even to our stodgy Mennonites. You can sing in oratorios and give lieder recitals all over the colonies."

Clara laughed delightedly. "Yes, yes, I'll make the rounds — just like a *reiseprediger* — and you'll be my manager, Gusha, and Vasya will design the posters for my recitals." In one of those lightening changes of mood characteristic of her, she had returned to her former gaiety. She remained that way for the rest of the trip.

3

In the spring of 1913, Moscow, like cities and towns all over Russia, was celebrating the tercentenary of the Romanov dynasty with a somewhat forced pomp and contrived display of patriotism designed to refurbish the badly tarnished image of the monarchy, especially the image of the "grace-of-God" tsar, Nicholas II. Streets and public building were festooned with flags and patriotic banners; parades during the day and fireworks at night enlivened the scene in cities and towns. There were special concerts everywhere, and in theatres all over the country newly commissioned plays and operas glorified the exploits of the Romanovs through the centuries. None of them, however, could rival the popularity of an older work, Glinka's *A Life for the Tsar,* with its unabashed nationalism and sentimental celebration of tsardom. Its great patriotic closing hymn "Slavsa," sung by tremendous mass choirs, brought tears even to the most cynical Russian eyes.

As their train rolled into Moscow's St. Petersburg Station, Wilhelm felt both excited and somewhat apprehensive. He looked forward to seeing the historic city, the traditional heart of the nation, in the company of Clara and August. His apprehension concerned Clara's mother. Mrs. Bock was said to be a very proud, sophisticated lady who came from a rich, well-connected family in Germany. He did not look forward to his first dinner with the family that evening. He knew he would be carefully scrutinized not as August's friend but as Clara's. In Mennonite terms the Bocks counted as aristocracy. Mrs. Bock could be expected to take careful stock of her daughter's new friend as a possible suitor. He did not think it likely that she would welcome a village teacher into the family.

Wilhelm's apprehensions turned out to be well-founded. August Bock Senior was as warm and affable as he had been in Petersburg, but Clara's mother greeted Wilhelm with a formality so distant and chilling that he felt like a clumsy intruder. Clara and young August tried valiantly to make up for their mother's rude aloofness, but Wilhelm knew he was in for a miserable evening. Not even the experience of dining in the the Hotel Metropole's famous dining room with its magnificent stone fountain and frescoes could compensate for the humiliation he felt.

A tall, slender, strikingly handsome woman, Mrs. Bock's every movement and gesture spoke of conscious breeding and refinement. Clara had inherited her mother's good looks and regal bearing. But while Clara had her mother's physical attributes, she had none of her mother's snobbishness and air of superiority. Instead, as he had already noted in Petersburg, the daughter had inherited her father's frank nature and gentle, unassuming manner.

Never once during dinner did Mrs. Bock address Wilhelm directly. When not pointedly ignoring him, she would coldly instruct Clara to "pass your dear friend the bread," or to "ask your young man if he would like some more tea" — all the while averting her eyes and face from him, as though fearing contamination. Clara, her small jaw set grimly, had apparently not expected this deliberate campaign of malice. Wilhelm was sure of that. Several times she tried, in near desperation, to draw her mother and Wilhelm into conversation, but without success.

Father and son did their best to create a normal conversational atmosphere, and Wilhelm gratefully joined their talk about politics and recent social events. His friend August gave his parents a witty account of a bizarre incident that had occurred in Petersburg in early March at the official opening of the tercentenary celebration in Kazan Cathedral. When Rodzianko, President of the Duma, arrived he found a gorgeously dressed peasant sitting in one of the seats reserved for members of the Duma. The peasant turned out to be Rasputin. Rodzianko ordered him to leave. Rasputin refused and tried to hypnotise the President. Rodzianko was so incensed he grabbed the priest by the scruff of the neck and tried in vain to heave him bodily out of the seat. Even Mrs. Bock smiled at the story, and murmured something in German about Russians being barbarians even in church.

After dinner they attended a performance of Tchaikovsky's *Sleeping Beauty* at the Bolshoi. It was a ballet Mrs. Bock had last seen as a girl in Germany, as she had already reminded them several times. It was a fine performance, and under its spell Clara's mother relaxed a little and even nodded with appreciation in Wilhelm's direction several times. Mr. Bock, however, had trouble staying awake. His massive head kept nodding, like a great boulder teetering on the edge of a precipice. Wilhelm smiled in the darkness. After his ordeal at dinner he was grateful for the dark anonymity of his theatre seat. He looked around the theatre, impressed with its size and splendor. He and Clara agreed in whispers that while its vast interior did not quite match the sheer elegance of the Maryinsky's, the Bolshoi fully deserved its reputation as the premier theatre in the country.

As soon as they returned to the apartment, Mrs. Bock announced that she was retiring, and with a significant look expressed her hope that her daughter would soon join her upstairs. Clara's anger and misery over her mother's behavior had made her sullen. At the foot of the stairs she whispered a quick apology to Wilhelm and marched grimly up the stairs.

The two Bocks, father and son, lit up cigars and invited Wilhelm to sit with them. Out of politeness he did so, although he would have preferred to go to bed directly in order to mull over the evening and Mrs. Bock's callous rejection of him. With a sinking heart he realized that between Clara and himself now stood a very determined and ruthless mother obviously used to getting her own way. Somehow he could not see Clara successfully defying her mother's will.

4

"Tonight, my dear Rembrandt, you will meet a fascinating man who loves talking about ideas and culture and things as much as you do. And he has even more to talk about," Clara added slyly, her eyes teasing, her head cocked in that graceful way she had. She was holding his wrists and swinging his arms from side to side in sheer delight. She seemed to have completely shaken off her shame and anger of the night before. As always Wilhelm was enchanted by her amazing knack for suddenly and unexpectedly transforming the whole mood and tenor of their relationship. They had spent a delightful day seeing the sights of Moscow and were now waiting at the door for August to take them out to dinner and then for a visit to a friend's house.

"All right, you imp, who is the remarkable man who knows so much more than I do?" He stiffened his swinging arms suddenly and she collapsed against him.

Laughing, she punched his chest. "Never mind, you'll find out when we get there." He knew this teasing show of secrecy could not possibly last for more than a minute or two. She was bursting to tell him, of course.

A few minutes later August led the way to the droshky he had ordered. As Wilhelm handed Clara into the carriage, August whispered, "Watch, she's about to play a guessing game with you."

As they got underway she leaned back, her eyes bright. "Vasya, who would you say are the three greatest men our Mennonites have produced here in Russia?"

Wilhelm's look was innocent. "Well, let me see now — Klaas Funk would be one." August tried to suppress a snicker.

"Who's Klaas Funk?" Clara asked blankly.

"What, you've never heard of Klaas Funk? He's the man who invented the *brommtopp* Mennonites use when they go mumming at New Yea—"

Clara shrieked and gave the deadpan Wilhelm a sharp jab in the ribs. "So, you'll make fun of me when I'm trying to be serious, will you?"

"All right, all right," he chuckled, protecting his side from further assault, "I confess August tipped me off just now."

Clara blurted out her secret. "P. M. Friesen, Vasya. Would you say he's greater than your Klaas Funk? We're going to his house. There'll be other students there. Peter Martinovich's house is a popular place for Mennonite students here in Moscow."

Wilhelm had heard a great deal about P. M. Friesen. He was, if anything, even better known among the Mennonites of Russia than Erdmann Lepp. Friesen had made a name for himself first as a teacher and minister, more recently as a scholar and author. His monumental source-history of the Russian Mennonites had been published a couple of years ago, the first work of its kind; it was a labor of love that "P. M." had worked on for twenty-five years. Wilhelm had read parts of it at the Halbstadt Central School, where Friesen had been a popular teacher in the closing decades of the last century. His father had told the family many funny stories about the colorful little teacher who had taught him there. What interested Wilhelm most about P. M. Fricsen was that he had, without ceasing to be a Mennonite, made a successful career for himself outside of Mennonite circles. P. M. had proved that it could be done, at least as a teacher and minister. Could a Mennonite artist also do it?

The door of the impressive-looking house on Nikitsky Boulevard was opened by a well-built young man whose thick, brown hair was neatly parted down the middle. He was Paul Petrovich Friesen, P. M.'s son.

"Ah, Clara and August Bock. Come in, come in" he invited affably. "How nice to see you again." Paul introduced himself to Wilhelm as he led them down the hall toward the babble of voices.

A dozen or more young people were assembled in the spacious, well-furnished Friesen parlor. Wilhelm saw at once that the room did not look at all like the traditional Mennonite *grootestow*. It was larger, more elaborately and more tastefully furnished, and its brightly papered walls were graced by a number of framed pictures, including several oil paintings. In one corner, near some handsome bay windows, there was a large piano — not the usual Mennonite harmonium — and there were several dark-wood, glass-fronted bookcases crammed with volumes. More books were scattered about the room and piled in crooked heaps on furniture and window ledges.

P. M. Friesen and his wife, the warm, gracious "Susanna Ivanovna" beloved by generations of students from Sevastopol to Moscow, were seated side by side on a long, curved divan at the far end of the room. Mrs. Friesen rose and came forward to greet the new arrivals. P. M. did not rise, but interrupted his conversation to cry a shrill greeting to Clara and August. Wilhelm was presented to "Peter Martinovich," who pumped his hand with vigor surprising for such a small, frail figure. P. M. was obviously not a well man. Behind his lively expression was the pale, drawn face of a semi-invalid. He was egg-bald on top and his droop mustache and wiry white full beard gave him the appearance of a patriarchal gnome. His almond eyes under heavy lids had the forward squint of the near-sighted, and his glasses rode low over his nose.

"Welcome, welcome, my young friends," he shrilled warmly. "Clara! Come sit down here Clara, my dear, and bring your friend — here, here — so, that's fine. Now then," he continued gaily, "we were just having a little discussion on patriotism, what it is and what obligations it imposes on all citizens of our motherland — especially on us 'silent ones in the land.'" P. M. began in German, then switched to Russian in mid-sentence, as though it was the most natural thing to do.

"But Peter Martinovich, allow me to ask a question," pleaded a fleshy-faced youth with an enormous thatch of unruly yellow hair. He spoke flawless Russian.

"Well, Redekopp, what's the question?" P. M.'s bullet head with its narrow, bulging brow bobbed encouragingly at the questioner.

"You said just now, sir, that we Mennonites here in Russia have enjoyed the special favor and protection of the tsars precisely because we are foreigners — non-Russians — a Christian people who can be trusted to remain loyal to the crown under any and all circumstances. But does that mean we should give our loyalty even to a bad tsar — another Ivan the Terrible, say?"

P. M.'s pinched face tightened. "That's a fair question, my boy. I needn't remind you of Christ's exhortation to 'render unto Ceasar,' or Paul's definition of rulers as 'God's agents working for your good.' We Mennonites have always lived under a monarchy, at least here in Europe. We know no other form of government. We've always believed that the monarch is the anointed of God, and as Christians we owe him our complete allegiance and obedience." The high-pitched voice trod air for a moment. "Now it's true, of course, that not all monarchs are equally good. Some, we know, have been more bad than good. For every David there is a Jereboam. But even a bad king has been anointed by God. Even an Ivan the Terrible is set over his people for a purpose — perhaps so that the subjects will not always take a good king for granted. Here in Russia we have on the whole been very fortunate with the Romanov dynasty. From the time of Peter the Great at least, we have with very few exceptions had a line of strict but just and responsible rulers; so that for us your question is merely a hypothetical one." P. M.'s smile was benign.

Young Redekopp, plainly unsatisfied with P. M.'s answer, was on the verge of rebutting, then thought better of it. He tried a different tack.

"I accept what you say, Peter Martinovich, but I can't help feeling that our people are obedient and loyal more out of ignorance and indifference than out of conviction. We sit behind our mulberry hedges in our closed villages not knowing or caring what is happening in the outside world."

"That's very true, Redekopp." It always made P. M. Friesen happy when he could agree with an opponent, especially after just scoring points against him. "I can't defend our isolation from the world, our cultural isolation in particular. I wrote in my book that the leaders of the migration to America in the seventies naively equated 'Mennonite' with 'German,' and that those leaders were shockingly ignorant of all things Russian — language, history, culture. Since then, of course, things have improved somewhat. Our children now learn Russian in school. I myself feel more at home in Russian at times than in German. But we have a long way to go. We still tend to hold ourselves aloof from the Russians around us. We still tend to look down on our non-Mennonite neighbors, an arrogance bred of ignorance, as you say."

August Bock had joined the group around P. M. just in time to hear the last comment. Russification was a favorite subject of his.

"Yes, exactly, Peter Martinovich," August chimed in. "Here we are with our sacred German virtues of piety, discipline, orderliness, hard work, and thrift. But are these really the highest virtues? For economic prosperity yes, but where is our cultural prosperity? Look at the Russian peasant. On the one hand we condemn him for his lice, his laziness, and itchy fingers. On the other hand, we praise him extravagantly — and patronizingly — for his passionate soul, his loving heart, his generosity, and hospitality. We wax sentimental over his beautiful folk songs, his stories, and art. But have we even considered that there may be a vital connection between the contradictory sides of the Russian nature? That the lack of order and industry in the Russian, his leisurely pace, his slovenliness, and lack of ambition may have a lot to do with his love for beauty and his power to express it in art? Where is our folk art, our great church music, our beautiful painting, our Pushkin, our Tolstoy?"

P. M. had listened to this outburst with approval at first, but then with growing impatience.

"August, August," he shouted, "I think you're getting a little carried away. The orderly, disciplined German nature you seem to disdain has also created great art and culture — perhaps not in us Mennonites; we are, after all, a tiny sect of farmers mainly. But your theory that a dreamy, impractical nation like Russia is more creative than a down-to-earth nation like Germany just doesn't hold water."

"But that wasn't exactly my point, Onkel Friesen," August said, his long, cold face as usual betraying no emotion. "I'm simply saying that the sooner we stop thinking and feeling like Germans and start thinking and feeling like Russians in a country in which we have now lived as strangers and aliens for over a hundred years, the better off we'll be socially and culturally."

The mop-haired Redekopp nodded agreement, but P. M. did not appear entirely satisfied. Before he could answer August, Clara spoke up, her clear voice quiet but firm.

"It's all very well for you to say we should become russified, dear brother, but how can we suddenly become like our Russian countrymen when our experience as a people has been so different from theirs?"

"Yes, yes," P. M. broke in approvingly, "our pretty Clara here has put her finger on the problem exactly. We have been a sheltered, protected people for a long time. We can't suddenly think and feel like Russians. We can read Russian literature and listen to Russian music, but what do we really know about the ordinary Russian except the part of him he shows when he works for us. Nekrasov said, 'Name one hut in which the Russian does not suffer.' What do we know about that suffering, the turmoil and brutality and despair of a peasant existence that has almost nothing of the security and stability ours has. All men are equally God's creation, my friend. The Russian peasant is born with a soul-ache, and no matter how often in life he says '*nichevo*,' it doesn't matter, he knows it does matter, but he also knows that there's nothing he can do about it. So he learns to suffer in silence, or he makes up beautiful, sad — or even happy — songs, and gets rid of some of the pain that way. In that sense, August, you're right about the peasant and his need to express himself in art."

P. M. stopped, his myopic eyes glistening. His frank, loving nature burgeoned into sympathy and compassion very easily. His love for and devotion to the underdog were legendary.

August, his tone less dogmatic than usual, made another attempt to get the discussion back to a more speculative, less personal level.

"But excuse me, Peter Martinovich, aren't you painting the Russian peasant in rather sentimental terms? One needn't be a peasant to know what spiritual suffering is. One need only read Dostoievsky or Lermontov. The Russian peasant may be soulful, but he is also a brute capable of the most inhuman and abandoned behavior. Embracing the peasant as an equal one moment and being abused and deceived by him the next is not my idea of how we should become russified. I believe —"

"Just what do you believe, August?" P. M., thoroughly aroused now, shot back. "That the only people who really matter are the educated, enlightened ones like you and me? No, no, my young friend, that won't do, that's a dangerous attitude.

August was about to reply when P. M. suddenly went very pale and seemed ready to collapse. Alarmed, Mrs. Friesen reached out to support her stricken husband. He tried to rouse himself, but the effort was too much.

He closed his eyes and sagged weakly in his wife's arms. Without uttering another word he allowed himself to be lifted to his feet and led from the room by his son Paul and one of the students. He looked very sick. Wilhelm's last glimpse of the old man was of the glistening white crown of his head between the husky shoulders of the two young men taking him away.

P. M.'s sudden departure brought the social evening to a rather premature close. The guests left the Friesen residence sad and subdued. Apparently P. M. had diabetes and was subject to such attacks of weakness and dizziness when he was tired or got over-excited. August was inclined to blame himself for having provoked the old man; Clara and Wilhelm tried to reassure him. Clara pointed out that P. M. was excitable by nature and just being with people, in his condition, could have a harmful effect on him.

August cheered up quickly. He was not one to wallow in self-accusations. "Friends," he said as their droshky jogged down a darkened side street, "we must not forget that this is Easter week. There are joyous celebrations going on all over this great city. Let's join them. It's too early to go home." His jaw glinted palely. "And I know just the place — a famous gypsy restaurant. You'll love it Clara — it's lively, colorful, and the gypsy singing will fire your blood, Rembrandt. The Yar in Petrovsky Park, that's where we'll go. That's where the exciting Panina performs. What do you say?"

Clara and Wilhelm looked at each other doubtfully, but August was so persuasive they agreed. Clara stipulated, though, that they must be home at about the time her mother was expecting them to return from the Friesens.

As August had promised, the Yar was crowded with happy, noisy, tipsy Easter celebrants, and certainly colorful in the hot, raffish gypsy manner. They were extremely fortunate to get a table at all, even with August's usual ruble-grease, let alone one with a tolerable view of the stage. August expansively ordered a "Pushkin" vodka with a white wine chaser, while Clara and Wilhelm settled for a glass of white wine. August also ordered *zakuski,* which came as a rich mosaic of caviar, anchovies, smoked salmon, smoked goose *en croute,* radishes, and several kinds of olives.

They had arrived at just the right time. No sooner had they received their refreshments when the stage suddenly swarmed with gypsy entertainers, the men dressed in dazzling white brocaded blouses, the girls in bright silk dresses of red, green, and blue colors. August was right; never had Clara and Wilhelm heard such intoxicating music. The songs formed a kaleidoscope of moods, from delicious, languid melancholy to fierce joy and unbridled passion. Wilhelm, sipping at his wine, felt his blood respond to the wild pulse of the gypsy singers and dancers. Clara, lips slightly parted, was raptly following each dip and swerve of the sensual bodies and earthy voices.

Then Vera Panina, a lithe, dusky beauty with enormous black eyes, emerged from the center of the ring of dancing choristers and began to sing in a way that brought a blush to Clara's cheeks. The great Panina sang with naked intensity, an elemental passion that made the men in the audience sigh and snicker and grope abstractedly for their wine or vodka glasses. August, enjoying himself hugely, called for another vodka between songs.

"What did I tell you," he said gaily, "with music like that and a singer like Panina even sober Mennonites can feel themselves warming up, eh Rembrandt? You know, I really did feel sorry for old Onkel Friesen tonight, but he was missing my whole point. What could be farther from the Mennonite spirit than this music, and yet more delight —"

"—*Yei Bogu,* what have we here?" The voice was deep and harsh, but strangely insinuating. A tall, fierce-looking man, starkly drunk, had stopped at their table. He was staring down boldly, lewdly, at a startled Clara. On each arm he had clinging to him a leering young trollop. One was dark, the other blonde, but both were equally drunk. Simpering drunkenly, the man continued his brazen examination of Clara's face and figure. She was horribly embarrassed, but could not tear her eyes from him. Even August seemed mesmerized.

Wilhelm stared aghast at the wild apparition. Though wobbly drunk, the creature seemed full of a wild energy, like some foul, drunken beast on the rampage. A kind of demonic force almost tangibly threatening emanated from the burly, black figure. The eyes, it was the eyes — strange, pale eyes glittering like a madman's, but with a cunning, deliberate concentration of enormous power in their pin-point depths. Those frightening eyes were set in a coarse brown peasant face bordered by long hanks of dank black hair and a greasy, unruly beard. His clothes were black like those of a priest.

Suddenly the man gave a low animal moan. "Matushka" — he was pointing at Clara — "this one looks like you Matushka — when you were younger. Oh, Matushka, I hear, I hear. You are calling me." He looked wildly at his two drunken companions. With a powerful wrench of his arms he shook them off. "Get away from me you filthy whores. It's a sign, a sign" —again staring at Clara — "Matushka, my empress, you are calling me back." Without warning he thrust a hairy paw at Clara, who shrank back with a sharp little squeal. Then, with a thick, half-strangled cry, he lurched away, bumping against tables as he made his way to the door.

Clara, her face white, her pupils dilated, was near hysteria. "Gusha," she whispered hoarsely, "home, take me home."

August and Wilhelm moved to her side as she rose unsteadily. August, looking shaken himself, turned to Wilhelm. "Do you know who that drunken beast looked like?" Wilhelm shook his head. "Like Rasputin — like the mad monk himself. But it couldn't be. This is Moscow, not Petersburg." August shook his head in bewilderment. "But I saw him once — from a distance. And that's what he looked like, I tell you."

Still shaken, they left the restaurant and took a droshky home. Arriving at the apartment earlier than expected, they received another shock. Mr. and Mrs. Bock were in the midst of a violent quarrel. They heard Mrs. Bock's furious voice as they reached the front door.

"And I tell you, August, I won't put up with him. He's simply not suitable as a —"

In the drawing room Mrs. Bock broke off abruptly as August pushed open the door to the entrance hall. There was an ominous silence as the young people took off their coats.

Mrs. Bock was standing stiffly by the fireplace as they entered. Mr. Bock, his great homely face ashamed and dejected, was seated in an armchair nearby. Mrs. Bock stared at them coldly, the wrath not yet faded from her face.

She took the initiative. "Well" — the imperious tone firmly in place again — "we didn't expect you home so early." It sounded to Wilhelm like an accusation. Then she saw the look on her daughter's face. "You look upset, child. What is it?" She reached for Clara's hand and pulled her closer.

"Oh, Mama, it's too awful." Her eyes filled as she spoke. "One shock after another. First Uncle Friesen's attack. He looked as though he might be, be — then on the way home another terrible thing happened. And now —" She gave her mother an anguished look of reproach mixed with self-pity.

Father Bock expressed his concern for P. M. Friesen, then asked what had happened on the way home. Young August looked a trifle uncomfortable as he explained where they had gone and what had happened. He said they had seen a man who looked a lot like the notorious Rasputin. The brute had stopped at their table for a moment and frightened Clara. August was careful, however, to leave out the lurid details. His father gave him a penetrating look but did not pursue the matter.

Mrs. Bock, her wrath flooding back, did pursue the matter in no uncertain terms. She turned on her son. "What, you fool, you took your sister to a low place like that — at this time of night?" She turned to Wilhelm, her voice barely under control. "There are some things I will not tolerate, Mr. Fast, and this, this shabby behavior is one of them." Her husband gave her a stern look of warning but she ignored him. "Let me make myself even plainer, now that we're on the subject. My daughter, young gentleman, is aiming for a singing career." She paused, her rage now icily controlled. "And nothing — no one — will interfere —"

"Enough, Melissa, that's enough," Bock Senior rumbled in a voice that shook the walls. He took his wife by the arm and guided her up the stairs. Clara threw herself sobbing on the sofa and young August looked more agitated than Wilhelm had ever seen him look. After some embarrassed apologies to Wilhelm, he too disappeared to his room.

Wilhelm did the only thing he could do — try to comfort the girl weeping with humiliation and outrage. They sat together on the sofa for some time in silence. Clara had stopped sobbing but her face looked devastated. Finally, she pressed her head against Wilhelm's shoulder and murmured brokenly, "Oh, I'm so ashamed, Vasya, so ashamed. How can she be so — ?"

"Hush, darling, it doesn't matter." He lifted her face gently, and for the first time their lips met. It was a sad, tentative kiss that awoke no strong response in either of them.

Clara raised only mild objections when he told her that under the circumstances he couldn't stay and would leave for Petersburg in the morning.

Vehemently she whispered in his ear. "I'll make it up to you Vasya, I promise. And I'll bring Mama around too. You wait and see."

They clung to each other for a long moment. Then they kissed again, deeply this time, with a passion that surprised them both. They were murmuring things to each other when they heard a movement on the stairs. Clara sprang up, whispered good night and started for the stairs.

They both knew who was waiting there.

CHAPTER ELEVEN

1
Daniel Fast Remembers: (4) "Like an Angel of Light"
Blumenau, August, 1852

Na, ja, everything has an end, as they say, except a *wurst,* which has two. My despair had an end too. Slowly, I came to myself again and my doubts about my leadership in the church no longer raged in my head like a bad toothache. I turned to my neglected *wirtschaft* again. I had always loved farming but my work with the church had been so heavy I had to leave the farm work to my son Peter, who wasn't really old enough to carry so much. And he didn't show much promise as a farmer anyway. All he wanted was to build things with his hands. He was a born carpenter — but more. He liked to think up new ways of doing things, so they would be less work. Machines, that's what he was interested in.

I threw myself into the farm work and with the help of Peter and my younger son Johann soon had the *wirtschaft* solidly on its feet again. But my success as a farmer did not bring me happiness.

My work with the *gemeinde* was at an end. I knew that. But somehow I couldn't bring myself to leave what I had started and go back, cap in hand, to the Old Church. I had put too much of my life and love into my vision of the pure church. Besides, the Old Church had been getting even farther away from the truth since I had left it with my small group. More groups were coming out from Prussia bringing with them new ideas and teachings that shocked me very much. One of these groups, led by Elder Peter Wedel, believed in the millenium, the thousand-year-kingdom, which I regarded as a misreading and misteaching of Scripture.

Satan knows exactly how to confuse idlers and fools. These people actually believed that Christ would set up an earthly kingdom for them lasting a thousand years so they could convert all the heathen and claim all the credit. And Christ would be living right in their midst helping them with their missionary work! Such people can never be brought to their senses. They are puffed up with pride and self-made holiness. Ach, *lieber Gott,* how terrible it is to see Satan on the loose, disguised as an Angel of Light, eagerly misleading us pilgrims!

My position as a servant of God was hopeless. My own *gemeinde* ignored me, though I hadn't been banned, and I was never asked to preach. But the Old Church was no place for me either, worldly as it now was. I was not surprised when it finally split apart like an over-ripe watermelon. My cousin Hermann Riesner of Blumenau wanted me to join the new congregation, but I had lost my appetite for Satan's bitter brew of strife and hatred. For the time being, at least, I would stay with our small *gemeinde.*

The next year, the year the Tsar paid us a visit, Johann Cornies came to see me one day. He had met with me a few times years before when we were having our fight with Elder Dyck and had urged me to make peace with the terrible elder. But Cornies had been mild and friendly and had not pressed me after I had given him my side. Now he came to see the strange new wagon my Peter had made. Cornies was interested in new things, and always on the lookout for young craftsmen who had skills and ideas that could help the colony.

He examined the wagon from tongue to backboard, worked the controls and asked Peter a lot of sharp questions. He kept shaking his head in wonder, and seemed particularly interested in the handbrake on the wagon: when you pulled a lever both rear wheels locked. But there was more, much more, on that wagon. On one side was a crank. When you turned it the front end of the box pushed up and the back end came down. That way the load of grain could shoot out the back without any shoveling. Peter had also built a big box with windows and a door that could be fitted on top of the wagon for winter driving. And there was a foot pedal on the floor in front. When you pressed it the wagon tongue and singletrees broke free of the wagon. The idea was to be able to release runaway horses so as to prevent serious accidents.

"Na ya, a very interesting piece of work," Cornies said finally, "but a little ahead of its time. And such a contraption, Oom Fast, won't help you with your *gemeinde*. I hear they're having a brotherhood meeting over Peter's wagon on Sunday."

I was stunned. A brotherhood meeting to which I would be called as the accused. Would it never end?

Cornies had more to say. "Oom Fast, bring your boy to see me at my place one of these days. I'd like to find out what other ideas he has. Perhaps he'd be interested in starting a wagon-making business here on your *bof* — not this kind of wagon exactly, but good, solid farm wagons and droshkies. There's a growing need for them, and good money in them too. Ya, with one or two of the ideas in this new wagon — the handbrake, perhaps, your wagons would sell very well."

That's how my friendship started with the remarkable man who later became the permanent president of the Agricultural Association which controlled the affairs of the settlement. Cornies became the most powerful and the richest Mennonite in Russia. Even in the mid-twenties, when I got to know him well, though still a young man he was already well off with his large herds of sheep on the open steppes, his horse-breeding and pig-raising, and what not. He was a man to be reckoned with. I made up my mind I would get to know this man so that if the worst happened to me I would at least have one powerful friend to help me.

A few months later Cornies helped Peter and me get started in the wagon-making business.

At the brotherhood meeting that Sunday I was prepared for the worst. And the worst happened. My father-in-law Johann M. Froese, now the elder of the *gemeinde,* seemed to have Satan riding on his back, with his terrible wife the Widow whipping them both on. Oom Johann never gave me a chance to explain about Peter's fancy new wagon. He just bellowed at me that such worldly ideas could only come from the Evil One. And because I had allowed my son to do such devil's work I was as guilty as he — if not more so.

The brotherhood voted to ban Peter and me, but they said nothing about poor Anna. Maybe they thought she was already in a shunned state with her weak head. I was all numb and didn't feel much of anything just then. But I knew the whole wagon business was just an excuse to get rid of me. They had been waiting for a chance. If it hadn't been the wagon it would have been something else.

Then next day I went to see Cornies in Ohrloff. He already knew what had happened. He told me Elder Bernhard Fast (Elder Dyck was dead by this time) would be glad to welcome me back into the Ohrloff congregation, but that my future as church teacher was clouded right now.

And so it was. I had come full circle. It was a bitter medicine for me to swallow, but what could I do? As a Mennonite and Christian I could not be without a *gemeinde.* So I swallowed my pride and asked Elder Fast, who was not related to me, to take me back.

It was the end of my dream for a pure church. From now on I would just do the best I could and try to live in peace and harmony with my fellow man according to my conscience and God's Word.

All this happened in the year 1825. Na ya, that was a year in more ways than one here in the Molochnaya. Even the weather seemed to be in Satan's hands. In winter we had terrible storms with the winds howling across the steppes like starving wolves and the snow piled up to the rooftrees. Many had to rip the straw from their roofs to feed their animals, if they could get through the drifts to the barns. When spring came at last the houses and barns looked like moulting chickens. More than one building had the roofribs sticking out bare. Many animals lay stiff behind barns and in the fields. Those still standing had the bones shining through their hides. Ya, that was a winter.

But the summer wasn't much better. First wet, then a long dry spell, then wet again in fall. But in November came something exciting for our people. The Emperor Alexander made a tour of our villages. That day we didn't care about the rain. We all stood on the street as the great monarch drove slowly by in his fancy calash, its red wheels dripping mud and the gold-trimmed sides splattered all over. The horses were good; they looked like Mennonite horses. Probably from up around Rueckenau.

Johann Cornies and other important men from our *gebietsamt* rode ahead of the Emperor's carriage to show the way. The Emperor's men rode behind. All the riders were splashed with mud from head to foot. Only the Tsar in his bright uniform and cape was dry. The hood of his calash was raised just enough to cover him but open enough so that we could see him. I remember how pale and sad he looked behind his little smile. The Empress Elizabeth was not with him. They said she was sick and that the Emperor had taken her to Tagenrog on the Sea of Azov for her health. A few weeks later we got word that the Emperor himself had died there . . . Ya, such is this life, even for the great rulers of the world.

Soon after the Tsar's visit, I went to Ohrloff to see Johann Cornies on business. He told me in his plump Low German what had happened when the royal party stopped in Ohrloff to change the monarch's horses. We were sitting in the *sommastow* which Cornies used as his office then.

"Just remember, Fast, I don't want this story to get around," he began. "The people here find enough to fleer at already. Well, we stopped at my place to change horses. What the cuckoo, I think to myself, there's just enough time to run in and change clothes. I'm soaked to the skin and mud all over. I run to the *sommastow* here without stopping to explain to my mumtje. *Na oba,* just as I'm reaching for dry trousers I hear a man's voice in the *grootestow.* What, I think, has he come into the house? I pull on my trousers as fast as I can. *Ach du lieber,* that would be something, to have the Emperor of Russia catch a man with his pants off in his own house. And how is my mumtje doing with the royal visitor? That's my next thought.

"I hurry into the *grootestow* just as my Agnes is stretching out her hand to the Emperor. She wants to shake hands with him, as a good Mennonite housewife does when she's welcoming guests! I stand and stare at them like a frozen sheep's head. The Emperor doesn't seem to notice anything wrong. He gives a little bow, takes my mumtje's honest red farm hand and raises it delicately to his lips. Agnes, startled by this unexpected gesture, staggers back and stares, mouth open. No one has ever done such a thing to her before.

"Quickly I step forward to the rescue. Agnes escapes to the kitchen, holding her hand as though she had burned it on the stove. The Emperor starts asking me about my place — why the house is bigger than the others in the village and how much it had cost to build. He says good things about my tree plantings, but wants to know why there are no acacia trees in the colony. I take this as a hint that we should start planting acacias. He also says some things about farming, but I have trouble paying attention. Do you know what, Fast? All the time the monarch is talking to me in his elegant clothes I can think of only one thing. Did I do up all the buttons on my trousers when I put them on in such a hurry? The moment he turns to go I check, and thanks be to God my buttons are all in place."

Ya, Cornies could tell a story broad and dry, even when it was on himself.

The next spring everybody was planting acacias. Cornies saw to that. That's when I planted this old friend here. Such a mighty one now. Then, it was just a frail little sapling. I was a big one then. Now I'm dried up and shrunken and this tree is still growing and spreading. So many summers it has put on its white crown for me . . . Ya, the queen of the steppe we call the acacia now. And we have that tsar and Cornies to thank for her. Like so many other things.

Na ya, Cornies. At that time he was a pleasant man to know. He wasn't so big yet that people were afraid of him. Like his acacias he grew and spread out slowly at first, so that you didn't notice for awhile. I was a lot older than he, but we got along well. He was so smart and knew so many things that I never felt older or wiser. We saw a lot of each other before he became the lifetime chairman of the new Agricultural Association and didn't have much time for visiting with friends anymore. He was always a very hard worker — that's how he was able to bring it to so much — but he also knew when to close off the day and relax on the *schaffott* with a friend or two. People didn't think of him as the Mennonite tsar yet. That came later.

He knew people envied him because his flocks and herds seemed to spring up on the wild steppe like grass seeds. Everything he touched grew and almost everything he tried worked. Purebred sheep and horses and cattle. Even grape vines for wine. Only the silkworms and the tobacco plants failed him in the long run. He was forever planning and trying out new things. A good farmer, he told me once, plans at least fifty years ahead. It was as if time and change whispered their secrets to Cornies.

One evening as we sat on the rough bench outside his office, he fixed his large, brown eyes on me and said earnestly, "Daniel, I'll tell you why I do better than others. I feel a deep urge to work as hard as I can while there's time. The night will come for me too, as it does for all men. Meanwhile, I rely on myself. I don't care a pig's hide if other people don't like my ideas or oppose them. I set my faith in God, and as long as I do that I'll never get lukewarm in my work or life."

Those words went right through me. I knew he meant them. Cornies had a will like a threshing stone — hard and heavy, and once it started moving it was not easily stopped. He was also patient and threshed very fine. When he took over the Agricultural Association he quickly showed us the difference between a plate and a ploughshare, as they say. He used the Association as a personal tool to control every part of our lives — not just farming matters, as had been intended. No, he started changing the whole Molochnaya from top to bottom. The new villages at the western end of the settlement had to be laid out exactly to Cornies' plan, straight as pins, all the *hoefe* bordered with mulberry hedges just so, gardens and orchards and woods exactly alike, so that the whole string of villages looked like so many peas in a pod. Everything regulated and controlled by the will and wisdom of one man. A farmer could hardly visit his backhouse without Cornies' knowledge and approval.

Nothing escaped his sharp eyes and ears. He seemed to be everywhere at once. Houses, barns, and fences had to be properly maintained and painted regularly. He stuck his nose even into the women's kitchens. The yards had to be neat and clean. Even the straw piles had to be put in a certain place so they wouldn't be a fire hazard. He would walk around a *hof,* shoulders hunched forward, poke with his walking stick, ask a few sharp questions and file everything in that strange brain of his for future use.

They said he never forgot and seldom forgave. He had offenders who broke his regulations flogged by the *gebietsamt.* And for all his patience, he sometimes flew into a rage or even gave a beating himself, on the spot. He did that once to a man who was trying to make a fool of him. That was a certain Harms — I knew him a little — a lazy farmer but stubborn as an ox. Harms couldn't be bothered planting the tree seedlings he got from the Association. When Cornies came to inspect the orchard the next summer, Harms tried to play a game with him. He pretended to be looking for the seedlings among the thick weeds. With Cornies right behind, Harms kept stooping and muttering, "They must be here somewhere. They can't simply have disappeared, *toom schinda.* I know I planted them somewhere in here."

Suddenly Cornies' stout stick whistled on the man's exposed backside. As Harms sprang up with a startled roar, Cornies calmly said, "Na ya, so you've found your trees. Good."

The more the farmers rebelled against Cornies, the tighter he pulled the bit. Nobody could outfox or defy him for long. The more serious cases, and there weren't many, he dealt with in a ruthless manner. Cornies always gave proper warnings, but if they were ignored the offender's farm was simply sold from under him by the Association and resold to someone of good reputation.

Na nay, I didn't like to see Cornies become such a mighty one, though I never hated him the way many people did. Some talked about sending him to Siberia and some of our ministers even called him the forerunner of the Antichrist. Foolish, wicked talk! I never held with such people, God be praised. I had faith in Cornies' good intentions even when I didn't like his methods. He had his faults, but he did many great things for us. Like the system of black fallow and four-crop rotation of fields after we had that terrible drought and crop failure in thirty-three. Who but Cornies could have come up with such a useful idea? Preserving the moisture and energy of the soil that way did more to improve our farming on the dry Molochnaya steppe land than anything else. And we have Cornies to thank for the way the government officials looked at us with special favor.

Hard Cornies could be, but he had a soft side too. Only a few people close to him knew how many poor people he helped — often with cash out of his own pocket, or found them jobs or set them up on farms. And he helped not only our own people but other groups too — the Hutterites, Nogaies, Molokans, even the Jews.

The thing I liked best about Cornies was that he wasn't proud or stuck-up. They say he refused all the honors and awards and promotions the government wanted to give him. He could have been the governor of a province at least and become a titled nobleman. Ya, old Cornies preferred to live in Ohrloff as a simple Mennonite *wirt,* even though he had vast model estates at Jushanlee, Taschenak, and Verigen. Imagine, a beautiful, handtooled coach from Prussia standing in his *schien* and he never used it. He drove around on business in an old droshky without springs. Once, I remember, I found him relaxing in his office after hours. He was sitting in his big horsehide chair dressed in an old housecoat but still wearing his boots. When I asked him why he hadn't put on his *schlorre,* he gave his dry little smile and said he didn't own any slippers. That's the kind of man he was privately, even in the later years . . . .

Ya, and now the good Lord has taken away Cornies too. Everything comes from God, the good and the bad. He's gone, the mighty man, dead before sixty — from overwork, many say. Na ya, large mountains cast large shadows, as they say. God alone must judge him and his works . . . . I sit here old and feeble. My life is used up. Soon God will call me home too . . . . But an old man at death's door should ask some hard questions about himself and the people in his life.

I often wondered what exactly drove Cornies to do all the things he did in his lifetime — more things than a dozen ordinary people could do. Was it simply a deep love for his people? Did God choose him as His special instrument to help our people here in Russia? Or was it perhaps, as his enemies claimed, just a big hunger for wealth and power? Was he, as some charged, a willing tool to make the government's land settlement policies look good? Everybody knew he was the darling of the Guardians Committee for Foreign Colonists, and that they gave him a free hand to run the affairs of the settlement. Can anyone but God answer such questions?

Maybe what drove Cornies was all these things — and more.

In my long friendship with Cornies I saw a few things in him I never told anyone. I could never get him to talk much about religion or his own faith, although he was a good church man. But once — that was in the later years already — he said something to me I have never forgotten.

"Daniel," he said, "I've read the Bible as much as the next man, and my favorite chapter in God's Word is still the very first one and His first words: 'Let there be light.' "

Something clicked in my head when Cornies said that. Ya, Ya, I said to myself, you would like those words. You think of yourself as a creator too. You say, and it is. You say let there be roads and hedges and forests in our colonies, and there are. You permit no interference, no opposition. You never raise your voice, but when you say something everyone listens, even the imperial court in Petersburg.

But it wasn't power for himself that Cornies was hungering for. I never felt that in him. He didn't enjoy lording it over others. What drove him was something higher. He was in love with order. And progress. His dream was of an orderly world where everything was in its place and everybody could be made to work fruitfully. He must have seen himself as God's agent for improving and perfecting His physical world. The Mennonite colonies here on the steppe would be like an extension of his own clear mind and will. His brain would direct the settlers' hands as they transformed the wilderness into a lush garden.

Maybe he wanted to go even beyond that. In his innermost vision, perhaps, he saw himself not as possessing the settlement but as *being* possessed by it — totally — so that he himself became the settlement. He was the thousands of acres of rich steppe land, the flocks of thick-fleeced sheep ripe for the shears, the millions of trees taking root in precise, controlled patterns of growth. He was the neatly lotted, prosperous villages strung in neighborly rows; he was the very people working, worshipping, planning, and building their kingdom on earth. In the end, his will and the land and its people would become one and the same thing.

That must have been Cornies' great dream, the dream that drove him beyond anything else. Juschanlee and his other estates were just the beginning, the rough drawings for the master plan. What he really wanted was to transform the whole Molochnaya into one big efficient, progressive estate. His estate? No. He would have said that it all belonged to God. That it was only held in trust by men. He wanted only to create, to shape and control, not to own. That's why he rejected the honors and rewards from the government. He didn't need those baubles. They would only show that he was a servant. He knew that in his own Mennonite world his position was as absolute as the tsar's in his world.

But the changes Cornies made were not all good. By changing the instruction in our schools, he was letting the world into the classroom. The Bible had always been our book of instruction. Cornies brought in other books — worldly books like geography and what not. Ya, he wanted our farmers to be God-fearing and morally pure and obedient. But he also wanted them to learn things about the world that would make them even better farmers. And that's where the danger came in. I tried to tell him that once, but he only looked past me and said that the church could not always control everything in this life. My hair rose up when I heard that. I knew then that Cornies wanted to change the whole direction of our people.

As always, he got his way, and not just in education either. There was that long terrible fight that started in my early years between the elders and the *gebietsamt,* and later the officials of the Association led by Cornies, to see who would have the final authority in the settlement. We elders lost in the end and I always suspected that Cornies had been working hard against us behind the wall, as they say, but I never had any proof and he never talked to me about his part in the long quarrel. Ach, what misery and calamity when Elder Jacob Warkentin was deposed and Elder Heinrich Wiens was banished from Russia! And that's only a few years ago. They were stiff-necked men, it's true, but they didn't deserve such harsh treatment. It must have been Cornies. Who else? Funny, but he never showed me that side of his hide. Ya, by now the Church's power is badly cracked and the officials are stronger than ever . . . . They have let Oom Wiens come back again from Prussia, but without his office. Now he is just a broken old man living out his days. Like me.

All in the name of progress. And what has that progress done for us? Na ya, we were a backward people before Cornies came. We have better farms now, richer colonies, that can't be denied. But more and more this very prosperity is drawing us into the world. I can feel it in my bones. I wanted to turn back the clock, bring back the pure Anabaptist church here in the Molochnaya. But I failed, and my failure has gnawed at me ever since. Did I fail because of my own weakness, or was God trying to teach me a lesson? Did he punish me because I had been following not His will but my own?

I didn't want progress like Cornies. I wanted purity. But if progress leads to worldliness, then maybe purity leads to spiritual pride. Stagnation. Cornies and I started out with the right intentions, but we both must have taken a wrong turning somewhere . . . . Ach, there is so much in the past that keeps sliding out of reach just as your mind touches it. So slippery, the past, you can't even get a good bearing on the present from it.

How could I have foreseen that our little church group would be so savagely persecuted by our own brethren? And then, after all that suffering, my followers turning on me and making such a scandal with their foolish, fanatical behavior? That was the end of my dream.

And now Cornies' Molochnaya has become a spectacle for visiting lords and ladies from Petersburg and Moscow on their way down to the holiday spas of the Crimea. We are a sight to see — like the Kremlin or a famous waterfall. We are like Potemkin villages, but real ones this time. Was that really all Cornies had in mind, to make the Molochnaya into a pretty showplace for the world to admire? I can't believe that! If that's all he wanted then he was following not God's will but the vanities of Satan.

No, I was not the savior of our people I wanted to be. But was Cornies? I failed because I was weak and self-willed. Cornies was strong and self-willed, but what will the future show about him? I wanted to build a quiet path to God. Cornies has built a highway to the world for us.

Ya, we Mennonites began by building separate little worlds for ourselves — first in Holland, then in Danzig, and now in an even bigger way here in Russia. Perhaps our big mistake right from the start was to think we could live in our little world like ducks on a pond, without ever letting the fox get near us. But the fox knows how to coax the ducks to the shore. Our Anabaptist forefathers — Menno, Marpeck, Grebel, and the others —stayed in their tight little circle because they expected Christ to come back soon to reclaim His bride the Church. And so they kept themselves pure for Him. But Christ did not come then. He still has not come, after all these years. We are still waiting for Him, but maybe with only one eye and one ear now. Our other eye and ear are on the world.

The world, ach ya, the world, Satan's kingdom. It sits there all around us. Waiting . . . . But doesn't it also protect us? Could we have even set up our separate church, kept alive our suffering *gemeinde,* without the protection of kings and governments? Ach, that is a hard thing for simple men to understand. No, I can't believe like some that the whole world exists for the sake of our tiny brotherhood . . . . If only You had come sooner, dear Lord, and saved us from our pride. Our little pond isn't enough for us anymore. The fox is calling oh so sweetly from the bank, and we are listening. We think we'll always be able to come back to the safety of our pond. But it won't work. We separated ourselves from the world so we could live for Him, not so we could build bigger *wirtschaften* and richer estates.

Ach, *lieber Gott,* I am too old and weak to hold in my grief . . . to carry the burden of guilt You, in your wisdom, have tied to me. I can no longer bear it . . . . Like Job's, my harp is turned to mourning. Give me release. From memory. From earthly life. I leave behind no monuments, no records to mark the course I followed. Like Cornies. Not even a broken pillar. His works will be remembered. His highway stands strong and broad. My narrow path has already vanished into grass. If only I could have . . . .

"It is a terrible thing to fall into the hands of the living God."

Ach, Heavenly Father, Thy terrible, loving will be done . . . .

CHAPTER TWELVE

1

Schoenwiese-Alexandrovsk, August, 1913

As the train clattered northward through the dazzling afternoon sunshine, Wilhelm kept his eyes on the freshly harvested fields rolling by and wondered anxiously how his weekend with the Bocks would go. He longed to see Clara again, but his misgivings about Mrs. Bock had made him reluctant to accept Clara's invitation. But she had persisted, either ignoring or explaining away his flimsily contrived excuses, until he said yes he would be glad to come. Perhaps the visit would settle things between himself and Clara once and for all.

It was the uncertainty of their relationship that bothered him. Clara's warmly possessive letters were exhilarating and reassuring when he read them, but between letters doubts rose in him like cold mists. She kept assuring him that her mother sincerely regretted her rudeness to him at Easter and that he would find her friendly and civil now. Wilhelm hoped she was right. Privately he doubted that Mrs. Bock had undergone a change of heart towards him, but for Clara's sake he was willing to give her the benefit of the doubt.

He had not seen Clara since the fiasco in Moscow. Mrs. Bock had not permitted her daughter to go back to Petersburg after Easter. Instead, Clara was forced to go home with her parents, while August was instructed to pack her things in the capital and send them after her. Clara was to resume her vocal studies closer to home. Mrs. Bock would take no more chances with her daughter's future. In her first letter to him Clara noted — in a brave attempt to be casual about it — that her teacher Mde. Slobodskaja was probably as relieved to see her go as her mother was to get her back.

Wilhelm had come home from Petersburg in May, his first and in all likelihood his only year at the Academy completed in a blaze of glory. Not only had he passed his courses with good grades, but had taken second prize in the water color competition for junior students. Best of all, he had been formally acknowledged as the first year student who had shown the most improvement during the year. He deeply regretted that he would not be able to go back to the Academy in the fall, but at least he had the satisfaction of knowing that he had been measured against some of the better young art students in the nation and had not been found wanting.

He had also gained greatly in the eyes of his family. Even Father seemed to have lost his contempt for art and artists, and now talked proudly of what his talented son had accomplished in only one winter. If only Willie could finish his studies and show those snooty Halbstadters what a boy from Blumenau could do! But, he sighed, it was apparently not God's will. Willie would have to set aside his ambitions and serve as a village teacher, which after all was a divinely approved profession too. Besides, who could tell what might happen in the future? Willie might yet get a chance to serve the Lord as a picture-painter. New churches were being built all the time. Some might want a blue heaven or something like that painted on the ceiling. There was an estate-owner near Schoenfeld-Brazol who had faces of famous poets and musicians painted on his ceiling. Willie could do things like that in his spare time and in the summer when he wasn't teaching. Then Father would sigh deeply and express the hope that his youngest son would finally come to his senses and also become a useful, God-fearing member of society, instead of leading a worldly, un-Mennonite life as some kind of clerk in Berdjansk.

The train rolled into the small but handsome Schoenwiese station. Clara and August Junior were there waiting. Clara had never looked lovelier, more vivacious. She rushed into Wilhelm's arms and they held each other in a fond embrace, but she did not raise her face to be kissed. He would have been shocked if she had, in public.

She released him with a happy sigh and surveyed him with dancing eyes. "Oh, Vasya, it's so good to see you again."

"Yes, good to see you, Rembrandt." August seemed a little reserved, even distant. He took Wilhelm's bag and led the way to the big family Daimler parked outside.

Clara was already going over the schedule for the week-end. Tonight they would have dinner at home and visit. Tomorrow morning Gusha would take him on a tour of the Bock and Riesen factory. In the afternoon they would show him around Schoenwiese and Alexandrovsk and perhaps go on a picnic to Khortitza Island. Sunday after church they were all to drive down by car to Selenaya, their country estate on the Dnieper about a dozen miles south of town.

"You'll love Selenaya, Vasya," Clara promised eagerly as she sat between Wilhelm and her brother in the front seat of the huge car.

As they turned into Station Street, the wide main thoroughfare of Schoenwiese, Clara said gaily, "Behold our own Nevsky Prospect, Vasya, and this time I'm the guide. Pay careful attention now." She was trying to imitate her brother's officious drawl. "Here on the left we have the well-known firm of Lepp and Wallmann. Note the architectural unity of the many fine buildings in this huge complex. Next we come to the equally impressive factory of A. J. Koop. And there, off to the right, dominating the skyline, the majestic flour mill of the H. A. Niebuhr firm, with the twin-domed mansion of J. H. Niebuhr right beside it. Ahead of you, you see the spacious main square of Schoenwiese, with the famous Tavonious *apteka* dominating the corner on the left." She looked up at Wilhelm mischievously. "And you will note, my discerning artist friend, that there is no vulgar metal ball on a tower here to spoil the view."

Smiling, Wilhelm acknowledged her sally. "But where is the most famous Mennonite factory of them all?"

"You mean Bock and Riesen?"

"No, I mean the Klaas Funk *brommtopp* factory."

August brayed loudly. "He's got you again, little sister."

"Yes," Clara said sweetly, "it's too bad we haven't got a *brommtopp* on a tower for him. With his superior taste, I'm sure he'd prefer it to the Singer globe."

They turned off the square into a side street with stately stone and brick houses on both sides. In a few more minutes they nosed into a neatly graveled driveway and pulled up in front of a large orange-red brick mansion whose fancy facade combined an odd mixture of styles, Wilhelm noted as they walked up to the steps. He wondered who designed these French chateau-Italian villa hybrids for wealthy Mennonites. Probably the same architects who created mansions and villas for Russian estate owners. They certainly looked more foreign than Russian.

The interior of the Bock residence was spacious but certainly not grand or pretentious. There were even some traditional Mennonite touches here and there: an old pull-out sleeping couch in one corner of the huge parlor or drawing room, and a beautifully painted Kroeger wall clock hanging demurely amidst lustrous oil paintings and smart water colors.

In a small, bright room off the parlor they came upon Mrs. Bock reading. Wilhelm tensed, not at all sure how he would be received. Mrs. Bock put down her book and greeted the guest with cool but not chilling formality. She trusted he had had a comfortable trip and invited him to make himself at home. She looked at Wilhelm directly for only a moment, but without the slightest hint of embarrassment, as though she had completely forgotten the incident in Moscow. As an afterthought she murmured that Mr. Bock would be home in time for dinner, then picked up her book again. Wilhelm breathed a sigh of relief as they left the room. He had a curious feeling that Mrs. Bock had dismissed him from her world, that she was as politely indifferent to him as she would be to a servant once in her employ whom she chanced to meet in the street months later.

The evening went by quickly, with Clara and August attentive and entertaining hosts. Clara was at her most talkative and Wilhelm relaxed and listened, as charmed by her bright presence as ever. August, however, seemed changed — no longer the bantering student always ready with a quip or irreverent comment. There was a new air of maturity about him. He had even begun to grow a mustache, a male affectation he had disdained in the past.

They were sitting in a comfortable screened porch at the back of the house overlooking a large, low, formal garden consisting of flowers and miniature shrubs in a cunning variety of colors in intricate geometrical patterns.

"Well, Rembrandt, what do you think?" August drawled. "I've joined the firm on a permanent basis. I'm not going back to Petersburg either. Papa thinks conditions being what they are I may as well start mastering the business before I'm called into the forestry service, assuming that I will be called in."

"Ah, so that explains the mustache. Will it be a full Hussar with waxed ends, to go with your exalted position?"

August rubbed the short nap under his nose. "So far it's not even big enough for an infantryman. I think my beard has too much chin to cover. There's nothing left for my lip."

"You should see him, Vasya, standing in front of the mirror pretending to twirl tips that aren't there yet," Clara teased. "He's growing it so the workers will take him for a real boss when he strides through the foundry." She looked with fond malice at her brother's long, bland profile. "He can't wait to be on the board of directors and have his picture taken in front of the factory with Papa and the other officials. He even wears dark, three-piece suits to the office now — exactly like Papa's."

August regarded his sister without expression. "Listen to the pampered child. She's got nothing to do all day except sing a few scales in the morning and practise a song or two, then spend the rest of the day idling away her time — amusing herself, she calls it, like one of Chekhov's bored country belles." His gaze shifted to Wilhelm. "What she needs is to settle down too, find a devoted, up-and-coming Mennonite husband who'll give her a large household to look after — and lots of babies to amuse herself with," he added wickedly.

"Listen to Mr. Playboy," Clara shot back, "dispensing advice about marriage and settling down. He won't get married before thirty, he says, but he wants me to be chained down before twenty! Vasya, have you ever heard such insufferable male smugness?"

Even as Wilhelm chuckled over the exchange between brother and sister he was aware of its possible implications. Were the casual references to "a large household" and being "chained down" at twenty intended to tell him something? Or was he being unduly sensitive?

With Bock Senior's arrival the family sat down to dinner. This time the atmosphere was relaxed and informal. Mrs. Bock was gracious and affable, and made Wilhelm feel completely at ease. Tonight she was a very charming lady and the perfect hostess. It was hard to believe she was the same person who had created such a scene in Moscow. But she had considered him a threat then, as she clearly did not now. He wondered why.

Dinner over, the young people went back to the porch to enjoy the cooler evening air. Wilhelm was looking for some time alone with Clara, but young August hovered about in a manner that seemed a little out of character for him. He was not insensitive. Surely he knew that Wilhelm and Clara would want some time to themselves their first evening together in months. Even when Clara suggested a walk in the garden in the fading light,

August tagged along. Wilhelm was on the verge of telling him to stop playing chaperone, but he was suddenly aware that some kind of signal had passed between brother and sister. Now he understood. August had been instructed to see to it that his sister and her friend were not left alone together.

It was a clever tactic. But the weekend wasn't over.

In the morning, August and Wilhelm had the breakfast table to themselves. The parents — both early risers even on weekends — had already had their breakfast and Clara, a notorious slugabed according to August, had not yet come down. She was to join them later, after their tour of the factory.

There was a marked change in August this morning. Not a trace of his guarded manner left. He was as bright and cheerful as ever. Over their fried eggs and bacon (August called it an American breakfast), he began telling Wilhelm the story of his father and the firm. Wilhelm had heard some of it before, but he listened politely. He was amused to note the seriousness and conscious pride with which August talked about his father. It was as though he had appointed himself Bock Senior's official biographer and was determined to do justice to his subject.

August Bock Senior had grown up in the village of Einlage, across the river from Alexandrovsk. He soon became known in the village for his remarkable mechanical ability. He could fix (and usually improve) anything from a Kroeger clock to a horse-drawn forage cutter. At seventeen he was hired by the Lepp and Wallmann factory in Khortitza as a machinist's apprentice. This was in the early eighties, about the time the reorganized firm of Lepp and Wallmann was beginning to expand rapidly.

The young mechanical wizard so impressed his employers that after two years Lepp and Wallmann sent him to Hamburg, where they had excellent business connections. Young Bock lacked the formal education to enter an engineering school; instead he was given an opportunity to study factory methods for the production of farm machinery at Wuetz and Company, one of the largest manufacturers in Europe.

Two years later he returned to Lepp and Wallman as a thoroughly trained technical assistant and factory trouble-shooter. The owners shrewdly gave him the time and opportunity to tinker and experiment with the company's production methods and with their line of products.

Bock's special status began to pay off almost immediately. He had brought back with him from Germany the rough design for a multiple-share plough known as a *bugger,* which would replace the traditional one-share plough. The partners gloated openly. With the *bugger* they would steal a march on their closest Mennonite competitors A. J. Koop and J. G. Niebuhr, and vault to top place among the leading Mennonite manufacturing firms.

The young inventive genius quickly perfected two- and three-share

ploughs. After they went into production he continued to experiment
—with four shares, then five and finally six — after which he realized that
adding further shares would create too many mechanical problems.

In 1890 young Bock took a brief but rather mysterious leave of absence
to go back to Hamburg. The two partners looked smug but said nothing.
There was much speculation about the mechanical ideas Bock would bring
back this time. When he returned two months later he brought back
something more tangible than ideas. He was accompanied by a bride, and
what a bride she was! She was beautiful and elegantly aristocratic, the
former Melissa Felsenburg, whose father was an executive with Wuetz and
Company. The two had met and fallen in love during Bock's first stay in
Hamburg. They had maintained a passionate correspondence (August Jr.,
lowering his voice coyly, said he had surreptitiously read some of the letters
kept by his mother) during which Bock Senior proposed and was accepted.

"Courtship via private letters is one thing, marriage quite another," said
August sententiously. The match was violently opposed by the Felsenburgs,
who were appalled at the very idea of their beautiful only daughter
marrying a completely unknown young barbarian from the wild steppes of
South Russia. Granted he spoke German, although with a peculiar accent,
and considered himself to be German and Protestant, even though he
belonged to that staid Mennonite sect, hardly one of your best churches
even here in Hamburg. Worst of all, at least in the opinion of Mrs. Felsenburg, was that while young Bock appeared to be a well-behaved, polite
young man, he was more than just ill-favored: he was downright repulsive
looking with his huge ungainly frame, monstrous face and jowls, and
cavernous voice. August chuckled without embarrassment when he got to
this part and said he got these details from his father, who of course got
them from his wife. The very idea of her precious daughter in the arms of
this ugly giant, Mrs. Felsenburg had desperately confided to Melissa one
day, was enough to give her nightmares. The match was preposterous and
out of the question.

But Melissa's family underestimated the steel in their daughter's character. In the end her will prevailed, although her parents played for time by
insisting on a two-year waiting period before the marriage.

While Melissa held firm, the Felsenburgs continued to oppose a son-in-
law whom they considered altogether unsuitable. They had too much
breeding to display open hostility, but they had subtle ways of showing
disapproval. One of the more effective, designed to throw young Bock on
the defensive, to make him feel guilty, was to express repeatedly their
doubts as to whether their darling daughter, raised in a sheltered and refined
atmosphere, would be able to adapt to the harsh climate and rugged setting
of a Mennonite colony in Russia. The harassed bridegroom vainly tried to
dispel their fears by convincing them that life in Khortitza was as comfortable, if less interesting culturally, as life in Hamburg. As for culture, Melissa

and he would sample the riches of Moscow and Petersburg as often as they could. Their daughter, he assured them with confidence, would adapt quickly.

But August Bock proved to be wrong, the Felsenburgs right. Melissa endured life in the wilds of Russia with aristocratic fortitude, but she never adapted to it. She truly loved her talented husband and believed in him and in his business career. But she hated almost everything about her new life, and as she got older her feelings of frustration and bitterness seethed within her like a corrosive acid. She stubbornly refused to become a member of her husband's beloved Einlage church, although her sense of social position compelled her to attend often enough to keep up appearances. From the beginning she disliked Mennonites and their ways, and rarely bothered to hide her contempt. For years now, August said, she had been conducting a determined campaign to persuade her husband to retire to Germany when the time came.

"End of part one," August announced and drained his coffee cup. "Let's get going. The plant closes at noon on Saturdays. I'll tell you the rest of the story on the way."

As they walked to the factory several blocks away, August continued his narrative. In the early nineties his father had decided it was time to go on his own. Lepp and Wallmann, understandably, were sorry to see him go, but they were astute enough to see that young Bock was cut out for big things in the industrial world. They even offered him a partnership in the end, but he was set on launching his own firm.

Bock began to look around for a partner with the necessary risk capital. He found one in Franz Riesen, a highly successful Mennonite entrepreneur from Halbstadt in the Molochnaya who had made money from such diverse enterprises as grain-selling in Berdjansk and a paint factory in Halbstadt. The diminutive but boundlessly energetic Riesen (he was, after all, a "Riesen," a giant, he liked to say, small only in body) was looking for new commercial worlds to conquer. A first-rate technical man like Bock, with fresh, inventive ideas, was just what he was looking for. Together they would be a *"Riesenbock,"* a giant ram, he boasted, from the beginning. And that was how the new firm's nickname got started.

After much planning and consulting the new partners decided to establish themselves in Schoenwiese, in direct competition to Lepp and Wallmann and to A. J. Koop, the next largest implement manufacturer. It was a bold, almost provocative move, but Lepp and Wallmann were not exactly novices in business. They knew they could only benefit from the establishment of another rival factory on their doorstep, especially if it proved as successful as they anticipated it would be. Mennonite and other farmers were growing insatiable for new machines. Besides, Bock's continual improvements to existing machines and his almost certain invention of new ones could always be adapted to their own line of products, patents notwithstanding. In a sense, their former employee would still be working for them. Yes, they were confident the new firm would be good for the whole Mennonite farm machinery industry, which was growing by leaps and bounds and already accounted for close to ten percent of the implement manufacturing in South Russia.

The firm of Bock and Riesen did indeed prosper from the beginning. Mennonite farm holdings, especially in the daughter colonies springing up in the east and southeast, were expanding rapidly. Farming methods were growing more efficient and mechanized all the time, and the golden streams of winter wheat were pouring from the Russian-Mennonite steppes in endless floods. The *Riesenbock* ran smoothly. While shrewd, dynamic little Riesen looked after the business end of the enterprise, the ingenious, methodical Bock worked tirelessly to improve production methods and to add mechanical refinements and new designs.

Bock once again raised eyebrows by devising a gear and pulley system for his *bugger* plough which made it possible to raise or lower the shares simultaneously by means of a hand lever at the back. But his biggest technical innovation, the one that set the industry on its collective ear, was a hand-forged steel frame to replace the wooden frame on the popular reaper known as the *lobogreika*. The new steel-frame reaper had far-reaching consequences. Not only did it ensure greater durability and longevity but it made possible bigger and wider-cutting machines. Almost overnight the familiar sight of reapers standing idly in the fields with broken frames became a rarity. Farmers were loud in their praise of the new steel machine.

Among Bock's later technical achievements was a *bugger* drill-plough with five small shares mounted under a four-wheel carriage bearing a narrow seedbox. The drill-plough enabled farmers to plough and sow in one operation in spring, instead of the much more cumbersome and costly double operation of ploughing in fall and seeding in spring. The new machine greatly facilitated the growing of the hard red wheat *Krimka,* for which there was an ever-growing demand from abroad. The latest refinement of the drill-plough was a seeder drill that used discs instead of shares and seeded the grain in neat rows through hanging tubes.

Fortunately for Wilhelm, who was getting a little bored by August's technical recital, they had reached the factory, a huge, sprawling complex of buildings covering an entire city block. The long, low, one- and two-story brick buildings formed a broken square around the block, and enclosed a large inner courtyard which, August explained, served as a storage area. They entered the courtyard through the main gate and August guided Wilhelm through a maze of machine parts stacked in neat rows — wheels, frames, gears, and pulleys in various shapes and sizes. Several long sheds, open on one side, contained piles of white and yellow lumber. There was also a row of newly completed reapers, their fresh green and red coats of paint glistening in the morning sun. The pungent smells of metal, freshly planed wood, and new paint permeated the hot summer air.

"We'll start with the foundry and carpentry shop," August said briskly as he waited for Wilhelm to finish his inspection of the courtyard. "Organized confusion, we call it. Hard to believe that all these separate parts end up looking like these sleek beauties, isn't it?" he grinned, fondly patting the end reaper.

They stepped into one end of a long shed teeming with activity. The air inside felt hot and steamy and close. An acrid smell of burning coal came from the furnace doors on one side. Placed at intervals on the sand-covered floor were what looked like metal vats of different kinds and sizes. Light came from a broad skylight that ran along the apex section of the roof.

"Those are the casting molds in which we cast the various pulleys, flywheels, and gears we require for our machines," August explained as they picked their way carefully along the loose, uneven floor. Dozens of Russian workmen dressed in loose or belted peasant shirts were busy pouring molten metal, prying open forms, mulling sand and working the overhead hoists that carried the finished parts to the exit at the far end. Wilhelm was curious to know why the men working inside in this heat were all wearing caps or hats.

"Out of habit, I guess," August said. "These fellows grew up on farms mostly, where they wore caps while working outside. But a cap or hat also acts as protection from falling objects in here."

As August and his guest passed by, the workers looked up and nodded respectfully to the owner's son. But many of the lean, hard faces were unsmiling and did not look friendly. In fact, they gave the impression of being morose and sullen. As he and August passed by, Wilhelm could feel hostile eyes boring into his back. The glowering looks and curling lips seemed to signal a hatred and contempt barely suppressed. It was a little frightening, although in his case there could hardly be anything personal —unless the veiled ill will was directed at August, who seemed oblivious to it. Or was he? Did he know or care how the workers felt about him?

As they left the foundry he asked August about the apparent unfriendliness in the workmen's faces.

"Oh that," August said disdainfully, "don't pay any attention. Your ordinary Russian doesn't exactly enjoy organized work. Most of these peasants still haven't got the undisciplined, procrastinating life of the village out of their systems. If you saw them a few hours from now you wouldn't recognize them. They'll be full of vodka and as happy and friendly as puppies. They don't hate me, they hate the job. Those glum looks are put on only during working hours."

Wilhelm was far from convinced by August's glib explanation. Those grim faces had more than job-hatred in them — much more. He was sure they reflected the malevolent class-hatred that was again beginning to erupt all over the country in strikes and acts of terrorism. And wasn't it true that men of August's class were usually blind to such signs of danger until it was too late?

After touring the carpentry shop, the assembling shed, and the painting shed they walked back to the office near the main gate.

"Well, Rembrandt, what do you think of it all?" Pride of ownership and bland self-satisfaction mellowed August's long face.

Wilhelm felt a perverse urge to say the wrong thing, to prick August's suave self-importance; he was, after all, merely the beneficiary of his father's hard work and skill. How like Snapper Loewen August was in this respect, but at least Snapper was eager and ambitious to improve and expand his father's estate. Somehow Wilhelm doubted that August would ever add much to his father's business. "It's all very impressive," he heard himself say (he was after all a guest), "no wonder you've become so absorbed in all this."

But August, seating himself at his father's big desk, was preening for more. He obviously wanted his guest to ask questions that would feed August's self-esteem, allow him to boast and show off his knowledge of the firm's operations. When Wilhelm remained silent, August went ahead anyway. One long leg draped over the arm of his father's chair, he smoothly reeled off company statistics. "We employ about 150 here in the main plant and another 100 in our branch plant at Osterwick in the Old Colony." He clasped his hands behind his head and leaned back with a little frown of concentration. "Last year we reached a production volume of just over 500,000 rubles. By now we've got capital stock of around a million rubles and we're still growing — rapidly, I might add. We're still a little behind Lepp and Wallmann and A. J. Koop, but ahead of J. G. Niebuhr, Neufeld and Company, Franz and Schroeder, and all the rest."

Wilhelm listened as he looked around the office. The furniture, heavy and darkly gleaming, looked expensive and solid. A massive, richly carved oak cabinet along the wall was filled with fancy glass and metal bric-a-brac — souvenirs of Bock Senior's business travels, he surmised. He glanced at the neat piles of papers on the desk, the inevitable abacus. There was even an elegant-looking silver telephone within easy reach.

August, having recited his statistics of success, passed a sheet of the firm's stationery to Wilhelm. The resplendently designed letterhead favored by Russian business firms completely covered the top third of the page. Beneath the ornate scroll-work name of the firm were lavish sketches of its two factories, flanked on both sides by reproductions of the various medals awarded to Bock and Riesen at exhibitions and industrial fairs.

August pointed to an oval insert on one side of the letterhead. It depicted a giant ram standing protectively over a multi-share plough. "That's the company crest. The nickname *Riesenbock* for the firm became so popular the partners finally decided to adopt it officially."

As they rose to leave, Wilhelm said in an offhanded way, "Let's just hope, old boy, that when you take over all this one day, the giant ram won't be reduced to a lost sheep."

August gave him a lofty stare. "Not a chance, Vasya, Bock and Riesen are just beginning to climb. Franz Riesen has no heirs. Someday I'll be sitting on top of the largest industrial complex in Ekaterinoslav Province. You wait and see."

In the Bock home the mid-day meal was always — even on Saturdays — a solid though not elaborate affair. The food was again served, as it had been the previous evening, by a Russian servant girl so striking in appearance that Wilhelm could not keep his eyes off her. Even her stiff maid's uniform could not entirely mask the freedom and grace of her movements, the touch of insolence in her bearing. The haughtiness in her broad, high-cheeked peasant face came from a pair of flashing black eyes and a nose that had the delicate sweep of a scimitar. There was nothing of the docile servant about her. Instead, Wilhelm thought he detected in her a smoldering resentment at her menial role. When she came close he was aware of a gathered energy in her, a physical intensity that struck him as almost masculine. Even her figure had a taut male flatness and angularity that denied passive femininity.

After dinner, at ease in the porch, he asked Clara about the unusual looking servant girl.

The girl was not, he found, in Clara's good graces. "Oh, so our proud Marusya has caught your eyes too, has she? She seems to be good at making men notice her, including my roving brother. You're right, Vasya, she's not exactly your typical Russian help. She must have more than one wild gypsy ancestor. I don't know where Mama found her but in the few months she's been here she's grown so lazy and impudent that I'm sure she won't be with us much longer. Even Mama can't break that stupid girl. She's a vile creature. I can't stand her, if you must know. And she hates me too. She'd do anything to spite me."

"Hates you? But why —"

"Oh, I suppose because of things I've said to her when she made me angry." Clara halted and blushed. "Also because of something that happened at Selenaya a few weeks ago. I — you see, I caught her there with the coachman — in the arbor — one evening. I told her what — what she was and that I'd have to tell Mama, but she just laughed and said she didn't care and would do what she liked in her spare time."

Wilhelm guessed the truth. "And why haven't you told your mother Clara? Are you trying to keep the girl — ?"

"No, no Vasya, you're wrong." She was agitated. "I'm — I'm just waiting for the right — oh, let's drop it. The creature isn't worth discussing." Suddenly she was smiling. "Listen, let's go for a little walk and then I have a treat for you. I've been working on Hugo Wolf's *Italian Songbook*. They're beautiful songs. You'll love them." She rushed on. "And later on Gusha is taking us by boat to the 'Monkey-head' on the Island for a picnic. It's a lovely spot. Very romantic, my dear Vasya."

She took him by the hand and led him out into the garden. "And tomorrow we'll be at Selenaya," she added, "the most beautiful place of all."

As he followed her down the steps he felt a sudden urge to grab her by the shoulders and tell her to stop running. But by then they were in the garden and she was stooping to pick a flower. For luck, she said, smiling for him a secret smile as she handed it to him.

The wealthy Bock family attended the Mennonite church in Einlage because that was the church Bock Senior had grown up in. The Einlage church was said to be the handsomest house of worship in the colonies. Even so, Wilhelm was not prepared for the un-Mennonite splendor of the building. Its neo-Gothic facade was dominated by a large, intricately carved rose window set in the end gable that fronted the street. The gothic effect was enhanced by crenellated stone work and by a heavy, decorated brick fence and a huge, triple-arched, fantastically ornamented entrance gate. The whole structure looked unlike any Mennonite church he had ever seen. Had sober Mennonites created this fanciful edifice? Even without towers or onion domes it seemed to have a touch of Russian flamboyance about it. It certainly didn't seem to reflect much *schlichtheit*, the modesty and plainness that Mennonites had always tried to practise. A Mennonite St. Basil's — yes, that's exactly what it was!

By comparison, the interior was almost plain with clean, simple lines, bright and airy, without the ostentation of the exterior. In the rear a broad, straight staircase led up to the center of a balcony that ran the length of the building. Light flooded through the plain-glass gothic windows and gave lustre to the fine dark wood of pews, stairs, and railings. The whole arrangement of the interior had a breadth and spaciousness that gave Wilhelm a devotional feeling as they waited for the service to begin.

But he lost that feeling once the sermon began. His mind kept wandering to Clara sitting demurely beside her mother on the women's side. Lapsing into daydream, he saw her standing beside him as his bride here in this sun-filled church. The church full to overflowing, his family proudly seated in the front pew, the Bocks, also beaming approval, on the other side. Clara looking up at him shyly as they exchanged wedding vows, smiling her secret smile for him. And then — but there his fancy snapped. With a soft little sigh he dismissed the daydream. That's all it was, an idle Sunday morning daydream.

The reality mocked him coldly. She had never seriously considered him as a lover and future husband. In her eyes they had simply been good friends temporarily drawn together in the big city away from home, making exciting intellectual and cultural discoveries together. That part of her life was probably already fading from her mind. She was trying to let him down gently with this visit. He was sure he would not be invited again. This entertaining weekend was merely her way of saying thank-you, my friend, *aufwiedersehn*. He glanced at her profile, sharp and delicate, lowered slightly in pious concentration as she listened to the drone from the pulpit — or pretended to. His heart ached with the nearness of her, and with her utterly unattainable distance. He felt depressed suddenly, and wished the day were over so he could go home and try to forget this entrancing, maddening girl who would never be his. Who would, he thought bitterly, be sold to the highest bidder when her mother decided the time was right.

But perhaps he was being too pessimistic. He had not lost Clara yet. There were moments, he knew, when they had been more than casual friends. And those moments would come again, he reassured himself as the service rustled to a close.

As they drove down to Selenaya that afternoon, the mighty Dnieper shimmering below them on the right, he was enjoying himself again. The half-hour drive through the countryside, Clara sparkling beside him, cleansed the morning's blackness from his mind.

The Bock *khutor* Selenaya proved to be everything Clara had claimed for it. The truly magnificent manor house, as were all the main buildings on the estate, was built of quarried stone and decorated with baroque opulence. The central row of windows was topped by handsome Roman arches and there was elaborately carved stonework with scroll-work between the windows and along the roofline. It was, Wilhelm remarked with a smile to Clara, almost as breathtaking and dramatic looking as the Einlage Church. But larger, she added with a laugh.

In the middle of the courtyard rose a spectacular rondell of flowers whose profusion of colors and patterns added an almost garish luxuriance to the whole place. The vast mound of the rondell was girdled by a low white fence and pierced at its apex by a tiny ornamental bell tower. He half expected fountains to shoot up at any moment.

In an ecstasy of proprietorship Clara conducted Wilhelm through the enormous house. It was her favorite place in all the world, and didn't he think so too? With a theatrical flourish she led him into a spacious drawing room. Two stately white Doric columns supported the center arch of the long, high-ceilinged room. Rows of broad French windows on two sides charged the room with the fierce light of August. Except for a round table in one corner, a row of elegant chairs, a divan, some potted plants and a grand piano against the inside wall, the whole vast room was bare, sun-soaked space. It was a veritable salon. One could hold formal balls here. He wondered if the Bocks ever did.

"You adore it, Vasya, I can tell. Wouldn't you like to paint in a room like this?" She dashed over to the piano. "I love practising in here. Somehow my voice always sounds best in this room." She mock-trilled a shower of glittering arpeggios and imitated the feverish laugh of a Puccini heroine.

"I can believe it," Wilhelm laughed. "Even my voice would sound better in here."

Clara flew to the phonograph resting on the table in the corner. She found the record she wanted, placed it on the turntable. "Come, Vasya, you must crank a little so that Signor Caruso will sound like his glorious self, not like a drowning monster."

Wilhelm turned the crank until he could turn it no more. Clara flicked the slim-necked playing head down and the liquid gold of the great tenor's voice poured out of the fluted horn, seeming to turn the sunlight itself into passionate sound.

She took his hand and danced him across the polished floor to the divan, while they listened to the melting phrases of *Celeste Aida*.

It was the moment he had been waiting for. It was now or never. The singer's vibrant tones were urging him. They turned to each other, their eyes bright with shared feeling, cupping and holding the moment, neither wanting to break the spell. Slowly, spontaneously their heads inclined, lips met trembling, then broke apart, their eyes still locked. But even as he opened his mouth to speak, she shook her head almost imperceptibly and with a movement of delicate finality placed her forefinger against his lips.

The moment had passed. The divine Caruso soared to and held a final, glowing high note, then fell silent, leaving only the hissing and crackling of the still revolving disc and needle.

Later August took him on a walking tour of Selenaya. The estate was so grand it made the Loewen *khutor* of Voronaya seem modest by comparison. Even the barns and stables here were built of the same stone as the manor, and harmonious with it in design. And yet, Wilhelm wasn't at all sure he preferred this estate. This grandiose display of stone buildings seemed deliberately designed to impress. The Loewens farmed on a large, profitable scale, but their *khutor* was also their home, a complete way of life. The Bocks' imposing estate seemed more important to them as a playground and retreat than as a working farm. They obviously used it when it suited them, enjoying its splendor and comforts. But they were not bound to it in the devoted way the Loewens were to Voronaya. No, this village of carved stone overlooking endless acres seemed more like a monument to wealth and power than a home to live and work in.

He did not think he could ever have fitted comfortably into all this.

Afterwards, as they sat in the garden over *faspa,* the conversation turned to politics, to Clara's visible disgust. The elder Bock bluntly expressed his concern over the deteriorating political situation in Europe. He saw growing prospects of a general war. That was being unduly pessimistic, August Junior objected.

"I know something about Germany, son," Bock said with heavy emphasis, "and Kaiser Wilhelm is an ambitious and restless leader, make no mistake about that. He wants more power and prestige for Germany in European affairs, and he'll stop at nothing to get them. You wait and see." He thrust his thick forefinger at his son. "And I'll tell you something else. The Kaiser doesn't like Russia. He's proven that many times; every time I go to Germany people tell me that."

Young August was well informed. "Papa, excuse me, but I think you're oversimplifying the issue. The Kaiser doesn't control Europe. There's a very complex balance of alliances to consider. It's true the Balkan squabbles seem to threaten that balance but I don't think the big powers will allow them to do that. The Treaty of London in May didn't solve things to everybody's satisfaction and Bulgaria started acting up again. But the peace-making talks are on again." He paused confidently. "And this time I think they'll work. The great powers just have too much at stake. They won't let the little fellows burn their soup for them."

Mrs. Bock had been listening to her men with a patrician frown. "I don't profess to know much about politics, my dear," she said as she refilled her husband's coffee cup, "but I can't agree that the Kaiser would ever lead Germany into a reckless course. We Germans have always been fortunate in having leaders whom we could trust and follow safely."

Bock Senior slowly sipped his coffee, then turned his massive face with a slight smile towards his wife. "Well, Mama, perhaps your feminine intuitions are more to be trusted than all this young whippersnapper's papers and journals. I hope you are both right," he rumbled amiably.

"There will be no general war, Papa, I'm confident of that. The big powers aren't fools. They know what damage modern weapons could do in a general war — to everybody." The underslung jaw tilted up, as it always did when young August knew he had silenced his opposition. He turned to Wilhelm. "Don't you agree, Rembrandt?"

Diplomatically, Wilhelm tried to straddle the fence between father and son, but his mind was elsewhere. Right now Wilhelm Fast was more concerned about a girl's finger sealing his lips than he was about the politicians' frenzied fistwaving in Europe.

2
Schoensee, Molochnaya, November, 1913

Wilhelm was in his third month of teaching at the Schoensee village school. The school had two classrooms; he taught the four lower classes in one while his senior colleague Martin Stobbe taught the three upper ones in the other.

Stobbe was an elderly, habitually morose bachelor whose tubercular pallor and rotting teeth caused the older boys to call him *Oolet Os,* Old Carrion, behind his back. His long thin figure curved in on itself as though trying to protect the bony cavity where his chest should have been. Even his hollow voice sounded cadaverous. Old Stobbe had a constant, phlegmy cough and his condition was obvious to everyone except him. He admitted only to hereditary chest weakness which made him, he said, liable to colds the year round. When it was cold or damp outside he kept a not very clean-looking handkerchief pressed to his mouth and long, sharp nose. Somewhere he had read about germs and saw legions of them all around, waiting to gain entrance to the besieged fortress of his throat and lungs.

Stobbe had long since lost interest in teaching and waited only for the day he could retire to his little cottage in the backyard of his brother's half-farm in Ladekopp. Old Stobbe had always wanted to farm rather than teach and only his fragile physical condition had forced him into a profession he despised and for which he was totally unsuited.

Wilhelm quickly saw that he would learn very little about the mysteries of teaching from his bored colleague. Fortunately, Jacob Priess had taken a teaching post in Fuerstenau, a few miles to the west. The two young teachers saw each other frequently to discuss preparation of lessons, teaching methods, and other things. Also, Jacob's senior colleague was an excellent teacher, enthusiastic and knowledgeable, who helped both of them in every way he could.

Once the excitement of the first few weeks had faded, Wilhelm knew his heart would never really be in teaching. Not this kind of teaching, at any rate. He had managed to avoid the forestry service, but he quailed at the thought of having to teach for the next five years. What would happen to him as an artist during that time? The same tedious routine year after year, until he would be as bored with it all as old Stobbe was. Already he felt trapped — and he had just started!

It wasn't that he didn't like his children. Mornings, as he surveyed the ruddy-cheeked, towheaded boys and rosy, braided girls standing before him in neat rows, sweetly singing the introductory hymn, he would feel proud, often elated, to be where he was. As the day wore on, however, he began to feel listless, felt himself withdrawing from his charges. He often finished the day's work depressed. Then felt guilty. He wanted to be a good teacher. He tried hard, but . . . .

He couldn't escape the feeling that his classroom with its whitewashed walls, its long wooden desks and benches with room for six pupils each, was really a prison cell to which he and his small prisoners were condemned for six long hours a day. He was the warden for thirty-eight little inmates ranging in age from seven to eleven.

Sometimes, as he waited for the children to finish their exercise, he would begin to sketch idly, almost cynically. Once he drew the classroom as an actual prison, the pupils as miniature convicts in striped prison garb, with leg irons chained to their desks, their faces pinched and empty and cowed. Another time he drew them as various wild animals in children's clothes, their sly, furred faces looking beleaguered, their slim, hard ankles also shackled. He never included himself in these sketches. He often drew to amuse his pupils, and they loved his sketches, especially the comical ones. But these private drawings he kept to himself. He thought the children would only be confused by them.

During lulls he could hear old Stobbe drone monotonously to the upper classes in the adjoining room. Stobbe, with his teaching motto of "Respect, fear, and love," with the emphasis, Wilhelm could hear him reedily intoning, on the first two. "Yaaah, Fast, Mennonite children are to be educated in the fear of the Lord, respect for their elders, and love for work and each other. If you pound" — "pound" was one of his favorite words — "those three things into them, you'll be a good teacher." It had apparently never occurred to Old Carrion that you couldn't "pound" love into a child. Wilhelm's contempt for his dour and insensitive colleague had grown to the point where he wondered how much longer he could stand living in the same house with him.

Sharing the little four-room teacherage with the old man was a constant source of irritation. Stobbe's domestic habits were as inflexible and deeply ingrained as his teaching methods. If in school he was a mindless martinet, at home he was a peevish old maid. At first they had shared their meals, but after Wilhelm had missed Stobbe's rigidly set mealtimes by a few minutes several times, the old man had surlily said that since they couldn't seem to agree on a common time for meals, they might both be better off if they cooked and ate separately. Wilhelm was glad to oblige. He preferred to be with his colleague as little as possible. Besides, Stobbe almost never deviated from a fixed menu: groats for breakfast, fried potatoes and ham for dinner, fried eggs and *bultje,* white bread, for supper. Every second weekend he brought his food supplies back with him from his brother's place in Ladekopp. And he would use up every scrap no matter how dry, hard, or rancid. Worst of all, the old man left behind in the kitchen a miasma of cooking odors, sour body smell, and foul breath that nothing could dispel.

Evenings they usually shared the small sitting room for awhile. After supper Stobbe took a short constitutional along the village street, but seldom stopped anywhere to chat or visit. Returning from his walk he would hang up his hat and cane in precisely the same way every evening, lower his emaciated frame with a mephitic sigh into his old armchair, and pick up his *Voice of Peace,* the twice weekly Mennonite Brethren German paper he deemed the only one fit for a Christian Mennonite to read. He was highly suspicious of the larger rival Mennonite paper *Messenger* and coldly disapproving of the secular *Odessa News,* both of which Wilhelm read regularly.

He was never quite sure whether old Stobbe was actually reading his paper or merely dozing behind it. At least the paper mercifully blocked the unbearable stink from his rotting teeth. Promptly at ten, Stobbe would lower his paper, yawn pointedly and rise to retire. He obviously disapproved of Wilhelm staying up later but had so far not actually raised the point. Wilhelm wondered how long the old bachelor spent on his bony knees in bedside prayers every night. He suspected it was a considerable time, judging by the belated creaking of his bed after he disappeared into his room.

It was after ten. There was no sound from Stobbe's room and Wilhelm guessed he was still at his devotions. Gusts of rain spattered the windows, and he was in a melancholy mood as he sat in the tiny room, the *Odessa News* spread out over his knees. It had been the same old story today. A burst of enthusiastic energy had carried him through the morning, then increasing ennui as the day wore on.

He stared glumly at the rain-darkened window. What was he doing here? He didn't belong here at all. He should be out in the world learning to be a painter. Instead he was playing nursemaid to farm children whose futures were inevitably set — the boys' sunburnt faces already wise in the lore of wind and weather, soil and animals, marking time until they too could be farmers. The girls, hair so tightly pulled back into braids they couldn't wrinkle their egg-shell foreheads if they tried, already dressed like matrons in their long print dresses and striped aprons, their lean flat little bodies waiting to swell with the certain destiny of home and children. Disdainful now of each other's sex, they were marked for coupling in the fertile feather beds, their unripe loins as destined for each other as the frozen earth of winter for the warm seeds of spring. Sow, grow, reap — what else was there in this world?

Not that they weren't lovable children. They were. Shy but friendly, in awe of the teacher, yet wanting to make human contact with him. Like tiny Greta Wiebe this morning during play period. Standing on the playground watching, he became aware of her edging, oh so gently, up to him until she was suddenly touching his leg — like a kitten wanting to be stroked, yet ready to flee at a rebuff.

And the art classes. If only he could have a free hand. He found it hard to accept that the curriculum allowed him only an hour a week for drawing. One hour a week! What could he do with that? Even if he skimped the weekly singing period, as he increasingly tended to do, it wasn't nearly enough. He couldn't even teach them fundamentals in the allotted time. And that ass of a Stobbe had actually asked him if he really needed all that time for "picture drawing"! It was the traditional Mennonite contempt for art as a "useless" activity. Would that attitude ever change?

He shook himself out of his gloomy reverie. Well, I've cooked myself a soup, now I'll have to spoon it up, he thought. I just hope it won't be a soup that'll choke me, as the Russian says.

He picked up his paper and turned to the "Letters" page. As he read the first letter he grew alert. It was a vicious attack on what the writer referred to as "the reactionary forces represented by the Mennonite leaders and men of wealth in the Molochnaya." He read the letter carefully, then reread it. It was harshly accusing and its tone dripped with irony as thick as sour cream.

Dear Editor:

Is it not fitting that in the very year we Russians are celebrating the tercentenary of our glorious monarchy, the reactionary forces represented by the Mennonite leaders and men of wealth in the Molochnaya are displaying their patriotism by (1) seeking permission to establish a seminary so they can spread their alien beliefs even more effectively; (2) opening another commercial school in Alexanderkrone in order to train young Mennonites in more efficient ways to exploit others, particularly their Russian fellow-citizens; and (3) paying hypocritical lip-service to their government while working zealously to make themselves ever more independent as a state within a state. Witness, for example, the disgusting spectacle of two Mennonite church elders proudly receiving medals and thanks from our beloved Tsar at the anniversary levee in Petersburg last February. There is Mennonite hypocrisy for you! Even the all-powerful Cornies in the last century refused to bow his neck to servilely accept medals and formal honors from the state.

The sooner these arrogant people of alien race and culture are brought to heel the better. Like parasites they have sucked themselves fat on the backs of the Russian peasant and worker.

And if war with Germany should come, where would their loyalties be?

Vox Populi

Wilhelm read the letter a third time just to be sure. The "Voice of the People" was his brother Nikolai. He recognized Kolya's ideas and style only too well. The letter was written with an insider's knowledge of the settlement. It could hardly have been written by a non-Mennonite. Kolya's black hatred for his own people was frightening. Where did it come from? From sullen boyhood Nikolai had grown to surly and rebellious adolescence, then to open, adult defiance and hostility towards everything Christian and Mennonite.

Had there ever been a blacker sheep in the Mennonite fold? After Kolya's disastrous first year at Halbstadt Central School Father had kept him home for a year and forced him to work like a common field hand. Kolya retaliated by idling away his spare time with hard-eyed Russian lads from a nearby village. But towards the end of the summer he suddenly changed his habits completely, stayed home, started studying on his own. Then he did something he had never done before: he begged, literally *begged* Father to let him go back to school. Father was so surprised he said yes, but only on the condition that Kolya would not repeat his first performance in Halbstadt. And he hadn't. He had finished Central School with better than average grades, although he still kept to himself as much as possible and conformed only as much as he had to.

Nikolai's long-range plan had become clear. He wanted to go to a private technical high school in Berdjansk, the one that had been founded there by the late Mennonite educator A. A. Neufeld. Again Father had surprised himself and the rest of the family by agreeing. Wilhelm had not been surprised that Kolya, removed at last from the Mennonite society he hated, had done quite well in Berdjansk. Their parents were pleased, although uneasy at having their wayward son so far from home.

They would have been more than uneasy if they had known that Kolya was getting a second, informal education in radical politics from some of his non-Mennonite classmates and from friends he made out of school. As Wilhelm had discovered later, Nikolai had never had any real intention of reforming according to his parents' wishes. He had gone back to school as the quickest and best way of setting himself free from parental control and a Mennonite environment. Kolya had graduated around the time Wilhelm got back from his year in Petersburg. He had found a clerical position in Berdjansk, a position about which he was characteristically vague when he came home for a rare — and brief — visit that summer. As far as their parents were concerned, Kolya was at last showing signs of reforming, although they did not like to see him living in Berdjansk on his own. But at least they now had some hope for him.

Wilhelm knew better, but could not bring himself to tell his parents. As always, Kolya was close-lipped about his personal affairs, but he dropped a few hints which enabled Wilhelm to piece together certain things. There was no doubt that his brother was steeped in revolutionary politics, perhaps even in revolutionary activities, God forbid. Wilhelm suspected that even his "clerical" job had something to do with "the worker's cause," as he called it.

A hopeless, self-defeating mixture of wild ideals and violent hatred, that's my brother Nikolai, Wilhelm sighed, and reached for a piece of paper. He tried to keep his letter restrained but to the point.

My Dear Kolya,

The "Voice of the People" in the *Odessa News* is too full of anger and spite to be a convincing spokesman for truth and justice. What blind fanaticism drives you to make such charges? From a few grains of truth you raise a vindictive harvest of accusations.

All my life, dear brother, I've tried to understand you, to see if I could justify your strange views and odd behavior. The ideas and ideals you profess are all twisted and warped by your ugly prejudices and destructive passions. You have already spat on everything our people stand for. Now you want to destroy them too, grind them into the ground like vermin. Why, Kolya, why? To uphold the "principles of freedom and justice" you are so proud of?

Oh, Kolya, Kolya, I can't believe it has to be this way. I mean, you turning on us so savagely, as though we have all betrayed you and must now be punishcd. Think of the suffering you have already caused our parents. Do you want to expose them to public shame too? What if you should be arrested and tried as an enemy of the state? Have you considered all those consequences?

I just hope and pray, dear Kolya, that no one else will guess the identity of "Vox Populi."

If you should ever want to talk things over, let me know. You will always be my brother, regardless.

In God's name, Kolya, come to your senses!

With love,
Vasya

Wilhelm studied his letter for a long time. Would it have the right effect — or any effect at all? Would Kolya at least feel in it the concern of a loving brother, or would it antagonize him even more?

He blew out the lamp and went to bed sad and perplexed. His brother's bitter denunciation of his people stuck in Wilhelm's throat like a bone. It was unfair and slanderous of course, but . . . He listened to old Stobbe's rasping cough coming muffled through the wall, his mind groping for something. No, he didn't agree with Kolya's charges, but his moral passion — yes, that was it, the moral passion — that was real, he had to admit. He could almost admire — even envy — his strange brother for the depth of his feelings. He really cared. If only he weren't so wrong-headed and vengeful. He grimaced to himself in the darkness. But Kolya was also shrewd. One couldn't take that away from him.

3

Nikolai Fast poured himself a large vodka and in the Russian manner downed it in one swallow. He proceeded to read his brother's admonishing letter with little snorts of contempt. Noble Willie, playing the role of concerned older brother. Smug bastard! Telling him to come to his senses. "What the hell do you know about anything, big brother?" he muttered to himself. Well, at least Vasya had guessed who wrote the letter. He wasn't completely stupid. You should talk dear brother (already he was composing a letter of rebuttal in his mind) about "ugly prejudices" and "destructive passions!" Sure, you've always played it cool, haven't you? Said all the right things at home, made people think you were with them when in fact you didn't give a damn about them. Don't preach to me about our people and what they stand for, you hypocrite. You don't care any more about "our people" than I do. You just haven't got the guts to let go, that's all. It's so much easier to keep wearing that safe Mennonite disguise, isn't it? Pretending you're still one of them, smiling inside your Mennonite skin while you're plotting how to use them, feed off them, and have them admiring and respecting you for it. Oh, Willie, you're easy to see through! Your trouble is you believe in nothing. You hear that, Mr. high and mighty Rembrandt? In *nothing,* not even yourself. You're a smiling, charming cynic. But not a nihilist. You haven't the energy or will even to want to destroy what you no longer believe in. You're not even a Rudin. At least Turgenev's talking fool of an intellectual did finally sacrifice himself on the barricades, even if it was a futile gesture. But you, Vasya? You're just an empty hypocrite. Even your attempts to be an artist are all sham and pretense. You have about as much of the real artist in you as a bourgeois school girl dabbling in water colors. Pretty pictures! I spit on your pretty pictures, dear brother. What do you know about real life, real people? You and your spoiled Clara Bock? And her brother, that oily serpent. I know about him too. He's even more contemptible and decadent than you are, but you two have one thing in common. You're both parasites waiting to suck on your father's inheritance. But remember, Willie, no matter how hard you suck you'll never fill up the hollow space inside you. Oh yeah, in the end you'll be a good Mennonite farmer. Better still, if you marry your little Bock you'll be an instantly made industrialist in a dark suit with a big gold chain across your well-fed guts. You'll forget all about your painting then, you'll be too busy being another big ram butting the Russian workers into place in the factory. Ah, yes, that's the future I see for you, my noble, self-righteous brother. Those are your precious Mennonite ways, your Mennonite Christianity!

Nikolai, pouring himself yet another vodka, was strongly tempted to set his mental diatribe down in a letter. But finally decided not to, as he knocked back the last of his vodka. No. Willie could never take that much truth about himself. A Rudin only talked, he never listened.

He sat there in his small room by the open window, letting the evening street noises filter unheard through his ears. He felt his eyes brimming after awhile and wondered whether it was the vodka or his rage at his brother's letter.

He turned finally to his scarred little desk and with quick, slashing strokes wrote a short, curt answer to his brother's letter.

4

"Jacob, it's about my brother Nikolai. I'm worried sick about him, but I can't tell my parents. I — there's only you" — Wilhelm was tense as he faced Jacob in his rented room in Fuerstenau.

"Is he in trouble?" Alarm showed in Jacob's gentle face.

"No, not yet — at least not that I know. But I do know he's playing with fire in Berdjansk. He's involved in radical politics. I haven't told you before because I wasn't sure. But now — here, read this, it speaks for itself." He drew out of his pocket the letter from the *Odessa News.* Jacob seldom read the paper and had almost certainly not seen the letter.

Jacob read the letter carefully while Wilhelm waited nervously. He handed it back with a shocked expression.

"Kolya making such bitter charges? He's always been a little — well, different — but how could a boy raised in a Christian Mennonite home come to such twisted, godless views? Are you sure it's him?"

"I'm sure, Jacob. I wrote him immediately when I saw this — you know, a letter expressing a brother's concern. Well, today I got this. Listen.

'Dear Brother,

You have sharp eyes and you're a good guesser. If only you had a character and a set of convictions to match your brain!

Well, Vasya, you and I must go our separate ways. My way leads —hopefully — to a new and better future for all Russians. Your way leads from an over-privileged past to a dead-end future — in other words, *no* future.

And when in God's name will *you* come to your senses, Vasya?'

It's signed 'Vox Populi.' "

"Does anyone else know who Vox Populi is?"

"I hope not. My parents certainly wouldn't guess even if they had read the letter, which is not likely."

"That's something to be thankful for —"

"Yes, of course, Jacob, but what's to be done with this young madman? He's a *revolutionary!* What if he does something — some act of terrorism — and gets arrested? What can I do to bring him to his senses before something happens to him?"

Jacob had never seen Wilhelm so distressed. But he felt helpless. He couldn't think of any practical advice to give. And the consoling words that rose in his mind would, he feared, sound trite. Wilhelm's concern was too urgent, his anguish too real. Jacob longed to express comfort directly from the heart, in prayer, on their knees together, but he was hesitant. He knew how Willie felt about such a personal outpouring of spiritual emotion. Embarrassed, he would withdraw into cold reserve. Jacob longed to console, but not at the risk of offending. Erdmann Lepp would know what to say, what to do. Jacob didn't. Helplessly, in mute love and sympathy, he rose and pressed his arm around his friend's shoulder.

Wilhelm looked up gratefully, his eyes full of tears. "He's crazy, but he's my brother and I love him," he whispered brokenly.

"Perhaps if someone like Oom Lepp talked to him — I happen to know he's going to Berdjansk later this month."

"No, Jacob, I'm afraid it's too late for anything like that. Besides, a long time ago when Kolya was just a boy he got very angry at Oom Lepp, said cruel things to him. He's hated him ever since — as he seems to hate most people," Wilhelm added, a tremor passing through him.

They continued to sit in the darkening room, Wilhelm drawing comfort from Jacob's warm, still presence. He was thankful for his friend's tact, the delicate reserve that offered the gift of silent compassion instead of solicitous advice. Jacob's love and loyalty were palpable. They required no words.

In the darkness, Wilhelm saddled his stall-relaxed bay Major for the ride home. As Jacob passed the cinch strap to him under the horses's warm belly their fingers fumbled together warmly for a moment and Wilhelm thought again how lucky he was to have Jacob as his friend.

Outside, under a pale sliver of moon in a darkly tumbling sky, Wilhelm swung into the saddle, spoke a low "*Aufwiedersehn,* my friend" and left. Jacob walked to the front gate and watched Wilhelm slowly move down the street in the direction of Schoensee. He seemed to sit his horse listlessly, as if he didn't care how long it would take to cover the three miles home.

In the brisk November night air Wilhelm felt somewhat revived. He was not sorry for having unburdened himself to Jacob. Jacob's intense, unreserved brotherliness was like a soothing massage. He knew his deeply religious friend would have liked to express his consolation more directly in scripture-reading and spontaneous prayer. Good old Jacob! His steadfast piety, which might have seemed strident in a less sensitive nature, was part of his quiet charm, made you want to bask in the warmth of his being.

Why couldn't there be more people like Jacob Priess in this world?

He thought of the two people who were causing him pain right now: Kolya and Clara. The same mail that had brought Nikolai's brusque, alienating note had also brought a long, affectionate letter from Clara. She wrote often, spontaneously, as though nothing had changed between them. She seemed to be trying to preserve their relationship as it had started — with a warm but innocent comradeliness. Didn't that show a degree of insensitivity in her, a willful blindness that made her seem shallow? In a museum once he had seen insects perfectly preserved in amber. Dead insects in transparent tombs. Is that how she had entombed their love when she gently sealed his lips at Selenaya?

Enough. Worrying about Kolya was making him morbid. He urged Major into a brisk gallop. Ahead was the tiny hamlet of Fabrikerwiese, which lay between Fuerstenau and Schoensee. Its handful of farmsteads silent and asleep in the darkness. There was not a stir or movement in the yards and not a single lighted window. The darkened farmsteads told him it was after ten, the traditional hour for rural families to retire.

He glanced up at the slice of lemon moon garnishing a salad of dark clouds. He was beginning to feel chilled from the raw autumn wind.

He welcomed the protection afforded on the far side of the hamlet by the avenue of giant poplars that ran the remaining mile to Schoensee. In summer the high, century-old poplars flung a thick green canopy over the road — from a distance it looked like a shimmering tunnel. Now, in mid-November, the tunnel was broken and gaping where wind and rain had torn away its dying leaves. A remnant of dry leaves still clinging to black limbs overhead rustled like showers of coins. But the dark trunks stood massively soaring, unaffected by wind or weather.

Major, as though aware of the sheltering trees, slowed down to a bare canter as they entered the avenue. Wilhelm was thinking now only of his warm bed and the blessed relief of sleep.

He felt rather than saw the dark shapes detaching themselves from the thick shadows on both sides of the road. Two riders glided out swiftly and met on the road, like a gate sliding shut. He was cut off.

"*Stoi!*" — from the left.

"Hands up, *njemets!*" — from the right.

Even in the dark he could tell they were mere boys — peasant boys a little unsteady in their saddles. Perhaps a little drunk. Their faces were indistinct under their peaked caps, but he could tell they were nervous. He caught the glint of a knife on one side, the outline of a cudgel on the other. He sensed they had no guns.

"Hand over your money and your watch," grated the one with the knife.

"And then get the hell off your horse," added the other, his voice sounding thick.

They still stood clear, making no move to grab Major's bridle. The instant he moved his hand down to his pocket he knew he would not obey. He let out a wild yell, slapped Major's rump, then threw his arms up for protection as the big horse sprang forward, catching the two boys off guard.

Major's sudden spring bulled aside the two horses. The knife-wielder twisted sideways and slashed out wildly. Wilhelm felt a searing tear in his thigh. The next instant the cudgel crashed heavily against his raised upper arm.

Then he was clear. He bent low, urging Major on with slaps and urgent commands, waiting for shots to crash. The well-rested bay knew he was homeward bound. He flew.

Wilhelm felt his panic subsiding. The drum of hoofbeats behind him was not getting louder. He knew they would not catch him and he was sure now they had no guns.

In what seemed no time at all he was passing the first farmstead of Schoensee. He glanced back. There was no sign of his assailants.

He was safe. Thank God, he had escaped! His right arm was throbbing numbly. He hoped it wasn't broken. He felt for the gash on his thigh and drew away wet fingers.

Old Stobbe would not be happy to be roused out of bed. But there was no doctor in the village and he knew he needed attention.

Dejection hemmed him in like a tightening net. What was happening to his world? A world that had seemed so inviting, so secure, so promising. A brother drunk with hatred, intent on bringing ruin to his own house; the girl he loved lost to him behind walls of snobbish wealth; he himself condemned to an isolated prison that was stifling his talent and wearing down his spirit.

And now this. To experience the savagery of violence on a peaceful Mennonite country road.

Feeling weak and light-headed, he guided Major into the bleak emptiness of the schoolyard.

Part II
The Great Commission of
Erdmann Lepp

CHAPTER THIRTEEN

All his life Erdmann Lepp had known himself as set apart from others, as consecrated to a sacred destiny. Like Samuel he was called early. Unlike Samuel he was never in any doubt as to who had done the calling. He was a vessel of the Lord. Now and always. As a small boy he had listened eagerly, had believed absolutely, as his mother told him over and over like a litany that he would someday do great things in the service of the Lord. Rapturously, she would remind him that he had been born on the sacred day —January 6, 1860 — that the revered founding fathers of the Mennonite Brethren Church, eighteen of them, had written their courageous, blazing letter of secession and independence, amidst day-long prayers, to the stony authorities of the Old Church. Yes, his birth was forever intertwined with that of the church he loved.

Not that he had ever shown any vanity over his unique role in the divine plan. Oh no. He never thought of himself as in any way superior to those around him. Only as different. As personally marked by the warm finger of the Almighty. Egotism and selfishness were equally foreign to his austere nature. His special feeling about himself had nothing to do with ego or consciousness of self-worth. It was based entirely on his view of service, service to God and His human creatures.

Lepp even took his considerable personal gifts for granted. He possessed them, they possessed him. God had lent them to him so that he, Erdmann Lepp, could help carry on the Great Commission in the tradition of the consecrated Christian servants who had gone before him. One man who influenced him directly was Johann Wieler, the first Mennonite Brethren minister to become a missionary among the Russian people. But it was the great preacher and poet Bernhard Harder who became his friend and mentor, who had the most lasting influence on him.

Like Harder, Erdmann Lepp was a native of Halbstadt, but there the similarity ended. Harder had come from a poor, humble family, the second youngest of nine children. The Lepp family was well placed on both sides. Erdmann's father rose to become chief secretary of the Halbstadt District Office, a position of considerable power and prestige. His mother came from one of the more prominent families in the Molochnaya, and was a remarkable woman in every respect. She was known for her intense piety and for her devotion to the Mennonite Brethren movement, in which she was as active as a woman was permitted to be.

Endowed with a good mind, an abundance of energy and ambition, she was in fact a woman who in a more open, more sophisticated society would have distinguished herself in her own right. As it was, she accepted her circumscribed lot with equanimity and concentrated her fine perceptions and creative vitality on the rearing of her gifted and only son. Her three daughters, all older, had inherited the cool, placid nature of their father Andreas Lepp, and neither needed nor wanted the constant attention she lavished on her remarkable little Erdmann.

He was a pale, slight lad with curly black hair and eyes in whose darkly limpid depths there was something that fascinated not only other children but adults as well. The slightly hooded lids even then added an enigmatic touch to his expression. His grave demeanor and graceful bearing were striking in a mere child. Never boisterous nor unruly like other boys, he was precociously self-possessed and deliberate in everything he said and did. He never seemed to get excited and seldom laughed or cried. He had a very early memory of shedding slow, heavy tears the day his favorite cat Felix was crushed under a ladder wagon full of harvest sheaves. And there was that terrible time his grandfather had frightened him with a story and he sobbed until he thought he would choke. As for laughing, only the Russian maid Anyushka, whom he adored shyly for her madcap Slavic nature, could sometimes coax delighted shrieks from him with her droll, outrageous folk tales. But he never let himself go like that with anyone else.

The solitary boy found his real world in books. He was fortunate to find such a world at a time when most Mennonite families owned no more than a German bible and perhaps a devotional book or two such as Menno Simons' *Foundation of Christian Ethics* and van Braght's *Martyrs Mirror*. The boy Erdmann eagerly devoured Jung-Stilling's popular mystical novel *Das Heimweh* and Schabaelje's *Wandering Soul,* which contained lengthy dialogues with such biblical heroes as Adam and Moses. He also found a German translation of Milton's *Paradise Lost,* which bored him, and of Bunyan's *Pilgrim's Progress,* which he liked. Father Lepp also owned a richly bound, three-volume edition of Fritz Reuter's *During My Apprenticeship.* The books were in Low German and very funny, but the boy never really warmed to them. They didn't seem to go anywhere, stayed on the earth, when all he wanted was to soar to spiritual realms.

That is what the *Martyrs Mirror* inspired him to do again and again. He read and reread the ghastly accounts of early Anabaptist martyrs who in their thousands were whipped, gouged, torn apart, smothered, buried alive, crucified, stoned, beheaded, drowned from boats, and burned to cinders for their faith, with horror and outrage that such terrible things could be done to true believers. But always his thrills of horror changed to surging jubilance as he saw how the true believers bore torture and death with their joy and faith shining like a golden nimbus high over the dark heads of their wicked tormentors.

But his favorite book of all was the Bible. Almost daily he returned to the stunningly dramatic world of the Old Testament. Best of all he loved the fearless old prophets — Samuel, Elijah, Elisha, Ezekiel, and Daniel. He sat immobile for hours under a tree in the orchard, reading and day-dreaming with a worn, heavy Bible spread out on his spindly thighs. His imagination leaped with the mighty exploits of his biblical heroes and fell to earth when they suffered pain and defeat. The awsome visions of Ezekiel and Daniel took possession of him until the real world seemed drab and unimportant. At such times he walked around with an expression of such transfigured gravity that even his mother was afraid to approach him.

His pensive, abstracted nature was accepted as saintly by the members of his family: they left him undisturbed for long periods, especially in summer when there was no school. The three placid sisters never doubted that their solemn little brother would grow up to do wondrous things for God and the church. The story of the boy Jesus sternly telling his family he must be about his Father's business was always in their minds when they looked at little Erdmann. They were struck dumb with pride and awe on those special occasions when the boy saw fit to emerge from his inner world to preach hot little play sermons in the orchard shade to them and their friends.

But the strange, self-contained lad who seldom laughed or cried had lodged within him, like an animal ready to spring, a terrible, guilty secret. His terror of that beast within — a terror he revealed to no one — was of a recurring nightmare which often made him cry out at night and left him pale and shaken in the morning.

And more withdrawn than ever.

It had all begun innocently enough. Once, when he was about six, his Grandpapa Hiebert, who lived in Gnadenfeld, had told him a fascinating story about the pagan Nogaies who had lived on the Molochnaya steppe when the first Mennonites came. Grandpapa Hiebert, big and grave and unhurried, was a natural storyteller with his rich voice and slow way of talking. Little Erdmann was transfixed by his vivid description of the fierce, small brown Tatars who flashed around the creaking, travel-stained Mennonite wagons like bolts of lightning on their swift, agile horses. Long greasy hair flying, feral eyes catching the waning light, they hurled their bunched horses at the wagons as though to crash right through them. All the while giving sharp yelps of outrage and making menacing gestures with sinewy arms sticking out from the short thick fur jackets they wore even in summer.

When the wagons finally stopped and the unloading began the swarthy Nogaies, in an ecstasy of rage, swirled in a black and brown vortex of thundering hooves and streaming manes round and round the stolid ring of covered wagons. The ferocious little riders cracked their whips like rippling serpents over the black-hatted, short-vested Mennonite men and boys who were straining and heaving their boxes and trunks off the wagons before sundown. But the exploding whips never touched even a hat brim, and the hollow-eyed immigrants seemed to sense that no blow would fall, no blood spurt. The short bows slung over shoulders, the wicked-looking knives and stubby swords dangling over bare dusky flanks, remained untouched and sheathed. But the women and children sat riveted with terror inside the wagons as the flood of heathen riders boiled around them.

So it had been when their people first came to the Molochnaya from faraway Prussia, Grandpapa said in his slow voice. Erdmann could see and feel it all just as Grandpapa told it. His pale skin shone and he trembled with delicious horror.

Then, just when the story seemed to be coming to a happy ending Grandpapa Hiebert told about the really horrible thing the heathen Nogaies had done. It was so cruel and wicked it took his breath away. One night some Nogaies had been caught trying to steal horses. They were soundly beaten and let go. A few days later Nogai horsemen surprised four Mennonite men who were out on the open steppe surveying more land for farming. All four were savagely butchered right there in the high grass. Grandpapa described the mutilated bodies as he had seen them when they were brought back. One of the murdered men had been Grandpapa's own papa, Erdmann's great-grandfather on his mother's side.

The boy was sick with shock. He had already decided, as he listened to the first part of the story, that it was God who had stayed the hands of the little heathens. They had not been allowed to hurt the peaceful new settlers. And then to be told that his own great-grandfather had been hacked to pieces by the fiendish monsters. They had dared to disobey God! He could not begin to imagine such a wicked sin. They had, of course, gone straight to Hell, those godless fiends. God would torture them for all eternity (which was much longer than long). He could see and smell them burning, their brown skins crackling and smoking, just like the ham that had once fallen into their oven fire and that Papa had finally pulled out all sizzling and smudged, its charred skin criss-crossed with smoke-oozing cracks.

The more he thought about the monstrous sin the Nogaies had committed, the more agitated he became. Grandpapa tried to soothe him and calm him down. But Erdmann got hysterical and sobbed and sobbed in uncontrollable spasms until he was racked with hiccups and his mother, close to hysterics herself, rocked him against her bosom like a baby. Gently, she shook some Haarlemer drops down his spasmodic throat and rocked him some more until, still shuddering weakly, he finally fell asleep against her shoulder.

That night the terrible nightmare came for the first time. At first he saw himself just watching with quiet satisfaction as the Nogaies burned and yelled with pain. He knew right away it was Hell. It was a very hot, noisy, orange-and-red place where nothing grew and there were no houses, only glowing rocks. Smoke came out of white-hot rocks and bright red devils with long, pointed teeth were walking around jabbing at the burning people with long pitchforks and laughing fiendishly. But then the terrible noise and searing heat moved closer and closer and he suddenly realized he was standing in Hell too, not just looking at it. Now there was nowhere for him to walk without burning his bare feet, and he couldn't breathe the fiery air.

In his agony he turned and saw the grinning devils coming towards him too; in a frenzy of terror he skipped over the bubbling, boiling stones until he finally reached a dense cloud of smoke and lost his pursuers. But now he couldn't see anything and felt himself choking, unable to breathe.

He woke up coughing and sputtering, his drooling mouth and nose pressed deep into his pillow. But he stifled the scream that rose in his burning throat because he knew it would bring his mother. He quaked and sweated under his thick quilt, but did not cry out; he did not even whimper. He just lay there trembling, his mind aflame with Hell.

The nightmare came back many times, always with gruesome refinements that convulsed him into a tight ball of quivering fright. As he got older, the dream came less often, but each time it was more frightening. Over and over he wished his Grandpapa had never told him about the fiendish Nogaies. He despaired of ever getting rid of them and the red devils of Hell.

When he was twelve, Erdmann went with his parents to hear the well-known revivalist Bernhard Harder. From the moment the mighty voice rolled over the congregation the boy was spellbound. That relentless voice stripped bare his quivering soul — those sharp accusations of hidden sins, those scathing revelations of guilt, those cajoling, whispered pleas for repentance. Then, when he thought he could not bear it a moment longer, came the mighty, ringing promise that purged and lifted him beyond anything he had ever known.

He found himself kneeling gratefully under the great man's uplifted hand, feeling the love and peace of the Lord Jesus Christ flooding his heart and soul, bearing him up far above this world until he was sure he would stay up there forever. In words that might have been uttered by an angel, he promised Jesus he would devote his life to Him. Only then did he dare to look up into the lustrous eyes and shining countenance of Onkel Harder, and knew that from this moment he was committed, a child no longer but come to man's estate like the boy Jesus taking his place with the wise men in the temple.

With his conversion and baptism the evil nightmare disappeared as if wiped away by a gentle hand. By the time he entered Halbstadt Central School as a tall, skinny lad of thirteen, his guilty secret was a mere ghost of a memory that occasionally flitted through his mind as he relaxed into sleep. He no longer worried about it. He was now safely in God's hands.

And then with terrifying suddenness one night the dream came back —only ten times worse! This time it not only frightened him but filled him with such self-loathing guilt that for the first time in his blameless young life the thought of suicide came to him. As before, the dream began with the accursed devils screaming vileness and prodding their broiling Nogai victims in the suffocating confines of the flaming, rocky pit of Hell.

Then suddenly the dream changed character, turning into something quite different from the familiar horrors of before. This time the cackling, gruesome red devils were suddenly joined by the tortured Nogaies themselves to form a wall of writhing, thrusting, naked bodies all around him. He looked down and saw shrieking female devils and witches, bared and shameless, rolling wildly on the smoldering floor, making lewd gestures to the male devils and to him. As he watched in horrified fascination the crazed females started doing things with the male devils, loathsome, obscene things he had never even dared to imagine. As he stood there, groaning, heaving, straining red flesh all around him, a plump, frog-white hag leered up at him and tried to pull him down on top of her gaping organs. He began to scream. No, no, no, I won't — and braced himself on the scorching rock, and then he felt the excruciating pain of the red-hot tines boring into his back and flanks as the devils tried to push him down to the sprawling hag. And then he felt something even more grotesque happening. He looked down at himself and saw that he too was naked and that there was a monstrous hard man-root rising grossly from his own innocent loins. In a panic of revulsion and shame he clawed at the terrible beast that had attached itself to his flesh and wouldn't let go. In a final burst of desperation he grasped the repulsive thing in both hands and pulled frantically while the depraved faces danced and bobbed around him glee-fully and the revolting females flaunted their secret parts ever more shame-lessly and tried to touch the red monster under his belly that he was futilely trying to extract. And suddenly a blinding shower of liquid fire engulfed him and the wild figures around him, and he felt himself yanked savagely off his feet and borne up and up through lurid flames and dense clouds. All at once he could breathe again and found himself in a small bare room he didn't recognize.

He was awake, lying perfectly still, trying to get his bearings. A wave of misery and shame flushed through him as he realized that his hands, wetly defiled, were cupped around his spent loins. The shame of his vile secret was too awful to think about. No one must ever know what had happened to him.

But Erdmann knew that God knew. Every day he spent hours on his knees — beside his bed, in the wood, on the river bank — beseeching God to lift the terrible curse of the unspeakable nightmare with its accompanying shameful physical pollution. But the nightmare kept returning at such regular intervals that he knew God must either have abandoned him completely or was continuing to punish him for reasons known only to Him. For awhile he saw himself as a disgraceful backslider, and that perhaps even his conversion two years earlier had been a sham, an abominable act of self-deception, a sacrilege against the Lord. He went through spiritual agonies that left him limp with exhaustion and full of despair.

As the weeks and months went by, he kept reading his Bible feverishly, concentrating now on the life-giving Gospels. Gradually his shame and despair wore away, and he felt himself reaching firmer spiritual ground again. He fervently rededicated his soul to Jesus and promised to devote himself to a lifetime of tireless, self-sacrificing service to the unsaved hordes of Russia. If only the Almighty would see fit to lift this utterly mortifying spiritual and physical shame from him, so that he would never again dream of the filthy Nogaies and the other demons in Hell, especially the depraved female demons.

And his passionate prayers were answered. His nocturnal plague came less frequently and finally stopped altogether. With God's help he had won! He had survived a hard spiritual test. Like Christ in the desert he had been toughened through ordeal. He felt stronger than ever. He was convinced that nothing ever again would be as humiliating and threatening to him as that satanic nightmare.

Young Lepp proved to be a brilliant student at Halbstadt. His superior abilities were recognized early by the better teachers in school. The gifted young P. M. Friesen, who taught Russian language and history, soon took him under his wing. Lepp was also inspired by the dynamic teaching of Johann Wieler, who a few years later was to become a fearless but ill-fated missionary. Even the older teachers agreed that they could not remember a more promising student in the school.

When Erdmann graduated from the Central School in 1878 he was admitted, along with eleven other candidates, to the new two-year pedagogy course which had finally been established in the school after years of planning and debate. He continued to do well in his studies, although he had no strong desire to become a teacher. But he knew that his best chance — perhaps his only chance — to have the missionary career he coveted was to prove himself as a teacher first.

That summer, just before he began his teaching course, he got to know the man who would become his mentor. That man was Bernhard Harder, the great preacher who had brought him to the Lord when he was twelve, and whose ministry had been an inspiration to him ever since. Erdmann understood at once that by bringing them together, God was letting him know that He wanted his young servant to follow in the footsteps of the renowned Molochnaya *reiseprediger*.

But God could hardly have chosen a more mundane and demeaning way for "Oom Bernd" to enter Erdmann's life. It filled him with indignation. His father came home one day and shocked him almost speechless by announcing that he had hired Bernhard Harder as an assistant in his office. Bernhard Harder the great man of God? Yes, the same. It seemed that the *reiseprediger* had fallen on hard times. After serving for years as a privately subsidized traveling evangelist, Harder's financial support had been suddenly withdrawn by his friends and supporters. With a large family to feed, he once again had to earn his livelihood as a teacher at Alexanderwohl. Now he had lost even that job and was forced to go back to the vocation he had started in as secretary in the *volost* office. Erdmann could not believe that this dedicated man of God, after all his years of inspired service to his people, could be brought so low in worldly estate, and seemingly treated with such callous neglect by the very people whom he had lifted up towards God in a thousand gripping sermons.

Nevertheless, Erdmann was eager to get to know Oom Bernd. Soon he was spending most of his spare time in the *volost* office, where Harder's duties were light enough to give him ample time to chat with the intense young Lepp. The two settled into the roles of master and disciple as though predestined to them. Under Oom Bernd's hearty, convivial guidance, Erdmann embarked on an ambitious program of devotional and theological reading. The extra reading and the lengthy discussions with his mentor did not affect the youth's regular studies adversely. Erdmann's father took secret pride in the attention Oom Bernd lavished on his son. He kept Harder's secretarial work unburdensome and treated him not only as an equal but with conscious deference. Oom Bernd's son Peter, a lively, sensitive lad of eleven, sometimes came to the office after school to see his father. Erdmann liked the boy, and envied him for being the great man's son. In October, after a lengthy illness, Mrs. Harder died and Erdmann did not see much of Oom Bernd for awhile.

Bernhard Harder had made it clear when he started that he regarded his secretarial post in the *volost* office as temporary employment. When he remarried the next year he was ready for a change. Shortly after Erdmann graduated from his pedagogy course (at the head of his class) in May, 1880, Oom Bernd announced one day that he had accepted an offer to teach religion at the Halbstadt Central School for the coming year. Erdmann was happy that his friend was on the rise once more, even though he would be seeing less of him from now on.

That September Erdmann began his own teaching career in Ohrloff. It was considered one of the best schools in the colony and Erdmann got the position mainly because of his brilliant scholastic record. He rose to the challenge of teaching with the easy confidence characteristic of him, but without the hearty enthusiasm expected of young teachers. The men in charge of school affairs in Ohrloff watched him with a growing sense of disappointment. Had the young teacher not done such a fine job with religious instruction, he would probably not have had his contract renewed for a second year.

In the summer of 1882 young Lepp was invited by Oom Bernd to accompany him on a trip to St. Petersburg. The colony was sending Harder to the capital to iron out some technical problems for a group of Prussian Mennonites who had emigrated to Russia several years before. Oom Bernd wanted Erdmann along as his secretary and traveling companion. The young teacher accepted eagerly. The prospect of spending several weeks in the exclusive company of his idol was exciting enough in itself. It would also be his first opportunity to go on an extended train trip and to see Moscow and the great Russian capital of Petersburg.

The trip proved to be everything he expected and more. Once the novelty of traveling by train had worn off, Erdmann and Oom Bernd immersed themselves in religious discussions. For hours that seemed to pass like minutes Erdmann was happily oblivious to the people around them and to the kaleidoscopic landscape flowing past their window. They made quick, simple meals with the bread, *wurst* and cold boiled potatoes they had brought in generous amounts. From the hot water provided for passengers they made tea, which Oom Bernd consumed till sweat beaded his brow. The train stopped frequently at both big and small stations where stout women in babushkas and their apple-cheeked daughters held up for sale crisply roasted chickens and pots of warm milk glazed with thick, yellow cream-skins. Only the more affluent passengers bought food from the peasant women. The rest had brought food with them, as there was none available on the train.

Except for the brief catnaps Oom Bernd took after his heavy meals, they talked all the way to Kharkov. He also insisted on getting — or trying to get — a full night's sleep on the hard, swaying seats. As for Erdmann, he would gladly have talked the nights through too. The second day they reached the city of Kursk, followed at intervals the younger man scarcely noticed by Orel, Tula, and finally Mother Moscow herself. In Moscow they changed trains for Petersburg. Another very long day of travel through seemingly endless northern tracts of sombre evergreens and graceful birch groves interspersed with small villages, their double rows of tiny *izby,* log cabins, looking lost and forlorn in the surrounding immensity, brought them to the capital at last.

And through it all they had talked and talked. For hours they followed the mystical mazes of Jung-Stilling's millenialism in his allegorical novel *Heimweh* and other books. In a general way, they agreed, the Book of Revelations did seem to indicate that Christ's Second Coming would be followed by a peaceful, thousand-year reign before the final destruction of the earth. In *Heimweh* the hero, Eugenius, after much wandering and searching finally discovered the "open door" and "place of refuge in the East, somewhere south of Samarkand." There, near the Aral Sea, he founded an oriental theocracy as a refuge from the Antichrist while waiting for the Second Coming.

Heimweh had become almost a second Bible for many Mennonites, Oom Bernd said. He himself had first read it when he was still at school and had been greatly excited by it. Later, he had become a strong supporter of the Mennonite movement in Russia to find a "place of refuge" in central Asia, preferably in Turkestan. In fact, in 1867 he had been sent to Petersburg to explore the possibilities of a mass Mennonite migration to Turkestan. But nothing had come of that. In the seventies the government had shown its good will on the conscription issue by allowing young Mennonite men to serve out their time in alternative service. That generous compromise had so impressed Harder that he began to doubt the truth of the millenialists' belief that the West was corrupt and the place where the Antichrist would appear, and that only the East, associated with the Holy Land, offered a haven for God's Chosen.

"As I became more familiar with our own Anabaptist fathers," Oom Bernd continued, "I discovered they weren't millenialists at all. They hardly ever even mentioned the thousand-year kingdom in their writings. I became convinced that millenialism is contrary to Anabaptist teachings."

Young Lepp was disappointed. He had not expected his mentor to take that position. He himself was already a convinced millenialist, although he was aware that he had not yet thought through all its implications.

"But Oom Bernd," he countered, "isn't it a glorious vision God offers: to make a new covenant with his Chosen, to prepare them with a new heart and spirit to be citizens of the Messianic Kingdom, the new City of God? It's such an inspiring fulfillment of God's glorious plan of salvation." His eyes shone as his square young shoulders swayed with the movement of the train.

Harder looked at his young friend with a twinkle of affection. "Yes, Erdmann, that would be a glorious fulfillment. Pray God it may come to pass." Then a cloud passed over the large, open face. "But any vision, no matter how pure and uplifting, can be corrupted into evil selfishness and used to enslave others. Take, for example, the prophetic book by Claas Epp Junior that has caused such a stir in the last few years. It's a mad, willful book, but some of our people believe in it fanatically, especially the people in Epp's Am Tract settlement. Now don't misunderstand me, I don't doubt that Epp is sincere, but he's a dangerous visionary nevertheless."

Erdmann wanted to protest, but Harder held up his hand. "Consider, Erdmann, what the consequences of this man's teachings have been.

Several hundred families — men, women, children of all ages — have placed themselves completely in the power of this ruthless, iron-willed leader. God grant he doesn't turn out to be a false prophet, an advance scout of the Antichrist with whom he's so obsessed. Wagon train after wagon train has left for Turkestan in the last two years. And by all reports those poor people have suffered unbelievable hardships, total fatigue being the least of them. They have been afflicted with internal dissensions, hostile natives, terrible diseases like typhoid, and the good Lord knows what else.

"But even Tashkent wasn't far enough for Epp. As you know, late last summer he pushed south with his group to the hostile khanate of Bukhara. There, in a little place called, of all things, Valley of the Carrots — in that exact place — Epp says the second coming of Christ will occur. That's to be the "place of refuge south of Samarkand" prophesied by Jung-Stilling. But apparently the Bukharan officials don't know that, or perhaps they're working for Antichrist." He smiled sweetly. "At any rate, they've kicked Epp's holy band out of there. Now those poor, misguided souls are apparently wandering around in a kind of no-man's land between Russian and Turkish soil.

"And can you believe it? Even after all those terrible reports of hardship and suffering filtered back from the first groups, more wagon trains left last summer. How can decent, Godfearing Mennonites be so blind and foolish? You know, Erdmann, when I was sent to Petersburg years ago I was excited by the prospect of settlement in Turkestan. But I never dreamt that it would happen in this manner — rash and wrong-headed. I could weep when I think of all those good, trusting people led into danger and perhaps destruction by a man who is committing the ultimate sin: presuming to know the will of God better than God himself."

Harder fell silent. He took out a tan handkerchief and mopped his brow, exactly as he did at the end of one of his rousing sermons.

Erdmann tried, timidly, to defend Epp. "But Oom Bernd, isn't it at least possible that Claas Epp is a true prophet? Perhaps we *are* closer to the Second Coming than we think. Surely there are many signs around us that confirm that the events predicted in Daniel and Revelation are near at hand." He stopped as he saw Harder becoming agitated.

"Yes, yes, my boy, there are many signs, and there always have been. And they can be interpreted in many different ways, and always have been. Epp's prediction of the end of the world is nothing new, of course, only the date is. Every new end-time prophet who comes along interprets the signs in his own way and sets a new date for Christ's coming. But when the day comes and the Lord doesn't arrive is the prophet humbled or ashamed? No, he calmly goes about finding explanations and excuses for having given the wrong date. Witness Melchior Hofmann and Bernhard Rothmann, those two strange Anabaptist prophets. Hofmann was convinced the second coming would occur at Strassburg in the 1530s. Poor old Hofmann clung to his idea through sickness and imprisonment, convinced to the end that he would yet be proven right. Rothmann, who thought the great event would happen at Muenster, in the end came to see the futility of trying to read God's mind.

"And that's the heart of the matter, Erdmann. Such end-of-time prophets presume to read the mind of God as easily as other men read newspapers. Now, as Christians we believe, of course, that human history is entirely in God's hand and has a definite beginning and end. But trying to anticipate that end is more than presumptuous: it's a dangerous act of spiritual pride. The only difference between Claas Epp, my friend, and all the earlier end-time prophets is that they have already been proven wrong while he still has a chance of being right."

"And what if he is right, Oom Bernd?"

"Then, my boy, we believers will all rejoice that we are privileged to be part of the most important event in history, and that we will go to our eternal reward sooner than we expected."

Harder smiled his innocent smile, then stretched and yawned. He reached for his food box under the seat. "It's time to take in a bite. So much talking has made me hungry as a wolf." He sighed heavily as he opened his box and took out the rump of a large, brown loaf. "What I wouldn't give for a thick, juicy *schnäd* of fresh watermelon right now."

They arrived in Petersburg late in the evening, but Erdmann was amazed, as they were driven to their hotel, to see that the sky over the dark-burnished dome of St. Isaac's Cathedral was almost as bright as day. Oom Bernd informed him he was looking at one of Petersburg's famous "white nights" of summer, when the sun dipped below the horizon for only a few hours every night.

In the morning Oom Bernd took him on a walking tour of the beautiful city and Erdmann was more impressed than he wanted to be by the endless display of worldly splendor the capital offered. Oom Bernd showed a hearty delight in the beauty and riches all around them. Erdmann nodded politely, but he did not share the older man's pleasure. All this wealth and magnificence, after all, belonged to Satan's kingdom, was designed to keep the Russian people in a state of spiritual enslavement to that "Great Whore" the Orthodox Church. With its opulent cathedrals and mumbo-jumbo ritual it kept the impoverished masses in a state of spiritual ignorance and superstitious obedience. He surveyed the glittering churches and palaces through hostile eyes. He was now in the very midst of the Enemy, the satanic state church that sucked the spiritual blood of the nation. More than ever, surrounded by these proud stone faces, he felt himself irrevocably commissioned to engage in soul-to-soul combat with the mighty state dragon of false religion. Seeing all this only strengthened his resolve to use all the force and cunning God had given him to help defeat this all-powerful foe.

But these thoughts and feelings he kept to himself as they plodded among the vast, costly vanities and monuments dedicated to the tsars, the princes of the church, and the other mighty ones of this world.

Yes, that trip to Petersburg had opened young Lepp's eyes — to the world, to Oom Bernd, to himself — as nothing had before. He returned from it knowing that his friendship with Bernhard Harder was mortised for life. He had learned to know the private man, had seen him from the inside as it were. In some ways it had been a disquieting revelation. On the return journey Oom Bernd had confided that he was far from happy with what he had accomplished with the notoriously vague and supercilious government officials in the capital, that perhaps his mission would have gone better if he had been firmer and more tenacious. He had been too timid and easy-going with those snooty bureaucrats. He could see that now. He went on to assess his own character in a manner so candid and unsparing that Erdmann was taken a little aback, wanted to defend Oom Bernd from himself.

"You know, my dear Erdmann," he began, "I'm a jolly, optimistic fellow by nature — always have been. I'm never sick, enjoy a good appetite — a sinful appetite, my first wife used to say — and am generally blessed with a sense of physical well-being. And yet, life has been anything but easy for me. I was born into a dirt-poor family and I've continued to live close to the brink of poverty ever since. And that's never bothered me much.

"But here's something else. I'm grateful that God has given me gifts that enable me to rouse and exhort large numbers of people, but my gifts are also of that kind that are distrusted, regarded as a bit subversive by certain people, the people who wield power in the world. Such people sense something unstable about me; they sense that I'm not really one of them, that what I say in my sermons somehow threatens them. And they're right, you know — on both counts. I *am* unstable, and the message I bring is not meant to comfort well-off, secure people.

"You see, people, in spite of what they may say to the contrary, really believe in power, feel comfortable with it, but only if that power is used to some practical end. My power is expressed through fervent words in the Lord's cause; my power is real without being useful in a practical sense. When you hold a handful of wheat you know exactly what you have, and when you listen to one of our old ooms reading a sermon even older than he is you know exactly what you have. But this Harder fellow doesn't read his sermons; he speaks without having anything written down. He says just what comes to him, makes up his message as he goes along (or so they think, these practical men of power), and then you don't know exactly what you have. It's unsettling for them to have me running around loose with my warnings and admonitions. They consider me impractical, a visionary, a performer with my verses and hymns. They respect me, yes, but they don't quite trust my kind of power. They can't quite measure and weigh it, and that makes them uneasy."

Harder looked shrewdly at his young friend, then smiled. "But I have an idea, Erdmann, that things will be different for you. You are serious, sober and dignified on the outside, to go with your zeal and dedication inside. You will always give people an impression of strength and stability of character. You will have the weight and balance I seem to lack. You want to pursue a Russian mission — against all odds and no matter what the cost you want to bring Russian peasants to Christ. The men of power will sense a will and strength in you to match their own, a practical sense of purpose they can respect. They will understand that you are out to win the souls of the lost — as many as possible — and that you are as realistic in your aims as they are in theirs. They will not feel threatened by you. They will see that you are trying to bring in a harvest, as big a harvest as possible. They will understand that."

Erdmann Lepp was young but he was not naive. He understood what Oom Bernd was saying, the distinction he was making between himself and his young protégé. Erdmann understood that while the veteran revivalist whole-heartedly embraced the sacred burden of the Great Commission, the burning desire and unswerving dedication to spread the Word, he was, when all was said and done, more concerned with renewal and unity within the Old Church than with winning souls among false believers and heathen non-believers. Harder's concern was for the Mennonite church as a whole, for group renewal and a pure fellowship of believers.

Erdmann had to admit that Oom Bernd was at his most eloquent and emotionally compelling when he was flaying the spiritual complacency and dead formalism he saw all around him in the narcissistic Mennonite villages. What he wanted was a proper tension between the church and the "world." When Harder hurled his verbal bolts against "false prophets" he actually meant not heretical preachers or spreaders of false doctrines, but rather the comfortable, conforming, sermon-reading ministers who consciously or unconsciously soothed their congregations into acceptance of the status-quo — both in the material and spiritual realms.

Everything considered, however, young Lepp could not escape the conclusion that the man he admired above all others, an evangelist of much more than local fame, was not employing his superior talents as fully as he might have done. So far as he knew Oom Bernd had never even tried to reach out beyond the Mennonite colonies in his ministry. He did not seem to share Erdmann's own aching hunger for new souls to win, to take the Word to the Russian masses no matter what the danger. Sometimes Erdmann thought he detected in Harder a kind of spiritual *gemütlichkeit*, a relaxed willingness to accept difficulties and unfavorable circumstances as from God rather than to attack them as from Satan.

Harder's disposition to leave things in God's time-shaping hands instead of forcing Satan's stubborn hand, had never been more evident than in the last conversation Erdmann had with him just weeks before his sudden death in the fall of 1884. Erdmann had resigned his teaching post that summer and had come to say goodbye before leaving for Switzerland, where he was to attend the St. Crischona Bible School at Basel. He knew that this was an important step for him and he very much wanted to leave with Oom Bernd's blessing.

It was a warm day in mid-August and they were sitting in the shade behind the Harders' modest home in Halbstadt. Beside Oom Bernd's wicker armchair lay a mound of freshly picked, green-mottled watermelons, the fruit he loved so well. Every few minutes his hand would drop down and mold itself around the top melon, as though to reassure himself that the fruit was still there.

As so often before, they were discussing various aspects of the Great Commission. For Erdmann there really was only one important aspect: "Go forth therefore and make all nations my disciples; baptize men everywhere in the name of the Father and the Son and the Holy Spirit." It seemed like such a clear, simple beautiful command. How could it be misunderstood by anyone who professed to be doing God's work?

Yes, Oom Bernd agreed, in principle it was indeed that simple, but in practice there were many things to consider: timing, method, the state of readiness of both the potential convert and the missionary, and so on. As always he advocated patience and an appreciation for various forms of evangelizing, including the more indirect means. In his own case the indirect means had taken the form of thousands of religious poems and hymns which he had written during his long ministry. Who but God could say what effect such things had on human souls by comparison with the more direct and dramatic arts of revivalist preaching and exhortation?

Erdmann could not restrain his impatience with what seemed to him Oom Bernd's rather indulgent self-justification for his verse-dabbling. The advice struck him as not very relevant in any case.

"But Oom Bernd," he expostulated, "what's the use of writing verses and songs when the real work is out there waiting. We all know the time is short and the fields white already . . . ." He stopped, sounding a little pompous even to himself.

Oom Bernd, smiling beatifically, quoted back: "He brings us unfailingly fixed seasons of harvest, Jeremiah 5:24." His eyes still looked benign, but his manner grew more serious. "Listen, my boy, I know how eager you are to win souls — and so am I — but to be as impatient, as impulsive as you are, isn't the right way. It smacks not only of immaturity but of a certain self-righteousness."

He reached down beside his chair once more and clamped his huge hand firmly around the fat watermelon on top. Effortlessly he held it up. "Behold this fruit, my friend. For me it's nature's masterpiece." His eyes sparkled. "I like to think that Mother Eve must have smuggled some watermelon seeds out of Paradise — it is the fruit of Paradise, surely. Now, let's cut it open."

He picked up the knife lying on the little table in front of him and with a few deft movements laid open the blood-red flesh of the melon. He held the slice up admiringly. "There! A finc juicy *schnäd*. But you know, it took time to bring this miracle to perfection. It took a seed and rain and the hot steppe sun — and time, the right amount of time. Look at those seeds —count them — each one perfectly formed and ready to become in its own good time another such luscious marvel as this one. Do you see my point, boy?"

He passed the slice to Erdmann, who received it awkwardly just as he was starting to speak. "Well, yes, sir, I guess I do, but I still think we have to 'bring in the sheaves' —"

"— 'for the night is coming.' Yes, Erdmann, but it's coming in its own good time, and nothing you, my earnest young friend, nor I can do will delay or speed it up one second. In the meantime, we do the best we can and trust God to lead us." He leaned forward and plunged his mouth into his thick slice of watermelon, his lofty brow shining from the heat, bold eyes and open face aglow with sheer enjoyment.

As Harder straightened up to chew he remembered something else. "Let me give you an example of how unexpectedly and casually the Heavenly Father can guide us in our work. Years ago when I was teaching in Blumstein, I woke up from my afternoon nap one Saturday with a strong craving for watermelon." He took another huge bite and chewed lustily. "Now everybody knows that the finest watermelons in the Molochnaya are those of Muensterberg, the neighboring village. I got up and set out immediately to satisfy my hunger. I decided to knock on the first door I reached in Muensterberg.

"A middle-aged woman I didn't know opened the door. She stared at me suspiciously when I told her what I had come for, but finally, looking nervous, she went to fetch me a watermelon. As I waited by the open door on the *schaffott,* I heard a gruff man's voice inside demanding to know what that 'pope' was doing here. Well, to make a long story short, I found a human soul in distress, a confused, bitter, frightened man on his sickbed, who could disguise his fear only with anger, contempt, and surly reproach. I won a soul for the Lord that day, and all because I had so shamelessly given in to my lust for the heavenly watermelon." He bent his head to nibble the last red remnants from his slice.

But even as Erdmann murmured polite approval of the anecdote, he felt welling up within him impatience, a disapproval amounting almost to contempt for such a random, unorganized approach to evangelism. It was important, of course, to reclaim the one lost sheep among the hundred. He acknowledged that. But it wasn't enough — not from someone like Bernhard Harder. If only he could persuade Oom Bernd to use his time and energy on a bigger scale, in a more organized manner. And now he was talking of going on a preaching trip to Sagradovka. Why there? It was just another Mennonite colony with maybe a few unsaved and backsliding souls among the many true Christians. Work any good minister could do.

In the last few years Erdmann had come to believe that the chief work of a *reiseprediger* was to search out souls in darkness in places where no one else dared to go — to Russian villages, to the far corners of the empire where people had never heard the true gospel in their lives. What did it matter that such a native mission was hazardous because it was illegal? It was not illegal in God's eyes to spread the gospel! Johann Wieler, his former teacher in Halbstadt, was showing in dramatic fashion what could be done in the Russian mission. When the Mennonite Brethren Conference had rejected his proposal to conduct evangelistic services illegally among the Russians, Wieler had bravely launched out on his own in the Odessa area. He was said to be in constant danger of arrest. But driven by the fire in his soul, he went about his Father's business and ignored all else. There was the hero whose fearless course he was burning to follow! Oom Bernd, sad to say, seemed to be getting more moderate and cautious with the years. He had opened Erdmann's eyes to many things, for which he would always be deeply grateful. But he knew already that he would never be content with the kind of ministry Bernhard Harder had followed.

Even during the three years of teaching which he had just concluded, and which he had regarded as a form of exile in the wilderness, he had done all he could to prepare and train himself for the kind of ministry he envisioned. He had waited in vain for a formal call from his church, refusing to believe he was too young, or that marriage would make him a more attractive candidate for election and ordination. He fretted impatiently, a lean, tense young man, coiled tightly like a steel spring waiting to be released. He had heard God's clear call long ago. Why couldn't others hear it too?

But young Lepp was not the man to wait passively, to sit brooding over a call that didn't come. He eagerly accepted and sought out opportunities to preach — to youth groups and Brethren church groups too small or isolated to have regularly ordained minsters. He was intent on honing his pulpit craft. But the work that brought him to a fever pitch of excitement was the preaching he was able to do among Russian servants in Mennonite homes, no matter how informally. He was fully aware of the risk. He knew that under Russian law anyone who "seduced" a member of the Orthodox Church would be exiled to Siberia. His mother had told him what had happened to early Brethren evangelists like Heinrich Neufeld, Abram Unger, and Gerhard Wieler, Johann's older brother, in the sixties for converting and baptizing a handful of Russian servants. All three had been cited in court for "spreading a sectarian doctrine," and Gerhard Wieler had been sent to prison for a time.

Erdmann was thrilled when he gained his first convert, a Russian field hand who had come down with a mysterious ailment, which probably made him more receptive than he would otherwise have been. When the youth went back to his village to convalesce he told everybody about the miracle that had come into his life. Erdmann received an invitation to preach in the village. It was an important breakthrough and he made the most of it. He led several more peasants to Christ, and received further invitations to preach.

His preaching in Russian villages soon became an open secret. The school board in Ohrloff summoned him and warned him that if he persisted with his illegal (and unauthorized) preaching he would be facing dismissal.

He knew the time had come to make a decision. He resigned at the end of the school year in 1884. All the hints he had dropped in the proper places that he would not be averse to a ministerial career were futile. He was well aware that it was considered bad form to show an open desire to become a minister. Now that his secret mission work had been discovered, he had fallen into disfavor with the more conservative members of his home church in Halbstadt as well as with those in Ohrloff. As things stood he could not expect to receive a call.

He decided to change his strategy. He applied to and was accepted as a student by the St. Crischona school in Basel, which was well-regarded by the select few Mennonite students who had attended it over the years.

Lepp's two years at St. Crischona proved to be a rich blessing, but he never lost his yearning to be back in the spiritual harvest field of his native Russia. He returned home in the summer of 1886 on the same train as another young Russian Mennonite who had been studying in Germany. The young man was August Bock from Einlage. The two young men, so different from each other in temperament and aspirations, took an immediate liking to one another. By the time the trip was over they had become friends, and would continue to see each other often over the years.

Erdmann arrived home to find the Mennonite community buzzing with the news that Johann Wieler was a fugitive in hiding. Some said he had already fled the country and reached Germany. Apparently his arrest had been ordered after he was caught baptizing a Russian woman. Even as he prayed for Wieler's safety, Lepp once again felt his soul singing the glorious challenge offered by the Russian mission. It was the Great Commission as it was meant to be. Men like Johann Wieler were following directly in the footsteps of the disciples and Paul in the dawning years of Christianity. That was the way the Christian ministry was to be conducted, as a bold war, a battle of wits between tough, fearless men of God and the brutal, repressive authorities of the state. It was the only kind of war sanctioned by the meek and loving Christ.

That perilous native ministry would be his in due course. But first he would master the language of the country as no Mennonite ever had in the century his people had lived in Russia. Both his Russian and Ukrainian were already very good, but he wanted to speak them like a native. His father promised to support him financially for a year of language study in Petersburg. After that he was to manage on his own.

Lepp's studies in the capital went well, and he soon found himself with spare times on his hands. He decided to use it by becoming active in the evangelical tract mission which had been started in St. Petersburg some years earlier by Lord Radstock, an English nobleman with good connections among the Russian aristocracy. It was a time of religious ferment in Russia, with Baptists, Stundists, Evangelicals and other radical sects gaining adherents among Russians from all walks of life regardless of official opposition and repression. It became fashionable and seemed to satisfy a deep inner need for members of the minor nobility especially to become ardent Western-style Christians and to promote militant Christian causes with typical Russian zeal.

The first time Erdmann Lepp met the Countess Mathilde Glazonova he realized, without giving the matter much thought, that she was the most beautiful and charming young woman he had ever seen. The Countess was reputed to be descended from the natural son of Count Rastrelli, the Italian architectural genius who in the middle decades of the eighteenth century helped transform Peter the Great's squat, raw swamp city into an elegant Venice of the north. Countess Glazonova herself neither confirmed nor denied her alleged ancestry, on the sensible grounds that it was nobody's business.

After being splendidly presented at Court in the late seventies, Mathilde Tashkova, as she then was, had married Count Konstantin Glazonov, a young favorite of Alexander II, who was destined, so everyone said, for a brilliant career in the diplomatic service. But in 1881, less than a year after the Glazonov marriage, Tsar Alexander was blown apart on the street by a home-made bomb. With his royal patron gone, young Glazonov's career fell into limbo when the new tsar, Alexander III, surly, suspicious, and reactionary, took over the reins of government.

Not long after, in a fit of black depression, Count Glazonov committed suicide. The young Countess took the loss of her husband hard, and came close to despair herself. But she was a strong young woman, and emerged from her prolonged mourning determined to give her new life some purpose and meaning. She had friends waiting to help her, friends who had themselves found spiritual fulfillment, if not always peace, in the Evangelical Christian movement. Reluctant at first, the Countess was soon won over by the deep sincerity and zeal of the people who were active in the movement. It was not long before she experienced a spiritual awakening that was to change her completely.

After her conversion, Countess Glazonova threw herself into the work of the Evangelical movement with quiet, effective devotion. She was ideally suited to help with the "drawing-room mission" which Lord Radstock and his friend the famed German-English evangelist Dr. F. W. Baedeker had been conducting successfully among the Russian nobility since their great revival of the mid-seventies. The Countess' excellent connections opened many new doors for the mission, and soon she was referred to everywhere as the "Holy Countess."

When Erdmann Lepp arrived in St. Petersburg in the fall of 1886, Countess Glazonova, more beautiful and radiant than ever, was an important but self-effacing guiding force behind the growing Evangelical movement in the capital. When young Lepp became an evening volunteer in the tract mission, the Countess immediately saw that the tall, slender young Southerner with the striking black sidewhiskers (rather provincial by Petersburg standards) and strange, hooded eyes, was someone quite out of the ordinary. She began to search him out, suggested challenging projects to him.

They became friends quickly, drawn together by the unusual qualities each possessed. From the beginning, the lovely, court-polished Russian noblewoman and the raw, shy, but self-confident Mennonite from the provinces hit it off perfectly.

Looking back later, Erdmann realized that the numerous personal contacts that had seemed so natural and innocent at the time had led inevitably through a series of small steps to an intimacy neither had foreseen nor consciously willed. When he finally discovered what was happening to him, he could not believe it.

While still an adolescent, Erdmann had decided that like Paul he would be better off without women in his life. He was serenely confident he would never fall in love and certain he would never get married. He was a vessel of the Lord; as such he had no need for a weaker vessel himself. For him carnal love and marriage would be a form of defilement, or at best a wasteful deflection from his true purpose in life. And yet he discovered, ironically, that he was exactly the kind of man who aroused the interest of females of all ages. His special curse was the demurely predatory Mennonite mumtje with one or more marriageable daughters. During his years as a teacher in Ohrloff he learned to detect the artless marital snares that were set for him on all sides by affable but determined mothers. He had learned how to take evasive action without giving offense, or so he thought.

And so he was not prepared for what happened when he met the young Russian noblewoman. He could not blame the Countess. Her behavior had been impeccable from the beginning. She had never stooped to the vulgarity of flirting with him, deliberately signaling her femininity to attract him. On the contrary, she made no attempt to set off her natural beauty, tried, if anything, to hide or at least to neutralize its effect on men. She dressed with almost severe plainness, put on no airs, and maintained a simple, almost austere manner. But her refined charm and warm elegance were so exquisitely novel in young Lepp's experience that he was overcome in spite of himself. For hours after each meeting with her, no matter how casual, he was left with heavy, unsettling feelings he dared not name.

For the first time in his adult life Erdmann Lepp felt bewildered and unsure of himself. His sense of self-betrayal was made more agonizing by his belief that the calm, gracious Mathilde, even if she knew his feelings, would never reciprocate them. And he simply could not believe that his sudden passion for a woman of alien race and culture was part of God's plan for him. Not that she wasn't a genuine, born-again Christian; he was as sure of that as he was of his own spiritual state. He would never meet a finer, more sincere, more pleasing and beautiful Christian woman in his life. He knew that. All the same, when he was not with her he often felt strong shame, felt himself cringing in defeat and self-revulsion. Since his troubled puberty he had never seriously thought that he could be defeated by anything. But to be defeated now from within, to be betrayed and overcome by his own base passions, was an ignominy too awful to bear.

Or so he thought at first. After much prayer and meditation, however, he resolved that this was another test — perhaps the supreme test — that God was sending his way. He would try to meet it decisively and without flinching. He would never declare his love nor seek to consummate it. He would close and cauterize the wound without anybody's help but God's. No one, least of all Mathilde, would even see the scar.

He never got to close the wound. Instead, he declared his love one day as easily and naturally as he said his prayers. And Mathilde responded in the same way. He was astonished that she could have dissembled so well. She told him with a tender smile that he did not know much about women. The rapture that spread through him then seemed at that moment to render all thoughts of sin or guilt irrelevant.

Even then he did not expect that their love would or could express itself in complete physical intimacy. And when in due course that happened as well, he knew at last that he lived in the flesh like other men and that he must be crucified in the flesh like other living creatures. And even as his senses sang their joy, his mind and soul darkened with self-knowledge. The arrogant, self-righteous boy he had been he would not be again. He saw now that the innocence of his young manhood had been sterile and self-serving. That his hot zeal and impatience had made him appear fatuous and intolerant (perhaps intolerable) to a mature, battle-wise soldier of God like Bernhard Harder.

Yes, the intensity of his passion for the adorable Countess had shaken him to the roots of his being. But it did not destroy him, as he at first feared it might. Another man of Lepp's uncompromising religious convictions might have been overwhelmed by the enormity of such a carnal sin, considered himself lost anyway, and abandoned himself to sinfulness. Lepp was not such a man. There was never any doubt in his mind about the sinfulness of his affair with Mathilde. They discussed in sorrow and with many misgivings their guilty love, their inability to resist temptation, and agreed that it must not continue. At the same time, both realized that what they shared was much more than a casual, furtive liason. They confessed undying love for each other, regardless of what might happen. They also discussed the possibility of marriage, but without much conviction. Both intuitively felt that marriage to each other would be wrong for them. What sustained them was their mutual discovery of human riches within themselves and each other, riches whose existence they had not even suspected.

Never had Erdmann been so aware of himself as a man. God had breathed life and soul into him at birth, but it was only now, filled with love for another fallible human being, that he felt fully created as a man doomed to live and die, to fall into sin and error on the way, but with an immortal soul redeemed by the blood of Christ, the unimaginable love of God. His virtue and chastity had been those of a lifeless puppet; now he had been miraculously changed into a flesh-and-blood man by the love of a woman. And Erdmann knew with certainty that for the rest of his life he would be a stronger man and a more understanding Christian as the result of his fall into the loving flesh.

Then, as easily and inevitably as it had begun, the physical expression of their love came to an end. It was never to be resumed, although their love for each other flowed on like a placid river.

Shortly after Lepp returned to the Molochnaya from the capital, the Mennonite Brethren Missions Committee appointed him an itinerant evangelist. It was understood that his work would be with Mennonite congregations. In fact, he was warned explicitly not to jeopardize himself with Russian authorities.

The young preacher went to work with a will. At last he had received the spiritual position he had longed for, even though he was not yet an ordained minister.

Now the years of arduous traveling began in earnest. His annual stipend from the conference was about that of a village teacher, which meant that even though he was single he had to be careful with every kopek, what with the incidental traveling expenses that cropped up constantly. But money was the least of Lepp's concerns. He was doing at last what he had yearned and prayed for since his youth.

His first notable success as an evangelist came during his first full summer as a *reiseprediger.* He made a series of "visitations" to four of the eight recently established forestry stations on which young Mennonite men were serving their four-year terms of alternative service. At all four stations Lepp's services produced dramatic results. Hitherto uncommitted young men came forward and declared themselves for the Lord. The rich harvest of souls was all the more remarkable considering the forestry boys' known antipathy towards *reiseprediger,* who were thought to have soft, prestigious jobs at their congregations' expense while they themselves had to slave away for years in the forests away from home and loved ones.

He had stood there, a long black-clad beanpole with the eyes of an eagle, confidently facing stiffly seated rows of uniformed forestry lads. To their amazement he spoke not as a *jegromda,* their derisive term for anyone with a higher education and an educated manner, but in their own deliberately homely farmer's language. He spoke in High German, the accepted church language, but he slipped into his sermons enough homespun Low German words and expressions to make the men feel at ease. This "pope," not much older in years than they were, seemed to understand their special problems and to be genuinely concerned about their spiritual welfare. Even the more cynical among them were impressed and several, to their own amazement, actually broke down under Lepp's quiet but deeply probing words.

Lepp immediately looked for new challenges. His first extended evangelical campaign was in the Kuban settlement up in the northern Caucasus in 1890. Kuban was the only daughter colony sponsored by the Mennonite Brethren; it had fallen on hard times due to both bad economic conditions and internal religious strife. A renegade Mennonite religious group known as "Friends of Jerusalem" had been winning young people away from the Brethren congregation in such numbers it had become a rarity for a Brethren baptism to take place. There was a mood of despondency, almost of desperation, in the villages of Wohldemfürst and Alexanderfeld. The leaders and older members of the colony had finally appealed to the mother church for help.

Erdmann Lepp and Wilhelm Loewen, a veteran evangelist, were dispatched to the Kuban to appraise the situation and to see if their ministry could bring the young defectors of the colony to their senses.

The two evangelists reached the settlement after a tedious, six-hundred-mile train and wagon trip that had taken three days. They arrived in the early afternoon, and though fatigued from the journey immediately announced that they would hold a meeting that evening. Lepp preached a rousing admonitory sermon that made a deep impression even though the short notice had failed to attract a full audience to the meeting house. Fourteen young men and women were brought to the altar as penitents that night. The church elders were overjoyed and promised all the cooperation and organization in their power for further meetings.

They stayed a week, with Lepp doing most of the preaching while Loewen looked after the personal counseling between meetings. By the end of the week more than seventy people, most of them young adults, had declared themselves for Christ and were received into the Brethren church through public baptism. The group of converts even included a few older people who had been excommunicated from the Brethren fellowship.

Lepp and Loewen left for home amidst general rejoicing in a colony that had been almost overnight rejuvenated spiritually, although its economic problems remained. Erdmann Lepp's ministry in the Kuban proved to be a turning point in the fortunes of the colony and was regarded as a divinely inspired event. Lepp's fame as an evangelist swept through the Mennonite colonies like a mighty wind. Soon his services were in such demand he could not keep up with the requests.

In spite of his success in Mennonite churches, Lepp still had his heart set on a native ministry. It became an obsession that preyed on him constantly as he conducted one successful revival campaign after another in such far-flung Mennonite colonies as Friedensfeld in the west, the Crimean in the south, and Memrik and New Samara in the east. In between such trips he diligently sought contacts among the Russian populace, preaching where he could, bearing personal witness to individuals where he couldn't preach. But these contacts were all too infrequent and abortive to satisfy him. Impatiently, he awaited God's command for a new type of ministry.

That command came in 1893 in the form of a call from Dr. Baedeker, the esteemed Baptist missionary whom Lepp had learned to know in Petersburg. Dr. Baedeker informed Lepp by letter that he had been granted permission by the authorities to conduct evangelistic campaigns in Russian prisons. He would need an interpreter, however, and everyone assured him that Erdmann Lepp was just the man to help him. Lepp recalled the affectionate joke in Petersburg Baptist circles that Dr. Baedeker's Russian vocabulary consisted of exactly one sentence: "*Isus ljubit tebya,*" "Jesus loves you."

Lepp was delighted by the offer and wrote his acceptance by return post. It was the voice of God. A door was opening at last, albeit a dangerous door. He had no illusions about that. In spite of receiving official sanction to preach to convicts, they would be closely watched by the state police. Lepp knew that inexorably the dossier on his missionary activities would grow until one day, in some office, an official would decide that the time had come. And then Erdmann Lepp, man of God, would be arrested. But the certainty of that fate caused him no more concern than the knowledge that he must some day die.

Dr. F. W. Baedeker was made of the same intrepid stuff. A small, delicate man, always formally dressed in dark suit and tie, his hair and Vandyke beard snow white, he looked like a retired teacher or petty bureaucrat timidly out of place in the sordid surroundings of a prison. Lepp, walking beside him, towered over him like a gaunt sentry, his stern countenance as fixed in resolve as Dr. Baedeker's seemed uncertain and flustered. The old man would begin to speak in German, softly at first, then with controlled intensity as Lepp hovered over him with precise, prompt translations that crackled in the prisoners' ears like a warm hearth fire under a bubbling pot of *shashlik*. The little evangelist was so thorough that he missed not a single prisoner in any of the prisons they visited. When guards or prison officials demurred about opening the cells of notorious criminals in solitary confinement, he would insist politely but firmly that they must be opened. Undaunted, he would step into the murky interior, Lepp on his heels, embrace the startled malefactor and, like a lover, coo his "*Isus ljubit tebya*" into his grimy ear.

The prison ministry lasted for several years and took them even into the endless reaches of Siberia along the newly built Trans-Siberian Railway. But by the fall of 1896 the strenuous schedule of traveling had become too much even for the doughty Dr. Baedeker. He was past seventy and severely arthritic, and so decided to turn over the prison ministry to his dedicated helper and companion while he returned to England for a period of rest and spiritual renewal. Lepp completed the remaining part of the itinerary they had made up when they started. Then he too decided to go home for a rest.

Erdmann Lepp was finally ordained in Halbstadt in 1897. He was reappointed as a conference *reiseprediger* and resumed his campaigns among the newer and more remote Mennonite colonies. He made a second visit to the Kuban, then traveled north to the settlements in the Don basin: Memrik, Naumenko, and Barvenkovo, the small Russian city which was rapidly becoming a base for enterprising Mennonites engaged in trade and industry, from highly successful steam-operated flour mills to factories and machine shops specializing in agricultural implements. From there he headed east to the Volga settlements of Am Tract, Old and New Samara, and finally to the newest and most easterly of all Mennonite settlements at that time — Orenburg, which had only existed since 1894. Everywhere he went he preached with the inspired power of an Old Testament prophet and won many new converts, including children and adult backsliders, for local congregations.

After completing this long and exhausting itinerary, which had kept him on the road for almost six months, he once again returned home for a well-earned rest. But his restless, driven nature did not allow him to relax for long. Soon he was preaching in Russian villages again, but with a growing awareness that he was being watched more closely than ever. He had no difficulty spotting the strangers among his village audiences, men who were dressed differently, and who wore expressions a little too knowing as they tried to blend in with the crowds. But Erdmann ignored these strangers as he went calmly about his Father's business.

Early in 1898 the inevitable happened, but in a manner he had not foreseen. He had always thought his arrest would come dramatically, in the midst of a service, or at night as he read in his room, or when he came home from a house visit. Instead, he arrested himself, so to speak. In Berdjansk, one day, he decided he could not bear a moment longer the tight surveillance he was under. God was urging him to force the issue once and for all. Boldly he walked into the police station and demanded to see the chief. In a firm, confident voice he asked the official for written permission to preach the gospel in the Berdjansk jurisdiction.

The chief of police, a burly chap with a florid face and a short, rug-smooth nap of graying hair, almost lost his professional poise. "Am I to understand, my dear sir, that you are asking me, an official of the crown, to break the law by giving you permission to proselytise Russian citizens who are members of the official church?" He glared at Lepp in disbelief. "That's a criminal offence, as you very well know."

"Yes, sir, I know it is," Lepp answered calmly, "but we are dealing here with the highest law of all — God's commission to spread the pure gospel over all the world." He paused for effect. "And what I preach is the pure Word of God."

The two men stared at each other in silence. Then the police chief reached into a desk drawer and pulled out a thick file. "This is your file, Mr. Lepp. We have been watching you for some time, as you no doubt are aware. The record is not yet complete, but since you have done me the honor of a visit today, you have, if I may put it so, completed the file yourself. As of this moment you are under arrest, and you'd be wise to use what time you have in preparing yourself for interrogation."

Lepp kept his composure and made no further attempt to negotiate with the police official.

After a few days in the Berdjansk prison, during which he was permitted visitors, he was sent to St. Petersburg for further interrogation and possible court proceedings. Inwardly, he was already preparing himself for exile to Siberia. Perhaps that would after all be God's way of allowing him to begin a full-time Russian ministry at last — with Siberian exiles. Wondrous were the ways of the Lord!

But exile was not to be his path. He was surprised one day by two visitors to his cell. They were his old friend and associate Dr. Baedeker, and J. S. Prokhanov, another important leader in the evangelical movement in Petersburg. After much tearful embracing and fervent greetings, the three men knelt in grateful prayer. The visitors informed Erdmann that Countess Glazonova was doing everything in her power to get him released. He accepted the news with mixed feelings, but with secret gratitude for Mathilde's continued devotion. He promised his friends that he would wait patiently and bear whatever was to come.

After three weeks in his cell he was abruptly released, but on the condition that he would never again proselytise members of the Orthodox Church. When he went to see her, Mathilde told him with tears in her eyes that she had been able to secure his freedom only with great difficulty and only on that one condition. She was sure that if he were ever again arrested for proselytising she would be unable to do anything for him. He promised only that he would be more careful in future. They gave each other a chaste but heart-felt kiss of peace.

Lepp returned to the Molochnaya expecting trouble. And he was right. The Missions Committee gave him a stern reprimand for what they called his "reckless, irresponsible, disobedient behavior." It was a low point in his life. One more false step and his career with the church would be over. He considered joining the Baptist church, where he would have considerably more scope and freedom. But he could not bring himself to take the step.

He was born a Mennonite and would remain one. Somewhat chastened, he bowed to God's will and the church's and resumed his itinerant preaching among Mennonite congregations of both Brethren and Old Church allegiance.

Sincerely resolved to avoid further controversy, unable to expand his ministry as he desired, Lepp turned inward and began to steep himself in the Christian mysticism that had always fascinated him. He diligently restudied the prophetic books of the Bible, intent on discovering in them more substantial clues for the pre-millenialist position he had favored for years. For weeks and months on end he pored over and pondered the books of Daniel, Ezekiel and Revelation. He read and reread all the apocalyptic literature he could find, including the writings of Jung-Stilling. He studied and meditated with a growing sense of excitement. He felt God opening up to him through secret signs and symbols the inner meaning and ultimate destiny of the human race. Carefully, prayerfully, he began to set down the revelations that were being vouchsafed to him.

The fruit of his intense studies was a book to which he gave the resonant title *The Symbolic Key to God's Glorious Plan for True Believers*. Published in 1901, the booklet was an instant success and completely superseded Claas Epp's popular but crude and naively literal prophetic key to the end-times. Lepp's book went through several printings in short order and became the definitive exposition of pre-millenialism not only among the Mennonites and Baptists of Russia but among Mennonites and Baptists in other countries as well. Lepp was invited to hold a series of meetings in Mennonite churches in America, but he declined. His new, ever-widening fame as a biblical expositor did not in any way lessen his keen disappointment and frustration over his failure to establish the permanent native mission that had been his dream for so many years.

As the years went by, Erdmann Lepp stoically tried to adapt himself to a wintry religious climate that seemed changeless. But spring did come at last, amid stormy political weather. The humiliating war with Japan in 1904-05, with its aftermath of internal violence and abortive revolution, finally shook the imperial government out of its long complacency. The October Manifesto of 1905 proclaimed, among other things, principles of civil liberty and religious freedom. To show the government's good intention, Count Witte, the new prime minister, had some 75,000 Baptists and other evangelical Christians released from Siberian exile.

The divine finger had finally nudged open the door. Lepp sprang to life like a man possessed. Under his urging, the Brethren Missions Committee early in 1906 appointed a team of nine evangelists to take the gospel to the Russian masses. The team included not only Mennonites but several dynamic Russian Baptist preachers as well. Lepp was designated as field co-ordinator for the group. He was assisted by Adolf Reimer, a gifted young evangelist who, like Lepp, had received a call to dedicate himself to the

Russian mission. For a while he and Reimer preached in a rented theatre in
Berdjansk, but Lepp found that his job as co-ordinator demanded that he
spend much of his time on the road.

Russia's religious springtime, however, was short-lived and brought no
summer. After 1907 the government, harassed by a fractious Duma, abro-
gated — or at least discouraged — most of the new freedoms it had granted
in a rare mood of unautocratic accommodation, including the new religious freedom. Lepp and his evangelists could not ignore the signs of state
disapproval springing up again. They worked harder than ever, aware that
they were on borrowed time.

The new Russian converts could not be baptized as Mennonites; to do so
would have been a dangerous violation of Russian law, and even Lepp saw
that it would be futile to take such a risk. The alternative was to form Baptist
groups which were to serve as the nuclei for regular congregations as
conditions warranted. But the rituals of baptism and church admission,
simple though they were, had to be carried out in a risky and covert
manner. Often the evangelists and their assistants worked through the
night, first preparing baptismal candidates in secret and then taking them
furtively along back roads to a remote stream or brook for the immersion
rite. They were then smuggled back to the secret meeting place for their
formal acceptance and first communion as baptized Christians.

During this uncertain time Erdmann Lepp accepted an assignment from
the Raduga Press in Halbstadt to edit a Russian version of their popular
German "tear-off" calendar used by Mennonite families as a daily devotional reading. It was a time-consuming task, but Lepp was excited by it. He saw
at once that the project would enable him to make valuable contacts in
numerous Russian and Evangelical centers. On the weekends he kept up his
preaching and accepted invitations to special conferences on estates like
Apanlee, Steinbach, and the one at Voronaya in August, 1908, where he had
his first ride in a motor car and saw in an unexpected vision how this new
kind of vehicle might serve in the distribution of tracts as well as for
evangelistic campaigns in distant colonies. From that time he had actively
looked for a personal assistant whom he could train and eventually entrust
with the work he himself would someday have to relinquish.

In the summer of 1909, after he had finished the Russian religious
calendar, Lepp went on a preaching tour of the Bakhmut region in the
north-east. One evening he preached in a Russian village where no evangelist had ever been. His audience in the school house was small and seemed
unusually tense, almost fearful. As he spoke the broad peasant faces kept
glancing back nervously at the door. When he made his call to come
forward no one moved. He called again, and still there was no response.
Suddenly the door opened noisily and four husky young men with clubs
took up stations just inside the entrance. He knew now why his audience
had been ill at ease. It wasn't the first time he had been confronted by local

toughs determined to break up his meetings. But he had never been hemmed in as ominously as this. The youths just stood there, grimly waiting for him to try to get out.

Lepp decided his only chance was to take the initiative boldly. In his heartiest manner he invited the young men to sit down with the others. Although it was getting late he would be glad to repeat the gist of his message for their benefit. When they just stared back at him impassively he repeated his invitation even more warmly. Again no response, although they were beginning to look less sure of themselves.

Without warning Lepp raised his burning eyes and black-sleeved arms dramatically heavenwards and in a voice throbbing with emotion called out, "Oh, God, you see before you stubborn young sinners who have hardened their hearts to you. Father, I beseech you, if it be Your will to send down a miracle, soften these stony hearts, sweeten these bitter souls —NOW, this MOMENT . . . ." The long gaunt figure vibrated with passion, straining upwards in an entreaty so inspired and august that he seemed about to rise aloft. He waited long moments in sculptured supplication. Suddenly his powerful voice rose exulting, "Heavenly Father, I see, I see the sign you send. Like Daniel I am to walk the lions' den under your protecting arm. Lord, Lord, I come — I come to embrace those who would do me harm. In your name, Almighty, I advance to embrace those whose arms are raised in violence."

Slowly he let his arms sink, fixed his eyes on the men at the door and in a slow, deliberate manner, still praying, began to walk up the aisle. As one the small peasant congregation sank to its knees with awed sighs. The four men at the door held their ground, but their eyes wavered before Lepp's burning gaze and they slowly averted their faces as though from a scorching fire. Then he stood before them, greeting them in a voice vibrant with love, inviting them to approach him. One by one, sullen-faced but passive, they allowed him to embrace them. When he had finished with them he turned and delivered a blessing to the congregation. Then he departed.

The following summer the indefatigable Baptist preacher Prokhanov came to Halbstadt with an exciting new proposal: the establishment in Petersburg of a seminary for the training of evangelists. He wanted Lepp and Adolf Reimer to join the teaching staff of the new institution. Countess Glazonova was the benefactress who was making the school possible; she had also agreed to sit on its board of directors. Lepp and Reimer accepted the call, as it came at a time when the itinerant ministry was at a low ebb.

With his teaching well underway in Petersburg, Lepp looked around for some form of part-time ministry that might serve also as practical training for his students. He decided to follow the example of his friend and colleague Ivan Fetler, who had been holding occasional evening rallies in the capital for years. Instead of holding general rallies, however, Lepp held late evening meetings to which he specifically invited the riff-raff and shady characters who infested the streets at night. These late meetings were always well attended and brought surprising results, considering the sleazy ruffians, thieves, and whores they attracted. When Lepp spotted policemen among his audience, as he frequently did, he would audaciously call on them to come forward too. When they didn't, he promised to pray for them — to the sardonic amusement of his underworld audience.

Lepp's incautious flouting of the authorities began to worry his friends and colleagues. He seemed to be indifferent to all danger, as though his missionary zeal had driven him beyond any consideration for his own safety, had burned away even his instinct for survival. Sometimes it seemed to Adolf Reimer and others who worked with Lepp that the impassioned evangelist acted more like a fiery archangel on a direct mission from God and thus secure from earthly dangers than as a weak and fallible man who was endangering his freedom and perhaps his very life by taking the risks he did. They feared for him, but they also regarded him with loving awe, as though they were living witnesses to the making of a holy martyr.

Erdmann Lepp saw himself in a very different light. He was not a madman and he knew that his daring, defiant ministry could come to a sudden or violent end at any time. What others took to be his divinely inspired courage and strength of faith he knew were spurred on as much by his growing sense of desperation than by his zeal and conviction. He lived with a constant fear of failure, a despondency of spirit that came from his awareness that no matter how hard he worked, it was never enough. The years were slipping by. It was now 1913 and his ambitious dream to set up a solid, expanding native ministry seemed as far away as ever. True, he had found an ardent young disciple — Jacob Priess — to carry on the dream. And there were others like Adolf Reimer, also younger and fresher than he, to labor in the Russian vineyard. The dream would not die with him, God be praised!

But at fifty-three he was getting a little tired. Already he was a year older than Bernhard Harder had been when he went so suddenly to his eternal reward. And what had he really accomplished? Increasingly, Lepp felt the need to take stock of himself, to account for the failures and missed opportunities that by now seemed to outnumber his successes. Had he really believed when he sprang into action as a young man that he could single-handedly win all Russia to Christ? Had he been as naive as all that? Or had it been a form of vainglory he had been too blind to see?

How little one man could do in his brief lifetime. And yet how large had been his desire, how seemingly inexhaustible his dedication and stamina. At times his memories of his many years of traveling in the Lord's yoke coalesced into one transcendent vision in which he saw himself covering the endless reaches of Russia, dotted with innumerable clusters of villages and towns, tirelessly ministering to the multitudes of ignorant, superstitious peasants yearning for a spiritual understanding forever beyond them.

As though their spiritual eyes were so near-sighted they could not see anything beyond their own little "beautiful corner," the pathetic little *khata* shrine with its meagre lamp flickering over painted icons of remote, unreal saints and patriarchs. What could those stiff, lifeless images do for the miserable, uncomprehending but trusting wretches kneeling before them?

Yes, he could drive himself into frenzies of frustrated zeal just by thinking of all those millions of unsaved peasants in their sprawling, muddy, dog-teeming, anonymous villages of white-washed *khatas* and scrawny chickens, gaunt cows and horses and free-foraging pigs, living forever in hopeless poverty, trying to escape briefly in bouts of drunkenness and debauchery and violence. How he longed to bring those simple, loveable people to the warm bosom of the living Christ — away from the meaningless church ritual and the worship of painted idols on shelf or wall.

If only he could have devoted his entire life to that precious work. But God had decided otherwise. And yet, the clarion trumpet of His command to "Go forth . . . and make all nations my disciples" had been so clear and compelling. Why had God not permitted him to answer it more often?

Deep within his soul, Erdmann Lepp still clung to the hope that God had something truly momentous in store for His servant, a grand, ultimate campaign or mission that would end all his frustrations, justify all his tenacious zeal, fulfill all his dreams and prayers for success in fighting His holy war.

He would wait as patiently as he could for that final call. There were loud rumors of war coming from the European countries these days. The frog-shaped evil spirits were louder and more venomous than ever. The sixth vial was nearly empty. It had to be. Then would come the seventh vial and Armageddon.

It must be now. War in the West, followed by the Final Battle in the East. Armageddon!

It would be now. In the midst of war and strife the Lord would issue the final command to "go forth."

Part III
Sword of the Oppressor: 1914-1919

CHAPTER FOURTEEN

1
August-December, 1914

God's ways are most mysterious, Erdmann Lepp was fond of saying, when there is most at stake. Who would have thought that war in the West, the prelude to Armageddon, would come as quietly as it did? It was precipitated by an act of terrorism that seemed at the time too random and isolated to be of much significance in the eternal scheme of things. On June 28, 1914, in the small Bosnian city of Sarajevo, a somewhat fleshy Austrian archduke with mild eyes and and a fierce handlebar mustache was assassinated in an open touring car by a young Serbian nationalist.

Archduke Franz Ferdinand's death, however, set off a chain reaction of political moves that led to general war a month later. And that war would in time have a scope and an intensity, release a mania for mass destruction, the likes of which the world had never seen before. Among its incidental victims would be the Romanov dynasty that had ruled Russia for three centuries.

In August, 1914, however, Russia mobilized for war against Germany with great optimism, never dreaming of the catastrophes to come. On the afternoon of August 2, Tsar Nicholas II delivered a formal proclamation of war in the grand Salle de Nicholas of the Winter Palace. Although no enemy soldiers had as yet crossed the Russian frontier, the Tsar repeated the oath sworn by Alexander I when Napoleon invaded Russia: "I solemnly swear that I will never make peace so long as a single enemy remains on the soil of the fatherland."

The whole vast empire of Russia erupted in an orgy of patriotism. The bitter grievances, strikes, and outbreaks of civil violence that had been plaguing the country for years ceased abruptly, as if by ukase. *Batushka* Nikolai, the Little Father, would lead them to victory against the hated Germans. The imperial anthem "God Save the Tsar" rang out across the land with long-neglected fervor. The peasant recruits in their new, ill-fitting uniforms joked about celebrating Christmas in Berlin that year.

There was no jubilation in the German-speaking colonies of South Russia. War between Russia and the ancestral homeland was bewildering; it split loyalties like the naked halves of an apple. Mennonite farmers looked up from their harvesting with faces aghast. How could God allow this to happen? They deeply resented the sudden disruption of their normal routine. The harvest was sacred, took precedence over everything else. War was evil, but war coming in the midst of harvest was an unprecedented sacrilege. They watched with helpless outrage as Russian fieldhands in the early days of war were plucked off the ladder wagons and hastily put on trains bound for military camps. Mennonite farmers were forced to do their own conscripting to finish the harvest: sons, older daughters, even wives and grandfathers were pressed into service.

Most Mennonites, however, did not let their shock over the outbreak of war becloud their sense of patriotic duty. As always, the Mennonite colonies were prepared to help their country in time of need so long as their young men didn't have to shoulder arms and march into battle. Even in the early days of war the Mennonite Brethren *Voice of Peace* was calling on young Mennonite men to enlist for service in the Red Cross, and the call did not go unheeded. Most Mennonites saw the medical service as an honorable alternative to military service.

During the first month of war no Mennonite men were called up because the government was trying to decide what type of service it would require of them. Russian families in nearby villages grumbled and complained as their own men were marched off while most young Mennonites continued to lead normal lives. Even when Mennonite harvest gangs moved in to do the threshing for the absent Russian farmers their wives and mothers were not appeased, though they accepted the help.

All that soon changed. In early September the first group of young Mennonites — over 700 of them — was ordered to Ekaterinoslav for enlistment. The government had decided, after consulting with Mennonite leaders, that Mennonite draftees would not be required to bear arms; instead, they could serve either on forestry stations or in medical units. In either case they would be serving in civilian organizations.

The largest of those organizations was the All-Russian *Zemstvos* (Municipalities) Union, which had been formed to provide hospital and ambulance train service to the Russian military. As early as mid-August a group of Mennonite volunteers from the Old Colony had gone to Moscow to join the AZU. They had been recruited by Paul Friesen, the son of P. M. Friesen, who had been appointed as a special recruiting officer for the medical service. The volunteer group was to form a training cadre for the throngs of Mennonite draftees shortly expected to arrive at AZU headquarters in Moscow.

Jacob Priess, who had been working with Erdmann Lepp in Petersburg that summer, decided to join the volunteers going to Moscow instead of waiting to be called up as a reservist. He returned to Fuerstenau just long enough to tender his resignation as a teacher and pack his belongings. Wilhelm was home in Blumenau and so missed seeing his friend before his departure for Moscow.

In Moscow the Mennonite volunteers reported to AZU headquarters on Nikitsky Boulevard. The Union, headed by Prince Lvov, had already received orders to equip and man fifty ambulance trains as soon as possible. Each train, depending on its size, would require personnel consisting of one or two doctors, up to half a dozen nurses, and from thirty-five to forty male orderlies and medics. The Mennonite personnel that would serve on these trains was to be housed in a four-story barracks on Tishinsky Street. The first volunteers found that the arrangements made for them were far from complete. They had to purchase their own makeshift uniforms from a clothing store. And the old factory that served them as a barracks would require considerable fixing up to make it fully habitable.

Once settled in, the volunteer group, augmented almost daily by new recruits, was put to work converting freight trains into ambulance trains. The men had elected Armin Lehn of the Old Colony as their *starshi* or group leader. Under his supervision they loaded three freight cars with enough equipment for five ambulance trains. These cars, along with several more for the medical staff itself, were then attached to a freight train headed for the western front.

These first ambulance trains were ready for the front barely in time to receive the first Russian casualties. The casualties, beginning as a mere trickle, would soon become a frightening flood.

Wilhelm was getting ready for the new school term when his conscription call came. He felt mainly relief at being suddenly released from a teaching job he had already tired of in his first year. Just to get out of the Molochnaya seemed like an exciting prospect, even if it meant facing the uncertainties and possible dangers brought on by war.

He decided that having rejected the forestry service once, he would not enter it now. No, it would be the medical service, preferably an ambulance train on active duty. Jacob had already written from Moscow, describing in detail the service he was helping to organize. He had urged his friend to come to Moscow as a volunteer. But Wilhelm had hesitated, feeling that with the new term about to begin his duty was to remain at his post until he was drafted. Snapper Loewen, who had been serving in the Old-Berdjansk forestry station for nearly a year, also wrote to say that he was applying for a transfer to the medical service in Moscow.

Old Stobbe was outraged when he heard of Wilhelm's call-up. "What, *now?* Just when school is opening? That's impossible! It's completely out of the question." He glowered at Wilhelm, long sharp nose a poised stiletto. "No, no," he repeated stubbornly, "it's completely out of the question.

Where can we possibly get another teacher now?" He threw his bony hands up in despair. "I can't take both rooms myself — running from one to the other." He sniffled and wheezed alarmingly over the unfairness of it all.

Wilhelm could not resist aggravating Old Carrion's self-pity. "Maybe they'll send you a nice, hearty Russian girl teacher from Tokmak or Melitopol." He knew Stobbe could not stand female teachers, especially if they were Russian. The old man was convinced that except for the nobility all Russians teemed with lice and disease germs, and he lived in terror of being contaminated by these human carriers.

"Never." Stobbe's straggly mustache quivered at its dunnish edges. "I'll quit myself if it comes to that. "I'll retire to my house in Ladekopp. Let the Russian *merjales* do what they like here."

"And have the authorities accuse you of being unpatriotic? Unsympathetic to the war effort? You wait, Herr Stobbe, we Mennonites will be watched closely just for being German if this war goes for any length of time."

So old Stobbe, looking more doleful than ever, fumed and fussed over what he considered an intolerable situation. But he vowed that no snippy Russian wench from a city gymnasium would boss him around in his own school. And if he ever found even one louse or germ in the school he'd quit, no matter what.

2

On a bright, warm morning in mid-September, several hundred Mennonite draftees gathered in Halbstadt for the trip to Ekaterinoslav, the mustering-in center for the area. Halbstadt was teeming with wagons, autos, and people on foot as more and more draftees arrived accompanied by their concerned families. Everybody headed for the churchyard, where the nervous young men, rucksacks beside them on the ground, were assembling with their families for an open-air farewell service conducted by Elder Heinrich Unruh.

The service was brief but emotionally gripping. Many of the onlookers and parents were moist-eyed, while the draftees tried to look manly and unconcerned. The atmosphere was reminiscent of the kind of funeral where the whole community came to mourn when a prominent person had died unexpectedly, or a child had been killed in an accident. Wilhelm glanced at "Hinkie" Klassen sitting near him and wondered with a sudden chill how many public funerals would take place here for these Mennonite boys about to leave.

Then it was over and the recruits picked up their gear and drove in droshkies, wagons, and autos to the station a few blocks away, their loved ones beside them. A train made up of some eight or nine freight cars waited to receive them. However, they were told that their train could not depart until the train bringing recruits from the Gnadenfeld *volost* to the east had arrived. The two groups of recruits were to travel to Ekaterinoslav together.

During the delay the ritual of leave-taking began all over again, with much embracing and eye-dabbing, as close-knit families surrendered to the ancient pain of physical separation amidst the dangers of war. Some of the draftees were family men approaching middle age. Mature and substantial-looking, they stood around somberly, surrounded by their families, including in some cases married children. These "graybeards" were mostly men who had already served their terms in the forestry service and did not relish the prospect of once again being separated from home for extended periods, even if it was a national emergency.

Like the rest, Wilhelm reeled under an onslaught of family goodbyes. His father's squat figure drooped dejectedly. He had removed his cap and was turning and squeezing it round and round as he spoke to Wilhelm in the hushed voice he used at funerals. Then, with a heavy lunge, he embraced his son one more time and gruffly ordered him to bear himself like a man no matter how God might test him. His mother pressed him again and again with such desperate strength that he felt tears springing to his eyes for the first time. Heinrich looked even more haggard than usual and, embarrassed, tried to stifle his chronic coughing as he pressed his brother's hand in mute love. Greta and Lenchen were alternately teary-eyed and starry-eyed. Several times Wilhelm caught Greta, a fresh-faced seventeen, looking around anxiously, as though searching for someone. He wondered who the young man was and whether he was even aware of Greta's interest.

The train from Gnadenfeld finally arrived with its seven cars of recruits and the Halbstadt boys embarked. The Gnadenfeld boys, already recovered from the agony of leave-taking, were in a cheerful, bantering mood and threw broad Low German quips at the people on the platform. Then the cars glided past the familiar faces and waving hands outside, and they were off.

In Ekaterinoslav the Mennonite draftees were taken to an old empty artillery barracks, a long three-story building that reminded Wilhem, oddly, of the Arts Academy in Petersburg. After they had been assigned bunks and had stowed their gear they were marched off to the mess hall at the headquarters compound nearby for the evening meal.

The long wooden mess tables were bare of everything except large wooden pots set at intervals. Seated, they looked at each other inquiringly, then spontaneously bowed their heads for grace, as they had done all their lives.

They looked with amused suspicion at the wooden spoons they had been issued. Those who were not satisfied blew on them and rubbed them clean on handkerchiefs or shirttails. Gingerly they dipped their spoons into the *kasha,* the buckwheat porridge that along with *khleb,* the hard, sour black bread of the peasant, was the Russian soldier's unvarying supper. Only the bread had not yet arrived at table. By the time it did they were halfway through the *kasha*. They found the *khleb* so hard they had trouble cutting it with their pocket knives. Chewing it enough to get it down made their jaws cramp. One man joked that his slice of *khleb* would make a good plate if only he had some food to put on it.

Never a fussy eater, Wilhelm was amused by the man on his left, one of the "graybeards" he had observed with his family in Halbstadt, who turned up his nose fastidiously and muttered something in Low German about being forced to eat rotten garbage out of a pig trough and chew on a piece of petrified cow pie. After supper some of the men discovered a small store nearby and stocked up on white bread and sausage.

The medical examination next morning presented no problems for most of the well-nourished, work-hardened Mennonite boys. A few were found medically unfit and given their release. The older rejects looked pleased and relieved, but a handful of younger ones were visibly disappointed or looked sheepish, as though they were letting their comrades down.

Wilhelm, standing naked with the others, accepted the Doctor's clipped *"godyen,"* which pronounced him fit for service, with a feeling of relief. Later he declared his preference for the medical service. Most of the older fellows who passed the physical chose the foresty service — the known evil over the unknown. As most of them had already served a three-year forestry hitch, they knew exactly what to expect.

Five days later they boarded a train for Moscow. First the station buildings, then the adjoining factories disappeared rapidly from view. As the train chugged through the autumn landscape, Wilhelm felt more depressed and apprehensive than he had when he left home. He stared disconsolately at the chequered gold-brown-black steppe flats, passive and bare, their crops harvested and carted away, and deliberately kept aloof from the groups chattering away in Low German all around him. The jokes were mostly about the food and medical examinations.

The more serious speculation concerned their immediate future. What would things be like in Moscow and what exactly would their war service be like? The more devout boys were ready to leave all in God's hands with a comforting "What He lets happen will happen." Others were less resigned and exchanged meagre bits of information on the various kinds of medical service. The consensus was that the ambulance trains going to the front constituted the most dangerous branch of the service. The safest would be base hospitals or, failing that, serving on the inland trains that took the wounded from places like Riga, Moscow, and Petrograd, as St. Petersburg had just been renamed, to cities safely inland.

Wilhelm listened to the discussion with disdain. Mennonite non-resistance ought to mean more than trying to stay as far away from enemy shells as possible. A lot more. And these fools didn't even realize that their most dangerous enemies might turn out to be disease and the anti-German campaign that was already underway in the Russian press against the country's German-speaking citizens. They would not be able to hide inland from those.

Well, let them find out the hard way, these innocent farm boys who had never been farther away from home than Berdjansk or Ekaterinoslav. They would soon get the ignorance and smugness knocked out of them! It would do them good, at least those who survived. The war would crack open those Mennonite shells, the shells that protected their view of themselves as a superior, privileged people in a land they still considered somewhat suspect after living in it for over a century. They would come back — if they came back at all — with their eyes opened to a world that would make the one they returned to seem small and dull by comparison.

But what about himself? Was he really any different? He had spent a little time away from the Molochnaya, had been exposed to a world these farm boys didn't know. His experience as an art student had enabled him to crack open his own protective shell, but had he really emerged from it? Could he honestly say that he had shaken off the accepted prejudices? Risen above church and community conformism rooted in a carefully prepared soil of custom, rules, and tradition? His thinking might be a little more sophisticated, but in his feelings and attitudes he was still very much a Mennonite. Certainly no Russian would ever take him for anything but German — a German alien and a potential traitor in this war!

He slumped down in his seat, closed his eyes wearily and tried to shut out the raucous Low German voices. And what was he as an artist? He didn't even have the right to call himself one. He was an apprentice who hadn't finished art school. Of the hundreds of things he had done, from rough sketches to finished oils, there wasn't one — no, not one — he could point to with pride as the real thing, as a work of art that could stand on its own. Shrewd old Burzev had urged him to get out into the world if he wanted to become a real artist. He had managed to do that, at least for a short time. He had tried, God knows he had tried. But had he ever really left Blumenau? Perhaps Kolya was right after all — at least in this — if you wanted to get out, really get out, you had to cut yourself loose, and not just see how far the rope would stretch.

Circumstances had been against him too. He had been forced to leave art school to avoid the forestry service. The monotonous routine of teaching had sapped his will to work seriously at his art. Even this summer he had been forced to put work on his father's farm ahead of everything else.

And now the war. Its demands were total. He would have to forget or at least postpone everything else for now. Even Clara. They still wrote to each other, but when would he see her again? Perhaps never. A shudder passed through him just as an explosion of laughter burst from the boys across the aisle. If only I could forget myself like these wisecracking yawpers, he thought bitterly. Well, he would have to try. He was in this with the rest of them and would have to make the best of it. He could already see that war was the great leveller — in more ways than one. He smiled to himself sardonically. In war the artist and the peasant stood shoulder to shoulder. Cannon fodder both.

The passing miles that were hurrying him to the war were also putting ever more distance between himself and Clara. The beginning of something was always the end of something else, it seemed. Already he was turning into a new man, one who could see the man he had been with much greater clarity. He saw himself as a young art student driven by vanity to cultivate a friendship with a charming girl who encouraged him to think of himself as someone special. He had talked to her a great deal about art, had tried to clarify the things that bothered him about himself as an artist. He could see now that most of it had been merely talk, the exuberant self-definition of a bumptious youth playing to an admiring, impressionable audience of one.

Worst of all, he had fallen in love with his pretty admirer. The ultimate vanity and delusion. Had fallen in love with a spoiled little rich girl making a winter's pet out of a naive farm boy dreaming a career as an artist. It hadn't been anything more for her. For all her giddy, flighty moods Clara was no fool. She was shrewd and realistic, especially about herself. She must have realized almost from the beginning that she was out of her depth as a serious singing student in Petersburg. Her talent as a singer was as charming but superficial as the rest of her. She had needed a diversion that winter, a distraction from her own failure as a singer. And she had been too proud or too stubborn to confess her failure until he had told her he was leaving the Academy at the end of the year.

Maybe it hadn't been quite that simple. Perhaps she had needed him not just as a diversion but as a support for her tottering career as a singing student. She had needed him as much as he had needed her. She had clung to him because he had faith in himself — the faith of ambition — which she had already lost in herself. She had fed on his artistic ego in a desperate attempt to sustain her own starved hopes. Well, why not? He'd had enough ego for both of them, he thought wryly. And she had after all been a brave girl to fight defeat for so long.

She had needed him, but she had not loved him. He was sure of that now. And when she no longer needed him she had bowed him out of her life with charming smiles, bright chatter, and cordial but one-time-only hospitality at her fairy castle of Selenaya. There the beautiful fairy had touched the magic wand of her finger to his lips and struck him . . . dumb. Had robbed him of the power to declare his love.

But then again perhaps she had done him a favor, knowing that she could not return his love. He could admit as much now. Yes, in the midst of his devastating disappointment he had felt a trickle of relief that she had spared him the humiliation of a formal rejection. She had the delicacy not to want to bruise his vanity. He supposed he should be grateful. It was a little like accepting the pain of a barked shin with relief when you realized how close you had come to breaking your leg.

He knew now he would never win her. He was done with her in a serious way. And the war, he hoped, would make it easier to forget.

And yet . . . Clara, bright golden Clara, his first and only love, the marvelous creature who had so entranced him. No matter how he tried to rationalize it, he felt sharp loss, an aching emptiness when he thought of her.

Wilhelm's low spirits persisted through the long, tedious hours on the train. Even his body felt sluggish and heavy. Like the others he dozed fitfully through the night, got out to stretch his cramped limbs whenever the train stopped briefly during the day. For the most part he kept to himself, making no effort to join the boisterous horseplay that was already fostering camaraderie among his fellow recruits.

Their train pulled into Moscow's Kursky Station in the early afternoon. The recruits were met by Armin Lehn, who was in charge of the Mennonite medical unit, and several of his assistants. Lehn and his staff had worked long hours to get the large Mennonite barracks ready for the influx of recruits. Chief Lehn was a brisk, business-like man who had already proven to be a masterful organizer. He and his men were smartly dressed in belted gray military tunics, black pants, and shiny boots. They wore high peaked caps complete with insignia, and their shoulder tabs bore the letters AZU. Each man also wore a large red and white Red Cross insignia on his left arm.

Promptly and efficiently the new men were lined up in four columns and marched through the streets of Moscow to the barracks on Tishinsky Street in the Pereulok district at the northern end of the Garden Ring. Most of the men, in the big city for the first time, their bodies stiff from traveling, marched with self-conscious awkwardness, aware they were drawing amused stares from the people they passed. After a while Wilhelm, like most of the others, didn't even try to stay in step. It was a march that seemed endless, although it was a warm, pleasant September day.

The barracks was a four-story brick building surrounded by a massive brick fence. Inside the main gate they passed a sentry-box manned by a Mennonite guard standing at rigid attention. Chief Lehn and his assistants saluted smartly as they came up to the sentry. A few of the recruits also tried to salute but most of them just stared stupidly at the guard.

They were shown through the main floor, which contained a large mess hall and kitchen in front and laundry rooms in the rear. On the second floor they passed by the administrative offices, a post office, and a small confectionary shop. Chief Lehn informed them there was also room on the floor for a barber shop and several much-needed workshops soon to be added.

As they were being ushered up to the third floor Wilhelm, glancing along the hallway, saw a familiar figure hurrying towards them. It was Jacob Priess with a sheaf of papers in his hand. The two friends greeted each other warmly. Jacob had been made Armin Lehn's administrative assistant, which meant he was second-in-command in the barracks. They would have time to visit at the supper table, Jacob said, and hurried off with his papers, his polished boots crinkling as he walked.

The dormitory on the third floor was filled end to end with densely packed rows of hospital cots separated by the narrowest of aisles. There was barely enough room to stand between the cots. There was no room at all for night tables, chest, or lockers. Personal possessions were piled on small wooden shelves crudely nailed to the rough walls. Clothes hung from nails everywhere. Boxes peeped out from under cots. There was apparently no fear of theft here.

They stood awkwardly in the narrow aisles while Chief Lehn said dryly that as they could see the dormitory was getting a little crowded. There were plans to replace the cots with double-tiered bunks as soon as possible. He instructed them to select their bunks and dismissed them with an order to report to the mess hall for the evening meal at seven sharp.

After their experience with military rations in Ekaterinoslav the recruits were pleasantly surprised by the food served for supper. It was like the food at home, consisting of good beef soup (left over from dinner), thick slices of fried ham, fried potatoes, and even some cold *plumemoos*.

Wilhelm and Jacob sat together. Jacob said grace for the several hundred men. As they ate their soup, Jacob explained how they could provide such familiar fare.

"When we first arrived we were given standard soldiers rations. Most of us couldn't stand the stuff so we petitoned headquarters to allow us to do our own provisioning. Now we're allowed fifty kopeks per day for each man. It's more than we need even for food like this. Our head cook Heinz Enns is an absolute wizard when it comes to buying supplies and planning menus."

"Well," Wilhelm drawled contentedly, mouth full, "if we can eat like this all the time, the boys will soon forget that buckwheat slop we've had till now."

Jacob's gentle face grew solemn. He put down his spoon, his voice grave with concern. "I'm afraid once you get on the trains, Willie, it won't be quite like this." His eyes went dark with remembered pain. "So much suffering this war is causing already. The slaughters at Gumbinnen and Tannenberg. Casualties piling up at stations, along the roads, in fields — we haven't got enough trains to fetch them. You can't imagine what those cloudbursts of steel at the front can do to human bodies — torn flesh, limbs shot off, wounds putrified and black with flies. Our boys came back from their first trips to the front in utter shock. Some just can't handle it. One of our corpsmen, a lad from Rosengart in the Old Colony, a Dirks, took a, took" — his voice faltered — "a revolver from a wounded soldier and shot himself through the head two weeks ago. It was only his second time to the front, but it was just too much for him." Jacob was struggling for control. "I don't know how God can let this terrible suffering go on like this. We try to console and counsel the boys whenever they come back here, but it's not easy."

He picked up his fork, poking abstractedly at the food on his plate. Then he looked up. "Too bad there isn't a place for you with the staff here. If an opening comes I'll try to get if for you." His eyes were warm with affection.

Wilhelm shook his head. Tremors of fear had passed through him as Jacob spoke. But he had made up his mind. "Jacob, I appreciate your concern. I know you're trying to help me, but I don't think I'd want to be in the office here." Embarrassed, he groped for the right words. "Please don't misunderstand me. I don't mean that I wouldn't like to be with you again, but . . . I, I feel — no I couldn't . . . here." His eyes pleaded for understanding.

"I'm frightened of what's to come, Jacob, and I know you're right —about the horrors of killing and maiming, I mean. The shock may be too much for me too. But you know, somehow I feel that I'm meant to go through it all. If I'm ever going to be an artist, my friend, than I've got to drink my cup — all of it — no matter what's in it." He stopped again, aware that he wasn't getting it right. It was coming out naively romantic somehow. He didn't feel it like that. He tried again. "I know one thing. I was slowly stagnating in Schoensee as a village teacher. I sketched only out of boredom, hardly painted at all, even this summer. I abhor violence and pain and suffering. You know how long it took me to get over what happened with those two hold-up guys. But now I feel I have to expose myself to all of it. If I don't I'll never develop the courage, the emotional toughness, a real artist must have."

It still hadn't come out right. He searched his friend's face, hoping he would understand, that he wouldn't feel offended or rebuffed.

Early next morning the recruits' training began. While an ambulance train was being prepared for them by the older hands, the new men were drilled in the military fundamentals of marching, identifying and saluting officers, and standing parade. They were, however, excused from handling firearms. Under the sharp eyes of Sergeant Ilyin they sweated in the warm September sun in the makeshift parade square behind the barracks.

For long days they marched, saluted, and stood at rigid attention, their muscular farm bodies trying awkwardly to adapt to the unaccustomed rhythms of regimented movements. Their Russian drill sergeant seemed to take cold enjoyment in putting these queer unarmed recruits through the harsh geometry of military drill. Wilhelm could read contempt behind his official parade square manner. Ilyin knew they were German and not real soldiers. Daily the papers screamed hatred for the Germans, including German citizens of Russia, who were branded as potential traitors. It was to be expected that a man like Ilyin would despise them.

After supper they were generally too tired to do anything but lie on their bunks exchanging quips and unkind remarks about Sergeant Ilyin. Wilhelm preferred to read or write letters. Some evenings he and Jacob sat in the latter's office and chatted comfortably as they used to when they were roommates in Petersburg. In any case, during their first month in training recruits were not permitted to leave the barracks unless they were required for service on the trains.

One evening Armin Lehn walked into the dormitory at the head of a new group of recruits. They were forestry boys who had volunteered for the medical service. And among them was Snapper Loewen! Wilhelm forgot his fatigue in the pleasure of greeting his old school buddy.

Snapper had lost none of his ebullience and brashness. "Pretty posh setup you guys have here, Rembrandt," he boomed as he surveyed the ludicrously overcrowded dormitory. "This is what I call cozy. Real cozy. At Old-Berdjansk our bunks were so widely separated by tables and cupboards and chests and just plain old space we had to shout to each other. This is so much more intimate. What happens when you stretch out your arm in your sleep and club your neighbor? Does he hit back, or does he thank you for shooing the flies away?"

The boys on their bunks nearby stared at Snapper. Wilhelm smiled. He knew about the forestry boys' habit of talking "through the flower," a form of conversational irony that pretended to find everthing, no matter how rotten, sweetly praiseworthy and reasonable.

"And I hear you have to march and drill all day. And in this autumn heat! I don't know if we forest children can take that. We're used to working in the shade."

But the forestry lads took to the training very well. They were already in good physical condition and used to a semi-military type of discipline.

After ten days of fairly intensive training Wilhelm's group was turned over to Mennonite instructors who were to familiarize them with their duties as orderlies and medics on the ambulance trains. When fully operational such trains consisted of thirty to forty cars, most of them *teplushki,* freight cars, roughly fitted out as medical wards with double tiers of bunks attached to the side walls, six to a side. There were usually several passenger cars as well with seats for the less seriously wounded who didn't require beds. There was also a first-aid car with an operation table and a kitchen car. The personnel normally consisted of two Russian doctors, half a dozen nurses, and thirty-five to forty male orderlies who were almost exclusively Mennonite. One of the orderlies became the *starshi,* or group leader, who was responsible for handing out work assignments and overseeing the orderlies generally.

Wilhelm and Snapper Loewen asked for and were granted permission to serve on the same train. They were assigned to train No. 188 under the direction of a crusty old army doctor called Barbarov (a fitting name, Snapper said). Their *starshi* was a Fritz Unruh from Osterwick in the Old

Colony. A quiet, decent chap whose lower lip was never without a stained cigarette stub, Fritz was one of the original group of volunteers who had come with the Lehn brothers in August. He had already made three or four trips to the front. Wilhelm was assigned to an ambulance car. Snapper, who claimed to have done some first-aid work at Old-Berdjansk, joined the staff in the antiseptic, neatly furnished first-aid car with its white-washed interior, its crisp linen, and locked supply cupboards.

3

Most of the newly fitted ambulance trains with their green crews were given several practice runs to hospitals in the interior before being sent to the frontier on a "live" mission. Train 188's first active run was a short, easy one. It was ordered to take wounded soldiers from a Moscow hospital to the Don city of Tambov. They began loading the bed cases in the afternoon and were ready to start at nine that evening.

Wilhelm had eleven men to take care of for the night. Several were severely wounded men recovering from operations and amputations who still required close attention. But at least they were properly disinfected and bandaged, which eased some of his nervousness. All he had in his car by way of supplies were bandages, iodine, and water. He fervently hoped that all would go well. He knew his crew was lucky to get such an easy maiden run. He had heard of green crews being sent directly to the front to pick up freshly wounded soldiers.

He was sitting in the rocking car reading at his tiny table next to his bunk. There was still a little gray light filtering through the two small, high windows in the car. So far everything was orderly and quiet. His patients were clean, deloused, and well-fed, and he foresaw no special problems. Still he felt a little nervous. Every few minutes he looked up from his book and ran his eyes over the inert forms under their neatly tucked gray blankets. A few were already asleep. The rest stared impassively into space or conversed sporadically in the spare, weary manner of the bedridden.

Before retiring, Wilhelm took his little oil lamp and made a final bed check for the night. He gave water to several, the bedpan to some, and pulled covers up against the early October chill. There was no heat in the car.

Finished, he pulled off his boots and lay down on the lower bunk reserved for him. He listened to the rattling of the wheels, the creaking of the darkened car. He had become part of the deadly routine that was war. That routine was beginning quietly enough for him, but he knew it wouldn't stay that way. For the moment he was safely removed from the bloody tempest. But the confusion and misery and terror were out there waiting for him. The broken, mutilated bodies around him were the victims of that insane storm. His turn would come too. On some as yet unknown battlefield he would be helping to gather up the messy human debris in a hail of bullets and shells. And then . . . .

He was just drifting into sleep when he was jolted awake by loud groans coming from the rear of the car. The groaning soldier was writhing in agony. He was one of the amputees. His bandaged leg, sheared off just under the knee, dangled awkwardly over the side of the cot. Dazed with sleep he must have been trying to get up for some reason and received a bad jolt from the swaying train. Even in the darkness Wilhelm could see a darker stain spreading around the wrapped stump. The young lieutenant looked up with fright-startled eyes. He was still straining to get up. Wilhelm said soothing words to him and pressed him gently down.

He tried to think through his alarm. What should he do? Since the freight cars that served as wards had no connecting passageways, he couldn't call a doctor or nurse until the train stopped. He was on his own and would have to do the best he could to rebandage the man's leg and hope the bleeding would stop.

He relit his little lamp with unsteady hands. But as he wound the fresh bandage tightly around the patient's stump he grew calmer. The sutures in the wound had not been torn and the bleeding was not as bad as he had feared. He covered the soldier carefully and went back to his bunk.

The rest of the night passed without incident, although Wilhelm could only sleep in fits and starts. Late the following day they arrived at the hospital in Tambov.

Back in Moscow, Wilhelm found waiting for him a letter with an Odessa postmark. It was a note from Kolya.

Dear Red Cross Brother,

Unlike you, I decided not to wait for my call-up. Have joined the army and expect to be sent either to the Polish or Caucasian front as soon as I finish basic training.

No doubt you and the family will write me off completely for this, but that can't be helped. I admit that serving on an ambulance train is less cowardly than hiding at home on the farm or on a forestry station. But it's not my idea of serving one's country in wartime.

I don't expect our paths to cross in this war. If I do get wounded I hope I don't end up on your train. You never were much good at giving aid and comfort to others were you?

Militarily yours
Kolya

4
Khodynka Field, Moscow, December, 1914

Train No. 188 made four more trips to interior cities, each time carrying between 300 and 400 patients to less crowded eastern and northern hospitals. The runs went smoothly enough and Wilhelm and Snapper and the rest of the newer orderlies began to think of themselves as veterans, though they had not yet seen any front-line service.

Wilhelm had felt sharp disappointment but little surprise at Nikolai's decision to become a fighting soldier. But he kept brooding over Kolya's references to him in the letter. What was Kolya accusing him of? Not caring enough? Not trying hard enough to understand the puzzling complex nature of his rebellious brother? And of not acting as a more diligent mediator between Kolya and his alienated parents? No, he would not allow his blacksheep brother to make him feel guilty, lay the blame for his hostility and alienation at his feet. Wilhelm longed to justify himself to Kolya. But he knew it would be futile.

Perhaps if they both survived the war they would have a chance to start all over again with each other.

But somewhere within him lingered a faint odor of guilt. And it bothered him.

When they returned in late November from their fifth run, a long one to Saratov on the Volga, they found the barracks buzzing with exciting news. In two weeks the royal family would be in Moscow for official inspections of military and medical installations. Their own No. Seven medical unit, a special AZU mobile volunteer group organized to serve on the Turkish front, had been selected for inspection. The unit was to set up a complete model field hospital on the huge military training ground known as Khodynka Field, on the outskirts of the city. It was the same field where several hundred over-eager peasants had been trampled to death at a gift-giving ceremony during the Tsar's coronation back in 1896. The field would now be a suitable place for a life-saving exercise, especially since there had been a trade exhibition on it that summer, and the great pavilion erected for it was still standing.

With the ground already frozen hard and raggedly covered with snow, the preparations for the royal inspection had to be elaborate and thorough. A work detachment from No. Seven cleared a large area in front of the pavilion and then thawed the frozen surface with great bonfires that looked oddly incongruous with the wintry surroundings. The high bank of snow cleared away from the pavilion formed a protective backdrop for the men who for days on end practised erecting and striking hospital tents until they could do so with smooth efficiency.

There was enough room for one very large hospital tent and four smaller tents that housed a first-aid station, an operating ward, a field kitchen, and a supply tent. The interiors of the tents were insulated with padded coverings and a stove installed in each one. They were fully furnished with cots, bedding, facilities, and supplies, just as they would be in actual field operations.

By the morning of December 8th, all was in readiness for the royal visit. Practically everyone from the barracks on Tishinsky Street managed to get to Khodynka Field one way or another. Even the walking sick and wounded from the infirmary refused to stay behind. The commandant of AZU headquarters in Moscow, B. N. Saltykov, stood at attention in the shelter of the pavilion along with an impressive array of uniformed officials. The route from the main entrance to the pavilion was lined on both sides by an honor guard of Mennonite corpsmen. Gathered around the main entrance but not permitted to enter the field were thousands of Moscow citizens who had heard or read about the royal visit.

Promptly at two in the afternoon a cavalcade of sleek, open limousines appeared at the main gate and slowly made its way to the pavilion. In the first car, standing at rigid attention in the frosty air, was the Governor General of Moscow. In the second car sat the Tsar, the Tsarina, and the Tsarevich Alexei. The third car bore the four pretty young grand duchesses. There was absolute silence as the cars glided between the rows of Mennonite men. There were none of the usual "hurras" as the Tsar's car passed by. Saltykov had decided that since they were only para-military personnel, they were to avoid the standard noisy military greetings.

Wilhelm and Snapper, whose train had returned the day before from a run to Nizhny Novgorod, had been last-minute additions to a group of corpsmen drawn up on the side closest to the kitchen tent. They had an unimpeded view as the cavalcade stopped and the royal party descended. After a brief opening ceremony the royal family began its inspection.

Wearing a simple combat officer's uniform, the Tsar looked diminutive and undistinguished. Seen at close range, his face appeared listless, pale, and creased with fatigue, and he had unsightly, bluish bags under his eyes. Wilhelm thought: This is the Emperor and Autocrat of all the Russias and I would not give him a second glance if I passed him on the street! The Tsarina, however, looked more properly regal. She was tall and bore her maturely rounded figure with an imperious air. But she too looked pale and fatigued around the eyes when Wilhelm got a closer look at her. There was a nervous guardedness about her, he noted, as though she was preoccupied with something, or protecting something from hostile eyes.

By contrast, the royal children looked fresh and animated, and obviously enjoyed being in the public eye. The Tsarevich Alexei, a lively lad of eleven, was dressed in a smart, dark blue naval uniform and greatcoat. The corners of his mouth quirked with mischief and he looked healthy and active, in spite of the ugly rumors that there was something odd about his physical condition. A step behind the Tsarevich walked a burly sailor with a long mustache who never took his eyes off the lad.

Wilhelm wondered why the boy was so closely guarded.

But he did not look at the prince for long. His eyes, like those of the other young Mennonite males, were irresistibly drawn to the four enchanting princesses. They were identically dressed in brilliant scarlet overcoats trimmed with fur and wore black fur hats set at smart angles. Wilhelm and Snapper agreed that Princess Tatiana, the second oldest and tallest of the four, was the prettiest. But all four were lovely, gracious-looking creatures who seemed to rise from the frozen ground like willowy red wands. Without acting in the least coquettish, they seemed to enjoy the admiring glances of the watching young men.

The inspection went quickly. The Tsar and his son stepped into the field kitchen tent, which was nearest to where Wilhelm and Snapper were standing. Through the open flap he saw the slight imperial figure frozen for a moment in profile, the short-bearded face dominated by the broad, snub Romanov nose he was known to detest. The Tsar took a step forward to the large, steaming soup kettle behind which chief cook Heinz Enns stood with an obsequious look on his long face. The Tsar murmured something and Enns produced a large wooden ladle, filled it, and passed it to his sovereign with a trembling hand. Nicholas took a tentative sip, gave a fleeting smile of approval and held the spoon for the Tsarevich, who also took a dutiful taste. Then they came out.

The Empress and her daughters emerged from the operating tent a few moments later. The royal party merged and headed for the large hospital tent. Suddenly Alexei gave his youngest sister Anastasia a playful little shove; she turned on him, annoyance in her eyes, ready to shove back. Immediately, the huge sailor stooped and gathered the Crown Prince deftly into his arms. He carried him the rest of the way to the tent. Wilhelm and Snapper looked at each other, wondering why the healthy-looking boy was being treated like a fragile child.

The royal visit was over before the assembled men even got their feet chilled, although it was a raw December day with icy gusts sweeping across the flat Khodynka grounds. The royal family and attending officials stepped back into their waiting autos and the cavalcade wound its way back to the entrance. Suddenly, spontaneously and against orders, the multitude of Mennonite corpsmen, quickly joined by the casual bystanders beyond the fence, broke into a long, sustained series of "Hurras." The Emperor and Empress smiled broadly in all directions and raised their white-gloved hands in fluttering little salutes. The princesses looked positively radiant as they smiled and waved. Then Princess Tatiana turned her head and for a long moment seemed to be looking straight at Wilhelm.

He would never forget that moment.

Then they were gone.

CHAPTER FIFTEEN

1
Schoenwiese, December, 1914

August Bock Senior, his coarse hippo face thrust forward, was waiting for the dozen men around the table to settle down. He was about to address the Administrative Board of Bock & Riesen Farm Implement company. The round, stolidly middleaged faces before him looked composed and alert. They were obedient "yes" men for the most part and knew it, but they were also shrewd. A special meeting meant trouble. Only youthful August Junior, haughty and studiedly casual as always, seemed unimpressed by the occasion. But then he already knew why the meeting had been called and was trying to hide his nervousness.

President Bock did not mince words. "I need hardly remind you, gentlemen, that the war is presenting us with problems we have never faced before — shortages in manpower, materials, transportation difficulties, and so on." He paused, then rumbled on without change of expression. "On the other hand, if we can weather the storm we may have new opportunities for growth and success. As the Russian says, when you fall into the river you find out how well you can swim.

"I want to give you the good and the bad together, though I don't claim they balance each other out. First, I'm happy to report we are now in a position to take care of our 200,000 ruble bank loan. The wartime government measure of shutting off bank credit to German-owned business firms may, in fact, have the beneficial effect of making us independent of bank financing in future. We've had an excellent year with record sales of binders and threshing machines, and we are in a position not only to repay the bank but to leave ourselves with an operating surplus that should carry us along for a bit in these uncertain times. The sixty days we were given in October are now up, and we are ready with our payment."

For the first time a glimmer of expression came into Bock's massive face. "Another piece of good news — for me personally, as you will appreciate —is that young August here has been exempted from the draft as an indispensible assistant in our operation."

The smooth, heavy faces turned towards August Junior with sedate expressions of congratulations which betrayed not a trace of resentment that their own sons had not been similarly favored. Young August nodded his long head and tried not to look smug.

"Also, all our factory hands have now been granted exemption from either military or alternative service for the duration of the war." Again murmurs of approval went around the room.

Bock leaned forward and scanned the faces before him intently. "The rest of my report is less pleasant. The Ministry of Defense for our province, of which I have the honor to be chairman as you know, met in Ekaterinoslav the day before yesterday. Gentlemen" — again the ponderous head swiveled slowly to left and right and the reverberating voice sank to funereal depths — "it is now certain that we'll be forced to go into" — he stressed the word carefully — *'real* defense production." He let the information sink in. "As you know, we are already producing mobile field kitchens — they present no problems. But the new order I've just received is for heavy wagons of another sort."

He surveyed his board with a look that would have made a Cossack quail. "The design of the new wagon is unmistakably that of a gun carriage." He stared straight ahead as the board members exchanged nervous glances. "As far as the public is concerned, we are still making only supply wagons, wagons to be used by the military. Under no circumstances are they to be identified as gun carriages. We must all agree on that point."

Jacob Riesen, Bock's partner, had assumed the fierce look of a bantam cock about to attack. He moved in with a rustle of feathers. He was the only man in the room who would even think of interrupting August Bock. "Let me add my word to that of our chairman," he crowed in his precise Molochnaya accent. "The last thing we want is to have a stink raised about violating our traditional Mennonite views against war and helping the war effort directly. "You know as well as I do," he added primly, "that nobody can afford the luxury of moral purity in a war. The government is taking our horses and our boys. Our horses will be used to pull the gun carriages we build. Our boys are nursing wounded Russian soldiers back to health so they can return to the front and shoot more Germans and Austrians." He glared around the table, his pale face glistening with righteous indignation.

August Bock, hiding his annoyance, moved in smoothly. "Yes, we all know we are caught in a situation not of our own making. All we can do now is to comply quietly and hope that there will be no serious consequences for the firm within the community. We are men of integrity and honor, so we must not be alarmist about this. Whatever happens, we must strive to retain the confidence and trust of our Mennonite people. Our customers will rely on us more than ever when this war is over. We here in South Russia are the breadbasket of Europe. Not even a war can change that."

Bock shifted uncomfortably in his chair. "However, I haven't yet told you the worst. We have been given another defense order that is potentially even more explosive" — Riesen looked startled at the unintended pun —"than the order for gun carriages. We are to begin casting casings for landmines and hand grenades as soon as possible."

This time the impassive faces around the table registered something close to consternation. Making munitions! They saw no way of keeping this order from becoming common knowledge.

Bock read their faces. "I know what you are thinking, gentlemen. Let me reassure you, however, at least partly. For the time being the casings are to be stockpiled here at the factory, pending shipment to other factories where they are to be loaded. We'll use the old warehouse in the back lot for that purpose. And we'll make sure our workers do not talk. The men will be sworn to silence on pain of dismissal. Our men consider themselves very lucky to have good paying jobs in this war instead of becoming cannon fodder at the front. I'm reasonably confident we can keep this whole operation a secret. When the time comes to ship the casing consignment we'll do it at night, secretly. In the meantime no unauthorized visitors will be permitted on the premises. I've already hired extra guards."

The massive jaw pushed forward like a battering ram. "It is absolutely imperative, gentlemen, that we protect our interests as best we can. Bock and Riesen must not be allowed to sink into disrepute — or even ruin" — the low thunder of the voice sounded like the last rumbling of a summer storm — "because of carelessness or lack of vigilance on our part."

The emergency board meeting was over. Chairman Bock left the room chatting affably with the members of his board, but he was more troubled than he had been willing to show before the others. August Bock took quiet pride in his personal integrity and in his reputation as a businessman.

Only he knew how deeply the dilemma the firm was in worried him.

2

Clara Bock lay sprawled on her bed feeling sorry for herself. She had excused herself from the dinner table as soon as possible. She was sick and tired of hearing about the stupid war and what it was doing to business and the German people in Russia. It was all so depressing and tiresome. Tonight her father had invited some of the members of his Board of Directors home for dinner — fat, middle-aged men in thick dark suits from hick places like Khortitza and Osterwick who smiled at her fawningly with their yellow teeth and bushy eyebrows and mustaches — and so there had been even more talk than usual about the war and business.

Why had the war come now, just when she was enjoying the best and freest part of her life, before she would have to marry, settle down, and raise a family like everyone else?

Her irritation flared into anger as she thought of that sly serving girl Marusya snooping around the dining table pretending to be helpful with her sarcastic face. Clara was convinced the girl was listening carefully to the conversation, that she could understand a lot more German than she let on. She could even — well, be a spy of some sort. Clara had mentioned this possibility to her mother, but Mama, as usual, defended the servant. "Pooh, Clara, shame on you. Marusya may think too well of herself for a servant; but she's too ignorant and slow-witted to be a spy for anybody. What a ridiculous idea."

But Clara kept her eye on the detestable creature. She was sure the girl was up to something. Sooner or later she would give herself away and then even Mama would be convinced. Could it be that there was something going on between the maid and Gusha? Several times lately Clara thought she had seen knowing looks pass between Marusya and her brother. But no, that couldn't be. The girl was a slut and though August was a bit of a playboy surely he was above that sort of thing. Not a Russian domestic — at home? She dismissed the idea from her mind.

She groped on the bed for the letter from Vasya and read it through once more. It was long and detailed, exactly the kind of letter she like to receive from him. He gave a colorful, witty account of barracks life in Moscow, and of his present service on the trains. But he made no attempt to glamorize his war service, and Clara thought she detected a deep sense of frustration, a dark streak of fatalism running through the letter. There was no real excitement in his tone, no sparks of discovery as he relived his experiences on paper. She couldn't quite understand his passive attitude. She herself, thirsting for a larger freedom, for novel experiences, would have welcomed the chance to exchange her safe, mundane existence for uncertain but novel trips into the unknown and encounters with people who were different and therefore exciting.

She noted again that the personal parts of Vasya's letter were carefully neutral in tone. He was no longer presuming anything about their relationship and its future. She felt a twinge of guilt as she realized how perceptively he had read the import of his weekend in Schoenwiese the year before. Since then, although they had not seen each other, they had continued to correspond on a more or less regular basis. In her letters to him she tried to recapture the free, bohemian feeling of camaraderie they had shared in Petersburg during their winter together, but Vasya's letters maintained a personal reserve which her warmer, freer letters could not seem to dispel. But whenever she tried to reassess her feelings for the intense young man from the Molochnaya, she becme confused. Even as she longed for his presence and the easy, confessional feeling of intimacy they had shared, she knew with sad certainty and a regret she knew would linger that Wilhelm Fast would not be a permanent part of her future. But in the meantime —

The soft knock on her door took her by surprise. Wasn't her mother still downstairs with her father's guests?

"Come in," she called puzzled.

The door opened and Marusya stood there, her expression for once more self-conscious than defiant or arrogant.

"Excuse me, Miss Cl—"

"What do you want?" Clara snapped, swinging her legs to the floor.

The girl looked around cautiously. "May I speak to you for a moment?"

"Why aren't you downstairs tending to your duties?"

The black eyes hardened. "They're all in the drawing room. I'm not needed just now." Her look grew bolder.

Suddenly it was Clara who felt a little uncomfortable. How did the girl dare come to her room? And why? "I'm not interested in your grubby affairs with the coachman and other servants, if that's what you want to talk about." She felt herself lifted on a wave of rancor. "I know what you are. And I don't like your snooping and listening to things that don't concern you."

She could not stare down the insolent black eyes. Her rage crested. "You won't be here much longer. I promise you." Her vehemence had brought her to her feet. She was shaking.

The black eyes flashed back hatred and the curved nose gleamed in the dim light of the room as Marusya tossed her head contemptuously. "I don't give a damn what you think about me or my conduct, *Miss,*" she hissed. "But you should care about the conduct of your high-and-mighty brother."

So, she had guessed right. Gusha had — she felt herself losing control. "What, you dare mention my brother, you slut? Get out of here" — she was screaming now — "get out, get out, or I'll call him right now. Then we'll see." She advanced towards the girl at the door, but Marusya did not retreat. "This time you've gone too far. I'll speak to my mother. You'll be gone from here within the hour." She stopped just short of the haughty creature and glared at her with loathing.

Marusya stood her ground calmly, arms folded across her slim breast. "More fool you, if you won't even hear what I've got to say. Listen, your precious brother isn't exactly a Mennonite saint. He's mixed up with some pretty —"

"Out, out, out," Clara screeched, waving her arms in a frenzy. "You're finished here, you filthy peasant. How dare you come in here with your dirty slander."

Still facing her coolly, the maid opened the door behind her back and took a parting shot. "You decadent bourgeois fools are all the same. You have a death wish — and you'll get your wish soon enough." She gave a mocking laugh. "There's an old saying: When the birds get into your fruit trees something drastic has to be done! And you foreigners have been pecking our fruit for too long."

Marusya shut the door before Clara could reach her. Clara stood there, staring murderous rage at the closed door. Gradually she grew calmer. At last that hateful tramp had given herself away. Here was her chance. Her mother would believe her now. Mama was strangely tolerant of what the servants did in their spare time so long as they were discreet and didn't neglect their duties. "The Russian peasant is a grown-up child," she liked to say. "He indulges his feelings and drives as spontaneously as a child. He likes to act out his feelings and desires as soon as discipline is relaxed or he is at play."

But Marusya Nikoforovna had gone too far. She was sent packing that same night by a stony-faced Mrs. Bock.

Not until the next day did Clara discover that her favorite necklace and matching earrings had disappeared along with the discharged servant.

3

Everything considered, August Junior was relieved to see Marusya dismissed from the house. But he felt uneasy as he listened to the family tirade against "that unbearable, thieving Russian wench." He knew Marusya had tried to tell Clara something about him, but his sister claimed she had cut the girl off before she could say anything. So, he was not betrayed. He didn't have to worry about that at least. The bitch! What was she trying to gain by talking to Clara? Was she simply trying to get back at him because he had told her it was too risky for them to get together again, that they better not see each other again?

It wasn't that he was tired of her — it wasn't that at all. Actually, she excited him more all the time. In bed she was a fiery creature with her supple boys's body, an elemental force that swept him to dizzying heights of passion. But that was the problem. She was so tempestuous she made him feel inadequate as a lover. No, it was more than that. She actually frightened him with the wild fury of her love making. She seemed driven by some savage instinct that turned her into a raging, thrashing beast. As though she wanted to destroy him — yes, that was it — take apart his body limb by limb with her hard, frenzied lover's blows. They weren't kisses and caresses so much as the lashings of an enemy, a punishing attack. Yes, yes, she hated him! That was it. In her wild sexual rage she violated him against his will, took his body as impersonally and brutally as though *he* were the hired whore.

And all the time he could feel her laughing at him. Yes, laughing at him, as though she were using him in ways he was too stupid to fathom. It had started when he rented that little room for them at the north end of Alexandrovsk, the other end of town from Schoenwiese. That's when she had started brazenly mocking the master-servant relationship.

The rotten bitch! And he had plied her with money and gifts — more than she'd ever had in her miserable peasant life.

There was something even worse nagging at him. Marusya knew far too much about his private life in general, about the dissolute habits he had so far hidden successfully from his family. What if she had been trying to blackmail him through Clara? Marusya was smart enough to know that Clara would do almost anything to protect her brother and the family name. What the bitch clearly hadn't reckoned with was Clara's quick temper, her harsh dislike for the Russian girl, which she voiced almost daily. He smiled to himself. Trust Clara not even to listen to a servant whom she despised so heartily. Come to think of it, why was Clara's hatred for Marusya so violent and irrational? Did she see something other than the servant in the girl? Did she feel threatened by her in some obscure way?

Whatever the reason, her fierce loyalty had saved him — this time.

Ruefully, he resolved to be more careful in future. But he had a sinking feeling that perhaps he had gone too far already. He knew Marusya was no fool; she was anything but the dim-witted peasant servant she pretended to be. He had early discovered that she was proud, belligerent, cunning, and determined to get her way. And he was sure they had not heard the last of her. Would she try to blackmail him directly now? What if she were pregnant?

He had been a fool to take chances with such a creature. Never again, he vowed.

4

In Blumenau the Fast family was sunk in gloom and shame. Nikolai's curt letter telling them that he was now a member of the Imperial Army, a fighting soldier soon to be sent to the front, had sent parents and children alike into a state of shock. No other family in Blumenau — in the whole Molochnaya, so far as they knew — had as yet experienced the disgrace, the deep shame of having a son who had callously, sinfully violated the sacred Mennonite practise of nonresistance. Mennonite refusal to bear arms had been an example for a quarrelsome world since Anabaptist times, Father Fast reminded his family at the breakfast table one morning after he had read a lesson on brotherly love and divine grace in the Kroeker "tear-off" religious calendar with which they began each day.

Only in his mid-fifties, Gerhard Fast had aged visibly of late. Always a stolid, prudent man who had built his life and that of his family around the order, stability, and purposeful routine of his time-consecrated *wirtschaft,* he was feeling more and more unsettled and threatened by the inexplicable events and changes swirling around him. His once thick, dark hair now looked grizzled and dishevelled, and the once powerful, squat frame was beginning to droop at the shoulders and hips, as though pulled down by an invisible force. His weather-blanched eyes had lost their confident directness, now wavering and blinking as though dazed by dark confusions.

Almost daily Fast and the other Mennonite farmers, respected pillars of the community, were subjected to some new war order calculated, it seemed, to deprive them of what was rightfully theirs and to humiliate them into the bargain. First it had been the horses. Within days of the declaration of war they had been ordered to take their work horses to the requisition center in Tokmak where they were graded and selected for war service by a commission of army officers. Today it's our horses, tomorrow it will be our boys, the men had agreed gloomily as they drove their sleek, carefully bred horses to Bolshoi Tokmak.

Old Anton the stableman, a little maudlin with age, was devastated by the "theft" of the horses. At first he flatly refused to let his "brave pigeons" go to be "shot down like old dogs in a ditch." He stood defiantly before the horse stalls massaging his dirty-gray stubble beard with one hand while pulling nervously at his frayed old rope belt with the other, all the while swearing warmly that Mennonite horses, like Mennonite boys, did not have to go to war, were not meant to do anything but work on the farm. Besides, Galya was as delicate and skittish as a schoolgirl, couldn't stand loud noises, and would bolt at the first sound of gunfire. And that old villain Vanya would refuse to work at all for strangers.

The old man was finally persuaded to step aside, but only after he had been repeatedly assured that there was a good chance that at least some of the older horses would be found unfit for service and returned. His rheumy eyes brimming with tears, Old Anton said an emotional farewell to each horse, lovingly repeating all the curses and threats he hurled at them daily in his trilingual patois. Gravely he told them all that they would now belong to *Batushka* Tsar, and that they were to work well and "show respect."

But when the old man saw his master moving towards the stall of Major, Wilhelm's own riding horse, he left the other horses and hobbled over to the stall weeping and beseeching "Papasha" to spare at least Major. Gerhard Fast, already affected by Old Anton's distraught state, quickly agreed to leave Major behind. After all, the order had not specifically called for riding horses.

After the horses had been taken away, Old Anton, sullen with grief, retreated to his box above the now empty horse stalls. Next morning he was missing. He was gone for a week, and when he returned early one moning he looked like a man who had lost a terrible battle with *samogon* and been forced to recuperate in cold ditches.

The war measures came thick and fast after that. An order was issued that German place names were to be replaced by Russian names. Thus Halbstadt was transformed into "Molochansk" and Blumenau became "Sadovoie." One weekend the Molochnaya villages were ordered to prepare masses of roasted buns for the soldiers at the front. Then came the order for all pigeons to be registered for possible use as carrier pigeons. Heinrich, whose hobby was raising fine homing pigeons, was alarmed by the possibility of losing his flock and could be heard coughing more than ever at night.

The death in October of P. M. Friesen seemed to many, including Gerhard Fast, to be another ominous sign of the times. His passing seemed to symbolize the end of an era for the Mennonites of Russia. Sadly, Father Fast paid his last respects to his old teacher in the village of Tiege, where Friesen had live in relative obscurity after illness had forced him into retirement the year before.

In early November, on top of the growing anti-German hate campaign directly aimed at German-speaking Russian citizens, came an imperial decree banning the use of the German language in the press or in public assembly. The penalty for violating the decree was a fine of 3,000 rubles or three months in prison. Although not completely unexpected, the Mennonite colonies were badly shaken by the prohibition. The language which for over a century had been their sacred language of faith and church teaching was now to vanish from their lips. What could take its place? To adopt Russian as a church language was unthinkable — even if all Mennonites had had a command of it, which was very far from being the case. It was sacriligious to even contemplate such a move, although it would undoubtedly have made a favorable impression on the government.

In the hastily called brotherhood meetings Mennonite congregations almost unanimously agreed to conduct their services, for the duration of the war only of course, in the homely, less than spiritually dignified Low German which most of them spoke almost exclusively on weekdays anyway. The case would be made to the government that *Plautdietsch* was really a form of Dutch, and therefore exempt from the decree.

Hardly had the language crisis been met when even more disturbing rumors of government measures began to circulate. The Tsar was about to sign the most draconian law of all: the dreaded property liquidation law that would force the Mennonites and other Russian Germans to sell their land and property at a fraction of their worth. They themselves would be forced to move, holus-bolus, to the East — perhaps even to Siberia! There were reliable reports that German colonists in the western province of Volhynia on the Polish border were already being dispossessed and sent east even before the liquidation law had been issued. It was only a matter of time before the authorities would get to the heart of South Russia and the main Mennonite colonies.

In late November Gerhard Fast suffered a severe personal blow when his close, life-long friend Dirk Peters, who owned a large steam mill in Halbstadt, was arrested for having spoken German to his foreman in the mill. It was unbelievable, but true! Peters must have been reported by one of the Russian peasants having his grain milled at the time. Dirk was being held in Tokmak while the authorities dithered and tried to decide whether to prosecute him or not. There was talk that Peters might wind up in Siberian exile for the crime of having spoken a few sentences of German in public!

Gerhard Fast could not comprehend such iniquities. They were entirely beyond the world he knew or recognized. He faced each new day with a vague sense of foreboding that gave him a tight feeling in the chest and made him forget at times where he was or what he was doing. He saw the world as suddenly gone mad, like one of the hideous nightmares he sometimes got when he overloaded his stomach with his wife's *wrennitje* or waffles with beet syrup. But this nightmare could not be digested away overnight. Only God knew how long it would go on. Now Christmas was coming and they had been notified that there were to be no decorated Christmas trees on display during the holiday season. Apparently Christmas trees were considered a decadent German custom and contrary to the spirit of Russian culture.

Father Fast looked around his once solid *wirtschaft* and saw it dissolving before his dazed eyes. Wilhelm was away serving in the war. Kolya was in the shooting army — even now perhaps on his way to the front. Of his three sons only Heinrich remained at home, and he had been spared from war service only because he was slowly dying of consumption.

Beset by worries and fears for the future, Gerhard Fast shrank into his ageing bulldog body and grew moodier and more peevish.

Even Mother Fast, talkative and outgoing by nature, lapsed into uncharacteristic silences and sometimes went to the summer room in the middle of the day. There she sat on the scarred old sleepbench and wept quietly and inconsolably for her absent sons. And for her failing husband and doomed son at home. She wept also for a world of violence and bloodshed which she could only picture as a kind of red mist or haze in which shadowy, silent figures ran, stumbled, and fell, brought down by a force she could not see. The picture had no sound. Her sobs the only voices she could hear.

CHAPTER SIXTEEN

1

Moscow, Spring, 1915

That first winter of war passed quickly for Wilhelm. Train No. 188 was kept busy transporting thousands of wounded soldiers from Moscow and Petrograd to cities and towns in the east. By the time spring arrived in late March Wilhelm's crew had ten uneventful trips behind them. Although there had been no serious incidents, he still dreaded the long hours between stops when he was completely isolated in his car from the rest of the train and the doctors and nurses. Often their station stops were so brief that the medical staff had time to visit only those cars where they were most needed.

Several times Wilhelm's car had been near the back of the train far removed from the medical staff car and so his patients had not been checked for the better part of a day or night. The neglect had caused him much anxiety. He dreaded the prospect of having a patient die on him as a result. Several of his patients had been in bad shape and he had feared the worst. One of them had been an aristocratic-looking young soldier with both legs amputated above the knees. He was still in a great deal of pain and delirious much of the time. In fact, he was lucky to be alive at all. Not many double-leg amputees survived Russian field surgery, he had been told. And yet this boyish amputee was being moved hundreds of miles on a jolting train with his stumps still raw from the knife!

Wilhelm often wondered whether he would ever get used to it. There seemed to be no respect at all for human life in wartime, even for the sick and wounded in one's own country. The doctors and AZU officials seemed to turn a deaf ear to the simplest and most sensible suggestions for improving the ambulance service and alleviating the needless suffering caused by neglect and inadequate facilities. The Mennonite first aid men had repeatedly suggested, for example, that the cars should have connecting passageways for the good of the patients, but so far nothing had been done.

Russia was rumored to be ready to launch a major spring offensive on the Polish front. The barracks in Moscow were now receiving new Mennonite recruits almost every day. Something big was up. The men agreed that for most of them the soft inland runs would soon be over. As the number of wounded mounted in the new campaign, more ambulance trains would have to be sent to the front lines directly. Wilhelm felt flutters of anxiety whenever he thought of their train moving into the orbit of slaughter at the front.

Snapper, however, remained breezy and unconcerned. "Can't expect to keep the cushy job forever, Rembrandt," he drawled one day when they were back in Moscow. "Got to give the new kids a chance to learn to play nursemaid without getting shot at. Our basic training is over, old buddy. It's the real thing for us now."

Wilhelm noted though that for once Snapper's eyes did not quite match the easy confidence of his words.

The next day, as he was passing by Jacob's office, Wilhelm thought he recognized the uniformed figure sitting there with Jacob and Armin Lehn. He was sure it was Paul Friesen, P. M.'s son, whose home in Moscow he had visited with Clara and August Bock. Paul Friesen was the AZU's special recruiting officer in the Mennonite colonies.

Later Jacob, who knew Paul Friesen well by now, invited Wilhelm to join them for afternoon coffee. Friesen remembered Wilhelm immediately. A shadow passed over his face as he recalled that evening, the last his father had spent with his beloved students.

"Father never recovered fully from the attack he suffered that night. Shortly afterwards we gave up the house in Moscow and my parents retired to a little cottage in Tiege. Father's diabetes was getting worse and he was going blind with cataracts. But he still insisted on working. Mother would prop him up in a chair in the morning and he would work hour after hour on the supplement to his history. When the war started he seemed to get a new lease on life. All his patriotic fervor came out and he complained constantly about not being able to help in some way.

"He was eager for me to volunteer for alternative service. He said he envied me. While I was helping to organize the Mennonite service here in Moscow he wrote me long letters encouraging me and demanding to know all the details of the work here. He also speculated about the war and filled whole pages with patriotic slogans and declarations. He was very proud of our Mennonite contribution to the war and of the good reception we were getting from the Russian authorities. 'You see, my boy,' he liked to say, 'we may be a tiny speck on the vast Russian landscape but they can see us. We have their respect. They know we won't let them down in time of need. They discovered that during the Crimean War.'

"When I got back to the Molochnaya to recruit last October he insisted on accompanying me to Halbstadt even though he couldn't walk unaided to the carriage. Even with his hearing going he was eager to attend all our sessions and seemed to follow every turn in our discussions. A week later he insisted on going to Halbstadt with me again. When Mother warned him he was courting death, he replied: 'At least I'll die with my loved ones nearby. What about the millions who are dying and will die in this war without anyone even caring?'

"Well or dying you couldn't faze the man. After I got back to Moscow he wrote and gave me detailed instructions about his funeral arrangements. At the same time he strictly forbade me to come home for his funeral, 'since so many fathers,' he said, 'were forced to die now without having their sons present.'"

Friesen's voice caught at this point. It was obvious that he had loved his father deeply and that his recent death was still very much an open wound with him.

He looked thoughtful as he drained the last of his coffee. "Perhaps it was a mercy for my father to pass away when he did. This war is sure to change everything for us Mennonites. P. M.'s safe, secure world is gone. No matter what the outcome of this war, my friends, things will never be the same for us here in Russia. This vicious anti-German campaign is just the beginning. We are now unwanted step-children of Mother Russia and must expect to be treated as such from now on. My father was able to take most of his illusions about this country to the grave with him. We won't be so lucky, I fear. The signs are there for us to read now. And they are all bad."

2

"Ah, my dear friend Fast. Here you are at last. I've been looking for you for weeks, but you always seem to be away on your train."

Above him on the stairs he saw the long, gaunt figure of Erdmann Lepp. Wilhelm, climbing with his head down, had almost run into the minister. Startled, he shot out his hand in greeting and Lepp pumped it vigorously.

"How well you look, Wilhelm. Life in the service of your country must be agreeing with you," Lepp enthused as he surveyed Wilhelm's trim figure. "I've been asking Jacob about you. He keeps telling me how happy he is to have you here, even if your work keeps you on the road much of the time."

Lepp paused and Wilhelm could guess what his next comment would be.

"I grieve for your brother, Wilhelm. But then we've all seen this coming, haven't we? We must continue to pray for him. May God grant that Nikolai will survive this terrible war. Perhaps the terrors of the battle field will shock him into facing the truth where all else failed."

Groaning inwardly, Wilhelm found his face shaping itself into the proper expression of gratitude for Lepp's sympathetic concern for Kolya. Why doesn't he say what he really thinks: that Kolya is irredeemably lost — beyond the pale — that there is no hope at all that he will ever change?

It was late afternoon and Wilhelm was just coming from a walk before dinner. He had felt tired and depressed after returning from his latest run —to Pensa — with a trainload of wounded soldiers. There seemed to be more serious cases on the trains all the time, and the suffering soldiers looked younger and younger.

And his secret fear was getting worse. He could not enter a hospital ward now without expecting to see Kolya in one of the beds. At first glance he thought more than once that he had actually seen him. He knew the odds of this happening in an army that numbered in the millions were slight, to say the least, but he was braced for it all the same.

Lepp, still talking, was accompanying him up the stairs to the second floor of the barracks. He gripped Wilhelm's arm firmly. "Come, my friend.

I've looked in on Jacob. He is just finishing for the day, and then we can have a nice quiet chat, the three of us." He looked at Wilhelm benignly. "The last time I saw you you were a carefree student in Petersburg hobnobbing with student friends. By the way, young August Bock is now in his father's firm and seems to be doing well. But I suppose you know that. And of course" —the voice turned delicately arch — "there is Clara, the beautiful Clara. I know you and she became dear friends in the capital."

Blushing in spite of himself, Wilhelm chose to ignore the older man's roguish glance as they reached the second floor landing. He noted though that climbing the stairs while talking had not affected Lepp's breathing at all.

They entered Jacob's office just as he was phoning in his daily report to AZU headquarters. He reported that he had telegraphed the military commandant in Ekaterinoslav for fifty additional Mennonite first-aid men to be sent as soon as possible. He also gave a brief account of how the training of new crews for service on the trains was coming along. Once again Wilhelm couldn't help admiring the brisk efficiency of his friend. Here in Moscow Jacob was showing qualities of leadership that Wilhelm had not detected in him before the war.

Having completed his report Jacob turned eagerly to his revered mentor Erdmann Lepp. Gone instantly was the easy, confident administrative manner. Jacob was again the devoted disciple, humble and pious, ready and eager to assist the inspired master. And Lepp accepted Jacob's gift of himself with a benevolent air that bordered on the complacent, Wilhelm noted critically. And then wondered guiltily whether he might be feeling a touch of jealousy. Not having seen the two men together since their first meeting in Petersburg, he had not been able to observe till now the closeness of their relationship.

Lepp was brimming with optimism over the way the "work" was going in wartime. He was the newly appointed official chaplain to the Mennonite medical unit in Moscow. The Baptist seminary in the capital had been forced to close its doors shortly after war began. August Reimer and several other teachers had been drafted. Lepp himself was too old for the service. He had, however, immediately seen the splendid new opportunities for evangelism that the war brought with it. He took his duties as spiritual counselor to the Mennonite draftees in Moscow seriously enough, but he also saw an opportunity to extend his ministry to Russian troops.

"God hates war and the suffering it brings," Lepp was saying, "but He wants us to use even that to advantage in our ministry. In the present situation our work is taking a new direction." Jacob's face glowed with an inner light as he listened to Lepp. "Everywhere there are soldiers — young men torn from their homes — who are confused and frightened and lost, including many of our own boys. They all need spiritual help and are hungering for it. The Russian peasant soldier especially. Illicit alcohol and women will not appease his hunger. He is open to the Word as never before. The village priest is no longer there to ward off true spiritual contact, to keep him in the old state of spiritual sloth. The young men are scared now and open to the truth." He banged his bony fist down on Jacob's solid oak desk. "Open, my friends. There has never been a more glorious opportunity for doing God's work here in Russia."

The passion that illumined Lepp's ascetic face was reflected in Jacob's youthful countenance like an image in a mirror.

"Yes, in the midst of devastation and carnage," Lepp continued in a blaze, "God has chosen to prepare the field for harvest." He turned to Wilhelm, his voice now soft and insinuating. "And you, my dear young friend, if only you could give yourself to the work too, as Jacob is doing with such rich blessings."

Caught by surprise, Wilhelm turned to Jacob, who was also regarding him raptly, as though both men were waiting for a sign from him, a sudden, spontaneous commitment.

Once again Lepp's intense voice was casting its spell over him. "Remember, my boy, God's love is centripetal, it pulls everybody to its loving center — saints, sinners, and ordinary men." He leaned forward, touched his long fingers lightly to Wilhelm's wrist. "You could begin by examining your own conscience. Is your relationship with the loving Christ what it should be? Have you experienced his cleansing grace yourself?"

Wilhelm felt himself unmoored once more by guilt and confusion under Lepp's relentless prodding. Then anger washed him back. Why did he allow himself to be put on the defensive every time he came into contact with this spiritual hypnotist? A clear, calm inner voice told him to hold on to himself, reminded him coolly that Lepp's burning words consumed as much truth as they illuminated.

But Lepp was not through. "If you are in a state of grace, Wilhelm, then you will want to share your joy with others. Your fellow orderlies — are they all committed Christians? Or do some of them live unclean lives now that they have been removed from the wholesome influences of home and church? That is a mission you can—"

"Onkel Lepp" — Wilhelm's resentment burst to the surface beyond his will to control — "please forgive me, but I don't consider myself a missionary and I don't want to be one. Whether I'm a Christian or not is for God and my own conscience to decide. I — I" — he looked at his friend Jacob for help, but saw in his face only surprise and chagrin at Wilhelm's impertinent rejection. He stumbled on with a sickening feeling that for the first time in his life he was publicly exposing the dark lining of his own soul, revealing his weak inner state for the world to see. The feeling that all was lost anyway, that he could not swallow back the offending words, made him even more reckless. "I want to be left alone, you see. I don't want to be pushed into a corner every time I meet you, Onkel Lepp — like a naughty schoolboy who is expected to confess on demand, whether he has committed a suitable sin that day or not."

He rose stiffly. "And now if you'll excuse me, there's something I have to do before dinner."

As he left Jacob's office he was already regretting his outburst. What would Lepp think of him? And Jacob? What if Jacob had asked Lepp to "speak" to his friend? He had no right to embarrass Jacob like that, to cast aside his loving concern in a public display of pique, whatever the aggravation.

He had stupidly burned another bridge he might want to cross again some day. How many more were left?

3
Polish Front, April, 1915

Wilhelm and Snapper were sitting together in the rear car of their train watching the unfamiliar landscape rolling by. It was a former passenger carriage used to transport the walking wounded or those who could at least sit up.   This time they were really on their way to the front — the Polish front. That was all they had been told.

It was their fifth day out of Moscow and the sheer tedium and weariness of traveling had made them listless and ill-humored. Even the usually loquacious Snapper was lapsing into long silences. They had long since readied their respective cars for the coming action and now had nothing to do but wait for their destination. Wilhelm had made up his twelve bunks so tightly they looked like gray table tops. His white rolls of bandages were piled on his little table with parade square precision, flanked by several large brown bottles of iodine. Snapper had prepared his first-aid car with the same meticulous care.

Wilhelm had spent the first couple of days sketching. When he tired of that he wrote some letters. Then he finished the book he had brought. In between he and Snapper engaged in desultory conversation or took naps that were rudely interrupted whenever the train stopped at a station for water or supplies.

Around noon they passed through the war-scarred valley city of Lemberg in the heart of Galicia. The front had already passed over this region twice. And still they headed west. They had long since left the everlasting, featureless steppes and were now crawling across the great northern flank of the Eastern Carpathians. All around them rose lovely green hills interspersed with the breathtaking, downsweeping curves of ravines and valleys. Behind the hills on the left soared hoary bald peaks, like white-topped grandfathers looking benignly down on upstart grandchildren. Periodically their towering grandeur was hidden behind noble forests of oaks, elms, and beeches.

Wilhelm feasted on the magnificent mountain scenery and found it difficult to believe that violence and destruction lay just ahead. Several times he and Snapper became conscious of indistinct rumbling sounds —more felt than heard above the clacking wheels. They agreed it must be the sound of big field guns somewhere to the west. Sister Tanya, one of the nurses who had been to the front before, agreed that the big guns could indeed be felt before they were actually heard.

In the late afternoon they coasted down into the San Valley and the town of Jaroslav. Fritz Unruh, their *starshi,* told them this was their destination.

Jaroslav reminded Wilhelm of Tokmak on market day. The whole town was awash with soldiers and horse-drawn transport. But the bustle and movement seemed random and disorganized. Was the army preparing to move forward or pulling back? The noise and confusion were so great that Wilhelm and Snapper decided that this disorderly mob could not possibly be on the attack. Everywhere infantry men in unbelievably filthy, tattered uniforms, many still wearing ragged greatcoats in late April, were standing or sitting around nervously smoking and talking, or moving about their horses and wagons as they loaded supplies.

Wilhelm's eyes were drawn to a lone soldier leaning against a wall, seemingly oblivious to the turmoil around him. He couldn't see the man's face clearly but he was reminded with a start of Kolya. Was it Kolya? That was the way Kolya would be even in the army — aloof, shutting himself off from it all, wrapping himself in his own private space like a blanket. But no, it couldn't be Kolya. His mind was playing tricks on him again. Why did he keep expecting to run across Kolya? This was getting to be ridiculous. He was creating phantom Kolyas everywhere he looked. The real Kolya would have laughed in derision at such sentimental fantasies.

As their train slid into the station on the far side of the town, the orderlies looked in utter consternation at the sight that greeted them. The station was in chaos. There were wounded soldiers everywhere, some sitting, some standing, but most lying on the bare station platform without beds or blankets, as if simply dumped there as human refuse. Unbearable sounds and stenches assailed their ears and noses as the train came to a stop with windows and doors open.

Starshi Unruh issued terse orders. They were to start loading the wounded at once, the litter cases first. With a rattle they unlimbered their canvas stretchers and went to work, preceded by the doctors and nurses whose job it was to sort out and grade the broken bodies piled side by side on the rough, filthy boards.

Numb with shock Wilhelm and Snapper carried their stretcher to the densely packed rows of groaning men lying in pools of their own or their neighbors' blood. Darkly stained wounds showed obscenely through ragged rents in the khaki uniforms. Wilhelm stared down in horror, overcome by feelings of outrage at these senseless violations of the body's privacy, of its right to remain intact and whole. Everywhere he looked he saw raw, gaping wounds — like huge black and red insects sucking life out of healthy young bodies, he thought with a shudder. At least some of the wounds were bandaged but so crudely they seemed to have been covered more out of decency than as effective first aid. Tourniquets and bandages had been applied so haphazardly that it was a miracle some of the men were still alive. Others, the luckless ones, were already stiffening in the casual postures of death.

Awaiting orders from the doctors, Wilhelm found himself kneeling beside a rugged-looking man with his chest laid open in the shape of some weird red and purple flower. The man's face was contorted with pain but he made no sound, not even while being lifted onto the stretcher.

It took four or five orderlies to hand the stretchers up through the doorways of the ambulance cars. The two doctors and the nurses were sifting calmly and rapidly through the seething rows, looking for the more serious but not hopeless cases. Some of the men whined piteously and cried weakly for water or for a doctor.

Wilhelm and Snapper fought down nausea and kept working. Every few minutes an ambulance wagon — just a wooden peasant cart — arrived with another load of human freight to be callously dumped on the platform. Many of the wounded had befouled themselves and the stink of faeces and urine, mixed with the stench of rotting flesh, attacked the nostrils like a poisonous gas.

Wilhelm was bending over a small, dark-bearded man with a hideous wound in his lower abdomen. The man lay on his back flaccid, eyes closed, sweat pouring into his beard. Only his hands moved. They kept fluttering to his belly as he moaned softly, like an animal in pain. Wilhelm was about to tend to him when he heard the voice of Dr. Stolupkin sharp above him. "Leave him, Fast, he's finished. He should have been left on the field. We're taking only men who have a chance." The doctor moved on impatiently.

"Leave him, he's finished," Wilhelm mimicked softly. An order — and a prayer for the dead. The words served for both.

Obediently he followed the doctor until he stopped and pointed. "That one. Hurry up. Where's your partner? We've got to finish loading before dark."

Snapper arrived as Wilhelm turned to look for him. They regarded each other dumbly then bent to their task.

They were done at last. The sliding door of Wilhelm's car clanked shut and almost immediately the train eased out of the station.

The long journey back to Moscow had started. Wilhelm sat at his little desk, trying to pull himself together.

His shoulders and arms ached from the lifting and carrying. He felt dazed and shaken. All his cots were filled with seriously wounded patients and he had three more men with lighter wounds sitting on the floor in one corner. They were to be taken as far as Lemberg.

He wanted only to put his head down and weep, but he knew he couldn't with those suffering men lying there watching. He prayed silently instead. He prayed for his patients, for himself, for Snapper, for the whole crew, then for his family, his friends, and finally for the whole mad world of God's mis-creation. He prayed for Russia and for the enemy, for mankind and for this stupid, bloody, confusing war. He remembered suddenly Erdmann Lepp saying that God's love is centripetal, inward-drawing. Yes, he thought with dull fury, and so is this Satan's war that sucks human lives into its hellish vortex. And whose centripetal force is stronger — God's or Satan's?

Then, emptied at last of all feeling and thought, he felt curiously at peace as he rose to start the long night's work of caring for the helpless men entrusted to him. What he had to do now was remove the emergency bandages one by one, cleanse each wound thoroughly with water and iodine, and then carefully rebandage it. The leg and arm wounds weren't so hard to do. But he shrank at the thought of dealing with belly and chest wounds.

The burly man on the lower bunk opposite Wilhelm's finally got the garish blossom on his chest swathed in white strips. He lay uncomplaining, his breathing labored. The man above him, face and hands almost as white as his bandages, had several blue-ringed bayonet slits just under his rib cage that kept oozing red and sticky — like fresh cherry *platz,* he thought incongruously.

There would be little rest for his aching body this night and in the days ahead. He knew that.

But it could be worse. Much worse. But for the grace of God he could be the man with the obscene cuts in his belly, or have a shell-sown flower blooming hideously in his chest. Come to think of it, was he enjoying the grace of God only because he was a Mennonite and didn't have to fight at the front? It was a disturbing question. What had he done to earn that exemption other than get himself born a Mennonite? He wasn't even sure that he was a good Mennonite, that he accepted everything the church taught, that he was, when he came right down to it, even a Christian in a sense that people like Jacob and Erdmann Lepp would accept. Kolya had repudiated military exemption as a Mennonite. Had Kolya been more honest with himself than he?

Sternly he told himself to put such thoughts aside. He must not give in to morbid feelings of guilt.

And then he thought of the soldier he had almost taken for Kolya. He felt a rush of blood to the head. But of course. He *had* seen Kolya! That *had* been his brother standing there. Not a phantom Kolya. A real, living Russian brother who had been there alone and frightened because he too wondered what he was doing in this place that he had not chosen. They were brothers in spite of the accident of birth that separated them. They had failed to recognize each other because they were strangers. Strangers and brothers. They could be both.

He and Kolya too. He would look for no more phantom Kolyas. He was a Mennonite by accident, but he would be a brother by choice — to Kolya and to all the other victims of war who had not chosen to be where they were.

And wherever you are in these mountains, Kolya, he promised, I will know you when I see you but I will not judge you.

Lest I be judged as I speed away from this hell to the safety of Moscow.

CHAPTER SEVENTEEN

1
Galicia, June, 1915

Along with thousands of other Russian soldiers in rumpled, mud-colored uniforms, Nikolai Fast sat in the middle of a vast field on the northern outskirts of the Galician city of Lemberg. They had been in the field for a whole day and night now, waiting. Just waiting. Ever since the relentless waves of *Germanzi* had forced them to surrender the city after weeks of fierce fighting.

The only men on their feet were the hard-eyed German guards in gray-green uniforms and brown spiked helmets, guns held lightly on their shoulders. Some were standing in small groups talking and smoking. Others were strolling around the perimeter of the huddled Russians, eyeing them warily or with open contempt.

Nikolai looked around at the impassive Slav faces and wondered how they felt about being prisoners. He supposed they were still too stunned by the fact of their capture to feel much of anything. He himself felt nothing —well, perhaps some relief that he was no longer trapped in the hell of a shell-torn city trying to fight off terror and sleep by turns, wondering dumbly whether he'd be alive tomorrow.

Here I am, he thought, a prisoner of the Germans and I'm as German as they are. No, he contradicted himself. I am not a German, I'm a Russian who happens to have German blood and can speak German. But I won't talk German to the bastards, he vowed. I'll listen to what they say, but I won't let on I understand them.

Home. Blumenau. The family . . . He squelched the familiar images. They don't matter, he thought grimly. All that matters now is me — my own fate. I don't even care anymore how the war is going. Let the Russian papers, blind drunk with chauvinism, blare the "Heroic Defense of Lemberg" and "Our brave troops went down fighting to the last man" — the diarrhea of lies will go on and on. Somehow, in the popular mind, defeat will become a noble victory. Or perhaps they'll simply keep the fortress city of Lemberg Russian by not even mentioning its fall. In the end what does it matter anyway? *Nichevo.* I have no faith left in the Tsar, or the Imperial Army — or anything else . . . .

It was still early morning but the sun was already beating down fiercely from a cloudless sky. As the earth warmed up, the stink of piss and shit in the field lay acrid in the nostrils. The prisoners were forced to relieve themselves within the perimeter, and there were no latrines. They were being treated like cattle in this godforsaken field.

Nikolai slumped down on one elbow, wishing for the hundredth time that he had some *makhorka* to smoke. He and his buddies had already turned their pockets inside out for the last fugitive grains. Together they got enough for two thin cigarettes which they had shared with deep drags. The rumble in his gut was getting worse. Yesterday they had received one small ration of stale bread. Nothing so far today.

He reached up and pushed gingerly at the filthy rag around his head. The bloody thing had slipped down again. The hot sun was making his head throb and his skin itched under the bandage where he had been grazed by a piece of shrapnel just before they surrendered. He took off his greasy peaked cap and examined it idly. It was blood-stained and rank with sweat and he noted that the regimental badge in front was half torn off. With a savage twist he ripped it off and tossed it aside. Where he was going he wouldn't need any more badges.

Where were they going? They hadn't been told anything. To Germany, he supposed. Land of his ancestors. His buddies were already kidding him about going "home." They were pestering him to teach them some German words. The words they wanted to know first were bread, water, and the smutty ones.

He glanced up as he heard the synchronized whine of several aeroplanes. High overhead, they seemed to hang in the air like painted dragonflies, three of the pretty red machines. They were triple-winged, flying in a neat row. For a moment he wondered if they had come to drop bombs on them. That would be a quick way of getting rid of so many prisoners.

But the planes kept plying the air, seemingly indifferent to anything on the ground. In their alien element high up they reminded him suddenly of the family of storks that used to come to the Fast farm in Blumenau in spring. Long legs laid straight back, their great wings moving with lazy grace, they would soar majestically over the village several times before settling on the barn. They always made him feel they were doing him and the whole village an undeserved favor by showing up at all.

Craning his neck awkwardly, he watched the planes until they had dissolved into the empty blue.

Following the minute specks in the bright sky, he found, had darkened his sight, made him a little giddy. For a few moments the sprawling figures around him were opaquely wavering blobs.

He wondered how many prisoners the Germans had taken in the summer offensive so far. It must be many thousands, perhaps hundreds of thousands. And maybe killed even more. Always they employed the same deadly tactics. Simple but oh so effective. They had started with an unbelievable hail of shells — for hours they flattened everything until you were ready to crawl under a leaf and die, if you could find a leaf. Then they started coming out of the smoke and fire — from all sides they came shooting and stabbing with their long rifles that never seemed to get empty, until they were on top of you with their thick bayonets to finish the job.

And you could do nothing, he raged, except take it. Half of us didn't even have guns, let alone enough ammunition the last week. How could you fight without arms? Over and over he and his comrades had pawed desperately through the mounds of dead after a battle — even during —looking for weapons and ammo so they could keep fighting. At the end, when the *Germanzi* stormed them they were lying behind walls of their own dead with empty guns, shaking and cursing with rage and fright.

What were the people back home doing? Why weren't they making enough guns and ammunition? Had the factory workers all been sent to the front, leaving the machines in the factories idle? Or were the women and children manning them now? He tried to picture a munitions factory, like the one in Berdjansk, with female workers clumsily doing men's work.

But the Mennonite boys in the Molochnaya, he thought bitterly, were still on their farms staying sleek on ham and fried potatoes, working with their greedy fathers to make more rubles from the war. Oh, yeah, they stuck a few in the forestry stations and the hospital trains just to make it look good. Fools like Vasya, who didn't have the guts to break away from the whole rotten system. Cowards and hypocrites, the whole damn pack! Thanking God, no doubt, for keeping them safe from the war while honest men were bleeding out their lives for them at the front.

His anger was making him fidgety on the hard ground. He jabbed his finger at a passing ant and vowed that if he ever got back from this lousy war he'd do anything at all to help change things. He'd work for any cause or movement that opposed power and privilege and exploitation, including the Mennonite kind. In Berdjansk he had listened to them all — the Socialist Revolutionaries, the Mensheviks and Bolsheviks, the Anarchists — and they had opened his eyes to what was really going on in Russian society. They had all agreed on one thing: that Russian society was rotten from top to bottom and only the most violent, fundamental upheaval could bring about real change. The whole rotten structure had to be brought crashing down like a decayed old building.

But the coming of war made us forget all that, he thought. Suddenly, miraculously, the tottering old building of Russia seemed transformed into a magnificent new palace. The would-be revolutionaries stopped orating in mid-sentence, the disgruntled workers started cheering, the students shouted patriotic slogans, the young men in their millions trooped gaily to the colors — all Russia forgot its ancient misery and guilt, and in one collective delirium eagerly directed its hatred at the Germans.

"For Faith, Tsar, and Country," we sang, "For the Defense of Holy Russia!"

What an idiot I was! We all were! The Little Father Tsar and all his friends and supporters in the capital must have been laughing their heads off as we dutifully marched off to fight the evil Germans. Like schoolboys we boasted that we would whip the enemy and be back in time for Christmas! The Germans were only good at making sausages, we jeered.

Now we know what else they are good at. The Prussians fight a war exactly the way Mennonites run their farms — everything planned to the letter in advance, only the best of equipment, then the iron discipline of hard work, of scrupulous thoroughness, of never quitting until the job is done. And doing it all with a feeling of righteousness and God's blessing!

The Hungarians and Austrians, he thought contemptuously, are more on our level. We could beat *them* all right. When we took the fortress of Przemysl from the stupid Austrians in March I still had some hope. Like the others I felt proud that day the Tsar came to Lemberg in early April to savor the Russian advances on the Carpathian front. He came in a long, shiny black limousine with the giant Commander in Chief of the Army Nicholas Nikolaevich, almost seven feet tall, towering beside him. The ludicrous contrast in size between the short Tsar and his gigantic cousin made our eyes glisten with suppressed smiles as they slowly passed up and down the stiff rows. And then the Tsar, looking warm in his long, beautifully tailored greatcoat, made a flowery little speech while we shivered in the April rawness. He thanked the men for their gallant exploits and assured them solemnly that liberated Galicia would remain a part of Holy Russia forever! The pompous little ass.

"Forever" turned out to be three months. Now it was June and General Mackensen's Eleventh Army was pushing them right out of the Carpathians. At this rate the Tsar would be lucky to keep any part of Holy Russia forever until the end of the summer.

Well, no matter what happened now, for him the war was over. If Germany won, at least the Mennonites would be happy. If Russia did win in the end, they'd all come back and send the Tsar packing. In either case, he would never go back to the Molochnaya again. He'd had enough hypocrisy and self-righteousness and piety to last him a lifetime. He'd—

"*Auf—zum Marsch!*" The guards were prodding them to their feet. They were being moved out — but where? To the station? To a prison compound?

This was it then. The end of the war for him and all these other poor bastards.

2
Polish Front, August, 1915

"They're sending up some pretty spectacular fireworks out there, my friend," gritted Snapper Loewen, his face pressed to the train window.

He turned and looked at Wilhelm beside him. "Not exactly meant for kids though, I'd say." The flippant words only underlined his nervousness.

Train No. 188 was moving through darkness that every few moments was eerily rent in ragged slashes of bursting flares and explosions that seemed to erupt on all sides. They could hear the deep whoosh-crump of artillery fire somewhere up front and, at longer intervals, even deeper, more rumbling explosions they could not identify. Their train seemed to be heading directly into a raging inferno, a front gone mad with shrieking, thunderous, random destruction. In moments of sudden hush they thought they heard the thin whine of aeroplanes overhead.

"If this keeps up we'll never make it to Kobrin," Wilhelm murmured. He could hear the dry rasp of fear in his voice.

The door connecting with the staff car up ahead swung open and their *starshi* Fritz Unruh walked in, his face tight with tension. His news was not reassuring.

"At our stop just now, fellows, we heard that Brest and the strongholds around it have been abandoned. The city has been evacuated and put to the torch. And the strongholds around it are being systematically demolished by our retreating troops."

"So that's what those deeper explosions are, the ammo dumps going up," Snapper said.

"Most likely," Fritz agreed. "I just hope we get to Kobrin and get our wounded loaded before the Germans get there."

"If we don't" — Snapper's grin looked forced — "we may get a free train ride all the way back to Germany."

They felt the train breaking speed, slowing down again. They looked at each other.

Fritz, dead cigarette stub dangling from his lip, couldn't hide his apprehension. "What's going on? We're not even close to Kobrin yet."

"Maybe old Barbarov has ordered a stop to see what'll happen," Wilhelm offered hopefully.

"Not likely." Snapper sounded dour. "If he's been ordered to go to Kobrin, he'll go. They'd have to explode the track before he'd order the train to stop."

Fritz Unruh blew away his dead butt. "I better go see what's up." He headed back to the staff car.

A few minutes later the train came to a grating stop. Snapper and Wilhelm searched the darkness for signs of a station. There was nothing on either side. They seemed to have stopped in the middle of nowhere.

Fritz was shouting from the front door. "Okay, boys, let's go. We've been flagged down by a Red Cross field unit. They've set up a first aid station nearby. There's a lot of wounded and they're expecting more."

They were surprised to find a neat, well laid-out dressing station differing markedly from the usual makeshift area with its jumble of hastily deposited, barely tended patients left lying in pathetic squalor on the bare ground. Here the more severely wounded were actually lodged in cots set up in neat rows inside a large field tent. The less serious cases were lying out in the open on the ground, but even they had been arranged in orderly rows and provided with ground blankets in most cases.

"Doesn't look like a Russian station somehow, " Snapper muttered in German as he and Wilhelm looked down at a field orderly who was dressing a patient.

"Heh, you guys, do I hear German? Where'ya from?" The kneeling corpsman rose with a grin, his cap pushed back over an unruly shock of curly black hair. He appraised them shrewdly. "You wouldn't be *Menniste* by any chance?" he asked hopefully in Low German.

Before they could answer, he stuck out his hand. "Friesen, Peter, from the Molochnaya, village Pordenau. Most of us are Mennonites in this outfit."

So that was why this station looked so different. There was little time for further talk, but in bits and pieces between trips to the train with their stretchers, Wilhelm and Snapper exchanged information with young Friesen. He told them he had been at the Polish front since January. His outfit had accompanied the advance that took Przemysl in March and had been at Lemberg when that was lost to the Germans in June.

"We lost a lot of good men in that one," Friesen said with a sad shake of his black curls. "Our outfit pulled back with some wounded just before the final German assault. When we left our fighting men were actually using their dead comrades as barricades — piled up stiff like logs." He shuddered at the memory.

Since the disaster in Lemberg they had been retreating slowly northwards, always closer to the frontier at the Bug — through Bilgorai, Zamose, Chelm, and a hundred little places in between — and finally across the Bug to Brest, then Kobrin.

"I tell you, boys, I've seen so many terrible things in this war when I get back to Pordenau I'll just pull my old *murratje's* apron over my head like a little kid and bawl my head off." He shook his curls again. "I joined the Red Cross Field Service because I wanted to see what war looked like close up, but without shooting like a regular soldier. Well, I've seen more than enough. I haven't killed anybody myself, but I've seen so much killing that sometimes I get this queer feeling that I'm part of it too — the killing, I mean . . . .I don't know . . . I can hardly tell the difference anymore between killing and being killed . . . ."

They left him still shaking his head dolefully, as they humped back to the train with another laden stretcher.

Fritz Unruh was bustling about, supervising the loading of the wounded. He came over to where Wilhelm and Snapper were lifting their stretcher into a car. He looked more harried than ever. For once his lower lip had no *poppeross* glued to it.

"I have a strange feeling, boys. The shelling's coming closer all the time, don't you think? We've got only about half our cars loaded. I don't know how much longer we can sit here a standing target. Barbarov thinks we'll have enough time to finish. I'm not so sure . . . What do you —"

The explosion ripped away time and space . . . .

Wilhelm saw and heard nothing, only felt himself disappear, sucked violently down a black maw. Out of nowhere space came back in horrible falling bits — showers of earth, steel, wood, and flesh. He was being buried alive, suffocating under a weight of things falling on him.

He lay still and wondered why he couldn't hear anything. Maybe he was dying — oh God, no, please don't let me die now — and opened his mouth to scream protest. But his mouth was filled up and he was choking. In a panic he tried to spit out whatever was in his mouth and felt his chest and throat heaving with a stifled cough. His nose felt dead too. He got one hand free and tore frantically at the filth lodged on his face, in mouth and nostrils.

At last he felt breath filtering thinly back into heaving blocked chest. Then terror flooded in as he became aware that he occupied only head and chest. His lower body didn't seem to be there anymore.

Oh, God, I'm cut in half, he thought. How can I still be alive? Then felt his mind sliding away too.

Blackness engulfed him . . . .

Far inside his head gray light. Moving. Distant pain. Pressure under his armpits. Nothing below that. He opened his eyes to a hazy impression of somebody bending over him . . . Then he was swimming again, swept down a tunnel . . . .

Very gradually his mind focussed on the roaring in his ears. He seemed to be floating, swaying in space. He opened his eyes to darkness, a dark surface just overhead. The surface clarified to wood — planks, rough planks and canvas. A bunk, he thought. I'm in one too. On the train. It's moving. Where are we?

He freed the hand at his side and ran it cautiously over the blanket that covered him. His hand stopped at his right thigh and he groaned.

At least his body was still there. He grew conscious of an ache. It came from his leg, the one he had just touched.

I've been wounded, he thought, awed. I'm one of the wounded. But how? He remembered no shooting, no explosions.

He heard, from a great distance, groans and stirrings around him. And voices. Voices from far away calling for something. *Voda.*

A closer voice. From a face above him. A familiar face. Snapper. Looking relieved.

"Well, old buddy, you're finally awake. I was getting a little annoyed with you. Sleeping on the job is *strengst verboten*. By rights I should report you to Barbarov."

"What, what happened, Snapper?" His own voice seemed to come from far away too.

"What happened? Our German brothers sent us a greeting card, that's what happened. A shell right in our midst." Snapper's voice went soft. "You and I are lucky to be here, Willie." He took a deep breath and his eyes filled. "Fritz wasn't so lucky . . . Fritz just disappeared, Willie . . . .I thought you had been blown up too . . . Then I saw your hand and arm sticking out of the rubble that buried you." He paused, brightened. "You have a pretty nasty thigh wound, and bruises and contusions, but I think you're all right otherwise. No broken bones. No sign of internal injuries, thank God."

Snapper straightened up, looked away at the other bunks for a long moment, then faced his friend again. "And me, nothing happened to me, nothing at all. All the concussion did was slam me down under the car, where I was protected from flying debris. The old Loewen luck." His smile was almost apologetic. "Nothing ever happens to me, pal. I'm always the one who walks away unharmed."

He looked thoughtful. "I don't know why. Either God is protecting me —or playing with me. I happened to be standing a few feet farther from the center of the blast, and that's what saved me. Fritz was a little closer, so he . . . ."

Fritz gone? So suddenly? He lay there stunned, too weak to grieve.

"And who else, Snapper? The station . . .?"

"Yeah, it was a direct hit on the station. I don't want to talk about that mess. There wasn't anything we could do. That Friesen from Pordenau, the others — they were just — vanished. We picked up our own wounded and dead, if we could find them, and moved out quickly, in reverse. We're still going with the locomotive in reverse looking for a station with a siding so we can get turned around properly."

Snapper's voice dropped again. "We lost three other men, too — Willms, Peters, and Jash Toews, the new guy. Eight others are wounded, but only you and Pete Ediger seriously."

"My wound, Snapper. How bad is it?" He felt a curious sense of detachment, almost as if he were asking about someone else.

"It's mostly a flesh wound on the outside of your right thigh, the way you were turned, but there may be some damage to the femur. Dr. Barbarov isn't sure yet. He said he'd search for shrapnel later." He stooped to feel Wilhelm's forhead. "Anyhow, I'm sure you'll walk again, my friend. Maybe you'll get a long recovery leave and the war'll be over before you report back, you lucky bum."

"I guess I'll be going to the Arbatt in . . ." He wanted to say more but felt his mind going dark again. He closed his eyes and surrendered to oblivion with a sigh, Snapper still hovering over him.

3
Moscow, August, 1915

Wilhelm, having propped himself up rather awkwardly in his white hospital bed, was trying to do some sketching. He was resting his sketch pad on his good thigh, carefully away from his heavily bandaged one. There was still a dull ache in it and sharper twinges whenever he moved, but on the whole he felt much better today than he had in the ten days he had been in the Arbatt Hospital.

The Arbatt was situated on the fifth floor of a large building in central Moscow. It was a hospital reserved for the personnel of the AZU. Most of the patients were Mennonite boys suffering various ailments while on active service. A few, like Wilhelm, had been wounded in action. Pete Ediger, the cheerful, freckled redhead from the Alexanderthal settlement on the Volga, was dozing in the bed alongside his. Young Ediger, on his first run to the front, had been hit by shrapnel in several places.

But he was recovering nicely. Wilhelm glanced at the sleeping lad and wondered, not for the first time, how he had managed to survive their tortuous five-day trip back to Moscow. He himself had been washed night and day by excruciating waves of pain as the train rocked and clattered its interminable course across the great plains. At least they had been brought to a hospital that was efficiently run, where the care of patients was exemplary and the food wholesome and plentiful.

He was working on a sketch of No. 188 nosing into the battle area near Kobrin, with the eerie, flickering light of flares punctuating the night sky and in the background a sinister tangle of burning and exploding fortifications. And aeroplanes buzzing overhead like lost insects.

But hard as he tried he couldn't seem to get things right. His pencil felt thick and awkward in his fingers; it did not move of itself, as it did when he was working well. The scene needed more depth, more realistic proportions and textures. He wasn't getting the hectic intensity, the ominous, chaotic quality he had experienced that night. But that was the trouble. He had witnessed the scene from the interior of the train only. And here he was trying to do it from the outside. He wanted to convey sounds too, but how could he do that when he had only visual images to work with?

He threw down his pencil, feeling suddenly dejected. He pushed aside his sketch pad and sank back on his pillow. He would try again later.

He kept his eyes expectantly on the door. It was time for Snapper and Jacob's visit. They had promised to come again on Sunday afternoon. Maybe they would have some mail for him from home. By now his parents would know he had been wounded. Good old Jacob had used his personal connections to telegraph the news to the regional office in Ekaterinoslav, from where it was relayed to Bolshoi Tokmak in the Molochnaya.

Snapper stood in the doorway, his greeting boisterous. "Look at him Jacob. It's disgusting. They must be feeding him five times a day here. His cheeks are fatter than ever." He came closer, peering exaggeratedly. "And who shaves you and trims your mustache? That pretty little nurse we just passed in the hall?" He winked broadly.

Jacob's warm smile enveloped Wilhelm as he handed him two envelopes.

"The blue one is distinctly feminine, old boy," Snapper boomed, "both in scent and handwriting. That Alexandrovsk postmark speaks for itself. The beauteous Clara Bock, the Mennonite gift to opera, has not forgotten her artist friend. Tra-a-a-la-la." His grotesque attempt at an operatic trill drew chuckles from near-by beds.

"Shut your trap, Snapper," Wilhelm smiled. "You can't sing any better than you can draw. You're just a farmer, old buddy. Stick to that."

"Right, Rembrandt, but first there's a war to be won. And when you get out of that bed," Snapper pounced in glee, "you'll be taking your orders from me."

"What —?"

Jacob broke in softly. "That's right, Willie, Snapper's No. 188's new *starshi.*"

"Im applying for a transfer," Wilhelm straight-faced. "The man will be unbearable. He likes nothing better than to run things and order people around. He can hardly wait to take over his old man's *khutor.*"

Wilhelm put the blue envelope aside for later. He picked up the other letter. It was from his parents but bore no postmark, which meant that someone had brought it to Moscow personally. He would open it now and skim it while talking to his friends. Later he would read it more thoroughly, along with his letter from Clara.

The letter was from home and began with jolting news. In his formal German style his father informed him that Kolya was missing in action, but was believed to have been taken prisoner in the fall of Lemberg in June.

"Oh, dear God, not Kolya," he murmured.

"He isn't — ?" Jacob's face finished the question.

"No, not dead — at least they don't think so — but missing in action at Lemberg and presumed captured," Wilhelm said disconsolately.

During the long, solitary hours on the train he had often tried to anticipate this moment, to prepare himself for it. But he wasn't prepared for it. And his family — how were his parents taking the news? This was an even more serious blow after his own bad news. He felt a sudden rush of compassion for them. They would be devastated. Forgotten would be all the shame and agony their wayward son had caused them over the years. They would think only of their loss. At least there was hope that Kolya was still alive. They would cling to that.

He tried to steady his voice as he began reading the letter aloud to the friends who were sharing his pain.

My dear, dear son,

I write to you with a heavy heart but with my faith in a merciful and loving God as strong as ever. At long last we have news of Kolya — bad news. He is missing in the fall of Lemberg, but — God grant it be so — believed to have been taken prisoner rather than fallen in action. You can guess how your dear mother and I, and Heinrich and the girls, are suffering from the shock of this terrible news. We have sent word to Maria and Franz in Arkadak.

If the boy is dead, we must hope that the Lord in His infinite mercy melted his heart into obedience and acceptance before the end came. If he is a prisoner in Germany then there is, of course, further hope for him. The agony is not knowing which fate he has suffered. Not being sure. All we can do is wait and pray that we will hear one way or the other soon. Son, I ask you to add your own prayers to ours for the safety of your brother. He has been a heavy cross for us to bear, but as parents we still love him and as Christians yearn to see him saved.

We were shocked to hear about your injury, but relieved that it is not a serious wound. We received your telegram the day before we got the letter about Kolya. You can imagine what the double news did to us. We pray fervently for your full recovery.

The rest of my news, I fear, can only add pain to the grief you will already feel over your brother.

The Land Expropriation Laws aimed at the German colonists of our nation are giving us great concern. Apparently all German-speaking citizens with land holdings in the western and central parts of the country are to be dispossesed and resettled in the East. Right now we don't even know whether we will get a fair price for our land or whether the government will simply confiscate it and send us to Siberia. The ten months we were given to liquidate our land are now almost up and we simply don't know what will happen then.

What is to become of us, dear son? There is so much happening right now that defies human understanding. Even the mighty Tsar's behavior seems strange and erratic. They say that terrible monk Rasputin is practically running the country now that the Tsar is with the troops at the front. And just think, Willie: a few days before the monarch signed those two cruel liquidation laws last February, he visited Ekaterinoslav and was personally handed 35,000 rubles from the Mennonites of the Molochnaya and the Old Colony to help the war effort. Can you imagine? Such lack of pity in the good Tsar Nicholas?

So far, no one here has lost his land. But apparently many German colonists in Volynia and other western provinces have already been uprooted and sent east. Innocent, loyal, hardworking Russian citizens treated like stateless gypsies. Shameful!

Recently a petition was sent around addressed to the Tsar himself which beseeches him to modify the harsh conditions of the expropriation laws. There is also a move afoot to persuade the government to reclassify our Mennonite people as of Dutch origin instead of German. That would be one way of getting around these draconian land laws. Personally, I can't see that happening. How can we have it both ways? Here in Russia we have always prided ourselves on our Germanness and our German culture. Now suddenly we claim a Dutch heritage. But then these cruel and unjust measures have made us desperate enough to try anything, I suppose.

The violence of war is coming home even to us now. The other day in Halbstadt (sorry, Molochansk now) I was accosted on the street in broad daylight by a drunken Russian soldier who waved his pistol in my face and even drew his sabre. He wanted money for *samogon,* but in spite of his threats I refused to give him anything. Then one of our local policemen came by and rescued me. Can you believe it? In Halbstadt? In broad daylight?

Well, I must end this dreary chronicle, dear son. I'm sure the news about Kolya will be hard enough for you to bear. Your dear mother sends her love and prayers for your speedy recovery. If only she could nurse you herself, she keeps saying. She is sure they are not feeding you properly in the hospital. Will you be getting sick leave to come home? How we all long to see you again. Heinrich and the girls send their love and prayers too.

Poor Heinrich is worse lately. He coughs all night and looks so gray and tired in the morning. He still tries to work but it is becoming harder and harder for him to do even the light chores. Pray for him also, Wilhelm. And write when you can.

Your loving father.

P.S. I am sending this letter with a young recruit from Halbstadt —Waldemar Barg — who is going to Moscow to join your service. He comes from a good family. I think he has eyes for our Greta. Befriend him if you get the chance. He is a fine young man and a sincere Christian. I would never dare send such a frank letter as this through the mail.

Later, still brooding over his father's news, he opened Clara's letter. Most of it was chatty and inconsequential enough to cheer him up a little, but she also had unpleasant news to report.

As usual she fretted about "this beastly war," but said she was trying to do her bit by serving as a part-time volunteer nurse's assistant in an Alexandrovsk hospital. She complained that she hardly ever saw her father and brother anymore, as both of them worked long hours and often didn't come home till late in the evening, especially Gusha. The factory, of course, was on a war footing and manufacturing mobile field kitchens for the army, or something like that. She wasn't sure because her father and Gusha said very little about the factory these days.

Clara's unpleasant news was that the Bock family was actually involved in scandal — not yet public knowledge, thank the Lord — but "so shameful" that she could hardly bring herself to set it down even to a "trusted friend." It was all the doing of "that horrid Marusya Nikoforovna, the thieving slut of a maid" whom they had turned out of the house last winter, if he recalled. Well, the creature was now a prostitute in Alexandrovsk, making her living off soldiers on leave. Exactly what one would expect. But that wasn't all. The nasty trollop was trying to blackmail the Bock family! She claimed to have been Gusha's mistress while she worked for them, and that she was pregnant at the time she was dismissed. She claimed to have had a child in June and now wanted support for it. In a letter to Clara's mother the brazen harlot had even threatened to "leave her brat on the Bock's doorstep" unless she got the money she wanted. That was too much for her father, who was now taking steps to have the girl silenced. Clara didn't know what steps.

Gusha, of course, had sworn innocence in the matter. He would have to be, he had told his family more than once, "a complete idiot" to have taken up with such a "filthy, lying trull." And Gusha was far from being an idiot, Vasya would agree.

The rest of her letter was "less sordid," she assured him. She was still singing, had in fact performed at a benefit concert for wounded soldiers recently. She hoped he would not scold her for doing something so "un-Mennonite," but she felt that singing for wounded soldiers, while not as important as "binding up their wounds on the battlefield," was at least something for a "mere girl" who was forced to stay home and "suffer passively" while the nation was "bleeding from this nasty war."

She fervently hoped that her "dear bohemian artist-friend of long-ago peacetime" was safe and healthy, and that he would not "expose himself to unnecessary dangers" in carrying out his "extremely important — sacred really — duties of saving life instead of taking it." She closed by urging him to write whenever he could, that she found his letters "utterly fascinating" and would he please, please keep decorating them with "those amusing personal sketches" he was so good at.

With much love and the hope of an early end to this war so he could come home, she remained . . . .

Wilhelm dropped the letter on the bed. He felt suddenly very tired. His despondency weighed on him like lead. He wanted nothing more right now than to drop into a long, dreamless sleep.

But he knew he would lie awake for awhile.

CHAPTER EIGHTEEN

1

Blumenau, October, 1915

It was almost a month before Wilhelm was discharged from the Arbatt Hospital with a three-month sick leave. His joy soon turned to frustration, however, when he discovered how difficult it would be to get home to Blumenau by train. Russia's train system, like everything else in the country, was being taxed to the limit by the demands of the war. Time after time he went down to Kursky Station only to find that there were no tickets left for south-bound trains, or that the trains were hopelessly late, or had been commandeered temporarily for military purposes.

Finally, after a week of frantic effort, including some shrewdly placed bribes, he was able to get his hands on a third-class ticket on a train bound for the Crimea.

The trip home was sheer torture. His third-class coach was filthy with neglect and his fellow passengers, many of them soldiers on leave, were a rowdy, drunken lot who quickly turned the train into a rolling den of noisy, chaotic revelry. It was a mystery to Wilhelm where they got hold of all the alcohol in a country that had been officially declared dry for the duration.

The air in the coach was foul with unwashed bodies, *makhorka* fumes, and putrid cabbage farts. It depressed him to think of the difference between the quiet, antiseptic interior of his hospital train and this cesspool on wheels. And the stations they passed had the same neglected, seedy, unswept, and abused look as the train.

What was happening to the country? Were the deteriorating conditions in evidence everywhere an indication that the war was gradually exhausting Russia, bleeding her slowly to death like a wounded soldier left lying on the battlefield?

Fortunately, his first night at home was a joyous reunion that drove all such thoughts from his mind. He was a little shocked by the cruel signs of ageing in his parents, particularly his father. But the fifteen months he had been away were, he reminded himself, a long enough time for visible changes to take place. And the virginal bloom of Greta and Lenchen, his young sisters, made the older members of the family look all the more faded by comparison. Especially Hein, who while still trying to lead a normal life, did not appear to be long for this world. His wan color and lacklustre eyes reminded Wilhelm of the two dying typhus victims he had seen in the Arbatt. Even freshly wounded soldiers looked less moribund than Heinrich. He made a mental note to spend as much time with his older brother as he could. It would probably be the last chance he would have.

Wilhelm had made good his vow not to come home on crutches, but by relying only on a cane he subjected himself to a good deal of teeth-gritting discomfort at first. He walked with a stiff, dragging limp which gradually diminished and became more bearable as his leg continued to strengthen. He did not tell his family that the doctor at the Arbatt had told him he would probably retain a slight limp permanently, as there had been more damage to his thigh bone than early examinations had revealed. The cicatrix on his skin formed a rough, jagged flap that made his thigh bulge out like a saddle. Even the bone under the skin felt bumpy and uneven. Whenever he looked at his wound he was stabbed by resentment at this irreparable mutilation of his young body.

The ageless Anton, waiting in the barn, was overjoyed to see his favorite again. The long, ragged coat was the same, but the slight shoulders now drooped almost straight down to the little mound of belly. The ancient black fur cap still sat rakishly askew, and the frayed old rope belt had been replaced by a stouter leather belt.

Old Anton's rheumy, close-set eyes beamed affection, but the polyglot words tumbling from his lips were abject with apology.

"Ah, Vasya, *min lieber* — Vasily Gerhardovich," he corrected himself formally, "I tried to save Major, that prince of the road, for you, that darling of the steppes, but I couldn't. They wouldn't let me." He sniffled loudly and drew his frazzled mitten across his eyes. "What could I do, a broken old man, against the papasha and the government? They took all the best horses for the army — to be shot like dogs in a ditch — even Mishka." He dabbed at his eyes again, snuffling. "Major they spared at first. But we knew they wouldn't let that handsome cock pigeon stay home long. So the papasha himself" — his voice broke entirely at the memory — "your own father, my master, sold Major to the cavalry." A glimmer of craft in the watery eyes. "So the artillery wouldn't get him. You understand, Vasya?" He squinted an eye at Wilhelm, looking for approval.

"Anton Mironovich, please calm yourself," Wilhelm said with gentle formality. "I understand. God himself will reward you for your loyal concern. But what do I need a horse for? I ride on trains now."

"On trains?" the old man echoed. "But the trains only go where the shiny, straight tracks go." He spat his contempt. "You still need a horse for the crooked places where the tracks don't go."

"You're right, my friend. But right now with this stiff leg I can't even think of riding." He tapped his thigh lightly. "Later, I can always take old Grishka here if I have to. At least they've spared him, the old grandfather."

Old Anton, delicately embarrassed by Wilhelm's physical disability, directed his gaze instead at the spavined old *kunta*. "Ya, Vasya, a crippled old *oomtje* that one. He still eats his share, but he'd cave in like a rotten barrel if you sat on him."

Wilhelm looked around at the familiar, now mostly empty horse stalls and mourned with Old Anton. What was a stableman without horses to tend? And where would his father find the needed horse power for seeding next spring? He thought suddenly of the magnificent Oldenburger stallion he had admired and drawn so often as a boy. Where was the numerous equine progeny he had sired for the village? Bred for the fruitful *wirtschaften,* his sons and grandsons were now pulling gun carriages and troops through the mud at the front.

And somewhere a young cavalry officer was proudly riding Major, another son of Blumenau victimized by war.

His first week at home Wilhelm luxuriated in the pampered treatment he received from his mother. He slept late in the old summer room he and Kolya had shared as boys. He gorged himself on his mother's cooking — the cottage-cheese *wrennitje* with cream gravy he loved, the liverwurst and boiled spareribs from freshly slaughtered hogs, the oven-fresh *tweeback* and warm *bultje* with melted butter — although he suspected the copious quantities of food she prepared were love-gifts to him which violated the frugality she normally practised in these times of growing scarcity.

In the mornings he sat relaxed and somnolent by the warm *piech,* the huge, enclosed brick fireplace-cum-stove that dominated the kitchen, and watched his mother and sisters at their household tasks. He was staying indoors as much as possible, reluctant to expose himself and his leg to the cold, rainy autumn weather.

He spent long, intimate hours with Hein, whose delicate condition also forced him to keep to the house during inclement weather. He had never really gotten to know his shy, introverted older brother very well. Hein had been a familiar presence, little more. Except for his uncertain health, which had always given him a special dignity in Wilhelm's eyes, Hein had never made much of an impression on him. Now, for the first time, he was deeply moved by the meek, perfectly serene way in which his brother accepted his unfair lot. There was not a trace of bitterness in him and his mind and nature were as untroubled as though he was looking forward to a long, happy life. What a deep well of faith he must be drawing from, Wilhelm thought enviously. The better he got to know Hein during their quiet conversations the less he pitied him. His admiration left no room for pity.

Everybody knew about his leg and the difficulty he had in getting around, so relatives and friends came to see him. They usually came in the afternoons for *faspa* or in the early evenings after the chores were done. All were eager to bring him up to date on what had happened during his time away, and he listened with resigned amusement to stories and reports told several times over in sometimes widely differing versions.

Most of the talk was about the war, of course, and what it was doing to life in the villages. Apparently the hate campaign against German-speaking citizens was unrelenting and growing in intensity on all sides. Some of the stories Wilhelm listened to as he sat in the big kitchen trying to find the most comfortable position for his tender leg were hard to credit, even after the gruesome war experiences he had gone through himself. In fact, the virulence of the anti-German actions here at home exceeded by far anything he had been exposed to in Moscow and elsewhere. So far he had encountered little by way of personal prejudice in the service. Here at home, he was assured repeatedly, Mennonites and Lutheran Germans were subjected to such prejudices daily.

One of the more macabre of these stories concerned a wealthy Mennonite landowner named Siemens, whose estate lay in the Schoenfeld-Brazol area not far from the Loewen *khutor* Voronaya. A rather dashing, enterprising young man, Siemens had become interested years ago in flying and the whole new field of aviation. Just before the outbreak of war he had purchased a light plane in Germany and learned to fly it at his estate. This past summer somebody had reported him as a German spy. After all, he was German-speaking and the "evidence" of the German airplane spoke for itself. Siemens was arrested, tried, convicted, and had just been banished to Siberia for life.

Another distressing incident much talked about had happened even closer to home. Several months ago a Russian student at the Halbstadt School of Commerce had found in the school two treasonable letters, which he promptly turned over to the authorities. The letters were full of the most loathsome insults to the Tsar and the Imperial family, as well as the grossest condemnation of the Russian people, the Orthodox church, and the Imperial Army. Charges of treason were brought against the school and its director, ironically a Russian himself. But the school authorities did not take the charges lying down. They immediately conducted their own thorough investigation and soon discovered that the youth who had "found" the shocking letters was also the culprit who had placed them there. He was found to be a member of one of the "patriotic clubs" that were springing up all over the country. He was arrested and jailed, but the members of his club openly threatened to avenge themselves against the hated German "foreigners."

After being confined to house and barn for several weeks, Wilhelm began to grow restless. As his leg grew stronger, he felt the need to exercise it more. Bundled up in warm clothes and leaning heavily on his cane, he went for short but leisurely walks down the village's main street. Neighbors greeted him warmly, hailed him from open doorways and invited him in. They asked eager questions about his experiences in the ambulance service and were eager to tell him about their own sons, brothers, and uncles who were in service.

Among the over two dozen Blumenau boys in alternative service, there was one who would not be returning. "Prayer" Martens' Hans, the pious boy who had been despised and hated by the other boys as a moral sneak, had died of typhus in September while serving with a field ambulance unit on the Caucasian front. And "Hinkie" Klassen, the school clown and low-minded windbag who could spot pregnancies among village matrons even before their husbands knew (he liked to boast), was apparently recuperating in hospital from an injury he suffered when a tree fell on him at the forestry station where he served.

On impulse, Wilhelm got out one day the old home-made portfolio of which he had been so proud. He found it exciting to look over his adolescent art work again, as well as the more sophisticated work he had done at art school. He was amazed at how much he had done over the years. Just looking at all his stuff released creative juices he had not felt in some time.

So he began to work. To his pleasant surprise, he found that now he was removed from the war and front-line service, he was able to capture on paper some of the sights and sounds and feelings which had eluded him when he tried to get them down at the Arbatt.

Day after day, his excitement mounting, he lost himself in his sketching. Often he became so absorbed he forgot about his leg until the ache from an awkward position reminded him.

At last he was drawing as he had always wanted to: easily, incisively, with dramatic flair yet economy of line. His pencil flew across the tracts of white paper, caressing into life dynamic outlines, molding three-dimensional shapes, giving black and white form to the flat void. Forgotten was the listless tedium of so much of his wartime experience, the heavy ennui that smothered mind and will like a musty quilt. He felt now only the sharp, jagged edges of his trips to the front, the raw, naked images of fear, compassion, and horror that his pencil limned on the page with a clarity and boldness like engraving.

He made dozens of sketches of his train at the front, of himself at his nursing tasks in his *teplushka,* of first-aid stations and their stricken victims, of Snapper and the others carrying and handing their human cargo into the boxcars. He drew young Friesen of Pordenau as he had looked — young-old with his springing curls and fatigued eyes and mouth — just moments before being blown away like so much dust. And with each finished sketch he felt that something more had been purged from him.

He worked feverishly in his room, hardly stopping to eat, as though afraid of not getting it all down before it faded forever from his mind, or dried up in the vital streams of energy that flowed through his pencil tip. That was it. His inner channels, his secret, vital channels had been opened at last, as though by some unbidden force.

So he drew and drew, often with tears in his eyes, always with fire in his heart and urgency in his hand.

The finished sheets piled up in his folder, and he hoarded them like a miser. He had them now; they could not be unmade. The sheets glowing with life (and death) would never be empty blanks again. He showed only a few of the milder drawings to his family. The rest were too personal; he did not yet feel ready to expose them to other eyes. His father wondered aloud how he could spend so much time in his room drawing a few simple pictures.

Every few days he stopped to catch his breath, and went through the growing pile of drawings with a critical eye. And each time he saw that what he had done was good. It was all very good.

At the end of the second week he stopped again, but this time he knew it was not just to catch his breath. He was finished, for now. He had exhausted himself, used up all his creative reserves.

But he smiled and smiled to himself as he eased his tender leg.

And knew himself to be an artist. He had confronted the confusion, the evil and brute terror that was war and had carved meaning out of it — a small, personal meaning, perhaps, but a meaning . . . .

It was a kind of victory. A sort of miracle.

2
Voronaya, December, 1915

The telegram, delivered from Halbstadt, read: "Home on leave. Order you to visit Voronaya before Christmas. Take Tokmak-Great Northern to Gulai Polye. Wire time of arrival." It was signed "Your *Starshi.*"

Wilhelm accepted the invitation with alacrity. His weeks of furious sketching had left him spent and restless. He assured his family that he would be back in plenty of time to help them celebrate the three holy days of Chistmas.

Snapper, as ebullient as ever, met him at the station in Gulai Polye in an open sleigh sporting high, baroquely curved runners; a liveried coachman wearing a resplendent fur hat sat stiffly on the raised front seat. Wilhelm found his friend's breezy manner and animal vitality as refreshing as always. He fondly observed Snapper's confident, clean-shaven face and submitted to his chaffing with an indulgent smile.

"I'm impressed with your elegant limp, Rembrandt. We'll have to get you an elegant cane to go with it. After the war you'll cut a dashing figure with your artist friends. How did you manage to get wounded in just the right place anyway?"

"Mind over matter, farmer. Making life imitate art. You don't think I'd let my drawing hand get injured, do you?" He jabbed his elbow into Snapper's side. "That would be like you getting a mouth wound and not being able to talk. You'd go crazy."

Snapper's booming laugh roused the coachman to snap the reins and urge the horses to a faster pace.

The eight-mile drive from Gulai Polye to Voronaya was pleasantly invigorating in the crisp, wintry air and passed quickly. As they approached the Loewen *khutor* Wilhelm again admired its fine setting, just as he had years before. Except that this time the fields and trees did not wear rich August colors of gold and green but the flat black of a December landscape laced with a gray-white tracery of snow, like inlaid ivory.

From behind the row of skeletal trees fronting the estate, smoke rose from the manor in silent greeting. This secluded spot was as remote from the war as the Siberian taiga. No ambulance train would ever speed to this place, then away again with its gory load. This was one of Old Anton's crooked places where the shiny, straight tracks didn't go. A place comfortably lost on the steppe.

Snapper's mother was still the same twinkly warm hostess as she scurried about giving the serving girl crisp orders for *faspa* preparations. Her tiny wire-rimmed glasses flashed as she chirped away, her trim *haube* perched on the back of her head like a black sunflower.

Mr. Loewen looked a little grayer and heavier than before: a substantial man, confident and aware of station, but not in the least self-assertive or overbearing. His short-clipped rug of coarse black hair was shot with gray, but his drooping mustaches hung thick and heavy like furry tails over the corners of his mouth.

"I was talking to Hermann Bergmann, our Duma deputy the other day," he said as they sat at the *faspa* table. "He told me our Mennonite boys are giving a fine account of themselves in the ambulance service, winning the respect and trust of their Russian superiors and comrades wherever they're called upon to serve. Oh, he admits there've been isolated cases of anti-German prejudice, even harassment by Russians — especially at the beginning; but by and large you boys in the service, it seems, are experiencing a good deal less of that sort of thing than we German civilians are." He looked at Wilhelm for confirmation.

"I agree, sir, judging from our experience. Snapper — er, Martin here —and I haven't seen much of that, though some of the lads coming to headquarters have complained about harsh treatment from Russian doctors — even nurses — on their trains."

Loewen had more information, facts, and figures. "Bergmann tells me there are now over 5,000 of our lads in the ambulance service — 3,000 in the AZU alone — and at least as many in the forestry service." His brown eyes under their bushy eyebrows beamed over his poised coffee cup. That's almost ten percent of our Mennonite population. I'd say we're doing our bit for the country, all right." He took a long sip. "And we're making our contribution without sacrificing our long-cherished principles. That's the important thing, God be praised." He added as an afterthought, "And look at the food and other supplies we're providing the nation with."

"True, Father," Snapper broke in as he reached for another of his mother's feathery light *tweeback,* "but if this war doesn't end soon, we'll be in a real pickle here. We've already lost two thirds of our horses and field help will be impossible to get next summer unless they let us use prisoners of war, as they did in some places this summer." Concern lay on Snapper's handsome face. "And what'll we do for scarce essentials like oil and binder twine?" He rested his elbows heavily on the table and shook his head. "But all that's nothing compared with the very real possibility that the *khutor* itself may be expropriated at any time. What then?"

Father Loewen tried to cling to the bright side. "Yes, yes, son, you're right up to a point," he conceded. "This war is hard on everybody. But I'm optimistic by nature. I believe God looks afer his own. And He never loads more on us than we can bear. Shortages we'll have to cope with — perhaps even scarcities — but I don't think our land will be taken. Private estates are specifically exempted from the liquidation laws, I understand." He looked at Wilhelm. "It's the village landowners who stand to lose their land." He paused to reflect. "We'll get through this, I feel, even if worst comes to worst and we lose this war. If only those socialist hotheads in the Duma would stop their defeatist talk of blaming the government every time there's a setback at the front."

Wilhelm and Snapper looked at each other. The conservative Deputy Bergmann was well known for his stubborn oppositon to any political opinion or party even a centimeter to the left of his own right-wing position. And his views were stongly supported by Mennonite estate owners like Jacob Loewen.

However, Loewen's next remark surprised the two younger men. "The radicals are right about one thing though: the shortage of arms and munitions at the front. According to Bergmann, August Bock and other Mennonite industrialists are predicting that the government may force them to manufacture armaments, or take over the factories completely. Can you believe such a thing? Mennonites being forced to manufacture guns for war?"

And so Loewen rose from the *faspa* table in a sombre mood after all, as did the others, even though their stomachs were comfortably lined with Mrs. Loewen's delicious baking.

Next day, when Katya Loewen arrived home for the weekend from her school in Schoenfeld, Wilhelm saw that the pretty, vivacious young girl of half a dozen years ago had developed into a young woman of stunning, self-assured beauty. The direct, incredibly pristine expression of her deep, widely spaced eyes almost took his breath away. Her strong, broad face struck him as pensive, but when she smiled at him he felt as if he was being lapped in something warm and soft. There was a freshness and radiance about Katya that was beguiling. Like her brother she breathed of health and vitality.

Intrigued, he listened to Katya talk that first evening, and watched her covertly. He couldn't help comparing her with Clara Bock. True, this girl lacked Clara's city sophistication, looked wholesome rather than elegant. But that didn't matter at all. Clara's beauty was of the quicksilver kind, depended on physical grace and animation, a dazzling variety of artful moods and poses, all instinctively, charmingly, feminine but ultimately —well, evasive, distancing, less than intimate, though fascinating enough.

They evoked the beauty and warmth of a skilled actress. A born coquette.

Katya was very different. Even on the surface, he discovered in the next two days. Her manner towards him was utterly devoid of coquetry or overt femininity, as though she didn't know such things existed. He guessed that his presence in the house didn't change her behavior at all: she was as natural and unaffected with him as she was with the members of her family. She spoke to him with a frank sincerity that drew him in, made him feel at ease with her. She treated him quite simply like another human being whom she found interesting enough to want to know better.

Again, how different this was from Clara, who had a spoiled self-centeredness, an avid narcissism which clutched everything to itself, made her spin tight webs of feeling around people she liked, but spurn the feelings of people she didn't like or whom she considered her inferiors. She could be spiteful and even ruthless when she felt she was not given her due, or her self-esteem was threatened. Look at the petty, vindictive little feud she had carried on with that sleazy domestic — Marusya, was it?

Katya's nature ran in deeper, calmer channels, he began to appreciate. Not that she was serious all the time. She was not one of those painfuly earnest girls one met in Mennonite homes of self-conscious refinement, the kind that plodded through classical pieces on the piano for company and practised the stiff art of *fraktur* drawing (learned at *maedchenschule*) in illuminated wall mottoes. She was naturally high-spirited and fun-loving and laughed easily. But she also had the gift of repose. When she stopped smiling or laughing and became serious her face and figure assumed a complete stillness, an immobility almost like that of a statue, in whatever attitude or posture she happened to be. Then she would listen or speak with a gravity that glowed from within, from a spirit, and mind which seemed to him to teem with inner riches he could not begin to comprehend.

And as if the depths of empathy and understanding he sensed in her weren't enough, he soon discovered that she had a sharp, well-stocked mind, a mind more disciplined and rigorous than her brother's.

Even that first evening they conversed together without any of the initial shyness young Mennnonite males and females often displayed towards each other — or felt they ought to display — when they were getting acquainted. Katya told him she was totally — romantically — dedicated to her teaching. She loved everything about it, she assured him with the full lustre of her deep brown eyes. She declared her intention of going to a state teacher's institute to qualify as a high school teacher. But first she wanted to gain a few years' experience as a village teacher. Some day she hoped to get a position in the Halbstadt Girls school, her alma mater, and teach under the direction of Mr. Benjamin Unruh, the marvelous teacher who had taught her German literature in her final year at Halbstadt. She respected and adored Oom Benjamin both as a man and as a teacher.

"And what subject will you specialize in?"

"Oh, literature, of course," she smiled. "I love German and Russian literature equally, but I'll probably have to make a choice between them when it comes to teaching. I know I could never compete with the enchanting Marina Petrovna Letkemann, who taught us the delights and mysteries of Lermontov, Pushkin, Nekrasov, Dostoievsky, and Tolstoy. So, I'll problably choose German literature. And work with Oom Benjamin, hopefully."

But Katya didn't talk about herself for long. She wanted to know all about Wilhelm's progress as an artist. Did he still find time to draw and paint in the service? What had it been like at the famous Academy of Art in the capital? She had never seen any of his work, except for the pen-and-ink drawing of Martin in uniform that her brother had sent her from Moscow as a gift for her birthday. It was, she told Wilhelm with a sincerity that thrilled him, one of her most cherished possessions. He began to regret that he had not brought along any of his work, especially the recent war sketches he was so pleased with. No one else had as yet seen them. But he would have no hesitation in showing them to this wonderfully sensitive and perceptive girl. He was sure she would understand instinctively exactly what he was trying to do in them.

He couldn't get enough of Katya's company that first week-end and watched her depart for her school early Sunday evening with keen regret. He would not be seeing her again till Friday and his last weekend at Voronaya.

The week passed slowly for Wilhelm. He spent most of his time accompanying Snapper and Mr. Loewen as they attended to the day-to-day business of the *khutor*. Some of the time he was left to his own devices as the two Loewen men discussed and planned the future of the fine *khutor* they both loved with a passion. He had brought his sketch pad with him, fortunately. To amuse himself, he drew Katya over and over from memory, trying to capture the subtle moods of her expressive face. One evening in his room he began a more formal portrait of her. He would surprise her with it.

And then Katya was home for the weekend again. And he did indeed surprise her. But himself even more. On the last evening of his visit Wilhelm felt such a rush of tenderness for her as they sat on the high-backed divan in the drawing room after dinner, that he was on the verge of blurting out his feelings. But the reticence and shyness in his nature were too strong. Avoiding her eyes, he adopted a light casualness that belied his true feelings. Strangely, Katya also seemed suddenly shy and uncertain of herself. Their conversation, which had flowed so easily, stuttered and died. They were suddenly self-conscious with each other.

After an awkward moment or two, Katya, picking nervously at the maroon plush of the divan with her strong, slim fingers, spoke softly into the silence.

"I've enjoyed our conversations about art and literature so much, Wilhelm. I only wish we'd had more time." "She raised her eyes and looked at him with such naked intensity he was startled. "Do you think you could find time to write to me occasionally when you go back to the war?"

"Oh, yes, Katya, I was about to ask you the same thing."

She smiled warmly and said more lightly: "I'm glad you and Martin are friends, although I've never quite understood what you have in common. Certainly not art and literature."

"You know, I've often wondered about that myself. At school we fought a lot but even that only seemed to bring us closer together somehow. There must be an inner magnet that draws certain people together, regardless. So that their lives intertwine almost in spite of each other."

It pleased him to see her blush. He found himself reaching for her hand, the restless hand that was still plucking at the cloth. Katya did not draw it away. There was no withdrawal in her, no girlish coyness. She only looked at him with that direct, wide-eyed candor, as if searching for his exact intention.

Still holding her hand, he drew out of his pocket a small picture and gave it to her, "Just a small Christmas token, Katya."

Artfully mounted on a stiff paper backing, it was the sketch of her he had done from memory during the week. He had worked on it for several evenings, always with the curious conviction, as Katya's face came luminously alive on the page, that he was creating a new being just for himself. His own Katya, the secret nuances of her lovely face known only to him. He had never had quite that feeling with a drawing before.

"Oh, Vasya, it's lovely — I mean . . ." She stopped in confusion. "I mean it's so marvelously well done. How could you get such a good likeness without my sitting for you?"

"But you have been sitting for me, Katya, without knowing it. I've spent hours looking at you, studying you. Or haven't you noticed?" Fondly, he watched her coloring again. "And don't you remember, Katya, years ago when I was here I said your face was worth drawing?"

"Yes, but you didn't do it then. And a vain young girl decided that boys only said things like that for effect. To remind you of your promise would have been unbecoming."

"I wish you had reminded me, dear Katya. We might have become friends much sooner."

Her eyes were bright as she said briskly: "Well, please don't think I've forgotten *you*. I have a token for you too."

She went to her room and came back with a gaily wrapped little gift. "There, open it. I want to see you laugh."

It was a fine set of sketching pencils. They both laughed over the coincidence. Katya did not tell him that Snapper had brought the set from

Moscow as a gift for Wilhelm from him. She had easily inveigled him into letting her appropriate the pencils as her gift to their visitor.

All the way home the next day Wilhelm was in a state of quiet rapture. He had no doubts at all about his feelings. He had fallen deeply in love with the dark, intense young woman he had found at Voronaya. And he was confident his love was returned. Katya had promised to send him a photograph of herself as soon as she could have a good one made, she said. In the meantime he would recreate that marvelous face with his own hand, as he had already done for her. And some day that enchanting face would be his in the living flesh.

3
Butyrki Prison, Moscow, May, 1916

My angel of light Katya Loewen lying in this black stinking hole chained to this everlasting stone wall nothing but cold stones steel bars damp darkness like a blind mole no at least a mole can feel warm earth around him not just this hard black cage alone.

Stretched on the floor he saw the bright wraith of a girl before him as he had so many times, her deep eyes holding him friendly and warm, her softly curved mouth speaking kind, inviting words to him alone. Always he saw her first as the innocent, laughing girl he had worshipped from a distance. But realized she was grown up now, her maiden stalk lush with the sweet bulbs and dark petals of woman. And then his mind ran riot as he caressed petal by petal the aching mystery of her. And wondered, in lusting envy, if she was married, his Mennonite *golubka* — yes, most likely to some big rich Mennonite farmer who mounted her grunting in the dark and filled her with blond *njemtsi* kids. His lovely, pure angel. Aroused by his lascivious, envious fantasy, he squirmed in the dark and brought his chain clanking dully to life. His hand moved down to his swelling groin and then he was writhing in an ecstasy of lust . . . .

His body was still again in the fetid stench of the punishment cell. Someday I'll be out of this hell-hole Butyrki, he thought again. For years now he had been confident that he would survive and get out. He let go a ragged volley of coughs. He'd have to leave with his cough, though, he thought bitterly. He couldn't leave that behind with the prison lice.

And when he got out he'd go straight back to Gulai Polye.

And this time things would be different, he vowed aloud in the dark. No matter how long it took he'd kill all the sons-of-whores who had put him in here — that big bastard Karachentsev, the police chief, and those slimy informers Ivanov and Tchurenko, if somebody else hadn't croaked them yet.

But he'd play it smart. The first thing he'd do would be to grab control. Nobody from a "movement" or party was going to boss him around, no not even Savva and Grishka, his brothers. He would form his own activist group, a pure anarchist group of peasants and workers. He was a peasant himself and knew what the peasants wanted, by the Holy Virgin!

No more half-assed factory strikes and ass-wipe pamphlets and leaflets and proclamations printed in somebody's basement. Thanks to his friend Pyotr Andreevich Arshinov he knew what to do now. Bakhunin, Kropotkin, he'd read them. Liberty, equality, solidarity! The sacred principles of revolutionary anarchism. A free brotherhood of peasants. He would settle for nothing less. No more factories where you broke your back for a few miserable kopeks, no more police clubs, no more taxes. They would live hidden at first, in the Dibrovka Forest where Nikolka's swine couldn't find them. They'd live off the fat-assed Russian and German *pomeshchicks,* the landowners like the big Loewen who had sweated the salt off their balls all these years. Now the fat-asses would sweat! They would make their raids at night. The stupid buggers would never know where they'd be hit next or when.

And all the time he'd be waiting, waiting for the big revolution all over Russia to come. Then he'd bust from the forest like a steppe *buran,* a storm that would sweep up everything in its path. He'd lead a mighty movement that would destroy the whole rotten system that had kept his people in bondage. They would become one great family of peasants living and loving and playing together. They'd all be kings equally, like the ancient Cossacks in their *siech.*

Nestor the Greek warrior, Nestor the monk of Kiev, Mamashka used to say to me. Will my boy be a warrior or a scholar? Hah! I won't be Nestor the monk when I get out of here, Mamashka. Not a monk and not a scholar, by Christ.

He'd be Nestor Ivanovich Makhno — no monk but warrior and savior. Savior of his people. Leader and soul of free peasant communes. Batko Makhno!

He glowed with pride and jubilation on the hard, sweating stones of the cell.

Batko Makhno.

And nobody was going to shit on his head. Ever again.

4
Schoenwiese, June, 1916

What August Bock and his partner Jacob Riesen had long feared came to pass. The secret was out. It was now common knowledge in the Old Colony and beyond that the "supply" wagons Bock and Riesen were manufacturing on government contract were really gun carriages. A Mennonite corpsman with battle experience home on leave had seen them lined up in the factory compound and recognized them immediately for what they were: two-wheeled carriages for field guns and ammunition caissons attached to front-wheel limbers which, to the inexperienced eye, made them look like ordinary four-wheel wagons.

Gun carriages! ammunition caissons! people said to each other in shocked tones, without being entirely clear just what they were used for. But they were for war, for killing, and that was enough. Just imagine! Supposedly Christian Mennonites actively helping with the terrible, devil-inspired mass blood-letting — and against German people too! And all for what? For money! It was too much. Bock and Riesen, who had been popular and highly respected figures in the Mennnonite community, were now branded as cynical war-profiteers, as opportunistic betrayers of the sacred Mennonite principle of nonresistance. They were reviled in private and shunned in public. There were dark mutterings of banning them from the church.

August Bock was concerned, but not as yet unduly worried. Characteristically, he kept his head and paid no attention to the attacks behind his back. The malicious gossip would, he knew, die down eventually. And there would be no action taken against him by the church in the matter of the gun carriages. Of that he was confident. He was, after all, a deacon in the Einlage church, and by far its largest financial supporter. No, the *bruderschaft* would not move against him. Not for the gun carriages. They could ride out the gossip and rumors. As long as nothing more got out.

Bock's partner, however, the feisty little Riesen, did not remain aloof. Discreetly at first, then more boldly, Riesen launched a counter-offensive against the rumor-mongers and detractors. He challenged people to tell him why the gun carriages he and Bock manufactured were a greater betrayal of Christian nonresistance than the Mennonite horses requisition-ed to pull them? When his opponents argued that they had no control over the uses their horses were put to by a government that had commandeered them, Riesen countered by pointing out that the firm of Bock and Riesen also came under the stringent wartime control of the government. The Ekaterinoslav Defense Ministry, like similar ministries all over Russia, had decided which factories in its jurisdiction were to go into war production and what kind of contracts they were to fill. Thus, individual factories had no choice but to comply and help win the war. Bock and Riesen, he affirmed in ringing tones, was an honorable firm and loyal to its country. As well as to the Mennonite community, in spite of appearances to the contrary.

Jacob Riesen's spirited campaign to silence the moral censure of the Mennonite community seemed to work. The criticism of the firm and its owners gradually subsided and other war news, most of it bad, captured the attention of the public.

Then, just when the whole affair had died down, came another revelation that quickly assumed the proportions of a major scandal that shook the firm of Bock and Riesen to its last brick outbuilding.

One of the foundry workers, a young peasant rapidly sinking into alcoholsim on his first steady job with pay, was severely reprimanded one morning for absenteeism and drunkenness, first by his foreman, then even more harshly by August Bock, Junior, who acted as a kind of trouble shooter in the factory. The factory hand, still stoked with *samogon,* flew into a violent rage and walked off the job. That night, blind drunk on the street, he told anyone who would listen, including a couple of Mennonite youths, about the growing piles of shell cases stacked secretly at night in the back sheds behind the factory.

Now the darker secret was also out. This time the righteous indignation of the people of Schoenwiese was too great to be stolidly ignored by Bock Senior or skilfully defused by the clever Riesen. August Bock sensed immediately that he and his partner were in serious trouble with church and community. To make matters even worse, the drunken workman, who had continued his binge after spilling the beans, was found unconscious two days later in a back alley in Alexandrovsk from a beating so savage it was feared at first he would not live. Immediately, the story went around that August Bock Junior, whose irregular life in town was by now well known, had hired thugs to teach the drunken "canary" a lesson he would not forget.

His heavy face a fearsome mask of anger, August Bock Senior faced his son across the desk in his office.

"August, let me tell you something. If you're responsible for this beating, you're not only a man of brutal violence and no Mennonite, but stupid into the bargain. Once that worker blabbed the damage was done. Did you really think the secret could be beaten back into him again?"

He scowled at his son in open contempt, the long curves of his jaw like slabs of granite.

Young August looked neither cowed nor crestfallen. He stared back at his father with the haughty air of well-bred self-assurance he had inherited from his aristocratic mother.

"You have no right to accuse me, Father. I know no more of the matter than you do. What happens to a drunken, dismissed workman is of no concern to me. He isn't the only one. Sooner or later one of them would have let his tongue wag with *samogon.* It was just a matter of time. I never believed we could keep the casings a secret." He flicked a trace of cigarette ash from his dark, striped vest front.

Father bock studied the insolent face of his son for a long time. Then words like heavy stones rumbled from his chest. "This is not a threat, but a warning, August. If anything like this ever happens again, I will have no choice but to demote you — or even dismiss you from the firm altogether." He stopped, his countenance more sad than angry now. "You're an only son, my boy, a too much loved and pampered one. But I wonder if you really know me. I fear the Lord, and try to walk in His ways. I am proud of this firm and its success, and I will not permit you or anyone else to bring it into disrepute. Through no fault of our own we have been forced to walk a tightrope. And if you have stupidly upset the balance then you are not the man I was hoping to groom for the future.

"I'm well aware that you're leading a dissolute life. And frankly your attitude here in the firm has been more high-handed than responsible. These are serious times. If we lose this war, son, there'll be a revolution. And men like you and me will be made short work of. Yes, conditions being what they are, its quite possible that you won't be able to live out your life as a spoiled and frivolous playboy. And I won't deny that I feel a touch of *schadenfreude* in knowing that."

The good will of the church and our Mennonite community may not mean much to you, August. But they do to me. They mean a lot to me, and if I lose them through a scandal involving the firm I will lose much of what I have lived for. I am moved to say that I would sooner give up this firm and all the money and power it has brought me, than lose the respect of our Mennonite people and — above all — the spiritual benefits of the church I have loved all my life."

Again he looked at the smooth, indifferent face of his son and heir and felt profoundly depressed. In the softest rumble he could muster he added, "I want you to think seriously about what I have said, August. As of now you are on probation in this firm. You will carry out your duties as usual, but you will keep in mind that you cannot afford any further missteps. If you want to hold the reins of this firm someday, you will have to earn the right."

It was the longest speech August Bock had ever made, and the most painful. After his son had nonchalantly removed himself from the office, Bock heaved a mighty sigh and slid a huge forefinger across his eyes. He feared for the future.

The next day Bock had another confrontation in his office. He faced a small delegation of church and lay leaders. Elder Thomas Unger of the Einlage church was the spokesman. He and Bock had been close friends all their lives.

"It's a serious matter, August," the elder opened, obviously uncomfortable. "There's no precedent for this sort of thing in our whole history." He was searching for words that would not sound intimidating or self-righteous. "We are all equally under God's eye, my friend. He alone knows the trials and temptations you have been subjected to in this distressing matter. But the argument that you had no choice cannot be accepted. No one can be forced to do evil or to disobey the will of God and the rules of the brotherhood."

August Bock, deeply moved, searched his old friend's furrowed face. "Thomas, what would you have me do? Resign from the church gracefully, before I'm thrown out? I—I can't do that. I'm willing to admit error, but I don't want to be rejected by my own church, my own people." The craggy features sagged in dejection.

"No, August, I think there are enough mitigating circumstances here to make such drastic action unnecessary, perhaps even lacking in Christian charity. At least I hope so." He looked steadily at Bock. "You need the church — I know that my friend." The elder glanced at the others sitting with him. "And we know, as you do, that the church and community also need you." He squared his shoulders, continued more briskly. "There will have to be a *bruderschaft* decision over this. But I think" — a wisp of a smile appeared at his lips — "that the brotherhood can be persuaded to let you off with a firm, public reprimand. You will be expected, of course, to make a confession before the full body of believers that you have sinned and that you will make a very sincere Christian effort to extricate yourself and your firm from this unholy business as quickly as possible."

Bock's direct gaze swept the four stern faces before him. "I accept," he said simply. "I'll do what I can. I'll make every effort to stall the delivery of the casings as long as I can. And I'll do my best to persuade the Defense Ministry to let us go into another line of production — perhaps field canteens, or something like that."

The delegation rose, much more relaxed than when they came in. Bock shook hands solemnly with the four and courteously bowed them out of his office.

He sat at his desk pondering. Yes, the Ministry might just go for the canteen idea, especially since the most recent reports showed that the production of munitions and small arms was at last beginning to improve substantially.

Who would have thought that things would ever come to this?

CHAPTER NINETEEN

1
Petrograd, March, 1917

In the Duma Alexander Kerensky rose and pointed an oratorical finger heavenwards. "Look up at the distant flashes that are lighting the skies of Russia," he thundered.

No one really believed the storm would strike so quickly.

The people of Petrograd, like so many others all over Russia, were sullen with cold and hunger. And utterly disillusioned with a war that had become hopeless. Made reckless by deprivation and enforced idleness, some began to shout slogans on the streets:

"Down with the War! Down with the Monarchy!" But most slouched passively in futile breadlines or milled about workless in the public squares. There was no more coal or wood to run the factories, and the bread stocks were dwindling rapidly.

The people did not know that the nation's lifeline, the railway system, was clogged, undermanned, and uncoordinated. That it was slowing down like the arterial system of a sick old man.

At the front the Tsar's personal train stood in his beloved *stavka,* the headquarters camp, snug and protected on its special siding under the curving birches and lofty pines. In its sumptuous interior Nicholas II ate simple but taseful meals with his generals and whiled away soothing hours discussing the intricate chess moves of war. That and reading and rereading the almost daily letters from his "dearest wifey," the fanatically unyielding Empress Alexandra.

The royal couple had come to a tacit arrangement: while he was running the war, she would run the country. Neither of them was aware of the portentous flashes of lightning Kerensky saw. The only flashes the Tsar saw were those over the distant front at night. The Empress could see only the lightning flashes in the mad eyes of Rasputin. When her holy man was finally assassinated in December of 1916 Alexandra stooped to mourn him, her faith in him sublimely unshaken. With revolution already rumbling she wrote to her "darling Nicky:" "The sun shines so clearly and I felt such peace and quiet at Our Friend's grave. He died in order to save us."

The death of the obscene *starets* from Siberia did not save the Romanov dynasty. Only a firm push was needed to bring it down — a push from the people.

By 1916 the war had settled into uneasy stalemate. The fronts were more or less stable, but the conditions inside Russia were deteriorating at an alarming rate. Growing shortages of bread, salt, kerosene, candles, and boots made life almost unbearable even for a populace inured to primitive conditions. In the cities there were strikes which made the shortage of staples even worse, if possible. Millions of soldiers, withdrawn from the labor force long before they were needed at the front, caused a further hemorrhaging of the economy. Their inactivity also made them receptive to political propaganda.

The Duma heard accusations against an apparently suicidal government grow ever more strident and open.

The climactic events that led up to a spontaneous outbreak of revolution began quietly enough. As more and more factories closed down, droves of workers gravitated to Petrograd's core around the Winter Palace. The crowds seemed remarkably free of bitterness, considering the ugly reality of their situation. They chatted and joked with the mounted troops, who were uncharacteristically polite and relaxed. True, there were isolated cases of violence, destruction, and looting, but it appeared as if once again disaster would be averted if the authorities kept their heads and did not overreact.

But the queues for bread grew inexorably longer as the supplies grew shorter. The women, bearing the domestic brunt as usual, grew angrier and more desperate each passing day. Then the women, quite spontaneously, began to march; they were joined rather sheepishly by their men. The Empress received the news calmly, although she admitted privately that when the people were hungry there was always some danger.

In his *stavka* at Mogilev the Tsar was distressed by the news that all four of his pretty daughters, as well as his adored son Crown Prince Alexei, had been stricken by measles.

It would be such a strain on poor, dear Alix.

What the swelling, marching crowds in Petrograd noticed first was that the mounted Cossacks with their tall fur caps and flashing sabres, who on command had ridden down the people for generations, were suddenly quite human and devoid of hostility. They rode carefully around people instead of over them. They even smiled under their bushy mustaches and touched their hats in friendly greetings.

The Tsar, satisfied that the measles were under control, finally turned his attention to the fractious capital. He telegraphed an order to General Khabalov, the Petrograd commandant, that civil disorders were "not permissible in a time of difficult war with Germany and Austria" and must be stopped at once.

Khabalov, sensing that something extraordinary was happening, hesitated to carry out the Tsar's command. The General was no longer sure of the reliability of his crack guard regiments, most of which were now filled with peasants and workers instead of young aristocrats.

His fears were well-founded. When he did order out several detachments, they fired on the mounted tsarist police, the hated "pharoahs," instead of on the people. Then they put down their guns and mingled with the crowds.

It was all over. The Romanov dynasty had fallen, although the confused, lethargic Tsar did not yet know it. On March 12 the Duma was dissolved and a "Provisional Committee" formed.

Nicholas bestirred himself at last and decided to return to Petrograd to clear up the whole bothersome mess once and for all. He did some unaccustomed hard thinking; then had a pleasant dinner on the way and played a relaxing game of dominoes.

But the telegram he received enroute on March 14 from his generals at the various fronts convinced the Tsar at last that he must abdicate. Without any fuss, maintaining his stolid composure as always, he sat in his railway car and signed the document of abdication. He thought he was abdicating in favor of his brother, the Grand Duke Michael. Actually, he was signing away the Russian monarchy.

For the first time in Russian history the peasant had beaten the tsar. With Nicholas and his family under guard at Tsarskoe Selo, the people celebrated their new freedom in a deliriium tremens of joy. The prisons were stormed and burned down and prisoners, including notorious criminals, were tearfully embraced and welcomed into a new-minted society.

Or at least the appearance of one.

In the Tauride Palace, seat of the now defunct Duma, Foreign Minister Miliukov gloated that this had been the quietest, most peaceful, and least bloody revolution in history.

Miliukov was unaware that in another wing of the Palace the Soviet of Workers and Soldiers Deputies were already planning ways of sweeping aside the Provisional Committee so that the next phase of the Revolution could proceed.

The bloody phase, led by iron-willed Lenin, was still to come.

2
April, 1917

From a distance the train resembled a huge, furry dark caterpillar. It crawled along slowly, its whole exterior covered with clinging passengers. They clung to the sides of the boxcars from crude handholds and footholds, lay or sat on the roofs. On the locomotive they stood pressed together all around the boiler platform and the buffers in front, dangled from the ladders at the ends of the cars. A writhing, wind-whipped but happy mass of humanity.

They were celebrating by passing bottles precariously from hand to hand in the punishing wind, the train whistle sounding raucous toots every few minutes, tipping back their heads and swigging, in dizzying danger of falling from their perches. They laughed and shouted and sang wind-torn snatches of song in their tipsy joy. Every few miles someone drunk past all caution forgot his handhold or lost his balance and dropped roaring and rolling away in the ditch.

Nobody seemed to care. Even the April chill could not numb the *samogon*-heated bodies, dampen the mood of revelry.

Not even when the train approached an overhead trestle bridge and three men sitting on the roof, too befuddled to duck, were swept screaming into the ice-strewn waters below.

Inside the train the scene, if less hazardous, was even more riotous. The makeshift plank seats were crowded to overflowing. Many sprawled on the dirty floor, some not of their own volition, not seeming to mind being shoved, kicked, stepped on, and spat upon amidst the deafening babble.

The majority of passengers were carousing soldiers and sailors heading home at last, but there were also sedate older civilians, men and women, and a sprinkling of eager-eyed high school and university students still wearing their black, brown, or blue student uniforms with big brass buttons, soiled and wrinkled though the uniforms were by now.

Samogon and brandy flasks passed up and down the rows and seldom got back to their owners. Who didn't care in any case. Especially the roistering sailors, who seemed to have an endless supply of bottles in their kit bags. Though the cars were unheated, the tightly packed, sweating bodies generated a fetid warmth that added coziness to the debauchery. Those whose stomachs began to heave with drink, heat, and the swaying, puked where they sat or lay without even trying to avoid their neighbors. There was much good-natured cursing over the vomiting, but nobody seemed to get incensed over it.

The loud, drunken talk was ribald and disjointed. Slogans were shouted constantly between swigs. "Land for the peasant," "Fair wages for the workers," "Down with the ruling classes," "All power to the people and their soviets." Over and over, gaggles of comrades shouted in ragged unison: "Long live freedom, long live equality, long live fraternity." Then they fell around each other's necks in the lurching train, smacked cheeks wetly and wept more drunken tears of joy.

Someone started a series of crude jokes about the deposed tsar and his family. "Where do you think he is now, boys? Hiding under his German whore's skirts?"

"There's no room for him down there," another roared, "she's still hiding the corpse of her murdered priest down there."

"I'd like to get under the skirts of the daughters," a third yelled in glee, "I'd soon show them how an honest peasant tills the soil."

As the hours went by and the drunkeness gained intensity, inevitably the jubilant celebrating began to degenerate into surly truculence and unruly behavior. Gibes and insults turned ugly and led to angry shoving and even exchanges of blows, where there was enough room for the combatants to maneuver.

A little rooster of a soldier, dangerously drunk, suddenly held a large pistol under his startled neighbor's nose and screamed: "You don't talk to me that way! You smell that, comrade son-of-a-bitch? That's not the smell of your old lady's dirty twat. That's the smell of death, you serpent."

Behind him a huge Tatar calmly reached over and grabbed the pistol out of the demented man's hand. Then he brought his other large paw down on the man's head and squashed him to the floor in a moaning heap. "No guns here, comrade," the Tatar bellowed. "This is a train of free citizens going home in a free land."

Huddled in a corner seat of the same car was a small, pale passenger who took no part in the orgiastic celebrations. He kept his eyes closed, pretending to be asleep. A burly sailor in the seat opposite, annoyed at the small man's aloofness, started baiting him finally.

"Comrade, you must be a *burzhuj* or something. You better have a drink and join in the fun or we'll start getting suspicious of you."

The sailor leaned forward and with playful roughness jabbed his flask into the man's belly.

Suddenly the man opened his eyes and gave the sailor a stare so piercingly malevolent that his jaw dropped and he pulled back his bottle with a nervous start.

"All right, comrade, it's a free country now," he mumbled hastily, "if you want to sleep, sleep." He turned away and took a long pull from his rejected bottle. "Son-of-a-whore," he muttered, but did not bother the man again.

When the train reached Gulai Polye the fragile-looking little man with the prison-pallor skin clutched his meagre bundle and got off. He stood on the station platform and looked around greedily, his thin body shivering slightly as the raw spring wind hit him. As he was not expected, there was no one to meet him. He hitched up his bundle and headed into town.

Nestor Makhno was home after eight long years in the Butyrki prison in Moscow.

3
Gulai Polye, April, 1917

That evening he got a hero's welcome in his home town. Their own little Nestor Ivanovich had returned from the dead. It was a miracle, they wept, as they embraced him again and again. To think that one of their own, said his old anarchist friends, had survived all those years in one of Nikolka's stone pig pens. A miracle! They shook their heads at the wonder of it as the *samogon* passed from hand to hand in the dingy Makhno *khata*.

Makhno, pallid boy's face glowing ruddy for once what with the *samogon* and heat of the crowded room, accepted the warm welcome graciously but with barely suppressed impatience. He chewed his full lips as he waited for the casual well-wishers to depart. He was careful not to drink too much this home-coming night. He wanted his head clear when the time came to discuss the political situation with his anarchist pals. Already he could sense something not quite right with local revolutionary politics from the casual remarks passed around him, but he couldn't quite put his finger on what was wrong.

"Savva," he turned finally to his older brother after the crowd had thinned out in the wee hours of the morning, "what exactly is this Communal Committee everybody keeps mentioning?"

"It's the all-party local organ of the provisional government in Petrograd."

Makhno's voice flared up in anger, so that the others in the room were compelled to listen. "What? Have you all gone crazy here? What kind of *duraki* are you? Supporting the Petrograd bandits, those slimy, big-city Bolsheviki? What about your Anarchist ideals? Have you swept those behind the door?"

The tigerish eyes swept the room, pounced on each man's will with a fury that startled them. They were impressed enough with the little man's anger to listen. Their punk of a Nestor had become a man. A fiery little man.

Makhno shrewdly sensed that he could make his will prevail here. They would put up resistance, yes, but in the end they would give in to him. He thrilled to the certainty of it. If he struck fast. And with authority.

"The first thing to do, comrades" — his steely glance leaped from face to face through the smoke — "is to get rid of this useless Communal Committee and form a real union of peasants, an organization with a will and purpose of its own — so we'll do something, not just talk like old women and fart around waiting for orders from the Petrograd swine."

He banged his slim fist down on the table for emphasis. The men facing him looked sheepish, but far from cowed.

"We can't do that Nestor, you old thief." It was Petya Serlenko, one of his old boozing buddies. "The Committee represents the Revolution. It's a legal soviet to carry out the orders of the new Constituent Assembly in the capital."

Makhno surveyed the swarthy Serlenko with open disdain. "Yeah, Petya, so what has the Committee done so far for you and the peasants in this town? Tell me, Petya." He leaned forward over the table, his red, chiselled lips sarcastically curved, his eyes not smiling at Serlenko.

"Well, Nestor, it hasn't had a chance to do anything yet except start planning, but —"

"—But nothing, Petya," Makhno cut him off savagely, "don't be stupid, it'll never do anything but talk."

Abruptly he rose to his feet, planted his fists on the table for support. His voice was urgent, pleading , quietly confident. "Comrades, I tell you there is no time to waste, not a day, not an hour, not a minute. We have to act while we can, while we have the freedom to act. We'll form our own committee of peasants and workers — a true union — and we'll move as fast as we can requisitioning land and workshops, cattle, horses, clothes, and goods from the lard-ass *pomeshchicks*. On our *own* authority. Not waiting for orders from Petrograd, if they ever come."

"But Nestor Ivanovich —"

They were stubborn *khokhols,* refusing to admit they were wrong. Not realizing that they were already harnessed to his will. That he was now holding the reins that would guide them.

At daybreak they were still arguing with him, bleary-eyed through the foul *makhorka* smayze, but feebly now. Damn it, this Makhno kid was worse than a priest. Once he started at you he wouldn't let go till you agreed with him. They looked at each other dazed, then at Makhno. He seemed to be growing bigger and older before their eyes. They could feel his strength, his harsh determination.

One by one they fell silent, submitted with a shrug, a mutter, more out of fatigue than conviction, perhaps.

It was done. They agreed to form the "Union of Peasants of Gulai Polye."

The fiery Makhno, now in his element, hardly seemed to eat or sleep. He was everywhere at once. In less than a week the Union of Peasants was a fact, with Nestor Ivanovich Makhno as its president. He went to work ruthlessly, ignoring or sweeping aside all other committees and parties.

Makhno now had his political horse and was firmly in the saddle. He was ready to begin his revolutionary career in earnest. Even his brothers regarded him with awe, wondered where this firebrand had come from. His mamasha fondly called him Nestor the Warrior and did not even think of Nestor the Monk.

His first order as president went out to local factories and shops and to large landowners within a ten-mile radius of Gulai Polye. The order called for complete inventories to be made and submitted as soon as possible. Materials, goods, and land holdings were to be requistioned. "For the purpose of providing the necessities of life for the working people, " the directive stated. Once the Union had the land and possessions, Makhno explained, they would set up peasant communes all over the area, about ten families per commune, where they could work and play, sing and tend their gardens. The communes would be self-governing and self-sufficient. They would be the "torch bearers of a new humanity," Makhno added with a pretty rhetorical flourish, his deep eyes glowing with pride.

But the reality unfolded less smoothly, he found. He was soon berating himself for a *durak* as he discovered that allowing the business men and landowners to draw up their own inventories was a little like allowing the fox to count the chickens in the henhouse. The inventories were suspiciously short, with all kinds of moveables having mysteriously disappeared or been "loaned out." At least they couldn't hide or take off with the land, he thought grimly. But he controlled his anger, showed the patience of a born leader. To his followers he said quietly: "Wait my friends, we'll find a way of kneading our little pigeons soft."

Makhno found a way quickly. "A good farmer," he told his men, "doesn't send the fox to count the chickens. He goes himself. And he stays till they're all counted." His fleshy lips parted with a grin. "And if we have to eat a chicken or two and sleep in the henhouse for a few days while we're counting what could be better?"

His men laughed in admiration. Their little Makhno was a sly little fox himself.

"A good soul and a man of gold," they agreed as they got ready to ride.

4
Voronaya, May, 1917

Jacob Loewen was standing just inside the arched brick gateway of Voronaya on a warm, rain-scoured Saturday morning in early May. His narrowed eyes followed the line of riders moving swiftly up the winding road that led to his *khutor*. He was not alarmed, although he suspected that these riders were not just making a casual social call. He had heard reports that Nestor Makhno (the youngest of the brood, wasn't he?) had organized the peasants of Gulai Polye and was taking over the countryside.

Makhno had served notice that the surrounding landowners were to make inventories of their estates so that the requisitioning and land distribution called for by the peasants could begin. Loewen had received the notice but had decided not to do anything about it just yet. He did not regard it as a legal order. But he knew there was danger in his defiance. He could only hope that these men would listen to reason and not resort to violence, as they had at several other *khutors* in the region.

If it was young Makhno himself, he didn't have to worry. He'd know how to handle him, provided the fellow knew how to keep his men in check. Loewen found the very idea of the pimply faced, skinny Makhno kid as a leader of men preposterous. He had thought the lad was executed years ago for robbing a bank or something, and here he was a leader in the revolution.

What upside down times.

The band of riders swept through the gate and quickly formed a fierce-looking circle around Loewen. Their sweaty horses snorting and pawing, they looked like a Tatar band in their wild attire. Over their gaudy shirts and jackets they wore wide red, white, or blue belts or sashes and all were loaded down not only with swords and pistols but with rifles and even hand grenades. A few looked bizare in top hats and fancy patent shoes. A grotesque bunch, but there was nothing funny about their faces.

"Well, Papasha Loewen, we meet again." Makhno swept his beautiful gray fur cap from his head in grandiose greeting. "We have come to pay you a little visit — for old times sake," he added with a sly grin on his boyish face. "It's a long time ago, but I can still feel your *nagaika* on my backside."

"You are welcome, Nestor Ivanovich," Jacob Loewen said simply. "Will you come in?" He looked dubiously at the mounted men, but Makhno gave staccato orders and the circle dissolved. Only two of the men accompanied their leader inside.

"We had expected to hear from you by now, Jacob Jacovlevich," Makhno remarked casually as he appropriated the velvet maroon divan in the living room.

"Yes, well, Nestor Ivanovich, these are unsettled times. I was waiting for things to settle down a bit. I suppose when the new Petrograd government has consolidated itself such matters as land redistribution will be handled in a regular and legal manner."

Makhno leaned forward, his hard eyes fixed on Loewen's impassive face. He did not raise his voice, but his tone was suddenly menacing.

"You do not seem to understand the situation, Uncle Loewen. We are the government here — the Union of Peasants of Gulai Polye. The Petrograd government doesn't exist here." He paused for effect. "Since you have not been your usual efficient self in making an inventory, we have come to make it for you."

He turned to one of his aides. "Petya, tell the boys to start with the stock. They know what to do."

Makhno leaned back, addressed Loewen again, his tone affable as before. "I remember the Mamasha Loewen's cooking with love. Of course, we were never invited to eat here in the big masion then." He swept his surprisingly long arm around the room. "The Mamasha Loewen, she is still well, yes?"

Before Loewen could answer, his short, round wife bustled through the doorway. She beamed at the visitors, her spectacles flashing. "Welcome, gentlemen, to our house. Dinner will be ready soon." She bustled out again, nodding agreeably.

Makhno was polite, at ease but missing nothing. "And your son, the student — uh, Martin Jacovlevich — he is away perhaps? Oh yes, and the young lady, your daughter, where is she? Married now, with little ones?" The deep eyes were not casual.

Loewen regarded his former stable boy and harvest worker with barely disguised distaste. He didn't like the familiarity in the questions.

"My son is serving in the war, the ambulance service. My daughter teaches school in Schoenfeld. She's not married yet."

He did not add that Katya was home for the weekend. He assumed she was in the house somewhere and hoped she would have the sense to keep out of these rough fellows' sight.

Makhno relaxed by putting his elegant boots up on the low glass-topped table in front of the divan. In doing so he knocked a glass object off the table. It rolled across the floor and stopped in front of Loewen, who bent over to retrieve it.

"Ah, so the young heir is not exactly fighting against the Germans then," Makhno observed slyly.

"You must know, Nestor Ivanovich, that we Mennonites do not believe in killing, even in war."

"Yes — well, it's always better to serve one's own interests first in any case. We Russian peasants believe that too, especially now that the revolution has finally arrived."

Makhno's aides chuckled approvingly. Loewen stared at them but said nothing.

"I'm sure you'll agree, Jacob Jacovlevich," Makhno continued smoothly, "that it'll take several days to complete our inventory here, so I trust you won't mind having us as your guests during that time."

He opened the top buttons of his well-tailored uniform. It was a gray law-student's uniform complete with crest. Loewen wondered whether it had belonged to a Mennonite student.

"I don't suppose the charming Miss Katya comes home for weekends, does she?" He looked at Loewen innocently.

"Yes, but not always." Loewen was beginning to feel uncomfortable.

Makhno rose and went over to the piano, upon which stood an enlarged photograph of Katya set in an elegant silver frame.

"So this is what she looks like now?" He hardly breathed as he studied the soft, tranquil face with its wide-spaced, luminous eyes and dark-tendrilled hair. By God, she's perfection, he thought. She's even lovelier than I dreamt her all those times in the stinking Bonterky. He heard someone entering the room.

It was the beauty herself. She looked neither startled nor embarrassed as she took in the scene. For a moment she stood there in the doorway, the vision of his dark cell in the radiant flesh. Her gaze lightly met his transfixed stare, but there was no flicker of recognition in her eyes. She murmured a polite apology to her father for having intruded and disappeared.

Loewen watched her leave, relief on his face. He had seen the look Makhno had given his daughter.

Makhno scowled at him. Wait, you proud old bastard, he vowed silently. Someday I'll train your prize *golubka* to fly to my hand.

Mrs. Loewen called them in for dinner.

Jacob Loewen slowly rose and for the first time in his life felt a gut-clenching fear so strong he was sure he would not be able to eat at all. He glanced at the skinny little man swaggering beside him, and his heart shriveled within him.

5
Moscow, May, 1917

Wilhelm Fast had been as shocked by the momentous news from Petrograd as the others in the Mennonite barracks in Moscow. That the Tsar had actually laid down his crown and meekly surrendered the nation to the rabble in the capital! He refused to believe it at first. In Moscow they had not even known that there was an uprising until that fateful day of March 14th. Oh, there had been the usual reports of marches and demonstrations and strikes. But revolution? Where had the army been? The Tsar's loyal-to-the-death guards? Surely they hadn't all been sent to the front?

He couldn't help recalling the tired-looking little man in khaki he had seen at Khodynka Field not long after the war began. He had not looked much like a ruler, but still when you saw him you were awed to think that this tiny man was the absolute ruler of one of the largest and most powerful countries in the world. And that his family the Romanovs had ruled Russia in an unbroken line for three hundred years. The Tsar and his family had simply disappeared, although they were reported to be in detention at their palace in Tsarkoe Selo. He could not imagine the beautiful young crown princesses as prisoners, especially Princess Tatiana whose eyes had bestowed on him an unforgettable moment of radiance that long-ago morning at Khodynka Field.

The revolution was now over two months old and the situation was more confused than ever. All they knew was that the war was going on as usual, that the new Provisional Government led by former Duma ministers like Guchkov, Miliukov, and Kerensky had vowed to fight on to victory.

But wasn't it all mere bluff and bluster? The rumors were that the Provisional Government was just a figurehead, that the real power in Petrograd was now wielded by the 2,500 member committee known as the Soviet of Workers and Soldiers. It was known to oppose the war and to favor withdrawing from it as soon as possible. The Petrograd Soviet, it was said, was mainly concerned with such issues as shorter factory hours and land distribution. So, in effect, there were now two governments with conflicting aims and interests. What a mess!

"Pity Holy Mother Russia," was the way Snapper put it, "the old gal's jumped from chaos into anarchy."

"Yeah," Wilhelm added, "looks as if the double eagle of the Romanovs is flying in opposite directions now."

There were ominous signs that worse was to come. Apparently Lenin, Trotsky, Stalin, and other revolutionary leaders were gathering in Petrograd like wolves for the kill. Already there were fresh acts of violence. Many people expected another coup before the summer was out. This time it would be the Bolsheviks who would come to the fore, it was said. And they were known to be a tough lot.

The day-to-day routine of the AZU had not changed, but it was becoming more difficult to maintain as conditions worsened. Russian forces at the front were being bled white not by the enemy but by massive desertions. The millions of peasant soldiers at the front were aware that back home other peasants were already seizing land for themselves and the soldiers were in a frenzy to claim their share. Nothing could stop them, neither threats by officers nor actual punishment. Not even the rousing, spell-binding oratory of Kerensky, who rushed from one unit to another trying to shore up the sagging army with patriotic words, could keep them at their stations.

Whole units, still armed, left the front. They commandeered trains at gun point. They insisted on the right of way, creating the most terrible transportation snarls. Ambulance trains were often forced to lay over on sidings, bereft of locomotives for days, while the wounded men in them died like flies.

Even Jacob Priess lost his gentle calm in desperate attempts to maintain a schedule, a semblance of order for his trains and men. Wilhelm, who was now Jacob's part-time assistant, worked long hours beside his friend as the two of them tried to sort out the horrible railway messes.

Because of his leg, Wilhelm had not been reassigned to his ambulance train as an orderly. Luckily, Armin Lehn and Jacob had been in need of another man for the office when Wilhelm had returned from his three-month sick leave near the end of January, 1916. Wilhelm was to spend half his time in the post office on the second floor, the other half doing clerical work for Jacob and Armin Lehn.

It promised to be a less taxing, less precarious way of spending the rest of the war and he had accepted with relief. He had not been anxious to serve on the trains again, even with the lighter duties of a secretary or doctor's helper. His injured leg had responded well to several months of rest, but he knew it would never be as strong as the other and that he would retain a limp. He could walk without a cane now, but there were still days when he felt more comfortable using it. In time, the doctor had promised, he would probably be able to discard it completely.

Wilhelm sorted the daily mail eagerly, looking for an envelope addressed to him in Katya's strong, bold hand, a masculine hand he had teased her. They wrote long, passionate letters to each other. He devoured her letters voraciously, not only for their frank, glowing sentiments, but for their overall interest. Katya had a natural gift for letter-writing. In a simple but vivid style she brought alive the small events of her life, as well as her thoughts and feelings about a whole range of things.

He no longer expected or received letters from Clara Bock. He had written Clara and told her about Katya Loewen. It had not been an easy letter to write, but he had written it as honestly albeit gently as he could. She had replied with a brief letter, carefully neutral in tone, in which she had congratulated him sincerely, told him she had heard of the Loewens of Voronaya and that she was sure Miss Katya Loewen was a fine young lady and deserving of his love. As for herself, she "remained his devoted friend" and wished him "happiness and fulfillment." She would follow his career as an aritist with "the greatest interest," even though conditions at the moment were not exactly conducive to "civilized things like art and music." She concluded with the hope that they would not lose touch with each other completely.

He had not heard from Clara since.

Katya's most recent letter had frightened him. In it she had expressed her alarm over the distinct possibility that their beloved Voronaya would be taken away from them — stolen from them by "that beastly little man Makhno," who was now marauding the countryside at will, making lists of things and taking whatever he wanted like a wild Cossack. She described how Makhno and his wild men had recently come to Voronaya, taken over as though the place was theirs, looked through everything — even the things in her room — stayed two whole days and demanded that her mother give them big, lavish meals as though they were honored guests. What she had found most repulsive were the funny looks that "brazen little thief" had given her, although she had tried to stay out of his way as much as possible that weekend. She still hadn't recovered from the dreadful experience, she concluded.

Wilhelm was deeply disturbed by Kaya's letter. The revolution, with its threats and violence had reached even Voronaya. And he was here in Moscow, helplessly sorting letters, not knowing what might be happening right now — at Voronaya or at Blumenau and the Molochnaya. He wrote back to her at once, trying to hide his apprehension, and promised her he would try to get a leave as soon as possible.

Snapper, also worried about the fate of his family and the *khutor,* had already applied for a leave, but so far it had not been granted. He had now decided to appeal to Commandant Saltykov himself. Failing that, he confided to Wilhelm, he would seriously consider going home without permission.

Erdmann Lepp was tremendously excited when the revolution broke out, even though his emotions were at first somewhat mixed. He deplored the bloodshed and destruction and was scandalized by the overthrow of the monarchy he revered. He had not expected it to happen in just that way. He was horrified by the state of godless anarchy into which the nation was sinking. He shuddered at the vulgarity and cruel opportunism of the new men who were rising to power. The Bolsheviks, especially, seemed to be without moral scruples or even common decency.

But he consoled himself that all this dreadful upheaval was a necessary part of God's carefully orchestrated plan for mankind. The sixth vial of wrath was now clearly empty. The seventh vial and Armageddon were at hand. This tremendous convulsion within Russia was a prelude to Armageddon. He felt his blood race as he saw himself privileged to play a part in these momentous events so clearly and powerfully prophesied in the Word.

The apocalyptic events now unfolding in the land, and in other parts of Europe, were a sign from God that the final harvest was at hand.

The final command to "go forth" was about to sound.

And Lepp's faith was dramatically confirmed when the new Provisional Government, in its very first decree, granted freedoms never seen in Russia before, including complete freedom of worship and the abolition of all religious distinctions.

Lepp was ecstatic. There would no longer be a state church which forbade proselytizing of its members! The gospel of Christ could now be preached freely and openly to all. The full-time Russian ministry he had yearned and planned for all his adult life was now his.

In his wartime mission in Moscow Erdmann Lepp had already demonstrated that young soldiers, dispirited, disillusioned, scared, confused, and homesick, were in the greatest need of spiritual counsel.

Now he declared to Jacob Priess: "The watchword all around us is 'organize, organize.' So we too, laboring in the Lord's vineyard, must organize a union." He permitted himself a smile at the pun. "Jacob, we must organize a Union for Christian Soldiers to spread the gospel here in Moscow and beyond. We already have the nucleous here in the AZU barracks. You have often heard me say that God's miraculous love is centripetal, pulling all to its living centre. But God's *mission* must be centrifugal and fly out in ever greater waves of grace. Our Mennonite boys here will be very receptive, I'm sure. With such a Union we can plan a proper division of labor with tract distribution, street meetings, hospital visits, and so on." His eyes twinkled again. "That's an idea we can safely borrow from the godless socialists."

Lepp was a skilled organizer. The Christian Soldiers Union immediately drew an enthusiastic response from devout young Mennonites in the ambulance service. Soon there were Baptist soldiers helping as well. "The preaching is only the most dramatic of our activities," he told his eager followers. "We must make informal contact wherever possible, on the streets, in barracks and hospitals, even on the trains. I have secured the cooperation of tract societies in Petrograd and here. I've also contacted Abram Kroeker's Raduga publishing house in Molochansk. Soon we'll have the materials to spread the Word wherever we can. And when the war is over and the soldiers go home we will follow them to their villages all over Russia, winning souls for Christ before the local priests can spoil them again.

It was a glorious vision, and for the first time attainable, praise God! Erdmann Lepp had never been happier or felt more alive. Daily, he pleaded fervently on his knees that God would make him equal to the task.

Wilhelm, although approached by both Jacob and the redoubtable Lepp, chose not to join the Christian Soldiers Union. He did not feel the conviction to do so, and he would not be a hypocrite and join because so many others in the barracks did. Jacob said he understood, but he was not able to hide his keen disappointment at his friend's refusal to become a part of a spiritual revolution that seemed so gloriously inspired by the Lord.

Lepp, to Wilhelm's surprise, did not exert any undue pressure on him either. Ever since Wilhelm's outburst in Jacob's office, Onkel Lepp had treated him with unfailing courtesy but with a shade less personal warmth than before.

Perhaps he was only biding his time in the conviction that Wilhelm was made of the right stuff and would come around finally of his own accord.

6
Alexandrovsk, May, 1917

It was exactly the kind of simple, relaxing evening August Bock Junior looked forward to now that he had reformed and given up his more strenuous playboy activities. He looked amiably across the table at his two dinner companions. Both were old school friends with whom he felt at ease. The ascetic-looking young man, Phillip Niebuhr, was the son of a Mennonite factory owner who like August had been exempted from service. The other was Captain Maxim Boldyakov, an officer home on leave, who came from a wealthy merchant family in Alexandrovsk.

They were making their leisurely way through a good dinner at the Maidan, the best Georgian restaurant in town. After some spicy Georgian wine, they were now topping off their meal with a superb bottle of vintage Crimean Muscatel Lyinell, August's personal favorite. He felt expansive as they discussed the rapidly developing political situation.

"You know, boys," August said confidently, "the man to watch is Kerensky. He may call himself a socialist, but don't be fooled. He's not a true revolutionary. He's got a solid bourgeois background. He'll be the man — just you watch. He's only the Minister of Justice and he's running things already. When he feels strong enough he'll come forward and put those filthy swine in the Soviets in their places. You wait." He deftly clipped the end off a fat cigar and winked at his companions through the cigar haze over the table.

"I'm not so sure, Gusha," young Niebuhr countered. He had hardly touched his wine and did not smoke at all. "There's something weak-looking in that fellow Kerensky's face, if you can judge from the pictures in the papers. I've a strong feeling he's nothing but an orator, a mere talker, and that when it comes right down to it he'll prove to be a paper tiger." His pale, narrow face turned to the military man for confirmation.

"I dare say you may be right about Kerensky," Boldyakov agreed, "but I'd also say that if the Provisional Government can last through the summer and show some definite improvement on the front, its chances of forming a stable government are pretty good, with or without Kerensky."

"Well, it was time for the Romanovs to go," said Niebuhr firmly. "What we're headed for, I hope, is a constitutional democracy like England's. And that's fine with me."

August snickered and nodded his head, "And there's no country in the world that has retained more class privileges than England." He took another sip of the sweet mellow Lyinell.

Later, as he walked down the almost deserted street towards the alley where he had parked his auto, August Bock was still savoring an agreeable evening spent in the company of amusing old friends. The somewhat coolish early May evening was pleasantly bracing. He jingled the coins in the pocket of his light English topcoat.

When he turned into the alley he got the shock of his life. The elegant French Charronette which he had imported just before the outbreak of the war and had been allowed to keep on a special permit since, had been reduced to a horribly battered wreck. The slim hood was crushed and mutilated, the windshield splintered and gaping, the doors smashed in and the tires viciously slashed. Even the upholstery had been hacked and gouged in the mad assault.

He stood there, mouth agape, surveying the obscene outrage perpetrated against his beautiful automobile. Tears of helpless anger blurred his eyes. And still he stood there. Then murderous rage welled up inside him and he came out of his trance.

Somebody would pay for this. Somebody —

He heard the footsteps, but too late. He half turned just as the knife ripped through the expensive tweed of his coat.

August Bock's body was discovered next morning propped up behind the broken steering wheel of his wrecked auto. His eyes were fixed in sightless horror on the shattered rectangle of the windshield, as though he was careening down the street and knew he couldn't stop in time to avoid hitting the brick wall that loomed beyond the flattened hood.

The robin's egg blue of the car was stained on the driver's side with dark smears and the black, torn upholstery glistened with red streaks. There were seven stab wounds in the body. There was no wallet and no money in the pockets not even coins.

A police investigation got nowhere. It unearthed no clues, found no suspects. Everybody talked about the bizarre murder, however, and rumors and speculations whizzed through Schoenwiese daily. One of the more persistent rumors had it that the man who had been fired from the Bock and Riesen factory for drunkenness and subsequently beaten up, had been seen lurking near the alley where young Bock was murdered. It was also whispered around that the fired workman was the brother of a Russian girl who had worked in the Bock household at one time and who had been dismissed under circumstances that had made her very bitter against the Bock family. The murder was clearly an act of revenge.

Sensible people in Schoenwiese dismissed the rumors as idle gossip. The motive for the grisly murder had been theft coupled with a drunken urge, most likely, for wanton destruction and bloodletting. In these godless times of violence you could expect anything. If only law and order would return to the land, they sighed. Things just couldn't go on this way.

After the funeral in Einlage, the Bock family closed up the big house in Schoenwiese and retreated to Selenaya, their estate on the Dnieper.

Shocked and grief-stricken, August Bock Senior saw his son's murder as a judgment from God. He began to make secret plans to liquidate his assets. He would leave this accursed country and take his wife and daughter to Germany the moment the war was over.

CHAPTER TWENTY

1

Petrograd, November 7, 1917
TO THE CITIZENS OF RUSSIA!

The Provisional Government is deposed. State Power has passed into the hands of the organ of the Petrograd Soviet of Workers' and Soldiers' Deputies, the Military Revolutionary Committee, which heads the Petrograd proletariat and garrison.

The cause for which the people were fighting: the immediate offer of a democratic peace, abolition of landlord property-rights over the land, workers' control over production, and the establishment of Soviet government — this cause has been secured.

LONG LIVE THE REVOLUTION OF WORKERS, SOLDIERS, AND PEASANTS!

Plastered all over Petrograd, the black-on-yellow proclamation officially announced the Bolshevik coup as an accomplished fact.

The proclamation was not only brazenly premature, but its briskly confident tone gave no hint of the more bizarre aspects of the events that were unfolding on November 7th.

They began with Prime Minister Kerensky waking up in the tsar's bed in the Winter Palace and finding his phone ominously dead. Through his bedroom window he could see nothing but Bolsheviks on the street below. For once he decided to take the prudent course. In an open Pierce Arrow borrowed from the British embassy, preceded by a Renault flying the Stars and Stripes, Kerensky raced through the dark, cold streets of Petrograd and out into the limbo of Russian history.

As for the people of Petrograd, they saw no signs of revolution that day. They shopped as usual in long, tedious queues, then took the streetcar home or to a place of amusement. There were no street demonstrations and no armed outbreaks. None. That evening the restaurants and theatres were crowded as usual and the great Chaliapin was in splendid voice at the People's Theatre as King Philip II in Verdi's *Don Carlos*.

The peaceful facade was an illusion. At the bright yellow Smolny Institute, once a finishing school for daughters of the nobility and now the headquarters for the Petrograd Soviet, Lenin and Trotsky had been frenetically busy since early morning. They were issuing orders for the takeover of such strategic buildings as the telephone exchange, the post office and telegraph station, as well as the railway stations.

By noon most of these buildings were occupied. The Bolsheviks, in fact, now controlled the city, although they were not yet fully aware of it. The only important holdout was the garrisoned Winter Palace, where Kerensky's Provisional Ministers (minus their leader) were closeted in aimless, futile discussion.

Lenin kept calling for the capture of the Winter Palace, the symbol of tsarist and bourgeois power. A plan of action was finally agreed upon. It would begin with an ultimatum for surrender delivered to the Palace. Should the ultimatum be rejected, a red lantern would be flashed from the Peter and Paul Fortress on the other side of the Neva. This would be the signal for the cruiser *Aurora* and the guns of the Fortress to fire blank rounds at the Palace to indicate that the final assault was underway.

But nothing seemed to go right. To start with, nobody could find a red lantern. The ultimatum was belatedly delivered by bicycle only five minutes before the half-hour deadline was to run out. It was promptly refused.

Instead of the promised attack another lengthy stalemate followed. Not until 10:30 p.m. did the red lantern appear at the Peter and Paul. The *Aurora* fired its blanks at the Palace, but the Fortress guns were found to be unfit for firing so the gunners lobbed shrapnel shells across the river instead. The insurgents in Palace Square opened fire from armored cars and with small arms, but without visible effect. The cadet defenders inside the Palace, augmented by the volunteer Women's Battalion (their heads militarily shorn against lice) repulsed the attack easily.

The Revolutionary Committee decided to step up the attack. They started shelling the Palace in earnest. The shells did little more than break some windows but they badly frightened the young defenders inside, especially the women. The attackers, sensing the uncertainty inside, did some shrewd parleying and soon the cadets and female soldiers were defecting from the Palace in droves. By midnight the thousand rooms of the Winter Palace were virtually undefended.

The moment had come to move in. But even now the attacking force looked and acted more like a visiting delegation than an assault unit. The insurgents passed unchallenged through Palace side entrances, dashed up the wide staircases and spread through the magnificent rooms until they finally reached the Malachite Chamber, where the ministers were waiting in near panic.

Engineered by Trotsky, supervised by Lenin, the Bolshevik coup, for all its bungling, had worked. The casualties in the final assault numbered only six men killed. Even the Women's Battalion had escaped relatively unscathed. None of its members had been killed, none wounded, and only three had been raped as the Bolsheviks primly pointed out later.

Lenin was jubilant, although still wary of the future. The revolution he had dreamt through long years of exile was now a reality. But the difficult and dangerous work of consolidation was still to come. The vast regions of Russia must now be swiftly and relentlessly colored Red if the revolution was to succeed.

The chief agents for that herculean task would be the Cheka, the secret police, the Red Guard, the workers' militia, and, most important of all, the newly organized Red Army.

2
Voronaya, November, 1917

Snapper Loewen had gone through an anxious, frustrating summer of trying to wangle leave so he could go home and assess for himself the danger his family and Voronaya were in. Repeatedly he had been told that he could not be spared from his duties during the summer campaign when battle casualties were at their heaviest. He had been desperate enough to consider deserting, as so many front line soldiers were rumored to be doing. "If the soldiers can get away with it," he demanded angrily of Wilhelm, "why can't a Mennonite corpsman?"

Only Commandant Saltykov's personal assurance that he would get an extended leave as soon as the summer rush was over kept Snapper at his post. He was finally granted leave in late October and had just arrived at Voronaya when news came of the Bolshevik revolution. That settled the matter for him. He told his father that he wouldn't go back to the AZU at all.

Jacob Loewen did not argue with his determined son. He was only too glad to have the young man's support in the grave crisis they were facing. Voronaya was in a perilous state. Makhno's men had already "expropriated" a good part of the stock and much valuable portable property. And they were certain to come back for more.

So far Loewen's land was intact, but he knew it was only a matter of time before all or at least most of that would be wrested away from him too. Sadly, he had already reconciled himself to the complete loss of his beloved *khutor*, although his son had not. Together they would stay and defend it as long as possible. The risks, he knew, including the danger of physical violence, were great. For the first time in his life Jacob Loewen knew fear of another man: he feared Makhno. And it made Jacob very uneasy to see that his son did not. Martin had a hot temper and a confident young man's sense of outrage over injustice and exploitation. Loewen prayed that his son would not have to learn caution the hard way.

Snapper did not take long to size up the situation and form a plan of action. He fumed daily over the plundered stock and property. Then he discovered an even more serious and brazen injustice that sent him into a towering fit of rage against Makhno.

What so incensed the younger Loewen was his discovery that Makhno, as president of his Union of Peasants, had impounded all the money held at the bank in Gulai Polye for the grain sold that fall by area farmers. The money had been transferred to the town bank for local distribution by the special commissariat in Alexandrovsk, which since the March revolution had been in charge of administering grain supplies in the region.

Snapper had been pleasantly surprised when he arrived home to find that in spite of the critical labor shortage, depleted horse power, and shortage of petrol and naphtha, not to mention the atrocious price of imported binder twine, his father had been able to harvest a respectable crop of rye and wheat. But inflation was now rampant and the harvest meant little unless they could get the money for it quickly. Without money they faced ruin. It was as simple as that.

"Who does that pimply-faced jailbird think he is?" Snapper raged. "Father, we've got to go to Gulai Polye and talk some sense into this peasant dictator. I remember the thieving runt and the dirty eyes he made at Katya when he worked here. I'm not afraid of telling him a thing or two." He balled his fist menacingly.

Jacob Loewen looked at his son in alarm. This was what he had feared most since the boy had come home. "Martin, I forbid you to talk that way. You remember Makhno only as a kid. You don't know the man. I tell you he's cunning and dangerous and you better be careful."

"But, Father, the man's a convicted thief and murderer. We can't let him get away with more crimes."

"I agree, Martin, we must go see him, and try to reason with him. If we approach him the right way he may let us have at least part of our money. But we must be very careful not to rub him the wrong way, son. I've watched him closely when he's been here and I'm afraid of him. I know he's capable of extreme brutality if aroused. And so are his men. I can show you what they've done in this district already. It's terrible." Jacob looked at his angry son with grave concern. "We'll go tomorrow, Martin, but you must promise not to lose your temper with Makhno, or threaten him in any way."

Next morning the two men drove to Gulai Polye. Snapper had reluctantly promised his father to be discreet and diplomatic with Chairman Makhno, that is if they even got to see him. He was reported to be a very busy man these days.

Half way to town they came upon a shocking sight: the burned out estate of Hans Balzer, one of their more distant neighbors.

"My God," Snapper blurted, "that looks awful. When did you say they did this to the Balzers' *khutor?*" His father had mentioned a raid on the Balzers, but Snapper was not prepared for what he saw. He had known the Balzers all his life, had thought of them as almost next-door neighbors. He and Willy Balzer had played together as boys, had eagerly explored and compared each other's *khutors.* In their teens they had experimented secretly with their fathers' cigarettes and cigars and on one memorable occasion with a bottle of Georgian brandy "borrowed" from Willy's father.

"Makhno's men set the red cock over it one night about three weeks ago," Loewen said, his walrus mustache twitching as he grimaced at the memory. The slang expression he used for terrorist arson was on everybody's lips these days. "Nobody was killed, but Balzer and the two boys were taken away and haven't been heard of since. Tante Balzer and the girls are staying with relatives in Schoenfeld. Balzer was accused of having buried vast amounts of arms and money and valuables — the old story. You know what a stubborn, tight-lipped old man Balzer is. I don't know if he had hidden away anything, but I do know that not even bandits holding guns to his head would have forced Balzer to talk or give up anything he didn't want to." He shook his head and added, "I'm not hopeful that he and the boys are still alive."

Willy Balzer, his brother Pete, and the old man — gone just like that. Snapper gloomily surveyed the desolate chasms and blackened ruins of the ravaged farmyard. Most of the buildings still had walls or parts of walls standing in gaping futility with no roofs to support. Even the stately elms and acacias that had framed the house and forecourt had been reduced to jagged, charred stumps.

Looking at the Balzer ruins Snapper began to understand why his father had grown so cautious and fearful. Well, he himself didn't feel cowed and Voronaya still stood. He would do everything in his power to keep it so.

At the door of the big, white *volost* building in Gulai Polye they were stopped by a burly guard, a peasant lad who appeared to be no more than seventeen or eighteen.

"What do you want here, *burzhuj?*" Rifle clamped around the breech by a huge, redmeat hand, he held it up against Jacob Loewen's chest as though handling a stick. "State your business."

"We'd like to see Chairman Makhno on an urgent matter, if it's possible," Loewen said politely over the gun barrel. "It's about our crop money. We've, we've come a long way," he added awkwardly.

"That's nothing to me, *burzhuj.* You can see this place is busier'n a whorehouse on payday. The Chairman's full up. I've got my orders." But he looked less certain than he sounded. Scratching the red stubble on his chin, he glowered at Loewen a long moment, then abruptly lowered his weapon. "*Khorosho,* if you're a *burzhuj* and a landowner maybe he'll want to see you right away. He enjoys dealing with your kind. Follow me, but don't be surprised if you get some curses and jabs in the ribs from the guys inside. They're honest peasants and don't like people like you snooping around here. And getting in ahead of them," he added sarcastically.

The beefy-faced guard opened the door and rudely thrust himself into the tight throng of peasants squeezed into the small anteroom. "Hey, comrade, watch your elbows," a middle-aged fellow almost as big as the guard said sharply. "We're all good souls and equals here."

"Shut your trap, *druzhok,*" the guard drawled amiably as he bulled by. "Dogs and lice are your equals, comrade. What would you know about good souls?"

As they pushed through the noisy tangle of men reluctantly making way for them, they were assailed by hostile mutterings and outright threats. "Wait your turn, *njemtsi tcherti;*" "death to the rich, you *burzhuj* blood-suckers." "Look at them slinking past honest men, the German parasites," one surly fellow hissed, stepping up to Snapper belligerently. Resentment and hostility thick as garlic fumes swirled around the lowered heads of the two Loewens.

Then they were through the tense gauntlet, and after a few minutes delay found themselves in Makhno's office. A large, sparsely furnished room, it was dominated at the far end by an imposing black desk behind which sat Makhno, slim face bent over his papers, looking from across the room like a boy impersonating a man. On the table on his right lay a huge pistol and a couple of hand grenades. On his left a tray containing a tea pot, several glasses, and the remains of a meal. Makhno was dressed in a blue Hussar's uniform trimmed with black. His almost shoulder-length mane of raven hair glistened in the light of the window behind him.

Makhno looked up abruptly, his pale, smooth face betraying no surprise as he studied the two men standing before him. When Snapper caught the glint of those dark eyes, he felt a cold shaft pass through him. The face was the same but this was no sneaky little *khokhol* making sheep's eyes at an innocent girl. This was a man in control of himself and others: a man primed to deal instant destruction, like the weapons poised by his elbow.

When it came, Makhno's smile was cordial and some of the deadly glitter faded from his eyes. "Well, well, my two Loewen friends of long ago." The eyes narrowed on Snapper. "And the student too. Back from the wars. This is indeed an honor. Excuse me for not rising." His grin was sarcastic now and the eyes mocking. He was enjoying himself.

He motioned them to chairs. "Shall we get down to business, comrades? As you saw out there, I have many deserving people waiting to see me."

In a simple respectful manner Jacob Loewen stated his case and made a dignified request for his harvest money.

Makhno listened casually, the slight smile never leaving his face.

"So, you've come for what you call *your* money, comrades? I can't believe my ears." He leaned forward on his elbows, the smile now unctuous on his fleshy lips. "Let me remind you that you raised this crop on land that belongs to the people. Which means, my friends, that the money for it belongs to the people too." The grin was palpably malevolent now. "Of course, you will get a small part of it later as wages, like everybody else."

Snapper ignored the restraining hand his father placed on his arm. In spite of his fear he felt anger rising harsh and thick. "Why do you play this game with us, Nestor Ivanovich? That land is ours — at least until somebody takes it away from us. You're not going to deny us what's rightfully ours with an argument like that, are you?"

He stopped, aware that his father, alarmed, was trying to silence him. He sat back breathing heavily, glaring defiantly at the little man behind the desk.

Makhno took the outburst calmly, remained unruffled. His smile did not waver, but when he spoke his voice was chillingly insolent.

"Well, well, *burzhuj,* you've learned nothing in your wanderings, have you? You were a cocky shit of a student when I slaved for your papasha years ago and you're still a cocky shit."

Jacob Loewen, his voice low and urgent, said to his son in German, "Martin, you must not talk that way. This man is in charge here and we need his good will not his enmity." He turned to Makhno, his manner obsequious in his apprehension. "Comrade Makhno, please forgive this outburst. My son is a little hot-headed sometimes — he, he has come home from the front for a much-needed rest. He has seen so much destruction and suffering. His nerves —" Loewen stopped, lowered his eyes in silent pleading.

Makhno looked at his old employer with amused contempt. "Jacov Jacovlevich, I know you to be a good man, but I have a job to do. I say again, there will be no money leaving here until I decide otherwise. Is that understood?" He locked eyes again with Snapper. "And I would advise you to keep a tight rein on your son's tongue." His grin was ghastly now. "I needn't remind you that I have the power to wring his neck like a sick rooster."

He made a gesture of dismissal. "Good day, comrades, I have much work to do." He reached for the papers on his desk.

On the way home Snapper gave free vent to his pent-up rage. "He's a monster, Father. He *enjoyed* having the upper hand over us, sitting there in his fancy stolen uniform. I agree he's dangerous. I saw those killer's eyes. But we're not through with him yet. We can organize and defend ourselves against this greedy peasant. There are enough of us German landowners around here to give these bloodthirsty *muzhiks* a run for their money. The next time Makhno comes to Voronaya he'll get a different reception."

Jacob Loewen sat slumped beside his ranting son. He did not argue with him. He remained silent, but his heart was heavy.

3
Blumenau, December, 1917

Through the long, earnest word-roll of the funeral Wilhelm sat with the rest of the family grieving for his dead brother. Heinrich's body lay before them under the pulpit in a shallow, open casket. Blanched profile sharp and pinched, arms lying stiffly by his sides, he looked as serene and accepting in death as he had in life.

Dear, gentle Hein. His fragile life had faded out like a puff of smoke. Wilhelm thought of Hein living with his hideous secret, the slow rotting of his lungs, feeling every waking moment the worm gnawing in his chest. But he had never complained or openly shown any anguish. He had accepted his condition as serenely as he accepted everything in life. His winsome nature would not permit him to brood, to lock himself into self-pity. Where his cruel condition might have driven him inwards, it had instead made him loving, kind, and outgoing towards others. His smile was melancholy, but it came easily and lingered at the corners with a child's freshness and intimacy.

Deeply religious, he had a passion for memorizing and reciting bible passages, hymns, and the religious verse of Bernhard Harder. In his soft, musical voice, as delicately textured as a girl's, he could recite by the hour, and as a boy Wilhelm had been fascinated by his older brother's stories and verses. Though shy by nature Hein accepted every invitation to recite at weddings, socials, even funerals. His sin of pride, he called it, an addiction as strong as a drunkard's — but less costly, he would add. Besides, he always hoped that his recitations would awaken a sleeping conscience or pierce a sinner's heart.

Heinrich's only other passion had been his homing pigeons. They were pedigreed birds of whose ever-expanding genealogies he kept elaborate records. Before the war he had ordered books from Germany on the care and training of racing pigeons. Unfortunately he was the only pigeon fancier in the immediate area, so he could only race his best birds against each other. He would release his birds at a neighboring village, then try to beat them back to Blumenau by horseback so that he could rate them when they arrived.

It broke Hein's heart when his beloved pigeons were requisitioned by the army as carriers. According to Father it was from that time that Hein's condition had begun to deteriorate rapidly.

And now he was gone. Not only Hein but Kolya too. Hein's death breathed peace and *gelassenheit*. But what about Kolya? Had he departed this life filled with murderous rage and spite, the black bile in his nature poisoning even his last moments on earth? It was too horrible to contemplate. If at least he were alive in a prison camp somewhere where he would have the chance to think things through for himself.

As he stared dully at Hein's coffin, Wilhelm felt a crushing despondency. It all seemed so bleak and hopeless. He had lost both brothers, his own future was uncertain — at least an artistic career seemed farther away than ever. And most intolerable of all, he lived in a mad land that seemed bent on destroying itself.

No wonder his parents were aging so fast, living as they did in a world they no longer understood. He glanced at them now, his mother dabbing at her eyes with a delicacy that wrenched him, though he knew she had long prepared herself for this grief. His father sat with head bent, his dark bulk humped dejectedly, as though suffering some public shame he was powerless to avoid. He looked baffled, uncomprehending. More and more, his mother had confided to him, Father was sinking into moods of silence and defeat that worried her. Now Hein's death was making him burrow even deeper into his darkening self. He's like a blind old bulldog, thought Wilhelm, who finds nothing to sink his teeth into anymore and pull at so he can feel alive and useful. He feels only the leaden weight of his aging body.

The tightening collar of mortality.

Wilhelm had been granted compassionate leave as soon as he had received word that Hein was dying, but had been unable to get home in time. He had barely made it for the funeral.

Now that he was home he had no intention of going back to Moscow. The ambulance service was at a virtual standstill, and the AZU seemed to be disintegrating. He had discharged his wartime service to his country to the best of his ability. Had carried out his duties, exposed himself to enemy fire, and had been wounded in front line action. He had done his part. Now it was over for him, as it was for Snapper. He had other things to do with his life, if this crazy revolution would ever settle down.

With a delicious pang he thought of Katya. He could hardly wait to see her. Being with Katya again would lift him out of the morbid state he was in. She was by far his best link to the future, the wise, loving force he needed to sustain him in a world that in some frightening way seemed already to have passed him by like a devastating storm. A world in which his dream of becoming an artist seemed irrelevant if not completely ludicrous. Well, he could live with that brute reality. But only if he had Katya. With her he could endure even a lifetime sentence as a village teacher.

As soon as possible he was going to Voronaya to lay claim to a bride. He had hinted at marriage in his letters, but now he would propose to Katya directly. And he had no doubts as to what her answer would be. If she agreed, they would get married in summer. No more waiting. He would suggest that they both apply for teaching jobs in Blumenau or in a neighboring village.

The funeral was over. Hein would now be taken to his final resting place in the cool, dark earth housing his forebears.

4
Voronaya, December, 1917

There was no space between them as they sat on the curved divan in the Loewen living room.

Katya Loewen's response was immediate, joyous. "Of course, I'll marry you, Willie. I've been waiting with maidenly impatience for you to ask me." Her dark eyes were as direct and radiant as he had remembered them. She smiled, her strong white teeth and firm chin flashing vitality — and amusement. "But I'm glad you waited to propose in person, instead of in a letter. Unless, of course, you had proposed in one of your delicious drawings —you know, you humbly down on your knees beseeching me — regally sitting in a chair — for my hand. I would have liked that. You can still do it, you know."

Delighted, Wilhelm fell in with her capering mood. "Don't think that didn't cross my mind every time I wrote. If you only knew how many times I drew your likeness in Moscow, and in romantic poses that would have made you blush, my darling."

"You know what convinced me that you really loved me — not your passionate words on paper, though I admit I was greedy for those too, but the little sketch you did of me as a Christmas gift. I used to look at that and think, this man already knows more about me — sees more in me — than I do myself. That I could give myself to this young man without fear, never doubt that he would understand me and cherish me for myself and not just as a prize to win, a property to own."

Touched deeply by her words, Wilhelm could only reach for that lovely, strong face and kiss her passionately, gratefully.

"My parents will be pleased too," she said more sedately when he finally released her. "You made a very good impression on them last Christmas. I wrote you that, remember? Mutti talked about you for weeks, and thinks you are a good influence on Martin, who will jump for joy at the news. And it can't be soon enough for Mutti, I'm sure, she's considered me an old maid for years now, with my chances for a good match dwindling rapidly." She regarded him with uncharacteristic coquettishness. "I trust, dear sir, your offer is motivated by more than simple compassion for a spinsterish school teacher."

His answer once again was to pull her towards himself and smother her with kisses. She was in no hurry to extricate herself from his embrace. When she finally did she had something else on her mind.

"You know what I would like for us someday — yes, that too, many children" — she blushed as she saw the expression on his face — "but I was thinking of something else just now. Someday I wish you and I could start a school together, a special school devoted to the finer things — you would teach art, of course, and I could teach such things as elocution, literature, perhaps even music. Wouldn't that be something new and wonderful for our Mennonite *bauernkultur* here in the Molochnaya?"

Wilhelm's heart leaped. For months he had been dreaming of the same possibility. That she had the same dream only made him more certain that they were meant for each other.

And after they had discussed at length their marriage plans and their dream for the future, he quite suddenly blurted out what he had never been able to mention in his letters to her, he told her about his old friendship with Clara Bock. He held back nothing, not his feelings for Clara nor his growing uneasiness that she had valued him only as a conveniently placed friend and not as a serious suitor.

"I can tell you all this now, Katya, because Clara and I are completely free of each other, and have been for some time." He smiled at her. "In fact, from about the time I informed her in my last letter to her how I felt about you."

Katya had searched his face avidly as he spoke, then cast down her eyes. Now she looked up and smiled back, her eyes moist. "I'm glad you told me, Willie, but I already knew about you and Miss Clara Bock. You see, she wrote to me herself after you told her about me. Wait" — she saw his surprised chagrin — "no, you mustn't think she was nasty or anything —perhaps just a bit condescending, but very gentle and kind in what she said about you and your 'innocent friendship.' "

Wilhelm was embarrassed, but knew he shouldn't have been surprised. It was, he realized, exactly the kind of thing Clara would think of doing, and enjoy doing in her spoiled way.

Katya snuggled closer into the curve of his arm and reached for his free hand. "I've been waiting to make a confession too, *mein lieber*. Remember when I wrote you that Makhno and his brutes had been here and taken over the place as though they owned it?" She frowned, seeing the apprehension on his face. "No, no, my darling, nothing terrible happened, but a little more than I wanted to say in my letter. I didn't want to alarm you any more than I knew you would be already. The truth is the little monster acted very strangely towards me. No, he never actually touched me, but he was always hovering about, devouring me with his eyes.

"One evening he came to my room where I was reading — just opened the door and walked in — I don't know where Mutti and Papi were at the time. I jumped up in alarm, but he was very polite and said he didn't want to disturb me at all. He just stood there and stared at me with a very odd expression on his face. If he took another step I was ready to scream — and fight." She stared past Wilhelm as she recollected the scene. "Then he recited something so strange I still can't quite understand it. Never taking his eyes off me, he said — I remember his words exactly: '*golubka, golubka,* fly to my hand, your wings are of azure, have never touched land; come down from your height, your elegant soaring, my heart is yearning to lock you up tight.' It sounded like a verse he had made up — a love poem. But I still don't understand why he said it to me. So far as I know, he had never seen me before. And still he kept standing there staring at me, as if he wanted something from me — an answer perhaps. I just stared back, too frightened to do anything else. Suddenly he turned to my dresser, looked over the objects on it, then snatched a lace handkerchief lying there, and grinning a ghastly grin at me he turned and disappeared as suddenly as he had come. And that was all." She raised her face to his. "What do you think got into the brute, Willie? Was he just drunk? I don't mind telling you I didn't sleep much that night and felt very nervous until I heard the last Makhno hoofbeat die away the next afternoon."

Before Wilhelm could offer any comments, Father and Mother Loewen, coughing discreetly, came in together from the kitchen, as though following some inaudible cue.

Wilhelm's formal request for Katya's hand in marriage was granted with dignified but obviously pleased approval first by Jacob Loewen and then, after the two men had finished their brief private talk, by beaming Mutti Loewen as well, her eyes behind her glasses shining with happiness and satisfaction.

5
Halbstadt-Molochansk, February 16-19, 1918

On an unseasonably mild, sun-washed Monday morning Wilhelm and his father drove to Halbstadt to do some shopping. They went first to the Mutual Credit Bank on Romanov Street, where Gerhard Fast withdrew some money. The bank was now controlled by the local Soviet, and the service was slow and inefficient.

They were on their way to Thiessen's store next to the bank when they were rudely accosted. "Halt, you filthy bloodsuckers!"

A riding whip whistled in the air, and Wilhelm instinctively threw a protective arm over his face while shielding his father at the same time.

"You're under arrest, you bastards," a hoarse voice bawled in his ear. "The Red Guards are in charge here now. I'm Pishklov, the new commissar. I'm officially charging you two as counter-revolutionaries."

Wilhelm stared in disbelief at a swarthy, evil-looking man in a black leather jacket and cap with rolled-up ear lugs. The brute leered drunkenly, waving his *nagan* with one hand and keeping his whip poised with the other.

Let's see what you got out of that bank, old serpent." He thrust the muzzle of his revolver against Gerhard Fast's forehead. Fast reached for his wallet without a word and held it out to the man with a shaky hand. The commissar, sticking his whip in his boot, grabbed it with a savage swipe.

Wilhelm glanced at his father's ashen face. There was a small red circle marked on his brow.

The commissar hefted the bulging wallet. "This is open theft of money belonging to the people. Impounded."

Slobbering drunken curses he ordered father and son across the street to the *volost* office on the corner. He marched them around the back to a much smaller building which served as the town lockup.

"More counter-revolutionaries," the commissar roared at the heavily armed man in sailor's uniform who was guarding the door. The sailor chuckled and prodded the two prisoners up the steps to the door.

"We'll make short work of you too, you vipers," he growled as he gave them each a violent shove through the door.

The small, one-room jail was dirty, dark, and cold. The only furnishing was a long wooden bench against the far wall. On it sat half a dozen dejected-looking men, all well-known Mennonite citizens of the town. In the middle of the room, haphazardly placed, were a few large boxes or chests which served as chairs for several other prisoners. A few more were seated on the floor. There were about a dozen prisoners altogether, which made the cell crowded.

The new prisoners were greeted with sombre questions. "And what are they charging you with, Gerhard?" It was old Jacob Sudermann, the retired owner of the model estate Apanlee, one of the wealthiest and most influential men in the Molochnaya.

"I don't know, Jacob, I don't understand. He called us counter —
counter-revolutionaries. I don't even know what that means."

"Yes, one of their favorite charges," murmured Herman Neufeld, a
prominent businessman in Halbstadt. "That's my charge too. And you know
why?" he asked plaintively. "Because I have my coachman sleeping in the
barn instead of in the house." He shook his head despairingly.

A third man spoke up in a quiet but firm voice. He was Peter Letkemann,
a teacher in the School of Commerce. Even in the gray shadows of the cell
his large, liquid eyes, close-cropped beard, and jaunty mustache gave him a
striking resemblance to the deposed Tsar Nicholas. Wilhelm knew Letkemann only slightly. He was said to be a brilliant teacher and was the
husband of Maria Petrovna Letkemann, the Russian teacher whom Katya
had liked so much.

"Our situation here is very grave," Letkemann explained quietly. "We've
been kept here since yesterday morning, in mortal danger every minute. At
first we thought they were holding us for ransom. We soon found out
differently." His voice faltered momentarily. "They shot two of us yesterday
afternoon — young Heinz Willms and a Russian lad who protested the
looting the sailors were doing." He hesitated again. "They've already made
up a list for today. Five names are on it, they say." Letkemann and old
Sudermann exchanged anguished looks.

"Uncle Sudermann," Letkemann continued, "tries to comfort us by
reading from God's Word."

Sudermann, a pocket Bible open in his hands, began to turn pages with
near-sighted concentration. In the faint light of the one small window, he
slowly began to read Psalm 121: " 'If I lift up my eyes to the hills, where shall
I find help? Help comes only' — "

The door crashed open and the drunken commissar stood scowling and
breathing heavily in the doorway. "Neufeld, Henry — where's the son-of-a-
bitch who tried to hop out of our hands yesterday?"

Henry Neufeld, his face a rigid disk of terror, rose unsteadily from one of
the boxes.

"Aha!" the commissar grabbed his arm and yanked him towards the door.
"Pigeons that try to fly over the wall are put against the wall." He guffawed
at his own ghastly joke and seemed surprised the others didn't join in.

At the door Neufeld turned and in a strangled whisper said goodbye to
his brother Herman and the others. He was deathly pale but dry-eyed.

Fighting nausea, Wilhelm got up and stepped over to the small dirty
window. Through its bars he had a partial view of the yard. He watched
mesmerized as Neufeld was placed against the wall of what appeared to be
a barn nearby. He could not see where the executioners were standing.

As the shots rang out there were loud cries of anguish behind him. He
glanced down and saw that the prisoners nearest him had fallen to their

knees and were praying fervently. The victim's brother was rocking on his knees in an ecstasy of terror, eyes closed, mouth working soundlessly.

Wilhelm looked out again and was astonished to see Henry Neufeld still on his feet, apparently unhurt. He was saying something to the commissar. The commissar waved his arm and a couple of Red Guards led the condemned man away.

"He's alive! They must have missed him intentionally. Now they're taking him away," Wilhelm reported to the others. "But why?" Several more prisoners were now crowding around the window.

"They must be taking him back to the store to make him hand over the money in our strong box" Herman Neufeld said weakly. Then consternation came over his round face. "But I have the key. Here in my pocket. Oh, my God, he won't be able to open —" His voice broke and he began to sob softly.

Again they waited tensely as the minutes ticked by. Suddenly, furious curses at the door as the commissar burst in and screamed: "He's gotten away again, the lousy bastard!" He glared murderously round the room, his chest heaving. "For that you all go to the wall!"

Old Sudermann shuffled forward, face and hands beseeching. "But comrade commissar, how can you hold us responsible for the man escaping? We're helpless here. We didn't have —"

"Shut your hole, old swine. You're next anyway. Save your stinking breath."

But after further pleading from Teacher Letkemann, Herman Neufeld, and Wilhelm the commissar calmed down a bit.

"All right, you *njemtsi* cockroaches. I'll let the people decide. What the people say goes." He swaggered to the door, his rage far from spent. "And I know what the people will want me to do, you *burzhuj* scum. You can all start saying your goddamn prayers."

For the next half hour Sudermann read some more passages from his Bible and they all prayed together several times. Then they lapsed into a tense waiting silence again.

Wilhelm looked with concern at his father, who sat on the bench without moving. He seemed to be in a trance, perhaps close to collapse. For some time now they had known that he was suffering from a heart condition. Looking at him Wilhelm felt stabs of pity for his stricken parent.

And then he thought about himself. And Katya. And felt the blood drain from his body. It couldn't end this way. Not like this. It was too randomly unjust. God would not permit it to happen. He and Katya were getting married in June. They already had schools for the winter, she in Blumenau, he in nearby Fishau. They would live at home the first while, in the summer room. It was all arranged. This couldn't be happening. He had survived a shell blast at the front. God had wanted him to live then. Only to be snuffed out now? It wasn't possible. It must not be!

God, you must not let it happen this way. It makes no sense. YOU CAN'T, he screamed through the corridors of his brain and was surprised the others hadn't heard. But no dejected head had been raised. They were all preoccupied with their own fate, he saw.

His father moaned softly and mumbled something. He seemed to be in pain. Wilhelm turned to him just as the door flew open again.

The commissar's face was flushed with triumph. "The people have decided, *njemtsi*. Justice will be done! The people's revolution goes forward. You have sucked our blood, you vipers. Now we suck yours." He held up a rumpled list. "Two of you every half hour till we find the cockroach that's escaped. Sudermann, Jacob — out."

The old man sighed, rose slowly, and said in a firm voice: "Brothers, I go to be with the Lord in glory. Pray for me and for each other — and for our murderers." He drew his stooped figure erect and faced the commissar. Remembering something, he drew the Bible out of his pocket and handed it back to its owner Herman Neufeld.

At the door he turned again, swept the room with a calm gaze. "Goodby, brothers in Christ. Till we meet again in a better world."

Wilhelm watched at the window as the veteran slowly walked towards the barn, his lank white hair riffling slightly in the breeze. He never got there. The swarthy commissar trotted up behind him and with a loud curse fired his *nagan* into the old man's head. Soundlessly, he crumpled forward and hit the ground face down. He did not move.

Wilhelm felt himself sinking into a numbing lethargy, as though his whole body had gone dead with only a faint flicker in his brain still alive and functioning. He sat down beside his father and put his arm around the slumped shoulders.

"Father, we mustn't give up hope," he whispered. "Our names aren't on the list yet." He could only hope it was so. "Something may happen out there to stop this. We must trust in the Heavenly Father." He stopped, racked by the futility of his words.

His father opened his eyes and looked at him dully, pain and incomprehension stamped visibly on his bulldog features. He looked defenseless, utterly beaten, nakedly devoid of all hope and assurance. "Willie," he muttered thickly, "I want to go — go home. I can't breathe here. My chest hurts; I feel cold, cold."

A minute later the name "Letkemann, Pyotr" rang through the cell. The teacher also kept his composure. He said farewell, then added, "Why my friends? What's the purpose?" His dark eyes were luminous. "I die with that question surging through my mind." He began shaking hands with those nearest him. "Well, God's will be done. Tell my darling Maria that I did not lose faith and that I will await her. Pray for me."

Once more Wilhelm forced himself to the window. He was afraid this time he would faint. But he felt compelled to witness the horror, to burn it all into his consciousness. If he survived he would record it for others. If not —

Letkemann, standing erect against the barn wall, was saying something to the commissar even as the latter raised his *nagan*. Wilhelm could not hear the teacher's words. A shot exploded and Letkemann lay in the dirt on his back, his tsar's face obliterated.

Again terror and panic lay like a thick, vile stench in the cell. The prisoners sat slumped, motionless, as though all their vital energy now went into listening for the dreaded sound of the door opening again.

Then it did open and the commissar, more swollen with maniacal self-importance than ever, confronted them again. "Well, *burzhuj* pigs, we got the little rabbit that hopped away. He won't be doing any more hopping."

There was a gasp from Herman Neufeld. He covered his face in his hands and moaned brokenly.

The commissar looked at him with baleful contempt. "And now we want the rabbit's brother. He's the son-of-a-bitch with the key to the strongbox and he hasn't said a word." The brute came forward and grasped Neufeld savagely by the collar, almost yanking him off his feet.

"Out you bloodsucker, out." He accompanied the order with a brutal kick that sent Neufeld staggering through the door.

For the rest of the day and all through the night the remaining prisoners were left to wonder who would be next.

Tuesday passed without further incident, though again they were given nothing to eat.

Late Wednesday morning the commissar, sober now but as foul-mouthed as before, released them from the lockup amidst a volley of threats and execrations.

Though weak and badly shaken by his ordeal, Wilhelm decided that before anything else he must get his sick father to the hospital in neighboring Muntau. Then he went home to comfort his mother and sisters.

Gerhard Fast would never be the same again. The two days and nights of terror and unbearable tension had reduced him to a feeble old man who quaked at the slightest sound. Wilhelm himself felt as if he had returned from the dead. He knew now how Dostoievsky had felt when he was led out to be executed, not knowing that he would be spared at the last moment. A cruel hoax to teach young university radicals a lesson they would never forget.

But this had been no hoax. Only by the grace of God had he escaped with his life. Yes, he was alive, but something, he knew, had been extinguished within him during those terrible forty-eight hours. Something he would never be able to rekindle.

He didn't quite know what it was that had gone out. He knew only that it had to do with innocence and hope, an inner radiance that had survived earlier fear and despair. Until now.

CHAPTER TWENTY-ONE

1

Spring, 1918

Nikolai Fast was on his way back to Russia. He had been released by the Germans in an exchange of prisoners of war with the new Bolshevik government. He was one of the first Russian prisoners to benefit from the arrangement.

He was coming back from Germany looking reasonably healthy and fit. Except for the first eight months in an over-crowded prisoner-of-war camp, he had spent his three years as a prisoner working on farms in West Prussia. He had welcomed the work outside in the fresh air, but he had also been subjected to treatment that had left him feeling humiliated and very bitter.

As he sat by the train window looking idly at the rolling, war-ravaged plains east of Warsaw, his mind wandered back to the early weeks and months of captivity. The temporary camp at Buitov near Lemberg hadn't been too bad. In the siege of Lemberg the Germans had not only captured masses of Russian soldiers but also huge stores of food. That was Imperial Russia for you, he reflected contemptuously, a fortress packed with mountains of tinned meat and vegetables but no arms or ammunition! So they were fed their own food in the German camp.

After a few weeks they had been shipped off to Camp Hammerstein near Berlin. There they got their first real taste of prison life. Their scanty rations consisted mainly of watery, flavorless soup with a thin slice of mouldy bread. Twice a week they also got a small salt herring which most of the men stuck in their pockets for later. Soon they all had hard white crusts around their pockets.

Camp Hammerstein had once been a cavalry depot. It was run by a crotchety old Prussian general whose idea of daily exercise was to put them every morning through two hours of quick march drill up and down the hard-baked parade square. The drill was murder in the muggy heat, without a break, their bodies weakened by the poor diet.

The rest of the day was devoted to moving huge piles of darkly rotted horse dung from the generations of cavalry horses quartered there before the place became a prison camp. They were given no tools for this job except primitive little wagons hardly bigger than toy wagons. In groups of six or eight to a wagon they had to dig up and load the manure with their bare hands and then pull and push the wagons out of the compound to be dumped in a nearby ravine.

It was useless, degrading work that drove Nikolai half crazy with frustrated fury. There were days when he knew himself to be close to the breaking point and about to go berserk, as more than one prisoner had already. What kept him barely under control was the rumor that well-behaved, farm-bred prisoners would soon be assigned to German farms to help ease the critical shortage of labor in the Reich.

For once luck had been with him. In March of 1916 he was assigned to a small farm in West Prussia, near Marienburg. Nikolai knew this was the general area from which his ancestors had migrated to Russia in the early nineteenth century. He was relieved to find, however, that his new boss, a man called Bemling, was not a Mennonite, although there were apparently still Mennonites living in the Vistula delta near Danzig. Fast was a North German name, and he had no trouble passing himself off as a Russian whose family had come from Germany a long time ago.

Herr Bemling was a tall, gaunt-stooped man in his early fifties. His wife, a good twenty years younger, had a pretty face and a plumply ripe figure. Her eyes had gone shy so quickly when she first saw him that he was on the alert at once.

When her husband was around Frau Berthe stayed in the house and ignored the new farmhand, but she became friendly, even flirtatious, when her husband was away. Which seemed to be often, especially in the evenings. One night she came to his room in the barn after Herr Bemling had left for town. Sitting carelessly on his hard bed, Frau Berthe told him that her husband spent his evenings with his cronies in a tavern, drinking and playing cards. It made her feel lonesome being left like that night after night; after all, she was much younger and would like to go out too — do something at least.

Such an open invitation could not be ignored, even by a lowly prisoner of war. In fact, the seduction had been so easy that Nikolai wasn't sure later who had seduced whom.

He couldn't believe his luck. Here he was a war prisoner in a foreign land with comfortable, familiar farm work to do, enjoying good food, and getting an eager, attractive partner for his bed almost nightly. It was all too good to be true. He soon grew suspicious of his master's lack of suspicion. Was he blind? How could he not realize the danger of leaving his hot-blooded young wife alone on the farm almost every evening with a vigorous young man deprived of women over a long period? His cot still warm and rumpled from his exertions with Berthe, he would listen smugly to the sounds of the old man returning late at night on horseback, stumbling and cursing drunkenly to himself as he led his horse into the barn. The man was either a fool about his wife or simply didn't care.

After a while Nikolai had reason to wonder about Frau Berthe herself. He had been so gratified at first by her eager responses that he had quickly lost all shyness and inhibition with her. He couldn't get enough of her demanding, torrid embraces. But it didn't take him long to sense that her ardor was not altogether spontaneous. She was impatient with any foreplay, even kissing, and left him abruptly and coldly as soon as they had finished.

And during the day she ignored him completely, as though he didn't exist. He was puzzled and hurt, felt somehow humiliated by their hurried bouts of love-making, as though he were being used in some way he couldn't quite fathom. He could feel her coldness, her distaste for him even as her hot limbs strained against his. It struck him finally that she was going through the motions as mechanically as a whore. Except he didn't have to pay her.

Then, without warning, she stopped coming to his bed. She must be sick, he thought, and doesn't want me to be disappointed — like last month. But the days went by and still she stayed away.

He decided to visit her. After old Bemling had ridden off to town one night Nikolai went boldly to the house, something he'd never done before. She was sitting in the kitchen peeling potatoes over a bowl in her lap.

She looked up without surprise, her full, ruddy face cold. "What do you want, prisoner? You have no business here in the house."

Her curt dismissal angered him. "I want to know why you have stopped coming, why you're avoiding me?"

"That's my business, prisoner. Now get out," she snapped. "I'm busy." She bent over her potatoes with a sneer, provoking him, despising him.

He would not be put off. "Look Berthe, all I want is an explanation. You owe me that much at least."

She raised her eyes, still mocking him. "I owe you nothing, you Russian peasant." Her insolence enveloped him, as her lust had once. Then she smiled sadistically. "All right, why not? I'll tell you then. You're asking for it." She leaned forward, her heavy thighs spreading under her weight. "I came to you because I needed your seed," she hissed. "My husband desperately wants an heir and can't get one himself. When you turned out to be of German stock, though a Russian, we decided you were the right physical type. Best of all, you'll have no claim on us later." She stared at him triumphantly. "Now it's done. I don't need you anymore, prisoner."

Anger hit him like a club. "You filthy bitch," he grated and raised his fist.

Her eyes widened in alarm but she stood her ground. "Get away from me. Don't you dare. If you so much as touch me" — her voice rose to shrill confidence —" your soft life here will end tomorrow. You'll never touch me again. Never. Understood?"

He glared at her in brute fury but did not touch her. He was helpless and she knew it. "I hope my seed rots in your belly, you unfeeling sow," he spat at her and turned on his heel to her squeal of curses.

In the middle of the night he was manhandled out of sleep by an iron-fisted giant he had never seen before, yanked to his feet and pummeled savagely. Dazed, his underwear half ripped off, he tried to fight back, but was pinioned from behind by a second ruffian who held him while the giant slammed his fist into his face again and again, then switched to his gut and finally kicked him in the groin just as he began to collapse.

Before he passed out Nikolai saw old Bemling standing in the doorway holding up the barn lantern, his scraggy face sadistic in the flickering orange light.

In the gray light of dawn he examined the swollen blue mass of his genitals, the throbbing pain so acute he almost passed out again. Then he felt the cuts and welts on his face and decided that his horribly bruised nose was not quite broken. He longed to drag himself to the well outside, but knew his battered body was not up to it.

That afternoon Bemling, drunk and snarling threats, came in with another man, gave him some water at last and told him curtly that the man was his new boss and was taking him to his farm.

Nikolai had remained on Herr Lampner's farm near Königsdorf until his release. Lampner was a hard man who worked him long hours and addressed him only when he had something sarcastic to say. He followed the progress of the war closely and his sarcastic insults grew exultant whenever the news was good for Germany. The Germans had stopped a massive Russian offensive that spring and Lampner enjoyed entertaining his prisoner of war, as Nikolai forked hay up to him on the haystack they were building, with gloating accounts of how "our gallant German warriors" had crushed "the Mongolian apes," who had "turned tail and fled with the shit running down their legs, the half-wit peasants." And when German troops knocked Romania out of the war that autumn Lampner hailed the victory as a triumph of "civilized men" over "your Slavic cousins, who are as dumb and primitive as you Russian turds, and even more cowardly."

Nikolai had nursed his hatred for Germans and all things German in private and was careful never to give his loutish boss the satisfaction of seeing him show anger or resentment. Only his powerful ache to get home to Russia again had kept him from laying violent hands on that cretin Lampner.

And he had been rewarded for his patience and self-restraint. He was on his way home at last. But his experience with the Bemlings and with Lampner was a festering sore that would not heal for a long time, he knew. The thought of his seed growing into a human being inside that fat cow always worked him into a silent frenzy. Now that baby was alive and kicking in this world, suckled by that German bitch, and would itself grow up into a smug German. He would never forgive that slut and her impotent husband, and he would hate Germany and its people for the rest of his life. Never would he have anything more to do with *Germanzi*.

And that included the Mennonite colony he had grown up in. He had no desire to go back there, not even to visit his family. As far as they were concerned he was probably dead, and that's the way he would leave things.

He wondered what effect the revolution was having on places like the Molochnaya — on the whole country, for that matter. He was excited by the revolution but had no idea of what to expect. Except that he would become a part of it in one way or another. He didn't like the idea of the Bolsheviks gaining power, though. He remembered them from Berdjansk before the war. They were big talkers, conceited, hotheaded, brutally intolerant. They were forever trying to put down the other revolutionary parties, especially the Anarchists. He had always favored the Anarchists. They opposed the very idea of a central state run from a faraway capital. They believed in people running their own affairs at home. He liked that.

Nikolai leaned back in his seat and closed his eyes. He was tired of looking at a landscape pockmarked by shells and littered with the ugly debris of war. They had long since passed the Bug and weren't too far from Grodno on the Nieman, and still they were traveling through German-occupied territory. He wondered just how far the Germans had penetrated into Russia. You just couldn't get away from the bastards. They were everywhere. He wouldn't be surprised to find them in Alexandrovsk.

No, he didn't trust the Bosheviks. Lenin and Trotsky and all that crowd were city intellectuals. All they were interested in was grabbing power in the big cities — control the workers and unions. They wouldn't do anything for the peasant, who needed help the most and always had. The peasant would never be able to do anything for himself until the exploiter was beaten off his back. Give the peasant some land, leave him alone, and he'd do all right.

That's the kind of society he was going to fight for, he vowed, a free, natural, self-contained agrarian society. Let the cities shift for themselves. The Mennonites had always pretended that they had that kind of system, but of course it was all sham and pretense. The church and the big landowners in the *volost* had all the control. And what about the landless Mennonites? Every village in the Molochnaya had side streets full of good, dutiful church members who had to work for pitiful day wages for the rich farmers and businessmen. And that's where they stayed, unless they agreed to go to some wild tract in the East and break their backs building a new colony.

That wasn't free choice. That was exploitation carried from one generation to the next. That was the kind of rotten system he'd fight against, if the peasants and landless people hadn't already taken matters into their own hands now the revolution was here.

Yes, he'd help the revolution. But on his own terms. He wouldn't fight for the Bolsheviks. Never. He didn't believe in clubbing one master off the peasant's back just so another could take his place.

2
Alexandrovsk, Spring, 1918

Having finally managed to make his way from Moscow to Alexandrovsk, Nikolai Fast decided to stay there, at least until he could get his bearings or something turned up. He steered clear of the Red Guards swarming all over. Instead, after running into his old friend Bro one day, he got a chance to make contact with revolutionaries more to his liking. Bro took him one evening to a meeting of a band of local Anarchists who were said to be well-organized and extremely active. Their leader was a young woman reputed to be as tough and ruthless as any male leader.

"Kolya, tonight you'll meet the most remarkable gal you've ever met in your life," Bro promised gloatingly, "She's always looking for more good recruits. I've told her about you." Bro grinned lecherously. "If she takes a shine to you, Kolya, look out. She'll swallow you like a snake swallowing an egg." He chuckled. "They say she's had more lovers than Catherine the screwing Great."

"I hear she calls herself 'Chaika.' What's her real name?"

"Marusya Nikoforovna. Nobody knows much about her, but she's some gal. You'll see."

And Nikolai did. Bro had not exaggerated. Chaika was indeed a most unusual young woman. For a moment when she strode into the room for the meeting he took her for a man. Her wide, high-boned face was dominated by a nose that flashed like a Turkish sabre and her black eyes had the wild boldness of a Cossack cavalry officer's. Her whole figure looked mannish and she walked and bore herself like a man. She was dressed like a man, too, in a white peasant blouse half hidden under a dark military cape, Cossack pants, and gleaming boots. He could also see that she was wearing a black bandoleer and a low-slung, holstered pistol on each slender hip.

For a moment he was nonplussed by Chaika's unfeminine appearance. Then he became aware of the luxurious sweep of dark hair flowing from under her military peaked cap down over her shoulders. That long, thick mane of hair and the wild eyes declared her woman.

Chaika was completely at ease with her "boys," basking in their obvious adoration, enjoying her easy dominance over this rag-tag collection of street toughs and mean-eyed peasant adventurers. She had them eating out of her hands even before she addressed them. She stood before them, making a sour face as she began to speak.

"What a filthy-looking bunch of bastards I've got here. And you call yourselves my 'faithful ones'? I could find better-looking guys in a Siberian chain-gang."

"That's were I come from," roared a coarse-voiced man, and the rest chuckled appreciatively.

Chaika's sharp eyes had already ferreted out the new men, including Nikolai, sitting with Bro. He felt her eyes on him for a moment, appraising him.

Then she got down to business. "Those of you who weren't with us last night missed something big." She paused dramatically. "Last night we captured a train-load of supplies. North of town. A whole train, I tell you. Including a stock of new rifles! What do you think of that, *khlopsey?*"

A chorus of hoarse cheers and footstamping. "It's what we've been looking for, comrades," she went on. "Now we can carry out some proper raids. What do you say, boys?"

Again they responded noisily, worshipfully. Good old Chaika! They congratulated each other for having thrown their lot in with her.

"But we've got to be on our guard. We don't want nobody else horning in on our operation." She stood erect, eyes stormy with indignation. "I met today with Comrade Makhno from out Gulai Polye way. You remember we helped him out with guns when he was organizing last winter. Well, listen to this. Now he wants us to join up with him." She threw back her head defiantly. "But I don't trust that sly little serpent. He's looking to take us over." She made a threatening gesture and her voice rose as the men leaned forward, straining to be unleashed by her passion. "And we ain't gonna let them do that, are we my cock pigeons?"

As one they roared "No! Never! To hell with Makhno!"

Her thin red lips parted in a wide grin, a lascivious grin that embraced them all. "That's right, boys, we don't need Makhno. Nobody's gonna lie down on top of us. We stay together. We're a family and I'm your *batushka* and *mamushka* both. Am I right?"

"Yeah, yeah, you're right, *Batko* Chaika, *Mamushka* Marusya," they chanted lustily, their laughter lewd, "Let Makhno go screw himself." Bro jabbed Nikolai in delight. "Well, what did I tell you?"

There were not many men in the room who had not been taken to Chaika's lean bosom at one time or another. In her cups, Chaika liked to boast that by "breaking in" her boys she was creating a mystical bond with them so they would be true "freedom fighters" and "loyal to the death."

Standing in the shadows behind Chaika as she spoke to her men was her "official" lover Shalakov, large and brooding, his close-set eyes fixed balefully on one after the other of the new men as he tried to spot a potential rival among them. Shalakov was unconcerned about Chaika's casual encounters with her boys. He feared only a serious rival. He had already singled out Nikolai, huskily good-looking with his Tatar eyes and luxurious mustache, and glared fiercely at him as Chaika talked.

She had more news. "Tomorrow night, boys, we ride again. There's an estate a dozen miles down river — a German estate — you'll enjoy visiting. It's quite a place, my lads. The man who owns it is one of the richest exploiters around here. And I happen to know he'll be there tomorrow night with his family. We'll have some fun and get some loot. Believe me."

Nikolai was arrested by something in Chaika's face as she described their target. There was something personal here, he thought, she was hiding something. Her face had gone tight as she talked about the raid, locked up, and she was no longer smiling.

The men again bawled their approval and after issuing precise instructions for the attack Chaika declared the meeting over. The men, relaxed and in a good mood, broke out their *samogon* flasks.

Chaika's eyes found Nikolai's and with a peremptory toss of her head she signaled for him to follow her out. As she turned away she muttered something to Shalakov beside her, who gave Nikolai a murderous stare as he approached and hissed something to him as he passed by. But the big man did not follow the two out of the room. Bro threw the departing Nikolai a suggestive wink and turned to the other men.

Nikolai followed Chaika down the dark, musty stairs and out into the dimly lit street. Neither had spoken a word. He did not know what was expected of him, what she wanted of him.

Outside, under a streetlight, she turned to him abruptly, her face and eyes softer than they had been upstairs.

"What's your name, comrade?" Her voice was husky and her lips barely moved.

He loomed over her, feeling awkward. "Fast, Nikolai Jegorivich," he answered formally.

She was frowning. "Fast? Is that a German or a Mennonite name?"

He was caught off-balance by her question. "Uh, Mennonite — both, actually — uh, uh —" He was not sure what to call her and came to a stammering halt.

She was amused now. "Well, well, you seem to be a shy one."

With a deft movement she reached up and ran her finger slowly over his heavy mustache, from end to end. "So — Fast — just as long as it isn't Bock." Her eyes had hardened again. She looked up at him intently, her fingers still on the soft nap of his mustache.

Close up, her cape still open, he got a faint whiff of her body's rankness. She even smelled like a man. But he didn't understand her reference to the name Bock. Did she mean the rich Bock family of Schoenwiese, the family Willie used to associate with? Clara and August Bock's family? He had never met them but he remembered their names.

"Kolya, I'll call you Kolya the —" She stopped, looked at him coquettishly. "Tell me Kolya, is everything about you as big and thick as your mustache?"

Before he could think of an answer she grabbed his arm and started pulling him along.

"Come my big Mennonite Fast." She glanced up at him coyly. "My place isn't far. Tonight you'll fold your hairy brown wings over me. Don't worry. Shalakov won't bother us." Giggling like a schoolgirl she squeezed his arm and rubbed her thigh against his as they walked. She added with a wicked laugh, "Tonight you ride me. Tomorrow night you'll ride for me."

Inside her room her voice was low and urgent as she discarded her cape and embraced him. "By day you call me Chaika, my fighting name. At night you call me Marusya, my loving name."

His excitement mounting, he helped her wriggle out of her boots, coarse Cossack pants and blouse, the sour-sweet stench of her unwashed body rising up like a miasma.

Then they were locked together on the bed. Nikolai felt himself gripped by a wild lust for this strange creature — half man, all woman — as she drew him over on top of her. Her muscular arms tightened around his back and her fierce, pounding kisses and animal moans forced him quickly out of himself in a frenzy of passion. But she continued to drive herself against him in a kind of fury, until he realized that she was testing him, that they were really in a strange struggle for dominance.

He was stubborn and matched her blow for blow, thrusting down at her brutally.

Finally her voice was rasping in his ear. "Enough, *njemets*. That's enough. Are you trying to kill me?" But there was no real anger in her, only a grudging submission.

3

Selenaya, Selenaya, Selenaya . . . The syllables throbbed in her temples until they merged with the pounding hoofbeats of her big black stallion. Beside her face stolid, jaws clenched against the wind, Nikolai Fast easily kept pace with her. He was looking straight ahead. A good rider this big German. She smiled to herself. What was he thinking, flowing gracefully beside her? So different from her other boys — rough, stinking peasants all, who would as soon slice a throat as an apple.

But could he be trusted, this handsome Fast? Bro vouched for him, and Bro was a good man. She glanced again at his profile; it looked dark and closed against the silvery bars of moonlight on the broad waters of the Dnieper below them. She raised her eyes to the bold April moon. That too served her purpose.

She leaned forward and ripped a resounding fart, startling Nikolai into turning his head and looking at her. She smiled unselfconsciously at him. He smiled back, amused now. Yes, my *njemets* Fast, I can see you trust me. Even if you don't know where we're going or why. But I know why. And that's enough.

Chaika was pleased with herself. Not only would she get her revenge at last, she'd also get some good booty for her boys. And test this exciting new recruit at the same time. From her spies in town she knew that the Bocks —all three of them — had gone to Selenaya for Easter. Trapped in their luxurious nest — father, mother, and daughter, the snooty bitch! Tonight, Miss Clara, you'll find out how the other half lives. You've always lived where there are no clouds and so no thunder, she quoted to herself. But tonight the clouds are moving in and you'll hear the thunder soon enough.

She listened with satisfaction to the clattering hoofs of the horses strung out behind her. She had brought twenty of her best boys. And the randiest. She stole another look at Nikolai and grinned again.

A few minutes later she pointed ahead and shouted: "There it is Kolya, behind the trees on the right." There was something almost manic in her voice.

Chaika's plan of attack was simple: ride full-tilt up the approach road, sweep through the main gate like a hurricane and surround the house before its occupants could get out. Barking dogs might give alarm, but if there were any guards or sentries neither they nor the dogs would last long.

The horde of riders was held up momentarily by the locked front gate. A well-placed shot and the gate swung free. Dogs were barking furiously in the darkness. Another shot rang out from the shadows of a building on one side of the courtyard and one of the raiders threw up his arms with a startled cry and slumped off his horse slowly, awkwardly.

"The sentry. In the barn! Take cover," yelled Chaika and wheeled her stallion into the shadows on the other side. "Vanya, Bro, Senya, go get him. Be careful, there may be more."

A short silence, followed by more shots as half a dozen men stormed the barn where the sentry was hiding. A second bandit sank to the ground. The rest were through the doors. Several muffled shots came from inside. Then silence.

Bro emerged. "We've got the Cossack son-of-a-whore, Chaika. There's no one else here."

"All right," she ordered, "now the house. But go easy. I want the old man, the old woman, and the girl out here. Don't worry about the servants. They'll keep out of the way." She turned to Nikolai. "I want you to stay with me, Kolya."

He nodded, waiting uneasily for what was to happen.

The full moon shed a preternatural light over the courtyard. As they waited, Chaika seemed preoccupied with the magnificent rondell at its center. The huge mound of dwarf ornamental shrubs, herbs and flowers formed darkly intricate geometrical patterns in the ivory light. Deeper glimmers of color came from the early flowers already in bloom — tulips, crown imperial, peonies. With nervous intentness she circled the miniature picket fence of the rondell, as though searching for something in its floral profusions.

Selenaya, Selenaya — the throb in her temples again. She kept pacing her horse slowly around the flower bed.

Then thudding noises and cries came from within the manor. Chaika stopped her pacing and faced the front door expectantly.

The big double door crashed open and the two elder Bocks were pushed out roughly, looking dishevelled and ghostlike in their white night clothes. Anger and defiance in his large face, August Bock loomed massive in long nightgown between his smaller captors. Like a stubborn old bull he looked around warily, unafraid, suffering himself to be prodded along, watchful every step of the way. There was a spreading smear on his brow, over one eye. His wife was brought up beside him, her long, graying hair unfurled; she looked outraged and terrified both.

The two were marched down the steps towards the rondell where Chaika was waiting in the saddle. She looked down at them, her face cruel.

"Well, here you are, Herr Bock. And Frau Bock too. My generous old employers." Her sarcasm was barely controlled.

Bock raised his bloodied face, studied her calmly. "If it's money you want, Marusya Nikoforovna," he rumbled, "you can have it. But I don't keep much here." He searched her face for signs of cupidity. Finding none, he made his offer anyway. "You can take me back to Alexandrovsk under escort. I'll give you a bank —"

"Shut your filthy, bourgeois yap, Big Face," Chaika hissed in cold fury. "I made a deal with you once for the brat I got from your son, the serpent. You gave me half of what I wanted and told me to shut up — or else. Now I'm telling *you*. We'll take what we want here. But first —" She looked around at her men. "Boys, I've got a little entertainment for you." She bowed in mock courtesy to the Bocks. "For you too — Sir, Madam."

As if on cue the front door opened again and a terrified Clara Bock was hustled down the steps her filmy nightgown only partially covered by a light open robe. Her feet were bare.

The death-pale girl, her mouth working in pathetic little whimpers, was roughly thrust in front of Chaika, whose wild eyes blazed to black hatred as she confronted the shivering figure.

"Welcome, Miss Clara, welcome. Now our little family circle is complete. Now we —"

"— For the love of God, Marusya Nikoforovna, can't we —" Bock got no farther. Chaika's sabre was out in a flash and poised at his throat.

"Enough Bock. I said no more deals. It's not you or your missus I want. I want the precious young lady here. First the playboy. Now the playgirl."

Mrs. Bock began to sob and moan — her eyes closed, she writhed helplessly between her captors. Clara looked at her mother in alarm, trembled violently, and appeared ready to faint.

Chaika, ignoring her victims' terror, casually swept her sabre towards the rondell, as though just discovering it. "Ah, yes, the Mamasha Bock's beautiful ornamental flower bed. I always had the urge to step over the little fence and pick some of the pretty flowers, but I never dared. Now I dare."

She nudged her horse and urged it over the foot-high fence. Slowly, deliberately, she walked her stallion around the mound, the hoofs crushing down greenery and flowers, sinking heavily into the deep, yielding loam. With easy grace she swung her sabre at the tulips and peonies still erect, expertly slicing off the heavy bulbs and blooms.

She made one complete round, then calmly emerged from the desecrated garden. Her face was now a terrible mask. They were all, even her men, staring at her in fascination.

Chaika turned to her victims again. "There, now we can begin." Without warning she bent down, her sabre leapt in her hand and slashed open

Clara's loose nightgown. The girl screamed in terror and struggled vainly to free her pinioned arms so as to cover her nakedness amidst the white tatters.

Old Bock started forward with an anguished roar but was again stopped by the point of Chaika's sabre. Mrs. Bock's tortured scream ended in a strangled groan as she sank to the ground in a dead faint.

Chaika's triumph was wolfish. "What, you don't like our entertainment? One more move like that, Big Face, and you'll never move again." She stared Bock down, then the sabre point flashed back to Clara, moaning and cowering.

"Now, Miss Clara" — the mocking sing-song servant's voice again — "shall we begin? After all, even refined ladies must learn to bear male burdens." Guffaws from the men. "You Mennonites have a saying: 'Love does not always land on the rose; sometimes it lands on the manure pile.' " Again there were loud snickers all around.

Keeping the sabre point at the whimpering girl's throat, Chaika forced her backwards towards the rondell. Still trying to cope with her nakedness, Clara stumbled against the low picket fence and fell sidelong into the ruined mound, where she lay on her side curled in a tight ball, sobbing piteously, her frail feet white against the black earth.

Chaika, breathing heavily, looked down at the helpless girl, hatred twisting her face. Then she waved her sabre high in the air and screamed, "Vanya, your virgin bride is waiting on her flowery bed. Take her!" The voice rose to an unearthly pitch. "Then Misha, Vasya, Senya — and a—a—a—ll of you. See how you like it with a real lady, you randy bastards." Raised to the moon her face was insane with rage and lust and her demented laughter shrilled over the courtyard.

"No, no, you filthy beasts —" Bock rushed forward, but was instantly felled by a rifle butt from behind. He crashed to earth like a mortally wounded animal.

Nikolai Fast sat there on his horse, watching in shocked revulsion. He had anticipated violence, even bloodshed, but not this. Not this cold-blooded barbarity, this sadistic act of vengeance. These were the Bocks of Schoen- wiese. There couldn't be any doubt. And that was Clara Bock lying there, Willie's Clara. But what could he do? He was helpless. A move on his part to rescue the girl — even trying to intercede — would be suicidal. Trying to reason with Chaika in her maniacal state was out of the question. There was nothing he could do but watch. There was no escape. He was here by his own choice. He was part of this —

Clara shrieked hysterically, lashed about in a frenzy as the first man fell on her, the others urging him on. By the time the second and third brutes had taken their turns she had gone as limp as a ragdoll and only her involuntary grunts and low moans told that she was still conscious and alive.

Mrs. Bock's crumpled form had not moved, nor had the massive shape of her husband. Suddenly, with a mighty bellow of despair, Bock staggered to his feet and lunged for the man covering his daughter. Before anyone could move he had his hands around the bandit's neck. With a ferocious wrench of his mighty arms and torso he heaved the man aside like a child, snapping his neck with a savage twist as he released him.

They were upon him then, clubbing and hacking at him until he sank with a sepulchral sigh to the ground, mutilated into a shapeless, dark-streaked mound that finally settled and lay still.

Nikolai, not daring to think, jumped from his horse and dropped down beside the violated girl. She seemed barely conscious. He put his arms under the slight form and lifted her to her feet, but she was too dazed to stand up. With a quick motion he swept her up again and carried her past the flailing arms and arcing sabres towards his horse.

"What do you think you're doing, *njemets?*" Chaika's voice slashed at him like a sabre. "Taking her for yourself?"

"It's enough, Chaika. If it's revenge you wanted, you got it. The girl is in shock. If there's any more, they'll kill her too."

"A German to the rescue of a German, eh my Fast?" She was measuring him, her hand on the *nagan* at her hip, knowing he had failed her test but wanting to spare him, waiting for him to save himself. For the girl she felt nothing now. A dead lust. To hell with her. But this big Fast had a nerve she —

"Chaika, the men came for the looting. Let them do it. It's pointless this — this personal business."

She flared again, her madness tensed to spring. "It's my personal business. You keep the hell out of it."

Not daring to say more he could only stare back at her, the girl inert in his arms.

Chaika had made her decision. Her mockery was forgiving but carried a sting. "All right, Kolya, save your little virgin. If that's what you want. To these bastards she's just another hole anyway. But don't try this again. Next time you may end up at the bottom."

She jerked her horse around and gave rapid orders to her men. The men spread out, intent on booty now.

Nikolai gently set Clara down with her back to the little picket fence. She seemed oblivious to what was going on around her. She looked at Nikolai without expression, vacantly, dazed with pain like a child that had just been punished. Her eyes flickered over the motionless figures nearby, but without interest or recognition. Nor did she make any effort now to cover her body, so Nikolai took off his jacket and draped it around her shoulders and breast.

Chaika and most of the men had disappeared into the house. Nikolai went over to examine Mrs. Bock. She was dead. Heart attack or stroke, he guessed. He did not bother to examine Bock.

He didn't know what to do with the girl. He couldn't take her back to town with him. He'd have to leave her here with the servants. Tell them to take her to a doctor. She did need a doctor, he could see that. Her parents needed nothing but burial.

He picked up the shivering, passive girl and started across the courtyard to some smaller buildings which looked as if they might be servants' quarters. No one bothered him. Chaika and her boys were inside the big mansion carrying out a systematic search for valuables, the carnage outside already forgotten.

Nikolai, having delivered Clara Bock into the care of a tearful female domestic, decided on his next step. He would go back to town with the gang and then clear out fast. And he would contact no one. If this Clara Bock was still Willie's girl he'd find out about her soon enough, poor devil. He felt a twinge of pity for his brother and wondered what this tragedy would do to him.

He watched several of the men — his friend Bro among them — come staggering through the big front doors, arms and pockets greedily filled with loot. No, he vowed again, I'm not staying with this female hyena and her filthy pack. I'm a revolutionary but not a ravening fiend like this bunch.

Makhno. Makhno was the one to follow. If not Makhno, then no one. Yes, it had to be Makhno.

4
Halbstadt-Molochansk, April 19, 1918

At last! This time it was true. The German liberators were actually in the Molochnaya.

Wilhelm Fast had just joined the large, excited crowd on the station platform on this Friday afternoon. But he kept to himself, did not rejoice openly with the others. Since hearing the tragic news about Clara Bock and her family he had not been himself. It had taken him a long time to get over his own cruel ordeal in Halbstadt in February. And then came the terrible news from Selenaya. His shock and grief over what had happened to the Bocks had settled into a deep depression that was affecting even his relationship with Katya. Especially their marriage plans. They had long talks that settled nothing. He was caught in a painful, delicate dilemma. He was desperately afraid of hurting Katya by revealing to her how deeply stricken he was by Clara's terrible fate. But much as he loved Katya, he simply couldn't face the idea of getting married right now. He had no right to seek his own pleasure and happiness when someone who had once been so close to him had been tortured beyond belief and robbed not only of her parents but of her very sanity, if the reports were true.

He had begged Katya to be patient with him, that there were a few things he must resolve within himself before they could make their final plans. She said she understood, but did she? They had been planning to get married around the middle of June, just before the harvest. But would they? All he knew was that he would have to make a decision soon. Too soon.

He had come to town today when he heard the Germans were coming at last. This was, after all, an event of much greater importance than his personal problems. The coming of the German army was a rescue mission that would bring relief and security to so many people who might otherwise suffer the same fate as the Bocks.

The townspeople assembled at the station buzzed with happy anticipation as the time for the arrival of the occupation train drew near. Two German officers had arrived in an auto just after dinner to report that the train had reached Lichtenau ten miles south and would be arriving in Molochansk within the hour.

The station platform had been carefully decorated for the long-awaited event. Sprigs of greenery graced the door and windows of the small station house and displayed prominently was a fancily lettered welcome in German. Someone had even dug up a German flag and run it up the flagstaff. Against the wall, in the shade, stood several tables covered with food carefully protected from flies by snowy white napkins and pillow cases. Teen-aged girls, dressed in their Sunday finery, their blonde hair immaculately braided, hovered around the tables ready to offer the German military liberators a welcoming *faspa*.

Like other peaceable inhabitants of the southern steppes, the Mennonites of the Molochnaya, harassed and oppressed for months by roving bands of peasant anarchists and ruthless, self-appointed "commissars" of the Red Guards, saw the arrival of German troops as an answer to fervent prayer. The new Bolshevik government, its army shrinking and in disarray, forced to cope with opposition and insurrection everywhere, had been forced in early March to accept the humiliating conditions of the Treaty of Brest-Litovsk. Even though the Bolshevik army had managed to snuff out Petlura's newly proclaimed Republic of the Ukraine by occupying its capital Kiev, Lenin and Trotsky were forced to accept peace conditions which deprived them of the rich Ukraine as well as the Baltic states. Most Ukrainians rejoiced to see the Bolsheviks humiliated, welcomed the Treaty, and accepted the coming of the Germans as much the lesser of two evils.

In the hard-pressed settlements of the Molochnaya, Schoenfeld-Brazol, and the Old Colony, the people were hopeful that more or less normal conditions would now prevail. Looting and the "requisitioning" of property and money had been heavy and many Mennonite farmers and estate-owners were determined to get back at any cost what had been taken from them. Wilhelm's blood ran cold when he listened to Snapper and other young Mennonites describing what they would do to local partisans and Bolshevik supporters once the Germans arrived. This eye-for-an-eye attitude, so completely contrary to Mennonite teachings, did not bode well for the future. Who could be sure that the German army would stay in the Ukraine for the next fifteen years, as called for in the Treaty? What if Germany lost the war? What then? In any case, the Russian peasant had a very long memory.

The troop train, after several unexpected delays, arrived just after 4:30 p.m. It came sliding into the station so slowly it's movement was almost imperceptible. A hush descended on the waiting people. Most of them had never seen the countrymen from whom they had been for so long severed. Real Germans! Come to save them from oppression and violence. By the time the train inched to a stop many in the crowd were misty-eyed, deeply moved by the solemnity of the moment.

It was a long, fully equipped troop train which contained, in addition to troop carriages in front, a number of flat cars loaded with heavy artillery and wagons, and box cars full of horses and small arms.

The train came to a stop, but nothing happened. Its doors remained closed and the only sound was the stuttering hiss of the locomotive. Then all the doors seemed to open at once and smartly uniformed officers emerged from the cars shouting crisp orders. Lines of soldiers flowed out of the forward cars and lined up in precise formations. The colonel in charge of the troop train, spruce in soft peaked cap, short jacket with fur collar, breeches, and gleaming brown leggings, stepped forward and saluted the Mennonite officials waiting to greet him. At the same time the mixed choir drawn up behind broke into a spirited rendition of "*Deutschland, Deutschland über alles.*"

The deposed mayor of Halbstadt-Molochansk, happily reassuming office, spoke warm words of welcome in which he expressed the gratitude of all the "German-speaking colonists" in the area to the "long-awaited German liberators," who had saved them in the nick of time from a dreadful fate at the "hands of the Red Guard and other terrorists." The German colonel, his lean hawk face missing nothing, answered in kind and promised that his troops would do everything in their power to bring strict order to the tyrannized countryside and to ensure that the civilian population would be protected from further oppression. He then issued orders for the unloading of the train.

Wilhelm listened to the singing and to the mayor's indiscreet remarks with embarrassment. Glancing around the station he could see only here and there a Russian among the Mennonite faces, but he knew the news of this enthusiastic reception of foreign troops on Russian soil would race through the surrounding Russian villages like wildfire. The peasants in the area would neither forget nor forgive this openly declared collaboration between German-Russian citizens and troops which had only recently stopped killing Russians. What would happen if the German occupation troops were suddenly forced to withdraw? The consequences were too horrible to think about.

The platform beside the train was soon stacked with neat rows of supplies. As each section of troops completed its unloading, the officer in charge declared a rest period and the men gravitated towards the refreshment tables. They were surprised and delighted to find themselves addressed in unfamiliarly accented but fluent German. They received thick slices of ham and delicately crusted buns, then stood around talking to each other or to the Halbstadt men.

"*Donnerwetter,* Hans," Wilhelm heard a soldier say to his buddy, "these Russians speak better German than we do. What goes on here?"

"They're German colonists," his more knowledgeable comrade said. "Apparently they've lived here for generations, but kept their German language and ways. Remarkable."

The trim young German soldiers in their field gray uniforms and flared pot helmets immediately confirmed the romantic notions most Russian Mennonites had about "real" Germans from Germany. The Mennonite girls, demure but stealthily observant, blushed with pleasure and importance as they shyly offered the uniformed men plates of ham and *tweeback* and accepted their politely murmured thanks and compliments.

"*Menschenskind,*" a corn-blond six-footer drawled as he squatted in the shade with his friends, "these rosy-cheeked *englein* could be straight from Saxony."

"Yeah, but do you see the way their mothers are glaring at us?" another laughed as he chewed. "It may be harder to get near these Saxon angels than to the angels of heaven."

Wilhelm saw that the German colonel was now conferring earnestly with the Halbstadt mayor and several other Mennonite officials. The mayor seemed to be objecting to something and pleading with the German officer, who shook his head curtly and seemed to be unmoved. Then he said something that made the mayor mop his brow in silence, as though conceding defeat.

The colonel made a signal with his hand to a soldier standing beside one of the rear passenger cars. Almost immediately the door of the car opened and three captured Russian partisans, hands bound behind their backs, were led down the platform toward the station. As they passed, Wilhelm recognized all three prisoners as assistants to Pishklov and Maslenikov, the two ruthless commissars who had fled Halbstadt after brutalizing the community for months.

The three kept their heads down, their faces impassive. Only one, a short, bow-legged hunchback called Taubele, Wilhelm seemed to recall, showed emotion as he kept shaking his head from side to side as though in disbelief at his predicament.

The people gathered on the station platform fell into a puzzled silence as the Russian prisoners were lined up at the far end of the platform beyond the station house, away from the crowd. Only when the three were being blindfolded did the watching Mennonites become aware of what was about to take place. There were murmurs of shocked dismay and parents pushed their children behind them, out of sight, to spare them the horror of seeing the obscene ritual unfolding before them. Wilhelm glanced at the slim, erect figure of the colonel waiting to give the order. He looked as cold and immobile as a statue.

The three men in the firing squad took their positions in front of the doomed prisoners. Sounds of wordless babbling came from the little hunchback but otherwise he and the other two beside him stood as rigidly as though tied to posts.

At the colonel's bark the rifles cracked in unison followed by shrill screams from the onlookers as the three partisans collapsed violently backwards, exploded off their feet. Two of them disappeared over the edge of the platform, the third, the hunchback, landed half on half off the platform and lay there twitching grotesquely.

The crowd surged back, trying to escape the scene they had just witnessed. Children and women were sobbing, some close to hysteria. The men looked dazed and bewildered, unable to believe that their festive mood had been so suddenly shattered by violent death.

The colonel stepped forward and calmly commanded the retreating Mennonites to attention. Without emotion, he told them in a few brisk sentences that the executions were designed as an "object lesson" for the Russian populace and partisans still at large. His friendly German-speaking cousins, however, had nothing to fear and were not to regard this act of military justice as in any way intimidating to them. He thanked them again for their hospitality and promised that he and his men would do everything in their power to round up the rabble that had plundered and harassed them for so long. Then he dismissed them.

The Halbstadters dispersed subdued and frightened to their homes. Most were offended and angered by the bloody display of German efficiency and justice they had been forced to witness. But not all. Once away from the grim scene, some recovered their composure quickly and commended the firm action of the liberators as just the kind of medicine the lawless elements overrunning the country-side needed. Now was the time to get back all the goods and valuables that had been stolen from the Mennonite villages.

Wilhelm rode home to Blumenau filled with disgust and outrage. Were these the superior, civilized Germans romanticized in Mennonite school books? No, these were real Germans, as hard and ruthless as the Russian oppressors were. And they seemed to assume that the "German" settlers would approve of everything they did. Even these clumsily inappropriate executions that would now be indelibly associated in the minds of local peasants with the already hated Germans of Halbstadt and Prischib.

Well, one had to be fair, he supposed. The German troops would at least uphold the law and keep the commissars and bandits away. There would be no more such gruesome incidents as had occured at Selenaya, thank God. But for Clara and her parents the Germans had come too late. Why couldn't they have come a month earlier . . . ? Had it really been God's will to let it happen that way? Lovely, radiant Clara Bock, broken now in body and mind — perhaps permanently — while he was free and healthy and in love with —

And at that moment he made his decision. He would not postpone the marriage after all. He and Katya loved each other and wanted to make a life together, even in these insane times. He could do nothing for Clara now except grieve for her. He had no right to drag Katya into that grief. It was selfish of him.

If only the sound of that firing squad would stop reverberating in his head.

CHAPTER TWENTY-TWO

1
Voronaya, April-May, 1918

The arrival of the Central Powers' army of occupation in the colonies was nowhere welcomed with more joy and relief than at Voronaya. For the Loewens things had gone from bad to much worse since their fruitless attempt the previous autumn to persuade Makhno to give them the money for their 1917 crop. They were short of seed grain for the spring and did not have enough cash to buy more and also take care of other routine expenses that could not be avoided if they were to operate the *khutor* as before. When Jacob Loewen warned that by spring they might lose Voronaya altogether, his headstrong son refused to listen to such gloomy talk and vowed to defend the *khutor* with his life.

He never got the chance. One day early in the new year when Snapper returned from Schoenfeld where he had spent the day trying to barter for some much-needed seed grain, he heard from his dejected father that Makhno had come to announce what Jacob had dreaded for months: Voronaya was being expropriated for a peasant commune. The Loewens, at least for the time being, were allowed to keep their buildings and one-tenth of their arable land, or less than a hundred acres. They were also allowed to keep eight horses, three cows, and a reasonable number of pigs and sheep. Makhno had told his old boss that he was treating him generously "for old times sake."

Snapper went into such a paroxysm of rage that his parents begged him to control himself for their sake. They would need his support more than ever in this crisis. If this was the will of the merciful Lord then it was a sin to complain so bitterly. Mutti Loewen pointed out that much of her furniture and household possessions were already gone, but that she would try to make the best of things as they all would have to do. She tried to comfort Snapper: "God will smile on us again, as he has in the past, my son, you wait and see." Snapper finally calmed down but he remained sullen and brooding for weeks and made dark plans of his own.

To add insult to injury the Loewens were forced to give up most of their carefully hoarded little stock of seed grain. But then, as Jacob wryly pointed out to his unhappy son, their need for seed grain had been as dramatically reduced as their acreage. Snapper stalked about the badly depleted *khutor* making the necessary preparations for seeding. But the deep surge of excitement and satisfaction he had always felt in spring was not there this year. His mood this seeding time matched the appearance of Voronaya itself, which already had an air of shabbiness and deprivation about it. And he was powerless to change anything. In his frustration and anger he pounded his fist raw against the rough boards of the back cow shed.

And then, in mid-April, they had been saved by a miracle after all. The

German occupation would rectify all the injustices, restore Voronaya to its former state, save the whole countryside from tragic ruin and waste. At the end of April the semi-socialistic Ukainian *rada* government was ousted, with German backing, by Hetman Paul Skoropadsky and his Democratic Peasant Party. Hetman Skoropadsky's puppet government immediately issued orders that all the property and land confiscated by local Soviets and commissars were to be restored to their rightful owners.

Snapper's jubilation, however, soon gave way to impatience and new frustration over delays in restitution. Reclaiming all the confiscated land was impossible. The German commander-in-chief had issued an order that whoever seeded the land could also harvest the crop. The Loewens could only get back the land that had been seeded with their own seed grain and even then they had to share the crop with the peasants who had done the seeding.

Getting back all the portable property, from farm machinery to household goods, also turned out to be next to impossible. In the Molochnaya, which was occupied by efficient, well-disciplined Prussian troops, the restitution proceeded in an orderly manner for the most part. Fearing swift and stern reprisals, many peasants returned property voluntarily. The Schoenfeld-Brazol area, by contrast, was only skimpily occupied by rather lackadaisical Austro-Hungarian troops. As a result, conditions there remained chaotic, with armed bandits thumbing their noses at the easy-going Austrians and the peasants stubbornly refusing to part with their newly acquired possessions; or else hiding them so cleverly that they could not be found by search parties.

Snapper Loewen sprang into action. In the early days of May he organized, with the tacit approval of the Austrian district commandant, a well-armed mounted troop made up mainly of other haughty and vindictive sons of local Mennonite and German landowners. To give it legal force the posse was usually accompanied by a few soldiers or local police militia. Snapper's troop now made almost daily forays into Russian villages to reclaim confiscated property, using force where necessary. When threats fell on deaf peasant ears and property could not be readily located, the young men resorted occasionally to public floggings, which usually produced results. There were rumors of several cold-blooded executions, but Snapper and his men vehemently denied that they had killed anyone.

Snapper kept hoping that in one of their raids they would have the luck of capturing Makhno, who in late April had been reported as still in the area with his band. Then the trail grew cold. For weeks no one admitted having seen him. Makhno seemed to have vanished, much to Snapper's chagrin. Finally, under considerable pressure, two young peasants who were suspected of having been with Makhno divulged that he was slowly retreating eastwards with a sizable "army" of partisans and fighting a stubborn rearguard action against the German and Ukrainian troops. He had fallen back to Tagenrog, they said, then Rostov-on-the-Don, and was now thought to be in or near the Volga city of Tsaritsyn. That was all they knew.

Snapper, eying the Russian youths disdainfully, scoffed at the report. "Fighting? That cowardly pipsqueak? With a peasant *army,* you say? Don't make me laugh. He's probably holed up in Dibrovka Forest north of here with a few buddies and their whores, quaking every time he hears a leaf fall. That's where you guys have come from, eh? To spy for him here! Well, you slink right back there and tell the little weasel we're waiting for him. Sooner or later he'll have to come out of his hole, and then we'll get him."

Foiled in their attempts to capture and mete out justice to Makhno and his terrorists, the military authorities occupied Gulai Polye and, among other acts of retributive justice, burned down the Makhno *khata.* They also captured Emilian, Makhno's brother who had been disabled in the war, and shot him as a partisan.

2

The two young peasants had, in fact, told the truth about Makhno's general whereabouts, although they had for their own partisan reasons given a grossly inflated account of his military activities. Makhno had retreated eastward with his band and joined up with Red forces led by Yegorov. Tagenrog turned out to be a nest of intrigue filled with Red Army detachments, deserters, civilian refugees, and elements of the Cheka, who were busy arresting Anarchists and other non-Reds. Makhno sensed at once that this was not a healthy place for him to remain in. But at least he was out of the Ukraine now and safe from the even more dangerous German army of occupation.

So, having agreed with his advisors that they would suspend further activities until the harvest season in late June and early July, the partisan leader decided to fill in the time by going on an extended tour of Russian cities to see for himself how the revolution was going while the Ukraine was occupied by foreign troops. Who knew, he might learn something useful; in any case it would be safer than remaining in the south.

He decided to make his way to Moscow in a roundabout way. From Tagenrog he went east to Rostov and then even farther east to Astrakhan on the Caspian Sea. From there he headed northwest to Tsaritsyn and Saratov on the Volga, and finally to Moscow via a brief stopover in Tambov. Wherever he went he tried to see firsthand just what the Bolsheviks were up to, and to determine whether he could expect help or hindrance from them in his own planned revolution in the south. What disappointed him everywhere he went was the disorganized state of the Anarchist movement. Not only did he find weak organizations lacking adequate funds, but no real will to do anything. The Bolsheviks, on the other hand, were everywhere engaged in frenetic activities, but they didn't seem to amount to very much.

By the time Makhno got to Moscow in early June he was more than a little disillusioned. The Bolsheviks were in power, but seemed to be conducting nothing but a "paper revolution," a vast printing enterprise which churned out reams and reams of empty slogans and meaningless resolutions. He stood in Red Square and listened to the endless flow of rhetoric. They talk and wave their arms wildly and scream, each louder than the last, and do nothing, he decided contemptuously and turned away.

But perhaps this was just the outside face of the revolution, he thought with peasant shrewdness. Now that he was here he would at least try to see some of the leaders and get their views. Perhaps they would be able to give him a better picture, inspire him, give him some reassurance that they knew what they were doing.

He had come to Moscow to see the revolution. Where was it?

3
Moscow, June, 1918

In a few minutes I'll be meeting Lenin himself, he thought proudly as he sat waiting. His hand moved nervously to the unfamiliar cravat at his throat. His pride was mixed with apprehension. What could he, a simple peasant from Gulai Polye, say to the great Lenin? Would he find the right words to tell Lenin what he thought and felt about the revolution, what he had dreamt of doing in the Ukraine?

His meeting with Lenin had come about unexpectedly, a lucky accident. Yesterday when he came here to the Kremlin to get a billeting card he was confronted with such a maze of corridors and offices he got hopelessly lost. The signs he was able to decipher, the directions he got, only added to his confusion. He could feel his old prison panic tightening in his chest. Then he blundered into the office of no less a man than Sverdlov, the secretary of the Bolshevik Party's Central Committee. This important man received him cordially when he learned that the lost visitor was a revolutionary leader from the unsubdued south. Sverdlov promptly arranged to have him meet Lenin the following morning.

Now he was actually shaking hands with Lenin in his office. Sverdlov had just made the introductions. Like a benign uncle Lenin patted his shoulder, took him by the arm, and guided him to a chair near his own.

Lenin seemed eager to ask questions. "Tell me, my young friend," he began, "what do your Ukrainian peasants make of our slogan 'All power to the local Soviets?' "

"They believe it just the way it sounds, that they now have complete control of their own affairs." He watched Lenin closely, not at all sure how his answer would be taken.

"So," Lenin continued smoothly, shifting slightly in his chair, studying him with his slit, gray-green lynx eyes, "then your peasants have been infected with Anarchism?"

He felt suddenly exposed. Was it a trap? He hadn't forgotten the Cheka giving Anarchists a hard time in Tagenrog. He would be cunning too. "Do you think that's bad, Comrade Lenin?" he countered.

The lynx eyes narrowed slightly. "I did not say that." The domed brow glistened, the tapered russet beard thrust forward like a weapon. "In fact, it may be for the good if it speeds up the victory of Communism."

So it was a trap. He moved his hands and glanced over at Sverdlov, who was all polite attention.

Lenin shrewdly pressed his advantage. "Unfortunately, past experience teaches us that peasant enthusiasm puffs up like smoke from a chimney, and disappears as quickly. No, no, my friend, unless they're properly organized and led the peasants amount to a pile of turds as a political force. They'd be blown away like leaves by a counter-revolution."

Lenin was moving too fast for him. Was he hinting a threat just now? "But Vladimir Ilyich," he objected awkwardly, "I — I — a leader can't permit himself to — to—" he couldn't find the words he wanted —" to lose hope, to expect defeat before it even hap—"

"— That's all very well" — there was a touch of impatience in the great man's voice — "but the worst sin for a leader is to live in a fool's paradise, to ignore reality, to dream about victory instead of acting to bring it about."

He felt himself falling under the spell of those penetrating eyes, and the smooth, confident voice that could spin words like golden threads. How could he argue with this man who saw everything, knew everything, understood everything.

"The Anarchists," the suave voice lectured, "starting with Proudhon and Bakunin, have always been more dreamers than doers. Oh, they have plenty of zeal and are even ready for self-sacrifice, but" — he felt the words shuddering into his brain like bullets now — "but they remind me of fat, silly priests with their eyes raised to heaven waiting for faith to move mountains while they stub their toes on the stones in their path. In other words, they neglect the present for the far-distant future, a fatal mistake if you really want to change society."

He tried to protest again, but couldn't seem to find a firm hand-hold for his argument. "But, but the Anarchists are thorough revolutionaries too, just as thorough as the Bolsheviks."

Lenin cocked his bald head delicately, screwed up his eyes, then regarded him with amused detachment. "Nestor Ivanovich," he replied, the wary eyes retreating a little, "we know the Anarchists as well as you" — he turned to Sverdlov for confirmation — "you can't wait for paradise to create itself. Thistles grow in the same soil as roses."

He would have given anything for words that would convince Lenin that Anarchists *did* concern themselves with day-to-day realities, that they knew how to act, that in fact in the south it was the Anarchists and not the Bolsheviks who had pressed the revolutionary struggle against Petlura and his Kiev *rada*. It was the Anarchists who did the fighting, he wanted to shout, not your cursed, paper-shitting Bolshies.

But he knew it was no use. He couldn't say these things properly, and even if he could Lenin would have counter-arguments ready like a loaded gun. Damn it, damn it, *damn it,* he seethed inwardly, here I have the opportunity of my life and I can't take advantage of it. If only my old friend Arshinov was here. He'd know how to argue with the great Vladimir Ilyich.

Lenin was smiling at him again, knowing he had won. "But you mustn't take my remarks personally, Comrade Makhno. I can tell that you yourself are a good man, a born leader. If more of our Russian Anarchists were like you, we Bolsheviks would be quite prepared to go along with such ideas as free organization of production and, er, other things as well."

He was gratified by the personal praise, but also understood that it indicated the interview was over and that Lenin did not want him to leave on a sour note.

As they rose and shook hands Lenin asked him if he would like help for his journey home and he accepted gratefully. Lenin turned to Sverdlov. "Phone Karpenko and ask him to provide passport and identity for our friend." He patted Makhno's arm lightly, the tilted eyes beaming affably now. "So, you see, Nestor Ivanovich, I'm not so ill-disposed towards Anarchists after all."

And with that he was ushered out of Lenin's office, confused between gratitude and resentment, like a schoolboy who has just been given a kindly talking to by a concerned teacher.

Now he knew where the Bolshevik revolution was. It was in the mind and will of the remarkable man he had just talked to. But not my revolution, he thought defiantly. That's locked up inside my gut, waiting to explode. And when it does even the great Lenin will sit up and take notice.

4
Voronaya, June, 1918

The wedding of Katya Loewen and Wilhelm Fast took place on a warm, clear Saturday afternoon in mid-June. Considering the straitened times it was a large wedding, with around 150 guests in attendance. Before the war there would have been easily twice as many. In those halcyon days guests coming from a distance would have begun arriving several days before the nuptials and the last of them would not have left until a week later. Now they were expected to arrive on Friday, in time for the *polterabend,* the bridal shower, that evening and to leave again on Sunday.

Even on a reduced scale, the preparations for the wedding had been a complex exercise in logistics run off with military precision by Mutti Loewen, who was everywhere at once. Her major concerns were to provide sufficient food and adequate sleeping arrangements for the guests. Again, in normal times the requirements would have caused no special problems, the *khutor* being virtually self-sufficient in everything. Now there were problems. Snapper had managed to recover much of the property confiscated by Makhno's men, but he had not been able to track down all the missing machinery, wagons, and household furniture. Beds especially were in short supply at Voronaya and had to be borrowed wherever possible. Food was also a problem. Traditionally a calf or heifer furnished the main meat for a large wedding, but the Loewen livestock was too severely depleted to permit such a sacrifice. Father Loewen suggested they butcher a sheep or young pig instead.

Mother Loewen indignantly rejected her husband's offer. "We will not disgrace ourselves by skimping on food and making do with substitutes, Jacob, not even in these bad times. We have only the one daughter, and she will be properly married if I have any say in the matter." For once her guileless eyes glinted obstinately. "I'm sure you can get the beef we need somewhere."

Jacob Loewen sighed, shrugged his shoulders, and promised his determined wife he would get her a heifer even if he had to steal one of his own back from a peasant. Mutti Loewen patted his arm and told him not to joke about serious matters.

As for the bridal couple, they would have been quite content with a smaller, less elaborate affair. But Katya got nowhere with her mother on this point and gave up trying. In any case, the bride was by custom not very directly involved in the wedding preparations. As tradition required, Katya and Wilhelm spent the two weeks preceding the wedding, the period of their official engagement, in an almost constant round of visits to relatives and friends all over the countryside. Father Loewen had placed at their disposal his best team of horses and his one remaining droshky, somewhat the worse for the wear it had received in Gulai Polye recently. After a week of visiting in the Schoenfeld-Brazol district, they took the train to the Molochnaya and spent another week visiting in and around Blumenau in a rig provided by Wilhelm's father.

The constant visiting became a little wearing and tedious after awhile, but it did afford the young couple brief periods of privacy in the droshky as they drove from place to place.

Katya still had twinges of guilt over the wedding. She asked Wilhelm for reassurance almost daily. She did not want him to feel that he was being pressured into something he was not ready for under the circumstances. Even before the engagement had been made public she had, with her usual candor, declared her willingness to let him decide their future. "Willie, my darling," she said, "my heart aches for Clara Bock and for your sorrow. I would consider you callous if you didn't feel the way you do. If you want to postpone our engagement and wedding I'll understand."

Torn by conflicting emotions Wilhelm had told her he wanted a little more time to sort things out. He would go home to Blumenau for awhile until he had come to terms with himself. She wanted only what would make him happy, she assured him. And she was perfectly sincere, though privately she could admit to herself that she did not want to begin her marriage in the shadow cast by the suffering, no matter how terrible, of another woman.

She had taken the wise course. Wilhelm came back from Blumenau in late April and told her that he loved her more than ever and wanted to marry her as soon as possible. "What has happened to Clara cannot be atoned for by us. I want you, *liebchen,* and need you. We've waited long enough."

The wedding ceremony and reception were held, as was customary, in the granary, the building that afforded the largest open space to seat guests. Snapper had emptied out and cleaned the spacious main granary on the estate. As he noted, it was not a big job; Makhno's men had already done most of the work. The day before the wedding a laughing, chattering bevy of girls and young matrons gathered at Voronaya to decorate the hall. Wagonloads of greenery and flowers were trundled over from the back garden and soon intricately woven garlands festooned the canvas-covered walls. With the help of several friends Snapper collected an ample supply of benches and chairs from neighboring farms and estates. These were set up in the granary in church-pew fashion.

Inside the manor, the kitchen and dining room had been converted into a busy catering service. The mounds of freshly baked *tweeback* and *eenback* grew more heaping by the hour. Not all were baked in the Loewen kitchen, but came from the kitchens of nearby *khutors* to which crocks of dough had been consigned. A heifer, acquired at a quite outrageous price by Father Loewen, had been butchered and the meat roasted or boiled to be eaten cold at the reception. Some of the boiled beef went into the rich *borscht* cooked in large kettles very early on the day of the wedding. Also made in generous quantities was *plumemoos,* the thick sweet compote made from dried fruits and eaten cold with the main course.

The *polterabend* Friday evening was a gay affair attended by all the younger wedding guests and many of the older ones. Snapper was in his element as master of ceremonies for the program of songs and humorous recitations. He had even written a brief skit and rehearsed it with several friends. It was full of outrageous puns and unsubtle, mildly suggestive jokes that elicited more groans than blushes from the bridal couple. Snapper presented himself in a completely fictitious role as cunning matchmaker between his sister and his best friend. Having successfully completed his work, he concluded with a broad smirk, he could now sit back and await the results.

The rest of the evening was devoted to the bride's acknowledgment of the wedding gifts stacked up on a long trestle table. This happy ritual was frequently punctuated by quips and sallies from the audience. The bride held each gift aloft like a trophy. The groom tried, unsuccessfully, not to look self-consciously superfluous and bored.

The wedding ceremony next day began at two. The bridal couple walked in together, Katya demurely beautiful in a floor-length white gown and off-the-face veil and train flowing down from a bright wreath of tiny blossoms perched on her crown, Wilhelm resplendent in an immaculately tailored morning coat and striped trousers. What the guests did not know was that these splendid wedding costumes were the altered and refurbished garments worn by Katya's parents at their wedding in the last century.

It was a lengthy but comfortable ceremony with a feeling of long tradition and social *gemuetlichkeit*. The bridal pair sat facing the minister in chairs gaily decorated with garlands and sprigs of green. Immediately behind them sat their unmarried friends of both sexes. They too had walked down the aisle in couples.

After the assembled guests had sung the traditional wedding song "Wilt thou take this man to thee, Oh bride in festive gown," Elder Funk rose to perform the exchange of vows, the only part of the ceremony for which the bridal couple as well as the audience stood up. The rotund elder then preached an earnest sermon based on Romans 12:12: "Let hope keep you joyful; in trouble stand firm; persist in prayer."

Outwardly composed and attentive, Wilhelm had difficulty concentrating on the elder's well-worn phrases. He was too conscious of the moment itself, of the sheer awesomeness of the step he was taking with the radiant young woman beside him. An irreversible step, that's what made it almost frightening to sit here being formally united for the rest of his life with this fascinating female. For the rest of their lives! And to start now when everything was so uncertain, so gloomily foreboding. But at least they both had teaching positions. And they would be together. At home in Blumenau, in the old summer room he and Kolya had once shared. He could not begin to imagine what it would be like to have this strange new bed partner. If only he didn't have to face the tedium of village teaching again. But he and Katya had their dream. As soon as conditions allowed, they would start their own special school in Halbstadt where he would teach art and Katya music, elocution, and the like. It was an exciting prospect. They would start saving for it right away. And wait for their world to grow sane again . . . .

After the wedding supper the festivities concluded with an informal social evening of singing, dancing, and folk games. This was where the single men and girls came into their own. For them this was by far the most exciting part of the wedding, one of the rare social occasions where flirtations could be carried on in the open and seemed, indeed, to be subtly encouraged by the very nature of the activities and rituals prescribed for it. It was in reality a discreetly disguised, carefully controlled courtship ritual, a decorous mating dance, and most of the young people innocently felt it as that.

The highlight of the evening came when Katya was led forward for the ritual unveiling. Her veil and wreath were removed by one of her young matron friends while the guests exhorted her in song to

> Give up your wreath, you need it not,
> You have achieved a worthier lot;
> You've chosen now the married state,
> God grant you then a happy fate.

The friend then pinned a small black *haube* to the back of Katya's head as a symbol of her new married state.

The bride and groom were now expected to choose their symbolic successors. For this the young people formed a double ring around the bridal couple, the girls on the inside. With her eyes bound, Katya was handed a plate which held her folded veil and wreath. Wilhelm then spun her around several times. With a giddy little laugh Katya, guided by Wilhelm, groped her way to the circle of girls and handed her plate to the girl she had selected in advance. Wilhelm then went through the same blindfolded pretense by handing his large, beribboned boutonniere to the young man Katya helped him find.

With that the bride and groom were at last free to withdraw, leaving the new symbolic bride and groom to act as hosts for the rest of the evening. The party would continue for several more hours.

They were upstairs in Katya's room at last. Hand in hand they sat down beside each other on Katya's bed. Their longed-for privacy, now that they had it, rendered them suddenly shy with each other. Still in their formal wedding clothes, both felt a little bedraggled after the long afternoon and evening festivities in the granary. Wordlessly they searched each other's eyes for reassurance, for reaffirmation of their love for each other in their innocence and inexperience.

Katya, her lovely face a little flushed above her high, tight collar, broke the silence then. "Well, my darling, I feel blissfully happy — and frightened at the same time. Can you accept that, Willie?" She leaned forward and brushed his cheek with her lips.

Wilhelm cradled her face in his hands and they kissed, deeply. "I'm nervous too, my love." He gazed into the trusting depths of her dark eyes between his cupped hands. "But, Katya, I will cherish this moment all my life. I know you are the greatest gift I'll ever receive, and I thank God for you."

He removed his morning coat and cravat, then helped her fumblingly but tenderly with the difficult parts of her gown. And as Katya undressed swiftly, coyly, he caught glimpses of her white mystery, of fragile, unknown female vistas that dazzled him so he forgot to breathe as she shrugged into her nightgown and slid between the covers.

In bed they turned to each other shyly, bumpingly awkward in their primal search for the strange other. And then suddenly all was smooth and warm and natural as their bodies dissolved and flowed into one. From deep within that dark bliss Katya whispered against his lips. "Willie, my darling, I know you'll be gentle, always, and treat my body with respect, but I want you never to stop showing passion — openly and honestly — even when I'm a broad-beamed matron with gray hair and have finished bearing your children."

To think of his adorable bride as an old, broad-beamed matron struck Wilhelm as ludicrous enough to make him snicker in the dark and snuggle even closer. "Katya, Katya, I love you body and soul, now and forever, and will never neglect you or take you for granted if we live to be a hundred."

He came to himself with the gasps of her pain in his ears, knowing himself to be lord and monster both. This miracle was happening now, this very moment, and it was more than he could believe. He clasped the glowing, mysterious female creature who was now truly his wife even more tightly and sighed with happiness. In the moist, intimate darkness she smiled against his rough male cheek and fiery mustache and exulted through her pain: Now he is mine, my man, and will be for the rest of our days till death do us part.

5
Bethania Mental Hospital, Old Colony, June, 1918

She likes to sit outside in the shade and watch the other patients work. Miss Koop is forever asking her if she wouldn't like to work in the garden too, to get some exercise. But she always gives the same answer. No, she says, I don't think so. I feel a bit tired today. Perhaps tomorrow. She doesn't like Miss Koop much anyway with her sour face and sharp voice. Just because she's the head nurse . . . Dr. Thiessen is different. He's a very nice man, and so handsome with his blond hair and dashing, upturned mustache. he reminds her of someone, but whenever she tries to remember who she gets the fuzzy feeling in her head again.

Some days she feels much better, but other days she just feels like sleeping and not thinking about anything. She knows there was something horrible that happened a long time ago but no one has told her what it was. And she can't remember herself. Oh, she's had many terrible dreams about it, but when she wakes up she remembers only her terror, nothing else. Dr. Thiessen and Miss Klassen keep telling her she will soon be well enough to go home again. Miss Klassen is young, plump, and pretty. Her cap and apron are as white and starched-looking as Miss Koop's but her face is always dimple-warm and smiling. Miss Klassen makes her think of fresh *bultje* just taken from the oven.

Miss Klassen takes her for long walks, right down to the river sometimes. They sit on the high bank in the long, sun-drenched grass and look at the bright, swiftly flowing waters far below. It makes her feel so soothed and clean to look at the broad, rushing river. But a little sad too sometimes. The river can't ever stop. It has to keep hurrying down to the rapids below. She knows it's the Dnieper. She knows that very well. She tries to remember again the song she knows about the mighty river. Something about the broad Dnieper groaning. The song runs smoothly somewhere in her head, like the river itself, but she can't quite seem to hear it yet. It's annoying not to be able to recall a song you know so well. Far to the right, beyond the rapids, looms the rock-faced island of Khortitza. Everybody calls it the *Kaump.* She has been there many times, but she can't clearly remember with whom. But it's quiet and peaceful there, she remembers.

She is staying in the Bethania. She knows that very well too. She knew all about this hospital long before she came here to live. Yes, she feels proud that Papa helped to establish Bethania and is still one of its directors. She came here with him when Bethania was first opened. But she can't remember when that was. It seems so long ago — everything does. And after that she came on other visits because she was interested. She can even remember that she once wanted to train as a nurse so she could work here. But Mama was horrified and said no daughter of hers would work with insane people. Besides, Mama had her heart set on her becoming a singer, an opera singer. But she didn't, and now she can't remember why she didn't. She still sings sometimes to herself, but only when she feels very happy or very sad. The nurses often ask her to sing for the other patients, but she says no. She only wants to sing for herself now.

But try as she will she can't remember when she came here to stay. Or why. She remembers something about being in Bethel House for a while. That's where they keep the violent women. She didn't want to stay there, so they let her come here to the main building where it's much quieter. She feels quite safe here. She doesn't think she's been here all that long, but whenever she asks Miss Klassen or one of the other nurses how long they tell her to try and remember how long and when. But she just can't.

What bothers her most is that Mama and Papa don't come to see her very often. She can't even remember when they were here last. And Gusha, he should have been here long ago. She knows he went away for awhile but he must be back by now. And he can't be that busy with the factory and his women. She'll have to give him a good talking to . . . .

And her dear friend Vasya, why doesn't he come? They always had such fun together — when was it and where? She knows she'll think of the place in a minute. Vasya is so clever and fascinating even if she does see less of him now.

Not that she doesn't get regular visitors. That nice old Elder Unger from the Einlage church comes at least once a week. But he can't tell her why her parents don't come either. Other friends and relatives have visited her, but often she doesn't feel like talking to them so she just sits and stares at them till they go away. It doesn't bother her. But most of them have tears in their eyes when they leave. She doesn't know whether they are angry at her for staring and refusing to talk to them or what. But last time her cousin Sophie from Belenkoye refused to budge. First she chattered like a magpie, asking questions about all sorts of things, and then all at once she shut up and just stared too. She finally had to be rude to Sophie and tell her to go away and mind her own business or she'd have to call Miss Koop. She had never liked Sophie much anyway, boasting about Belenkoye all the time and about how rich their other relatives the Bergmanns are. Belenkoye is a pretty little *khutor* but it hardly bears comparison with — with —

Selenaya! The name bores through her brain like a hot needle. She feels faint. She doesn't want to think about Selenaya — now or ever. She begins to shake violently in her chair. Her head feels funny again and it hurts, it hurts. She begins to whimper and moan. I didn't want to go there Papa not then but you said . . . And Mama, what did I tell you? You should have listened. Gusha, why weren't you? . . . They said, they said — no, no, no I don't believe it . . . it was just a nightmare . . . but I couldn't wake up they stood there grinning wolves I screamed but they grabbed me in the closet — no, no, no — wait you're hurting me — who? Dear Lord protect me — Papa, Mama, help me — they're taking me — no Marusya I didn't tell any-one . . . Why are you? Help she's cutting me open . . . if only — Papa? He's coming — oh my God — a man he's — NO, NO, NO, aaaaahh — Pap —

"Hold her down, hold her — she'll hurt herself. I'm getting the needle ready. She's finally broken through. She remembers. Poor girl. All right now. Try to hold her still."

CHAPTER TWENTY-THREE

1

September-October, 1918

Nikolai Fast would never forget his first impression of Makhno. It had been in the village of Pokroskoie in early August, after the harvest. Makhno was methodically going from village to village, virtually under the noses of the occupation troops, exhorting the peasants to rise up, recruiting them and organizing his raw and undisciplined peasant volunteers into a fighting force poised to strike wherever and whenever it could against large landowners, German occupation troops, and elements of the Volunteer Army.

It had taken Nikolai a long time and much effort to find the elusive partisan leader. After the raid on Selenaya Nikolai had fled in disgust from Chaika, had lain low for weeks in Ekaterinoslav, then cautiously made his way eastward searching in such places as Tagenrog and Tsaritsyn. There was a rumor he had gone to Moscow for the summer, but would be back by harvest time.

So Nikolai, like many others, became a freebooter drifting from place to place, joining local partisan groups when he felt like it, soon moving restlessly on again. In late July he picked up Makhno's trail. He was back from Moscow but not yet in Gulai Polye, which was occupied by Austrian troops. Instead, he had gone farther north to organize the peasants around Dibrovka Forest. It took Nikolai another week of discreet inquiries and hard riding before he caught up with Makhno's dazzlingly mobile guerrilla force, which could cover up to sixty-five miles a day.

He had found Makhno standing in the village square of Pokroskoie, a slight figure dressed in a simple but well-cut gray uniform set off by a long, straight mane of black hair and gleaming black boots. The smooth schoolboy's face was unimpressive, except for the remarkable eyes. When Nikolai saw the expression in those eyes he knew he had found his leader, a man whom he could follow without question. A poet's soft eyes turned to steel, a relentless idealist who would never flinch at reality. A fanatic, yes, but a tough-minded fanatic born practical. A dreamer for whom the truth would always have the force and finality of a bullet through the brain.

Nikolai was aware that he had not read all these qualities in Makhno at first glance, that he had only felt the force of his complex nature that first day. The understanding had come gradually after he had been around the man for weeks, observing him at close range, listening to his laconic talk, trying to discern how his strange mind worked. Casually self-contained, the little man had an air of authority that daily contact did nothing to dispel. There was something unfathomable, inscrutable about Makhno that everybody around him took for granted, that aroused no envy, not even curiosity. It was just there and set him apart from his followers as completely as though he'd come from some other part of the world.

What surprised Nikolai when he heard Makhno speak in the square that day surrounded by eager, enthusiastic peasants hanging on his every word was his curiously flat voice, his rapid but unassertive delivery. Whatever else he was, Makhno was no flaming orator. And yet the overall effect of his staccato sentences was compelling, almost hypnotic. Somehow, it was the burly peasants hulking over him who seemed fragile, vulnerable, in need of protection, as in a sense they were. He radiated a quiet, gathered strength at the center of that human ring. Nikolai had the distinct impression that Makhno was the tallest and most powerful man there by far.

"Conquer or die, my friends," he began in a matter-of-fact voice that had none of Chaika's leering cynicism or theatrical brutality in it, "that's the choice for us steppe peasants and workers at this historic moment." He stopped abruptly, licked his fleshy lips, and suddenly smiled with the radiance of a boy enjoying an innocent joke. "They can't kill us all, comrades, there are too many of us. So" — the high clear brow reflected upwards — "we will conquer — some of us anyway. We will conquer! And we'll never again make the mistake of placing our heads under the boots of new masters. No!" For the first time some dramatic resonance. "No! We will stand up on our own hind legs. We'll live as *we* see fit, by our own will and decisions. We'll decide for ourselves what's true and what isn't. We know the difference between butter and bullshit." Another radiant grin. "I say death to all who try to take away from peasants and workers what they've gained through revolution. Do you agree, comrades?"

And that was all. A mighty cheer went up from the villagers. They laughed and thumped each other in approval. This smart little dandy from Gulai Polye was one of them. He understood the peasant and his needs. They would help him smash the rich *pomeshchicks* and the Hetman's hated *varta,* his guards, and the *njemtsi* soldiers. Then they would have land, lots of land.

Makhno had been intrigued to discover that Nikolai was a Mennonite.

"Well, well, comrade, and what will your family and people say when they know you're riding with the notorious partisan Makhno? They'll disown you." Behind the laughing sarcasm lay a shrewd appraisal of the new man. Makhno seemed to like what he saw.

"I don't consider myself a Mennonite anymore, Nestor Ivanovich, and I don't give a damn what other people think of me, including my family," was Nikolai's blunt answer.

Nikolai saw that Makhno was impressed with him from the beginning. He was gratified but not surprised to be singled out quickly for extra responsibilities and important duties in spite of his limited experience as a guerrilla fighter. Now, after only six weeks, he was already a trusted member of Makhno's inner circle, always at his side as a special aide, along with Tchus and a few other favorites.

Makhno's energy, daring, and military skills seemed to grow with every passing day. Nikolai was as impressed by his chief's organizational skills as by his military wizardry, his uncanny ability to mold an unruly, greedy peasant rabble into loyal, disciplined partisan warriors. Was it sheer instinct? Would Makhno prove to be a revolutionary leader in the heroic tradition of a Razin or Pugachev? Nikolai watched him closely and his assurance grew that Makhno's partisan activities were a means to an end, not an end in themselves as with that wild bitch Chaika and her vile hyenas. Makhno had a mission: peasant freedom was his cause.

Before the German occupation Makhno had been just another local insurgent leader, with influence only in and around Gulai Polye. There had been a dozen more like him in the southern steppes. Now he was absorbing more and more local bands of insurgents along with their leaders and was rapidly becoming the dominant leader in the south-central Ukraine. With his boldness, cunning, and common sense, Nestor Makhno was winning the support of predatory gangs devoid of political purpose or even a strategy for survival. The more influential regional chieftains like Kurilenko, Petrenko-Platonov, and most important Fedor Tchus had already been won over and were helping Makhno build an effective insurrectionary army that would, hopefully, soon be able to control the entire region and ultimately the whole Ukraine.

But Nikolai could see that Makhno's position was not entirely secure. As yet, the other leaders accepted his leadership warily, a bit grudgingly, still jealous of their own jurisdictions and prerogatives as chieftains. Their men also made it clear that their first loyalty was still to their own leader and not to Makhno.

Fedor Tchus, the powerful ex-sailor, seemed to pose a special threat to Makhno. Next to Makhno, Tchus was the most popular of the regional leaders, admired for his courage and innovative daring. In fact, they were operating on Tchus's home ground, the vast Dibrovka Forest, which was now the headquarters for their rapidly growing "army." That in itself made Nikolai uneasy.

Nikolai did not trust Tchus, looked for signs of treachery in him. Physically he was the exact opposite of Makhno. Tchus was tall and husky, with the broad shoulders and corded neck of an athlete. He was also a swaggering bully who enjoyed inflicting physical pain. He took pride in his naval service and liked to boast that he had served on the *Aurora* when it attacked the Winter Palace to touch off the October Revolution. Nikolai was certain that Tchus had never been within a thousand miles of the former capital.

Tchus's face with its pencil-line mustache was handsome, but there was a wild light in his eyes that reflected the basic instability of his character. He was immoderately self-indulgent even in the way he dressed. A flamboyant dandy, he chose his costumes with the vulgar taste of a third-rate actor. Even here in the depths of the forest he wore ludicrously incongruous naval dress uniforms — the fancier the better — tricked out with fancy belts and pistols, hand grenades, and his special trade-mark, a brilliantly ornamented Caucasian dagger suspended over his chest like some Oriental medal or talisman. He played with it constantly, depending on his mood, fondling, stroking, caressing it, running his fingers over it wildly when he was excited.

Much as Nikolai had come to loathe the foul-mouthed sailor, he also feared him. Tchus was ambitious. And he was smart. Very smart. Makhno kept his opinions and feelings about his top aides and leaders to himself, but Nikolai could see that he treated Tchus in a special way. Makhno was wary of the big man. Outwardly there was an easy comradeship between the two. They were always together. But Nikolai was convinced that they had joined forces mainly to keep a closer eye on each other. In public Tchus always deferred to Makhno, but Nikolai suspected that was an act. Tchus treated everyone else with a crude insolence and arrogance that had enraged more than one of them to near-violence.

A showdown between the two was sure to come. Makhno needed to assert his leadership in some decisive and dramatic manner or the uneasy alliance he had with Tchus and the other leaders was sure to break apart, perhaps violently. Makhno, Nikolai was confident, was aware of the internal danger and was waiting for the right moment.

On the last day of September Makhno and a handpicked detachment of thirty men, including Tchus and Nikolai, were returning at a leisurely pace from a recruiting expedition south of Dibrovka in the villages lying between Pokroskoie and Gulai Polye. Along the way they were warned several times by friendly villagers that a large unit of Austro-Hungarian troops, augmented by the local *varta,* was rapidly moving north towards the town of Dibrovka. Makhno was not unduly concerned. His main army was securely encamped in Dibrovka Forest several miles north of the town. He did not think the *njemtsi tcherti* would be foolish enough to attack him in his own forest lair.

He was too alert a leader, though, to ignore the warnings. He decided to stop overnight at a small village south of Dibrovka rather than risk running into a night ambush enroute to his camp. Within minutes his men and their horses were so cleverly dispersed among the *khatas* and barns — never more than two per hut — that no one would have guessed there were partisans hidden in the village.

It was still dark when two peasant youths came to the *khata* where Makhno was sleeping. Their information was precise and alarming. Dibrovka was occupied by a *Germanzi* force of at least company size. Most of the troops were quartered out in the open in the main square and they had over a dozen mounted machine guns.

Makhno knew he was trapped. There would be strong road blocks on every route to the forest. Pale and dishevelled, his black eyes gleamed as he considered his options. In crisp, clear terms he presented the picture to his senior aides.

"Well, comrades, we've stepped into a viper's nest. We can do one of two things. We can hightail it out of here back the way we came and hope they haven't already cut us off. Or" — his eyes shot fire in the half-light — "we can do what the sons-of-whores will least expect — attack them right now while they're still dreaming of their German bitches." He looked at them one by one, the fury in his face like a demon's. "I say attack," he hissed. "What the hell. The Cossacks say 'Nobody can die two deaths, and the first one comes no matter what.' It may as well be now as later."

There was silence as the others stared at the impassioned face and burning eyes.

Tchus, his wild eyes on Makhno's as though hypnotized, broke the silence. "I say yes, Nestor Ivanovich. We've got nothing to lose. We're not going to slink around the countryside like whipped curs waiting to be caught. Let's rip the bastards apart!" His big fingers slid up and down the shimmering dagger on his chest as though playing an instrument he couldn't finger fast enough.

Dibrovka was a town of about 10,000. Makhno's plan of attack was so bold and daring as to verge on the suicidal. Its main element was surprise, to catch the Austrian troops asleep in the square. Tchus and seven men were to infiltrate the village from the rear and launch a flank attack on the square while Makhno and the rest of his men made a sweeping frontal charge along the main street leading to the square. They would take care of lookouts as they needed to. The youthful spies had not seen any outposts. The double attack would not only have to be precisely timed, but would require a colossal amount of luck. If the townspeople came to their assistance they had a chance. But would they? Nikolai felt his insides rasping like a grindstone.

Makhno and his riders came hurtling down the main street just as dawn was breaking. Seconds later Tchus and his squad opened a ferocious fire from the deep shadows of buildings fronting one side of the square. Startled out of sleep, the dazed soldiers and militiamen assumed they were being attacked by a sizable force. Many of them never got to their stacked rifles or machine guns before they were mowed down in a hail of cross-fire. In the ensuing melee, Makhno's men, being mounted, were able to use their sabres with devastating effect.

Then the Austrians got their bearings and began to fire back. They now realized how small the attacking force was. They were beginning to press a counter-attack when the peasants started emerging from their *khatas* wielding not only firearms but knives, axes, even scythes and hammers. They chased down unarmed foes and cut them mercilessly to pieces. Those who got away and barricaded themselves in buildings were soon forced to emerge like rats when flames shot up the dry *khata* walls.

It turned into a massacre. The fury of the peasants, who had been extremely reluctant hosts to the Austrian troops, was so great that they refused to take prisoners; a number of helpless men managed to escape the town only to be rounded up later by the aroused peasants and savagely drowned in the nearby Volchya River.

When it was all over Makhno, breathing heavily, his skin sallow in the gray new-light, stood in the square and surveyed the carnage around him without a flicker of emotion. He might have been a boy standing in a meadow of flowers. He was soon joined by Tchus and Nikolai, who reported that at least ten of their men were dead and half a dozen more wounded, two critically. Makhno muttered something under his breath, but his expression did not change.

Only eight prisoners had been taken, one a *varta* guard. Makhno looked him up and down with loathing. He was a thickset young fellow with a broad, fleshy face and a shock of unruly blond hair that sprang up from his head like steppe grass. In a thick, barely controlled voice Makhno asked him for his name. The man, looking unsteady on his feet, answered "Terelenko" in a low, slurred voice.

"You rotten *khokhol* filth," Makhno ground out, lips barely moving, "you would hunt down your own people like rabbits in the field. For foreigners!" He reached for his *nagan* and without hesitation shot the guard squarely in the face.

Three of the soldiers began to whimper, fell to their knees, and fervently pleaded for mercy in a glutinous mixture of German and broken Russian. The other four remained standing and silent. All seven had already been divested of their boots and military jackets, or possibly not had time to don them when the attack began.

Makhno calmly holstered his *nagan* and ordered the kneeling men to get up. He turned to Nikolai.

"Tell them I'm letting them go. Tell them to go home and inform their people that the Ukrainian peasants are fighting only for their freedom, not against the workers and peasants of other countries. Tell them Nestor Makhno is a fighter for freedom and justice, not a murdering adventurer."

Nikolai translated and watched the prisoners' faces light up with relief and gratitude. They thanked the partisan leader profusely and walked away as though they had just experienced a miracle.

And so they had. Tchus looked thunderstruck. He couldn't believe what he had just witnessed. Shock and bewilderment clouded his face, and for once he forgot to play his fancy dagger as he continued to stare at Makhno.

Suddenly Tchus let out a roar that startled even Makhno, and with a bull-like rush threw his long arms around Makhno's thin shoulders and kissed him strenuously on both cheeks.

"Nestor Ivanovich," he rumbled in his deep voice, "you are not only a brave fighting leader but a brilliant and merciful one. From this sacred moment you are our *Batko,* our Little Father." His feral eyes warm and direct for once, he beamed long and proudly at Makhno. "Yes, you will be our *Batko,* and we your sons. This day you have shown us all what courage and determination and — yes, and mercy — really mean." He looked to the others for support, found it and pushed Makhno forward for them to embrace too. "From this day," he continued emotionally as the other men took turns embracing their new *batko,* "we freedom-loving peasants and workers vow to fight by your side in the ranks of the insurgents under your command until victory or death."

Then Tchus scooped Makhno up like a child and hoisted him to his shoulders, knocking his sailor's cap askew, his grin a broad slash, and his crazed eyes shining.

The rest of the men, including Nikolai, shouted lusty "hurras" and enthusiastically repeated Tchus's vow of allegiance.

Wearing a slightly embarrassed smile, *"Batko"* Makhno rode silently above his cheering men and the grotesque shapes of the dead and wounded that littered the square.

Nikolai watched the elevation of his chief with pride and infinite relief. Makhno had done it! He was now the undisputed leader of a united force of insurgents. His only serious rival had publically hailed him as *batko* and sworn an oath of fealty.

His elation was also for himself. For having survived a battle against fierce odds. *Batko* was not only good but lucky. By joining Makhno he had committed himself to a leader and a cause that would give meaning to his life as nothing ever had. Now the way was clear. He still wouldn't trust Tchus completely, but for now the problem of command was solved. Long live *Batko* Makhno!

2
Schoenfeld-Brazol, October, 1918

The Treaty of Brest-Litovsk called for the Central Powers to occupy the Ukraine for fifteen years. The occupation, however, lasted a scant six months. With the collapse of Germany and her allies on the Western Front in early November, the Austro-German troops were recalled post-haste. They departed in some disarray, leaving behind in the Molochnaya considerable stores of arms, ammunition, and supplies. They even left behind a few soldiers, but for a special purpose.

The Bolshevik government in Moscow, after the severe pressures of the summer, gradually took a new lease on life. The Volunteer or White Army, formed in February by tsarist officers, landowners, university students, and various other factions opposing the Bolsheviks, had effectively forced them out of the east and southeast. In the Ukraine the army of occupation had set up the puppet regime of Hetman Skoropadsky. The Bolsheviks had been left with control only over the central part of European Russia.

With the Germans gone, the new Red Army organized by Trotsky could concentrate on Deniken's White Army and the "Greens" of the Petlura regime which filled the political vacuum in Kiev created by the sudden collapse of the Hetman's government after the Germans had withdrawn. The Reds also became aware that a brash young guerilla leader by the name of Makhno was rapidly expanding his sphere of operations in the region around Gulai Polye. In the Bolshevik press he was praised as a promising leader working for the common revolutionary cause.

Makhno neither knew nor cared what the Reds said about him. The drummer he marched to was himself, always himself. And he had his hands full with the revolutionary activities he triggered even before the Germans left. A few days after Makhno's stunning victory over much superior forces at Dibrovka, the Austrian district commander sent a sizable force of Austro-Hungarian troops and Ukrainian *varta* back to Dibrovka to wipe out Makhno once and for all. An intense artillery fire practically leveled the town, killing a lot of people and leaving it in smouldering ruins.

Makhno was back in his forest stronghold plotting his next move; the punitive raid against Dibrovka roused him to a cold fury. He went on the rampage in a series of ferocious raids fuelled by the slogan "Death, death, death, to all on the side of the Hetman." With lightning speed he wheeled south out of the forest and brazenly occupied Gulai Polye with the Austro-Hungarian garrison only a few miles away at Pologi.

Next day the Austrians counter-attacked and forced Makhno to retreat. That night he was back, his ranks swelled by several hundred Gulai Polye peasants who dared to help him only under cover of darkness. The Austrians were driven off once more. The local Makhnovites then returned to their homes so that their participation would not be discovered in case the town changed hands once again.

After four days of this strange see-saw battle the Austrians, having lost their commanding officer in the fighting, had enough and left Gulai Polye in Makhno's hands for good.

Makhno now had the free hand he wanted. His favorite targets in the area were large, isolated *khutors* and Mennonite villages, which offered an undefended supply of horses and food, as well as valuables and money. Everywhere he left a gory wake of death and destruction. Estate owners and their families who had been too complacent or too stubborn or simply too undecided to flee were murdered without compunction in the most gruesome manner. Makhno allowed his men to plunder and rape at will, and they were usually well primed for their bloody nocturnal work by the *samogon* they carried with them in copious quantities. Makhno himself began to drink heavily, although his energy, guile, and decisiveness as a military commander seemed to be unaffected.

At Voronaya the Loewens knew they could not long escape Makhno's depredations. Their past association would mean nothing to Makhno now, Jacob Loewen knew, and he needed no convincing that the time had come to flee the terror. Mutti Loewen, enclosed in her domestic world, was harder to convince, but she too became alarmed after hearing about atrocities committed against people she knew. Snapper was anxious to get his parents to the Molochnaya and if need be to the Crimea, where his mother had close relatives. He himself was determined to stay and fight, if he could get enough men together in the district for a vigilante or self-defense force. The nucleus would be the mounted troop he had led that summer, most of whom were still around and eager to go against Makhno. The trouble was there weren't enough of them. They needed more men, including older men, to join them. They would also need more arms and ammunition, and they could expect no real help from the Austrians, who seemed to be getting ready to pull out in any case.

In mid-October Snapper took his parents to Schoenfeld; from there they were to travel with friends to Blumenau, where Katya and Wilhelm had arranged accommodations for them. In Schoenfeld Snapper heard that Makhno was already reported heading for Schoenfeld-Brazol from Gulai Polye. Voronaya lay in between; he could not go back there now. That afternoon he talked to some of his young friends and within minutes they decided to call an organizational meeting for that evening. The word was spread around Schoenfeld and the surrounding villages and *khutors*.

Over a hundred determined Mennonite men showed up for the meeting. All showed grim-faced determination to take direct action against predators who, they knew, would show them no mercy. They also knew that Makhno was completely unpredictable in his movements. He might take the most direct route to Schoenfeld and fall upon them this very night, or he might take his time and carry out raids in other places first. They would, in any event, get only short notice of his coming — if they were lucky — from the mounted lookouts who were now stationed at intervals between and just outside the villages.

Snapper Loewen, already known as a proven leader, was asked to take over the group. He did not demur. Snapper was devoid of false modesty and knew he was the best man there for the job.

With the help of three Schoenfelders who knew the local men, Snapper hastily divided the volunteers into squads and appointed squad leaders. Then they took inventory of their weapons and ammunition. Snapper's heart sank as he looked over the pitiful array of small arms — shabby rifles, rabbit guns, and antiquated pistols for the most part. The supply of ammunition was even worse: some men had brought no more than a single cartridge clip, a few no more than a handful of cartridges. There wasn't even a machine gun, though he knew that Makhno had machine guns mounted on his horse-drawn *tachankas*.

They were still assigning weapons and apportioning the ammo when Defehr, one of the outposts, came in, looking highly perturbed. He reported that Makhno was at Gaichur Station, only eleven miles away. There he and his men had apparently held up a train and shot several Austrian and Russian officers. The bandits were reported to be heading for Silbertal now, only five miles from Schoenfeld.

They had waited too long! Makhno was at their doorstep and they weren't ready. They had no training, only a meagre supply of obsolescent weapons, and not even a battle plan. Snapper saw at once that concerted action was now out of the question. There simply wasn't time to get ready to attack Makhno in force before he got to Schoenfeld. It would be folly to try. They could fortify themselves within the village, of course, and try to hold Makhno off when he came. But that would endanger not only the men involved but the women and children as well. Makhno was quite capable of exterminating every last inhabitant in a village that resisted.

No. Armed defense was now impossible. Flight or passive submission were the only alternatives — unless Makhno decided to make a detour and thus give them more time to organize.

Snapper had an idea. "Look," he told the nervous men, "I'll take Defehr and three others out on patrol towards Silbertal. We'll try to find out exactly where Makhno is. There's always a chance he's headed off in another direction. Give us about an hour. If we're not back by midnight, bury your arms and ammo as carefully as you can, then either get ready to move out or stay in your homes as quietly as possible. Under no circumstances should there be any weapons in evidence anywhere."

Just before midnight Snapper and his patrol were back. They had ridden all the way to Silbertal. The villagers there were gravely worried, but there were still no signs that Makhno was heading their way. They had lookouts in two different places, but so far they had reported nothing. All they could do was wait and pray, they said.

There was still no panic in Schoenfeld. Some families were getting ready to leave. A few had already left. Most, however, would stay where they were and hope for the best, with God's help.

Snapper and six of his friends, all estate owners' sons, decided they would head for the Molochnaya immediately. There was nothing more they could do here. And they were too well known for their raids on Russian villages a few months ago to be able to escape detection when Makhno arrived in Schoenfeld.

Snapper had heard that in Halbstadt there were secret plans underway for a Mennonite *Selbstschutz,* a Self-Defense that would really amount to something. Already German officers and noncoms were reported to be training Mennonite recruits in secret and equipping them with proper weapons. In a very short time the German occupation troops would be gone and then they would be on their own, God help them!

That it should finally have come to this, Snapper thought grimly as he rode through the night with his companions. Everything was at stake. They must fight to save the colonies. Snapper had never been surer of anything in his life. Makhno and his men were marauding wolves, and like wolves they would have to be hunted down. Soon there would be no higher power to protect them. They would have to do it themselves.

3
Silbertal, October 16, 1918

Like the other riders in the band, Nikolai Fast was half drunk as they moved towards the next village in the dark. He no longer cared what village it was. And the *njemtsi* troops no longer bothered them. They wouldn't be here much longer anyway. They could hit any village they liked now. They were in the Schoenfeld-Brazol area, but just where he wasn't sure. All he knew was that the sprawling settlement lay before them like a loaded fruit tree; he smiled to himself, and they were going to pick it clean, every last *yablochko,* little apple.

"*Yablochko, yablochko,*" he began to croon his favorite song in a monotone over the pricked ears of his horse. Sung to their own words, the old tune was a favorite with Makhno's men.

> Little apple,
> Little red apple
> In Makhno's white hand you are,
> Rolling about,
> And you'll never get out.
> Rolling about
> In Makhno's white hand,
> And you'll never get out.

His head buzzed pleasantly from the fiery *samogon* they had drunk around the frightened *pomeshchick's* big table a few miles back. And singing their favorite songs. The sour bugger hadn't even joined in, until Tchus with an evil grin had kicked him right in his gutsack. That got him wheezing along fast enough.

They'd been dying for some grub and drink after knocking off that train in Gaichur and giving those cocky German officers the works. That rich Mennonite bastard hadn't even wanted to give them supper, said he didn't have enough for all of them. But *Batko* had put on his faraway smile and gently nuzzled his *nagan* against the man's fat cheek. That did it. His plump wife jumped to the stove and a big meal appeared as if by magic. Mennonite magic. He chuckled into the wind. When it came to grub you couldn't beat the Mennonites.

Nikolai glanced idly at the sprawled form of a young man lying by the roadside as they passed by. Those punks, he thought contemptuously, never learned that Makhno had advance guards who knew how to clear the road so no alert signal could go back to the village. A mile farther on there was another youth lying faceup in the ditch staring at the clouds.

They were well into the wide, deserted street before Nikolai realized where they were. No, it couldn't be. He peered at the homesteads on both sides, then spotted the village school with its depressed gable ends. It was Silbertal all right. The village his mother came from. As a small boy he had sometimes spent part of his summers here with Oopa and Ooma Sudermann. They were dead, years ago. But damn — Silbertal. Did it have to be Silbertal? His uncle and aunt, so far as he knew they still lived on the old Sudermann farm. But he'd been away so long, maybe they were dead too.

He was sober now. He glanced at Makhno and Tchus riding slightly ahead of him, looking intent. He couldn't arouse their suspicions by staying out of it. He'd have to participate as usual. Make it look good, at least. And hope that no one would recognize him . . . .

Taking two men with him he carefully chose a house he did not recognize. He crashed his rifle butt against the door. It opened within moments and a young man with a long, terror-frozen face stood before them.

"Checking for arms," Nikolai said brusquely. It was their standard excuse for inviting themselves in. He pushed past the man and strode into the kitchen. A slender, pallidly pretty woman stood petrified at the brick stove, obviously the wife of the man who had let them in. An elderly couple were sitting at the table. They looked as if they had just gotten out of bed. All three stared at him in frightened silence. The kids must be in bed — or hidden.

The young man was struggling for composure. "We — we have no arms — nothing. Why do you — ?"

"Shut your yap, *burzhuj*."

"But we have done nothing to you."

The *samogon,* subsiding, was leaving him irritable. He wanted to slam his rifle into this stupid horse face.

"You've done everything to people like me, you lousy cur." Anger spurted from him like pus. "You've stuffed yourself with the best of everything and you don't give a good goddamn for any fellow creatures except other other fat Mennonite pigs grubbing in our Russian soil."

The young man, head down, stood meek but uncowed. He did not believe a word, clung grimly to his own innocent martyrdom, just waiting.

"All right, outside you." Nikolai canted his rifle over the table top. "You too, old man."

The young husband and wife exchanged quick, anguished glances, but did not speak. The grandfather got up heavily, his wife steadying his arm. Nikolai prodded the two men to the door.

From farmsteads on both sides of the street old and young men, some scarcely more than boys, were being herded into the street. Nikolai escorted his two victims over to a dazed-looking group of prisoners on the street and turned back towards the next house. Then he changed his mind and left his two partners on their own. He would stay in the street near his horse for a bit. No use taking chances. Something told him this would be no ordinary roundup, a search for loot, and a quick getaway.

There was blood in the air tonight. He could smell it. *Batko* had been drinking for days and was in a foul mood. He'd been short with the men all day, even Tchus, and there was that wolfish look in his eyes. He didn't have to say much. The men picked up his mood and will quickly. They looked for the signs; they didn't need explicit orders for work like this anymore. They knew how to satisfy their *Batko*.

It looked like these stupid Mennonites were in for it tonight. Already the first batch was being marched across the street to a big-looking yard where no doubt the specialists, led by Tchus, were eagerly waiting to take care of them with sabres or bullets, depending on how the whim struck them.

Two mounted men, sporting ill-fitting dark suit jackets, were cursing and prodding more victims to the place across the street. Nikolai hadn't heard shots, which probably meant the sabre artists were at it tonight. Maybe *Batko* had given orders to save ammunition.

That was Makhno for you, always thinking ahead. He could sit up for hours at night without moving, just staring at the flickering tongues of the campfire, planning his next move. He looked like some kind of holy man then, his eyes holding serene inner depths that fascinated Nikolai. Even Tchus didn't dare disturb *Batko* when he was in one of his mystical moods. Makhno's ideas and strength came from some deep well within him. He hated advice, especially from people who thought they knew more than he did. He was not taken in, he liked to say, by "conference tables" and the "scribblings of intellectuals," all of which didn't amount to a pile of turds.

Back on his horse, Nikolai helped round up men trying to hide behind mulberry hedges, in back orchards, and more remote hiding places. The herded prisoners were beginning to show signs of panic as they guessed what was happening to those taken across the street. Nikolai, back with another prisoner, eyed the group watchfully, wondering whether the more nervous ones might be foolish enough to make a break for it. And then he tensed as his eyes picked out a familiar figure standing a little aloof on the edge of the crowd, as if ashamed of the animal fear around him. His Uncle Hermann, his mother's older brother!

His uncle raised his glance straight at him, but betrayed not a flicker of recognition. Only a long, level stare that tested Nikolai's nerve. Was the old man playing a game with him? But how could he possibly recognize his nephew? They had scarcely met since Nikolai grew up, and that was years before he had raised his thick cavalry mustache. Besides, nobody in the family knew he was back in Russia, or even that he was alive. And who in the Fast family would believe that even their black sheep would ride with the notorious Makhno? Certainly not Uncle Hermann, who had always liked him. But why that long accusing look?

He felt his anger rising. Damn the stupid old man. Why hadn't he left Silbertal while there was still time? And Aunt Tien, she must be here too. What were these people thinking of? Did they really think that praying to their Mennonite God, their heavenly tsar, would protect them from hot lead or cold steel?

But then Uncle Hermann had always made a habit of ignoring reality, even in the old days. Childless himself, he kept trying to win the affection of his only sister's sons. Especially his, Nikolai remembered. His uncle kept inviting him to his farm in summer. Said he needed Kolya as a *schetjbenjel,* an errand boy. But he could have hired a *russejung* for a ruble a month. He just wanted Nikolai there for himself and for his stringy aunt with her big teeth and bad breath. He wouldn't have gone if Father hadn't made him. He hated the way they kept touching him, trying to please him. They made him feel he owed them something. After two summers there he had refused to go back, even though his father had given him a hard beating.

Nikolai jerked his horse aside to avoid a long, thin Mennonite reeling towards him under the blows of that huge Cossack Zharkov, pursuing him with drunken fury.

Damn them, damn all Mennonites — the fat ones living on the front street, the thin ones on the side streets. They deserved to be exterminated, the stupid sheep, with their pious airs and bulging granaries.

Eerily quiet at first, the scene was growing noisier and more chaotic by the minute. Flames and clouds of acrid smoke were pouring out of houses on both sides of the street. The looting was in full swing. There was much riding and running about. The raiders, many now bizarrely dressed in sober Mennonite Sunday clothes, were carrying food, clothing, and even furniture out of the houses, some staggering weak-kneed from *samogon* under their heavy loads. When a farmstead was more or less cleaned out someone usually put a gunny-sack torch to it. The red cock. Women and children, forced out of burning homes, added their terrified cries to the screams and groans of wounded victims of both sexes who lay unattended and helpless where they had been felled.

Batko Makhno seemed to be everywhere, calm and alert to everything that was going on. He watched the looting and butchering impassively, but took no part himself. Darting about on horseback he was rejoined by Tchus, who had for the moment sated his lust for blood at the execution yard. Riding together, the two conferred and observed the men closely.

Nikolai knew that what he was about to attempt was sheer madness. He cursed himself for even considering it. What did an old man with only a few years left matter anyway? He looked at the prisoners again. There were fewer of them now, but Uncle Hermann still stood there, tall and still, as though somehow removed from the terror around him.

Nikolai, keeping his voice cold and impersonal, ordered the old man and three other prisoners to step forward. Again the appraising stare from his uncle. Did he know? The three others looked ready to beg for mercy. Not Uncle Hermann. He did not look ready to bargain his dignity away for anything, even life. A tough old mule, for sure. He better cooperate when the moment came, or all would be lost.

He glanced across the street. The farmstead on the left was burning and dense billows of smoke were rolling thickly to the right over the yard directly across the street. To the right of that was the yard where the executions were taking place. If he could get his uncle across the street without arousing suspicion, he might be able to hide him and give him a chance to escape. It was worth a try. Now was the time. The noise and confusion were at their height and the sharp-eyed *Batko* and Tchus not around at the moment. It was now or never.

His heart pounding, Nikolai ordered his four prisoners to start moving across the street. But instead of bearing right towards the execution yard, he prodded his prisoners bit by bit to the left. He kept waiting for a shouted challenge and approaching hoofbeats. He did not dare check over his shoulder to see if he was being watched.

Slow and calm, he told himself, keep the prisoners moving. They were approaching the gateway, and still he had not been challenged. They passed the brick gateposts and were almost immediately engulfed in black, suffocating masses of smoke. Nikolai pushed and goaded his coughing, staggering men forward until they got through the worst of the smoke.

He'd made it! On the left bulked the wood and brick length of the house-barn. Directly in front was the granary, running off the barn at right angles. he ordered one of the men to slide open the granary door. Then he dismounted, grasped his uncle's arm, and thrust him inside.

"I'm giving you a chance to get away, old man. Hide here until everybody's gone. If they set fire to this place, you'll have to escape through the back."

Uncle Hermann's face was white, but his eyes remained calm. "Why are you doing this?"

The familiar, raspy voice caught Nikolai off guard. "Don't you know me, Uncle?" he asked in German.

The old man looked puzzled and shook his head.

"It's me, Nikolai."

"Nikolai? Greta's Kolya? *Our* Kolya?" For the first time he lost his calm look. He clutched at his nephew. "But why — ?"

Nikolai wrenched his arm free roughly and quickly shut the granary door. The three remaining men looked more bewildered and apprehensive than ever. Curtly, he ordered them to walk around to the back of the granary. He remounted and followed them.

In the dark shadows in the lee of the granary he stopped them. They looked up at him anxiously, ashen-faced. All three seemed to understand that the moment was critical. Before they could start pleading, Nikolai said quietly, "The old man can't run. I'm giving you the chance to try it. Get going."

The three upturned faces turned in relief. A moment later they began to trot awkwardly, pudgy, middle-aged men not used to running, towards the haystacks shouldering each other in the field just beyond the back fence.

He raised his rifle and without a pause shot all three.

The man in the lead had just enough time to turn and open his mouth to scream before a bullet slammed him into the weeds.

In a flash Nikolai had spurred his horse through the smoke and dashed back into the street. *Batko* and Tchus were following the last of the prisoners being herded across the street for execution. Nikolai guessed that Tchus intended to dispatch the last few captives himself. The sailor was inordinately vain of his sabre work and liked to cut his victims to pieces with what he fancied as true Cossack artistry. Nikolai's loathing for the sadistic butcher lay in his gut like a coiled snake.

In the middle of the street Nikolai pulled up beside Makhno in feigned triumph. "*Batko,* I just caught three of the swine trying to hide behind that place across the street." He pointed to the yard he had just left. "They won't be doing any more running."

"Good work, Kolya." The full lips curled with distaste and the deep eyes glowed contempt. "They're all cowards, these big-bellied sausage-eaters. They don't want to fight, and they don't even know how to die. All they can do is squeak and blubber."

Nikolai felt Tchus's shrewd eyes on him from the other side. The deep basso boomed sarcastically.

"What, you caught only three, comrade? Are you sure there weren't more hiding back there, the serpents? What did you do with the others? Let them get away?"

A fresh stab of fear. Was the ever-suspicious Tchus just fishing or had he seen him crossing the street with the four men? Tchus was a cunning bastard always looking to discredit him in *Batko's* eyes.

Tchus bored in with more spite. "How do you like seeing your people get what's coming to them, Fast? Don't you feel just a little sorry for them right now? Come on, sweetheart, admit it. We won't blame you if you do."

Nikolai tried to relax. He was on dangerous ground. He must not allow himself to be nettled into self-betrayal by Tchus's offensive baiting. And *Batko,* in his self-absorbed way, was listening too.

"I wouldn't be here if I felt sorry for these bloody exploiters, Fedya, would I? I know as well as you what they deserve, the bastards."

"Yeah, just as long as you don't get soft on 'em, comrade." Tchus snorted derisively and moved alongside *Batko,* who was already turning away.

More and more buildings were blazing in the night sky. The red cock rising. The low-lying smoke was a nuisance to the looters but it did not stop them. Nikolai kept an anxious eye on the farmstead where he had hidden his uncle. So far it hadn't been fired. He fervently hoped the old man would have the sense to sneak out the back if the place did go up.

The men who had worked off their blood-lust in slaughter now turned their attention to the women and girls. Hearing a terrified shriek coming from the yard to his right, he turned to see a young woman, her dress and most of her underwear ripped away, frantically trying to elude her pursuer, a short, bandy-legged fellow with a huge mustache whom the men called the Crab. Laughing fiendishly as he caught up with her, the Crab wrestled her brutally to the ground. Her scream suddenly stopped. She had either fainted or realized the futility of further resistance. He wasn't sure, but Nikolai thought he had recognized the victim as the young wife in the first house he had entered.

Poor wretch! He couldn't help feeling sorry for her. It always disturbed him, this part of a raid. Liquidating the exploiters was one thing, but the bestial violating of the women was senseless. That is what bothered him the most, the savage raping of girls scarcely into puberty and helpless old women. He had witnessed with revulsion women in their sixties and seventies viciously gang-raped and then hacked to pieces, sometimes in front of their husbands or sons. He had seen women dragged out of sick-beds and ravaged into unconsciouness. He'd taken his share of women, but he'd stayed away from that sort of thing.

Mindless brutality disturbed him. And the destruction of property, the fine Mennonite *wirtschaften*. Why burn them? Why not save them for new owners? Destroying them was stupid, almost criminally wasteful. Anarchy didn't mean destroying everything in sight. It meant destroying the system and removing forcibly the people who had built the system and exploited it.

If only *Batko* could see it that way, but he believed destroying the human part of the system was not enough. Makhno argued, persuasively Nikolai had to admit, that you could only destroy *burzhuj* society by ruthlessly eradicating everyone and everything in it. Hack it to pieces down to the very roots. Wipe out all physical traces. For him that was the only way.

Nikolai didn't dare argue openly with Makhno over this crucial point, but he wished he could. If only *Batko* and the others weren't quite so radical, so fanatical on this point. Why not make the old system serve the new? The rich Mennonite farm villages, for example, why not just take them over instead of plundering and destroying them? From Tchus and others you couldn't expect any more, but *Batko* saw so much why couldn't he . . . .

His thoughts were interrupted. The band was preparing to move out. He took a good look around. Many of the buildings were still burning fiercely. Some had already crashed into fiery ruins. The smoke and heat and stench of burning was getting uncomfortable. The dead and wounded lay strewn around like abandoned sacks. The looting had been carried out with the usual messy greed and spilled waste. Food, clothing, items of furniture, lay about everywhere. The *tachankas* were heaped in teetering mounds. Someone had left a beautiful piano leaning crazily against a tree, abandoned at the last minute for want of room in the wagons.

The terrified female screams had subsided to moans and pitiful gasps for help. Small children were wandering about sobbing, lost, and dazed. Nikolai had seen it all before, but felt himself stripped again to naked pity. And Uncle Hermann, was he able to get away? The farmstead where he was hiding was now also in flames, one of the last to go.

And Aunt Tien. He wondered about her also, but hadn't dared look for her. Peering down the street he could see that the old Sudermann place was still intact. Miraculously. If she were still alive, his uncle could save her from this mess.

Nikolai resisted the urge to look back as they left the dying village. The *samogon* had long since worn off; he wished he had some now to blot out the night's horror and tension.

He felt drained, empty. What was it all for, this killing and destruction? When would it end? What would he do when they got to the Molochnaya, to Halbstadt, and Blumenau? How would he feel then?

He ran his hand over the silken neck of his horse. The warmth and vitality of an animal trained to respond obediently to the touch of its rider.

Any rider at all.

4
Molochnaya, Late October, 1918

The Molochnaya, with its sixty villages and hamlets spread over an area forty miles by twenty, was the largest and most prosperous Mennonite settlement in Russia; a rich agricultural jewel adorning the southern steppe above the Sea of Azov. It was a proud colony, not one to submit meekly to spoliation and destruction even in a time of political anarchy and civil war. But the rumored withdrawal of the occupation troops would leave the settlement as unprotected and vulnerable as a farmstead with its doors open to thieves at night. For the first time ever many began to regard the hallowed Mennonite principle of nonresistance as at best an irrelevant Christian ideal, at worst a craven surrender to the forces of evil let loose upon the land.

The only chance to save the colony, the militants argued, was to create an armed force to protect the villages, an effective militia large enough to form a protective ring around the settlement and keep the lawless elements out until there was a legitimate government controlling the country again. Already during the summer months Self-Defense units had been formed in Halbstadt, Gnadenfeld, Tiege, Tiegenhagen, and Lutheran Prischib. The training began covertly under the leadership of Lieutenant Leroux and

Sergeant-Major Sonntag of the 182nd Saxon Regiment stationed in Halbstadt. By October it was rumored that if and when the Germans withdrew they would leave behind some of their officers and men to lead the Mennonite Self-Defense now being trained.

When Snapper and his friends arrived from Schoenfeld-Brazol in October, they promptly joined the First Halbstadt Company under Sergeant Sonntag. Snapper was quickly promoted to squad leader and spent his days drilling his men or engaging in mock battles with squads from other village units — all under the supervision of experienced soldiers like Sergeants Sonntag and Goebell and Corporals Henschel and Wollrich of the 182nd Saxon.

Snapper wasted little time trying to get Wilhelm to join the Self-Defense too. Sitting in the Fasts' big kitchen one evening with Snapper, Wilhelm and Katya argued that nonviolence, based on the love of Christ in the New Testament, was at the very heart of Mennonite beliefs. That principle must be followed even in these perilous times — especially now.

"You're wasting your breath, Snap," Wilhelm said, Katya nodding approval, "I may not be a good Mennonite in all things, but I believe that it's wrong to kill under any and all circumstances whatsoever."

Snapper regarded him with a tight smile. "That's easy to say, Rembrandt, when we're sitting here safe and relaxed after a good dinner." He leaned forward, the smile gone. "But would you still feel that way if you saw your father shot, Katya and your mother raped and sliced open before your eyes? That's exactly the kind of thing that's already happening and could happen here in the next little while, you know."

Katya was offended. "Look, Martin, there's no need to be gross. You won't persuade us that way."

Wilhelm tried to restrain himself. He disliked getting drawn into this kind of futile discussion, but he would not allow Snapper to score cheap debating points against him. "Okay, Snapper, let's not confuse the issue. Let's at least agree that nonresistance is biblical and that we Mennonites have practised it for almost four hundred years." He saw Snapper was eager to interrupt. "No, let me finish. I admit I don't know what I'd do in the unthinkable situation you raise. I might go berserk and try to kill too. But I do know that even if I pick up a gun and kill a dozen men I won't stop others from killing. I'll only be violating my own conscience and condemning myself in the eyes of God. Fighting just breeds more fighting, it doesn't settle anything. Can't you see that, Martin?"

Snapper, listening with growing impatience, decided to take another tack. "All right, Willie, but aren't you being a little self-righteous? You were at the conference with me in Lichtenau last summer where all this was discussed by the wisest men in the colony. And you know what happened. In the name of the Mennonite church they passed a resolution leaving it up to the individual conscience whether —"

"— Yes, yes, I know," Wilhelm conceded impatiently, "but they also passed another resolution which reaffirmed the principle of nonviolence, my friend. A typical Mennonite compromise, I grant you."

Snapper was not to be deflected. "Look, Willie, the Self-Defense we're organizing is not an army. It's no more than a local militia, a police force formed for the sole purpose of defending innocent lives and property against thieves, outlaws and murderers bent on grabbing and destroying everything."

Wilhelm was not impressed. "Snapper, you can call it a police force or anything you like, but it's still a military force that violates the Mennonite belief in peace and non-resistance as clearly as —"

"— any other army does," Katya jumped in against her brother. "You're just playing with words, Martin. That way you can argue that every armed force in the world is a defensive one trying to protect loved ones and property at home — even if it's in a foreign country a thousand miles from hearth and family."

This was too much for the volatile Snapper. His frustration with the counter-arguments boiled over. "Damn it all" — Father and Mother Fast, sitting quietly near the stove, looked over at the fierce Snapper in alarm —"will you both listen to reason, just this once? We have no state to protect us now; there is no government in control here. Even the Germans will soon be gone. This whole land is aflame with violence, bloodlust, and greedy lawlessness. We're living in hell, there is no protective state, no police force or even an army to maintain law and order — certainly not the Whites, or the Reds, or the Greens. Only the Blacks, Makhno's fiendish anarchist hordes, are in control here, murdering us in cold blood, raping our women, looting and destroying our property. Don't you understand dear sister and brother? We're fighting for our lives, or soon will be. Makhno is getting stronger and closer every day. You know what happened in Silbertal the night I came here. And those people were doing just what you want — turning the other cheek, don't forget! Their meekness didn't save them. If we don't defend ourselves we may be wiped out to the last man, woman, and child. Can't you get that through your thick skulls?"

There was tense silence. Snapper's angry outburst had embarrassed all three young people. His reference to Silbertal had been cruel and tactless, and he knew it. He kept his eyes averted from Mrs. Fast, whose brother and his wife were presumed to have been killed in the massacre.

Snapper broke the silence awkwardly. "I'm sorry, I shouldn't have shouted. And I shouldn't have —"

"It's all right, Martin," Katya said, conciliatory now, "we shouldn't have pushed you like that."

They left off arguing then, and avoided the subject of the Self-Defense for the next few days. But Wilhelm knew his brother-in-law too well to think that he had given up trying to get him to join the cause to which Snapper now gave all his time.

Then something happened that completely changed Wilhelm's mind about joining the Self-Defense. Something that moved him to surrender cherished principle to brute reality — even over Katya's angry remonstrances — as Snapper's passionate arguments could never have done. What changed Wilhelm's mind utterly was the unexpected appearance in Blumenau of two survivors of Makhno's terror and the shattering news they brought with them. Aunt Tien and Uncle Hermann Sudermann showed up at the Fasts' door one evening looking as though they had returned from the dead, as in a very real sense they had. They were on their way to seek refuge in the Crimea.

Uncle Hermann related in his calm, meticulous way how he himself had actually been saved from certain death by a member of Makhno's gang — he did not at first say who it was. When the granary he was hidden in had started to go up in flames he had escaped through the back door and run out into the field, where he had stumbled over the bodies of three of his friends. He dug himself into a haystack and waited till all was quiet. Then he had crawled out and headed for home, passing such gruesome sights on the street and in the yards that his heart almost failed him. But what faced him at home was even worse. He found Tien, his beloved wife for forty-two years lying on their bed moaning and delirious. Uncle Hermann stopped at this point in deference to his wife, who was softly weeping beside him. He would say no more of that except that he had tried to comfort her and nurse her back to health for a whole week. The neighbors — those that had survived — had helped too, as much as they could in that mortally wounded village. After ten days Tien had finally been well enough to get up. And then they had locked up the house and barn (although there wasn't much left to steal) and got out of Silbertal as fast as they could.

Then for the first time Uncle Hermann became agitated, acting like a man who wanted to say something but didn't know how to say it. Haltingly, as delicately as possible, he told them who had saved his life that dreadful night. But urged them not to be too quick to judge and condemn the boy. That he himself accepted what Kolya had done as an act of love, as a miracle sent from God for which he could only be humbly grateful.

Hearing that their Kolya was not only alive but actually riding with Makhno's murdering band left the Fast family almost paralyzed with dismay and shock. Having long given him up for dead, or at least lost to them, they could not now comprehend his reincarnation as a criminal outlaw, a thief and possible murderer. Even his daring act of saving Uncle Hermann's life could not mitigate the shame and horror that overwhelmed them. It only added to their emotional confusion. When they trusted themselves to talk about it, Father and Mother Fast sorrowfully agreed that it would have been ten times better if the boy had fallen in the war. Their son with Makhno!

That dreadful secret must never go beyond the family.

Wilhelm, as stunned by the news as the others, spent a sleepless night of soul-searching that brought him to a decision. A decision he knew Katya would oppose bitterly. But he was convinced now that Snapper was right: they were living in a hell that called for desperate measures. Who could live honorably by principle in such a chaotic world? And how could he ever have thought the moral issue was as simple as the principle of nonresistance he had upheld so confidently — fatuously — to Snapper? True, Kolya was a terrorist, maybe a rapist and murderer, and yet he had saved his uncle's life at the risk of his own. His uncle would be dead if Kolya hadn't been in Silbertal with Makhno that night. Who but God could explain such a moral enigma? He had oversimplified everything, deceived himself into a state of self-righteous, hypocritical passiveness. Perhaps as a member of the Self-Defense he too would be able to do something positive and beneficial for others, instead of sitting by in moral purity letting evil happen unchecked.

In the morning, over breakfast, he told Katya about his change of heart, nervously bracing himself for an argument, aware that she would find his reasons inadequate, a form of betrayal. The vehemence of her opposition shook him nevertheless.

"Oh, Willie, you're not going back on your own moral principles, are you? How can you? You have no right — it's indefensible."

She was grim with anger. He had never seen her that way before. Suddenly he saw an abyss opening between them and it frightened him. But her anger forced him to retreat, confused, into stubborn justification.

"Katya — I — sometimes the terrible things that happen to people make principles seem unreal somehow, beside the point. You heard Uncle Hermann's pitiful story last night, and yet it was my bad, sinful brother Kolya who saved his life. In times like these good and bad are too hopelessly mixed up to allow them to be neatly separated according to principles —whether religious, moral, or whatever." He stopped, aware that he was not convincing her.

Her indignation was scathing. "You can't possibly believe that, Willie. You're too intelligent, too honest. Principles of faith and belief are always clear-cut. We're supposed to be a *suffering* church, my heart, that's what the Mennonite church is all about, that's what makes it different from others churches. You know that as well as I do."

"Yes, yes, the quiet in the land and all that — I know, Katya, but Mennonites have never faced this kind of situation before, a complete breakdown of law and order — Snapper's right about that. To remain passive in the face of this evil threat may be evil and sinful itself. Have you considered that?"

"Willie, Willie" — she leaned across the kitchen table, sliding her cup of *prips* forward — "you're sounding more and more like my brother. And that angers me because Martin has always acted more on impulse — the superior impulse of his class of landowners, the privileged ones — than on principle, at least on such principles as nonresistance and Christian love, even for one's enemies. And now you want to follow this example." She looked down at her cup, gripped tightly in both hands, trying to control herself.

Wilhelm, feeling more miserable by the minute, stared into the abyss between them and unable to stop himself took a desperate leap. "When you come right down to it, I'm not sure it's possible to live a life of complete nonresistance in a world where conflict and strife seem to be at the center of everything. Can we speak of passive suffering without seeing that it's a form of resistance, a not-giving-in to the evil that causes the suffering? Wasn't Christ's conscious suffering, his sacrifice on the cross, the ultimate resistance to evil, a deliberate defensive action to save us all from perdition?"

He had plunged into the abyss, he knew, and dared not meet her eyes.

She raised hers slowly to his face and studied him without expression. But when she spoke at last her face softened and her voice was quietly resigned. "I have nothing more to say on the subject, *lieber*. For me, moral hair-splitting is self-defeating. You are my husband, Willie, and I love you dearly. I know you to be a decent God-fearing man, honorable and compassionate. I must accept your motives, although I don't understand them, and let you do what you think best. I accept that without reservation."

She reached across the table for his hand and smiled at him through her tears.

Wilhelm rose from the table with an ache in his heart but with the conviction that he must go through with his decision. But to himself he could admit that he understood his own motives scarcely any better than Katya did.

That evening he let Snapper enroll him in the First Halbstadt Company and was introduced to Sergeant-Major Sonntag, a tall, leathery-lean regular of the German Army who was planning to stay behind to command the Company after the German troops' imminent withdrawal. Wilhelm was still teaching in Fischau, so he was free to train only in the evenings and on weekends.

5
Chernigovka, December 6, 1918

The town rose above the steppe like a ghostly, eerie mirage in the early morning mist: indistinct clusters of steep-thatched *khatas* half-hidden behind lumpish straw stacks and crooked wattle fences, and the broad, empty main street stretching towards the square in the distance.

Swiftly, with a minimum of commotion, the men of the First Halbstadt Company fanned out from their columns in lateral lines. Wilhelm joined

Snapper's squad in the middle of the line. His guts tightened even more as he realized that their squad was expected to advance directly up the street where there was no cover. In the event of an ambush they would get it first. As they approached the first *khatas* his legs and arms felt wooden and he had trouble breathing normally. He glanced at Snapper beside him. There was grim concentration on his face but no sign of fear or panic. Even the sudden yelp of a dog nearby did not seem to startle him.

They had come from Halbstadt by train early last evening, disembarked at Stulnievo Station near Waldheim, then marched to Konteniusfeld and Sparrau, the villages on the eastern border of the settlement, for the night. And a very short night it was. By 3:00 a.m. Sergeant Sonntag had them up and ready to march the eight miles to Chernigovka, where Makhno was reported getting ready to assault the Molochnaya. They had been joined in the pre-dawn march by a Major Popov with two other White officers, a pair of machine gun wagons, and a squad of White soldiers.

The attack plan called for the Halbstadt men to launch a frontal attack on Chernigovka under the covering fire of the White machine guns and infantry. A company of Self-Defensers from Gnadenfeld were to form the right flank and a Mennonite cavalry detachment the left. The trouble was that neither flanking force had as yet arrived on the scene.

And still the street was devoid of life or sound except for the yapping of shaggy Russian mongrels skulking in the shadows. They were approaching the square and its big white church when a stout old woman in a big babushka came waddling out of the *khata* beside the *volost* building on the corner. She was visibly excited and shouted over and over:

"They've got one of yours in there" — pointing to the *volost* — "one of yours — a prisoner — one of yours."

Major Popov grabbed her by the arm to calm her down. "Listen, mamasha, are they here — Makhno's people?"

She beamed with self-importance. "Yes, yes, they're here." She pointed again, towards the church. "There, over —"

A pistol cracked and the old woman shuddered, as though hit. But it was a dog nearby that sank down dead. One of the Mennonite students, in his nervousness, had taken a pot shot at the savagely barking cur.

With a curse, Popov gave the order to spread out and take cover.

And not a moment too soon. As the men scattered and dove behind walls and haystacks, the metallic chatter of a big Lewis gun filled the air.

Snapper and Wilhelm were hugging the clay wall of a *khata*. "The bell-tower," Snapper yelled, "they've got a machine gun up there. Where's the sergeant?"·

Sonntag, on the other side of the street, was already calling for the machine gun wagons. But the two White machine gun wagons were not in sight. They had either remained behind or taken cover somewhere.

There was no time to wait for their covering fire. "All right, men,"

Sonntag shouted in German, "concentrate your fire on that tower and don't let up till you've got the bastard."

A ragged volley of rifle fire cut through the staccato noise of the Lewis gun. A minute or two later the machine gun fell silent. The gunner had either been hit or had retreated.

The advance resumed slowly, cautiously. The heaviest enemy fire was now coming from the left, where the cavalry detachment was supposed to be holding down the flank.

Wilhelm edging around the corner of a *khata,* saw riders moving up on the left and opened his mouth to yell that the cavalry had come. Nothing came out. A whining explosion struck him dumb. Dazed, he glanced up and saw that a big, ragged bite had been taken out of the corner a foot above his head. He was enveloped in an acrid cloud of powdery clay and lime. He removed his fur cap and stared at the white frosting on it in wonder.

"For God's sake, Willie, keep your head down. You almost got it shot off." Snapper had just run up behind him. He was breathing heavily.

"Our cavalry, Snap, did you see it?"

"It's not ours. It's theirs."

Then Sonntag was ordering them to attack the windmill up ahead to the left. Heart pounding, Wilhelm followed Snapper from cover to cover under sporadic firing, which became more concentrated as they closed in on the mill.

Snapper and his squad crept behind a granary close to the windmill. He turned to Wilhelm and the others. "Listen, keep me covered. I'm going to run behind that manure pile next to the mill. From there I can lob a grenade or two at them." He thought of something else. "Yeah, and keep your eyes on that open space beyond the manure pile. It looks like a cemetery. They may be hiding in there too."

Snapper slipped around the corner and was gone. For the next few minutes the squad kept up a steady covering fire at the mill, from which firing was returned. Nothing from the cemetery though. "I guess there's no life left in the old cemetery," Wilhelm muttered to the man beside him as he reloaded his ancient rifle.

There was a dull explosion in the vicinity of the mill, followed closely be a second one.

"He's got the mill," somebody in the squad shouted. Then they heard Sonntag's urgent order to advance.

Wilhelm ran with the others. He had no time to look back to see if Snapper was catching up with them.

They dove behind a low fence or wall that consisted of wattles daubed with manure and clay. Hardly an adequate cover against bullets, but at least they were out of sight for the moment. Shots were coming from several places in the farmyard directly ahead of them. Wilhelm, lying as flat as possible behind the flimsy wall, waited helplessly for the fatal bullet he was sure would strike him at any moment. Never in his life had he felt so dangerously exposed, not even at the front. Out of one eye he watched the German Corporal Henschel nearby coolly tie together two hand grenades. Suddenly he bolted upright and hurled the grenades into the middle of the farmyard. His body still extended, arm outstretched in a follow-through, Henschel suddenly stiffened, then seemed to leap violently backward and landed with a thud face-up, just as his grenades exploded with a shattering crash in the yard.

The firing from the *khata* and barn ceased in a cloud of smoke and flying debris. In the silence that followed the men peered behind the wall at the fallen Henschel. He had not moved and there was nothing left of his face.

Again the hoarse voice of Sonntag. "Get moving, lads. We've got them on the run. We'll meet in the square."

It was true, the enemy firing grew weaker then ceased almost entirely. Wilhelm looked around in vain for Snapper.

From all directions the men were gathering in the square, looking dirty and bedraggled, especially the commerce students in their black school uniforms, but all were flushed with victory.

Amazingly, apart from Corporal Henschel they had suffered almost no casualties. Braun, the Halbstadt *volost* assistant secretary, had taken a shot through the fleshy part of his forearm. He was stoical about it as it was being bandaged and kept saying it was a good thing it wasn't his writing arm. One of the students, supported by a comrade, appeared hobbling on one foot, bleeding profusely from the calf under the gaping hole in his pantleg. Several others had bruises and minor cuts from the action, but no bullet wounds. And that was all.

Snapper was still not there and Wilhelm was getting uneasy. He had not seen him since they had attacked the mill. He decided to go back that way to look for his brother-in-law. He had walked no more than a hundred yards when he turned a corner and saw two of his comrades awkwardly bearing a sagging weight between them.

Wilhelm went cold with dread. He knew who it was being carried towards him. Please God, he prayed silently, let him be alive.

But when the men stopped in front of him and put down their burden Wilhelm saw that Snapper was dead. He had been shot in the back of the head and killed instantly. That could only mean one thing: the shot must have come from the cemetery behind Snapper. And we were supposed to cover his back, Wilhelm groaned in agony as he bent over the inert form.

Snapper Loewen looked as unconcerned in death as he had in life. "Nothing ever happens to me, pal. I'm always the one who walks away unharmed." Wilhelm remembered Snapper's jaunty boast on the Polish front.

And then, for the first time, he thought of Kolya. Had his brother been here during the battle? Helping Makhno against his own people, his own brother? But then he might have been shooting at Kolya too. And here lay Snapper, the blood sacrifice.

He knelt on the ground beside his dead friend and brother-in-law and could not accept the reality. Not Snapper, God not Snapper. How would he face Katya and the family bearing home the lifeless body of their Martin.

In his desolation he did not even hear Gerhard Toew's tardy cavalry detachment clattering up the street towards the square. Major Popov immediately ordered them to pursue the fleeing Makhnovites and make every effort to capture Makhno himself.

The cavalry detachment thundered through the town in the direction of the railway station at Verkny Tokmak. But they were too late. Emerging from the town they saw a line of *tachankas* tearing across the fields towards the station. The *tachankas* had too big a lead. They could see a steaming locomotive and several cars waiting in the station. The bandits would be well on their way to Pologi before their Self-Defense pursuers could even reach Verkny Tokmak.

Makhno had escaped again, although he had left at least a dozen of his men dead in the streets of Chernigovka.

In a daze of grief and apprehension, Wilhelm examined every one of the enemy corpses. To his vast relief, Kolya was not among them.

Later, on a borrowed wagon, he drove Snapper back to Halbstadt through a soft December rain that fell without letup all the way home.

From wagons in front of him carrying returning soldiers, he heard over and over through the drizzle the little victory ditty the boys had made up and were lustily singing to a familiar tune.

> Short was the fray;
> Makhno ran away
> On St. Nicholas day.

Already the raucous Halbstadt students seemed to have forgotten their dead comrade. It occurred to Wilhelm that this might be the first time ever that Mennonite soldiers were celebrating a military victory. That depressed him even more. He glanced over his shoulder at the uneven surface of the horse blanket gathering little pools of water in its folds, and realized with a pang that the young man lying under it, had he survived the battle, would have sung this silly victory song as lustily as the rest.

CHAPTER TWENTY-FOUR

1
Molochnaya, December, 1918

Snapper Loewen and Corporal Horst Henschel, late of the German Army, were buried in Halbstadt-Molochansk with full military honors. The town had never seen a military funeral before. It drew so many mourners, not only from Halbstadt and nearby villages but from Prischib across the river, that the church could not begin to accommodate them all. So it was decided to move the service outside, with the speakers presiding from the front steps. Teacher Benjamin H. Unruh, his ample figure even bulkier in a furcoat, made a simple but moving opening. The bright blue eyes in his cherubic face were sober with the pain of shared loss as he surveyed the masses of dark-garbed mourners before him.

Then Erdmann Lepp, who had been conducting revival meetings in town all that week, delivered a brief and reconciling eulogy based on part of the Lord's Prayer.

"Dearly beloved and bereaved ones gathered here today: Christ taught us to pray, 'Forgive us the wrong we have done, as we forgive those who have wronged us. And do not bring us to the test, but save us from the evil one.' True, these two young men lying before us departed from this earth in violence. They chose to take the sword and they died by the sword. We all know that as Anabaptist Christians we Mennonites believe it wrong to live by the sword. But, my friends, these are perilous times, bitter, abnormal times for us all. Instead of sitting in judgment on these brave young men —we can safely leave the judging to our Lord and Savior — let us honor their memory with love, respect and compassion. For greater love has no man, as we well know.

"Yes, our message must be one of compassion and forgiveness. These willing young sacrifices, and there may well be others who will be put to the supreme test, did not die cynically or indifferently, but in the firm belief that what they were doing was for the good of us all. That is as much as our earthly understanding of this sad issue will permit us to say. We who mourn here have not been put to the test — not yet — as these dear departed were, and so we can only pray for them and for ourselves and leave the rest to God. We can do no other. Amen."

As the funeral cortege left the church it passed slowly between an honor guard of Self-Defense comrades from the First Halbstadt Company. At the cemetery another group of black-uniformed student members of the First Halbstadt sang in rather subdued, self-conscious voices "*Ich hatt' einen Kameraden.*" By the time they finished there were few dry eyes among the assembled. Erdmann Lepp, bony hands clasped tightly, spoke a final prayer over the open graves and the funeral service was over.

Through it all Wilhelm marvelled at Katya's strength. All the long, drizzling way home with his covered burden he had dreaded the moment he would have to tell her. She spared him that. She was sitting on the *schaffott* as though waiting for him when he turned into the Fast *hof.* She rose to meet him as he stopped, her deep eyes on the back of the wagon. "You've brought him home, *mein lieber,*" she murmured, and he couldn't tell whether her term of endearment was meant for him or her dead brother. When she looked up and saw the anguish and guilt in his eyes, she reassured him gently. "It's not your fault, Willie, you mustn't blame yourself."

In the bleak days before the funeral they talked, she solemn in her grief but without tears, he more agitated, wretched with remorse and loss. He had returned from Chernigovka resolved to quit the Self-Defense immediately, to have nothing more to do with the obscenity of hunting down and killing others or being killed. One sacrifice in the family was enough he told her. "And what if I'd shot my own brother, even if he has become a savage wolf?"

"Willie, darling, you mustn't torture yourself like that," Katya said passionately, her dark eyes troubled. "I agree with you. I want you out of this madness too. Let others go fight if they feel they have to. You've done your share. And so has Martin," she added bitterly.

He took her in his arms then, grateful beyond any words that her woman's heart had already forgiven them both — her brother for dying and himself for letting him die.

But even her healing love could not still the voice within him. The voice was insistent, and it was Snapper's. He heard that voice at night between waking and sleeping, and he heard it at quiet moments in the days that followed the funeral. A relentless voice, full of Snapper's old cajoling bluster. What, pull out now? You can't do that Willie. There's too much at stake. You have a wife and two families to protect, my friend. A whole community. Somebody's got to do it, pal. I'm gone. Your brothers are gone. Our fathers are too old. You're here, Rembrandt: you and the others. Somebody's got to stop that madman Makhno before he butchers us all.

The trouble was Katya did not hear her brother's voice. She did not share her husband's doubts and fears. How could she? When he tried to explain they got into the same old argument over principle. To her the moral issue was so clear and simple. To him it became more beclouded with ifs and buts all the time. They went through tearful scenes and sleepless nights over the issue, nights which left them feeling enervated and estranged from each other. But Wilhelm knew he had already made up his mind. And when Katya knew it too she sensibly stopped fighting him. She only made him promise to get out of the Self-Defense the moment his conscience would let him. She trusted him to know when that would be.

With full-time military duty a distinct possibility, Wilhelm began to look around, as Christmas and the end of the school term approached, for a substitute teacher to take over for him in the new year. He did so at the request of the Fischau school board, which was willing to give him a leave of absence if a substitute could be found.

The only substitute teacher he could find on such short notice was his old Schoensee colleague Martin Stobbe. "Old Carrion" had been living in retirement in Ladekopp for several years. He was more cadaverous looking than ever, but the flaccid ease of retirement had soothed away much of his former moroseness. When Wilhelm visited him in his little hut in his brother's garden, he was actually friendly and receptive. He seemed to have forgotten all his old complaints against his young colleague and had even forgiven him, he said, for having "abandoned him to the *russemerjales*" when Wilhelm was mobilized. Yes, he was prepared to "do his bit" in this terrible emergency, but only with the understanding that as soon as "that black butcher had been taught a lesson and things got back to normal again" he would be allowed to "come back to my little nest and wait for eternity to gather me into its bosom."

Wilhelm felt guilty for abandoning his pupils to such a teacher, but told himself that in this case the need was greater than the deed.

He was now free to join his unit full-time. There were persistent rumors that the First Halbstadt and other Self-Defense units would soon be sent north, where Makhno was reported getting ready for a major thrust at the Molochnaya.

The successful skirmish at Chernigovka had been eagerly hailed as a major victory by the frightened inhabitants of the Molochnaya. Their brave Mennonite boys with God's help had routed Makhno's band and come within a shot or two, they believed, of capturing or killing the monster himself. Biblical precedents sprang to their thankful lips: Abraham and his servants rescuing Lot; David defeating Goliath; Gideon and his God-selected 300 stampeding the Midianites; Joshua's conquest of the Amorites, although the Halbstadt boys had not needed such miracles as hailstones and a stopping of the sun. Many who had been dubious about the Self-Defense now became strong supporters. Village assemblies were called and more Self-Defense units organized for the conflict ahead. The voices of opposition, coming mainly from spiritual leaders and teachers, were drowned out by roaring militants, and even some of the ministers began blowing the trumpet for battle.

The rapid growth of the Molochnaya Self-Defense was viewed with approval by elements of the White Army now in effective control of much of the southern region abandoned by the Germans. Colonel Malakov, appointed commandant of the Molochnaya, correctly gauging the political and military naiveté of the civilian Self-Defense leaders, sent some of his officers on a delicate mission: to help the Mennonites with their military preparations while applying subtle pressures to persuade them to integrate their troops with the White Army. These officers were everywhere, giving expert advice, offering arms and training officers, persuasively seeking cooperation for joint military operations. Before the Mennonite leaders realized what was happening, their forces were being effectively, albeit unofficially, laced into the larger White military and administrative structure. In alarm they drew up a resolution stating the independent and limited nature of their "police" action. But it was too late to undo the damage. The Mennonites of the Molochnaya had innocently allowed themselves to become part of a loose alliance with the Whites for which they were to pay dearly later.

As for Makhno, his set back at Chernigovka had only made him more determined to bring the Molochnaya to its knees. His thrust at the eastern end of the settlement had been blocked, but he would find another opening. Of that he was confident. Moving northwest away from the Whites by a leisurely, roundabout route, he holed up in the village of Kopani, hard by the German Catholic village of Blumental thirty miles north of the Molochnaya. He was now poised on the main route to the settlement.

White units quickly moved up to invest Blumental, thus forming the nucleus of what would soon become a thirty-mile wide "front" designed to hold Makhno's forces at bay. Actually, this frontline never consisted of anything more than an irregular series of local outposts and battle stations with nothing but empty winter steppe between them.

In this paper-thin shield stretched across their northern perimeter the people of the Molochnaya now put their prayers and their trust.

On Christmas morning Makhno's forces launched a bloody assault on the Whites at Blumental. They were repulsed, with fairly heavy losses on both sides. Expecting further attacks, the Whites sent out a call to Halbstadt for reinforcements. Three squads of the First Halbstadt, including Wilhelm's, were dispatched to Blumental the following night.

Through the long hours of darkness they sat on the floor of jolting, springless farm wagons, huddled together for protection from the raw, gusty winter wind. This time there was no bravado, no nervous display of high spirits with the bantering and joking that had enlivened their train trip through the Molochnaya on the way to Chernigovka. They knew what to expect now and preferred to brood in silence or doze through merciful minutes of forgetfulness.

They arrived in Blumental along with a bleak, windswept dawn that did little to warm up their chilled, cramped limbs or lift their spirits. The village had a forlorn, abandoned look as though all its inhabitants had either fled or fallen victim to the black serpent coiled to strike less than a mile away. The villagers living in the upper half of the village facing the enemy line had indeed deserted their homes and either moved in with others at the lower end or fled southward. The empty houses now served as temporary fortifications and quarters for the defending troops until forward trenches could be dug and an earthen barricade thrown up.

Looking around, Wilhelm could see very little by way of military preparations. He saw no gun emplacements and only here and there a shallow forward dugout, used most likely as listening and sentry posts. His gaze swept the road and level fields to the north, but he saw nothing, no movement or activity to indicate the physical presence of the enemy. Even Kopani, what he could see of it from this distance, seemed devoid of life or movement. But they were there, he knew, and would choose their own time to strike. This time we are the defenders, he thought grimly.

A White officer led their squad to one of the empty farm houses near the northern perimeter and told them this was to be their defensive position. The house was cold and dirty and almost bare of furniture. The two remaining beds had been stripped of sheets and blankets and the mattresses despoiled, probably in a search for money and valuables. The large *piech* was dead and there was no proper wood for fuel, though somebody had apparently been hacking up chairs for fire wood. Most of the windows in the house were broken and in a few even the wooden frames had been shattered or ripped out.

And they were expected to live here. What a depressing prospect. This would be no surprise raid at dawn, a short hot skirmish then back to the warmth and comfort of home. Here they would have to wait it out. They might be here for weeks — even months — God forbid! Standing in the middle of that big, empty kitchen Wilhelm closed his eyes and tried not to think of what might happen here. How he needed someone like Snapper to rally him out of this mood of utter hopelessness and futility. Well, it was Snapper's ghostly voice that had brought him here. Perhaps his spirit would be with him here as well.

He was exploded out of sleep by shots reverberating through the house. He sprang up from the corner where he had been dozing fitfully sitting up against the wall, his field blanket tugged around him. Dazed, he groped for his rifle leaning against the wall. It must be an attack! "Schnaps" Wiebe, the squad leader, was shouting frantic orders to man battle stations. Wilhelm moved tensely to the side window overlooking the orchard, his position. Dawn was breaking but he could see nothing but the black limbs of trees outside and bare mulberry and rose bushes. His head was clear and alert but his body felt strangely numb and weightless. Then he was startled by more firing from the front of the house and he rammed his rifle tightly against his shoulder, slowly moving the muzzle from side to side through the open window, waiting for he knew not what.

Then it was there: a noise and movement on his side. The distinct sounds of a rider coming from in front somewhere, slowly, deliberately hugging the wall of the house. Instinctively, trying not to expose his face, he took a quick peek. Then ducked, the dark bulk bearing down on him too fast. He had only a second or two. In a desperate motion he thrust his head out, tilted his rifle at the looming figure above the horse, and fired.

A startled cry as he ducked his head inside, then the thud of a body hitting the ground and the plunging shape of the riderless horse filling the window.

He became aware of Wiebe's frenzied order to fall back — get out of the house! With covering fire from the front windows, the rest of the squad moved swiftly to the back door knowing that the house would be surrounded at any moment.

They were lucky to get out in time. One of the two men at the front windows was not so lucky. He had been hit and was calling for help. But they were already out and running in panic from the shots falling around them. They zigzagged through the back garden, heaved themselves over a fence and made for the next row of houses where they could expect to find shelter for the moment at least.

Wilhelm ran as desperately as the others, but the horror in his mind was for what he had just done. He had killed a man! Shot another human being at point-blank range, giving him no chance to defend himself. Just like that he had snuffed out a life. He was alive, the other man dead. Why? It made no sense. He followed the others into the first house they reached. The gasping pain that seared his chest would pass quickly. The self-revulsion over what he had done would not.

Nikolai Fast found himself lying in the dirt, trying to clear the fog from his brain. He knew he had been shot, but where? He tried to move and gasped as unbearable pain jolted through the shoulder he was resting on. He felt a dull pain somewhere else but it took him seconds to realize it was coming from his hand, his left hand. Gingerly, so as not to aggravate the hell-fire in his shoulder, he raised the hand: it was a mess of bubbling gore. He had been shot through the hand! Where else? The only other pain was coming from his right shoulder. He tried to remember the attack, the shots coming from the houses as they bore down on them in the half-light. They had tried to work in close, catch the bastards inside off guard. There had been no warning — just the shot exploding in his face. He must have thrown up his hand instinctively at the last second, and landed on his shoulder when he was knocked off his horse. He fought nausea, wondering how he could stanch the flow of blood from his hand without disturbing his shoulder, which felt broken. He didn't dare shout for help. He didn't want to rouse the bastards inside. He was too close to the house. They could finish him off with one shot. His horse was gone too. He uttered a long string of obscenities under his breath. That this should happen to him now, after all he'd been through. He tried holding his shattered hand tightly clamped against his thigh. Maybe that would stop the blood. Somebody would be along to help him. He was aware of heavy firing, cries coming from inside. Good. His men were blasting those goddamned Whites out of the house. They'd take this bloody German village . . . get to the Molochnaya . . . then . . . .

2
Molochnaya, March 6-10, 1919

The desolate, bitter months of January and February, 1919, would always be remembered by the survivors of the Molochnaya Self-Defense as an endless nightmare of bone-numbing cold, endless waiting, sleeplessness, and stale, tasteless rations; a nightmare cruelly punctuated by sudden eruptions of frantic action at dawn or dusk as the Makhnovites began their wild shelling again before thundering in to attack their positions. Even under almost constant harassment they had managed to throw up a barricade of earth to shelter behind, but their flanks remained pathetically vulnerable.

Day after day, week after week, reality was defined for them by the noise and confusion of brutal skirmishes, the screams of the wounded, and the accusing, astonished faces of the dead. Why they had not thrown down their antiquated rifles and pistols when they first saw the much larger, more effectively equipped enemy force and run all the way back to Halbstadt probably perplexed them as much as it did their antagonists. All they knew was that they were to hold Makhno's hordes at bay as long as possible, that if their line of defense broke those hordes would swarm through their villages killing, plundering, and violating their mothers, sisters, wives, and sweethearts. Also, they were proud sons of the soil, with the stubborn streak of a dissident people and German feelings of superiority towards the Russian peasant. For all that, they could scarcely believe that for two months they had actually managed to keep the fierce Makhnovites from overrunning their positions and trampling them underfoot to the last man.

No experienced military man would have approved of the way the Self-Defense troops were deployed along their so-called front. It wasn't even a broken line. Just a number of unstrategically placed outposts — except for the Blumental sector — without even communications links between them. At the western end the Anarchists controlled the Ekaterinoslav-Melitopol railroad at Prischib station, bringing in men and supplies under the very noses of the Prischib Self-Defense stationed there. The uncooperative Prischibers seemed intent only on holding on to the Lutheran villages of Gruental and Andreiburg, even though they were of no strategic importance whatever. Worst of all — fatal if it had been exploited by the Makhnovites — was the six or seven mile gap between the Prischib units in the west and the Mennonite units in the salient formed by the Blumental sector farther north. At any time during those two months Makhno's forces could have moved through the gap without firing a shot and rolled up the two main defensive sectors on each side with ease. For some strange reason, however, they kept stubbornly making frontal attacks against the two pressure points, especially the one at Blumental that was being defended with so much tenacity. Several times in bloody, close-quarter fighting, the Makhnovites captured the battered village only to have the dogged Self-Defensers and Whites take it back again in furious counter-attacks.

That the Self-Defensers' spirited resistance was able to hold up the Blumental front for so long owed something to circumstances. What they did not know was that Makhno was fighting on other fronts as well that winter. In fact, he himself had been in Kopani only long enough to set up the campaign against the Molochnaya. Then he had taken most of his best officers and most experienced men north with him, leaving his brother Savva in charge against Blumental with Nikolai Fast as his second-in-command. The Molochnaya could wait; he had a more urgent operation in mind. He needed more arms, and he had a plan for getting them. In a daring maneuvre in mid-December Makhno, having first allied himself with local Bolshevik leaders, launched a successful attack against Ekaterinoslav by sending a train load of his men into the city disguised as workers. It was a typical Makhno operation. In fierce fighting he was able to hold the city for four days, then retreated with a huge supply of fresh arms and other booty. The weapons went to the fresh troops he raised in the Gulai Polye area in the weeks that followed. With them he was able to commit large detachments to the fighting in the southeast against the Whites, who were trying to break out of the Caucasus.

By the end of February, however, it was clear to Makhno that he had overextended himself in trying to fight on several fronts. In the east his forces were unable to keep the Whites from pushing slowly northwards. On the other hand, the Red Army was moving into the central Ukraine from the north, so that he was in danger of being caught in a vice between his two foes. He was aware that this was hardly the time to make good on his oft-repeated boast that he would "beat the Reds white and the Whites red."

But as usual Makhno's luck held. General Dobenko, the astute commander of the rapidly advancing Red 42nd Division, invited him to ally himself with the Red Army for the final push south against the Whites. The hard-pressed partisan leader accepted, but on the condition that his forces would retain their own identity and command and not be absorbed into the Red Army. The black Anarchist flag would continue to fly at their head.

Makhno had bought time. Smelling a kill, he returned immediately with much of his staff to the Blumental front. That front, which had become increasingly unstable through February amidst reports that the Red Army was coming, became critical for the Self-Defense in the early days of March. When they suddenly found themselves opposing regular Red Army troops along with the Makhnovites they knew their cause was hopeless. The best they could hope for now was an orderly retreat that would cover the evacuation of civilians from the Molochnaya, at least those who wanted to flee south.

That retreat was made possible by the dramatic appearance of a remarkable German officer who seemed to the panic-stricken Molochnaya Mennonites God's answer to their fervid prayers. Lieutenant Heinz von Homeyer was a romantic adventurer with an exalted sense of destiny. In fact, he regarded himself as a bit of a mystic. A professional soldier, Lieutenant von Homeyer had been stationed in the Molochnaya with the German troops and had returned to Germany with them. Following some inner prompting, however, he had on his own initiative returned via the Crimea to see whether he could be of help to the beleaguered German and Mennonite colonists in southern Russia. He now offered to take over the leadership of the Molochnaya Self-Defense with the serene self-confidence of a man on a sacred mission. The offer was gratefully accepted by B. H. Unruh and the other civilian leaders who made up "Menno Centre," the executive council in Halbstadt which served as the staff headquarters responsible for organizing civilian defense and security in the colony.

Menno Centre's attempt to hand over the military command to Lieutenant von Homeyer was, however, deemed high-handed and improper by the Prischib command and the regional White commandant. At a most critical time von Homeyer lost valuable days waiting to be officially confirmed as commandant in the field. But that did not prevent him from making daily inspection trips to the front to familiarize himself with the deteriorating military situation. Finally, with the front already collapsing and senior White officers leaving their posts in retreat, he was confirmed as commanding officer. The Whites' spiteful act of treachery did not faze von Homeyer. He worked feverishly around the clock guiding his men to an orderly tactical retreat from the Blumental sector, thus saving them from encirclement and almost certain annihilation.

Wilhelm was no longer marching, but hobbling along with a dragging shuffle like a decrepit old man. He cared nothing for that. His fatigue-sodden mind was wired only to the dull ache in his bad leg, a persistent hammering of pain like a raging toothache. How long was it since he had slept? He tried but couldn't remember exactly. The man beside him stumbled, then caught himself — falling asleep on his feet. It would be sheer bliss to sink to the ground and rest. But he knew he couldn't.

This was the end, his brain told him, but his body didn't know it yet. It concentrated only on the next agonizing step, then the next. He must not fall behind. The strong swamp smell rose to his nostrils again and he knew they were still in the long marshy hollow through which the tiny Tchingul ran — hardly more than a creek even now in spring. And no cover around them. Where was the enemy? They couldn't be far behind. He tried desperately to concentrate through the steady throb in his thigh. What day was it today? Friday, Saturday? He'd been home from the front for a few blissful weeks with Katya, then they'd been called up again, Sergeant Sonntag's reserves in Halbstadt, to help cover the retreat from Blumental. How many days ago? Three, four? He wasn't sure.

Tiefenbrunn. The village below Blumental, facing the road north. That's where Sonntag had made them dig in to cover Corporal Wollrich's withdrawal from the front line. A staged withdrawal through the gap, Sonntag had explained. The attack began just after dusk. Mortar fire, machine guns on *tachankas,* cavalry everywhere. They had kept up a murderous fire from their trenches, which stopped the advance in front of them and drove the enemy back finally. But the enemy had come very close, close enough to reveal that they were shooting at men in regular uniforms — the Bolsheviks!

They barely had time to pull themselves together before the enemy was back. This time the attack was concentrated on their pathetically exposed flanks. If Sonntag had not ordered them to fall back, they would have been surrounded within minutes. They retreated towards the village in haste, not knowing how they would escape.

An old mine tunnel saved them. A friendly old man led them to the local brick works and showed them a tunnel that had been long since mined out for its clay. The tunnel led directly to the Tchingul valley below the village. They raced through the dark, clammy shaft not knowing whether they were headed for freedom or a trap at the other end. They emerged gasping from the running and the foul air and began quick marching south over the marshy fields. What bothered them most was that they had been forced to leave their dead and wounded behind. He didn't know how many casualties there had been, but he had seen enough of them to know they were heavy.

They had moved straight through Walldorf, the next village, where Corporal Wollrich and his men were dug in to cover them. They had marched — stumbled along, more accurately — through the rest of the night. Now it was daylight and they were past the two Russian villages that lay before Prischib and Halbstadt. Corporal Wollrich, on horseback, had already caught up with them. His men, a little fresher than Sonntag's, were still behind them but also catching up. They had broken off contact with the enemy, but knew it wouldn't be for long. To make things worse, it had started to rain just as dawn broke, a steady, penetrating drizzle.

"Halt, men," Sonntag bawled suddenly, "and gather round." They shuffled together awkwardly and stood squinting through the gray rain at a stern-looking officer facing them on horseback, water trickling down his long army mantle. This had to be von Homeyer, the German officer who had taken over. Wilhelm had seen him from a distance at Blumental.

The Lieutenant was brief and to the point. "This is it, lads. When you get up there on the ridge" — he twisted in the saddle and pointed towards the Colonists Hill — "you dig in. From up there you'll be able to see down along the valley behind you and cover the Russian village on your left. By with-

drawing you've closed the hole between your front and the Prischibers,' "
His voice went even harder. "Now we have to get the civilian population
out — your families — you know that. Just remember one thing: every hour
counts now. The longer you can hold out here the better their chances of
getting away safely. For you there's only one more stop — Halbstadt. From
there you're on your own. Your job will finish here. So, good luck, boys;
stand fast up there as long as you can. God be with you."

Then he turned and rode back towards the settlement, his aide beside
him. Sonntag gave the order to march and they started up towards the
ridge. There they would try to find enough strength to dig the holes that
Wilhelm fervently hoped would not prove to be their graves.

Leaning heavily on the stick he had picked up a few miles back, he
dragged along as fast as his almost useless leg would let him. Oblivious to
pain and fatigue, he just wanted to get to Blumenau before Katya and her
parents were gone. He knew Katya would wait for him as long as she could.
If he could only avoid capture till he had seen her he didn't care what
happened after that. He had long since ripped the black and white Self-
Defense band off his arm and he couldn't even remember where or when
he'd abandoned his rifle.

He didn't remember much of anything that had happened since they'd
dug in up there on the bluff above Halbstadt. Confused images and impressions jostled each other in his fevered brain, but he had lost grip on time
and sequence. He recalled the exposed terror he had felt as he lay in his
absurdly shallow position, with the Reds coming at them firing and
shouting. They had fired back frantically until their ammo ran low — he
didn't even want to think about that — and then Sonntag had given the
order to move down from the ridge and make the descent to Prischib and
Halbstadt.

After that, events blurred in his mind. He couldn't remember how he'd
made it down the Hill, but he knew he'd been hoisted up to the back of a
horse behind the rider — somewhere — with shots whistling around them.
Then he had found himself in Neu-Halbstadt, on the street in front of his old
school, with people walking and loaded wagons everywhere heading
south. He had joined the rout, keeping cautiously to the very edge of the
road for fear of getting jostled or falling under a team of horses. But his pace
had become agonizingly slow. He couldn't even keep up with the women
and children anymore. South, always south. Please Katya wait for me. I'm
coming . . . .

When he got to Muntau he knew he was about finished. And he still had
two miles to go. And then, as he was about to sink down in utter exhaustion,
a wagon stopped beside him and a familiar voice urged him to climb up on
the box. But he could only stare up helplessly at the driver, whom he
recognized as Jils Friesen from Fischau. Friesen had to get down and boost

him up, his bad leg dangling like a piece of rope. And he was so weak and dizzy sitting there on the box that Friesen had to hold his arm with one hand while driving so he wouldn't fall off.

And then they were in Blumenau at last and he half slid, half fell off the wagon in front of the Fast *hof*. It was still raining and he slipped and slithered in the mud on the driveway, but he was aware only of the fire in his breast, his panic that Katya would be gone.

"Katya, Katya, I'm here, I'm back," he shouted hoarsely from the big brick gateway.

A droshky was being loaded at the front door. Katya, just coming out of the house with her arms full, heard him and gave a joyful cry. She dropped her box and ran to meet him.

"Oh, darling, darling, you're here — and just in time. We were about to leave." She flung her arms around him and squeezed him so hard she overbalanced him in his weakness and with desperate strength had to pull him erect.

"Katya, dearest Katya," he whispered brokenly and buried his face in the fragrance of her hair.

His parents met him at the door, vastly relieved to see him safely at home. And Lenchen clung to her exhausted brother until Katya gently pried her loose. Katya's parents, the Loewens, were there too, dressed for travel. They were about to leave for the Crimea with their daughter. They would go in the droshky as far as Melitopol and take the train the rest of the way. Father and Mother Fast, however, had decided to stay in their house. Gerhard Fast, his bull-dog body limp and wasted, was not well enough with his weak heart to make the long journey. Mother Fast said she was not afraid to stay behind as long as they had Old Anton in the barn to do the chores and God to protect them from the Reds. She would not allow Lenchen to stay, though. Greta and her husband Waldemar Barg from Halbstadt would be stopping for her on their way south.

Wilhelm slumped down wearily at the kitchen table, glad to rest his overstrained leg at last. Mechanically, he began to eat the cold fried sausage and boiled potato Katya set down before him.

Her dark eyes bright with concern and love, she sat down beside him. "I packed things for you too, Willie, hoping against hope you'd be here in time. If not, I was going to leave word for you." She squeezed his arm. "Now I don't have to. You're here." She turned to her father happily. "Papa, now we have another driver. You won't have to do it all yourself."

Wilhelm groped for Katya's hand, not trusting himself to look at her. "Katya, darling, I'm sorry but I can't go with you. Please try to understand. It would be too dangerous. The enemy is right behind us. They'll be rounding up all the Self-Defensers they can find. And the road south to Melitopol is where they'll look first — that and the houses here."

He saw the shock on her face. "Oh my God, Willie, I can't bear to leave

without you. Not now, after seeing you again; and you with your poor leg."
She rose and threw her arms around him. "You must come, my darling.
What will you do? Where can you go? Oh my God, my God." She was
weeping as she buried her face in his hair.

He kept his head down, his voice a harsh whisper. "I'm going to head
southeast to Mariental at the other end of the colony. Maybe I can rest up
for a day or two there. Then I'll go south, perhaps to Berdjansk where the
Whites are still in control." He looked up at her agonized face, trying to
transmit a hope he hardly felt. "Please don't worry, my dearest, I'll find you.
You'll be at the Goerzs in Spat. I promise I'll be there with you long before
our son arrives." He forced a smile and patted her rounding belly. She was
nearing the end of her fifth month.

They were startled by a loud knock on the kitchen door connecting with
the barn. The door opened and Hans Goossen from down the street came
in. Young Hans was also in the First Halbstadt and had been in the retreat
from Blumental. He was no longer wearing his black commerce school
uniform. Wilhelm had not seen him since they came down from the Hill.

"Sorry to butt in, folks," Hans said, urgency in his voice, "But Willie,
there's no time to lose. I knew you were here. I've got a horse for you. Your
leg was giving you trouble I noticed, and I thought" — he looked across the
room at Lenchen Fast and blushed — "I thought you might want to come
with me and a few of the other boys — Enns, Koop, Andries, and Hans
Reimer are coming too. We thought we'd head for Mariental first." He
stopped, looking for Wilhelm's approval.

Wilhelm felt a relief so great he dared not show it in front of Katya. He
had not allowed himself to think of how he was going to get to Mariental
alone on foot, across country, avoiding roads. Even riding would be hard on
his leg, but he suddenly realized he would never have made it by himself.

It was time to go. He embraced his ailing father and wondered if he
would ever see him again. His mother tried to be stoical, but broke down.

At the door Katya clung to him with such silent desperation that his
resolve almost snapped.

"Oh, Willie, Willie, must you go?" she sobbed piteously and pressed her
face to his again and again.

Gently, he removed her arms and whispered, "Katya, I love you, I love
you; I don't want to go, but I have to. I want to stay alive Katya, for you and
the baby. *Aufwiedersehn, liebchen.* In Spat."

He turned, desolated, from his weeping, clinging wife and closed the
kitchen door behind him.

3

Normally a placid, patient man, Jacob Loewen was becoming more impatient and irritated by the minute. And it wasn't just the drizzle that was
soaking him, exposed as he was on the coachman's box of the droshky. At

least the two women behind him were sitting dry under the makeshift canvas top. It was now late afternoon, hours since they had left Blumenau and they weren't even up to Lichtenau, the third village south.

The rain that had started up again last night had continued all day and the ruts in the crowded, churned-up road were becoming deeper and more treacherous. The heavy Molochnaya mud clung to the wheels stubbornly. Even the mud doesn't want us to leave, he thought wryly. Even worse than the mud was the wheel-to-wheel traffic. This main road south was clogged with wagons of all kinds, most of them badly overloaded, and with walking refugees, including whole families with little children, slogging through the mud on the shoulders. At the rate this mob of refugees and mired vehicles was traveling it would take the rest of the day and all night to cover the twenty miles to Melitopol. And there was simply no way he could go any faster, even though he was driving a light droshky with a pair of fast young horses, compared with the heavy, lumbering farm wagons all around him. That was the trouble. There was just no room to pass anybody. All the traffic was going one way — south — and the wagons, horses and people covered the entire road in one densely packed, heaving mass.

Loewen's fear, a fear he did not want to alarm his women with, was that they would get to Melitopol too late. He had heard that the rail line going south might be cut by the Bolsheviks at any time, might already be cut as was the northern half going to Alexandrovsk. And what would they do then? He had some money, but precious little else. He had decided they should travel light so as to get to Melitopol quickly and then take the train to Spat. But he had not anticipated these terrible conditions, and he was getting worried. Clearly it had been a mistake to choose Melitopol when so many others had chosen the same destination.

An idea struck him. He could still rectify his mistake. When they reached Lichtenau he could turn off the main road and go east to Ohrloff instead. From there they could go up to Blumenort then take the road straight east to Kleefeld. They could overnight at his friend Wilhelm Klassen there and tomorrow drive through the southern line of villages all the way to Mariental. Of course, to Mariental! He also knew people there who would be glad to put them up. And hadn't Wilhelm said he was heading for Mariental and that he might rest up there for a day or two? Yes, with any luck at all they would see Wilhelm again by tomorrow afternoon. And they would be away from all this snail-slow traffic. He felt better already. And Mama and Katya would be overjoyed at the change in plans. They could stay in Mariental until things had settled down and then they could decide whether to go back to Blumenau or on to the Crimea. A good plan. Yes, it would do nicely.

He glanced over his shoulder at his two women huddled together under the canvas top. "Mutti, I have come to a decision, a change in plans. Katya, it will chase the sadness from your face when I tell you."

4

Halbstadt-Molochansk, March 10, 1919

General Ivan Serifimovich Dobenko, commander of the 42nd Division, Red Army, had a fearsome temper which the powers and responsibilities that came with military command had only made worse. And nothing set his temper on edge more quickly than dealing with two-faced civilian officials. He looked with undisguised contempt at the two Mennonites standing before him in the *volost* office: one tall, gaunt, and a bit smug-looking; the other short and thick with a bluff, hearty face that looked respectful but composed. He could guess that these two were here to beg for their damned treasonous soldiers and turncoat *njemtsi* people. This wasn't even his job. Malarenko, that slimy serpent, should be doing this. He was the political commissar attached to the division. But the bastard had stayed behind in Tokmak.

"General Dobenko, *prostite nas, prostite nas,* forgive us, forgive us, but we —" the beanpole started, but Dobenko heard no more as he erupted.

"Forgive you, forgive you, you damned apostates from your fathers' faith? Why should I forgive you? I know about you, you miserable hypocrites you. You couldn't take up arms for your own country — oh no, but for your bloody Kaiser Wilhelm —"

"*Gospodin* Dobenko, we beg you to understand" — the tall one had the gall to interrupt him —" our plight. Yes, you are right, we have sinned. We have relied on our fleshly arms to protect our lives and hearths. We should have put our trust completely in God, but —"

"But," Dobenko overrode Lepp angrily, "you couldn't wait for your German God to save your precious farms, you miserable apostates. The farms given to you by a German empress who was a foreigner on Russian soil too. Now that we Russians are trying to build a new and better society you shoot at us, your own countrymen."

The fat one had been clearing his throat nervously, waiting to speak. "General Dobenko," he began mildly but firmly, "we don't want to argue with you. We only wish, respectfully, to explain to you that our Self-Defense was never meant to be a counter-revolutionary force —"

"Tell that to my dead lads shot by your so-called pacifists. In open combat your damned Self-Defense opposed the forces of the legally constituted government of this country. And for what? To help those triple-damned *burzhuj* Kadets and Whites. Damned traitors that you are." He tried to stare down the fat one, who looked determined, but not self-righteous like the other one.

The fat one took a paper out of his coat pocket. "General, I have here —with your permission — a declaration signed last December by the leaders in Menno Centre as well as by Colonel Malakov, commandant of the White Army in this district. May I read it to you?"

Dobenko's anger subsided as the man spoke. At least this one had the sense to get down to business and not just whine and make excuses. He nodded and the fat one — Unruh was his name? — read his declaration.

"We, the Mennonites of the Halbstadt and Gnadenfeld *volosts,* have organized an armed Self-Defense during this period of violence, robbery, and molestation against us by lawless, roving bands. Our Self-Defense is not a military organization designed to wage war or counter-revolution, but merely a police force designed to protect our lives and possessions. We Mennonites have no revolutionary designs and do not wish to exercise either political or military power. As soon as a stable government emerges in Russia, we solemnly declare that regardless of its political persuasion we shall lay down our arms and submit to that government peacefully and gratefully as we always have in the past."

Dobenko, listening carefully, felt his gorge rising again. "So, you call it a police force. And does a police force take the field against the army of its own country?" He glared at them accusingly.

"But with all respect" — Unruh again — "we didn't know we were facing your army until it was too late. We thought only of Makhno and his brigands. We regret that mistake more than we can say."

"And do you also regret becoming part of the army of traitors and murderers who call themselves the Volunteers?"

"Excuse me, General, but our declaration was specifically drawn up to prove that we were not allowing ourselves to be absorbed into the White Army." Unruh shot a shrewd glance at him. "Though I confess we have, perhaps rashly, accepted their assistance at times just as you have accepted Makhno's help."

It was a bold thrust, but Dobenko now had himself under control and contented himself with sarcasm. "We use Makhno when it suits us, you allowed yourselves to be used by the Kadets when it suited them — that's the difference."

He could tell the two were studying him closely, more hopeful now that he had calmed down that they would be able to negotiate with him. *Khorosho.* He would listen, but they would not get off as lightly as they hoped.

He was brusque. "All right, state what you came for. I'm pressed for time."

Unruh again. "With respect, General Dobenko, we have been delegated to ask you to show mercy on two points. Firstly, that our young men who served in the Self-Defense, many of them mere students, will not be arrested and punished for doing what they were asked to do, namely, to protect their homes and loved ones. Secondly, that you give us your word that our people in general will be protected from looting and reprisals, especially from the Makhnovites." Direct and to the point, this rosy cherub.

Dobenko waited for the beanpole to add his two kopeks. "We admit, sir, that from your point of view it's probably more than we deserve." The deep eyes looked guileless. "But there is One — a Higher Authority — who judges human motives and actions more justly than we humans can. And in His eyes we trust we can be forgiven for our well-meant transgression against earthly authority."

Dobenko studied the man contemptuously. Oh no, my pious friend, he thought, you won't squirm out of it as easily as that. Oh no.

He snapped out his answer. "Both requests granted conditionally, subject to Commissar Malarenko's approval. You'll have to present your petition to him in Tokmak." He savored the moment. "These are the conditions. All weapons and ammunition — and I mean *all* — are to be collected and surrendered to me in three days. Understood? Also, I will allow my men three days in which to collect a few things for themselves as compensation for the tough campaign they have gone through thanks to you. Do I make myself clear? Oh, and one other thing. During those three days my men will also have the right to arrest and execute any Self-Defense men who may fall into their hands."

Erdmann Lepp and B. H. Unruh left the General's office with heavy hearts, but knew they had done the best they could. They had not expected more. Had, in fact, braced themselves for less.

5
Molochnaya, March 10, 1919

The scar was in the center of his left palm and shaped like a many-pointed white star where the skin puckered around the wound when it healed. Nikolai often looked at it. He was fascinated by it, found it rather pretty, and was beginning to think of it as a kind of personal good-luck charm, like an amulet or a rabbit's foot. Tchus had his Caucasian dagger, he had his star. Better a hole through his hand than his head, he liked to remind himself. The shoulder he had at first feared broken had only been badly bruised. It also had healed quickly and he had been back in action for over a month now.

They were finally in the Molochnaya. He had to admit that those Mennonite and Lutheran bastards had put up a tough fight. He had never expected them to be that stubborn. And *Batko* hadn't either. Since coming back here from the east a week ago he had become so furious at the spirited resistance and the counter-attacks around Blumental that he had sworn to kill every Self-Defense pig personally once they had cornered the cocky buggers. Nikolai wasn't sure they would have beaten these German farm boys even now if the Reds hadn't helped them. Where did those Mennonite boys learn to shoot like that with their old rifles, and almost no machine guns to help them?

He couldn't help feeling nervous here in the Molochnaya. Sooner or later he expected someone to recognize him. This afternoon they had ridden through Blumenau, at a brisk trot fortunately. He had made sure he was in the middle of the pack where no one could spot him. Not that there were people on the street in any case. He had not been able to resist looking at the old Fast *hof* as they rode by, but had seen no signs of life at all. Seeing it again, he had to admit, did give him a bit of a turn. That and some of the other village landmarks he knew so well.

After sweeping down the Colonists Hill on the heels of the retreating Molochnaya defenders, they had ridden through Halbstadt without stopping and headed south. As always, *Batko* was thinking ahead. He guessed that the area around Halbstadt and Gnadenfeld would be tightly controlled by Dobenko and Malarenko. "But we'll fool the bastards," *Batko* said with a bright smile. "We'll head southeast to the other side of the settlement. There won't be any Reds down there for a few days at least. And there are some nice fat villages there waiting to be plucked."

They had left the main road on the other side of Blumenau and struck off across country in the gray drizzle. *Batko* said he was damn-well tired of being slowed down by refugee wagons full of scared Mennonite sheep and their fat wives. They had routinely relieved some of the dumb sheep of their watches and money, but Makhno was impatient to put distance between himself and his allies, the Reds. They smelled too much of the city, he said, just like the Kadets.

But the rain-sodden countryside had made for tough going too, even the meadowland. Then they had struck the road to Tiegerweide which though muddy afforded a more solid footing for their tired horses. By the time they reached the narrow Juschanlee River and Tiegerweide it was late afternoon. Batko decided it was time to stop for some grub and rest the horses. They clattered over the little wooden bridge on the outskirts of Tiegerweide and picked out some likely looking houses.

Now it was early evening and they were cantering along the broad old post road going south. The drizzle had finally stopped and the men were in a good mood after a big Mennonite dinner in a large, comfortable farmstead with the family, eyes big with fear, watching them in stiff silence. Some of the men had dug *samogon* bottles out of their saddlebags and were singing lustily as the horses sloshed through the muck.

Just beyond where the crossroad from the west met the post road they came upon a droshky abandoned by the side of the road. The one remaining horse was lying on its side, still in its traces, in a pool of blood, not quite dead. In the fading light they stopped to take a closer look. A man's body was crumpled against the front wheel, probably shot down from the coachman's box. An elderly woman was sitting in the back seat, her head back as though asleep. Her face was unmarked, but her eyes were open behind little wire-rimmed glasses. Lying on the road behind the wagon they found a third figure: a young woman on her back with legs sprawled apart and exposed right up to the gentle mound of her belly. She had been raped, obviously, and her throat was cut.

Makhno stopped beside the dead man, a strange expression on his face. Finally he dismounted and bent over the man, examining his blood-stained face. "The big Loewen — papasha," he muttered and glanced up at the woman in the back seat. "And the mamasha too." There was fright in his eyes as he turned to the body on the road.

His hoarse cry startled Nikolai and the other men. The cry keened into a long wail, a wolf's howl. "Katya, Katyaaa, Katyaaaaah —" on and on, and then he fell to his knees in the mud and scrabbled and pawed at the woman's clothes as though demented, pulling them down over her exposed flesh, muttering incoherently, smoothing and patting her skirts into place.

Nikolai's blood ran cold as he watched *Batko* in his crazed grief. Who were these people and what did they mean to him? They must be Mennonites: they looked like Mennonites, were dressed like Mennonites. But then why was Makhno carrying on like this? Loewen, he said. Where would he have known them? And the dead girl, he was acting as if she belonged to him in some way. He had never mentioned having a Mennonite woman anywhere.

The men looked at each other in puzzled embarrassment.

But Makhno's furious grief was not spent. He staggered to his feet, glared around opening and closing his raised hands as if looking for someone to choke. Suddenly he became aware that loud, rasping breaths were still coming from the stricken horse. He rushed around the wagon, jerked out his sabre and stood for a moment looking down at the spasmodic equine belly. With a strange little squeal he plunged his sabre into it with both hands, viciously, like an angry child jabbing a spoon into a bowl of *kasha*. Then he drew his *nagan,* aimed carefully and shot out the dead horse's brain.

His storm of rage over, he returned to the young woman's body. He squatted down beside her, tears streaming down his cheeks. Then Nikolai observed him making a curious gesture. His hand moved absently down between his thighs and pressed against his groin. As though hugging his grief there, thought Nikolai.

CHAPTER TWENTY-FIVE

Blumenau, June 30, 1919

Wilhelm Fast sat at the old family table in the kitchen listening to his mother's delicately circumspect account of what had happened to his wife and her parents in March. Mama was trying to spare him the pain of grisly details. As they would have been graphically related to her. Many times. And she was right. He didn't want to know. Or rather, he knew them already. Knew them all. More than there ever could have been. As he had imagined them a thousand times since that day in Simferopol when he had started talking to a Self-Defenser who had still been at home in Kleefeld when it happened.

That was in April. A whole month and he had not known! His life had ended on that Molochnaya road with Katya's and he had not known. Had been waiting impatiently for their lives to be renewed again in the Crimea. And he had been so close when it happened — no more than fifteen miles down the road at Mariental, sleeping off his fatigue and resting his leg. Near Kleefeld, a little west of the village, Mathies, the Self-Defenser, had told him. Kleefeld? He couldn't comprehend that at first. Kleefeld was miles off the route to the Crimea. And then it came to him with a shock that stunned him. Katya and her parents, for whatever reason, had been on their way to Mariental to find him! And he had known nothing. Even as their bodies —no, even now he couldn't think of Katya as a lifeless body — were being taken back to Blumenau the next day for burial, he was already riding south with the other Self-Defense fugitives towards freedom.

Towards freedom, to join Katya and his soon-to-be son. In the welcoming springtime of a land as yet untouched by war they would be together again. Instead . . . .

With an effort he listened to his mother again. Poor Mama. She looked so worn and faded, so utterly lost and useless in her own spacious kitchen, her reason for living gone with Papa, who had died confused and uncomplaining only weeks after . . . .

"Just imagine, my dear boy," she related in her tired, plaintive voice, "they kept coming back to search for firearms and hidden gold and jewelery, they said, and Papa already too weak to walk out of the house by himself. At gunpoint they forced him to go with them behind the barn, in the orchard, the pig pen even — all over the *hof* — trying to force him to tell them where he had buried things that didn't exist." He noted that even the tears that wet her wan cheeks at the memory of her sick, abused husband looked old and feeble. "When he kept stumbling and falling they prodded him up roughly, pointed their guns at his head. Ach, dear Lord, it was pitiful to see. For Old Anton too. The third time they came he tried to tell them it was enough. But they just laughed and made him dance while they shot at his feet. When he finally fell down, one of them just shot him where he lay. I cried and cried and pleaded with them. And then at last they didn't come back anymore."

Wilhelm caressed the nodous veins on his mother's thin hand where it lay on her apron and mourned with her for Papa and Old Anton. Her gentle outflow of grief made a communion between them. He understood that she cherished him all the more intensely now as the last of the four men in her life. He knew that Kolya did not count. Though alive, he had forever forfeited his place as one of her men. And he himself had always been her favorite, the one to whom her sensitive nature turned in moments of introspection and reflection when her shy being uncurled like a fragile flower. She had always had ambitious but unspecified dreams for him, dreams that included and at the same time transcended her down-to-earth expectation that he would be the one, finally, to work and preserve the time-mellowed *wirtschaft* she loved so passionately.

That dream had been shattered by violence and death, trampled by the boots of barbarians. Seeing her favorite so unexpectedly today, had brought it all back to her again. Her losses, her never-to-be-retrieved losses. Her men. He wasn't sure she even noticed his White Army uniform. She saw only the last of her men, the only one left to whom she could pour out her grief-laden woman's heart.

He had told her that his visit would be brief. That he really shouldn't be here at all. That his unit could at any moment be ordered north to follow the retreating Reds. At least he had the consolation of knowing there was a man on the place again. Greta and her husband Waldemar, the young Halbstadter Wilhelm had befriended in Moscow during the war, had moved in after Papa's death. The Bargs and Lenchen had fled south in March but like most of the refugees had returned a few days later, just in time for Katya's funeral. Waldemar, who had refused to join the Self-Defense, was running the *wirtschaft* this summer. He had even put in a small crop, as much as conditions permitted. Lenchen too was still living at home. At the moment she was at the Goossens' down the street with her Hans, who served in the same White company as Wilhelm.

Hans and he had become close friends, he told his mother, in spite of the difference in age between them. For one thing, he owed his life to Hans. He would never have made it on his own in March. Not only had Hans supplied him with a horse for the escape, but had looked after him like a nursemaid until Wilhelm had recovered his strength and the use of his leg again. With four other Self-Defensers they had ridden from Mariental down to Berdjansk. But only for a few days. When it looked as if Berdjansk would fall to the Reds too, they had retreated with many other refugees westwards towards the isthmus at Perekop. They were careful to stay well south of Melitopol, though, which was already occupied by the Reds. On the road down to Perekop they joined up with a long, ragged cavalcade of refugees streaming down towards the Crimea.

Like the opening to a large, dark sack, Wilhelm had thought as they passed through Perekop. And how long before the Reds would pull tight the top of the sack and seal them up? For all his eagerness to be reunited with Katya, this southern paradise, now that he was in it, seemed more ominous to him than welcoming. The closer they got to the snow-capped mountains dark with pines and long, deep valleys that rimmed the bottom of the peninsula, the more shut in he felt. Nor was there much comfort in knowing that the one hole in the Crimean sack through which escape might be possible was in the southeast corner at Kerch, which only led to the wild fastnesses of the Caucasus.

But he would soon see Katya, and for the moment nothing else mattered. Still accompanied by his five friends, he went directly to Spat, to the Goerzs. But Katya and her parents were not yet there and the Goerzs had not heard from them. His keen disappointment turned to apprehension as he tried to imagine what might have happened to delay them. He knew they intended to take the train from Melitopol and had expected them to reach Spat long before he could. Now he was told that the train from Melitopol had stopped running a good ten days ago, about the time he had left home. His hope now was that they would come by road through Perekop as he himself had. But why was it taking them so long? Had something happened? As the days went by he began to think they must have changed their plans and gone back to Blumenau, as so many others had when they heard that it was relatively safe to do so. But then why hadn't they sent word to Spat somehow?

Hans and the others had gone on to Simferopol. After waiting anxiously at the Goerzs for two weeks he had become so restless and conscious of imposing on his wife's relatives that he had decided to follow his friends to Simferopol, but with the promise that he would maintain regular contact with the Goerzs.

And then one day in Simferopol he had struck up an acquaintance with the Self-Defenser from Kleefeld, who had innocently told him about Katya and her parents.

Crazed with grief, he had lost himself in the refugee-swollen city. For days he had wandered aimlessly, sometimes resting on a park bench, then stumbling on again. He confessed to his mother that he could still not recall those terrible days with any clarity. In his despair he had wandered into a tavern and ordered a bottle of vodka, which he proceeded to pour down his throat with the desperation of a man dying of thirst. It was the first time in his life he had tried to get drunk. But it had not worked. Unused to strong drink, he had made himself violently ill and had fallen asleep in an alley after heaving up the last drop of bile in his empty stomach.

Finally, weak from hunger and fatigue, he crawled back filthy and stinking to his friends, who had been scouring the city for him. Passively, he ate the food they set before him and then lay down to a long, fitful sleep. He did not tell his mother that before he had fallen asleep he had decided that he did not want to go on living.

Late the next morning he awoke with a raging headache only to find Hans and the others excitedly discussing a new development: Lieutenant von Homeyer, the officer who had engineered their withdrawal from Blumental, was here in Simferopol organizing a new unit of German and Mennonite colonists to be known as the Sharpshooters Brigade. For now the Brigade would be attached to the Whites and serve under White officers, but von Homeyer was privately assuring his recruits that he had something up his sleeve, a secret plan that would ensure the men's safety even when, as expected, the Reds took over the Crimea and pushed out the Whites.

Wilhelm had listened to all the talk and the new plans with deep-seated indifference, a weary lethargy of spirit. He consented to sign up with Homeyer's brigade along with his friends only because there was nothing else for him to do and he was afraid of being left alone again. But he had no enthusiasm for this new military project and told himself that if it came to more fighting he would just as soon stop a bullet as send one. He blurted this out to his mother before he could stop himself and felt guilty as he saw the pain in her face. What would she say if he told her about the man he had shot point-blank in Blumental, and possibly others?

But there hadn't been any fighting against the Reds then. Homeyer lived up to his word: he had a dramatic plan and it worked. Gambling that he could rely on the loyalty of his Russian-German troops (many of them Self-Defensers from the Molochnaya), von Homeyer staged a carefully timed command coup in which the White commanders were disarmed and escorted from the city. Already in possession of the military barracks in Simferopol, Homeyer and his 4,000 men took over control of the city and surrounding region and calmly waited for the Reds to arrive.

When they did Homeyer, in an even more desperate gamble, offered his brigade to them for continued garrison duty in Simferopol, with the request that the brigade be peacefully disbanded when no longer needed. The Bolsheviks accepted the offer, but only on condition that the Sharpshooters Brigade surrender all its weapons as soon as the city had been secured.

Once again he and his companions had been footloose without really being free. They did not want to join the Reds, nor did they have the slightest inclination to try crossing the line to the Kerch region where the Whites were said to be holing up. So they simply continued to mark time, homesick, bored, listless with inactivity, pooling what little money they had left for food now that they were deprived of their army rations again.

All that changed in early June when the Whites broke the Red line at Kerch and began pushing the Reds out of the Crimea. When the Whites reached Simferopol they began conscripting everyone on sight, particularly the former members of the Sharpshooters Brigade. He and Hans and the others had also been caught in the net. They were rudely interrupted at breakfast one morning by a White sergeant and two privates and forced to accompany them.

Wilhelm skipped over the rest — the sporadic fighting as they pushed the Reds across the semi-arid steppe in the northern half of the Crimea up towards Perekop. Mostly the retreating Bolsheviks avoided even rearguard action as they tried to get out of the Crimean sack as quickly as possible. The closer they got to the Molochnaya, he told her, the more their moods lifted. All six of them planned to defect from their units at the earliest opportunity to escape a military life they found ever more demoralizing and oppressive. In the meantime he would have to serve and hope for the best.

It was time for him to leave. "Mama," he said to the frail woman facing him, "you must be brave. You still have a life to lead. Papa would not have wanted you to give up after he was gone. Greta will have children, and Lenchen later, if Hans has anything to say about it." He saw she was too intent on him even to comprehend his little joke. "You will have many grandchildren to gladden your old age." He felt a sudden chill in his heart.

Her eyes were still on his. She was intent on reading him, whatever he felt inside. She did not need his words of comfort, did not even hear them, wanted only to hold his presence there before her. "And you, my dearest son, will you go on too in your sorrow and bitter disappointment? You are still young, Willie, you are the one whose heart must be comforted."

He rose to go, forced to stoop because she would not relinquish her grip on his hand. He pulled her up gently and they embraced, clinging to each other tightly, wordlessly.

CHAPTER TWENTY-SIX

1

April-September, 1919

Having helped General Dobenko push Deniken's Whites out of the Molochnaya and other southern regions, Makhno became the darling of the Bolshevik press. In the hyperbolic style of the day he was hailed as an intrepid military hero, a matchless peasant leader, and a true champion of the socialist cause. But relations between Makhno and the Reds began to deteriorate even as the tributes flowed. The Bolsheviks soon discovered that Makhno and his supporters were stubborn, independent-minded *khokhols* who resisted all efforts to be absorbed into the Red Army or to allow the Cheka to infiltrate and control the villages in the area around Gulai Polye. Indeed "Makhnograd," as Gulai Polye was now often called, was becoming a centre for Anarchist activities and propaganda under the leadership of urban intellectuals like Makhno's old prison teacher Arshinov, and the writer Voline.

Towards the end of May, with Deniken already pushing northwards from the Caucasus, the Cheka tried to assassinate Makhno. The attempt failed because one of the two Cheka killers lost his nerve at the last moment and confessed the plot in Gulai Polye.

Once again Makhno was facing a perilous crisis. The Reds were withholding much-needed supplies and ammunition from him in what amounted to a blockade at the very time that the Whites were advancing towards Gulai Polye from the south. When Makhno tried to call another workers and peasants congress to consolidate his position, Trotsky himself sent an order from Kharkov forbidding the congress as illegal.

By early June the White Cossack army under Gerneral Shkuro was sweeping back Makhno's partisans. On June 6, Shkuro's Cossacks occupied Gulai Polye. Under pressure from the Reds, the beleaguered Makhno agreed to relinquish his command annd turn his troops over to them at Alexandrovsk. He himself, however, was not about to be caught in a Red trap. With his personal squadron of picked cavalry, he crossed the Dnieper and disappeared. He knew he had become *persona non grata* with the Red Army command.

The cunning steppe fox had again eluded the hunters. In revenge the Reds summarily executed the staff officers whom Makhno had left behind with his troops when he gave up his command. But as usual Makhno had no trouble attracting fresh fighting men in the villages through which he moved. As he retreated westward, he fought skirmishes with both the retreating Reds and the advancing Whites. In doing so, he picked up adherents among the disgruntled Red Army units, while systematically butchering White prisoners and taking their arms. Gradually, Makhno's Insurrectionary Army swelled its ranks with hordes of peasants from devastated villages as well as with several complete, well-armed Bolshevik regiments.

Thus began a slow, four-month retreat westward for Makhno's rag-tag army, his "kingdom on wheels," with its thousands of peasant families, including women and children, complete with livestock and belongings, in flight from their villages burned down by the advancing Whites where the job had not already been done by the retreating Reds. The summer of 1919 was a dry one even for the southern Ukraine and the ragged columns of soldiers, horses, wagons, people, and cattle moved along the dusty roads and across the wispy fields, stretched out for miles in a haze of dust-laden heat. When not fighting, the infantry, riding *tachankas,* led the march with the artillery bringing up the rear and the peasant wagons and supply vehicles in between. And always over the lead *tachanka* floated a huge black flag made from a priest's hassock with the slogan "Liberty or Death" and "Land to the Peasants" embroidered in silver on its respective sides.

Makhno now found himself in the province of Kherson, a region controlled by Grigoriev, his chief rival as a counter-revolutionary adventurer. His retreat impeded by Grigoriev's guerrilla forces, Makhno again concocted the kind of bold and brutally treacherous plan that never seemed to fail him in times of crisis. He invited the guerrilla chieftain to a parley of accommodation at his headquarters. After allowing the swaggering Grigoriev to harangue the insurgents assembled from both sides, Makhno coolly accused him of being an enemy of the people. "Scoundrels like you," he shouted, "are the shame of all Ukrainian freedom fighters: they can't be tolerated in the ranks of honest revolutionaries."

Grigoriev was vainglorious, but no fool. Wildly signaling his aides to do the same, he reached for his *nagan.* He was too late. Simon Karetnik's Colt was already blasting. Makhno screamed "Death to the Ataman" and pumped more shots into the collapsing chieftain. It took only seconds more to dispatch Grigoriev's horrified staff.

Makhno was elated. Not only had he rid himself of a long-hated rival, but had also provided himself with much-needed fresh troops and arms. Grigoriev's willing forces were immediately incorporated into the Insurgent Army.

Every man of them was desperately needed. Deniken's cavalry harassed Makhno relentlessly and more than once threatened to surround his unwieldy, swollen hordes completely. Only Makhno's superb special cavalry was able to stave off Deniken's mounted Cossacks in savage, close-in sabre combat. Through a cruelly parched August the Whites, always superior in numbers and weapons, pressed Makhno's army mercilessly. To make matters worse, Makhno had by now thousands of wounded soldiers, without medical aid, clogging the rear of his train.

His situation was again getting desperate. At the end of August he was forced out of Elisavetgrad northwest into the province of Kiev, controlled

386   My Harp is Turned to Mourning

by the Petlurists. Once again, Makhno had a potential enemy at his back with another facing him. In mid-September, in savage fighting for the city of Uman, Grishka, Makhno's brother and member of his staff, fell before White bullets. Makhno avenged himself by personally butchering all his captive White officers.

Makhno and his staff knew that time was running out for them. In a matter of days they would be completely encircled and then annihilated. But his uncanny sixth sense did not desert him. On September 25th a reconnaissance patrol intercepted a messenger from White headquarters. Makhno called together his War Council and calmly read them the message: "Makhno's bands are surrounded. They are completely demoralized, disorganized, starving, and without ammunition. I order that they be attacked and destroyed within three days. General Slaschoff, Commander-in-Chief."

His sensuous lips pursed thoughtfully, Makhno looked past the heads of his "Monks" at the scarlet disk of the setting sun. "We attack tonight," he said softly. "In force. This is it *bratsy*. We'll show the swine how demoralized and starved we are. The real war begins now."

An hour later, after sunset, Makhno's army, spearheaded by an advance guard, began moving back in an easterly direction straight towards Deniken's main forces. After a late evening skirmish with the Whites, Makhno's advance guard withdrew in the darkness.

In the middle of the night Makhno headed his main force towards the enemy just outside the village of Peregonovka. He knew the Whites would regard the earlier skirmish as a mere feint and assume that his main force was still retreating westward.

The Whites were taken totally by surprise. The fighting began around 3:30 a.m. and reached its peak at 8:00 a.m. in deadly streams of machine-gun fire on both sides. An hour later the outnumbered insurgents began to fall back on the village. The villagers came out to help them. There was no sign of Makhno and his special cavalry anywhere.

The moment was critical. The Makhnovites were now backing up into the streets of Peregonovka. The Whites were streaming in, Lewis guns chattering. Suddenly the Whites heard cavalry charging at their backs. Makhno had led his cavalry detachment through a deep ravine that skirted one side of the village and around to the Whites' rear.

The charge broke the ranks of the Whites. Makhno's men leaped forward for the hand-to-hand "hacking" they relished. The Whites' First Officers Regiment of Simferopol was made up of seasoned soldiers, but they had never met foes who fought with the desperate ferocity of these peasants. They gave way slowly, then more quickly, and finally fled towards the Sinuikha River nearby, where most of them were ruthlessly dispatched by Makhno's cavalry.

Makhno had, incredibly, broken through the Whites' encirclement. Like a whirlwind his advance army swept back into the native territory it had been forced to abandon months earlier. On the third day after the crucial battle, Makhno's forward troops took over the important Dnieper bridge that connected Einlage-Kitchkas with the city of Alexandrovsk. In the next two weeks the Makhnovites reoccupied most of the central Ukraine, including the Old Colony, the Molochnaya, and Gulai Polye. By October 20th Makhno had again captured Ekaterinoslav.

From near-catastrophe, Makhno had in one daring leap reached the zenith of his power.

2
Khortitza, Old Colony, September 23, 1919

Nikolai Fast, having pulled off his rancid boots, stretched out on the soft Mennonite bed and wiggled his toes in sheer contentment. He had a blissful feeling of unreality, could scarcely believe that he was getting a chance to rest up in this comfortable house in Khortitza, in a real bed, eating good food again, not living on his horse and sleeping only in snatches. Most of all, he had survived the long, hard summer's campaign, the scores of bloody battles, the unbelievably vicious hand-to-hand fighting without a scratch as a member of *Batko's* elite cavalry squadron. Not even a scratch. He held up his left hand and looked at his lucky star. God, he couldn't believe it. Here they were back in the Old Colony living off Mennonites again. Even in this house, the house of a teacher — Epp was his name? — they had found shelves of preserves and other foodstuffs in the basement pantry. And clothing! This Teacher Epp must be getting a good salary to have all this. They never saw the bastard. He got away. Somebody must have tipped him off. But the men gave his wife and grown daughters a good scare before letting them go. He chuckled as he recalled the scene in the living room last night. And that teacher — Neufeld — the snooty bastard, trying to play the protector to those Epp girls. What an ass! He was lucky the guys hadn't cut him to pieces.

Of course, without *Batko* they wouldn't have come through at all. He had created the miracle that saved them. All the same he was worried about Makhno. He had changed since last spring. And not for the better. Something very strange had happened to him when he found that dead woman on the road. Since then he'd been even tougher, harder, more ruthless than before. But also more erratic. He drank all the time now, and even if he didn't show the effects most of the time he often flew into terrible rages, became violent and obscenely abusive even to his closest comrades in arms, like Tchus and Karetnik and Foma Kozhin, not to mention himself. His blood still ran cold when he thought of what *Batko* did to those three peasants, the old man and his two sons, when he found out through his spies they were the ones who killed those people on the road after raping the young woman. In that deadly voice of his he ordered them to get down on their knees and plead for mercy — the old man was a bit stubborn on that point — and then stepped up to each of them in turn and solemnly, as though administering the sacrament, shot him in the mouth. Then, still showing no emotion, he took out his sabre and mutilated the three corpses in the same manner as he had the dying horse on the road.

One evening, relaxed with *samogon* around the campfire, he had asked *Batko* who those people really were. The sharp stare he got went through him like a sabre-thrust. "They were *Menniste* like you, Fast, but they were rich and respectable. And clean-living too. Too good for a hardened sinner like you. Real Mennonites, prayers and all. Not fallen off like you," he added with a short, mirthless laugh. Nikolai knew better than to pursue the subject. It wasn't his business anyway.

He had to admit though that in the field that summer *Batko* had been nothing less than superb. In a crisis he was calm and clear-headed, even when he had been drinking heavily. The men marvelled at his stamina and determination. He often drank instead of sleeping during their hard-pressed weeks out west and it only seemed to make him steadier, more alert. All summer he had slept only in winks, until his piercing, black-rimmed eyes made him look like an over-worked demon in hell. As their situation became more desperate, Makhno grew more relaxed, as though simply carrying out business as usual. He seemed to know, even without scouting reports, exactly where the enemy's strong and weak points were and how and where his own inferior forces could be most effectively used. They had all, even that serpent Tchus, come to believe that *Batko's* military sense was infallible.

That big battle at Peregonovka had been the most terrible experience of his life. He didn't want to remember how many men he had shot and hacked at during that confused nightmare. And when it was all over and he and the other survivors had ridden back to the village from the river, he had looked in dumb awe at the heaps of male bodies strewn for a mile and more along the road under a star-studded sky, distorted into grotesque shapes and positions, like a fantastic troupe of acrobats frozen in mid-performance, many undressed to their underwear, some completely naked, all covered with dust and blood and horribly mutilated.

Seeing that monstrous harvest of corpses, some of them his own comrades, had unnerved him even more than the battle itself.

Where was *Batko* leading them? Did he know himself? Dead men casually littering a roadway like discarded refuse. Even the *samogon* and women couldn't make you forget them. Nothing could. His eyes focused on a large, framed photo hanging on the wall above the bed. The three blonde Epp girls. Looking very handsome, very proper, very soulfully at the camera. *Batko's* clean-living, respectable *Menniste*. He could have had one like that, maybe. Willie would have one like that by now — yes, like that rich Bock girl, Well, if he married her after what had happened to her he was taking damaged goods, poor bugger. But then Willie would know how to keep up appearances. He'd always been good at that.

3
Feodorovka, Old Colony, October 25, 1919

Fuddled rage filled him as he stood spraddle-legged in the middle of the yard, messily bepissing himself. His ears rang dully with night silence and the *samogon* he had consumed. He tried to focus his eyes on the clear dark sky and the stars stuck close together like those shiny things on gypsy dancers' dresses. The effort made him stagger giddily and he felt something warm as he looked down and saw the mess he was making, dribbling down the front of the smart guards uniform he had put on for the party. He tried to steady himself, to keep from stumbling.

He forced his mind back to what Tchus and the others had just told him inside. His fury mounted. The rotten bastards. He'd show them, the cowardly cockroaches. They'd squeak! He swayed unsteadily. Shooting down good men, *njemtsi* serpents. With wet clumsy fingers he tried to button up. Looking down owlishy, he tried to concentrate. To hell with it! He tottered back to the house, feeling nauseous.

Inside, the hot, noisy din washed over him, made him even more confused and nauseous. Nobody was paying any attention to him. Mother of God, he'd make the bastards listen . He clawed for his *nagan,* waved it around, fired it into the ceiling.

Sudden silence. He grinned wickedly, advanced weaving into the room. The hard, flushed faces were turned to him now. They followed the shifting angles of his *nagan* warily.

"*Bratsy,"* he shouted angrily into the silence, "I've made my decision. *'Sobake sobatscha smertj,* A dog deserves a dog's death.' The *Germanzi tcherti* who shot the soviet in Dubovka yesterday — tomorrow we teach them a lesson." He glared balefully at them, his *nagan* carelessly held. "*Tarakani,* cockroaches, *tarakani,"* he spat at them in his rage, "tomorrow we squash them all, all the bastards sixteen and over — tomorrow, *proklatie njemtsi."* They stared at him as his frenzy climbed. *"Duraki,"* he screamed insanely, "what does the War Council say? Heh?" His wild sarcasm was hurled their way now. "Monk Nestor's Apostles — are you here *drusia,* my little friends? You agree? He aimed his pistol at the nearest man. "Brother, yes or no? Are you with me *durak* or do you need a little coaxing?"

"With you, with you, *Batko,"* Kolyada, member of the Council, answered quickly, keeping a nervous eye on the gun pointed at him.

But Makhno's drunken fury was not appeased. "Call yourselves officers and leaders, you lazy devils? You sit around squashing lice while good men are being murdered under your eyes. Do I have to make all the decisions around here myself? Because you idiots won't take any responsibility? Those three men should have been avenged before the sun went down.

Instead you do nothing, wait to tell me, *duraki* — swill *samogon* and stuff your yaps." He was swaying dangerously. "You're nothing but a rotten bunch of cow —" Makhno's eyes suddenly went blank and with a twisting motion he collapsed to the floor as though his bones were dissolving. His *nagan* went skittering across the floor.

Relief was palpable in the room as the men looked down at their leader sprawled in drunken stupor.

From the table where he was playing cards, Nikolai regarded the crumpled figure with a mixture of pity and distaste. The *Batko's* behavior was becoming alarming. Since they had come back from Ekaterinoslav a few days ago he'd done nothing but drink and abuse everybody. Yesterday he had gone after Tchus so brutally Nikolai was afraid the burly sailor was going to turn on him. Why? Was it just inactivity that made him this way? Or was something eating at him that nobody knew about? Now he was ordering another senseless slaughter of Mennonites because of what was bothering him. It wasn't the three guys killed in the soviet. Batko didn't care about those bastards. He didn't even know them. They were placed there by the Reds, for God's sake.

It just didn't make sense. He turned back to his card game with a feeling of cold futility in his gut.

4
Eichenfeld-Dubovka, near Old Colony,
Saturday, October 26, 1919

Erdmann Lepp surveyed with a full and thankful heart the devoted brothers and sisters seated around the breakfast table. Never had he felt more blessed, more fulfilled in doing the Lord's work than in these past four months of their new tent mission, a mission that had overflowed with an abundance of God's blessings. A rich harvest of souls gathered in the gospel-starved peasant villages to the north, in and around Paniutino where they made their summer headquarters. They had taken with them five large tents, a God-inspired gift from the Red Cross negotiated by Brother Priess, who seemed to know every Red Cross official in Moscow.

And the Lord had led them to recruit a wonderful team of spiritual workers — not one, but two sets of disciples, one male the other female, twenty-four in all. Only God's hand could have supplied them, this dedicated group of evangelists made up of Mennonites, Latvians, Russians, and even a converted Jewess, Sister Rosenberg. After receiving the blessing of the congregation at a special service of consecration in the Mennonite Brethern meetinghouse at Rueckenau in the Molochnaya, they had traveled north ablaze to start work in the Russian vineyard. In groups of four and five they had gone from village to village, setting up their tents (most Russian villages had no building suitable for public meetings except for a small, usually inadequate school house), holding services, counseling those who came forward, talking to people on the streets, visiting homes, and even dispensing homeopathic medicines where needed.

Lepp had never been happier in his life. The long years of official harassment, the frustration, and disappointment dropped away as though they had never been. This gloriously busy, intoxicating summer in the Lord's vineyard made up for everything he had ever been forced to endure or suffer in the service of the Lord Jesus Christ. And this was only the beginning. With a leap of joy in his soul he already saw a vision of the years ahead, the masses of human vines waiting for the water of life, the tender care of the Gardener and His helpers.

He still cherished his old dream of widening his ministry by means of that wonderful invention the motor car. The war was over, and once this terrible revolution had run its course surely peaceful, stable times would come again. This Armegeddon would be followed by the promised Messianic Kingdom, and the Lord's work would proceed without interruption, without let or hindrance for a thousand fruitful years. With no violence, no death to plunge unprepared souls into perdition. Yes, that was his greatest desire, that he would be able to carry his ministry as one of King Jesus' Righteous Ones right through the thousand-year Sabbath. Though Satan would no longer be there to tempt them, mortal beings would still be capable of sinfulness, would even then "have to choose between light and darkness and need to be reborn through faith in Jesus Christ." So he had expressed it in his prophetic book many years ago.

Mrs. Peters, the widow in whose house in Dubovka their team was staying, brought in a big platter of fried eggs and potatoes. A fine Christian woman, Mrs. Peters. She had assured them when they arrived that she was one of the few saved ones in this fallen-off Mennonite village. There had never been a revivalist campaign here before, she said, and the field was ripe.

He studied his co-workers as they ate and chatted quietly about their work. Always sedate and earnest, they struck him this morning as more reserved than usual. They had all been warned of the danger of traveling through the Makhno-occupied region of the Old Colony on their way back to the Molochnaya and winter quarters. But not for a moment had they considered changing their plans, he recalled proudly. All were ready and eager to make stops along the way, to work their way south in slow, carefully chosen stages.

This team was more precious than pearls to him and his heart embraced them all with a deep and abiding love: Jacob Priess, his loyal and indispensible assistant, always by his side ready for any job no matter how difficult or menial. Brother Jushkevich, a Latvian of soaring faith and sunny dispositon, in his youth a pipe organist good enough to go on concert tours. Sitting next to him was Regina Rosenberg, dark and aristocratic looking, but filled with a child-like zeal for her risen Christ. Sister Regina reminded him so often of Mathilde Glazonova. Next to her Sister Louisa Suckau from

Rueckenau, who had dedicated herself at an early age to the native ministry, as he himself had so long ago. And at the foot of the table sat Brother Golitzen, a small, dynamic Ukrainian peasant who had the most wonderful rapport with the villagers he knew so intimately.

They were still sitting over their *prips* going over their itinerary for the day when the door burst open and three wild-looking men stood there, weapons drawn. One of them, a Cossack-looking fellow, glared at them brazenly and demanded to know who they were.

"We're traveling evangelists here in God's service with the tent mission," Lepp answered calmly, refusing to quail before the man's crude hostility.

The Cossack looked at the remains of food on the table. "In that case you won't mind sharing your grub with us hungry sinners, preacher," and without hesitation the three brutes fetched chairs, squeezed in at the table, and demanded to be served.

Lepp was alarmed only enough not to want to lose control of the situation. He offered to say grace for the men but they paid no attention as they scraped clean the left-over plates and platters while waiting for Mrs. Peters to fry more eggs and potatoes.

The uninvited guests ate wolfishly amidst utter silence. Finished, the Cossack belched loudly and rolled himself a *poppeross*. He turned expansively to the young female evangelists and asked them to sing or play some dance music. The two looked over to Lepp for guidance. Suavely, he suggested they sing a gospel duet for the visitors. The girls rose in their places, moved together and began singing, somewhat quaveringly, "For God so loved us" in Russian.

They continued to sing with determined miens as more Makhnovites entered and formed a noisy crowd. Some of the men were making crude jokes and suggestions as they crowded around the singers. Lepp could feel the atmosphere getting tense. As the girls finished their second song he stepped forward decisively and cheerfully thanked them for their witness. Then he face the leering intruders as though addressing a congregation.

"Brothers," he began resonantly, "listen to me for a moment. I have a wonderful story to tell—"

"Save your stinking breath, preacher," the Cossack cut him off, "we know you *njemtsi* evangelists from away back. We didn't come here to be preached at by *burzhuy* whores like you. We're on important business, right *bratsy?*" He was supported by roars of derision from his comrades.

Lepp stood calmly waiting for the hubbub to subside, but they ignored him utterly as they began moving through the house looking for booty.

Before they left the Cossack, obviously in charge, stepped up to Lepp with *nagan* pointed for emphasis. "A friendly word of advice, pope. Stay right here in the house with your people. If you try to hold any meeting in this village today, we'll give you and yours safe conduct to your heaven with this." He patted his pistol. "We have a harvest of our own to bring in here today." With a ferocious grin he combed the muzzle of his *nagan* through one of Lepp's broad side-whiskers and told him again to stay put in the house for the rest of the day.

It was a threat that would go unheeded by Erdmann Lepp and his team. By noon the last of the looters had left the house, taking with them most of the Widow Peters' belongings and leaving her with a filthy mess. Lepp and the others tried to comfort the distraught woman and spent some time in prayer with her. Then Lepp, Jacob Priess, and the two young women set out for the local school house, where they had arranged to conduct a prayer session with the teachers and to speak and sing the gospel to the children. Brothers Jushkevich and Golitzen were to go to the tent to prepare for the evening meeting and to witness to people on the streets.

Twenty minutes later Lepp and Priess were down on their knees in the teachers' room praying with the two young male teachers; Sisters Suckau and Rosenberg were singing gospel hymns with the children in one of the two classrooms. Suddenly the devotions were interrupted by rough faces at the windows and loud banging at the door. For the second time that day the four evangelists were confronted by hostile, half-drunken ruffians who were clearly beyond any appeal to reason or mercy. Lepp sensed that this time they were in mortal peril, especiallly when he saw the Cossack who had warned him not to leave the house coming towards them. They barely managed to rise to their feet before one of the bandits started flailing at them with the flat of his sabre. One of the teachers, trying to protect himself by throwing up his arms, stumbled backwards over a large floor globe and collapsed on the floor. He had the sense to stay down.

"All right, you filthy priests," the Cossack roared, "I warned you. You still want to spread your rotten propaganda, so let's see your permit. If you haven't got that you're as good as dead."

Lepp promptly produced the authorization paper he had managed to get with considerable difficulty the day before.

The Cossack, taken by surprise, peered at the form uncertainly, turned it over, apparently looking for a signature or seal. The seconds went by. The more he stared at the paper the more ferocious his expression. "This shit is useless," he grated finally. "Not properly signed. I don't see *Batko* Makhno's name here. What are you trying to pull, you viper?"

Lepp grimly held his ground. "This is a valid permit to conduct meetings here in Dubovka. It was signed by the district soviet in Nikolaipol yesterday morning." He pointed at the signature on the bottom. "There, see, right there."

"Without *Batko* Makhno's signature this is worthless," the Cossack rapped out. He was sure of his ground now.

"Makhno?" Lepp was incredulous. "Makhno is not the legal authority here. He's —"

He got no further. With a roar the Cossack was on him, beating him against the wall with his fists, then grabbing him by the throat. "*Morda,* shut your yap, you cur, you holy bloodsucker, or I'll squeeze your windpipe shut. You deny Makhno's authority, *burzhuj?*" He gave the evangelist a vicious swipe across the face. "You're finished, *njemets.*" He released his grip on the shaken Lepp. "All right, you serpent, we'll give you a chance to tell *Batko* in person that he ain't the legal authority here." He looked around, winking at his men, who were enjoying the scene. "*Khorosho, bratsy,* let's take these cocky popes to *Batko.* Fedya and Sasha come with me. The rest of you know what to do with these other two bastards and *njemtsi* bitches in the other room."

His head throbbing and nerves thrumming from last night's revelry, Makhno sourly looked over the two *njemtsi* brought before him: one tall, skinny, with deep, fearless eyes, the other shorter, younger, but also with no fear in his eyes. Those calmly defiant faces scratched him into irascible impatience. The Cossack hadn't done his job. Makhno did not like prisoners brought to him still defiant, in command of themselves, and unmarked. Well, these two were not quite unmarked. The tall one had a bruised cheek and a smear of blood under his nose; the short one's face also looked a little kneaded. But not kneaded enough, these pigeons, not yet. He took a bracing swig from the bottle beside him on the table.

"So you're the son-of-a-whore who says Makhno doesn't have legal authority here?" he demanded bluntly of Lepp. "Take care how you answer, pope." Just talking made his head hammer harder.

"Legal authority is said to come from Moscow. Higher authority only from God," the scarecrow said in his clear preacher's voice.

His temples jumped wildly. He couldn't believe his ears. "You want to bandy words, you scum? Moscow? God? Your God is a bureaucrat like Lenin, only higher?" He laughed harshly, his throat on fire. "Even Lenin would howl over that one, *burzhuj.*" He took another long, noisy pull, trying to numb the pounding. The scarecrow was looking right at him with his burning eyes. He took another swig of *samogon,* trying to remember something.

But this scarecrow wouldn't shut up. His high voice came boring in again, like a steppe wind. "God will not be mocked, not by the godless Lenin, not by you, my friend. The Bible says 'He that leadeth into captivity shall go into captivity: he that killeth with the sword must be killed with the sword.' "

His rage now pounded at him like a heavy surf. His fingers itched for his *nagan.* He should blow this stinking old goat full of holes — like Grigoriev. Why didn't he? It was too easy. He wouldn't let this crazy *njemets* priest off that easy. He'd make him squirm first, scare the cocky look out of his eyes. Beat him at his own game — yes! Words? He'd give him words. Bible words too, the pious bastard.

"Now listen to me, preacher, you have the gall to condemn me from your

Bible? Well, I know some scripture too. And I didn't learn it from you *fromme Menniste* either. Where is that part about the rich getting what's coming to them, their flesh eaten by fire — the ones who kept wages back from their workers and lived in luxury, condemning the innocent and murdering them? Where are those words in your holy black book, pope? Where, where?" He was screeching his rage now, willing his bullet words to demolish this scrawny black scarecrow with the scalding eyes.

"Epistle of James, Chapter Five," Lepp answered quietly. "Yes, you're right, my friend, the selfish rich have much to answer for. Christian faith should live not only in the heart but in the hands and feet too. But there's another verse there you didn't mention. James also says 'any man who brings a sinner back from his crooked ways will be rescuing his soul from death . . . .' Are you ready to carry out that part too Nestor Ivanovich? With your swords and guns and brutal followers?"

The sarcasm bit into him like a lash. This long black devil wouldn't let go. He understood now. A fight to the death. He was locked in mortal combat with this, this *starets* — yes, that's what he was trying to remember. The long hair and sticking-out whiskers and voice sweet as a bell — like that old *starets* long ago in the village . . . . But he wouldn't be made to look stupid by this cunning pope, in front of his own men. He shot back fire, his mouth a sardonic slash.

"You want to talk revolution now, preacher? *Khorosho.* I'm an Anarchist. We have our bible too, holy man. '*Staroye rasrushim, novoye postroyem,* We destroy the old to build the new,' — that's the holy text for the revolutionary. Ask the Reds. But we Anarchists have our own prophets — Bakunin, Kropotkin, and the others. Bakunin is *my* God, Kropotkin my Christ. Have you ever heard of the *Revolutionary Catechism,* priest? That's *my* bible. You mock my weapons and tough riders. Let me tell you something. Bakunin teaches that the peasant-brigand is your only true revolutionary, *Mennist.* And the true revolutionary knows that your so-called civilization with its cities and governments and churches and *burzhuj* culture is nothing but exploitation based on greed and hypocrisy. All those fine buildings and smooth words and nice feelings are nothing but chains and prison cells to keep people from being free. Day and night, Bakunin preaches, the revolutionary 'must have one thought, one aim — merciless destruction.' We Anarchists have just one duty, to exterminate and destroy rotten filth like you and your civilized prisons and churches and mansions and governments in cities and towns. Our holy struggle uses every method — bullets, sabres, the rope, and the red cock. To clear the ground. To sanctify it for the people."

That should hold the snotty old bastard. He grinned in triumph, walked up to the scarecrow and gave one of his long sausage whiskers a non-too-gentle tug.

But this Mennonite serpent only stretched up taller, wouldn't admit defeat, did not even seem to notice the shame of having his beard pulled. "You consider yourself a true revolutionary," he shot back, "an Anarchist? You don't even begin to understand what revolution is — you and your Bakunin, whoever he is." Scorn flashed from his eyes like sparks from a pitch torch. "Revolution, my erring friend, has nothing to do with the things of this world, with destroying people and their paltry possessions. Destroy to clear the ground? For what? So you can erect more things for other people to use until somebody else — another so-called revolutionary — comes along and starts destroying all over again? No, that's just Satan's work to confound and confuse. That's not revolution at all. True revolution is of the spirit" — the high voice rushed like wind through tree-tops — "the living Christ is the only true revolutionary, the divine force that can transform people's lives forever."

He heard the words like fire and in his blood-shot mind saw again the ancient *starets* who had come to the village when he was a boy. An old, old man, dry as a stick, half-blind, skin like old oak bark: but his voice, Mother-of-God, his voice. Like melted honey, like a cathedral bell, then like a strong steppe wind, a rushing spring flood. A miracle, that voice coming from that smelly old shit-pile. He and the other boys had stared at the decayed apparition in fascination. The villagers had gathered around to hear the old man talk, to hear him prophesying the future of Holy Mother Russia. Bad times were coming, he said, violent times that would shake the steppe like a thousand *burans*. The mighty Dnieper would not be able to hold the torrents of blood. Evil men riding high on horseback would crush good men broken into the ground. All this would surely come unless all breathing souls repented. Repent, repent your sins, all Russia must repent its sins or die lost, he had wailed, lifting high his mighty voice and withered arms.

And though he was feeble and half-starved, not till he had washed them all in the flood of his words and blessed the awestruck peasants had he accepted food and drink. This scarecrow, this roaring fool with his bible verses and his warnings, could he be such a holy man too? Didn't he even care that with every hard word he was scooping deeper his own grave?

And still he went on, unafraid, confident, as though he was in charge here. "I say again, Nestor Ivanovich, there has only been one true revolutionary on this earth, and that is Jesus Christ, the life-giving Redeemer. And he said just the opposite of what you're saying. He said: 'When a man hits you on the cheek, offer him the other cheek too.' The doctrine of love — that's the only revolutionary doctrine that works, the only one with the power to transform individuals and societies alike."

Makhno's laugh came out as a fiendish giggle. "Well, well, preacher, so you're an expert on revolution too, are you? You know what true revolution is. You want me to turn my other cheek so my enemy can knock off my head." He stood before Lepp, almost dancing in his excitement. "Yes, my saint of meekness, that's revolutionary all right. That's so revolutionary it's too good for this sinful old earth. Priest, you are so insane with your twisted talk you should be shut up in a nut house. You're, you're like a rabid cur running around infecting everybody and not even caring what happens to him."

The rage in Makhno's eyes blazed as fiercely as the holy passion in Lepp's. "So you want to turn the other cheek, sweet Jesus? *Khorosho*. Here's your chance."

With a deft upward movement he slapped the side of Lepp's face so hard that he staggered and started to go down. But Makhno grabbed his arm, steadied him, and pulled him awkwardly back to his feet. His grin was ghastly. "Now turn the other cheek, preacher."

Head bowed, blood oozing from his nose again, Lepp slowly turned his face so as to expose his other cheek. He raised his eyes and stared into space.

For long moments Makhno stood facing his victim, stiffly, as though at attention, his hands clenched at his sides. Then his head jerked back abruptly and he spat wildly up at the exposed profile. The spray of spittle was lost in Lepp's dense side-whisker. He had not moved a muscle. He turned his head finally and looked fixedly at the smaller man. Then a deep, pent-up sound, half moan half snarl, parted his lips and his hands lifted slightly and curled into claws.

Startled, Makhno studied his antagonist. Something close to exhilaration shot through him. Suddenly he was released from all rage and passion. The passion of words. They had both fired off a whole arsenal. And neither had won. The words had settled nothing. This crazy *starets* seemed to know it too. They were both through with words now. He wants to attack me with his bare hands. I can feel it, Makhno thought. Eyes still locked with Lepp's, he took a step to the side, as though feinting. Lepp, too, moved sideways, still facing him. Heads forward, shoulders hunched, they began to circle each other warily, the tall, skinny man and his short, slim-hipped opponent, as though engaged in mortal combat.

Like two dogs at bay, looking for an opening, thought Nikolai Fast as he stood with the others watching this strange spectacle. He was astounded that *Batko* was still toying with this defiant preacher, that he had not yet stretched him dead or ordered Tchus to carve him up. Instead captor and prisoner were playing some sort of weird game he didn't understand but found deeply disturbing. First they had hurled angry arguments at each other, now they looked as if they wanted to kill each other with their bare hands. What was going on?

Nikolai had recognized the preacher Lepp instantly, but it had taken him a while to identify the younger pope as Willie's old school buddy Jacob Priess. He wasn't quite sure even now that it was Priess. Not that he was concerned either man would recognize him. Nor was he overly concerned with their fate. Let them get what was coming to them, the bastards. But the whole scene made him uneasy. Why didn't *Batko* get it over with? They had other things to take care of here. He knew what was happening at this very moment to the Mennonites in Dubovka. Why was Makhno making a fool of himself here and wasting time?

Makhno suddenly stopped circling, his eyes still on Lepp's face. "Tchus," he called sharply, "give him twenty and let him go."

For a moment there was dead silence. Tchus looked at his chief in disbelief, then for some sort of sign, at least a signal, of ironic amusement. Nikolai saw that Tchus simply couldn't believe that *Batko's* order was to be carried out literally. Whip this mad preacher and let him go? Tchus could only assume that the real command was to kill him, of course, to shoot him or cut him to pieces.

Already Tchus was snickering in anticipation. It would be a pleasure to shut this windy old shit up for good. He grabbed Lepp roughly, and reached for his sabre.

Makhno stopped him, eyes hard. "I said whip him and let him go, Tchus."

Tchus was dumbfounded. *"Batko,* I —"

"Do it," Makhno screamed and turned away.

For some reason Tchus turned and threw a murderous look at Nikolai, then led Lepp out with muttered curses.

Outside in the yard Lepp, at Tchus's command, stripped down to the waist without protest, then lowered himself to his knees, the knobby ridge of his backbone prominent on his narrow back as he bowed his head, his lips moving in prayer. He uttered no sound as Tchus's heavy *nagaika* hissed and bit again and again into his gray, shuddering flesh. The fiery hissing ended at last and Lepp remained kneeling on the ground, proudly erect, blood staining his shredded skin.

Makhno stepped forward, pulled him to his feet, not gently but not roughly either. He draped the minister's shirt and coat around his trembling shoulders and said, not unkindly, without a trace of his earlier rage, "Now go old shepherd, and tell your *njemtsi* sheep that you owe your life to *Batko* Makhno. The lashes are for your rash words and false accusations — and for something else. The mercy, the mercy is for you — and me . . . . Now get, before I change my mind."

Lepp, his face expressionless, looked at Makhno. "And my friend and co-worker in Christ, are you setting him free too?"

Makhno's boyish face was open, guileless. "For now we keep him. He'll follow you soon enough."

Hands holding his shirt and coat in place in the cold autumn air, Lepp staggered as he started walking but caught himself quickly. He limped stiffly towards the road. He did not look back.

Makhno, his eyes on the retreating figure of Erdmann Lepp, was aware of

Tchus at his side.

"Batko, I don't understand. That man is dangerous. His tongue is a machine gun."

"But his words don't kill, Fedya. They don't kill. Never mind. You don't have to understand. Yes, I've let the old fool go. But he won't be going very far or for very long. There's no need for me to kill him. Others will do that soon enough, soon enough." His eyes were still following Lepp.

When he turned to Tchus, the murderous rage was back. "But where's that other son-of-a-bitch? I want to see him cut to pieces bit by bit, Tchus. I want you to carve that *njemets* pope like a boiled chicken, slice by slice. And any others that old scarecrow had preaching with him in Dubovka. The boys should have finished crushing most of those cockroaches by now. We'll go take a look."

Nikolai Fast had also watched Erdmann Lepp limping away. He felt nothing for the man, not even relief that he had escaped with his life. In another existence this man had frightened him badly, a long time ago when he had talked about the end of the world and his missionary work. On that day the boy Kolya had been the angry, defiant one, and had paid for his defiance with the worst beating his father had ever given him. He had never forgotten or forgiven this Erdmann Lepp, so-called man of God.

But that had happened a long time ago. Now he felt nothing against this ghost out of the past, or for him. He felt nothing anymore. Not even for *Batko.* Two strong, stubborn men testing each other's wills. That was what he had just witnessed. That was what it came down to in the end, in spite of all the passionate and holy words. Lepp's Mennonite God was laughable. The man was brave, yes, but he was also a fool. But was Makhno's Anarchism any better? Words in the wind, both of them. They were just two animals in the end trying to defeat each other. But first to humiliate, to heap contempt on the other.

If there was nothing more, then he was free. Of it all.

Part IV
Let Others Weep: 1919-1924

CHAPTER TWENTY-SEVEN

1
Khortitza, Old Colony, December, 1919

Tired. To the very bone tired. Clara Bock pressed her finger tips to her temples in a vain attempt to squeeze out fatigue and depression. She was alone in the small room off the main hallway where no one could see her weakness. She was glad she had closed the door. They mustn't see her like this, trembling with exhaustion. They all depended on her strength, the scores of burning typhus patients and the three orderlies — frightened high school boys who had been conscripted by the Makhnovites and herself to help tend the sick soldiers. It was pathetic the way they all depended on her, to the last man. She, the only woman here, was supposed to be the strong one. But they didn't know how close to the edge she was herself. At times she felt more like a patient than a nurse as time and place kept shifting away from her, confusing her, making her forget what she was to do next, or even what she was doing at the moment.

She raised her head abruptly, flattened her lips in determination. She refused to give in to the clamor of her mind and body. Human beings were dying all around her. She was powerless to prevent that. Her job was to be there, to help ease their stupefying pain, to comfort them in their terrible passage. And to minister to those who did survive.

She stared around the room, bare of everything except the battered little desk beside her and the chair she was sitting on. In one corner there was also some straw on the floor with a tattered old blanket over it that she and the orderlies took turns to catch some sleep on at night. Every second or third night she went to a friend's house for a fuller night's rest. How different from the old days when this had been the teachers' room, the inner sanctum which students rarely got to see. She tried to imagine it with her old teachers in it. How it must have rung with their bright female chatter. And the one male teacher in the school: dear, gentle old Mr. Klassen — Jacob Abramovich. How the girls had loved him for his courtly manners, his fine, melancholy eyes, his pink poet's face, and immaculately trimmed white van dyke. The school building itself had been almost new when she started in the fall of '06, and she had spent four delightful years here.

She had loved everything about the Khortitza Girls School: the demure order of the place, the precise classroom routine, and yet the wonderful new sense of freedom she had experienced in living away from home, at least from Monday to Friday each week. And getting to know a hundred other girls from all over the colony, all as excited and eager to launch their young lives here as she was. She had even loved the simple but smart school uniform, a gray-blue skirt with white stripes for summer and a green and blue woollen plaid for winter. Black pinafores and capes for weekdays, white ones for Sunday, completed the costume worn by students at all times. In class she had stoically endured arithmetic and science, loved German and religion from Mr. Klassen, adored the singing and music with effervescent Miss Gloekler, but positively hated needlework with fussy "Miss Kornelia," as Miss Thiessen insisted on being called.

And the *vechera,* dear God what pure enchantment the *vechera* had been, those special evening programs of musical and theatrical entertainments given in the spacious assembly hall upstairs several times a year. She had always been asked to sing one or more solos at the musical concerts, and in her junior year she had won the lead role in a one-act play. From time to time there were also plays put on by the boys from the Central School across the street or by older students from the Pedagogical Institute up the street. The girls would giggle with delight whenever they heard that the boys from the two other schools vied for tickets to the girls' concerts.

During the school week Clara had boarded with the Wallmanns in their big "castle" up on the hill behind the school. Mr. Andreas Wallmann Senior of the Lepp and Wallmann firm was an old friend and associate of her father. Her father had worked for Lepp and Wallmann for many years before establishing his own farm implement factory, and the old gentleman often came to visit them in Schoenwiese. Mr. Andreas Wallmann Junior ran the original factory in Khortitza while his father spent most of his time at the other Lepp and Wallmann factory in Schoenwiese. Young Mr. Wallmann was newly married the first year Clara had stayed in the red stone mansion.

Helene, his bride, was the most beautiful woman Clara, at the age of twelve, had ever seen. She had large, lustrous brown eyes, rich masses of deep auburn hair, and the long, elegant neck that Clara passionately coveted for her own coming womanhood. Just like the Empress's in the portrait of her that hung in their classroom. Clara worshipped Helene openly but mutely, struck shy and awkward in her dazzling presence. Without being asked she would do little favors and tasks for Helene, not realizing until years later what a nuisance she must have been and how funny Helene must have found her solemn, graceless adoration.

In the evenings Clara liked to look up from her homework in her third-story room and gaze down at the backyard of her beloved school. Looking at the neatly kept playground and the back of the school made her feel she was in touch with her school even after school hours. It was her favorite view. The front end of the school, facing the main street, had a splendid facade and main entrance, but they were more formal, like a parlor kept for special occasions. The back was homey, like a kitchen, where you felt at ease under the young acacias and protected on the street side by the trim brick house in which two of the teachers lived. Beyond the school, across the main road, bulked the square, blunt facade of Dyck's flour mill and beyond that, shimmering whitely on a rise at the edge of town, the graceful blue-onion-domed Orthodox church which Mennonite factory owners had years ago built for their Russian workers.

With a start she came back to herself and her fatigue, the dull ache of her body, her head threatening to spin out of control again, as it had in that spaceless void she now thought of as her "illness" at Bethania last year. She could face getting typhus, but the very possibility of those cruel black wings flapping through her brain again filled her with terror. It had taken her most of the summer to recover fully, and by that time she realized she had developed a deep attachment to Bethania and its staff and that she had no inclination to leave.

And where could she have gone? Her whole family was dead; she no longer had even a home. The family mansion in Schoenwiese, she had been told, had been looted and later commandeered by the Reds — or was it the Whites? — along with the factory. She had gone back to the house once while the German occupation troops were still in control, but she had found nothing but wanton destruction and emptiness. Her personal possessions had all been stolen and the desecrated house aroused such revulsion in her that she knew she would never go back. She didn't know what had happened to Selenaya. And she didn't care. She never wanted to see that place again — ever!

And so she had begun to work at Bethania as a volunteer nurse. At first she had only helped out, under the stern scrutiny of Miss Koop the head nurse, but to her pleasant surprise she discovered that she had a natural aptitude for working with mental patients. She found she was able to soothe and pacify some of the worst cases, the patients with whom other nurses could do nothing. She talked to them gently and sang to them until they were tranquil. Her friend Gretchen Klassen, the chubby young nurse who had been so good to her during her own dark time, said it was a gift from God and that she had been led in this way to discover and use it. Dr. Thiessen encouraged her too. And she in turn had worshipped the handsome young doctor. For the first time in her life she felt fulfilled, needed, even though the patients were difficult to handle at the best of times and sometimes so unruly that she feared for her nerves. But on the whole she was at peace with herself and wanted nothing more than to stay and work at Bethania.

Until Makhno's hordes had suddenly struck the Old Colony in late September like fiends from hell. She happened to be in Khortitza that weekend visiting Helene Wallmann and other old friends. Like wild Tatars the terrorists overran the town and district, looting, plundering and tormenting the petrified villagers at will. Clara waited anxiously to see how things would develop. For the first few days nobody even ventured out into the streets. The third night a drunken bunch of ruffians stormed into the Wallmann mansion where she was staying as a guest and after pillaging the beautiful home arrested Andreas Wallmann Junior. Now she had her hands full trying to console the distracted Helene. She had given up the idea of going back to Bethania altogether when she heard that it too had been overrun by the Makhnovites.

Instead, after the immediate crisis was over, she offered her services to Dr. Hottmann at the District Hospital a block away from the Wallmanns'. He accepted her offer gratefully, as the hospital was already full to overflowing with victims of the Makhno reign of terror.

Six weeks later with the typhus epidemic in full fury, Makhno's men came to the hospital one morning and demanded that Dr. Hottmann send a doctor or an experienced nurse to take charge of the emergency hospital they had set up in the Girls School down the street. Reluctantly, avoiding her eyes, Dr. Hottmann asked her if she would be willing to go — just for a few days, he added lamely. She did not hesitate. She said she would go for as long as they needed her. The dear old man had given her a guilty but grateful look, then quickly given her a few instructions she didn't really need. They both knew what might be in store for her among the Makhnovites.

She walked down to her old school immediately, feeling more than a flutter of apprehension as she approached the familiar back entrance. She had experienced human beastliness at its worst. And survived. Would she again be driven into terror? Could she possibly endure a second time what those male animals had done to her that first time?

She was in God's hands. She looked at the familiar door, then pushed it open.

Whatever it was she had steeled herself to, she was not prepared for what she actually found when she entered the school. The filth and stench were so overpowering, the utter lack of even the most primitive facilities expected in a hospital so appalling that she looked around in bewildered horror, her firm resolve to take charge here suddenly gone. There was nothing, simply nothing anywhere she recognized, could connect to the past. Nothing at all. The whole interior had been gutted of every familiar object. Not even the noble white pillars in the back entrance hall looked the same. They were as filthy and begrimed as a pigsty. The floor was squelchy with a nauseous, inches-deep layer of slime made up of mud and human waste. Several overfull latrine buckets stood in the hallway, their contents oozing onto the floor. She picked her way up the staircase to the classrooms, trying to avoid the worst of the disgusting paste underfoot.

The first classroom she entered made her gasp. On the floor lay dozens of fever-ridden Makhno soldiers, wasted and hollow-eyed, in ragged rows on wet, filthy straw, the live ones distinguishable from the dead ones only by their feeble movements and pitiable moans. No beds, not a stick of furniture anywhere. She had become used to sick people, but never had she seen anything like this. As she stood there and stared a moment of pure dread struck her that once she had stepped inside that fetid mass of suffering humanity she would never get out again. She forced herself to move forward, and then she was down on her knees in the middle of the room, engulfed in a miasma of burning flesh, wringing her hands in despair, her eyes clenched shut.

When she dared open them again she looked down at the packed bodies more closely and saw the obscene masses of lice everywhere, oh God, the lice, seething in hair, on clothing, on bare flesh. Most of the men lay naked from the waist up. Feeling faint and dizzy, she began to examine the nearest patient, a pathetically emaciated young boy with mouth agape, swollen, slime-covered tongue lolling, chest heaving for air. At least it was warm enough in the room. She could hear the hiss of the steam radiators. Thank God for the heating system at least.

Without a word she began to work, after looking around in vain for any signs of staff — nurses or orderlies — anybody at all who was not on the floor helpless. She found half a bucket of stale but usable water. She had brought some potassium hydroxide crystals from the hospital, and some home-made swabs. Mixing the crystals with water she began to swab and scrape off the thick coats of slime on tongues and gums, tried to cool off feverish faces and chests with the wet cloths she had brought.

She was on her third patient when a young man came in, startled to find her there.

She rose to her feet. "Are you an orderly here?"

"Yes, I'm Hans Harder." He looked at her hopefully, already wanting to rely on her, needing her pity and understanding. "There are only two of us here now — me and Jasch Harms. He's sleeping in the teachers' room right now. I was in the far room, I didn't hear you come in. We had the Schroeder sisters here too, but they ran away yesterday. They were afraid of the men who were bringing in more patients. We were all forced to come by those men. They tried to find more, but most of the young people are hiding. Especially the girls, they're so scared."

Clara studied young Hans. He was plainly scared himself, but he would have to do. The main thing now was to keep him so busy he wouldn't have time to worry about the risks.

She moved towards him with a reassuring smile. "Well, Hans, I'm Clara

Bock. I've come from the hospital to take charge here." She gestured at the floor. "This is a horrible mess, yes, but we must do the best we can. I know you'll help me. Now here's what I'd like you to do first, while I look at some more patients." His face was eager to please. "Try to persuade two or three of your friends — boys preferably — to come help. Tell them it's a Christian duty to help our fellow men, no matter who they are." She paused to let this sink in. She sensed that he would be her persuasive advocate. "And two more things: we need hot soup for the patients who are getting better. I don't know what they've been getting, if anything, but they need hot soup — any kind — every day. Get your mother and other ladies to make it and send it over. Also, you must make arrangements to have men come for the corpses regularly, and see that they get buried. And if the Makhnovites won't do it for themselves then we must do it for them." She held his gaze. "Can you do all that for me?"

Hans nodded vigorously, gladly bending to her will. She was taking over, telling him what to do. Now he could function. He would do everything this strong, lovely lady wanted. He would get a couple of his classmates to come, even if he had to drive them here with a club . . . .

Well, it had been a start at least . . . . She sighed heavily, postponing the moment she would rise and return to the sickrooms. She had made things work here, but only barely, and she didn't know how much longer she could make them work. Every day seemed harder, more hopeless than the day before. Hans Harder was still her right-hand man. Without him she would have been helpless. With him and the three friends he had brought she had managed to establish a primitive, barely workable routine in the four classroom wards: delousing the patients, washing them, and sometimes wrapping the most feverish of them in cold-water-soaked sheets — if they could stand it — an emergency treatment that brought down their temperatures a bit and helped their breathing. Endlessly they washed off and scraped the ugly yellow slime in the patients' mouths and moistened the dry, yellow parchment skin of their faces. And when all else failed, she would simply hold their parched hands and talk or croon soothingly to them while their skeletal faces glared up at her in dumb gratitude. Poor, poor wretches, who had once been the murderous enemy but would murder no more, most of them.

Hearing a commotion in the front hallway, Clara rose quickly. More patients? Where would she put them? No matter how fast they died and were removed from their straw deathbeds, there were always more to take their places.

She stood at the head of the stairs waiting. This one, at least, was still walking, supported by two comrades. He looked up at her as they mounted the stairs, and she felt herself go numb. She knew this man! For a moment she thought it was Vasya Fast, but she knew he wasn't. Who was he? By the way he abruptly dropped his eyes she knew he had recognized her too.

Puzzled, she led the way into the nearest classroom and cleared a space on the straw between two other patients for the man.

Resting on his back, eyes half closed, he looked gaunt and wasted but not yet in an advanced state of fever. As she took his temperature she couldn't take her eyes off his face. He reminded her so strongly of her old friend Vasya: the same broad face, high cheekbones pushing against the skin, and a thick, brown, upward curling mustache. She couldn't see his eyes clearly but they seemed slightly Tatar-shaped. Again like Vasya's.

With practised movements she divested him of his jacket and shirt, then stripped off his boots and pants so she could wash his whole body. To her surprise he wore underpants. and relatively clean ones at that. His upper body and limbs were densely stippled with the dreaded crimson flecks, and there already appeared to be a slight swelling of the spleen. Having noted the cleanness of his uniform, she was not surprised that he had few lice. He seemed different, somehow, from the scores of filthy Makhnovites she had examined.

She removed his underpants against his feeble squirming, and immediately his hands fluttered down to cover his bared loins. He was different all right. When she raised his left arm to wash it she caught a glimpse of the curiously shaped scar in the palm of his hand. It looked like a puckered white star.

The man opened his eyes fully for the first time and twitched her a weak smile. "I guess we're even now, Miss Bock. I did what little I could for you once. Now you're doing the same for me. I'm Nikolai Fast, Wilhelm's brother. You won't remember me, but I was there that night at Selenaya."

For a moment Clara lost her professional poise as she gaped at her newest patient. That's who he was! The images came flooding back. How often she had tried to remember the face of the man who had carried her away from those fiends at Selenaya that night. Vasya's brother! It didn't seem possible. She owed this man her life, and here he was fighting for his own with only her hands to help him. And she could do nothing to save him. How could God lay this extra burden on her?

She could see his crisis coming, perhaps tonight. Day after day she had been at his side, trying to keep alive his will to live. The nights were the worst. She had hardly slept for a week. He was usually delirious at night, hysterically reliving his worst experiences with Makhno, his guilt and fear spilling out in broken phrases and frenzied jabbering of which she understood very little. Some nights he became so wild she had to restrain him physically. One night she lost control of him and the orderlies were asleep somewhere and didn't come when she called. He sprang from her half naked, staggered clumsily through the door, skidded grotesquely on the filthy floor in the hall and pitched headfirst down the stairs. She found him lying in a crumpled heap, unconscious, his phlegm-choked chest laboring weakly, blood dripping from his nose. Sobbing with pity and exertion she dragged him inch by inch back up the stairs until the two orderlies, sluggish with sleep, finally emerged to help her get him back to his place on the straw. Sure that he was dying, she cradled his head tenderly and tried to stanch the flow of blood from his nose. That would soon stop; if only he wasn't bleeding internally.

Towards morning he had rallied and come to himself. But since then he had been getting a little weaker every day. His crisis could not be far away. There were now traces of blood in his stool, a very bad sign.

She was no longer just a nurse to him. They had become friends, drawn together not only by what had happened at Selenaya but also by the strong feelings which their shared memories of Wilhelm evoked in each of them. Kolya's rancor and bitterness towards his brother shocked her, but the more they talked about Wilhelm the more convinced she became that Kolya's contempt was more pretended than real. She encouraged him to talk about the past, trying to get at the roots of his fierce animosity towards Wilhelm and the rest of his family. And she confessed to him finally her own regret at having once so callously denied the dictates of her own heart where Wilhelm was concerned.

And then, on one of his better days, Kolya had at last poured out his real feelings to her, although his swollen tongue made speech slow and awkward. "Clara," he began, "if I . . . die, you must explain for me to Vasya . . . tell him I was sorry for what happened between us. You must make him see that I — I wanted his approval — even when I pretended to despise him. . . ." He gazed for long moments at the ceiling. She watched his long accumulated bitterness begin to break up like river ice. "He — they — never understood my real motives." His fever-cracked lips were working painfully. "I'm not proud of the horror and destruction I've taken part in" — he struggled to go on — "but, but you must make him understand, Clara . . . I always thought — I always thought I was helping to bring about a new order, a better world. It's why I joined that evil bitch Chaika . . . it's why I rode with Makhno for so long. Almost to the end I believed in Makhno, thought he was the leader to make the changes I was fighting for. . . . I always believed Mennonites — our people — had grown fat and selfish by exploiting their own poor and the Russian peasant. And to end all that . . . put them in their places, I was willing to put up with all the cruelty and violence and destruction of Makhno and his peasants as a . . . realistic price to pay."

"But Kolya," she objected gently, holding his hot, dry hand between hers, "how could you believe Makhno's terrible acts of destruction could result in anything good or positive?"

"I didn't see it that way, Clara. I thought violence was necessary. Had to come first. That it would end in time. And then Makhno's love for freedom, his dream of a peaceful communal life would happen. I kept waiting for that natural anarchy to, to be controlled by responsible . . . disciplined organization . . . . But it never was, except in a military sense." His bitterness, she saw, was now directed at his own blasted hopes. "I know now that it never could have been . . . ." His breathing was becoming labored again and she stroked his hand to soothe him. But he would not stop now. "We Makhnovites are simple steppe wolves who love hunting together, but we could never have built up anything together. I thought I was a serious revolutionary . . . but I can see now that Makhno . . . was just a brigand. Wanted to steal what he could from a bourgeois world he despised but also feared. Tried to destroy it because he didn't understand it. His talk . . . setting up free village communes . . . just that — talk! Empty Anarchist rhetoric . . . ." He sighed and brought up his free hand shakily to look at the star in his palm. "What a fool I was, Clara . . . what a fool."

He lay back exhausted, his unwieldy tongue and parched mouth allowing no more.

She had soothed and comforted him then, just as years ago she had tried to defend Vasya from himself when he accused himself of things that couldn't be undone. How alike these two brothers were under the skin, in spite of everything, she said to herself more than once.

He was very bad now, slipping in and out of delirium, so feeble and spent she feared he couldn't last much longer. He was also fighting pneumonia. She could tell. She watched him struggling for breath, his eyes frightened little animals deep in their burrows, and her spirits sagged. It was all so utterly hopeless. She had the feeling that the world outside was about to explode and blot out her and everybody else in these squalid rooms. For days now there had been a growing rumble of artillery fire from both north and west. Several shells had already exploded here in Rosental. At any moment the school could be hit, and then what?

How much worse could things get? She was almost alone here now. Poor Hans was down with typhus at home and she had only two other very reluctant boys to help now.

And no one seemed to know what was happening anymore. Khortitza-Rosental had been cut off for over two months now from any contact with Alexandrovsk across the river or with Ekaterinoslav in the north. The Makhnovites were keeping the colony in terrorized isolation. And the typhus was raging through the entire colony. A terrible black monster that was devouring more lives every day had been let loose among them by these same savage men she was devoting all her energy to saving. It didn't make any sense at all.

But the artillery barrage that was threatening their lives might also force the Makhnovites to leave at last. That was her hope, her only hope. This afternoon when she had stepped out the front door for a breath of fresh air she had seen thick columns of terrorists on horseback and in wagons moving down towards the Dnieper, presumably to cross over to Alexandrovsk. Were they fleeing or attacking? And who and where was the enemy? Would they get rid of one brutal horde only to fall prey to even worse devils? Would it be the Whites or the Reds? At least those were regular armies, not just undisciplined masses of blood-thirsty bandits like Makhno's people.

Kolya was slipping into delirium again but she could make nothing of his monotone mumbling. With alarm she noted that his fever was mounting. His whole body seemed to be enveloped in invisible flames. The cool wet cloths she pressed to his forehead and chest turned tepid within minutes. She considered bundling him in a cold wet sheet but decided the shock might be too much for him. Every few minutes he was racked by dreadful spasms of coughing as his weakened lungs tried to expel the phlegm that was drowning them. . . .

Each breath now was a rattling sob torn desperately from the mephitic air. His whole body shuddered, and in a panic she raised his head and shoulders in her arms. His eyes were rolling wildly, his mouth a black gaping hole. In horror she clung to him, heaving with him. His eyes suddenly focused and he stared at her in stark terror, trying to say something. She couldn't bear it. She lowered her cheek to his head, rocking him gently. And then a violent rasp came from his tortured throat.

She felt him still and slack in her arms. Weeping, she continued the rhythm of her rocking, postponing the moment she would have to release him to death.

2
Blumenau, Molochnaya, July, 1920

Tired and dispirited, Wilhelm Fast had come home from the front for a brief visit with his mother. Since joining the Self-Defense in '18 he had never really been out of uniform. Month after month, season after season, he had been pulled and pushed like a child's toy soldier, always under others' control, never knowing what would happen to him next.

Last summer his regiment, the Third Kornilov, had pushed up from the Crimea with Deniken's White Army. After a long and bitter struggle in which he had been slightly wounded in the arm and come close to death several times, they had been pushed down again for the winter. This summer they had started later — in June — with their new commander General Wrangel, and here they were again in the Molochnaya in hand-to-hand fighting with Trotsky's Bolsheviks. Endlessly back and forth, chasing each other out of Mennonite and Russian villages. For weeks now they had fought for the northern row of villages he knew so well from his teaching days there, in and around Fuerstenau, Schoensee and Liebenau. Now he was home on a two-day leave before going back into the line again.

For several days they had occupied Schoensee, where he had taught a lifetime ago. He had gone over to his former school one day when he noticed that its roof was damaged from shellfire. His old classroom was in a shocking mess, the front end raggedly open to sky and weather, broken benches and debris all over and every single window blown out. But the teacher's desk had remained miraculously intact. He cleared off the broken plaster and wood splinters and stood over it as he had so often when facing his class. Idly, he bent down and began pulling open the long deep desk drawers one by one. All were empty except for one at the bottom. It contained some loose sheets of paper. He pulled them out and examined them. They were lesson notes written in a hand not his, but the very last sheet brought a thrill of recognition. It was one of his own drawings, one of the many pencil sketches he had done while waiting for his class to finish this or that assignment. This one showed his boys and girls sitting passively hunched over their desks, but he had (cynically?) given them various animal faces, and their slim beast ankles were shackled to desks or benches. He himself was not in the drawing.

He studied the drawing carefully, trying to reconstruct the real faces as they looked behind the animal disguises. They were grown up now, these children, and dispersed to the winds. But their animal faces, he thought sardonically, might not be so inappropriate even now, living as they did in a world more animal than human. His drawing had proved to be prophetic in a way he had not intended.

Sadly, he pushed the lesson notes back into the drawer. His drawing he held up over the desk as though demonstrating something to a class, then ripped it slowly and precisely into pieces. Gathering them up from his desk, he tossed the fragments in a white shower towards the broken windows. Then he left, obscurely satisfied with his childish gesture.

Sitting on the *schaffott* now while his mother and Lenchen washed the dinner dishes, he thought of all the drawings and paintings stored under the bed in his old room. He decided to get them out and look at them again.

He went through them all, feeling more and more depressed. Not because he found them bad, but because they glowed with such a vibrant life of their own, especially the war sketches he had done after coming home wounded from the Polish front. They mocked him now with their very excellence. He recalled the excitement with which he had done them, barely stopping to eat or rest until he had been creatively spent and completely exhausted. And how happy he had been knowing that at last he had done something really first-rate, drawings brilliantly alive and dynamic even if, paradoxically, their subjects were images of violence and killing in war. But now as he studied them again he could only feel affronted by their confident air of assertion, by the bold faith in life that was affirmed even in the chaotic details of war's insanity and ruination.

Charged with that faith and optimism he had fallen in love with Katya, and his love had carried him through all his grim months in the Self-

Defense, including Snapper's death at Chernigovka and the horrors of the Blumenfeld front.

That strong current of love had suddenly dashed him aside and left him in a back eddy going round and round like a chip of wood. When he lost Katya he lost himself, the self that believed that through his art he could make something of lasting beauty and worth for his world. Now he knew better. He looked down once more at the bulging portfolio on his lap. Of what further use to him were these brash and posturing children of his brain and hand? Who would give a damn for them in a world where human life was worth no more than a stone kicked underfoot?

He sat there for a long time, lost in gloomy thoughts. Resolved at last, he rose and gathered the loose drawings on the bed together and stuffed them into his portfolio with the rest. Then he clamped the thick bundle of sheets under his arm and headed for the corridor leading to the barn. He was careful not to let his mother and sister see him from the kitchen. He did not feel like making any explanations.

He took the old familiar path down to the river. He was relieved to find that nothing here had changed. The place still had a soothing effect on him. As always, the willows dropped lazily over the bank in the July heat and even his old hermit oak was still there. He sat down against its rough bole in his old place and stared at the tawny waters. Then his gaze lifted to the brow of the Colonists Hill and to the spot where they had made their last stand against Makhno and the Reds.

It all seemed so long ago and yet retained a sharpness to lacerate his memory. Like an old man, he realized ruefully, he kept sending his memory into the past to distract himself from the present. Perhaps that was the one way to hang on to his sanity.

He pushed himself to his feet and proceeded slowly and deliberately to do what he had come here to do. He walked to the water's edge, opened his portfolio with both hands and heaved its contents — all his sketches, drawings and paintings — into the murky brown waters of the little Molochnaya.

Impassively, he watched the masses of sheets submerge, rise, float and slowly become gravid with water.

3

Kherson Province, near the Ingulets River, August 23, 1921

He could not stand the pain. Mother-of-God it would kill him, this horrible agony. The terrible jolting of the careening *tachanka* in which he lay hammered red hot spikes through his neck and jaw. His other wounds —his whole body — were on fire too, but the bullet that had ripped through his neck and out through his cheek yesterday had made his pain unbearable. He was finished. He knew it. He could not survive, could not twist and dodge away from his enemies and death this time.

He was lying in his dirty, tattered uniform on an old army blanket spread over straw on the floor, his jouncing head to the rear, facing the back of his driver up front, his two faithful "Lewis boys" sitting behind him, legs dangling over the end, hanging on to their mounted Lewis machine gun. Dead loyal, they would never desert him. But how could he hope to stay alive with all these holes in his body? Misha, his driver, said he had five new flesh wounds from yesterday's action. And he'd already had a nasty thigh wound in one leg and a shattered ankle bone in the other that he got two months ago and that hadn't knit enough for him to walk. Hell, he could barely stand it in the saddle with that foot.

And now, mother-of-sweet-holy-jesus, he was dying. His mouth and throat were burning up and he could barely swallow water in feeble little jerks let alone eat anything. He couldn't even raise himself the last time they stopped he was so weak from all the blood that had poured out of him yesterday and they had to chase miles and miles away from the battlefield before they dared to stop and bind him up . . . .

Those Red bastards had not let up. Just kept coming, coming, wave after wave of cavalry. And his own outnumbered mounted men trying desperately to hold them off.

He had insisted on getting up on his horse, though his ankle and thigh made him gasp with pain when they hoisted him into the saddle. Then he led the counterattack against the Red cavalry force from Nikolajev and forgot his throbbing ankle. With their usual lusty cries of "Live free or die fighting" they had hurled themselves at the enemy, firing fiercely and trying to get close enough to use their sabres. The *tachankas* with their deadly Lewis guns came flying alongside on their flanks, providing fire cover.

The hacking was unbelievable. Knowing they were badly outnumbered, his boys had fought with a desperate ferocity that had startled the Reds and made them give way within minutes. They hacked and hacked like wild demons, ignoring the bullets fizzing everywhere, exploding into men and horses. He saw one of his boys neatly slice a Bolshie's cap off, part of his head still inside. He himself was completely surrounded several times, but each time his comrades came to his rescue like avenging angels.

Suddenly he had found himself knocked clean off his horse, hitting hard turf amidst flying hooves, unable to breathe with the blood pouring into his mouth, drowning frantically in his own gore. He knew he was a goner just before everything went black.

When he came to he found himself propped up in his *tachanka* behind the driver's seat, so he could breathe better. They had wrapped a rag around his neck but his mouth was still filling up, so that he had to let it hang open to let the blood dribble out to keep from choking. Misha told him that when he was thrown off his horse one of the new guys — that punk Krilenko — yelled "Batko's down! He's finished." That did it. They barely had time to pick him up and toss him into the *tachanka* before the bastard

Reds had them on the run. . . .

And now he was flat down, his head and body burning up, so weak he could hardly breathe. Trying to hold on. God, he had to try and hang on. He mustn't give in to the raving darkness again. He had to think, plan. He still had troops to command, good loyal troops. But what could they do now, where could they go, the blasted Reds all around them, horsemen as good as his own — and more, so many more? And behind them came the infantry, masses of them. And most frightening of all those armored cars the Commies had, whole units of them: like big gray turtles they just came crawling, crawling, spitting fire. And you couldn't kill them. What could horses and *tachankas* do against armor-plated cars? Even machine-gun bullets just rattled off them like hail off a tin roof.

He groaned in pain and despair, tried moving his tormented head and neck ever so slightly to ease them. What could he do, what could he do? He was helpless, finished. Finished. That kid Krilenko was right. . . . He'd lost too many men. The odds had become impossible. He was surrounded on all sides. His only chance was to get across the Romanian border — save himself at least. But where, how? Where were they now? Heading for the border? Could they even get to the Dniester before the Reds cut them off? God, it was all useless. He would just lie here, slowly bleeding to death — if the Reds didn't get him first. . . .

His head was exploding. He could hear the sound of his own voice somewhere in the distance. He was raving again . . . So many lost . . . old comrades . . . gone down fighting or captured and finished off — like Karetnik and his whole staff at Mariupol. All my brave comrades. Even Petrenko, my best field commander. And Ivanyk — Bad Yashka — who could laugh more and drink more and screw more than any man alive. Not any more . . . So many gone . . . My brothers — first Grishka at Uman, then Savva, shot by the Bolshies in his own *khata*. And only because he was my brother, the rotten whores! Kolya . . . Kolya Fast my loyal, sober Mennist . . . taken by the spotted fever like so many others. And Tchus, good old Fedya, once my enemy. God, he would've gone through fire for me — did too, many times. Ruthless bastard, Fedya, but he never crossed me. My enforcer, shot through the head at Poltava, still wearing his old sailor's uniform . . . . And Foma Kozhin and Zabudko, two of my best officers, left behind wounded, maybe dead by now . . . .

What about me? How can I still be alive? Bullets and sabres only wound me. Can't kill me. Not yet . . . Even a tough bugger like Marchenko thought they couldn't get him. Ha! That Marchenko! Hacked his way up from the Reds' trap in Crimea with my best cavalry — 2,500 picked men — till he had only a couple hundred left. And when he met me at Kermenchik he said, "I have the honor of announcing to you the return of your Crimean army." The cheeky bastard! "I have the honor" — like one of those fat-assed Gold Epaulets, those White officers trained in tsarist military colleges. Two hundred men, out of 2,500! My Crimean army. I could have wept when I saw those poor scarecrows, half of them with blood-stained rags, but just happy they'd made it.

No, no, they couldn't get me . . . all those schemes to assassinate me the Cheka kept dreaming up. They never worked. Too smart, too many loyal men around me. They were bunglers anyway. . . . Like that kid Glushchenko that time in Gulai Polye coming up to me looking nervous and scared: "*Batko,* I've got important information for you . . ." Yeah, the bitch, he and his buddy were sent to kill me, but the kid couldn't see it through, said they'd forced him, the Cheka, but he knew he deserved to pay anyway, the little son-of-a-whore. Coming right up to me like that, loaded down with a Mauser and a Browning and a couple of bombs yet . . . and Kurilenko boldly going up to him and disarming him and his stinking buddy. What a fool that kid. Kept blabbering he'd made a mistake and was ready to pay for it. Even when we put him to the wall he kept jabbering and crying he deserved to die and even yelled "God save you!" to me just before Tchus gave the order to fire. . . .

The flames in his wounds leaping out of control, he opened his raging mouth to scream . . . And his mind screamed, I can't stand it any more. Give me my *nagan,* I'll put myself to sleep, by God! The *tachanka* was still lashing him with its pitiless bouncing over the rutty road. Why couldn't they stop, mother-of-God, for a bit? He tried to call out to Misha but the bouncing back ignored him.

His fevered brain was heaving as wildly as the wagon. He was drifting again . . . Oh God, where's it all gone? My dreams, my revolution, my communes to get away from the shit of cities. *Volnitsa!* Good times, comrades. Free — free forever not like that stinking Butyrki God help me the freezing dark cell in the Pugachev Tower no not that . . . they threw me . . . I couldn't . . . Arshinov they won't let me out and I'm freezing on these stones mother-of-God I can't stand it I just want to go back . . . village . . . home . . . not just this hacking and killing and shooting and always being hunted where do all the Reds come from thick as lice in a whore's crotch lousy stinking bastards they'll get me Misha get me to the border they're coming Oh God they're behind us Misha they'll . . . .

To hell with it . . . Katya, my angel of light, where are you? They wanted to kill you too but I wouldn't let them, the bastards . . . and now, and now . . . *O Bozhe moy! Nye mogu, nye mogu,* Oh my God, I can't, I can't . . . .

CHAPTER TWENTY-EIGHT

1

Blumenau, May, 1923

Erdmann Lepp had come to Halbstadt on important business. It had to do with the proposed Mennonite emigration to Canada which had once again kindled the hopes and will to live of a people hammered into lethargic despair by terrorism, disease, and famine, not to mention bewildering political and social changes. Lepp was on the executive of the recently formed Union of Citizens of Dutch Lineage, a Mennonite agrarian society charged with the enormous task of rebuilding the economy and social welfare of the Mennonites of the Ukraine and restoring them to their former levels, if possible. If possible. Lepp believed with God's help all was possible, so long as faith came first. Had God not sent Alvin Miller and the Mennonite Central Committee from America last year with enough food kitchens to keep alive hundreds, perhaps thousands, of Mennonites who would otherwise have starved?

Lepp knew, of course, that one miracle may only create the need for more. In this case the many destitute Mennonites whose lives had been saved still had no means of helping themselves and were a millstone around the already choking economy of the colonies. The UCDL executive had come to the decision that emigration was the only way out for Mennonites who had lost everything in the bad times. If enough of them could be placed in countries like Canada, then those who preferred to remain would have a better chance to build up the colonies again.

That was how the idea of emigration had taken root. By now it was a plant growing faster than the magic beanstalk in the old fairy tale. Emigration fever was the new epidemic that infected all alike, the destitute as well as those who still had means. Benjamin B. Janz, the energetic president of the UCDL, already had over 20,000 names on his application lists. But up to now neither the Kharkov government of the Ukraine nor Moscow had granted a single exit visa. The UCDL was coming under severe pressure to get the emigration started.

Many people were getting desperate. Six months ago a large group of people from the Gnadenfeld and Halbstadt *volosts* had sold everything and fled to the Black Sea port of Batum where, the rumor went, exit visas were readily obtainable. They had found otherwise. Most of them had been forced to wait indefinitely, living in utterly squalid conditions. As a result, several hundred of them had been struck by malaria or typhus, and many had died. Some of these poor wretches were still there suffering and hoping against hope to get out. A few had actually managed to escape by ship, the rest were doomed to remain.

His work of compiling emigration lists finished for the day, Lepp had accepted the offer of a ride to Blumenau this evening to pay a visit to the widow of his dear, departed old school friend Gerhard Fast. He also wanted very much to see Wilhelm again, who had suffered such tragic personal losses and was said to have gone through very rough times as a conscript in the White army.

Gaunt as ever, a little stooped, and much grayer, Lepp sat in the now seldom-used Fast living room with Wilhelm and his mother. He told them he was trying to visit all his old friends who were getting ready to emigrate. Since he worked with the lists, he knew exactly who was planning to leave. It was a pleasant duty he said as Greta handed him a cup of hot *prips,* but also saddening because he knew he would probably not see them again on this earth.

While Mother Fast snuffled decorously into her handkerchief at these solemn sentiments, Wilhelm studied their guest with interest. He had not seen the old *reiseprediger* for a long time, not since Snapper's funeral he recalled. He was relieved to find that he no longer felt uneasy with Lepp. For the first time he felt warmth for this remarkable man who had done so much for his people and given himself so courageously to a hazardous native ministry. Through what seemed like a divine miracle he had survived the terrible massacre at Dubovka, having been spared by Makhno himself with no more than a savage beating. Unfortunately, there had been no miracle for poor Jacob and the other missionaries.

Wilhelm was eager to find out from Lepp how the emigration plans were going. He had placed his own name and his mother's on the list months ago. Lenchen and her husband Hans Goossen had also decided to go, but Greta and Waldemar had not yet made up their minds. He himself was ready to leave for Canada tomorrow. He wanted to get away from this accursed country, the farther and sooner the better, away from the pain of loss and the personal woes he could never hope to bury in this ancestral soil. He could not believe that Lepp would want to stay.

"But surely," he asked directly, "you're planning to emigrate yourself, Onkel Lepp?"

Lepp had an air of tranquility now, Wilhelm observed, very different from his severity and intensity in the old days.

"No, my friend, I'm afraid not," came his gentle reply, "I've examined the matter earnestly in prayer. The dear Lord has laid upon me the duty to remain here in Russia — our Soviet Union now — to try and carry on the work He gave me to do in the Russian ministry many years ago."

"But the conditions are worse than ever," Wilhelm objected. "Soon they may be completely impossible."

"Yes, you may be right. But I can also see God's light on the horizon. Not everything in these end times is black and threatening. Lenin's New Economic Policy is certainly a step in the right direction. And I'm convinced our own UCDL can help our people here, even though our total and individual land holdings have been drastically reduced. The economic situation will improve with time, I have no doubt of that. What concerns me much more for the long haul is the spiritual and cultural damage that has been inflicted on us. As you know, most of our private schools have already been taken over by the state and many of our teachers dismissed. And our spiritual life is also in a sorry state. Yes, our moral and religious lives are at a low ebb. There is much work to be done in those areas, and that's the other reason I'm staying. We must never allow ourselves to be completely absorbed into Russian society. The danger, I admit, is great but I think it can still be averted if we work hard together in brotherly love. Brother Benjamin Janz and others disagree. They think it's already too late."

Lepp's courage and determination had to be admired, but Wilhelm couldn't help agreeing silently with Janz and the others. Emigration was the only answer.

"Can you tell us how the plans for emigration are going, Onkel Lepp?" He took another sip of his sister's raw-tasting *prips*.

"We are ready to move whenever the government allows us, though there are still technical and bureaucratic problems to be resolved. The Foreign Commissariat in Moscow has sanctioned group emigration in principle, but we haven't yet informed them of just how many want to leave. The large numbers may shock them a bit. We hope not enough to make them change their minds. Our biggest problem right now is to find a place for the medically unfit emigrants once they are out of Russia. Our government won't allow the rejects back in and it won't allow Canadian medical inspectors to conduct the examinations on Russian soil. We're hopeful of finding a centre in Germany where the rejects can find temporary shelter while being treated for trachoma and other curable ailments. It's a very serious problem that may result in the breaking up of families for long periods of time and causing much anguish and anxiety."

Wilhelm glanced at his frail mother. If he had to leave her behind in some foreign place it would kill her. He was sure of it.

"That sounds rather unhuman. Is there no other way?"

"Well, we haven't found one, and our people are getting extremely impatient to leave. Brother Janz and J. P. Klassen of Khortitza are in Moscow right now trying to push through the final arrangements for the first group from the Old Colony."

"And when will it be our turn here in Molochnaya?"

"It's hard to say right now. The Old Colony people are scheduled to leave first, about 3,000 of them. We're hoping that the Molochnaya lists will be approved for this summer as well, but right now we simply don't know." Lepp gave Wilhelm a keen glance. "By the way, an old friend of yours from your Petersburg student days will be in the first contingent of Khortitza emigrants: Clara Bock."

The unexpected name caught him by surprise. "Is she really? I'm very glad for her." He set down his cup carefully. "She nursed my brother Nikolai in his final illness, you know. Afterwards she wrote Mother a fine, compassionate letter. Her account of Kolya's sad end was very moving and came as a great comfort — especially to Mother."

"Yes, Clara has told me about Nikolai. God works in wonderful ways. Your troubled son seems to have found peace and understanding at the end, Mrs. Fast."

Mother Fast had said very little, content to listen to the two men. "Yes," she murmured huskily, "we are very grateful to Fräulein Bock and thank the Lord for leading our Nikolai to her when He did."

Lepp had expressed a desire to get back to his lodgings in Halbstadt for the night so he could get off to an early start in the morning. Wilhelm was glad to take him back. It would give him a chance to talk to him alone and at greater length. They sat together on the box of the rickety old droshky he and Waldemar had cobbled together from odds and ends and derelict wagon parts long ago abandoned in the far corner of the yard behind the barn. As they creaked into the street under a full moon Wilhelm slapped the lines down on the bony rump of old Turk and felt a pang of regret for the old days when he would have driven his guest home in a smart black droshky and a pair of fast pacers.

He had been waiting to ask Lepp about the grisly encounter with Makhno at Dubovka, a subject that would have upset his mother. He wanted to know how it had come about that Lepp had escaped with a beating while the other missionaries, including his dear friend Jacob Priess — loyal, loving devout Jacob — had all been savagely murdered. It didn't make sense. Could Onkel Lepp explain why he, as the leader, had been let go and the others . . . ?

Erdmann Lepp was not offended by Wilhelm's rather pointed question. He had often asked it of himself since that nightmarish day. He did not need to be reminded how close the two young men had been. He had gotten to know both of them well in wartime Moscow, and Jacob especially had become the son to him he had never had. But he had loved this young man too, so different from the simple Jacob who had lived so eagerly, so trustingly for his Lord and Master. Perhaps he had been drawn to Wilhelm for opposite reasons, for the very qualities that made him so unmalleable: his stubborn aloofness and unwillingness — perhaps inability — ever to give himself completely, to surrender his artist's ego and allow himself to be submerged in a Higher Will. Yes, that unyieldingness in this proud young man had excited and challenged him. And Lepp surmised that in spite of the calamities that had buffeted him, Wilhelm's nature had not changed. If only he did not grow hard, make himself invulnerable to suffering and sorrow. That would be the danger for him.

"Only God can answer that question, Wilhelm. All I can do is make guesses. When I was brought before that butcher I feared the worst naturally. I quaked, I can tell you, when I saw the fiend's dark rage flaming in his eyes. I smelled his drunken lust to squash me. His lashing contempt as he cursed and threatened cut me to the marrow. But in my soul I also knew that Almighty God would contend with the foul fiend possessing Makhno. And that gave me the courage to face up to him.

"And as we stood there roaring at each other, hurling angry arguments and counter-arguments back and forth, something else was happening that I didn't really understand until much later: God's words were in my voice and the Fiend's in Makhno's. I understood that we were a mighty battle-ground at that moment, he and I. And that the words and arguments were mightier than we, directed by forces beyond our control at targets far beyond us. We were just there, he and I, weak things of flesh with only our human feelings to use as weapons."

Lepp stopped, turning to look at his companion. "I must confess to you, Wilhelm — and I have never told anyone else this — when Makhno slapped my face and spat at me to show his contempt for Christ's law of love, I felt only the human outrage of a man being humiliated and degraded beyond endurance. An urge to kill him overcame me . . . . I say it to my everlasting shame. His murderous rage had leaped over to me, so that I wanted to grab him, sink my teeth into his throat like a wolf, suck his blood . . ."

Lepp was silent for long seconds as they swayed on the wagon box and the wheels and floor boards groaned with the uneven motion. "And then I saw something else so strange it left me bewildered. As we circled each other like wild beasts I saw that if I, as a life-long follower of Christ, could still feel such murderous rage if provoked enough, then Makhno, my evil, sadistic provoker, must finally be only a man too. Like myself. I tell you that came like a revelation to me. Not just a fiend possessed, but a human being with an immortal soul."

"But a soul doomed to hell," Wilhelm, shocked, blurted out in the darkness.

"Yes, perhaps, but we are not to judge. All I know is that at that moment a vital spark passed between Makhno's soul and mine. We had a clear moment of understanding. A wordless message had been flashed. I think we both realized in that instant that we were not really enemies, that in a strange way we were even allies, or at least bound to each other not as victim to captor, but as victim to victim, as sufferer to fellow sufferer."

Stunned though he was by Lepp's strange confession, Wilhelm couldn't help being moved by it. "Onkel Lepp," he demanded, "how can you find it in your heart to make such excuses for an inhuman monster responsible for untold suffering and the cruel snuffing out of hundreds, perhaps thousands, of human lives?"

Lepp took his time answering. "I don't for a moment condone what the butcher Makhno has done, my friend, and I'm not trying to explain away his unspeakable acts of barbarism. I'm simply trying to tell you that in my moment of illumination God showed me something else about him too, and about myself. Look, Wilhelm, you know what he said to me just before he let me go, half dead, with my back shredded? 'The lashes, the lashes are for your false accusations — and for something else. The mercy is for you and me both.' "

The venerable preacher and the younger man stared at each other in the pale moonlight, then Lepp continued in his slow and measured way. "After we have tried to account for all the terrible things Makhno has done to us, we mustn't stop there. We won't really know anything about this terrible man if we don't go on to understand something else about him. By the way, did you know that he escaped to Romania, then to Poland where he was reported to have been tried, convicted, and executed? Well, now there are even rumors that he is still alive after all somewhere in western Europe. Who knows? I suppose whether he is dead or alive is no longer important. He will in any case be arraigned before the Supreme Judge.

"What's important to all of us now who suffered at his cruel hands is to try and understand him. I say this to you in confidence, my boy, because I know you will understand where others wouldn't. Our worst enemy, you know, was never Makhno. Bad as he was, Makhno was not the Antichrist. He was sent by God as a scourge to us, a vicious dog to snap at our heels so we would change direction, a catalyst to stir us to a new spiritual awareness. I'm convinced that God intended something creative in this prolonged ordeal of violence against us. Yes, Makhno destroyed the innocent and defenceless, but he and his wolves could not of themselves have destroyed us. Most of us, at any rate, would have survived.

"And don't you see, Willie, we needed the suffering and persecution. The greatest sin of temptation for Christians is to avoid exposure to hostility and oppression, to seal themselves safely off from the world, as we Mennonites have done here in Russia. I sometimes think that what we have created here is not really an image of God's will but an illusory world created by the collective Mennonite will in defiance of God's will . . . . Yes, I concede that we thought we were obeying God's will by retreating into ourselves, living peaceful and productive lives as the quiet in the land. Blessed are the peacemakers, yes, but for us that has too often meant being content to be passive peace*takers*. We just took our non-violence for granted here in Russia; we didn't even teach our children what that precious heritage meant as a creative spiritual force. And so, when the crisis came, our young men were willing to throw aside a half-dead principle and form a Self-Defense. And by doing that we became peace*breakers,* like everyone else around us."

Lepp was lost in thought again, as though having forgotten that he was talking to someone else. "The most Russian things that ever happened to us in this country in over a century," he continued in a voice that shook with emotion, "are the destruction and violence we have suffered since the Revolution. Through a cruel twist of irony, the bullets and sabres that have pierced our flesh have made us 'Russian' finally. We have shed blood for our motherland, become God's reluctant martyrs of the sword. We should have gone out to meet persecution and suffering as our ancestors did a long time ago, but we didn't. We waited terrified and passive in our nests, hoping that the storm would pass us by once more."

He fell silent again as they drove through the long deserted main street of Muntau, with only a light showing here and there in the houses facing the street. When Lepp's voice came again it was a harsh whisper. "Yes, there was always a much more dangerous enemy than Makhno, Willie, and we are in his power now. The real Antichrist Satan let loose among us."

"Yes, the masters of our shining new Red Paradise."

"Our masters, yes, and will be for as long as God permits and until He intervenes by sending His Son down to establish the Messianic Kingdom. The Reds are building a machine, a vast impersonal machine of tyranny and oppression that may eventually crush down our Mennonite brotherhood as even Makhno could not do. Makhno was himself the baffled victim of that soulless machine. I think he knew all the time that he was only a minor force let loose for a little while, like a spring torrent that briefly turns a sleepy little creek into a raging river. But the creek knows it will inevitably be reduced to a midsummer trickle again.

"In his mad innocence Makhno created martyrs by the sword, and for that God will punish him. But the Reds won't even bother creating martyrs, at least not visibly, out in the open, because martyrs are irrelevant to their system. A martyr is not a marketable commodity in our new Soviet Union. The Bolsheviks have done with all that. They are tuned only to the future, to the building of an even bigger, more efficient state machine of which, they hope, we will all be small, impersonally functioning parts."

Wilhelm had to ask the question. "Then why, Onkel Lepp, have you decided to stay here to carry on your work? When by your own admission you won't have the freedom to be fully human, much less to be a Christian witness and missionary."

"You are right to ask that, Wilhelm. It's a question I've often asked myself and God on my knees before Him. All I can tell you is that I have received the clear call to stay and work here. As I said earlier tonight, in my more optimistic moments I do see at least some light on the horizon. In any case, I've fought man-made darkness and flouted benighted state religious laws most of my life. I know only too well that I'm an anachronism in Soviet society now, a cog in the machine as obsolete as Makhno. He's already disposed of and I may be too. But until that happens I must continue to work where and when my Lord and Savior directs. Besides, we are living in the end times. Our Savior may appear at any moment. And then all violence and persecution will be at an end and we shall all enjoy the fruits of His peaceable thousand-year Sabbath, no matter where we live or who our masters have been."

They were in Neu-Halbstadt. To the right the cream-colored columns of Wilhelm's old school looked blanched in the moonlight. Lepp had finished, but he looked as though still deep in thought. Wilhelm glanced at him and noted that the grizzled cones of his side-whiskers swerved out as assertively as ever. There was no doubt about it, Erdmann Lepp was the stuff martyrs were made of all right. But not even Makhno had bothered to make him one. And who now would?

2
Lichtenau, Molochnaya, June 23, 1924

The bright June sun streamed down from a cloudless sky. A festive sky, the air singing clear, the fields beside the road from Lindenau vibrant with cicada shrilling. The crops looked promising, the light green shoots of early summer rapidly swelling and stretching into the long lush stalks of harvest time. The kind of summer day that made a farmer walk through his fields with a surging heart.

Wilhelm Fast's farm-bred mind registered the sights and sounds without thought. He was preoccupied with weightier, more immediate things as he walked slowly, lines in hand, beside the ramshackle droshky he and Waldie and Hans had managed to extend into a crude ladder wagon so they could transport all their stuff in one trip to the station. Young Hans was walking on the other side, keeping a careful eye on their top-heavy cargo, while Waldemar Barg kept watch behind the wagon. His mother and Lenchen, dressed in their Sunday best, were sitting on the box up front with Greta, who was not going, squeezed between them in fond embrace.

They were on their way at last. Today they were leaving the Molochnaya forever: he, his mother, Lenchen, and Hans Goossen. In fact, the whole Goossen clan was emigrating and would share a car with them. Only Greta and Waldie were staying, at least for the time being. They would try to sell the old Fast farm and leave for Canada with a later group. Mama had insisted that the farm be sold to the right people, and not to some shiftless day worker or Russian peasant who would allow her fine home and *wirtschaft* to become "filthy, neglected eyesores in the sight of the Lord."

As they turned into the Lichtenau station they beheld a remarkable scene. On the tracks stood their waiting train, dozens of shabby, weathered freight cars massed in a line stretching well beyond the station. The marshaling area along the tracks was tightly jammed with people, horses, and every type of farm vehicle from long, straw-lined ladder wagons to droshkies of every size and style, and even a few elegant-looking covered buggies and fourgons. Men, women, and children were milling around or talking in groups, thousands of them. From a distance it was hard to tell which of them were leaving and which were staying. All were dressed in whatever decent clothes they still possessed — mostly drab and makeshift — men and boys in dark, rumpled jackets or light shirts and blouses, and the usual peaked caps; women and girls in dark dresses, or skirts with white blouses, and cheap, plain hats or kerchiefs on their heads. The younger children were skimpily dressed, for the most part, and almost all were barefoot. The men and women wore mainly home-made wooden clogs or open sandals. Generally, these people had the listless, worn-down appearance of people fallen on hard times.

The sliding doors of the freight cars were open wide to receive the personal possessions that were already being loaded. Wilhelm was astonished to see what some of the departing people were taking with them: not only large wooden chests, portmanteaus, boxes, canvas bags of food and the like, but items of furniture like small tables, chairs, Kroeger wall clocks, and even a folded up sleeping bench here and there. Would they actually be permitted to transport all that stuff across Russia and the ocean to Canada? He himself had carefully packed a few dozen of his favorite books in a strong wooden box. They were books he could not bear to leave behind, though they had been warned that non-religious books might be confiscated at the border. They were worth taking the risk for, he had decided. Perhaps they were all following some deep impulse to take at least a small part of their homeland with them, something tangible that would remind them later of what they had once had.

As the afternoon lengthened, the solemn and tearful farewells were repeated over and over again in a ritual that grew ever more intense. The scene reminded Wilhelm of Halbstadt station when he and other young Mennonite men had gone off to war. But this was also different. Here whole families were leaving for what they knew in advance would be forever. The most pathetic farewells were those between members of the same families where one or more members had been found medically unfit by Dr. Drury, the medical examiner sent from Canada for the preliminary inspection. All these medical rejects — a mother, perhaps, or a grandfather or daughter — could do was hope that they would be able to join their loved ones at some later date. And even those who had been cleared here faced a much more rigid inspection either in Riga or in Antwerp. And the rejects there would face an even more uncertain future. Wilhelm was particularly concerned for his mother, who had barely passed scrutiny in Halbstadt.

It was late afternoon when the first train bell sounded. The signal for boarding. They embraced Greta and Waldie one last time and headed for their car, Wilhelm and Lenchen guiding their mother through the crush. The leave-taking was getting frenetic as passengers began to move and jostle towards their assigned cars. Then the last desperate handshakes, sobbing embraces, wet, tense faces murmuring last-second endearments and exhortations to write, as the second and final bells sounded. A tremulous voice started singing "God be With You, Till We Meet Again" and soon everyone joined in. "Auf wiedersehen, all! Please, please, follow us soon." A man's deep bass boomed up at the people standing jammed together in the open doorways as the cars creaked into motion: "Reunion in eternity." And then only the outstretched hands and straining faces slowly receding and the boys and young men running alongside, panting goodbyes as long as they could.

Inside the cars tense silences as the passengers, dazed by the leave-taking, felt only the ache of parting and the shock of their narrow, swaying prisons taking them away from the land and people they loved to a world they could not yet imagine as real. They huddled on the rough planks that served as benches or sat down cautiously on the crude double-decker bunks attached to the walls on both sides and sought each other's faces for reassurance. They had tried so desperately to escape from their ruined world, but now that they were actually underway they gave way to the despair of leaving and the panic of going. Many of the younger passengers continued to stand at the open car doors, dully watching the familiar scenery rolling by.

Wilhelm, perched on his bunk, smiled reassuringly across the aisle at his mother and Lenchen. Hans was talking to his brother Fritz a few feet away. Mama looked so fragile and bewildered, as though heading for a grim fate she was powerless to resist. Even though the air was close and hot in the car, she had a woolen shawl wrapped tightly around her shoulders. She might look weak, but Wilhelm knew she would never despair. Her faith was a shaft of bright steel that would brace her even against her body's weakness. And she was free of all self-pity. He never doubted that. Her thoughts would concern themselves only with the welfare of her children. She would keep worrying about how Greta was managing at home. And of what would finally happen to the *wirtschaft* she loved almost above life itself, that had been in the family, as she never tired of saying, "ever since Blumenau had sprung from the steppe in the spring of 1804." He prayed that she would be able to withstand the rigors of this long journey. He had heard that there was some sort of nursing care available on all emigrant trains. That was some comfort at least.

At ten p.m. they reached Federovka, where they stopped for several hours while their train was shunted to the north-south line. Well after midnight they began heading north towards Alexandrovsk. As the train picked up speed and the wheels clacked more insistently, someone at the other end of the car struck up "If Thou but Suffer God to Guide," and in a moment the familiar old German hymn soared harmoniously above the din from the tracks. That was followed by "Holy God We Praise Thy Name," and "For God so Loved Us." As naturally as breathing, hymn after hymn rose sheer in the darkening box that enclosed them and all found strength and security in the well-worn sounds of worship. There were two dozen of them, including the children, and they all sang from memory, even the smaller ones. Gradually, voices began to drop out of the singing as drowsiness from fatigue and tension overcame them. Preacher Heinrich Bartel from

Muntau, who was married into the Goossen clan, said an evening prayer and they tried to compose themselves for sleep in their noisy, rocking beds. But tired though they were, the trauma of their new circumstances kept most of them awake long into the racketing night.

To Wilhelm the night noises of the train were familiar enough. He thought of all the nights he had spent in cars like this one, listening to the groans and muttered oaths of wounded soldiers. He recalled vividly the ache of loneliness and the scratching fear of what might lie ahead. At least now he had family and friends to share the isolation and uncertainty. But hadn't there also been something he had then that he didn't have now?

Lying there fully dressed on his bunk he knew what it was. Then, in spite of war's horrors and the thumping panic of danger and possible death, he still nursed live hopes for the future, had dreams to incarnate, an artistic vision to pursue . . . . He had none of that now. All that had been wrenched away from him by malevolent forces that gave no warning, had shown no mercy in their fury. The measure of his defeat was the cynicism he licked like a wound. He had nothing left to clutch to himself. Neither the impervious blanket of faith that warmed his mother, nor the mystic trust that kept an Erdmann Lepp following God's pillar of fire in an insane land. He could never do that. He had neither the faith nor the will . . . .

He held up his right hand, contemplated its blurred shape in the darkness, the hand that had so effortlessly done his bidding with pencil and brush. No more. He regarded it now as a menial thing of sinews and flesh fit only for guiding a plough and doing farm chores. No more pretensions to art. He smiled at the memory of his father relegating art to an idle pastime for schoolgirls. In Papa's world it had been so. And now in his as well. In Canada he would be too busy carving out a new life — as a farmer probably — to concern himself with such chimeras as drawing and painting. He would settle down on the western Canadian steppe, in that province with the long Indian name — Sas-ka-vatch-che-von — or something like that, perhaps marry again, and live out his life as an ordinary farmer going dutifully to church, trying to forget he had ever had such foolish dreams . . . .

The train made stops throughout the night. Picking up speed for a while, it would slow down again, whistle shrilling, and come to a grinding, lurching halt at another station. And each time the passengers would be rudely jolted out of uneasy sleep or somnolent reveries, the small children whimpering in fright, their elders shushing and grumbling. At one such stop the train bucked to a halt so violently that there was a sudden cry followed by a crash and a splintering of boards, then a hue and cry and much commotion. Han's grandmother, the old Tante Goossen, a heavy woman, had rolled off her bunk and landed on a fragile wooden chest in the aisle. The force of her fall had staved in the cover of the chest. Luckily, she herself suffered nothing more serious than a few bruises and considerable fright.

Morning had broken by the time the train came to a panting stop in the Schoenwiese station at the southern end of Alexandrovsk. Wilhelm knew at once where they were and jumped at the chance to stretch his legs and look around the familiar station. Their car was already well past the station platform and he and Hans jumped down to the gravel grade beside the track. They walked back towards the station platform wondering how long their stop would be. J. J. Thiessen, their group leader, was standing on the near side of the platform talking to the stationmaster, who kept pointing to a man and woman standing on the far side with a chest and several bags beside them.

When the fat little stationmaster spotted the two young men approaching he threw up his short arms in a shooing motion and shouted, "Back to your car, please, or you'll be left behind. This is a special stop to let on a passenger. No one gets off here. Go back to your car!" His round face was red with outrage, as though his authority had been flouted.

They stopped dutifully, but Wilhelm's interest had been aroused by the couple standing on the platform. The two were in animated conversation and he couldn't see their faces clearly but they looked familiar. The man was tall and thin and his companion was a young woman dressed in what looked like a nurse's uniform. Now the officious stationmaster was shouting at them again and making his shooing motions even more vigorously. Then he took Thiessen by the arm and walked him over to the waiting pair. When the couple turned to meet them, Wilhelm saw that the man was Erdmann Lepp and the young woman with him Clara Bock. He was astonished. Hadn't Lepp told him that Clara would be leaving with the first contingent last summer? He watched as the stationmaster pointed to a nearby car and shouted instructions to two young men, who jumped down from the nearest car. They picked up the chest and carried it to the designated car. Clara followed, with Lepp and Thiessen carrying her bags. Her things stowed aboard, Clara embraced Lepp warmly, then climbed the wooden steps placed under the door and disappeared inside the car. Moments later she reappeared in the doorway, waving and saying goodbye to Lepp as the train began to move.

Startled, Wilhelm turned and ran to catch up with his own car. Hans, already aboard, was waiting in the doorway to help him up. Wilhelm came abreast and threw himself at the doorway. Hans and Fritz grabbed him and pulled him up just in the nick of time. The train was picking up speed fast.

Clara Bock on this train! Till this moment he had not known how much he wanted to see her again. She must be the nurse assigned to the train. He would go to her car at the first opportunity.

"Vasya, do you remember that train trip we took together to Moscow for Easter? So long ago now it seems . . . How different things were then . . ." She trailed off, lost in reminiscence, her face soft and luminous under her severe nurse's cap.

Of course he remembered! And she still called him Vasya, as though time had not dimmed or changed anything between them, in spite of what she had just said. He did not think to answer her, he was too busy studying her, absorbing her bright presence again, as in the old days. They sat facing each other across the small first-aid table in her car.

"How could we have known then that our comfortable, secure world would soon come crashing down on our heads," she continued in wonder, as if just now discovering the magnitude of their youthful innocence. "You know, even when the war was on, I kept thinking of it as just a temporary inconvenience, like a sudden drenching electrical storm in summer, something to be endured and then everything would be even fresher than before . . . ." She closed her blue-gray eyes tightly, then opened them and gave Wilhelm a brilliant stare. "I can't believe now how naive I was — we all were — criminally naive, so stupidly trusting."

"You're right, Clara, we were, but I suppose blindness to coming disaster is very human. We weren't the only ones who failed to see what was coming. Disastrous events can begin so gradually that most people are barely aware that they're sliding downhill until they suddenly face a yawning chasm."

She smiled, remembering his youthful seriousness in Petersburg, and his endearing habit of generalizing personal concerns to a philosophical level. "But that makes it all the more horrible when you get to where the bottom should be, doesn't it?"

They had met earlier in the day because of Wilhelm's ailing mother. Concern for his mother's condition had compelled him to seek Clara's professional help even before he had a chance to visit her on his own. An hour out of Alexandrovsk Mama had begun to complain of a severe headache; soon she was also suffering dizzy spells and nausea. There was little they could do for her except apply wet cloths to her forehead. They had no medicine with them at all. When they stopped in Sinelnikovo in the early afternoon, Wilhelm went to fetch Clara. He found her in her car, looking crisp and efficient in her nurse's uniform, ready to dispense services where needed. She greeted him with surprised but unfeigned warmth, without a trace of selfconsciousness or reserve. She had come at once to look at his mother and as he walked back to his car with her he found it difficult to believe that this brisk, self-assured young woman was really Clara Bock of Schoenwiese.

After Clara had taken a careful look at his mother and given her a mild sedative to make her sleep, Wilhelm accompanied her back to her car. Then they had begun to talk as of old, and when the train had suddenly gotten underway it had seemed entirely natural for him to stay with her till the next stop. He assumed that his family would guess where he was and not worry. Clara was explaining to him now why she had not emigrated with the Old Colonists last summer.

"Another nurse was assigned to look after the hospital car for that first group. When she got sick just days before the departure date, Onkel Lepp of the UCDL asked me if I would substitute for her and emigrate with a later group. Well, one thing led to another, and before I knew it I had made the trip twice, with the first group and the third." She smiled happily at him. "But this time I'm crossing the border too. I feel I've done my share."

Later, her eyes brimming with compassion, voice tremulous with feeling, Clara talked about Nikolai. "You know, Vasya, I really got to love him very much before he . . . died. He was so very tough on the outside, so vulnerable inside. I only knew him those two weeks, but he must have been that way always, even when he was so difficult as a boy. I remembered some of the things you had told me about him. And he told me much more, about later too, so that I began to feel as if I had known him for a long time too. And you must believe me when I tell you he never made excuses for himself. Weak and sick as he was — delirious much of the time — he seemed intent only on understanding, understanding exactly what he was, had come to, what had made him do the things — some terrible things too — he confessed he had done."

Wilhelm listened intently, trying to see his dead brother through her eyes, the Kolya he himself had never been able to understand, but had tried to keep on loving. As she talked, he began to realize just how little he had really known about his brother; worse, what a snobbish fool he had been towards him because he had dared to be different, had defied the family, broken through the protective shell of the village and boldly walked out into the great world. It was the final step he himself had never had the nerve to take; he had only taken a tentative step that winter in Petersburg and then drawn back again into the security of the colony. What an unfeeling, smug clod he had been towards a brother who had yearned for understanding and support, and received only lofty criticism and disapproval in return.

"He had a curious, star-shaped bullet scar in the palm of his left hand, Vasya; he regarded it as a sort of lucky charm, a talisman. He said he got it on the Blumenfeld front the winter they were fighting against the Molochnaya Self-Defense. I guess he considered it lucky because the bullet could just as easily have gone through his heart or head as his hand. It was the star shape that fascinated him. He stared at it constantly, ran his finger around it even when he was burning up with fever and half-delirious."

Wilhelm started when he heard this. Kolya had been on the Blumenfeld front facing them? Where he himself had shot a Makhnovite through the head at point-blank range, and he didn't know how many more besides? At any time he might have shot his own brother! At least Kolya hadn't been the man at the window that night. That was too horrible to think about.

"There was another reason I felt close to your brother, Vasya." She stopped and searched his face to gauge the depth of his understanding and sympathy. In a flat, low voice that betrayed neither embarrassment nor shame, a voice naked only to her need to make him understand what this was costing her, she related what had happened to her that night at Selenaya, the night her parents were murdered in the pale courtyard, and what unspeakable things had been done to her by their former maid Marusya and the fiendish reptiles with her. She left out nothing, hid behind no false modesty, indulged in no self-pity. The hell she had been through had purged her of all that, he saw, and left her free even of bitterness and hatred. Only when she came to Nikolai's part in the story did her calmness desert her as she tried to express her gratitude for his courageous — magnificently foolhardy — rescue of her from that "hell-spawned bitch and her filthy hyenas."

"He risked his own life for me, Vasya, and he told me that even he didn't know at the time why he was doing it. You see, he and Marusya were lovers just then, and she saw his interest in me as black betrayal. But he did it anyway . . . . I don't know" — her voice broke for the first time — "when I was taking care of him in his last days there in my old school, I wanted so much to save his life in return — even at the risk of my own — but it was not to be." She took out a handkerchief, covered her face and tried to disguise her sobs in a gentle sniffing and nose-blowing. But she composed herself again.

"And Marusya Nikoforovna — I still call her horrible things, but I don't really hate her anymore. I don't even know if she's still alive. People like that don't seem to last very long, in any case. Much later, when I began to pull out of my . . . illness, I began to realize just how much reason she had to hate me. I'd been insufferably wicked towards her, treating her as a despised inferior, flaunting the wealth and power of my family in her face. With deep shame I recalled that I had *enjoyed* being nasty to her, playing on her weaknesses, treating her with a spiteful meanness she had every reason to hate me for. I also realized that those nasty rumors about her and my brother were probably true — or most of them, the rumors I had stupidly refused to believe. In the eyes of God I probably deserved —"

Clara broke off abruptly as the car lurched wildly and the wheels began to screech. The train was braking to its usual abrupt stop for the station ahead. They were coming to Lozovaya.

Wilhelm went to one of the small, high windows and saw that it was beginning to get dark. He looked down at Clara and felt the kind of joy and excitement leaping in his heart that he thought he had forgotten long ago.

And then he realized that he had not said a word to Clara about Katya. She would know about his marriage, of course, from Erdmann Lepp and about Katya's death, but she had been tactful enough not to ask about her. He appreciated her delicacy. She had the right to hear the story from him, but not just yet. To tell her would be to bare his lacerated heart and to expose himself to her pity. And he would need all his courage to do that.

On June 29, in the afternoon of the sixth day after leaving Lichtenau, train Nr. 22/70928 pulled into the border town of Sebesh opposite the Latvian border. The tension and suppressed ferment in the fifty freight cars loaded with anxious Mennonite emigrants were so great that it seemed as if the very walls that separated them no longer existed and that twelve hundred and fifty passengers were all pressed together in one large room waiting for their fate to be decided by some dreaded court. Their anxiety had been given a further twist each time they passed through another large town or city along the route. Kharkov had been the first important milestone. Then, still heading north, on to Kursk and Orel. From there the train began its long northwest swing through Bryansk, Smolensk, Vitebsk, Poltesk, and now, at long last, Sebesh.

Here their fate, they knew, would be decided. They were still on Russian soil. Now they faced the unpredictable gamut of the customs officials and the final inspection of the border guards at the so-called Red Gate straddling the tracks on the frontier a short distance beyond Sebesh. They had heard that many things could still go wrong there, that the border officials had been deliberately nasty to earlier groups of emigrants. They were nervous and apprehensive as they began to unload their bags and possessions and deposited them on the ground beside the tracks. Nothing was to be left in the cars during the customs search. Wilhelm could see already that some cherished personal possessions would remain behind here on Russian soil, far from the Mennonite villages of the south from whence they had been brought, but even farther from where their owners were going across the sea.

With the customs inspection well underway, J. J. Thiessen emerged from the station office with an odd request. The chief inspector was appealing for literate volunteers among the emigrants to help register all the passengers in the official border log. Thiessen called on teachers and high school graduates to step forward, and within minutes he had a team of sixteen recorders. With a shrug and a disbelieving shake of his head, Wilhelm had indicated his willingness to help. Doing something routine would at least pass the time and perhaps help relieve some of the tension of waiting.

They wrote for hours, page after page of familiar names, ages, and Molochnaya addresses. Finally, with their fingers growing cramped and sluggish, they were relieved by another team of recorders. Tired out, Wilhelm retreated to his bunk for a rest. He fell asleep wondering what Clara was doing through all this. He had not seen her since the train stopped.

It was late evening before the customs inspection and the registration of names were completed. Only then were their precious exit visas handed back to them. To his consternation Wilhelm found that his box of books had been confiscated, except for the family Bible and his mother's treasured hymn book. The secular books were state property, he was told, and not permitted to emigrate.

Just as the train began moving again Wilhelm's mother remembered with a wail of anguish that the cherished daguerrotype of their ancestor Daniel Fast had stayed behind in one of Wilhelm's books. Mistakenly thinking that religious books were more likely to be confiscated than others and that personal pictures might also be taken from them, she had hidden the portrait in one of Wilhelm's large art books. Her distress was great and Lenchen, fearing she would get another of her terrible headaches, made her lie down immediately with a cold compress.

Around eleven p.m. the train stopped again. They had reached the border. The Red Gate of Freedom! Wilhelm and Hans pulled open the door and looked around in the darkness. All around them they saw dark masses of pine forest inscrutable and still. Looking down, Wilhelm saw that their car had come to rest on a small bridge. Below them he heard the lively gurgling of a small stream. Up ahead, garishly illuminated in the headlight of their locomotive, loomed the beckoning border gate with its angular, asymetrical shape rising to a peak surmounted by a fiery red star in the night sky. The annunciation of a wondrous new birth for all of us, he smiled to himself. High above the watchtower on one side, the new red flag of the Soviet Union flapped in the cool night breeze. Long may it wave, he thought sardonically — here.

All was quiet, peaceful looking. How ironic it was, he thought, that their last moments in the old homeland would breathe only peace and tranquility in a gentle, empty landscape far removed from the strife and hatred and oppression that had forced them to abandon all hope for the future in this unhappy land. The vast land of promise that had been so eagerly embraced by Daniel Fast and his pioneering kind over a century ago. And they might perhaps have come by this very route, their heavily loaded wagons grating their impatient snail's pace towards the promised land waiting like a bride for consummation. And then he thought of all those he was leaving behind dead in the womb of the past. Katya and their unborn child — and all the others. And his career as an artist stillborn, also dead before it ever started. The past like an ugly, spreading stain in his soul. He wanted only to get away now, to blot it out with time and distance.

With a jolt he was brought back to the present. The stillness was suddenly rent by the harsh, hostile voices of the border guards bawling up at the emigrants lining the wide open car doors.

"All boards and planks out of the cars, you thieving bastards — now! Come on, get a move on or we'll kick your *njemtsi* arses. State property remains here."

They were dumbfounded. The boards and planks were their seats and beds. Without them their discomfort would be acute, and they still had hours of tedious travel before them before getting to Riga and then the port of Libau.

Under the guards' brutal prodding the men and boys grudgingly dismantled the bunks and benches and slid the boards and planks outside. They would have to make do with boxes and chests for seats . . . .

And then, finally, the train did begin to move through the Red Gate on its way to Riga.

Epilogue
The Bread Of Exile: 1933

1
Waldheim, Saskatchewan, 1933

They had laid their plans with great care so that nothing would go wrong. No one could say that they had rushed into a decision; they had taken years to decide that this was what they would do. In the evenings after the work was done and the children were in bed, they would discuss their plans for the future over endless cups of *prips* at their modest, oilcloth-covered kitchen table. This was, after all, a land of opportunity where hard work and perseverance were bound to pay off. Look how well Lenchen and Hans had done since getting off the land and moving to the city. They now ran their own grocery store in Saskatoon and already had their own house and car.

True, the country was in the grip of a depression that everyone said would get a lot worse before it got better. All the more reason then, they argued, to get off the farm now and try their luck in the city too. The gloomy talk of their dispirited English neighbors did not deter them. To move from a farm in rural Saskatchewan to the city of Winnipeg in Manitoba did not seem as venturesome to them as it did to the untraveled farmers around them. They had lived in cities before, in the Old country, they said quietly.

For seven years they had worked hard on their rented farm and saved their money. Neither of them really liked farming but they stuck to it this long because it seemed like the only way they could establish themselves in this strange new land. He sometimes joked that they could certainly use some of her father's money now, and she retorted that what would really come in handy was some of the farm machinery her father's factory had made in such abundance. At least he had made his mother happy by farming, before her death five years ago.

For years now he had spent all his spare time in drawing and painting again. When they first got married, for all her pleading he refused to go back to his art. But shortly after his son was born he started to draw again and had been at it ever since. Recently he had begun sending his better stuff to commercial art firms in Winnipeg and one of them had responded by inviting him to come for an interview.

The result had been an offer of a part-time job with a good possibility for a full-time position in the future. The offer fitted in so precisely with the plans they had been making they could hardly believe it. In Winnipeg he also planned to paint portraits for Mennonites of means and others who could afford them. She planned to give private singing lessons and perhaps fill out at first with a part-time job as a practical nurse. Both of them had worked hard on their English and spoke fluently, although with heavy accents, of course. Best of all, they would be able to raise Nickie (they still liked to call him Kolya at home) now six, and little Katya, going on five, in better schools and in a more cultivated atmosphere, so that they would grow up feeling completely at home in this peaceful Canada.

While they agreed that they would probably never feel completely at home here themselves, they had never regretted turning their backs, along with so many others, on their old homeland. And they had been even more fortunate, they never tired of saying, in having found each other again when they did. Their love for each other had brought serenity and purpose to their lives, and they thanked God for it.

The disturbing ghosts from the past that sometimes haunted their dreams made them cry out and cling to each other in the dark. But with dawn's budding they would rise together to face the inexorable light that swept them forward from day to day.

2
Paris, France, 1933

A small, hunched figure in a dark, baggy suit, he sat alone at a sidewalk table off in a corner in the shadows. He sat motionless, his body slack, passive, as if the effort to move was not worth it. Knobby and scarred, one hand lay inert on the table beside his glass of white wine. With the other he propped up his shaggy head and choir-boy face now puffy with layers of sallow flesh. His drooping lower lip looked unnaturally red below the scrubby salt-and-pepper mustache.

"Monsier desirez un autre?"

Opaque, expressionless eyes looked up at the polite young waiter. He shook his head. He couldn't afford another glass today. He wanted just to sit here and drift vacant, weightless, to feel the soft wine creeping through him like a morning mist. A single glass of wine could lull his failing body now as surely as the buckets of vodka and *samogon* he had swilled in that other life had fired him out of his body and made him immune to weakness and fatigue.

He was falling apart. He could feel it. His lungs were rotting like a carcass in the sun, and night after night he coughed himself into sleepless exhaustion in his airless little room. And when he wasn't coughing and spitting his old wounds drove him crazy. Last week he had composed a tribute to his old comrade Rogdajev, dead in exile somewhere behind the Caspian Sea: "And you, dear friend, comrade and brother, sleep; even though it is the heavy sleep with no awakening, it is a peaceful sleep."

How he longed for that peaceful sleep himself.

But first he had to finish his writing, the history of his revolutionary struggles in the Ukraine. That ocean of words into which he threw himself every morning. Words, words, words. He wrestled with them in despair, more frightened of them than he had ever been of enemy bullets. Every morning he felt himself drowning in them; every morning he tried desperately to set down on paper his experiences, trying to find clarity and sense in those nightmare years from which he would never fully awake. With a growing sense of futility — sometimes near-panic — he fought to control the rebel words, but they were tricky devils that wouldn't do his bidding. They turned on him, changing shape, threatening him, or else sliding away out of reach, tantalizing, mocking his dull clumsiness, his thick-fingered incompetence. What had happened to him? In prison many years ago the words had flocked to him like eager lovers, he had written poems endlessly. What frightened him most were the long black gaps in his memory devoid of any words at all, the places and events that came back to him only as puzzling shadows without form or substance. His memory was rotting away like his lungs.

And he had no one to help him. His so-called friends avoided him much of the time now, and even when he was with them they often ignored him by jabbering in French. Berkman, Voline, even the charming Emma Goldman, talked incessantly about things he didn't understand — revolutionary politics, always politics, more fancy words and words. Plain anarchism wasn't enough for them anymore. They had to tart it up like a painted whore with all kinds of fancy notions. He always felt depressed and betrayed after spending an evening with these fast-talking city intellectuals. Even his old friend and teacher Pyotr Arshinov, the bastard, had betrayed the true cause by advocating a policy of recognizing the Stalin regime.

He picked up his glass finally, jiggled the few drops remaining in it, and drained it. He was suddenly warmed by remembering the dream he sometimes had during those rare nights when he was able to sleep a little. In his dream he was back in Gulai Polye again, just an ordinary young peasant who had married plump, laughing Natasha, the girl who lived three *khatas* away. Only her face wasn't Natasha's but the beautiful, dark-eyed face of that other girl he had dreamt about so often. Katya. And what he desired more than anything else in his dream, and Natasha-Katya too, was to save enough money so he could buy a fine carriage and a pair of matched, black carriage horses . . . . Then he would show them all . . . .

3
The Solovetsky Islands, 1933

In the summer of 1923, five hundred years after the monks Savaaty and German landed on the uninhabited northern island of Bolshoi Solovetsky in the White Sea and proceeded to establish a monastery there, Soviet commissars kicked all the terrified monks off their "holy soil" and established on it another enduring institution: the Special Purpose Camp system that was designed to keep the new Soviet state forever secure from the threat of political dissidence and internal revolt. During the rest of the twenties thousands upon thousands of political prisoners (most of them prominent people like noblemen, professors, artists, and priests) were sent there to work under conditions so barbarous but effective that the place became the prototype for hundreds of subsequent punishment camps. As the camp system began to spread like a horrible cancer through the vast stretches of northern tundra, "Solovki" became a name so dreaded that it was uttered only in whispers by the inmates in other camps. Admittedly, there were only rumors; no one had any exact or first-hand knowledge, and no one wanted to acquire it at first hand.

By the end of the decade the sinister rumors about Solovki began to be confirmed by the few — the very few — inmates who had either escaped from there or been transferred to other camps on the mainland. There were eye-witness reports of such sadistic treatment as punishing prisoners in winter by pouring water over them outside, tying them to stumps to be devoured by mosquitoes in summer; or forcing a whole work detail to remain in the woods through a whole winter night because it had failed to fulfill its work norm during the day.

Among all the stories of inhuman torture and bestial cruelty there was one surfacing persistently among the survivors of Solovki that was startlingly different. It was the strange story of a wild-eyed, half-crazy *starets* who had eyes like the mad monk Rasputin but who preached like an angel to anyone willing to listen, including the hard-bitten guards. Thin and long as a flail, he was afraid of no one, and bore the savage curses, blows, and kicks from the guards as though he didn't hear or feel them. He had been there for years, tortured and abused, the witnesses said in awe, and should have been dead long ago. But by some miracle he was still alive. He was seldom seen working and by now most of the guards either ignored him or treated him with good-natured contempt and surprising mildness as a harmless madman who simply refused to die.

This stinking old scarecrow, they said, was not an orthodox priest. If he had been he wouldn't have lasted very long. He was said to be some kind of German pope, a Baptist or one of those other queer Christian cults from the old days. In a voice you couldn't help listening to, he preached the love of Christ and the peace that passes all understanding in the barracks every evening. And such a light would come into his mad eyes as he spoke that the hardened prisoners who listened to him looked at him and at each other in amazement. He had become to many there a living symbol of hope. As long as this *starets* lived and poured out the honey of his words, they knew that not everything was lost for them either.

Of course, no one could say with certainty that the old man was still alive and preaching now.

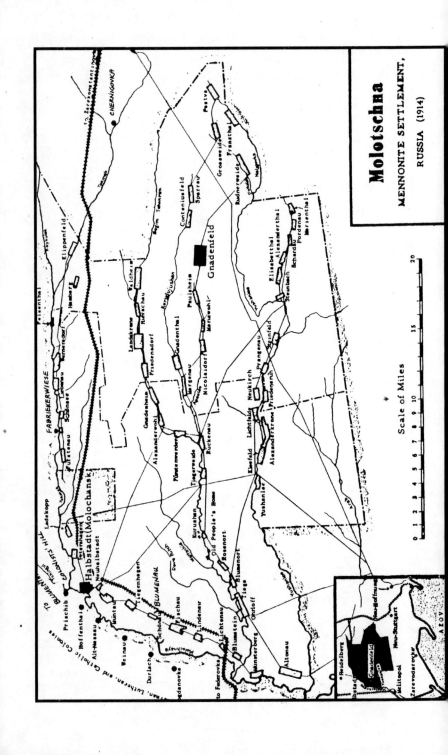

Molotschna

MENNONITE SETTLEMENT,
RUSSIA (1914)

Scale of Miles

0 1 2 3 4 5 6 7 8 9 10   15   20